2016 NHL DRAFT BLACK BOOK
PROSPECT SCOUTING REPORTS & DRAFT RANKINGS

by HockeyProspect.com

© 2016 by The Hockey Press

ALL RIGHTS RESERVED.

The Hockey Press

ISBN-13: 978-0991677573
ISBN-10: 0991677579

TABLE OF CONTENTS — 3

2016 NHL DRAFT RANKINGS	11
2016 NHL DRAFT PROSPECTS	17

★ Abramov, Vitalii 18
★ Aho, Sebastian 19
★ Alexeyev, Dmitry 19
★ Allard, Frédéric 20
★ Allen, Sean 20
★ Allison, Wade 21
★ Almari, Niclas 21
★ Andel, Lukas 21
★ Anderson, Joseph 22
★ Anderson, Josh 22
★ Ang, Jonathan 23
★ Armstrong, Jamie 23
★ Askew, Cam 24
★ Asplund, Rasmus 24
★ Babenko, Egor 25
★ Bajkov, Patrik 26
★ Balmas, Mitchell 26
★ Barberis, Matt 26
★ Barré-Boulet, Alex 27
★ Barron, Travis 27
★ Bastian, Nathan 28
★ Bavaro, Vito 29
★ Bean, Jake 29
★ Bellows, Kieffer 30
★ Benson, Tyler 31
★ Berdin, Mikhail 32
★ Berglund, Filip 32
★ Bernhardt, David 33
★ Betts, Kyle 33
★ Bilodeau, Gabriel 34
★ Bily, Shaun 34
★ Bitten, Will 35
★ Biro, Brandon 35
★ Bison, Bartek 36
★ Bjork, Marcus 36
★ Björkqvist, Kasper 37
★ Blichfeld, Joachim 37
★ Bliss, Trenton 37
★ Bobyk, Colton 37
★ Bobylev, Vladimir 38
★ Boltanov, Artur 38
★ Borgström, Henrik 39
★ Boucher, Matthew 39
★ Bourque, Trenton 40
★ Brassard, Matt 40
★ Bratt, Jesper 40
★ Brazeau, Justin 41
★ Brizgala, Adam 41
★ Brooks, Adam 42
★ Brown, Logan 42
★ Budik, Vojtech 44
★ Buinitsky, Dmitri 44
★ Bunnaman, Connor 45
★ Burgess, Todd 45
★ Burghardt, Luke 46
★ Burke, Brayden 46
★ Byrne, Mitchell 46
★ Caamano, Nicholas 47
★ Cairns, Matthew 47
★ Campoli, Michael 48
★ Candella, Cole 48
★ Carcone, Michael 49
★ Carlsson, Lucas 49
★ Carlsson, Lukas 50
★ Carroll, Noah 50
★ Carter, Cole 50
★ Cederholm, Jacob 51
★ Chernyuk, Konstantin 51
★ Cholowski, Dennis 52
★ Chuard, Leo 53
★ Chychrun, Jakob 53
★ Clague, Kale 54
★ Clarke, Cameron 55
★ Clurman, Nathan 55
★ Coghlan, Dylan 56
★ Coleman, Luke 56
★ Colton, Ross 57
★ Commisso, Domenic 57
★ Cormier, Evan 58
★ Corneil, Johnny 58
★ Cranford, Ryan 59
★ Culina, Mario 59
★ Dahlen, Jonathan 60
★ Danielsson, Hugo 61
★ Davidson, Dawson 61
★ Day, Sean 61
★ DeBrincat, Alex 62
★ De Jong, Brendan 64
★ De Mey, Vincent 64
★ DeNoble, Logan 64
★ De Wit, Jeff 65
★ Dhillon, Stephen 65
★ Dineen, Cam 66
★ Dmytriw, Jared 67
★ Dostie, Alex 67
★ Doudera, Lukas 68
★ Dube, Dillon 68
★ Dubois, Pierre-Luc 69
★ Duehr, Walker 70
★ Duhaime, Brandon 71
★ Dunn, Sam 71
★ Eder, Tobias 72
★ Egan, Taylor 72
★ Eisenmenger, Maximilian 73
★ Eliot, Mitchell 73
★ Elynuik, Hudson 74

Name	Page
★ Eriksson, Filip	74
★ Fabbro, Dante	75
★ Falkovsky, Stepan	76
★ Fallstrom, William	77
★ Felhaber, Tye	77
★ Felixson, Oliver	78
★ Field, Sam	78
★ Filipe, Matt	78
★ Finoro, Giordano	79
★ Fitzgerald, Casey	79
★ Fitzpatrick, Evan	79
★ Fontaine, Gabriel	80
★ Fonteyne, Matt	81
★ Fortier, Maxime	81
★ Fox, Adam	81
★ Fox, Trent	82
★ Frederic, Trent	83
★ Friend, Jacob	83
★ From, Mathias	84
★ Galipeau, Olivier	84
★ Gambrell, Dylan	84
★ Gardiner, Reid	85
★ Gauthier, Julien	85
★ Gerlach, Max	86
★ Gettinger, Tim	86
★ Gignac, Brandon	87
★ Girard, Samuel	88
★ Gleason, Benjamin	89
★ Gosiewski, Matt	89
★ Graham, Michael	89
★ Grametbauer, Mark	90
★ Grannary, Colin	90
★ Grant, Owen	91
★ Green, Luke	92
★ Greenway, James	92
★ Gregor, Noah	93
★ Grundstrom, Carl	93
★ Gustavsson, Filip	94
★ Hall, Connor	94
★ Hagel, Brandon	95
★ Hajek, Libor	95
★ Haman Aktell, Hardy	96
★ Hancock, Kevin	96
★ Hanley, Jack	97
★ Hannoun, Dante	97
★ Harrogate, Brendan	97
★ Hart, Carter	98
★ Harvey, Samuel	99
★ Hawerchuk, Ben	99
★ Hebig, Cameron	100
★ Hellickson, Matthew	100
★ Helvig, Jeremy	100
★ Henderson, Eric	101
★ Henrikson, Arvid	102
★ Hirano, Yushiroh	102
★ Hotchkiss, Matthew	102
★ Howden, Brett	103
★ Howdeshell, Keeghan	103
★ Hrenak, David	103
★ Hronek, Filip	104
★ Huber, Mario	104
★ Huether, Kenny	105
★ Hultstrand, Tim	105
★ Ilomäki, Valtteri	105
★ Ingram, Connor	106
★ Isokangas, Severi	106
★ Ivanyuzhenkov, Artyom	106
★ Jääskä, Juha	107
★ Järvinen, Ville	107
★ Jensen, Robin	107
★ Jerry, William (Billy)	108
★ Jette, Tyler	108
★ Johansen, Lucas	108
★ Johnson, Kenny	109
★ Johnson, Will	110
★ Jonsson, Joseph	110
★ Jonsson Fjallby, Axel	110
★ Johnstone, Dane	111
★ Jones, Max	111
★ Jordan, Zachary	112
★ Jost, Tyson	112
★ Jozefek, Grant	113
★ Juolevi, Olli	114
★ Jurusik, Matthew	115
★ Kachyna, Ondrej	115
★ Kalapudas, Antti	116
★ Karafiat, Jiri	116
★ Karlstrom, Fredrik	116
★ Karrer, Roger	117
★ Katchouk, Boris	117
★ Kayumov, Artur	118
★ Kaspick, Tanner	119
★ Kehler, Cole	119
★ Keller, Clayton	120
★ Khaira, Sahvan	120
★ Kiersted, Matt	121
★ Kirwan, Luke	121
★ Kislinger, Max	122
★ Klavins, Erlends	122
★ Knierim, William	122
★ Koch, Davis	123
★ Kodytek, Petr	123
★ Koivula, Otto	123
★ Kopacka, Jack	124
★ Koppanen, Joona	124
★ Korenar, Josef	125
★ Korshkov, Yegor	125
★ Kosorenkov, Ivan	126

Name	Page		Name	Page
★ Krag Christensen, Nikolaj	126		★ McLeod, Michael	153
★ Krassey, Evan	126		★ McPhee, Graham	155
★ Krempasky, Martin	127		★ Mendonca, Mitchell	155
★ Krikunenko, Roman	127		★ Mescheryakov, Mikhail	155
★ Krys, Chad	127		★ Mete, Victor	156
★ Kryski, Jake	128		★ Middleton, Keaton	157
★ Kunin, Luke	128		★ Mieritz, Christian	157
★ Kuokkanen, Janne	129		★ Miranda, Marco	157
★ Kurovsky, Daniel	130		★ Miromanov, Daniil	158
★ Kutkevicius, Luke	130		★ Mityakin, Yevgeni	158
★ Kuznetsov, Vladimir	130		★ Mizzi, Joseph	159
★ Kyrou, Jordan	131		★ Morrison, Cameron	159
★ Laberge, Pascal	131		★ Moverare, Jacob	160
★ Laberge, Samuel	132		★ Murdaca, Joseph	161
★ Laczynski, Tanner	133		★ Murphy, Liam	161
★ LaFontaine, Jack	133		★ Murray, Brett	161
★ Laine, Patrik	134		★ Murray, Justin	162
★ Lajoie, Maxime	136		★ Najman, Ondrej	163
★ Lakatos, Dominik	136		★ Nassen, Linus	163
★ Larsson, Filip	137		★ Neuls, Donovan	163
★ Lauzon, Felix	137		★ Neveu, Jacob	164
★ Lazarev, Maxim	137		★ Niemelainen, Markus	164
★ Leskinen, Otto	138		★ Noel, Nathan	165
★ Lestan, Filip	138		★ Nother, Tyler	165
★ Lindgren, Ryan	138		★ Nurmi, Markus	166
★ Lindholm, Max	139		★ Nylander, Alex	166
★ Lindstrom, Linus	140		★ O'Brien, Brogan	167
★ Lochead, William	140		★ O'Leary, Michael	168
★ Lockwood, William	141		★ Olischefski, Kohen	168
★ Luce, Griffin	141		★ O'Neil, Kevin	169
★ Luff, Matt	141		★ Olsson, Oliver	169
★ Lyszczarczyk, Alan	142		★ Osmanski, Austin	169
★ Magwood, Zachary	142		★ Ottenbreit, Turner	170
★ Maher, Jordan	142		★ Paquette, Christopher	170
★ Mahura, Josh	143		★ Parsons, Tyler	171
★ Makeev, Nikita	143		★ Pasichnuk, Brinson	172
★ Mäkinen, Otto	144		★ Pastujov, Nick	172
★ Maksimovich, Kyle	144		★ Peeke, Andrew	172
★ Malenstyn, Beck	145		★ Pelton-Byce, Ty	173
★ Maltsev, Artem	145		★ Pethrus, William	174
★ Maltsev, Mikhail	145		★ Pezzetta, Michael	174
★ Marmenlind, Daniel	146		★ Philips, Brock	175
★ Mascherin, Adam	146		★ Phillips, Matthew	175
★ Mattinen, Nicolas	147		★ Picard, Miguel	176
★ Matthews, Auston	148		★ Pickard, Reilly	176
★ Mattson, Mitchell	149		★ Pilon, Garrett	176
★ MacNab, Jack	150		★ Pitlick, Rem	177
★ McAvoy, Charles	150		★ Point, Colton	177
★ McDonald, Kody	151		★ Poirier, Zach	178
★ McEwan, James	151		★ Polunin, Alexander	178
★ McGing, Hugh	151		★ Popugayev, Nikita O.	179
★ McInnis, Luke	152		★ Priskie, Chase	179
★ McKenzie, Brett	153		★ Pu, Cliff	179
★ McKinstry, Ryely	153		★ Puljujärvi, Jesse	181

★ Quenneville, David	182
★ Raaymakers, Joseph	182
★ Raddysh, Taylor	183
★ Rasanen, Aapeli	184
★ Rathgeb, Yannick	184
★ Reichel, Kristian	185
★ Reichenbacher, Grant	185
★ Repo, Sebastian	185
★ Reunanen, Tarmo	186
★ Reynolds, Keenan	186
★ Riat, Damien	187
★ Rifai, Marshall	187
★ Rhodes, Kyle	187
★ Ronning, Ty	188
★ Rossini, Samuel	188
★ Rubins, Kristians	188
★ Rubtsov, German	189
★ Rymsha, Drake	190
★ Ryczek, Jake	190
★ Rykov, Yegor	191
★ Saigeon, Brandon	191
★ Salinitri, Anthony	192
★ Salituro, Dante	192
★ Sambrook, Jordan	193
★ Samuel, Antoine	194
★ Sanchez, James	194
★ Sarthou, Evan	194
★ Sawchenko, Zachary	195
★ Sergachev, Mikhail	195
★ Sevigny, Mathieu	196
★ Shevchenko, Vyacheslav	197
★ Shoemaker, Mark	197
★ Shvyrev, Igor	198
★ Sicoly, Nicolas	198
★ Sissons, Colby	199
★ Sjolund, Nicklas	199
★ Smith, Givani	199
★ Soderlund, Tim	200
★ Sokolov, Dmitry	201
★ Solensky, Samuel	202
★ Somppi, Otto	202
★ Soy, Tyler	202
★ Stadler, Livio	203
★ Stallard, Jordan	203
★ Stal Lyrenas, Oskar	203
★ Stanley, Logan	204
★ Staum, Casey	205
★ Steel, Sam	205
★ Steen, Oskar	206
★ Steenbergen, Tyler	206
★ Stewart, Dean	207
★ Stillman, Riley	207
★ Stransky, Simon	208
★ Stukel, Jakob	208
★ Sukhachyov, Vladislav	208
★ Suter, Pius	209
★ Suthers, Keenan	209
★ Svetlakov, Andrei	210
★ Sylvestre, Gabriel	210
★ Tetrault, Levi	211
★ Thompson, Tage	211
★ Thurkauf, Calvin	211
★ Timleck, Adam	212
★ Timms, Matthew	212
★ Timpano, Troy	213
★ Tkachuk, Matthew	213
★ Topping, Jordan	214
★ Tufte, Riley	215
★ Tuulola, Eetu	215
★ Twarynski, Carsen	216
★ Vala, Ondrej	216
★ Vehviläinen, Veini	217
★ Verbeek, Hayden	217
★ Volcan, Nolan	217
★ Wahlgren, Tim	218
★ Wall, Tyler	218
★ Walker, Jack	219
★ Walker, Zachary	219
★ Walli, Juuso	219
★ Weissbach, Linus	220
★ Wells, Dylan	220
★ Werner, Adam	221
★ Westlund, Gustaf	221
★ Wikman, William	221
★ Woll, Joseph	222
★ Yakovenko, Alexander	222
★ Zachar, Marek	222
★ Zelenak, Vojtech	223
★ Zimmer, Max	223

NHL DRAFT TOP 30   **225**
2017 NHL DRAFT PROSPECTS   **229**

★ Abate, Joseph	230
★ Alexeyev, Yaroslav	230
★ Almeida, Justin	230
★ Anderson, Matt	230
★ Anderson, Mikey	231
★ Anderson-Dolan, Jaret	231
★ Andersson, Lias	231
★ Aucoin, Yan	232
★ Auger, Kyle	232
★ Ball, Jacob	232
★ Baribeau, Dereck	233
★ Barratt, Evan	233
★ Bellerive, Jordy	233
★ Bishop, Joel	234
★ Bjugstad, Jesse	234
★ Bodak, Martin	234
★ Boqvist, Jesper	234

★ Boudrias, Shawn	235		★ Ivanov, Georgi	254
★ Bowers, Shane	235		★ Jokiharju, Henri	255
★ Brannstrom, Erik	235		★ Joly, D'Artagnan	255
★ Brook, Josh	236		★ Karow, Michael	256
★ Bucek, Samuel	236		★ Keating, Austen	256
★ Burt, Robbie	236		★ Keyser, Kyle	256
★ Carson, Macauley	237		★ Kneen, Nolan	257
★ Caufield, Brock	237		★ Kofron, David	257
★ Chainey, Jocktan	237		★ Kostin, Klim	257
★ Chmelevski, Sasha	238		★ Kousal, Pavel	258
★ Clarke, C.J.	238		★ Krief, Alex	258
★ Comtois, Maxime	239		★ Lapierre, Jacob	258
★ Coskey, Cole	239		★ Lauzon, Zachary	258
★ Côté, Louis-Philip	239		★ Le Coultre, Simon	259
★ Crête-Belzile, Antoine	240		★ Leschyshyn, Jake	259
★ Davidsson, Marcus	240		★ Liljegren, Timothy	260
★ Davis, Hayden	241		★ Lind, Kole	260
★ DiPietro, Michael	241		★ Lipanov, Alexei	261
★ D'Orio, Alex	241		★ Lodnia, Vanya	261
★ Duchesne, Samuel	242		★ Luukkonen, Ukko-Pekka	261
★ Durandeau, Arnaud	242		★ Lyle, Brady	262
★ Durocher, Jeffrey	242		★ MacIsaac, Keenan	262
★ Durzi, Sean	243		★ MacLean, Kyle	262
★ Entwistle, MacKenzie	243		★ Maksimov, Kirill	263
★ Farrance, David	243		★ Maniscalco, Josh	263
★ Fleury, Cale	243		★ Martin, Luke	263
★ Foote, Cal	244		★ Mattheos, Stelio	263
★ Fraser, Cole	244		★ McGregor, Ryan	264
★ Frost, Morgan	245		★ McHugh, Nick	264
★ Fulcher, Kaden	245		★ McIndoe, Ethan	265
★ Gadjovich, Jonah	246		★ Meireles, Greg	265
★ Gagnon, Anthony	246		★ Mendel, Griffin	265
★ Gallant, Zach	246		★ Mersch, Dominick	266
★ Garreffa, Joseph	247		★ Messier, Simon	266
★ Gildon, Max	247		★ Messner, Mick	266
★ Gilmour, Brady	247		★ Minulin, Artyom	266
★ Glass, Cody	248		★ Mismash, Grant	267
★ Gourley, Jarrod	248		★ Mitchell, Ian	267
★ Grima, Nick	248		★ Mittelstadt, Casey	267
★ Guay, Nicolas	249		★ Morand, Antoine	268
★ Hamblin, James	249		★ Necas, Martin	268
★ Hague, Nicolas	249		★ Neumann, Brett	268
★ Harrison, Jake	250		★ Noel, David	269
★ Hawel, Liam	250		★ Oettinger, Jake	269
★ Hedberg, Tom	251		★ O'Grady, Reagan	269
★ Heiskanen, Miro	251		★ Oksanen, Emil	269
★ Hischier, Nico	251		★ Paquette, Jacob	270
★ Hoefenmayer, Noel	252		★ Paré, Cédric	270
★ Hollowell, Mac	252		★ Pastujov, Michael	271
★ Hoyt, Peyton	253		★ Pataki, Brady	271
★ Hugg, Rickard	253		★ Patrick, Nolan	271
★ Hughes, Aidan	253		★ Pettersson, Elias	272
★ Ikonen, Joni	254		★ Phillips, Markus	273
★ Isaacson, Nick	254		★ Plouffe, Dylan	273

★ Poehling, Ryan 273
★ Popugaev, Nikita A. 274
★ Rasmussen, Michael 274
★ Ratcliffe, Isaac 275
★ Reedy, Scott 275
★ Reifenberger, Marko 276
★ Roberts, Elijah 276
★ Robertson, Jason 276
★ Rondbjerg, Jonas 277
★ Rule, Caleb 277
★ Ruzicka, Adam 277
★ Salo, Robin 277
★ Samorukov, Dmitri 278
★ Sandhu, Jordan 278
★ Semchuk, Brendan 278
★ Shaw, Mason 279
★ Shore, Baker 279
★ Sillinger, Owen 279
★ Sirota, Jakub 280
★ Skinner, Stuart 280
★ Smart, Jonathan 280
★ Sparkes, Sullivan 281
★ St. Cyr, Dylan 281
★ Stevens, Liam 281
★ Strome, Matthew 281
★ Studenic, Marian 282
★ Studnicka, Jack 282
★ Suzuki, Nick 282
★ Tarasov, Danil 283
★ Teasdale, Joel 283
★ Teravainen, Eero 283
★ Thilander, Adam 284
★ Thomas, Robert 284
★ Tippett, Owen 285
★ Tolvanen, Eeli 285
★ Tortora, Jacob 286
★ Trepanier, Maxim 286
★ Vaakanainen, Urho 286
★ Valimaki, Jusso 286
★ Verity, Daniil 287
★ Vesalainen, Kristian 287
★ Vilardi, Gabriel 288
★ Voyer, Alex-Olivier 288
★ Walker, Samuel 289
★ Wejse, Christian 289
★ Walford, Scott 289
★ Welsh, Matthew 289
★ Williamson, Jagger 290
★ Yamamoto, Kailer 290
★ Zablocki, Lane 291
★ Zetterlund, Fabian 291
★ Zhukov, Maxim 291

2018 NHL DRAFT PROSPECTS   293

★ Addison, Calen 294
★ Aucoin, Yan 294
★ Alexeyev, Alexander 294
★ Antropov, Danil 294
★ Bahl, Kevin 295
★ Beaudin, Nicolas 295
★ Bernard, Xavier 295
★ Bouchard, Evan 296
★ Bouchard, Xavier 296
★ Bouthillier, Zachary 296
★ Bucheler, Jeremie 297
★ Burzan, Luka 297
★ Busby, Dennis 297
★ Chisholm, Declan 298
★ Corcoran, Connor 298
★ Coxhead, Andrew 298
★ Dahlin, Rasmus 299
★ Damiani, Riley 299
★ Dellandrea, Ty 299
★ Der-Arguchintsev, Semen 300
★ Desgagnés, Mathieu 300
★ Dobson, Noah 300
★ Dudas, Aidan 301
★ Dunkley, Nathan 301
★ Emberson, Ty 301
★ Forhan, Rhys 301
★ Fortier, Gabriel 302
★ Foudy, Liam 302
★ Gilhula, Owen 302
★ Gogolev, Pavel 303
★ Gravel, Alexis 303
★ Groleau, Jeremy 303
★ Grondin, Maxim 304
★ Groulx, Benoit-Olivier 304
★ Hayton, Barrett 304
★ Hillis, Cameron 305
★ Holmes, Hunter 305
★ Houde, Samuel 305
★ Hughes, Quinton 306
★ Ingham, Jacob 306
★ Jenkins, Blade 306
★ King, D.J. 306
★ Kovalenko, Nikolai 307
★ Laferriere, Mathias 307
★ Lalonde, Owen 307
★ Levin, David 308
★ Lundestrom, Isac 308
★ MacDonald, Anderson 308
★ McBain, Jack 309
★ McIsaac, Jared 309
★ McMaster, Adam 309
★ McLeod, Ryan 310
★ McShane, Allan 310
★ Merkley, Ryan 310
★ Nizhnikov, Kirill 311

★ Nielsen, Tristen	311
★ Noel, Serron	312
★ Poirier, William	312
★ Popov, Sergey	312
★ Popowich, Tyler	313
★ Rippon, Merrick	313
★ Roberts, Connor	313
★ Robertson, Carter	314
★ Rodrigue, Olivier	314
★ Roman, Milos	314
★ Schmidt, Colin	314
★ Skarek, Jakub	315
★ Smith, Ty	315
★ Stratis, Peter	315
★ Struthers, Matthew	316
★ Svechnikov, Andrei	316
★ Thomas, Akil	316
★ Tkachuk, Brady	317
★ Tucker, Tyler	317
★ Vallati, Giovanni	317
★ Veleno, Joseph	318
★ Villeneuve, Gabriel	318
★ Wahlstrom, Oliver	318
★ Wilde, Bode	319
★ Weiss, Tyler	319
★ Wismer, Jack	319
★ Woo, Jett	320
★ Zabransky, Libor	320
★ Zadina, Filip	320
SCOUTS GAME REPORTS	**323**

2016 NHL DRAFT RANKINGS

2016 BLACK BOOK

RANK	PLAYER	TEAM	LEAGUE	DOB	HEIGHT	WEIGHT	POS	G	A
1	MATTHEWS, AUSTON	ZURICH	SWISS	17-Sep-1997	6' 1.5"	210 lbs	C	24	22
2	LAINE, PATRIK	TAPPARA	FINLAND	19-Apr-1998	6' 4.0"	206 lbs *	RW	17	16
3	PULJUJARVI, JESSE	KARPAT	FINLAND	07-May-1998	6' 3.5"	203 lbs *	RW	13	15
4	DUBOIS, PIERRE-LUC	CAPE BRETON	QMJHL	24-Jun-1998	6' 2.25"	201 lbs *	LW	42	57
5	TKACHUK, MATTHEW	LONDON	OHL	11-Dec-1997	6' 1.5"	200 lbs *	LW	30	77
6	JUOLEVI, OLLI	LONDON	OHL	05-May-1998	6' 2.0"	182 lbs *	D	9	33
7	BROWN, LOGAN	WINDSOR	OHL	05-Mar-1998	6' 6.0"	220 lbs *	C	21	53
8	SERGACHEV, MIKHAIL	WINDSOR	OHL	25-Jun-1998	6' 2.25"	208 lbs *	D	17	40
9	KELLER, CLAYTON	USA U-18	USHL	29-Jul-1998	5' 9.5"	168 lbs *	C	33	60
10	JOST, TYSON	PENTICTON	BCHL	14-Mar-1998	5' 11.25"	191 lbs *	C	42	62
11	FABBRO, DANTE	PENTICTON	BCHL	20-Jun-1998	6' 0.25"	189 lbs *	D	14	53
12	NYLANDER, ALEXANDER	MISSISSAUGA	OHL	02-Mar-1998	6' 0.5"	180 lbs *	LW	28	47
13	MCAVOY, CHARLES	BOSTON U	H-EAST	21-Dec-1997	6' 0.25"	208 lbs *	D	3	22
14	CHYCHRUN, JAKOB	SARNIA	OHL	31-Mar-1998	6' 2.25"	205 lbs *	D	11	38
15	BEAN, JAKE	CALGARY	WHL	09-Jun-1998	6' 0.75"	173 lbs *	D	24	40
16	RUBTSOV, GERMAN	TEAM RUSSIA U18	RUSSIA-JR.	27-Jun-1998	6' 0.25"	178 lbs	C	12	14
17	KUNIN, LUKE	U OF WISCONSIN	BIG10	04-Dec-1997	5' 11.75"	193 lbs *	C	19	13
18	BELLOWS, KIEFFER	USA U-18	USHL	10-Jun-1998	6' 0.0"	196 lbs *	LW	45	28
19	MCLEOD, MICHAEL	MISSISSAUGA	OHL	03-Feb-1998	6' 2.25"	188 lbs *	C	21	40
20	JONES, MAX	LONDON	OHL	17-Feb-1998	6' 2.5"	203 lbs *	LW	28	24
21	ASPLUND, RASMUS	FARJESTAD	SWEDEN	03-Dec-1997	5' 11.0"	176 lbs	C	4	8
22	KATCHOUK, BORIS	SAULT STE. MARIE	OHL	18-Jun-1998	6' 1.25"	192 lbs *	LW	24	27
23	TUFTE, RILEY	BLAINE	HIGH-MN	10-Apr-1998	6' 4.75"	205 lbs *	LW	47	31
24	DAHLEN, JONATHAN	TIMRA	SWEDEN-2	20-Dec-1997	5' 11.25"	176 lbs	C	15	14
25	GAUTHIER, JULIEN	VAL-D'OR	QMJHL	15-Oct-1997	6' 3.5"	225 lbs *	RW	41	16
26	CHOLOWSKI, DENNIS	CHILLIWACK	BCHL	15-Feb-1998	6' 0.25"	170 lbs *	D	12	28
27	HOWDEN, BRETT	MOOSE JAW	WHL	29-Mar-1998	6' 2.0"	193 lbs *	C	24	40
28	THOMPSON, TAGE	U CONN	H-EAST	30-Oct-1997	6' 5.0"	185 lbs *	C	14	18
29	ABRAMOV, VITALY	GATINEAU	QMJHL	08-May-1998	5' 9.25"	175 lbs *	RW	38	55
30	STANLEY, LOGAN	WINDSOR	OHL	26-May-1998	6' 7.25"	225 lbs *	D	5	12
31	PARSONS, TYLER	LONDON	OHL	18-Sep-97	6' 1.25"	184 lbs *	G	2.33	0.921
32	HAJEK, LIBOR	SASKATOON	WHL	04-Feb-1998	6' 1.75"	196 lbs *	D	3	23
33	DEBRINCAT, ALEXANDER	ERIE	OHL	18-Dec-1997	5' 7.25"	163 lbs *	RW	51	50
34	BENSON, TYLER	VANCOUVER	WHL	15-Mar-1998	5' 11.75"	201 lbs *	LW	9	19
35	GUSTAVSSON, FILIP	LULEA JR.	SWEDEN-JR.	07-Jun-1998	6' 1.5"	184 lbs *	G	3.22	0.893
36	GRUNDSTROM, CARL	MODO	SWEDEN	01-Dec-1997	6' 0.0"	194 lbs	RW	7	9
37	WOLL, JOSEPH	USA U-18	USHL	12-Jul-98	6' 2.5"	198 lbs *	G	2.23	0.915
38	JOHANSEN, LUCAS	KELOWNA	WHL	16-Nov-1997	6' 1.5"	176 lbs *	D	10	39
39	BITTEN, WILLIAM	FLINT	OHL	10-Jul-1998	5' 9.75"	167 lbs *	C	30	35
40	HALL, CONNOR	KITCHENER	OHL	21-Feb-1998	6' 2.5"	190 lbs *	D	2	7
41	SMITH, GIVANI	GUELPH	OHL	28-Feb-1998	6' 1.5"	204 lbs *	RW	23	19
42	NIEMELAINEN, MARKUS	SAGINAW	OHL	08-Jun-1998	6' 4.5"	198 lbs *	D	1	26
43	HART, CARTER	EVERETT	WHL	13-Aug-98	6' 0.5"	180 lbs *	G	2.14	0.918
44	MASCHERIN, ADAM	KITCHENER	OHL	06-Jun-1998	5' 9.5"	206 lbs *	LW	35	46
45	CLAGUE, KALE	BRANDON	WHL	05-Jun-1998	5' 11.75"	177 lbs *	D	6	37
46	RADDYSH, TAYLOR	ERIE	OHL	18-Feb-1998	6' 2.0"	203 lbs *	RW	24	49
47	BASTIAN, NATHAN	MISSISSAUGA	OHL	06-Dec-1997	6' 3.5"	205 lbs *	RW	19	40
48	LABERGE, PASCAL	VICTORIAVILLE	QMJHL	09-Apr-1998	6' 1.0"	172 lbs *	C	23	45
49	BERNHARDT, DAVID	DJURGARDEN JR.	SWEDEN-JR.	01-Dec-1997	6' 3.0"	203 lbs	D	10	28
50	MORRISON, CAMERON	YOUNGSTOWN	USHL	27-Aug-1998	6' 2.25"	200 lbs *	LW	34	32
51	BORGSTROM, HENRIK	HIFK JR.	FINLAND-JR.	06-Aug-1997	6' 3.0"	176 lbs	C	29	26
52	GETTINGER, TIMOTHY	SAULT STE. MARIE	OHL	14-Apr-1998	6' 5.25"	200 lbs *	LW	17	22
53	ALLARD, FREDERIC	CHICOUTIMI	QMJHL	27-Dec-1997	6' 1.0"	179 lbs *	D	14	45
54	FITZPATRICK, EVAN	SHERBROOKE	QMJHL	28-Jan-98	6' 2.75"	206 lbs *	G	3.42	0.896
55	STEEL, SAM	REGINA	WHL	03-Feb-1998	5' 11.0"	178 lbs *	C	23	47
56	GREGOR, NOAH	MOOSE JAW	WHL	28-Jul-1998	5' 11.25"	175 lbs *	C	28	45
57	KUOKKANEN, JANNE	KARPAT JR.	FINLAND-JR.	25-May-1998	6' 0.75"	175 lbs *	C/LW	22	31
58	ALLISON, WADE	TRI-CITY	USHL	14-Oct-1997	6' 1.75"	205 lbs *	RW	25	22
59	SAMBROOK, JORDAN	ERIE	OHL	11-Apr-1998	6' 1.5"	187 lbs *	D	9	18
60	DUBE, DILLON	KELOWNA	WHL	20-Jul-1998	5' 10.5"	182 lbs *	C	26	40

2016 NHL DRAFT RANKINGS — 13

RANK	PLAYER	TEAM	LEAGUE	DOB	HEIGHT	WEIGHT	POS	G	A
61	PEEKE, ANDREW	GREEN BAY	USHL	17-Mar-1998	6' 2.75"	205 lbs *	D	4	25
62	MAHURA, JOSH	RED DEER	WHL	5.May.98	6' 0.0"	170 lbs	D	0	1
63	LINDSTROM, LINUS	SKELLEFTEA JR.	SWEDEN-JR.	08-Jan-1998	5' 11.25"	164 lbs *	C	14	30
64	LAJOIE, MAXIME	SWIFT CURRENT	WHL	05-Nov-1997	6' 1.0"	183 lbs *	D	8	29
65	EDER, TOBIAS	BAD TOLZ	GERMANY-3	04-Mar-1998	5' 11.75"	176 lbs *	C	9	13
66	MATTINEN, NICOLAS	LONDON	OHL	05-Mar-1998	6' 4.5"	220 lbs *	D	4	6
67	FOX, ADAM	USA U-18	USHL	17-Feb-1998	5' 10.25"	185 lbs *	D	8	41
68	HRONEK, FILIP	HR. KRALOVE	CZREP	02-Nov-1997	6' 0.0"	163 lbs	D	0	4
69	KYROU, JORDAN	SARNIA	OHL	05-May-1998	6' 0.25"	175 lbs *	C	17	34
70	GIRARD, SAMUEL	SHAWINIGAN	QMJHL	12-May-1998	5' 9.5"	162 lbs *	D	10	64
71	GREEN, LUKE	SAINT JOHN	QMJHL	12-Jan-1998	6' 0.25"	188 lbs *	D	10	25
72	MOVERARE, JACOB	HV 71 JR.	SWEDEN-JR.	31-Aug-1998	6' 2.5"	198 lbs *	D	5	16
73	STRANSKY, SIMON	PRINCE ALBERT	WHL	21-Dec-1997	5' 11.25"	178 lbs *	LW	19	43
74	CARLSSON, LUCAS	BRYNAS	SWEDEN	05-Jul-1997	6' 0.0"	189 lbs	D	4	5
75	KAYUMOV, ARTUR	TEAM RUSSIA U18	RUSSIA-JR.	14-Feb-1998	5' 11.0"	176 lbs	LW/RW	12	19
76	ANDERSON, JOSEPH	USA U-18	USHL	19-Jun-1998	5' 11.0"	192 lbs *	RW	20	29
77	CAIRNS, MATTHEW	GEORGETOWN	OJHL	27-Apr-1998	6' 2.0"	202 lbs *	D	9	24
78	ELYNUIK, HUDSON	SPOKANE	WHL	12-Oct-1997	6' 4.75"	201 lbs *	C	19	25
79	BERDIN, MIKHAIL	TEAM RUSSIA U18	RUSSIA-JR.	01-Mar-1998	6' 1.5"	163 lbs	G	2.07	0.928
80	LINDGREN, RYAN	USA U-18	USHL	11-Feb-1998	5' 11.5"	198 lbs *	D	4	16
81	STILLMAN, RILEY	OSHAWA	OHL	09-Mar-1998	6' 0.5"	180 lbs *	D	6	15
82	GREENWAY, JAMES	USA U-18	USHL	27-Apr-1998	6' 5.0"	213 lbs *	D	4	16
83	MIDDLETON, KEATON	SAGINAW	OHL	10-Feb-1998	6' 5.5"	233 lbs *	D	1	6
84	PU, CLIFF	LONDON	OHL	03-Jun-1998	6' 1.5"	192 lbs *	RW	12	19
85	FREDERIC, TRENT	USA U-18	USHL	11-Feb-1998	6' 1.75"	203 lbs *	C	16	17
86	FROM, MATHIAS	ROGLE JR.	SWEDEN-JR.	16-Dec-1997	6' 1.0"	187 lbs	LW/RW	6	15
87	DINEEN, CAM	NORTH BAY	OHL	19-Jun-1998	5' 11.0"	183 lbs *	D	13	46
88	TUULOLA, EETU	HPK JR.	FINLAND-JR.	17-Mar-1998	6' 2.0"	227 lbs *	RW	9	5
89	KASPICK, TANNER	BRANDON	WHL	28-Jan-1998	6' 0.25"	200 lbs *	C	13	18
90	GLEASON, BENJAMIN	HAMILTON	OHL	25-Mar-1998	6' 0.0"	168 lbs *	D	7	25
91	BERGLUND, FILIP	SKELLEFTEA JR.	SWEDEN-JR.	10-May-1997	6' 3.0"	209 lbs	D	19	22
92	CEDERHOLM, JACOB	HV 71 JR.	SWEDEN-JR.	30-Jan-1998	6' 3.5"	187 lbs *	D	1	4
93	GIGNAC, BRANDON	SHAWINIGAN	QMJHL	07-Nov-1997	5' 10.5"	173 lbs *	C	24	37
94	BURGESS, TODD	FAIRBANKS	NAHL	03-Apr-1996	6' 2.0"	178 lbs	RW	38	57
95	ZIMMER, MAX	CHICAGO	USHL	29-Oct-1997	5' 11.75"	187 lbs *	LW	16	21
96	LAFONTAINE, JACK	JANESVILLE	NAHL	06-Jan-98	6' 3.0"	197 lbs *	G	2.16	0.921
97	WELLS, DYLAN	PETERBOROUGH	OHL	03-Jan-98	6' 1.5"	185 lbs *	G	4.59	0.871
98	STALLARD, JORDAN	CALGARY	WHL	18-Sep-1997	6' 2.0"	188 lbs *	C	21	28
99	COMMISSO, DOMENIC	OSHAWA	OHL	19-Feb-1998	5' 11.0"	178 lbs *	C	18	24
100	BRATT, JESPER	AIK	SWEDEN-2	30-Jul-1998	5' 9.75"	171 lbs *	LW/RW	8	9
101	KUZNETSOV, VLADIMIR	ACADIE-BATHURST	QMJHL	18-Feb-1998	6' 2.0"	210 lbs *	RW	25	33
102	BUDIK, VOJTECH	PRINCE ALBERT	WHL	29-Jan-1998	6' 1.0"	189 lbs *	D	3	13
103	DAY, SEAN	MISSISSAUGA	OHL	09-Jan-1998	6' 2.0"	228 lbs *	D	6	16
104	FORTIER, MAXIME	HALIFAX	QMJHL	15-Dec-1997	5' 10.0"	177 lbs *	RW	31	46
105	SAMUEL, ANTOINE	BAIE-COMEAU	QMJHL	17-Sep-97	6' 2.5"	187 lbs *	G	3.52	0.889
106	PEZZETTA, MICHAEL	SUDBURY	OHL	13-Mar-1998	6' 1.0"	204 lbs *	C	10	18
107	CORMIER, EVAN	SAGINAW	OHL	06-Nov-97	6' 2.75"	202 lbs *	G	3.72	0.89
108	METE, VICTOR	LONDON	OHL	07-Jun-1998	5' 9.5"	174 lbs *	D	8	30
109	KARLSTROM, FREDRIK	AIK JR.	SWEDEN-JR.	12-Jan-1998	6' 2.0"	185 lbs	C	13	20
110	COGHLAN, DYLAN	TRI-CITY	WHL	19-Feb-1998	6' 1.75"	190 lbs *	D	4	20
111	BAJKOV, PATRICK	EVERETT	WHL	27-Nov-1997	5' 11.5"	175 lbs *	LW	18	28
112	SOMPPI, OTTO	HALIFAX	QMJHL	12-Jan-1998	6' 0.5"	180 lbs *	C	13	33
113	POINT, COLTON	CARLETON PLACE	CCHL	04-Mar-98	6' 3.5"	219 lbs *	G	2.16	0.915
114	ANDERSON, JOSH	PRINCE GEORGE	WHL	29-Aug-1998	6' 2.25"	221 lbs *	D	1	5
115	MURRAY, BRETT	CARLETON PLACE	CCHL	20-Jul-1998	6' 4.25"	216 lbs *	LW	14	32
116	VALA, ONDREJ	KAMLOOPS	WHL	13-Apr-1998	6' 4.5"	207 lbs *	D	4	17
117	SOKOLOV, DMITRY	SUDBURY	OHL	14-Apr-1998	5' 11.25"	220 lbs *	RW	30	22
118	KORSHKOV, YEGOR	YAROSLAVL	RUSSIA	10-Jul-1996	6' 4.0"	180 lbs	RW	6	6
119	ZELENAK, VOJTECH	SPARTA JR.	CZREP-JR.	12-Jun-1998	6' 5.5"	223 lbs *	D	2	11
120	KOPACKA, JACK	SAULT STE. MARIE	OHL	05-Mar-1998	6' 2.0"	185 lbs *	LW	20	23

RANK	PLAYER	TEAM	LEAGUE	DOB	HEIGHT	WEIGHT	POS	G	A
121	PITLICK, REM	MUSKEGON	USHL	02-Apr-1997	5' 9.25"	196 lbs *	C	46	43
122	CAAMANO, NICHOLAS	FLINT	OHL	07-Sep-1998	6' 0.5"	188 lbs *	RW	20	17
123	CARROLL, NOAH	GUELPH	OHL	02-Dec-1997	6' 1.0"	178 lbs *	D	3	11
124	DUHAIME, BRANDON	TRI-CITY	USHL	22-May-1997	6' 0.5"	198 lbs *	RW	15	27
125	ANG, JONATHAN	PETERBOROUGH	OHL	31-Jan-1998	5' 11.25"	165 lbs *	C	21	28
126	KRYS, CHAD	USA U-18	USHL	10-Apr-1998	5' 11.0"	185 lbs *	D	3	23
127	BARRON, TRAVIS	OTTAWA	OHL	17-Aug-1998	6' 1.25"	195 lbs *	LW	13	24
128	FILIPE, MATT	CEDAR RAPIDS	USHL	31-Dec-1997	6' 1.5"	196 lbs *	LW	19	17
129	MITYAKIN, YEVGENI	YEKATERINBURG 2	RUSSIA-JR.	24-Dec-1997	6' 3.0"	202 lbs	RW	15	13
130	SAWCHENKO, ZACHARY	MOOSE JAW	WHL	30-Dec-97	6' 0.5"	185 lbs *	G	3.04	0.916
131	MALTSEV, MIKHAIL	TEAM RUSSIA U18	RUSSIA-JR.	12-Mar-1998	6' 3.0"	198 lbs	LW	11	12
132	BUNNAMAN, CONNOR	KITCHENER	OHL	16-Apr-1998	6' 1.0"	207 lbs *	C	16	22
133	TWARYNSKI, CARSEN	CALGARY	WHL	24-Nov-1997	6' 2.0"	198 lbs *	LW	20	25
134	NAJMAN, ONDREJ	JIHLAVA JR.	CZREP-JR.	30-Jan-1998	6' 1.0"	187 lbs *	LW	18	26
135	RASANEN, AAPELI	TAPPARA JR.	FINLAND-JR.	01-Jun-1998	6' 0.0"	196 lbs *	C	19	19
136	MALENSTYN, BECK	CALGARY	WHL	04-Feb-1998	6' 1.75"	191 lbs *	LW	8	17
137	STEWART, DEAN	PORTAGE	MJHL	12-Jun-1998	6' 1.5"	170 lbs *	D	8	14
138	GAMBRELL, DYLAN	U OF DENVER	NCHC	26-Aug-1996	5' 11.75"	179 lbs	C	17	30
139	LACZYNSKI, TANNER	LINCOLN	USHL	01-Jun-1997	6' 0.5"	190 lbs *	C	24	39
140	MAKINEN, OTTO	TAPPARA JR.	FINLAND-JR.	21-May-1998	6' 0.75"	178 lbs *	C	11	19
141	CANDELLA, COLE	HAMILTON	OHL	13-Feb-1998	6' 1.0"	189 lbs *	D	4	16
142	NEVEU, JACOB	ROUYN-NORANDA	QMJHL	12-Jan-1998	6' 1.5"	206 lbs *	D	2	14
143	KORENAR, JOSEF	JIHLAVA JR.	CZREP-JR.	31-Jan-1998	6' 1.5"	172 lbs	G	3.28	0.901
144	LYSZCZARCZYK, ALAN	SUDBURY	OHL	17-Feb-1998	5' 10.25"	184 lbs *	LW	17	33
145	QUENNEVILLE, DAVID	MEDICINE HAT	WHL	13-Mar-1998	5' 8.0"	182 lbs *	D	14	41
146	SAIGEON, BRANDON	HAMILTON	OHL	14-Jun-1998	6' 1.0"	197 lbs *	C	4	10
147	MATTSON, MITCHELL	GRAND RAPIDS	HIGH-MN	02-Jan-1998	6' 4.0"	186 lbs *	C	17	29
148	HENDERSON, ERIC	OSHAWA	OHL	23-Apr-98	6' 1.0"	170 lbs *	LW	8	16
149	KRAG CHRISTENSEN, NIKOLAJ	RODOVRE	DENMARK	12-Aug-1998	6' 3.0"	201 lbs	C/LW	2	2
150	HARROGATE, BRENDAN	MISSISSAUGA	OHL	13-Feb-98	6' 1.0"	174 lbs	RC	3	6
151	LOCKWOOD, WILLIAM	USA U-18	USHL	20-Jun-1998	5' 11.25"	172 lbs *	RW	12	14
152	STEEN, OSKAR	FARJESTAD JR.	SWEDEN-JR.	09-Mar-1998	5' 9.0"	188 lbs *	C	8	24
153	MARMENLIND, DANIEL	OREBRO JR.	SWEDEN-JR.	14-Nov-1997	6' 1.0"	191 lbs	G	2.93	0.921
154	BLICHFELD, JOACHIM	MALMO JR.	SWEDEN-JR.	17-Jul-98	6' 2.0"	176 lbs	RW	15	13
155	MAKSIMOVICH, KYLE	ERIE	OHL	10-Mar-1998	5' 8.5"	172 lbs *	LW	27	44
156	GRANNARY, COLIN	MERRITT	BCHL	24-Sep-1997	6' 0.0"	170 lbs *	C	28	48
157	CLARKE, CAMERON	LONE STAR	NAHL	15-May-96	6' 1.0	170 lbs	RD	9	41
158	WALKER, JACK	VICTORIA	WHL	30-Jul-96	5' 11.0"	179 lbs	LW	36	48
159	RONNING, TY	VANCOUVER	WHL	20-Oct-1997	5' 8.75"	163 lbs *	RW	31	28
160	VERBEEK, HAYDEN	SAULT STE. MARIE	OHL	17-Oct-1997	5' 9.25"	177 lbs *	C	14	20
161	COLTON, ROSS	CEDAR RAPIDS	USHL	11-Sep-1996	5' 11.5"	190 lbs *	C	35	31
162	MCINNIS, LUKE	YOUNGSTOWN	USHL	29-Jul-1998	5' 9.5"	167 lbs *	D	6	22
163	FONTAINE, GABRIEL	ROUYN-NORANDA	QMJHL	30-Apr-97	6'1.0"	185 lbs	LC	20	25
164	INGRAM, CONNOR	KAMLOOPS	WHL	31-Mar-97	6' 0.5"	212 lbs	G	2.61	0.922
165	MCPHEE, GRAHAM	USA U-18	USHL	24-Jul-1998	5' 11.25"	176 lbs *	LW	8	5
166	SANCHEZ, JAMES	USA U-18	USHL	25-Feb-1998	6' 1.25"	184 lbs *	LW	7	9
167	SEVIGNY, MATHIEU	DRUMMONDVILLE	QMJHL	12-Mar-1998	6' 0.75"	175 lbs *	LW	12	10
168	WESTLUND, GUSTAF	THE GUNNERY	HIGH-CT	12-Dec-1997	6' 0.25"	166 lbs *	C	10	18
169	SYLVESTRE, GABRIEL	SHAWINIGAN	QMJHL	22-Jan-1998	6' 3.0"	190 lbs *	D	1	12
170	DAVIDSON, DAWSON	KAMLOOPS	WHL	07-Apr-98	5' 11.0"	181 lbs	D	6	33
171	BURKE, BRAYDEN	LETHBRIDGE	WHL	01-Jan-1997	5' 9.75"	160 lbs *	LW	27	82
172	ARMSTRONG, JAMIE	AVON OLD FARMS	HIGH-CT	07-Aug-1998	6' 0.0"	183 lbs *	LW	22	29
173	LUCE, GRIFFIN	USA U-18	USHL	10-Mar-1998	6' 3.0"	217 lbs *	D	2	7
174	MURRAY, JUSTIN	BARRIE	OHL	22-Aug-1998	5' 11.5"	179 lbs *	D	3	10
175	CULINA, MARIO	WINDSOR	OHL	12-Jun-97	6' 2.0"	174 lbs	G	2.64	0.902
176	FALKOVSKY, STEPAN	OTTAWA	OHL	18-Dec-1996	6' 7.0"	224 lbs *	D	9	23
177	PASICHNUK, BRINSON	BONNYVILLE	AJHL	24-Nov-1997	5' 10.0"	190 lbs *	D	20	45
178	KARAFIAT, JIRI	ZLIN JR.	CZREP-JR.	07-Jul-1998	6' 1.75"	169 lbs *	RW	14	15
179	JONSSON FJALLBY, AXEL	DJURGARDEN JR.	SWEDEN-JR.	10-Feb-1998	6' 0.0"	170 lbs	LW	13	16
180	HAGEL, BRANDON	RED DEER	WHL	27-Aug-1998	5' 11.75"	160 lbs *	LW	13	34

2016 NHL DRAFT RANKINGS — 15

RANK	PLAYER	TEAM	LEAGUE	DOB	HEIGHT	WEIGHT	POS	G	A
181	RYKOV, YEGOR	SKA ST. PETERSBURG 2	RUSSIA-JR.	14-Apr-1997	6' 1.75"	205 lbs	D	3	7
182	RIAT, DAMIEN	GENEVE	SWISS	26-Feb-1997	6' 0.0"	172 lbs	LW	9	12
183	HELVIG, JEREMY	KINGSTON	OHL	25-May-97	6' 3.25"	195 lbs *	G	2.13	0.929
184	CAMPOLI, MICHAEL	USA U-18	USHL	21-Jan-1998	6' 2.25"	195 lbs *	D	0	1
185	NURMI, MARKUS	TPS JR.	FINLAND-JR.	29-Jun-1998	6' 4.25"	176 lbs *	RW	19	17
186	REICHEL, KRISTIAN	LITVINOV JR.	CZREP-JR.	11-Jun-1998	6' 1.0"	167 lbs *	C	17	7
187	PRISKIE, CHASE	QUINNIPIAC	ECAC	19-Mar-1996	6' 0.0"	185 lbs *	D	4	22
188	SHOEMAKER, MARK	NORTH BAY	OHL	28-Sep-97	6' 2.0"	209 lbs	RD	4	9
189	PASTUJOV, NICK	USA U-18	USHL	21-Jan-1998	6' 0.0"	202 lbs *	LW	10	7
190	BROOKS, ADAM	REGINA	WHL	06-May-1996	5' 10.25"	174 lbs *	C	38	82
191	MIROMANOV, DANIIL	ACADIE-BATHURST	QMJHL	11-Jul-1997	6' 3.5"	185 lbs *	LW	22	20
192	DE WIT, JEFFREY	RED DEER	WHL	14-Mar-1998	6' 3.25"	189 lbs *	C	7	15
193	KOIVULA, OTTO	ILVES JR.	FINLAND-JR.	01-Sep-1998	6' 3.75"	219 lbs *	LW	26	32
194	RYCZEK, JAKE	WATERLOO	USHL	19-Mar-1998	5' 10.0"	181 lbs *	D	7	27
195	WALL, TYLER	LEAMINGTON	GOJHL	14-Jan-98	6' 3.0"	202 lbs	G	1.49	0.941
196	SARTHOU, EVAN	TRI-CITY	WHL	24-Sep-97	6' 1.0"	186 lbs *	G	3.46	0.888
197	LESTAN, FILIP	HV 71 JR.	SWEDEN-JR.	26-Nov-1997	6' 5.0"	191 lbs	LW/RW	3	2
198	BETTS, KYLE	POWELL RIVER	BCHL	17-Sep-1997	6' 0.0"	174 lbs *	C	23	20
199	SVETLAKOV, ANDREI	CSKA	RUSSIA	06-Apr-1996	6' 0.0"	200 lbs	C	7	3
200	FITZGERALD, CASEY	BOSTON COLLEGE	H-EAST	25-Feb-1997	5' 10.5"	186 lbs	D	4	23
201	KNIERIM, WILLIAM	DUBUQUE	USHL	22-Jan-1998	6' 2.75"	210 lbs *	RW	14	13
202	GRAHAM, MICHAEL	EDEN PRAIRIE	HIGH-MN	25-Nov-1997	6' 1.5"	193 lbs *	C	14	29
203	SISSONS, COLBY	SWIFT CURRENT	WHL	15-Jan-1998	6' 1.75"	172 lbs *	D	3	19
204	PHILLIPS, MATTHEW	VICTORIA	WHL	06-Apr-1998	5' 6.5"	140 lbs *	C	37	39
205	PILON, GARRETT	KAMLOOPS	WHL	13-Apr-1998	5' 10.25"	175 lbs *	C	15	32
206	BIRO, BRANDON	SPRUCE GROVE	AJHL	11-Mar-98	5' 11.0"	161 lbs	C	32	25
207	PHILLIPS, BROCK	GUELPH	OHL	10-Mar-98	6' 5.0	205 lbs	RD	4	0
208	RAAYMAKERS, JOSEPH	SAULT STE. MARIE	OHL	17-Mar-98	6' 0.25"	185 lbs	G	3.61	0.891
209	LAKATOS, DOMINIK	LIBEREC	CZREP	08-Apr-1997	6' 0.0"	178 lbs	C	7	4
210	RIFAI, MARSHALL	HOTCHKISS SCHOOL	HIGH-CT	16-Mar-1998	5' 11.75"	180 lbs *	D	3	16
211	JORDAN, ZACHARY	DES MOINES	USHL	12-Nov-1996	6' 3.0"	213 lbs *	RW	32	12

2016 NHL DRAFT PROSPECTS

Abramov, Vitalii
LW – Gatineau Olympiques (QMJHL) 5'10", 170
HockeyProspect.com Ranking: 29

Vitalii entered his first full season in the QMJHL as he was selected in the CHL Import Draft in 2015 coming over from the Russian Jr. league. He did not look out of place at all where in his 1st game he scored 4 points and finished the year with 93 points tied for 5th in league scoring.

Vitalii is an undersized forward with great speed and high hockey IQ that creates a lot of offensive chances for himself and his teammates. He is a good skater and is really good on his edges and has good mobility to get out of tight areas, and has quick acceleration to separate himself from defenders. He has a quick and accurate release with his shot and is really good at coming off the half boards or off the rush and cutting into the slot and taking shot on net. Vitalii has very good stickhandling ability where he can handle the puck at top speed coming into the zone and can stickhandle in a phone booth. He has high hockey IQ, he is really good at anticipating how the play is going to develop in front of him, where his teammates are going to be on the ice, he is also very good at finding the open areas of the zone to get set up for an offensive chance. He hockey sense really shows on the power play where he can be very creative and seems to always find the open man, or taking the proper shot on net. Vitalii also can be very creative coming into the zone of the rush, whether it's stopping and finding the trailer or making a move on the D, he always seems to slow the game down. We would like to see him go hard to the net or to the dirty areas of the rink; he tends to do a lot of his work on the perimeter.

Vitalii defensive of game would be the thing he has to work on for the next level, he needs to get stronger along the boards, there were a lot of times in our viewings he was losing the puck along the boards for the break out or if the defensemen pinches down. He also tends to run around too much in his own zone, instead of focusing on his own man and staying with them. Once he does get the puck along the boards he's good at those touch passes to his center curling or touch pass of the boards. Vitalii has 1st round talent and hockey smarts, he just needs to focus on getting bigger and stronger and working on the little parts to the game away from the puck, he could be a very good hockey player at the next level and be very effective.

Quotable: "Vitalli is an undersized forward with good skating ability and High hockey IQ, he can create a lot of offensive chances, whether it's coming down the wing and stopping to wait for the play to develop in front of him, or coming down the wing and cutting into the slot using his quick release and accurate shot" - HP Scout, Justin Sproule

Quotable: "He is a hard working forward that competes every shift he is on the ice, seldom takes a night off" - NHL Scout (April 2016)

Quotable: "Vitalli's vision on the ice is outstanding, he somehow finds the open man that nobody could find. I love his ability on the power play to control the puck and understand where and who the puck should go to" - HP Scout, Justin Sproule (April 2016)

Quotable: "One of our top interviews, he knows his game and gave great answers to our questions." - NHL Scout (Combine week)

Quotable: "(Laughing) He was good (combine interview), I liked the kid. His english was fine and he was group oriented, he spoke to everyone in the room. He said he knows he's 5'9" but it doesn't deter him and that he uses different ways to get to the net. He had some inner drive in him. Good kid. He knows what he is." NHL Scout (Combine week)

Aho, Sebastian
LD – Skelleftea AIK (SHL) – 5'10", 176
HockeyProspect.com Ranking: NR

This is now Aho's third year of eligibility. There is no doubt that Aho is a solid blueliner, however the same question persists and that is whether his game is something that's going to bring value at the NHL level. Aho took another step forward in his production this year for Skelleftea which certainly won't hurt him.

Aho is an undersized puck-mover that has good instincts with the puck and is good at starting the transition. Starting the transition is probably Aho's best asset, as he finds options with passing lanes but can also skate the puck out of danger on his own. Aho also is a good defenseman in the offensive zone. He distributes the puck well and can run the PP. The first issue that Aho has is the fact that even though he has smart offensive decision-making, he simply isn't quite that dynamic with the puck nor a huge shot threat. For an undersized defenseman that can be a problem. Aho also reads the rush well and can defend zone entries well, in his own zone his positioning is on point and he will engage as much as his frame-size will allow him. Here, his second issue pops up and that is the fact that Aho is simply an undersized defenseman. If we were to project him to the NHL level, the reality is there are NHL power forwards he would struggle with simply as a function of his size.

Once we combine the fact that Aho isn't a huge shot threat or elite with his dynamic ability, there is real concern that Aho might simply be too much of a vanilla undersized puck-mover to hold down a role on an NHL blueline. There is no doubt that he is a good player, but whether he can make it at the NHL level remains a question mark. The fact that his production improved this year is at least one of the positives he has going for him as far as being a draft-worthy overager goes.

Alexeyev, Dmitry
LD – Team Russia U18 (MHL) – 6'00", 191
HockeyProspect.com Ranking: NR

Alexeyev was one Russia U18's better defensemen this season. He has shown a decent defensive game while also being a threat to put up some offense with his shot. Alexeyev also displays some physicality on occasion, he has average height but a reasonably solid frame.

Alexeyev likes to take care of his end first, but he will need to develop certain parts of his defensive zone game further than they are at this point for his defensive game to be consistently effective. While his ability to pick up forwards and detect where the danger is coming from is good, his gap can be inconsistent. He can be prone to getting too close and turned by the forward or lets too big of a gap develop which he then has to over-react to. While his gap control isn't always perfect, he is a good competitor and we have seen him display a physical brand of hockey. He also makes sure he has an active stick when defending. He doesn't really stand out with his mobility or size, which could make it a bit challenging for him to be a defensive presence at the next level.

He doesn't struggle with making basic passing plays but doesn't show anything too advanced as far as puck skills or creativity go. One way he manages to get offensively involved is through his powerful shot from the point. He however isn't someone that is going to skate with the puck much or be the type of defenseman that excels in transition. Alexeyev will need to continue to define his identity as a player, as right now he tends to fall too much in-between not being a strong offensive presence or a puck-mover, yet being only an average defensive zone player.

Allard, Frédéric
RD – Chicoutimi Saguenéens (QMJHL) – 6'01", 178
HockeyProspect.com Ranking: 53

Allard was in his third season with the Saguenéens after being selected 18th overall in the 2013 QMJHL Draft. As a late birthday, he had the opportunity to play three seasons in the league before being eligible for the NHL Draft. After a disappointing season in 2014-2015, Allard bounced back this year with a strong season, as he became the go-to guy on a young Chicoutimi defensive squad. He was among the highest-scoring defensemen in the QMJHL, finishing the season with 59 points. Allard is a smart defender who makes a good, accurate pass out of his zone, moving the puck quickly to his forwards in the neutral zone. On the power play, he has improved his shot over the last two years and he's much more of a threat to score from the point now as a result. He's not a physical player, but we love his compete level in his zone. He's a good competitor who still needs to get stronger physically, but showed a lot of improvement with his off-ice training since last year. He's not afraid to block shots in front of his net and plays with a lot of courage. This season, Allard played on a very young defensive corps, often with three 16 year olds on his team. He showed good leadership qualities and led by example on the ice. Allard is not a flashy defenseman but he's a player who makes a lot of smart plays all over the ice, has a good hockey sense and is very efficient on the ice. He's a player that a coach can trust in any situation.

Quotable: "I got a late look at him in Chicoutimi vs Dubois and friends in the playoffs. I think he's made strides in his game. I have heard very little chatter on him from NHL Scouts this season. - HP Scout Mark Edwards

Allen, Sean
LD - Oshawa Generals (OHL) 6'01.75" 187
HockeyProspect.com Ranking: NR

Allen was picked in the third round of the 2014 OHL Draft by the Kitchener Rangers. Allen played last season with the Kitchener Jr. B Dutchmen while playing a handful of games for the Rangers. He played 9 games this season for Kitchener despite being caught behind a deep, veteran blue line in Kitchener before being dealt to the Oshawa Generals.

Allen is a physical, defensive minded defensemen who is at his best when he plays a simple and composed game. He shows intriguing foot speed and mobility for his style of game. The rugged defensive defensemen can be difficult to play against. Defensively speaking Allen has inconsistencies to his game. He close gaps effectively and shows good contain in tight, Allen will often over commit to a play looking for a big hit. Allen improved his transitional play throughout the season as began to take better angles to the opposition, which allowed him to hold the blue line and take away the middle of the ice effectively. He struggled with high end speed attacking the offensive zone as he often got his hips turned and was unable to readjust accordingly. With the puck, Sean has shown the ability to make the smart, simple first pass up ice. He protects the puck well when carrying it up ice and has the skating to bring it up on occasion.

Allen is a highly competitive defender who likes the physical game. He projects as a defensive first defenseman with limited shutdown ability. Despite having a bit of a rocky draft year, he still remains as a potential late round prospect and has NHL level potential.

Allison, Wade
RW - Tri-City Storm (USHL) 6'02", 205
HockeyProspect.com Ranking: 58

Wade has become somewhat of a late bloomer in this year's draft class, after a pretty average Rookie season In the USHL last season, and fighting the injury bug early in the 15/16 season, Allison had really come on in the 2nd half of the season and became a key piece to Tri City's Post Season run and was the Team West's MVP of the USHL Top Prospects game in January.

Allison likes to play a physical Power Forward style that will go into any puck battle and plays with an edge and physicality that his teammates feed off of, create energy and can get under the opponents skin. Wade likes to drive the net and bang home dirty goals but also possesses a lethal shot that comes off his stick quickly. He likes to push the pace and come into the offensive zone with speed and drive straight to the net, he doesn't like pulling up with the puck or trying to find the soft area's to get a pass, even when that might be the play that's warranted in that situation. On the fore check Allison is a pest, always finishing his checks and working to keep pucks alive and create turnovers. Allison doesn't just work hard in the offensive zone; he battles in his own end and takes pride in blocking shots. Wade is a energy player who does all the little things well to help his team win but can also bring a level of skill and finishing ability. He will be off to Western Michigan next year where he will join a very talented recruiting class.

Quotable: "I always look for hockey sense and although he has good size and some great tools I just didn't see the smarts on the ice I like to see, so thats a bigger stopper for me." - HP Scout Mark Edwards

Almari, Niclas
LD – Jokerit (Fin U20) – 6'01", 167
HockeyProspect.com Ranking: NR

After a promising rookie year in U20 league Niclas had a rough start to the 2015-2016 season. He played 12 games with Espoo Blues U20 team and struggled to find a spot on the team. He also had to play with the U18 team just to get ice. During the fall he transferred to Jokerit and found his game again. He's a tall defenseman with good mobility and tools that allow him to play a solid all-around game. He is physically immature and doesn't play a particularly physical game. He makes a solid simple outlet and defends mostly through his positional sense rather than physicality.

Andel, Lukas
LW - HC Dukla Jihlava (CZE) 5'09", 163
HockeyProspect.com Ranking: NR

Andel plays like a seasoned veteran despite being late '97 birth. He spent a majority of the season playing on the men's team and helped them win the second tier championship. When he came down to the U20 team, he played like an over-ager - lots of confidence and leadership. Playmaker with skilled hands, he can generate scoring opportunities with his speed and passing ability. Good legs, generates lots of speed. Biggest area of improvement is finding his consistency, which was tough as he was used in different roles with the men's team and the U20 team. Even though he can play at the U20 level again next season in Czech, Andel could benefit from a change of scenery.

Anderson, Joseph
RW – USNTDP 5'11", 192
HockeyProspect.com Ranking: 76

Anderson has spent the majority of the year playing right wing on a line with the Bellows-Keller duo. While Anderson is less heralded than the other two, he still possesses qualities that made that line as successful as it was.

With Keller and Bellows dominating the play to a larger degree, Anderson excelled in playing a complementary role. He showed good ability to position himself without the puck, often on the weak side of the ice, where he would receive the puck for scoring chances or look to clean up on rebounds and loose pucks. He has also shown the ability to surprise goalies by skating into the zone as a trailer, then pick up speed, skate into a pass and release a powerful shot from further out, beating goalies clean. Anderson isn't the tallest player, but has a solid frame and will do his own work in the corners. With Bellows and especially Keller having the bulk of puck possession, there was not as much opportunity for Anderson to show off his playmaking skills, but he has shown good enough vision in keeping up with the other two, doing the dirty work and can make a nifty pass on occasion. He had no problem understanding what a highly intelligent playmaker like Keller was thinking and his ability to receive and make quality plays with Keller serves as an indicator of Anderson's own hockey sense.

There are some concerns on whether Anderson does enough on his own. He doesn't make bad decisions with the puck, however it is questionable whether he can create offense when not playing with high-end skill players. That said, Anderson has upside as a complementary player that has the timing, the sense, and the shot to take advantage of opportunities presented to him in the offensive zone.

Quotable: "He's smart, might be a guy that can play some PK and play on a 3rd line someday but I'm not 100% sold that he will. I'm not crazy about his physical play and he's not huge at 5'11". - HP Scout Mark Edwards

Quotable: "A few scouts told me his combine interview was below average." - HP Scout Mark Edwards (Combine week)

Anderson, Josh
LD – Prince George Cougars (WHL) 6'02", 221
HockeyProspect.com Ranking: 114

Selected third overall by the Prince George Cougars in the 2013 WHL Bantam Draft, Josh Anderson plays a fairly quiet and responsible defensive game, logging top four minutes for his club and playing as a key penalty killer. He immediately stands out as as big but a bit sluggish. On the plus side, Anderson is blessed with a sizeable frame and superior lower-body strength. He's a fairly disciplined player on most nights, but he can be occasionally provoked, finding himself involved in more than a couple fights this year. His skating is fairly subpar at this point, but he arrives to the draft table with a ready-made NHL frame.

Anderson saw only a bit of time on the powerplay this year, but was definitely a go-to on the penalty kill. Both his shooting and passing will have to undergo some improvements if he wants more assignments on the man advantage. On the defensive end, however, he does a good job of blocking shots. He also has the size and meanness to clear the space in front of his net with little mercy. His ability to tie up the opponent's stick in a net-front scrum is a bit of a speciality at this point. While strong in his own zone, Anderson will need to improve his footwork to be better at defending zone entries and against rushes.

Superior size and strength allows him to assert his dominance in all the important areas: in front of the net, behind the net, and in the corners. Furthermore, Anderson possesses a great reach and uses it well to protect the puck or to poke it out of danger. There's definitely room for improvement here, especially in terms of his skating, his stamina, and his stickhandling skills. However, from a pure defensive standpoint, there's a lot to like.

Quotable: "Not our best combine interview." - NHL Scout (Combine week)

Ang, Jonathan
RC - Peterborough Petes (OHL) 5'11.25" 165
HockeyProspect.com Ranking: 125

Ang was selected in the 1st round, 9th overall in the 2014 OHL Priority Selection Draft by the Peterborough Petes out of the Markham Waxers Minor Midget program. Ang had a decent rookie season and more than doubled his point totals across the board playing a more consistent top six role for the Petes.

Ang possesses high end speed and is a very offensive minded forward. He uses his speed very well when attempting to create offensive opportunities. He will challenge defenders one on one consistently and regardless of the result, he will keep coming back at defenders using his speed to try and get in for scoring chances. He has good puck skills and good offensive creativity. While Ang effortlessly gains the offensive zone off the rush and often gains a stride on his opposition, he still shows hesitation to drive the net, avoiding high traffic areas. Ang has a shoot first mentality and likes to take the puck to the net and try to create scoring chances. He has good passing ability but would often look off an open linemate to take his shot. Defensively, he utilizes his excellent speed but can sometimes over skate the play and miss his assignment. Ang played secondary minutes both on the power play and on the penalty kill. Despite his excellent speed, he had a tendency to lose puck races against players known to play a physical style of game.

When it comes to speed, Ang is among the top of the class in the 2016 NHL Entry Draft. He has the skill to have some potential as a top six forward at the next level. He needs improvement defensively, but it's not for a lack of trying, or backchecking. Over the next few seasons this area should improve because he displays a willingness to improve. What should hurt his NHL chances is his unwillingness to engage physically, combined with his individualistic mindset with the puck. He will either need to get his teammates more involved in the play or, he needs to get tougher and show a willingness to get involved in battles in order to reach his potential.

Quotable: "He's very talented but I've seen guys like him so many times, they don't suddenly change and become tougher. He plays scared and I doubt it changes." - NHL Scout (April 2015)

Quotable: "I didn't like his game last year at all. I thought he improved this season but he lacked playing at a high level on a consistent basis. I also thought he relied to much on his linemates to get him pucks." - NHL Scout (March 2015)

Armstrong, Jamie
LW – Avon Old Farms (NE Prep) 6'2" 195
HockeyProspect.com Ranking: 172

He is a decent sized winger that could develop into the power forward if the foot speed and lateral mobility improves. The skating has improved over the last two seasons as he is a determined individual working hard on and off the ice, it needs to keep getting better.. He is still physically maturing and hardening rather than just being tall. He competes hard all over the ice and plays a very determined game. He handles the puck fairly well as will try the toe drag move and shoots the puck hard. He excelled on a line with fellow draft prospect, Patrick Harper (BU), as he showed well in big games and gave his centerman room to operate with his physical play. He will play in Sioux Falls (USHL) where he should continue his growth before moving onto Northeastern (Hockey East) where he should continue his growth. Armstrong is probably worth a late round flyer. He produced solid numbers over the past two seasons at AOF in the New England prep league, although keeping pace in his skating will be the key to his future.

Quotable: "The son of St. Louis Blues Director of Amateur Scouting, Bill Armstrong, is a player who doesn't lack in the work ethic department. He competes hard, finishes checks and will go to the net. Skating still needs to progress some more." - HP Scout Mark Edwards

Askew, Cam
RW – Moncton Wildcats (QMJHL) – 6'04", 212
HockeyProspect.com Ranking: NR

After going un-drafted last season, Askew was back in the QMJHL for his 3rd season and 2nd with the Moncton Wildcats. Statistically, he had his best season yet, hitting career highs in goals, assists and points. The big American forward, who took part in the New York Rangers' rookie camp, managed to turn some heads before his return to Moncton. Askew is starting to figure out his game and understand a bit more what kind of hockey player he will become. He has become quite good at handling the puck down low as well as in terms of making passes for his teammates deep in the offensive zone. His playmaking abilities have always been underrated, as he sees the ice well. He possesses a good wrist shot with great velocity, but is a bit inconsistent with his accuracy. Ever since joining the QMJHL, we always found him to be a smart player who knows where to go in the offensive zone to create scoring chances. He does need to be more involved on the ice, as often he floats around without getting involved and battling for pucks. He's a big forward, but doesn't really play that big physical game that you would like to see from a power forward. He's more of a skilled guy. He can play a physical game if needed and can lean on guys along the boards, but lacks consistency there as well. That's one of the drawbacks with Askew: he lacks involvement in the game and he's inconsistent with his physical game. The same goes for his skating, which is average at best. He had some up and down playoff, score some important goals but was also healthy scratch as well, again consistency from game to game needs a lot of work. Going into his 2nd year of eligibility for the NHL Draft, it should be interesting to see if a team will take a gamble on him, as he does have tools to work with (shot, puck skills) and has great size.

Asplund, Rasmus
LC – Farjestad (SHL) – 5'11", 176
HockeyProspect.com Ranking: 21

Asplund is a left shooting center who can also line up on the wing. He spent this entire past year with Farjestad in the SHL and it was already his second season playing in the top Swedish league after logging 35 games last year. Rasmus is also internationally decorated, being a mainstay feature for Team Sweden in various age-groups over the past few years.

Asplund isn't the tallest guy and his frame will need some filling out to do, but what immediately catches the eye with him is the fact that he has very good skating ability and plays with energy. The combination of his work-ethic with his ability to get around the ice is one of his better features. He is a player that is consistently involved in all three zones on the ice and is effective with and without the puck. With some added power he has become stronger on his skates and can compete better that in the past when engaged by defenders, his consistency has also improved and is not a concern at this point.

Asplund is a multi-dimensional offensive player. He has very good on-ice awareness and opens up for plays properly, but also sees his linemates well. His passing game and his ability to be involved around the play is already really good and he rarely has a "quiet" shift where he doesn't contribute anything positive to the play, regardless of the situation. In the offensive zone, he can do a bit of everything. He reads the play well and it is natural for him to select the right choices. He understands how to get involved on the cycle and extend possession, he reads the holes well and can set himself up in the slot for a scoring chance. He has the hands to stickhandle under pressure and with the puck on his stick he quickly recognizes open linemates, his ability to take advantage of coverage break-downs is very good as he can both set up a linemate or finish on the play himself. One of the more impressive aspects about Asplund is that he also works hard around the net and in traffic. Although not a power forward, he does a very good job at gaining position and beating the defensemen with his compete level and skating ability. His reads on rebounds and in chaotic situations with plenty of traffic are quite good as he consistently arrives first on loose pucks. He's also got a quick stick in-tight and often manages to get it on the puck before the defenseman can react.

Defensively he's made impressive strides from last season and Asplund now plays a fairly mature two-way game, he is already a good forechecker and backchecker. He is committed to moving his feet and has a good active stick. He is capable of causing turnovers with it as he pressures the puck-carrier. Asplund is one of those players that will often hound the opponent on the backcheck and work until he gets the puck back. As a center he will need to get bigger to defend down-low in the defensive zone, sometimes he can also come out towards the blueline more than is needed because he is focused on pressuring the puck, especially as a center he should pay more attention not to expose the area behind him.

Quotable: "Really liked his game this year. I don't think I had a subpar viewing of him all year long. He brings something positive to the table each shift. I loved his willingness to work for pucks and him not shying away from playing in high-percentage scoring areas and through traffic. Played a pro-game". - HP Scout Nik Funa

Babenko, Egor
LW/RW – Lethbridge Hurricanes (WHL) 5'09", 160
HockeyProspect.com Ranking: NR

Egor was the Lethbridge Hurricanes Import draft pick, who they selected fifth overall in the 2015 edition. Egor is an electrifying offensive presence who has hand and footwork to burn. He's a good all-directional skater and a pure offensive force past the blueline.

Egor is a hard player to read because he does everything at a high pace and switches gears in the blink of an eye. He's very slippery coming out of the corners or off the walls. His ability to sneak into the dirty areas and to score was a big asset for the Lethbridge Hurricanes. At five-foot-nine and less than 160 pounds, he'll obviously need to get bigger and stronger. Mobility, creativity, puck skill, and pure offensive prowess are qualities that come to the forefront when watching Babenko. His movement off the puck is unpredictable but his passes have a soft touch and are easy to receive.

His defensive game leaves much to be desired. Babenko clearly lacks the size to be effective but that is compounded by the fact that he is also not the most engaging player defensively. As a second time NHL draft eligible, Babenko produced at a point-per-game pace.

Bajkov, Patrik
RW/LW – Everett Silvertips (WHL) 6'00", 175
HockeyProspect.com Ranking: 111

Bajkov is a winger with decent wheels and good hockey IQ who possesses good shooting ability. Bajkov was only able to match his point totals from last season, resulting in a bit of a disappointing campaign. With that being said, he was forced to reinvent his game and to make improvements to his passing game, resulting in a more well-rounded player than we saw last season. Known for his shot, Bajkov really improved his passing game this year.

Patrik is very dangerous when left in open space as he has a good shot from above the circles. Last year, we questioned his ability in the corners. This year, his game became more physically robust as the season progressed, even though he remains a bit undersized on the whole. Bajkov is at his best when operating through open ice and using his instincts to create offense. He can still be neutralized when he gets pushed to the wall, although some improvement was made there this year. Playing in Everett has also helped Bajkov round out his defensive game, Bajkov has an easy time tracking the play and knowing where to be on ice, it is unlikely that he will miss coverage. However, even though he is smart, he doesn't quite have the physical tools to really break up plays in one on one battles at a consistent level. Bajkov has been used on special teams and is a regular contributor on both the powerplay and the penalty kill.

Indeed, able to play multiple positions, and logging big minutes in all situations, versatility is one aspect of his game that can't easily be overstated. Although the offense didn't flow as much as some had anticipated, Bajkov finished the year with decent numbers.

Balmas, Mitchell
LC/LW – Charlottetown Islanders (QMJHL) – 6'00", 180
HockeyProspect.com Ranking: NR

Balmas was Charlottetown's 1st pick in the 2014 QMJHL Draft (7th overall) and after a tough first season in the league, he started making some noise this season. The Nova Scotia native scored 20 goals this season and started showing the potential of a goal scorer. He split this past season by playing down the middle and on the wing. Balmas is a goal scorer; he possesses a real good shot and can beat any goaltender with it. He's a bit of a streaky scorer, however, as he didn't finish the regular season on a high note with only two goals in his last 21 games. He doesn't have a lot of explosiveness in his strides, but has decent agility and is not a bad skater. Adding an extra gear could do wonders for him. Since coming into the QMJHL, he has worked hard on improving his defensive game and becoming a better two-way player. Going forward we see him more as winger than a center, as he struggled in the faceoff circle this season with a 46% rate and he's a much better shooter than he is a playmaker. In the playoffs, he scored some key goals for the Islanders. Balmas still needs to add strength to his frame, as there's not much in terms of a physical game with him. The chance are slim he gets selected this year but we could see get a look with a training camp invitation and look for a big increase in production next season with Charlottetown.

Barberis, Matt
RD – Vancouver Giants (WHL) 5'10", 186
HockeyProspect.com Ranking: NR

Matt Barberis is a right shot defenseman who has lined up mostly on the left side of the blueline. Barberis has been utilized on the PP where early in the season we noted his ability to unload dangerous point-shots. Barberis can move the puck out of his zone, though he can be a bit overly enthusiastic with some of the passing, as he could allow himself to wait an extra second to analyze his options better. Barberis also has some bite defensively, he competes against bigger players and is willing to play them physical once engaged in a battle but will need to work on his gap control and control the space around him better with his positioning. A minor flaw of his is also the fact that he sometimes doesn't bother to offer an easy option out to his defensive partner for a D to D pass. Barberis has shown some upside with his shot and an engaging game, but will need to work on quite a lot of details in his game going forward.

Barré-Boulet, Alex
LC – Drummondville Voltigeurs (QMJHL) – 5'10", 165
HockeyProspect.com Ranking: NR

Barré-Boulet went un-drafted last season after his rookie season with the Voltigeurs. This year, in his second season in the league, he was among the most productive players in the league and formed one of the best duos with Michael Carcone. There were not many positives in Drummondville this year, but their chemistry together was definitely one of them. For his size, Barré-Boulet doesn't possess an elite skating ability, but is at his best when he keeps his feet moving in the offensive zone. This makes him tough to counter. If he's not moving his feet, at his size, he's a lot easier to neutralize for opposing defensemen. He still lacks ideal strength to play at the pro level and will need to keep getting stronger over the next couple of years. Versus bigger players along the wall, it's tougher for him to win puck battles. Offensively, he sees the ice very well and makes his teammates around him better. On the power play, he controls the play from the half-wall and can create scoring chances with his vision. He loves to rush the puck into the offensive zone and quickly distribute it to his teammates. Defensively, he started seeing more ice time on the PK unit this season, as his anticipation and smarts are his best assets while shorthanded. Not likely to get selected in the draft but would be worth of summer invitation for a NHL camp.

Barron, Travis
LW - Ottawa 67's (OHL) 6'01.25" 195
HockeyProspect.com Ranking: 127

Barron was selected first round, third overall at the 2014 OHL Priority Selection Draft by the Ottawa 67's out of the Toronto Jr. Canadiens Minor Midget program. Barron had a decent rookie season but struggled to live up to the lofty expectations considering where he was drafted.

Travis has the body and skill to be a power forward at the next level. He is a north south type of player, he needs to be more consistent with his game on a night-to-night basis. Barron is a good skating forward; he has good speed when he is in full motion with the puck. Travis has really good balance, as he is very hard to knock off the puck and is hard to control down low. Travis has a heavy shot, when he uses and his accuracy is ok. He misses too many shots wide, needs to bare down with his shot and hit the net. Travis is a hard nose player who is effective on the fore-check and finishes all his checks. He can create separation for himself with his size and strength. His game is very effective when he is working down low on the cycle with the puck and driving hard to the net with the puck using his size and reach. The biggest thing for Travis is he has to compete hard every night and keep his feet moving, when he wasn't skating you didn't notice him on the ice and looked like an average player at best.

His defensive game is responsible, he understand systems and where to be on the ice in the defensive zone and what man to pick up. Travis is an effective penalty killer because he will block shots, get in lanes of the defenders and work hard along the boards to get the puck out. Travis is a character player and has shown good leadership on and off the ice. He sticks up for teammates on the ice and isn't afraid to fight if needed. Travis could possibly be a good role player at the next level but he will need to focus on getting faster, stronger and competing hard every game and shift to be an effective player.

Quotable: "I'm surprised he was selected that high in the OHL Draft." - NHL Scout (October 2015)

Quotable: "I saw him play a few good games but the average ones outweighed the good ones." - NHL Scout (February 2016)

Quotable: "Travis struggled a bit coming out of the gates at the start of the year, but ended the year on a good note by playing his in your face type of style." - HP Scout Justin Sproule

Quotable: "Travis is an effective player when he is skating hard every shift and engaged physically on the forecheck, winning 1 on 1 battles down low and driving hard to the net." NHL Scout (April 2016)

Bastian, Nathan
RW - Mississuaga Steelheads (OHL) 6'03.5" 205
HockeyProspect.com Ranking: 47

Nathan Bastian was selected in the 7th round of the 2013 OHL Priority Selection Draft by the Mississauga Steelheads out of the Kitchener Jr. Rangers Minor Midget program.

Bastian is a big power winger who possesses a great compete level below the dots. Bastian does an excellent job down low in the offensive zone to win battles and use his size and strength to overpower opponents. He protects the puck very well down low and is excellent at the cycling game. Nathan does a great job getting himself open in the offensive zone and it provides himself scoring chances. He has a powerful shot but has a terrible time trying to hit the net, even sometimes while at point blank range. If he had good shooting accuracy with his power and his positioning gaining the chances he had, he could have more than doubled his goal output. Bastian's biggest concern is his skating ability. He has heavy feet and struggles in transition or when the pace of the game picks up. He performs much better when the game is slowed down for him and he can grind it out. He has decent passing ability.

Bastian has some NHL upside as a power winger nut his offensive upside is up for debate. If he ever becomes more accurate, he could post some respectable point totals in the NHL, but as it stands now, he struggles to finish on a number of chances he gets. He plays the game below the dots as well and has value as a player who will succeed on the cycle. He gets pucks deep and does a lot of those little things well, but his skating needs to get better so he can get to the puck on those races.

Quotable: "I like him, he's at the end of my top 30." - NHL Scout (November 2015)

Quotable: "I thought he would be a solid mid round pick but the draft is so weak that I have him in the late 2nd round now." - NHL Scout (November 2015)

Quotable: "Find me 45 guys better than him. I'm listening." - NHL Scout (January 2016)

Quotable: "I don't get all this first round talk...3rd or 4th rounder for me. - NHL Scout (February 2016)

Quotable: "I've watched this kid going back a while because I know his billets. I coached their son years ago. When the season began, I thought Bastian would be a 3rd or 4th rounder and a guy I would be happy to select in that range. I like his work ethic and he's not a dumb player. He contributes with some grit and physical play and chips in with some nice puck movement as well. My issues with his game are his skating and his lack of finish. I attended at least 15 Mississauga games this season. I saw him miss too many of what I would deem 'sure goals' for players with scoring ability. He got a lot of opportunity this season, he played with McLeod and Nylander and got a ton of PP time. In my opinion, his numbers back up what I saw in my viewings." - HP Scout Mark Edwards

Quotable: "I have him as a late 2nd." - NHL Scout (March 2016)

Quotable: "I have him in the 40's." - NHL Scout (January 2016)

Quotable: "Had some hope for him earlier this season. The more I watched the more I soured on him." - NHL Scout (May 2016)

Quotable: "There's a lot to like about Bastian, I love the game he plays down low. He's an NHL prospect, but he needs to finish his scoring chances, he needs to work on his skating and I don't think he's a first rounder." - HP Scout Ryan Yessie

Quotable: "His interview good. Kind of a quiet kid." - NHL Scout (Combine week)

Bavaro, Vito
LW – Brooks School (NE Prep) 6'2" 190
HockeyProspect.com Ranking: NR

He is a sleeper for the draft as he plays a heavy game down the wing as he is an athletic player, with heavy NHL-calibre shot and strong on the puck and makes good use of his body. The skating isn't a strength but has improved. Even with an unconventional stride he gets from point A to B alright. He will need to keep improving on his lateral footwork and alteration of his speeds to show more deception and tools in the box. Bavaro also needs to play a less selfish game and utilize his teammates around him in order to be more effective. He is still somewhat raw, yet has some attractive pieces to his game.

Quotable: "I don't like the skating. He's just a drive the net and shoot it kid, lacks vision. Might go really late." - NHL Scout (May 2016)

Bean, Jake
LD – Calgary Hitmen (WHL) 6'01", 173
HockeyProspect.com Ranking: 15

After going un-drafted in the WHL Bantam Draft, Bean has been one of the biggest surprises in the WHL this season. He had a solid rookie campaign last season, but took his game to the next level this year finishing with 64 points. He played on a veteran laden Calgary Hitmen team and was a huge part of their success this season. A left shot defenseman, Bean has spent significant time playing on the right side of Calgary's blueline.

The first thing that strikes you when you watch Bean, is his poise and intelligence. He thinks the game on a very high level and has very good skills to complement his smarts. Bean is a great skater that has very good acceleration and mobility. He is not the fastest skater but a very efficient skater and can use his smooth stride to join the rush as the 4th attacker. Bean has great puck skills and more specifically is a great shooter from the offensive blueline. He does not have an overpowering shot, but with his good vision and great instincts he is great at getting pucks through crowds and more importantly getting pucks on net. His ability to both find seams for his accurate shot and to distribute the puck around is high-end which makes him a strong offensive producer. Bean is also a terrific powerplay contributor as his first pass, the ability to start the transition, puck-distribution from the offensive blueline, shooting, and the ability to spot weak-spots in PK coverage all rank very highly.

The biggest strength that this player possesses is his ability to think the game at a high level. He is very composed and uses his skills to make simple yet effective plays. He has a lot of poise to his game and very rarely panics or makes risky decisions. Bean is also a very good passer and with his great vision this makes him dangerous on the powerplay. He has both an excellent forehand as well as backhand pass. His passes are smooth and on-tape, make it very easy for forwards to control them. He is also very good at dishing passes into space and allowing forwards to skate into the puck with speed. One of the areas he will need to work on is his core strength and adding some weight which will allow him to be much more effective in the corners and in one on one battles, which is currently his greatest weakness. Some improvement will also be needed in Bean's ability to defend against players that go wide on him as he can allow too big of a gap to develop giving forwards time and space to make plays.

Bean has been a great story after going un-drafted in the WHL, his body of work speaks for itself. Bean has the upside to become a strong offensive defenseman at the NHL level and he will most likely hear his name called in the first round of the 2016 NHL Entry Draft.

Quotable: " Bean showed me control for game in each viewing, he skates with an air of confidence to make plays and doesn't let mistakes deter him from trying again. He wants to dictate the pace of the game, which is something I value in a defenseman. He's not in this years drafts top defenseman grouping for me, but his ceiling is really high in my eyes" - HP Scout Andy Levangie

Quotable: " He will make some ugly plays out there but he is loaded with talent as far his offensive game goes. One of my top defenseman in this draft. - NHL Scout (May 2016)

Quotable: " I spoke to Bean at the NHL Combine. He knows his game. He will need some time to get his body ready for the NHL but he mentioned that to me himself. He measured in officially at 6'0.75" - HP Scout Mark Edwards

Bellows, Kieffer
LW – USNTDP 6'00", 196
HockeyProspect.com Ranking: 18

Kieffer Bellows is a shoot-first ask questions later winger with a pro-ready frame and a knack for finding soft spots on the ice. A strong competitor, Bellows scores in multiple ways. From his quality quick-release to getting his nose dirty around the net, Bellows will make sure he gets his opportunities to score.

He is also a high-volume shooter. While getting pucks on net is never a bad idea, Bellows can at times be guilty of almost shooting too much from anywhere. His game can range from him being a consistent scoring threat, to a winger that is overly-reliant on his shooting game and fails to bring other offensive dimensions. The latter can be excusable at lower levels of hockey but won't necessarily fly to the same extent playing with and against pros. One thing that works in Bellows favor is that even when he is not having a good game, he seems to wind up with a scoring chance or two. Bellows is also a good skater and will play a physical game without the puck. He doesn't mind throwing his body around on the forecheck, and is more than willing to establish physical contact in battles. However his physicality sometimes lacks purpose, he will go out of his way to lay a hit without considering the in-game applications of it as those hits don't always improve his team's chances of obtaining the puck.

Bellows is also willing to attack the net and we have seen him score some greasy goals where he manages to find a way to get the puck into the net, even while off-balance or with bodies draped on him. As he moves up the ranks, Bellows will have to continue developing his ability to provide different dimensions of offensive play, as he can be overly-reliant on his shooting game. He will also have to find ways to make a consistent impact in his own zone and in the neutral zone.

Quotable: "He and Keller were quite the duo. I don't think the 18's would've w many games without those two on the team. - NHL Scout (May 2016)

Benson, Tyler
LW/LC – Vancouver (WHL) 6'00", 201
HockeyProspect.com Ranking: 34

Highly touted in the early goings of his WHL career, Benson was selected first overall in the 2013 Bantam draft and was a standout with Kelowna's Pursuit of excellence hockey academy. Injuries have hindered him throughout his career and ultimately his season was shut down in February to fully recover from a nagging groin ailment. A tough situation in Vancouver and a pile of injuries have affected the ability to see Benson perform at his peak level.

A captain of the Giants since he was 17, Benson is not the speediest of skaters but does have above-average acceleration and ability to create space with a powerful lower-body. At times he can look choppy and will need to improve the efficiency of his movements to fully maximize the natural strength he possesses. He shows an ability to fend off body contact, using his body positioning well to hold off defenders and keep them on his back and away from the puck. He more often than not comes out of scrums with the puck. This flows from strong edge work where above average strength is obvious. When he digs in, he uses edge work and body movement making him tough to defend, especially near the wall.

At times can show flashes of high end puck handling but doesn't consistently show the skill that we expect from a top end prospect. The strength of Benson's game is his high-end accuracy on both his forehand and backhand passes. He exhibits soft hands and heads up play with a quick strike mentality. Sometimes he over handles pucks looking for a great play and ends up lacking synergy with his teammates. A whipping wrist shot springs off his blade quickly and is hard to read. Benson is also willing to set up directly in front of the net to provide screens and tip in passes or rebounds.

Benson shows a strong compete level with a bulldog mentality. He's the type who would rather go through you than around you. He plays with emotion and goes over the edge at times showing frustration. While we like him when he plays his power game, it was a somewhat inconsistent occurrence this season, something that was likely impacted by the nagging injuries. Bensons possesses good upside, but his stock was hurt by a very tough year all around, as the forward struggled both with injuries as well as having the responsibility of captaining a team that went through a tough situation with several players walking away from the Giants mid-season.

Quotable: "I left the rink a few times wondering if his lackluster games were a result of his battles with injuries, for me he was way more consistent in his rookie season and I always wanted to give him the benefit of the doubt in that regard. He has the ability to take over games with physicality and skill, but it didn't happen enough for me this year" - HP Scout Andy Levangie

Quotable: "Combine interview reports from multiple teams were positive. One scout mentioned his medical feedback will dictate if he is a first rounder or not." HP Scout Mark Edwards

Berdin, Mikhail
G - Russia U18 (MHL) 6'02", 163
HockeyProspect.com Ranking: 79

Berdin has a nice blend of proper technique and unorthodox style that is fun to watch. His technique starts in his well balanced stance that allows him to move with ease around the crease. He tracks long shots in well to his body and his rebound control has improved throughout the season. Plays the puck well and knows when to come out and make tape-to-tape passes.

Not a physically dominating presence in the crease, but his angles are consistently right and he knows when challenge or hold back on plays. Berdin has a terrific butterfly but tends to lift his legs up too early. He is so light on his feet that he likes to pop up too early at times, which has lead to some goals sneaking through him. Needs to trust in his positioning and technique. He has shown creativity in the crease doing anything he can to get some part of him in front of the puck. Like a lot of young goalies, Berdin needs to work on being mentally focused for the full 60 minutes.
Berdin has great athleticism and can make the saves necessary to change momentum in a game. There is a lot of upside with Berdin and if he continues to develop his strength and mind, he could be a high-end goaltender.

Berglund, Filip
RD – Skelleftea J20 (SWE) – 6'03", 209
HockeyProspect.com Ranking: 91

Filip Berglund is a pro-sized right-shot right-defenseman who significantly improved his last season's total from 11 points to 41, especially notable however was the increase in goals from just 1 to an impressive 19 this year.

Despite the large frame and not the fastest stride, Berglund actually has good finesse with the puck. He controls the puck very well and uses his size to protect it. Berglund has good instincts both when starting the transition out of his own zone as well as in the offensive zone. Not only does he not struggle with starting the transition, he looks pretty comfortable for a big man in those situations and will handle the puck without any panic in his game. He has good vision and can regularly execute accurate passes. This allows him to complete accurate outlets, he also has enough puck-handling skills not to get flustered if he is pressured. In fact, Berglund isn't afraid of making a one on one move. Offensively, he can surprise with a high-end offensive zone pass on the occasion. He also has the ability to find lanes for his shot and get it on net. When defending Berglund's size helps and his defensive instincts are decent, but he is not a very physical player when considering his frame. His skating will also need to get better, he doesn't have the prettiest stride in the world and he could stand to further improve his footwork along with his acceleration as he can be slow getting to pucks.

Berglund is a second-time eligible that had a great developmental year in 2015-2016 season showing significant progress and putting himself firmly back on our map for the 2016 NHL draft.

Quotable: "He's one of the better second-time eligibles coming from Europe, had great progression from last year. Has the makings of a big two-way defenseman, I like that he has some skill and vision with the puck on top of that big frame, there's some offensive upside in him." - HP Scout Nik Funa

Quotable: "One of many possible 2nd or even 3rd time eligibles we expect to get drafted. I think he has a chance to go off the board higher than some might expect." - HP Scout Mark Edwards

Bernhardt, David
LD – Djurgardens IF J20 (SWE) – 6'03", 203
HockeyProspect.com Ranking: 49

Bernhardt is a defenseman who has good physical tools and turned in quite a productive season for Djurgardens J20 as he was one of the better producing draft eligible defensemen at that level. Bernhardt has decent forward skating ability and also skates reasonably well with the puck. His lateral ability while defending will need to improve though as he can struggle to get good angles and body position against forwards with speed. Bernhardt will occasionally use his body to be physical, but it is not a consistent part of his game at this point.

His first pass can also be quite inconsistent. He can be prone to making no-look passes out of his zone that get easily intercepted which is something that he will need to fix. His passing in the offensive zone and on PP is however pretty good. Bernhardt does a good job offensively and on the powerplay. Bernhardt actually shows flashes of offensive instincts both in offensive zone puck-distribution and his ability to find angles for his shot. Particularly his wrist-shot can beat goalies from further out and he finds ways to get it through to the net. He also utilizes a slap-shot but it is his wrist-shot that specifically stood out as something that he uses particularly well.

Bernhardt has a good frame, decent forward skating stride with the puck and the ability to create offense from the offensive blueline in. However, he is raw around the edges and will need some improvement in his defensive zone decision-making, especially on his outlets, and an improvement in the ability to defend laterally. Nevertheless, his tools make him an intriguing prospect with good upside and with considerable room for growth.

Quotable: "I like his upside, but just when I feel like I'm finally settled on him he does something dumb with the puck in his own end. The tools are there, but I didn't see consistent quality decision-making in my viewings. I think if he polishes his game more, he'll have a chance at being a player." - HP Scout Nik Funa

Betts, Kyle
LC – Powell River Kings (BCHL) 6'00", 174
HockeyProspect.com Ranking: 198

Betts is a smart opportunistic center who has completed his first BCHL season after spending last year playing GOJHL hockey. Betts' best quality is his hockey IQ as he anticipates the play very well both with and without the puck. Betts can see what's going to happen a move ahead, and consistently sets himself up into correct positions. He's an intelligent defensive player that supports his defense and has a natural understanding of when he can exert himself physically without taking himself out of position.

Offensively, Betts understands that skating into the correct place at the right time is more important than trying to force plays. He is a good playmaker as he regularly spots open linemates and will get opportunistically involved as a scorer. Betts looks a bit light at times and will need to work on his strength as he continues to develop, his skating is also just decent.

Quotable: "I have some time for him. He works his tail off and plays a hard nosed game despite being a bit weak and light." - HP Scout Mark Edwards

Bilodeau, Gabriel
RD – Gatineau Olympiques (QMJHL) 6'01", 172
HockeyProspect.com Ranking: NR

Gabriel finished his first full season with the Olympiques this year, as he came in a trade with the Val D'or Foreurs last year. He had an up and down season this year, where he showed glimpses of his potential at the beginning of the season and slowed down near the end of the season, as he was in and out of the lineup as healthy scratch.

Gabriel is big bodied 2 way defensemen that has shown some offensive upside in our viewings and also showed he could be a shut down D. Gabriel is a good skater, he doesn't have that burst of acceleration coming out of the zone with the puck, once he is full motion he can be deceiving. His mobility is average at best, where he struggles and gets in trouble is when there is an offensive player coming wide with speed on him, he is not quick enough with his pivots and loses a lot of battles with speed. He is good at reading plays on the ice and understanding what is going on, he tends to hesitate with his decision making whether it's to pinch at the blue line or where to move the puck which most of the time turned into turnovers or chances the other way. Gabriel has shown some good hockey smarts on the offensive side of the game. He has a good hard first pass out the zone, but again he sometimes hold onto the puck too long trying to make that perfect pass instead of just moving it quick. He has a good shot from the point as his accuracy is good, and he always seems to get pucks through to the net for tips or second chances. Gabriel was to inconsistent in the viewings we saw this year, he came out and look really good for a couple games and then the next couple games you wouldn't notice him.

He isn't an overly physical defenseman, but he's not afraid to make players pay when they go in his corner or in front of the net. His body position was ok; he sometimes was on the right side of the man and other times on the wrong side. He has a really good stick in his defensive zone, he is really good at getting in the lanes and breaking up cross crease passes, he anticipates the play well. With more time in the off season to get himself bigger, stronger, faster and with more ice time next year and to gain more confidence, Gabriel could end up being a solid defensemen in the league next season.

Bily, Shaun
LC - Erie Otters (OHL) 5'10" 185
HockeyProspect.com Ranking: NR

Shaun Bily was selected in the third round of the 2014 OHL Priority Selection Draft by the Erie Otters out of the New Jersey Jr. Titans U16 program. Bily Made the decision to join the Erie Otters and played about half the season on a very deep and talented Otters line up. He suffered a terrible shoulder injury losing about six months this season.

Bily is a little on the smaller side but plays a fearless style of game. He is aggressive on the forecheck and finishes his checks. He is capable of forcing turnovers and has a relentless motor. He is a very good skater which helps him battle in all three zones. Defensively, Shaun will block shots. He has decent puck skills and is capable of creating scoring chances. He has an ok shot but also has the hands and speed to beat defenders. Bily was a potential prospect going into the season. He only played 11 games between regular season and playoffs and likely didn't have enough time to make a case for himself. His speed, work ethic and offensive upside should make him appealing and may ultimately earn him a camp invite.

Bitten, Will
RW - Flint Firebirds (OHL) 5'09.75" 167
HockeyProspect.com Ranking: 39

Bitten was selected out of the now non existent Ottawa Jr. 67's Minor Midget program, 7th overall by the Plymouth Whalers in the 2014 OHL Priority Selection Draft. He quickly integrated himself in their top six and when the franchise moved to Flint, he became a critical part of his teams' offense.

Bitten is a speedy forward with excellent skating ability and good puck control. He is a skilled forward who split time this season at both Centre and Right Wing. He has the speed to burn defenders and excellent hands to deceive goaltenders. He is very dangerous on the breakaway and scores at a high rate when in alone. He does a great job utilizing a variation of speeds to affect opponents who try to match up with him, which gives him that extra edge in one on one situations. Despite his size, he will go up against bigger opponents. He is a very aggressive forechecker and has an excellent ability to track where the puck is going and take the best lane to get there in a hurry. . Bitten drew penalties with his forecheck pressure He has a great backcheck and utilized his speed to help his team defensively. He was also an excellent penalty killer this season, using his quickness and tenacity to get on the puck carrier quickly and get into lanes quickly. His presence put pressure on opponents because one puck mistake and he's gone on the short-handed rush.

Bitten is an offensive threat in the OHL and is likely to be one of the best players in the league over the next few seasons. As far as projecting him at the next level, he's a bit of a boom or bust prospect due to his size and lack of elite skill. He has the tremendous work ethic which will help him earn extra ice time, but will need to play bigger than he did at times this season to reach the NHL.

Quotable:" I was a huge fan of Bitten is his OHL Draft year. Fast forward to this season and it was interesting hearing the varied opinions on his game from scouts. I still like him but I don't think his toolset translates as well from the OHL to the NHL as it did from AAA to the OHL." - HP Scout Mark Edwards

Quotable:" Just when I thought I had him figured out I'd see him again and change my mind. When I like him he was showing grit along with some skill, when he was off it was because he played on the perimeter and made me questions his finishing ability. NHL Scout (April 2016)

Biro, Brandon
LW/LC – Spruce Grove Saints (AJHL) 5'11", 160
HockeyProspect.com Ranking: 206

Biro is a competitive scoring forward with good offensive instincts both on the playmaking and shooting side. He has enjoyed a productive season for Spruce Grove in AJHL, appeared internationally for Team Canada at the WJAC and also had a strong showing at the CJHL Top Prospects Game. He is committed to Penn State University.

Biro can play both wing and center positions and what immediately jumps out with him is his combination of smarts and a high-level compete. That along with the fact that he is an above average skater allows him to be buzzing around the play. Biro boasts good offensive instincts, he has the innate sense for finding positions to get his shot off. Has a hard to read quick-release shot that he snaps with almost no wind-up at all, that consistently creates rebounds. He is a good playmaker that can make plays at high pace, likes to draw in a checker out of his position before throwing an accurate dish to a linemate. Biro plays hard in traffic and doesn't mind taking physical contact, even though he lacks size at this point in time. Biro hasn't played at the highest level this season, but had a solid showing for Canada at the WJAC and also looked strong against higher level of competition at the CJHL top prospects game. He has shown that he brings some upside through his compete level and offensive instincts

Bison, Bartek
LW – Prince George Cougars (WHL) 6'03", 187
HockeyProspect.com Ranking: NR

Bartek Bison was selected by the Prince George Cougars in the 2016 CHL Import Draft, Bison arrived to North America with a huge frame and a reputation for playing a robust game.

Predictably Bison didn't put up the type of points he did in the Dutch leagues, but he still completed a full-season of North American major junior hockey, and didn't look a touch out of place. Playing in a depth role and fairly limited in his ice-time, Bison played an up-tempo and physical game.

He's still limited in what he can do with the puck, and his skating is a bit clunky at the end of long shifts, but he has a good sense of how to forecheck effectively and to not be a liability in his own end. He stands out as a crasher-and-banger who might have a chance as an energy guy at the higher levels if he develops particularly well. The North American game suits him.

Bjork, Marcus
RD – Lulea HF J20 (SWE) – 6'03", 203
HockeyProspect.com Ranking: NR

Bjork is a late '97 born pro-sized defenseman with good physical tools. Size is one of the first things that jumps out, but he also has some offense to his game and put up decent numbers at 31 points in 47 J20 games. Bjork likes to throw his body around and will play physical. His physicality is going to need a bit more control as he is prone to chasing players down and putting himself out of position. In fact, he is a bit like a wild-horse out there. His positioning will need quite a bit work. He can leave the front of the net empty and go behind the net to check the player his partner is already checking. He is also prone to dragging himself too far out of the position chasing a player. Bjork can skate reasonably well for his size but when defending he has the tendency to follow the puck too much and not pay enough attention to the space on ice.

Bjork shows the will to engage offensively, sometimes he will even jump up the play and try to get involved as an offensive defenseman would. He's also willing to join the rush and not afraid of taking a chance in order to create an out-numbered attack, but we don't expect Bjork to be a big offensive producer at the next level. Bjork is a toolsy defenseman, has size, physicality, some offensive instincts, but will need to considerably polish out the details in his game in order to be successful at higher levels of hockey.

Björkqvist, Kasper
LW – Blues (Fin U20) – 6'01", 198
HockeyProspect.com Ranking: NR

After going un-drafted in 2015 he decided to stay one more year in Finnish U20 league. In his first U20 season he recorded almost point per game and played an important role in Finland's U18 national team which won silver medal at the 2015 U18 World Championships. This year he was one of the best players in U20 league, showed significant improvement and was ready to move to professional level, but he didn't want lose his college eligibility. Kasper was also part of this year's Finland U20 national team and had a good tournament as a useful depth role-player. He's a quick winger with great two way ability. Plays a smart game and can grind in the corners which gives him some upside as a checking bottom 6 forward. His puck skills and vision are average, they don't stand out but Bjorkvist can make a play when needed and has decent smarts.

Blichfeld, Joachim
RW/LW – Malmo Redhawks J20 (SWE) – 6'02", 176
HockeyProspect.com Ranking: 154

Blichfeld is a lanky wing with a nice frame-size to build upon that can play both the right and left side. Not an impressive top-speed at this point, though he gets around well and his stride suggest there is room for growth as he gets stronger. Has surprising ability to make plays in-tight. Even though he doesn't look the most skilled or elusive, he does a good job dragging a player onto him and then making a subtle pass to an open linemate. He uses this well on the wall where he's willing to take physical contact in order to make plays. Has good vision to see linemates, but he is primarily a scorer. He can score in a variety of ways. Can tip pucks in front of the net and has an accurate quick release on his wrister that he doesn't telegraph to goalies. Blichfeld is raw but there is some potential there. He has good smarts, a frame-size that can be built upon, can get around the ice and has scoring prowess.

Bliss, Trenton
LC – Appleton United/Team Wisconsin U18 (WI-HS) 6'01", 190
HockeyProspect.com Ranking: NR

Bliss ran away with the Wisconsin's Mr. Hockey award this year. Bliss is a smart two-way center who finds a way to contribute on a nightly basis. Bliss isn't going to be the first guy in on the fore-check but he supports the play well, knows where to be to receive the puck in a scoring area and has good finishing ability. He isn't afraid to go to the front of the net and battle for goals but also has a good amount of skill to score some pretty ones as well. While Trenton's skating is not at the elite level yet, he has good straight line speed and good wedge work, as he gets stronger we'd expect to see a little more jump in his first few strides, his fundamentals are there but just needs to get stronger to bring it all together. Bliss will be off the Green Bay (USHL) next season and is committed to the University of Wisconsin the year after that.

Bobyk, Colton
LD – Red Deer Rebels (WHL) 6'02", 200
HockeyProspect.com Ranking: NR

Bobyk is a pro-sized defenseman with a big shot from the point. He is in his third year of eligibility and enjoyed a break-out year scoring 20 goals from the back-end. As a 20 year old, Bobyk knows what his strengths are and plays to them. Bobyk is a chippy, physical defenseman in his own end who likes to finish checks and battles well around the net and in the corners, though he can start chasing the play at times. He's got a long stick that he uses to swat at pucks and take away possession. His poise with the puck in his own end is just average, he'll try to move the puck away but is not the most natural at handling the puck and waiting for plays to open up. Offensively, Bobyk can use his sturdy frame to pinch up wall and keep the puck in the offensive zone. By far his biggest asset is his big shot from the point, he can be utilized on the PP to unload it from his off-side and is a threat there. As a third year draft eligible, Bobyk might have shown enough upside with his physical tools and big point shot for a team to take note of him.

Bobylev, Vladimir
RW – Victoria Royals (WHL) 6'02", 202
HockeyProspect.com Ranking: NR

Bobylev is a pro-sized forward who has compiled an impressive statline in his second year of NHL draft eligibility. What immediately stands out for Bobylev is his heavy frame that he actually gets around the ice fairly well. His first few steps and straight line speed aren't too bad at all for a player his size and he can look quite daunting while skating down the ice at top speed. He does have a bit more of a lumbering motion through his turns though. Bobylev had a giant improvement on his rookie season in North America, improving from mere 9 points in 52 games to hovering around PPG this season. Bobylev also showed good chemistry playing right wing with Tyler Soy and Jack Walker, which was quite a productive line overall. Along with Bobylev's size his best asset is also his powerful wrist-shot which goalies and defenses have to respect, it's not the most accurate but can cause troubles if given room. Bobylev also shows some upside with puck-protection and has improved his playmaking which has allowed him to excel on a line with two smaller skilled forwards. As a second time eligible, Bobylev brings to the table an interesting combination of physical tools and has proved that he does have some upside with a much improved second-year in North America.

Boltanov, Artur
LW – Metallurg Magnitogorsk Jr. (MHL) – 6'02", 172
HockeyProspect.com Ranking: NR

The glimpses of potential were already there in previous seasons, but this is the year Boltanov put it all together at least from an offensive standpoint at the MHL level. His 1.68 PPG ratio in the regular season more than doubled his past productions and was the best in the league among regulars. He managed to score 29 goals in 40 games (playoffs included) without much of a supporting cast. This Russian winger is hard to stop on the big ice once he gets going with the puck, can beat players and enter the offensive zone with ease at the junior level. He is shiftier then he might look at first glance, is a deft stickhandler and possesses the hands to remain effective in tight spaces. He is able to carry the puck to dangerous shooting positions, it's impressive how he can maneuver and find a lane for his release. Furthermore, his wrist shot needs very little room to get off. Artur also shows the ability to quickly stickhandle to the net from down low when given the room and is dangerous around the net. The part of his offensive package that looked more improved this season was his passing game, now a clear strength of his.

A '96 born, Boltanov had a stint at the senior level, but despite being draft eligible for the third-time, his game was still not mature enough to get proper icetime against men. In the past, a lack of intensity along with physical immaturity really hampered his game and he will still need to further improve on both counts. His good frame has yet to fill out and adding more strength could help him getting stronger on the puck among other things. Artur shows the will to initiate contact here and there along the boards, but is a finesse player and should probably focus more on improving his compete level to make more consistent use without the puck of his good mobility and reach. He is pretty good at stealing pucks, but still has defensive laps in coverage. His odd stride when he accelerates straight doesn't help on the backcheck, he seems to accelerate better when carrying the puck than without it. The fact his success was so far limited to his domestic junior league means Boltanov will be fighting against the odds on draft day, but at this point his upside would warrant a selection.

Borgström, Henrik
LC – HIFK (Fin U20) – 6'03", 176
HockeyProspect.com Ranking: 51

Henrik has always been a talented kid but he had a growth spurt where he grew a lot in a short period of time which affected his game. He is a second year eligible and this was his first season in the U20 league. After dominating at the U18 level, this year he impressed with a strong performance at the top Finnish junior level and he might have been the best player in the whole league. He scored 55 points in 40 games. Borgström is a centre with nice vision and great playmaking ability. He has become more than just a playmaker however, as he can also play a straightforward game and use his shot which is pretty accurate, especially his wrist shot. He possesses noteworthy puck-handling skills and can complete creative plays. He is a tall kid who has been improving his skating technique a lot and now that he's become more comfortable with his frame he is playing up to his capabilities.

Henrik is strong on faceoffs and plays a two way game, but on both sides of the puck only on rare plays he gives the impression of trying his hardest. Furthermore, even if he can go after the odd big hit along the boards, he often doesn't engage like he should and skates away instead of battling for the puck. Next season he will be playing at the University of Denver and moving forward he will have to improve his compete and intensity level to have a better chance to fulfill his obvious potential.

Quotable: "This is a player to watch, Our scout in Finland loves him. He has a ton of talent and has put it all together this year. I'd guess he could go off the board as early as the second round." - HP Scout Mark Edwards

Quotable: "Very non committal and bland answers to our questions. Love his game but interview was far from great." - NHL Scout (Combine week)

Quotable: "This will be an even more interesting player to watch at the draft. I had a few teams tell me his interview with them was on the weak side but he is trending way up for his play on the ice." - HP Scout Mark Edwards

Boucher, Matthew
LW – Québec Remparts (QMJHL) – 5'09", 175
HockeyProspect.com Ranking: NR

Boucher had his breakthrough season in his first year with the Remparts, leading the team in goals and points. Boucher is the son of Philippe Boucher, head coach and general manager of the team who made his acquisition last summer. Already on his 3rd team in the league, Boucher was originally drafted by Blainville-Boisbriand in the 7th round of the 2013 QMJHL Draft and was later traded to Drummondville. Boucher didn't get a lot of ice time last year in Drummondville and was seen more as a depth player. This season, with a lot more ice time on the power play, he produced over a point per game. However, he missed close to a month of action in February and struggled to keep his scoring pace after his injury. The Remparts had traded a lot of key veterans during the QMJHL trade period; because of that, they had one of the worst records in the 2nd half of the season and were quickly swept in the first round of the playoffs by Gatineau. Boucher is undersized and has above-average speed, but at his size, you wish he had another gear to be even more explosive on the ice. He can create scoring chances with his speed and has a great work ethic. Boucher is more of a shooter than a passer, and he has a shooter's mentality. He has a good compete level and brings some energy to his team with his hustling. Boucher may have showed this year that he could score at the QMJHL level, but we're not sold on him as a scorer at the next level and his size is a concern as well.

Bourque, Trenton
LD - Owen Sound Attack (OHL) 6'02" 194
HockeyProspect.com Ranking: NR

Bourque was drafted in the third round of the 2014 OHL Priority Selection Draft by the Sudbury Wolves out of the Hamilton Jr. Bulldogs Minor Midget program. Early this season he was traded from Sudbury for Jarret Meyer and played a more consistent, but minimal role for the Attack.

Bourque has good size and plays a steady shutdown role. He was decent in one on one plays, using both his stick and his body to shut down the opposition. He has average skating ability, which helped him defensively against speed, but also in plays along the wall winning his fair share of battles. Trenton doesn't display a great deal of offensive upside but his first pass is exactly what you would hope for a defense first defenseman. He chooses the smart, highest percentage option to advance the puck and has a high pass completion rate due to that. Trenton is showed a lot of upside in Minor Midget. He has yet to realize that potential in the OHL and while he still has more in him than he's shown thus far, he's probably a longshot to be selected at the 2016 NHL Entry Draft.

Brassard, Matt
RD - Barrie Colts (OHL) 6'02" 197
HockeyProspect.com Ranking: NR

Brassard was selected in the fourth round of the 2014 OHL Priority Selection Draft by the Barrie Colts out of the Barrie Jr. Colts Minor Midget program. Brassard made the team out of camp but was in and out of the lineup all season long due to the depth of older defenders on the Colts blueline. Despite this when injuries came up Brassard was a steady defender for the Colts when needed.

Brassard showed the ability to make a good first pass and for the most part his defensive positioning was solid. Brassard has a big wide frame which allowed him to protect the puck when rushing it and got pucks deep. In the offensive zone he moves his feet on the line opening himself up as an option. On occasion he will jump up in the rush, which is how he scored his one goal this season. Defensively he lost more puck battles than he should have and could stand to add more muscle to his frame. He does not play a physically assertive game either along the boards or in front of the net. He has a good stick defensively and this has been his strongest asset when defending.
Brassard has shown some upside but simply didn't get enough of an opportunity to progress enough to warrant a pick at the 2016 NHL Entry Draft. If he puts in work during the offseason, he has the desirable size and the potential to make himself a notable re-entry player as other Colts have done in recent memory.

Bratt, Jesper
LW/RW – AIK (SHL-2) – 5'09.75", 171
HockeyProspect.com Ranking: 100

Bratt is an exciting winger that plays a high-paced game with the ability to execute at top speed. He is one of the biggest one on one threats in the draft in transition, has a rare capability to deke out defensemen and tremendous agility. He gets up to speed in a hurry and can be very quick turning with the puck on his stick, is a deft stickhandler but usually doesn't hold onto the puck for too long. His quick decision making keeps up with his great skating ability, and together with patience and vision allows him to be a good playmaker. His accurate wrist shot is definitely a legit threat, but Jesper is a passer more than a goal scorer.

Has a high skill level and is elusive with the puck, but on the smaller rinks he would need to be stronger on the puck. We would like to see him more involved in puck battles, his focus is obviously on creating offense but he'll have to compete harder to get the puck. It looks like he doesn't like getting his nose dirty, especially along the boards. Defensively doesn't go beyond keeping his position and staying ready to jump on loose pucks with his quickness. When he tries to get physical and throws the odd hit he often gets called, should bother about engaging more consistently along the board instead. Bratt was fairly productive as a 17yrs old in the second tier Swedish men league, but as an undersized player his compete level will need to improve significantly for him to have a chance to eventually succeed at the NHL level.

Quotable: "There is some upside with his skating and skill but he will need to figure out his game. In my viewings, I came away with the impression of a winger who thinks he can make a couple of fancy offensive plays and decide the game with two or three flashy efforts. For me, he's just not quite skilled enough for that to fly at the NHL level anytime soon" - HP Scout Nik Funa

Quotable: "He catches my attention with some flash and dash but he's a guy I liked less with every viewing. He's got skill but needs to be a more complete player. Not competitive enough. One of our Euro scouts called him this year's Bracco." - HP Scout Mark Edwards

Brazeau, Justin
RW - North Bay Battalion (OHL) 6'04.25" 192
HockeyProspect.com Ranking: NR

Justin Brazeau is a big bodied, extremely raw two-way winger. The 6'04" winger showed some improvements throughout the 2015-2016 as he began to show more and more confidence in his game. While Brazeau's physical attributes are undoubtedly intriguing, he is still extremely raw and lacks ideal strength to his frame. With that being said Brazeau showed an effectiveness in a bottom six role for the North Bay Battalion this season. A player who fore checks effectively, Brazeau's anticipation skills along with tenaciousness in puck pursuit allowed the lanky winger to force turnovers throughout the season. While Brazeau isn't overly physical for a player of his stature, he relies on his competitiveness. A player who does his best work off the rush and below the hash marks, Brazeau works the half boards and cycle with effectively. Brazeau is below average in both skating and strength. He lacks ideal foot speed and explosiveness to his stride. While his stride is long and powerful it takes far to many strides for him to reach his top speed, allowing the opposition to close in on him and separate him from the puck.

Brazeau lacks the scoring upside of a top six forward and lacks the strength and skating needed to succeed in a bottom six role. If a team does take a shot at Brazeau, they will be looking at him as a long term project. North Bay has a recent track record of late blooming big wingers and Brazeau has a chance to be the next one if he puts in the effort. We are not expecting him to be selected at the 2016 NHL Entry Draft.

Brizgala, Adam
G – HC Sparta Praha U18/U20 (CZE) – 6'00", 209
HockeyProspect.com Ranking: NR

Brizgala has a very unique style that doesn't rely on proper technique and structure. Relies on being positionally sound and creative with his save selection. When on his knees, he generates lots of power, but can over push at times. He is a great competitor and never gives up on a shot. Very athletic and scrambles well. Had health issues this year as he only played in three games with his club this season and missed the U18s as well. Was selected by the Muskegon Lumberjacks in this years USHL Phase 2 draft

Brooks, Adam
LC – Regina Pats (WHL) 5'10", 174
HockeyProspect.com Ranking: 190

Brooks is a third time NHL draft eligible who has progressively improved with each year. This culminated with a league-leading 120 points in regular season and a terrific 23 points in 12 playoff games output. While Brooks is already 20 years old, he did everything he could do to put himself on map in his third year of eligibility.

Brooks has clearly been one of the biggest offensive threats in the WHL this season. His game is based around skill, solid skating, quick hands and offensive zone timing and sense. Brooks' stride is well above-average as he has good acceleration as well as top speed. He possesses good agility and balance on his feet and can use his footwork to create separation against defensemen, especially in-tight. Brooks has nifty hands and controls the puck well and can produce offense both off the rush as well as from controlled possession. While he is both skilled as well as fast, he doesn't necessarily wow you in that respect. His hands and skating are both quite good but neither aspect would classify as elite at the next level. Brooks creates most of his offense through his instincts. He reads soft spots and breakdowns in coverage well and will consistently find spots with the puck on his stick in high-percentage areas. There he is smart enough to find open linemates or finish on his own. His shot is above-average, certainly good at the junior level as the release is fairly quick and his wrist-shot is accurate, however that shot would look just OK against pro-players. Brooks doesn't lack in compete, however he isn't a true puck-hound on the forecheck and will also still need to get bigger in his own zone. Defensively, his reads aren't problematic but there isn't much there that spells out an above-average defender at the next level. Brooks could be a bit more physical and do a better job tying up guys moving across the slot. To Brooks' credit, he did see PK minutes and was one of the bigger shorthanded threats in the WHL.

Brooks is an interesting prospect from an offensive standpoint. While in our opinion he does not project to be more than an average all-around player, his league-leading season has certainly put him into the spotlight and allowed him to be one of the prospects worth checking out for the 2016 NHL draft. As a 20 year old he has succeeded against junior-aged players, but while he has a varied arsenal of offensive weapons, it is concerning that there is a lack of that one skill that would truly project as high-end at the next level.

Brown, Logan
LC - Windsor Spitfires (OHL) 6'06" 220
HockeyProspect.com Ranking: 7

Logan was selected sixth overall at the 2014 OHL Priority Selection Draft by the Niagara Ice Dogs out of the Indiana Jr. Ice U16 program. After being deemed non-committal by the Ice Dogs, he was traded to the Windsor Spitfires, where he began his OHL career and performed ok as a 16 year old.

This year has been the tale of two seasons for Logan Brown. It started with Logan being cut from Team Canada's U18 Ivan Hlinka team due to a lackluster performance. His season ended with him joining Team USA's U18 team at the IIHF World Under 18 Championships, where he impressed scouts with a fantastic performance.

Logan has very good offensive tools for such a big forward. He has an excellent shot that quickly snaps into the back of the net. Brown has shown good passing ability through traffic to set up scoring chances. His offensive strengths are pretty well rounded when he's set up in the offensive zone. Both passing and shooting skills are strong. He will need to improve 'off the rush' as he hasn't had great results when trying to beat defenders one on one in our viewings. His skating has shown steady improvements over the course of this season and like any player, he will need to continue to progress in this area. Logan protects the puck well down low and can get himself out of tight situations by protecting and cutting towards the net. He will need to get better and be a bit tougher in battles. Adding muscle to his huge frame will be important. He also needs to improve on his defensive urgency, as he isn't as strong on his own side of the red line as some of the other centres near the top of this draft.

Going back to his OHL Draft year, we felt Brown had shown an inconsistent compete level. This season was a different, as he seemed to flick a switch mid season. If this current version of Logan Brown is an indication of things to come, Logan could be one of the best players to come out of the 2016 NHL Entry Draft as a talented top six forward.

Quotable: "He left me wanting more in his OHL Draft season. It started out that way this season as well. All of the sudden in January he cleaned up all the things I didn't like in his game. He was outstanding in my last 9 or 10 viewings of him. He always showed me he had great vision and passing ability, but he began to use his great shot more often as well, I saw some absolute lasers. Brown's compete level was the key for me though. He transformed himself from a 6'6" kid who frustrated me with an almost lazy look to his game, to becoming a 6'6" monster with skills and smarts who began to compete as much as any player on his team. I said on radio early in the season that he is kid who could make us look like idiots for our then, late 1st round ranking of him, if he ever started to compete harder. Thankfully Logan started before his draft season ended. We adjusted our rankings again for our final list. I think he could go as high as 4th and no later than 7th." - HP Scout Mark Edwards

Quotable: "He was the worst player in camp." - NHL Scout (after Ivan Hlinka camp in August 2015)

Quotable: "So much potential but he is invisible on too many shifts." NHL Scout (October 2015)

Quotable: "I've only seen him twice so far but he was excellent both times. I know that I'm in the minority though." - NHL Scout (December 2015)

Quotable: "I interviewed him and asked him point blank why almost every scout watches him and then comes away thinking he is lazy or disinterested. He was shocked to hear that. He didn't see himself as playing that way." NHL Scout (December 2015)

Quotable: "He's like a different player." NHL Scout (March 2016)

Quotable: "He will be gone in the 12-14 range at worst. We have no chance." NHL Scout (February 2016)

Quotable: "I'd be shocked if he slid past 7th or 8th after his play these last 8 weeks." NHL Scout (April 2016)

Quotable: "His interview was really good." - NHL Scout (Combine week)

Quotable: "Multiple teams raved about his interviews. I also spoke to Logan one on one at the NHL Combine. It was less than a five minute chat but I'd rank it up with my best conversations I've had with a prospect. I spoke to him about the highs and lows of his season and his answer was both intelligent and very honest. The kid gets it. Since I was born in Montreal I've had a lot of people ask me about him to Montreal...I'd be surprised if he makes it to them. His second half combined with his great interviews has his stock very high." - HP Scout Mark Edwards (Combine week)

Budik, Vojtech
LD – Prince Albert Raiders (WHL) 6'01", 189
HockeyProspect.com Ranking: 102

Vojtech came into North America possessing already a quality body of work over in Europe and in international appearances, but while his season was decent, he perhaps wasn't quite the presence his last year's performances suggested he might be.

Vojtech is above all a very good skater for his size in terms of overall fluidity. His straight-ahead acceleration speed could use some improvement, but in all other areas he looks well ahead of the pack. Budik's backwards skating, in particular, is a step above, allowing him to maintain really tight gaps and to force a lot of plays offside at the blueline. Budik is well advanced in using his backwards mobility and stick to steer the play to the outside and force forwards to skate into low-percentage situations or outright strip them of the puck.

Budik's play with the puck, meanwhile, leaves something to be desired. He's not a natural puck handler and he has a tendency to panic under pressure at times, especially when he's handling the puck at the offensive blueline during an offensive possession. Thus, while he's an adept penalty killer, he's probably not a defenseman that is the most natural fit for an offensive quarterback or a PP option.

Budik plays his best hockey when he plays a simple defensive shutdown game, as he excels in the corners and when traveling in reverse. He has good defensive hockey IQ and reads the play well. He's got decent size and might look more comfortable in his play with the puck next year as this was his debut season in North America. Certainly, that would be one area to look for where he could make improvement. Right now Budik projects as a mobile defensive defenseman who is particularly good at using his backwards mobility and stick to defend. Budik is a smart player and there are inklings of offensive ability in his game, but that is not something that he managed to master in his first year of North American hockey.

Buinitsky, Dmitri
LW/RW – Madison Capitols (USHL) 6'01", 179
HockeyProspect.com Ranking: NR

Dmitri played 24 games for Madison (USHL) and was a decent offensive producer for his team with 6 Goals and 16 PTS. Dmitri made the Capitols a better offensive team upon his arrival after they traded away a lot of their top talent at the trade deadline. He is a gifted offensive player who can really skate and can make plays at a high speed. He plays a very skilled game, avoids contact and tries to create space using his offensive skills. Dmitri still needs to develop his defensive play and be more engaged in puck battles. In a lot of our viewings he seems to avoid the tough area's if there isn't a scoring chance involved and his play can come across as Lazy when he doesn't have the puck on his stick. Dmitri is a 97' birthday and his 24 games for Madison (USHL) was his only experience in North America so we are willing to give him more time to sort his complete game out on the smaller ice. Dmitri's options are completely open for the future as of now, he could return to Madison or he was drafted in the KHL draft by Dinamo Minsk in 2014 and the CHL may also be an option, however no team owns his rights as of now.

Quotable: "A really skilled player who could be selected by a smaller market team in the CHL Import Draft." - NHL Scout (May 2016)

Bunnaman, Connor
LC - Kitchener Rangers (OHL) 6'01" 207
HockeyProspect.com Ranking: 132

Bunnaman was selected in the second round of the 2014 OHL Priority Selection Draft by the Kitchener Rangers out of the Guelph Jr. Gryphons Minor Midget program. Bunnaman made the team as a 16 year old and did an excellent job playing a bottom six role with the team and developed well last season. This year he didn't show the same progress as his first season but with most forwards returning he played a similar role this year.

Bunnaman has great size and although he doesn't possess much of a mean streak, he is a tenacious forechecker and will finish the hits required of him. He does a good job getting into passing lanes and taking away time and space. Positionally sound two-way forward. Bunnaman has an awkward skating stride but gets ok speed after his first few steps. He protects the puck well down low and is effective at cycling the puck. His positional awareness is very good. Bunnaman has a good shot but his overall offensive ability is average at best. Defensively Bunnaman plays his biggest impact. He gets down and blocks shots he takes away options and breaks up chances.

Connor has upside as a very solid two-way player at the NHL level. He does all the things right to be a role player but lacks the skill to be a big impact player. The team that selects Bunnaman at the 2016 NHL Entry Draft is getting a player who will be excellent on the cycle, take away passing lanes and can play an effective penalty killing role.

Quotable: "Not much feedback on his interviews with the exception of one scout who made a point of saying how good his interview was." - HP Scout Mark Edwards

Burgess, Todd
RC/RW – Fairbanks Ice Dogs (NAHL) 6'02", 178
HockeyProspect.com Ranking: 94

Todd Burgess is a third time draft eligible who has spent the last three seasons playing for Fairbanks in NAHL. He is a playmaking center with a decent frame-size that probably still has room for a couple of additional pounds. He has good vision with the puck, plays a physically engaging game and is a smart player.

Burgess is a player that uses his frame well to gain beneficial body position against defensemen and make plays off it. He wins his 50-50 battles, gains body position against defensemen and can either look to cut inside or make a pass back to the point and then head to the net. Burgess is good at planting himself in the low-slot area or in front of the net and opening up his blade looking for a pass or a rebound. He is quite adept at fending off defensemen in those situations. He's a decent stickhandler and can handle the puck on his forehand or backhand while getting good reach out of it but his puck-skills from a purely technical standpoint don't necessarily project as better than average at the NHL level. He does have good vision with the puck though and utilizes it accordingly as a playmaker. Burgess competes well without the puck and likes to finish his checks on the forecheck. He also has a good stick and manages to get it on pucks. This gives him some ability to cause turnovers. As he moves forward, Burgess could make some improvements to his skating and also improve his defensive zone play. His defensive gaps and awareness in his own-end aren't perfect and his coverage there could be better.

Quotable: "*I've had my eyes as open to 2nd and 3rd times eligibles this year as any year previously. He stood out when I saw him along with the Dman Clarke in Texas. They are North American Hockey League guys but I though they showed themselves well when they got the chance.*" *- HP Scout Mark Edwards*

Burghardt, Luke
RC - Guelph Storm (OHL) 5'11" 170
HockeyProspect.com Ranking: NR

After being selected in the 6th round of the 2014 OHL Priority Selection Draft from the Clarington Toros Minor Midget program, he surprised many by making the Storm out of camp. This season he elevated his game to another level, gaining plenty of time on the top two forward lines.

Luke is a hard working forward with a ton of energy. He has a consistent work ethic and his compete level is among the best you'll find across the OHL. He gets his stick in passing lanes and can break up plays. His skating is above average and he uses it in both directions. Burghardt contributed in all game situations. He has good patience with the puck and can create offense. He also has some decent moves and an effective shot which lead to 17 goals on the season. Defensively he back checks hard and pressures the puck carrier negating offensive chances.

Luke is a tough one to project at the next level. We love his work ethic and should turn out to be a very solid two-way, top six junior player, especially for a sixth round pick. But as an NHL prospect he lacks the size or the offensive upside preferred. In the end, his off the chart compete and flashes of puck skills may be enough to hear his name called late.

Burke, Brayden
LW/LC – Lethbridge Hurricanes (WHL) 5'10", 160
HockeyProspect.com Ranking: 171

Burke is a smallish offensive-minded forward who is most dangerous on the powerplay thanks to high hockey IQ, quick scoring instincts, and an ability to place the puck below the dots. Thanks in part to his diminutive stature, Burke is quick-footed and slippery around the net. To call Burke a playmaker would be an understatement. He's so first-pass by mentality that there are games where it seems like he hardly even considers to shoot.

Another speciality is Burke's zone entry ability. Strong crossover technique gives him advanced east-to-west quickness and allows Burke to put opposition defensemen off balance. Burke manufactures a lot of zone entries with his quickness and is known for distributing the puck quickly and smartly. He's especially dangerous on the powerplay.

Burke is a second time-eligible who put up fantastic point totals this season. The skills that stand out for him are his ability to set up players in the offensive zone and passing ability in general, strong vision with the puck and a good skill level. Ultimately, Burke will have to answer how much of his game and production is translatable to the pro level. Undersized and not particularly the strongest defensive player, Burke's situation means that he will almost certainly have to play on a scoring line if he wants to make the NHL.

Byrne, Mitchell
LD - Erie Otters (OHL) 6'00" 192
HockeyProspect.com Ranking: NR

Mitchell Byrne was selected in the fifth round of the 2014 OHL Priority Selection Draft, by the Erie Otters out of the Toronto Jr. Canadiens Minor Midget program. Byrne spent last season with the Brampton Jr. B Bombers, playing a top six role. He then made the Erie Otters out of camp and played his first full junior season in the OHL this year.

Byrne has a decent frame and is a smooth skating defenseman. He is capable of skating the puck out of trouble and taking it up ice. However at the OHL level he's playing it a little safer getting the line and putting the puck deep the majority of the time. Defensively he had a little trial by fire but has played primarily on the third pairing and has been able to improve without being consistently tested against the best the league has to offer as this area of his game develops. He usually makes good passes but can serve up dangerous puck mistakes on occasion. Mitchell has some upside but has not realized his potential yet at the junior level. He has decent size, good skating ability but hasn't performed to the level we expect of a defenseman to be selected at the 2016 NHL Entry Draft. If he continues to improve he may make himself an opportunity down the road.

Caamano, Nicholas
LW - Flint Firebirds (OHL) 6'00.5" 188
HockeyProspect.com Ranking: 122

Caamano was the second round selection for the Plymouth Whalers out of the Hamilton Jr. Bulldogs program in 2014. He made the Whalers out of camp as a 16 year old and showed some real upside in his rookie season. His first season in Flint got off a little slow at first, but he recovered and posted a very respectable second OHL season hitting the 20 goal mark.

Caamano is a competitive and positionally sound forward for the Flint Firebirds. Nicholas reads the play and positions himself well in both the offensive and defensive zones. This allows him to get open for a quick shot in the offensive zone and react quickly to developing plays in the defensive zone. With this said, we could handle him being a little more aggressive while on the penalty kill. He has a bit of an awkward stride, but moves well laterally and can develop speed deceptively. He has a good, powerful shot with pretty good accuracy, but his playmaking ability in regards to setting up teammates with passes is below average.

Caamano is a good two-way player. He is capable of putting up good offensive numbers at the junior level. His positional game and his shot should help him increase his goal totals consistently through juniors and with a few adjustments could also become an effective penalty killer. However, Caamano isn't a player we expect to come off the board early, if at all at the 2016 NHL Entry Draft.

Quotable: "I had hope after a few shifts but he lost me pretty quickly after that." - NHL Scout (October 2015)

Quotable: "I thought he might have something but the more I watched the less I saw him as an NHL prospect. Too often I found that he seemed to be in too much of a rush to get rid of the puck. I didn't see puck confidence. I can't see his game translating well to the NHL." - Mark Edwards

Cairns, Matthew
LD - Georgetown Raiders (OJHL) 6'02" 202
HockeyProspect.com Ranking: 77

Cairns has experienced a lot of winning over the past few years. After winning the 2014 OHL Cup with the Toronto Marlboros Minor Midget program, Matthew joined the Toronto Jr. A Lakeshore Patriots where he won the OJHL Championship and competed for the Dudley Hewitt Cup. Cairns moved on to the Georgetown Raiders this season where his team made it to the OJHL Finals.

Matthew is a big defenseman with a good frame. His skating has experienced some improvements but his first few steps are still a little choppy. Simple has been the key for Cairns. He does a good job playing his man one on one letting the play come to him and attacking at the right time. He moves the puck well when he has time, choosing high percentage options instead of trying to make the big play. He has had some struggles when he doesn't have time and space. He will jump up in the rush and did a good job on the power play with more open ice to occasionally carry the puck. He moves the puck well in the offensive zone and has a decent shot. Defensively, he plays with an edge without having a huge mean streak he can land some solid open ice hits.

Cairns is a big bodied two-way defender that will probably lean more towards the defensive side of the game when he gets to the professional level. He plays a good game at both ends of the ice, albeit without having to face the high end scorers that he would have faced at the OHL level. Cairns has some options for next season. He was drafted by the Peterborough Petes in the third round of the 2014 OHL Priority Selection Draft. He was also selected in the 11th round of the 2015 USHL Entry Draft. Matthew is committed to Cornell University for the 2017-2018 season.

Quotable: " I watched him quite a bit last season and he played for my buddy. He had some good games. His best game I saw this year was in January at the Top Prospects game in Surrey. The only thing about that game is that it was on the big ice and in my opinion Cairns biggest weakness is mistakes when he's under pressure. On the big ice out west he had more time." - HP Scout Mark Edwards

Quotable: " We did interviewed Cairns from the Qj, he was just ok...he's going to play in the USHL next season." - NHL Scout (Combine week)

Campoli, Michael
LD – USNTDP 6'02", 195
HockeyProspect.com Ranking: 184

Campoli is a sturdy defenseman who takes care of his own end. Campoli is best described as a stay-at-home defenseman as he is solid at breaking up plays and protecting the middle of ice but does not exhibit much offensive upside. Campoli plays a reliable game and tries to minimize his mistakes with the puck. He makes a decent first pass but that's about where his strengths with the puck end. Campoli keeps good gaps in his own end and pushes the play to the outside. There he can seal players off and remove them from the puck. Campoli is the type of defenseman who might not be very noticeable but can be a solid defensive presence without looking flashy. The offense might never come, but he could be a useful PK player.

Candella, Cole
LD - Hamilton Bulldogs (OHL) 6'01" 189
HockeyProspect.com Ranking: 141

Candella was selected by the Belleville Bulls in the 2nd round of the 2014 OHL Priority Selection Draft out of the Vaughan Kings program. He made the jump as a 16 year old and endured some growing pains. He put up solid numbers this season, but every time he got a little momentum, injury struck.

Candella has decent size on the back end for an offensive minded defender. He displayed a good first pass, but when moving the puck in other situations he can sometimes overthink the play which would result in misplays with the puck. He has a good shot from the point and is very effective putting it on goal. This resulted not only in some goals for Candella, but also helped him rack up some assists on rebounds. He has a good size/skating combination and carries the puck up ice effectively. He can exploit skating lanes and use them effectively. He knows when to pass off, but the accuracy is sometimes hit or miss. In transition he can get ahead of the play leaving his defensive partner on an island and needs to make himself available until the puck starts advancing, unless he is the one carrying it. He struggled in one on one situations. He is a good skater but sometimes when defending he can stop moving his feet and this has gotten him in trouble on multiple occasions.

Candella's injury shortened season will be a bit of a concern. He did show a good boost in offensive productivity, showing that offensive potential he has and what he might develop into. However he has a lot of room to improve. His skating, size and shot are all very positive tools to build on but he doesn't appear to read the game that well at times, which is a tough concern to overcome.

Carcone, Michael
LW – Drummondville Voltigeurs (QMJHL) – 5'10", 170
HockeyProspect.com Ranking: NR

Carcone was a breakthrough player in the QMJHL this season, jumping from 12 to 47 goals. The 19 year old had a stellar season with the Voltigeurs, finishing 2nd in the league in goals and 8th in points. The Whitby, Ontario native was in his 2nd season with the Voltigeurs. With Alex Barré-Boulet, he formed one of the top duos in the league. Carcone is a good skater with a good burst of speed and great agility, making him tough to contain for opposing defenders with his ability to make quick turns to avoid opponents. He's a shooter first and has a good wrist shot that is very accurate, and he knows how to pick his corners. There's a good, quick release on his shot and he can score from different locations in the offensive zone. On the power play, he can score in front or at the side of the net, even from the half-wall. His vision is underrated, as you always think goal scorer with Carcone but he sees the ice well enough to make quick decisions with the puck. He has good puck skills and is good in one-on-one confrontations; his quick agile hands handle the puck well. He's not big and his size could be a problem at the next level, as he will need to add some strength. He struggled at the end of the season and lost his goal scoring title following a scoring drought in the last stretch of the year. He's a bit of one-dimensional player, as he will need to score at the next level to achieve success. He could potentially play pro hockey next season, depending what happens with him at the draft, or he could sign as a free agent. But more than likely he should be back in Drummondville for his overage season.

Carlsson, Lucas
LD – Brynas (SHL) – 6'00", 189
HockeyProspect.com Ranking: 74

Contrary to our expectations Lucas was passed over at last year's NHL Draft, but it's hard to see him going un-drafted again this time around after the season he completed. He played almost 40 games for Brynas at the SHL level, was able to bring his all around game contributing in every area and finished strong in the playoffs. Carlsson is a great competitor and already showed his strong personality playing against men as an 18yrs old defenseman, consistently trying to make a difference on the ice.

He has grown considerably since one year ago, his decision making has improved and he looks bigger than what he is currently listed at. He likes to engage along the boards and use his body to win possession, he shows good strength in battles already and is very strong on his legs for his age. Has nice instincts and can recognize if there is an opening when pressured, he is able to transition the puck and actively helps his team doing so. Carlsson saw time on both special teams and is a threat on the powerplay, he loves to shoot and possesses a heavy slapshot as well as a legit wrister. Stickhandling is a strength and allows him to make plays while he moves forward, he likes to join the rush and is surprisingly good for a defenseman when he has a chance to get close to the net.

Lucas has clearly improved his overall mobility, has good power, but could still become quicker. His backwards skating is not an issue, but he needs to keep his feet going when opponents have the puck not to get caught flat-footed. Carlsson doesn't play a mistake free game but is someone who has the potential to impact the games in different ways from the back-end.

Quotable: "There have been games this season where he has looked really good and I'd guess more than one NHL team will be on him this time around." - HP Scout Mik Portoni

Carlsson, Lukas
LD – Sodertalje J20 (SWE) – 6'02", 200
HockeyProspect.com Ranking: NR

Lukas Carlsson is an interesting package as a defenseman. He is a defensive defenseman but one with quite good puck-instincts. While there is not a lot there currently in his offensive zone game, Carlsson is actually a surprisingly solid transitional player. He makes very heady outlets and isn't shy about holding onto the puck an extra second longer. He can also rather atypically for a defensive defenseman excel in re-groups and organize neutral zone puck-movement. Defensively, Carlsson keeps a good gap and body position, he will engage physically when he has a chance but he defends mostly through his positioning rather than a physical component. His body position is intelligent and tends to push opposing forwards out of high-scoring areas. He has good defensive anticipation. The downside to Carlsson's game currently is the fact that he's a bit slow on his feet. He can be flustered by up-tempo fast physical forwards as it can be challenging for him to keep up. While he is not soft, he is also not a particularly physical player in front of his net, something that would help a player of his ilk to project better at the next level.

Carroll, Noah
LD - Guelph Storm (OHL) 6'01" 178
HockeyProspect.com Ranking: 123

After being selected in the fourth round of the 2013 OHL Priority Selection Draft out of the Elgin-Middlesex Chiefs program, Noah played for the Jr. B Guelph Hurricanes in his first season before joining the Guelph Storm over the last two years.

Noah came into the season with high expectations from our staff. However he struggled to find his stride on the last place Storm this season long. Constantly we'd see some great decisions followed by some questionable ones. Some great defensive plays to shut down the opposition, then getting walked for a scoring chance or a goal. As a puck rusher, he doesn't have explosive speed, but he does choose smart lanes to carry up ice. He has a good wrist shot from the point. He commonly gets it on net, but will sometimes fire into blockers instead of passing off or putting it deep. He has made some passes that show he has impressive vision. But will make some risky plays, commonly when facing a lot of pressure. For Carroll it comes down to taking a look and not rushing his decisions, because when he does he has been more successful. Defensively he has a good stick and showed a moderate amount of physicality. With that said, he lacks strength, which showed down low in the defensive zone.

Noah has some upside and it wouldn't be a shock to see him break out of his slump and have a breakout season next year. The potential is there. However too many mental errors and misplays at both end of the ice will likely drop his draft stock, possibly right out of the 2016 NHL Entry Draft.

Carter, Cole
RW - Windsor Spitfires (OHL) 5'08" 156
HockeyProspect.com Ranking: NR

After being passed over at the 2014 OHL Priority Selection Draft, Cole was selected in the fourth round of the 2015 OHL Priority Selection Draft by the Windsor Spitfires out of the Stittsville Jr. B Rams of the EOJHL.

Carter had a successful rookie season posting one point for every two games playing on the second or third line regularly. Cole has good speed and agility to beat defenders but doesn't have that separation gear that you like to see out of small skilled forwards. He's a pass first player with good creativity and likes to set up his linemates. He has above average passing ability and below average shooting ability, and rarely puts the puck on net. Cole struggled down low in puck battles showing a lack of strength and will need to get stronger to be more effective in battles, increasing his ability to create more chances. Carter projects to be a solid junior player who can play top six lines plus power play and help contribute offense. However, he doesn't project as an NHL talent at this point and isn't expected to be selected at the 2016 NHL Entry Draft.

Cederholm, Jacob
RD – HV71 (SWE Jr.) – 6'03.5", 187
HockeyProspect.com Ranking: 92

Jacob is a defensive defenseman with a pretty impressive frame. Has been a leader of his age group with the national team for a while and is the kind of player that immediately catches the new viewer's attention. He is a sound skater and his overall mobility paired with his size is the foundation of his game. Has a long reach and takes full advantage of it making good use of his stick defensively. Is a strong skater backwards and putting those elements together you get a defenseman that is hard to beat one on one and off the rush. He is a steady competitor in his zone and can be a physical presence here and there, but mostly uses his body to prevent opponents to get on rebounds and inside tracks to the net. He should further improve in battles in front or along the boards as he fills out his frame. He makes good reads defensively and is fairly reliable in his zone.

The limitations in Cederholm's game arise when he has the puck on his stick. His breakout passes can be rough at times and he doesn't have an offensive dimension to his game. He should be able to improve his shot in the future, but his hands are average and he struggles to make plays as he moves towards the other side of the rink as soon as he's taken away space. To his credit, he consistently does a good job at keeping things simple, can protect the puck to move it out of danger and is able to limit turnovers.

After making his pro debut in the previous season already, this year Cederholm appeared in 9 SHL games early on, but things were still happening a bit too fast for him and he spent the rest of the season at the junior level. He should be more of a steady presence with HV71 senior team next year, as it is probably time for him to face regularly more challenging opponents.

Quotable: "He has three things: the long stick, the mobility, and the size. Competitive enough, but I wish he had more snarl. I think his puck-movement is good enough for a coach not to panic, but he has no real offensive upside to speak of" - HP Scout Nik Funa

Chernyuk, Konstantin
LD - Kingston Frontenacs (OHL) 6'05" 181
HockeyProspect.com Ranking: NR

Chernyuk was selected 27th overall at the 2015 CHL Import Draft by the Kingston Frontenacs out of the Wichita Falls Wildcats of the NAHL. Chernyuk had a tale of two seasons, the first half saw the development of his intriguing upside as an NHL prospect. However by late January the Frontenacs had several veteran defensemen and their 16 year old defenseman was playing above and beyond expectations which saw Chernyuk spend most of the second half in the stands.

A big bodied defender with strong physical attributes, at 6'05" Chernyuk plays aggressive along the walls but lacks the physical strength and the technique to be as successful in these situations as he otherwise could. Reacts quickly from the slot to get down low when necessary. In one on one situations Chernyuk relied on his large wingspan and active stick to defend. His skating helps him stick with his opponents. He struggled with long distance passes and generally moving the puck two lines or more but consistently showed effectiveness with shorter passes and D to D passes. Got his shots through most of the time.

Chernyuk is a very interesting prospect. He has great size and good skating. His lack of games played on a stacked Kingston blueline should hurt his draft stock. Regardless, he is a player who may very well earn a selection late as he is a true sleeper pick for this draft class and may pay off if he is able to reach his full potential.

Quotable: "Our Scout Ryan Yessie saw him early and had time for him. It became a struggle to see him later on in the season when I started seeing Kingston more often." - HP Scout Mark Edwards

Cholowski, Dennis
LD – Chilliwack Chiefs (BCHL) 6'00", 170
HockeyProspect.com Ranking: 26

Dennis Cholowski possesses almost all the qualities you look for in a defensive prospect, including size, skating ability, skill with the puck and high end hockey IQ. He's very mobile in all directions and can make you pay on the breakout with either his passing game or his skating skills. Fairly good at defending in his own end and moving pucks out with control, this is a player with a lot of raw skill and no glaring weaknesses.

Cholowski received assignments in all situations this season, looking particularly talented and dangerous when patrolling the point on the powerplay. A really good passer, he shows a penchant for sliding the puck into the prime scoring area when least expected. His shot isn't bad either, but doesn't really stand out as a big strength of his. He has the intelligence to make smart reads and pinches that hem the opposition in their own end and can be an offensive factor when he plays an active game.

On the defensive side of the puck, good upper-body reflexes and a wide reach allows him to close gaps quickly and to excel with the pokecheck when defending on his own blueline. He's got good mobility and an active defensive stick which is a real factor in preventing forwards from cutting towards the middle and defending against speed. He can throw his body around a bit too if necessary, but could definitely be meaner on a more consistent basis. He defends better with his stick and positioning, filling out his frame, adding strength and using his body more to engage deeper in his own end is something that he has to improve on. Cholowski is committed to St. Cloud State University.

Quotable: "I liked him at the Junior A Challenge but my trip out west in January was when he sealed the deal for me as first round talent. Great skill, and I love his puck moving ability. I think he's a smart player. He reads the game, has great vision and anticipates well defensively. His physical game could be better. I think that he's one of the best puck movers in his draft class. The only slight drawbacks for me are that he needs to get stronger and he had the odd shift where I didn't think he worked hard enough." - HP Scout Mark Edwards

Quotable: "I spoke to him with a media guy for quite a while. Nice kid who gave a good interview. He interviewed with every team except Pittsburgh and I got zero bad *reviews. A few teams made a point of saying they really liked him. This kid was 5'6" 120 pounds in his WHL Bantam Draft year. Shockingly he went un-drafted.- Hp Scout Mark Edwards (Combine week)*

Chuard, Leo
G – Geneve-Servette Jr. (SUI Jr.) – 6'01", 187
HockeyProspect.com Ranking: NR

Chuard is a very technically sound goaltender. Gets square and over the puck consistently. He is very mature in his movement, meaning he has good body awareness and control of himself. He has strong legs and a strong core which allows him to have patience in his legs, doesn't drop too early. He tracks pucks into his glove well and doesn't cough up rebounds. Good technique on his post, knows when he should be in his reverse VH and is very quick off is post, sealing up the ice very well. He challenges, holds the top of his crease and is calm under fire. One serious concern is his puck playing. It's not that he doesn't come out of the net, he does and he comes out at proper times, but he mishandles and turns the puck over.

Chuard has below average size by nowadays NHL goaltenders' standards and had weak numbers in limited international exposure this season, so it's unlikely he'll be selected in June. He will need to prove in the future he can remain effective when playing at a higher level too and against better shooters than the ones he usually faced in Swiss juniors, but overall he is an intriguing prospect with a solid foundation who is only eligible for the upcoming draft by five days.

Chychrun, Jakob
LD - Sarnia Sting (OHL) 6'02.25" 208
HockeyProspect.com Ranking: 14

Jakob was selected first overall at the 2014 OHL Priority Selection Draft by the Sarnia Sting out of the Toronto Jr. Canadiens program. Right from his first OHL game, Chychrun has been a big minute defender for the Sarnia Sting. After an outstanding Minor Midget season, Chychrun had a great rookie season in the OHL and was Sarnia's top power play defender from the trade deadline on.

Through no fault of his own, Chychrun entered this season with some high expectations, as he was already a top defender as a rookie. He remained one of the top offensive defensemen in the league, but was often trying to do too much, which in our opinion got him into trouble. Chychrun likes to carry the puck up ice but sometimes needs to read his routes a little better. His outlet passes are accurate and skilled most of the time. On the power play he is able to move the puck but can make some poor decisions as well. He likes to shoot the puck and has a very powerful slap shot and a smart wrist shot. He will sometimes fake out the penalty killer and walk in and unload his wrist shot that commonly hit the net. Defensively Jakob needs to improve. He has the size but looks a little apprehensive at times, one of our scouts speculated early on that it could be due to the numerous shoulder injuries incurred over the past few seasons. He is hit or miss one on one. He's made some solid, smart plays showing the ability to shut down defenders but can be sometimes slow to react against some bigger skilled forwards and can get beat.

Jakob has excellent upside as a potential top pairing defenseman, but still has some room to improve. This has been his first injury free season in three years, which is promising for teams who may be concerned about his shoulder. He looks like he will need a little extra seasoning to further build his strength and improve his defensive ability. He is expected to be one of the first few defenders taken off the board at the 2016 NHL Entry Draft.

Quotable: "What's wrong with Chychrun this year?" - NHL Scout (November 2015)

Quotable: "I've changed how I'm looking at him now. I'm not even looking at him as an offensive guy anymore. I'm just evaluating the other facets of his game because I don't think he projects as a PP guy in the NHL." - NHL Scout (January 2016)

Quotable: "I've got him 12th now." - NHL Scout (March 2016)

Quotable: "There are probably a few guys that have him as their top D." - NHL Scout (January 2016)

Quotable: "I think he's Zach Bogosian." Three different NHL Scouts

Quotable: "He's dropped behind McLeod on my list." - NHL Scout (March 2015)

Quotable: "I thought he had good shifts today but got himself into trouble when he tried to do too much. Don't drop him too far though...he can still play." - NHL Scout (At the U18 in Grand Forks)

Quotable: "Great kid, I liked him a lot. Love the size and tools but he lacks pace to his game and skates himself into trouble a lot." - NHL Scout

Quotable: "I hate dropping players we had previously ranked higher. For me there was an initial drop based on his play, but it was combined with players passing him as well. In the end, Chychrun has great tools but I just think there are a few Dmen in this draft who think the game a bit better than he does." - Mark Edwards

Quotable: "Chychrun had a great interview, it stood out for me." - NHL Scout (Combine week)

Quotable: "I'd rate Chychrun's as one of our best interviews this week." - NHL Scout (Combine week)

Quotable: "I liked Chychrun's interview a lot. He was very honest and it made for a good back and forth." - NHL Scout (combine week)

Quotable: "Chychrun was really good, he was way too hard on himself about his season though. I finally had to stop him." - NHL Scout (combine week)

Clague, Kale
LD – Brandon Wheat Kings (WHL) 6'00, 177
HockeyProspect.com Ranking: 45

Clague's main and most obvious asset is his top-end, elite skating skill set. He has unbelievable acceleration and quickness which allows him to separate himself from his check or lead the rush. His quick feet and elite speed allows him to be a solid defender as well as a threat offensively. He is very good at exiting his own end as his speed and agility allows him the time and space to make plays. Clague can change directions on a dime, he is very tough to contain and is very good at escaping the fore checkers with elusive moves that come very natural to him.

Along with Clague's skating ability and speed is his vision and puck skills. He is a heads up hockey player who is constantly reading and analyzing the play and what his available options are. He is very good at controlling the puck at high speeds. He is a great passer and is very good at moving with the puck to open passing and shooting lanes. His ability to walk the line and attack the seams as a offensive threat stands out as a big plus. He does a great job of making quick decisions at a high pace and limits high risk decisions that can lead to chances against. He is a solid defender who will engage in battles along the wall and in the corners. We would like to see him continue to work on his strength and put on some weight so that he would be much more effective in these situations.

There is no denying that Clague is one of the better offensive puck moving defensemen in this year's draft. He was injured much of last season which limited his point production, and his statline over the course of this year is also not all that impressive as he scored 43 points in 71 games. In many respects, it was a tale of two half-seasons for Clague. Clague's first half was rather underwhelming. While his upside was evident, we felt he was at times too content to get lost among a deep Brandon team and settle for being just one of the guys instead of working to establish authority on the ice. Ultimately, Clague came back with a strong second half and continued his strong work in the playoffs and finished the season on a high note.

Quotable: " A tale of two seasons for him. He was a big faller in our rankings in the first half of the season but recovered a bit with a better finish." - HP Scout Mark Edwards

Clarke, Cameron
RD – Lone Star Brahmas (NAHL) 6'01", 170
HockeyProspect.com Ranking: 157

Cameron Clarke is a 1996 born and thus a third time NHL draft eligible. Moving on from Sarnia Legionnaires of GOJHL, Clarke has spent the 2015-2016 season playing for Lone Star in NAHL where he has produced 51 points in 63 games. Clarke has decent size. Although he has some filling out to do, he has good reach and uses his stick intelligently. Possessing above-average mobility in all 4 directions, Clarke does a good job maintaining his gaps and exhibits high amount of control over the space on the ice with his reach. He is good at keeping inside body position and steering the forwards to the perimeter. He uses that especially well while skating in reverse and defending in transition. While not small, Clarke could engage physically at a more consistent level and he isn't a big physical presence on the ice.

Clarke is an intelligent puck-mover that plays with no panic in his game and does a good job finding solutions. He can start the break-out and also has good skating ability, making him a strong player in transition. Although we have seen him use his shot from the point, he is more of a puck-distributor than a big threat with his shot. The fact that Clarke is already 20 years old playing in what is not the strongest league does raise some questions, but we can't ignore the fact that Clarke does possess legitimate upside as a smart, mobile blueliner that has some room to fill out.

Clurman, Nathan
RD – Culver Academy (IN-PREP) 6'02", 190
HockeyProspect.com Ranking: NR

Nathan shows good anticipation in his defensive zone, especially on the Penalty Kill and is really good in transitioning from defense to offense. He isn't shy about jumping into the play if he feels it will give his team numbers but is smart in picking his spots. His straight line forward and backwards skating is very good and shows decent agility and edgework in the tight areas as well. Nathan comes out of his own end with his head up and makes solid outlet passes. Clurman doesn't do anything at an elite level but has a pretty steady all around game. The Notre Dame Commit looks to be off to the USHL next season where Tri City currently holds his rights.

Quotable: "He's got NHL tools. He's 6'2" and a great skater but he doesn't seem to want the puck enough." - NHL Scout (March 2016)

Coghlan, Dylan
RD – Tri-City Americans (WHL) 6'02", 190
HockeyProspect.com Ranking: 110

Coghlan is a mobile blueliner with an emerging two-way game. Coghlan has spent his second season with Tri-City and although his production doesn't quite stand out, there has been some progress made on the offensive side of the puck. Coghlan possesses an elongated fluid stride, which is quite appealing at his frame-size. The size and mobility allows him to recover well, on dump-ins he can beat his man to the puck and with his size he doesn't mind taking a hit to move the puck forward. Also uses the combination of skating and size well to pinch in the offensive zone and keep possession for his team. He can skate the puck out of his zone and while he doesn't regularly do it yet, he is good at observing the play and using his reach and forward speed to skate around the first forechecker before dishing the puck, if he can't find a passing option.

Coghlan has been used on both PP and PK. He has shown improvement in his ability to be involved offensively and get shots on the net. Defensively, he uses his skating well but will need to improve his play in the defensive zone. He could be more physical at his size and needs to do a better job of keeping forwards to the outside. His angles will need some work, as he tends to lose inside body position against forwards and can be also prone to letting a forward sneak behind him by losing sight of him. Coghlan had a year where he showed offensive improvement and the ability to take on a bigger role. With continued development he might start looking like a solid two-way defenseman.

Coleman, Luke
LW – Prince Albert Raiders (WHL) 6'02", 193
HockeyProspect.com Ranking: NR

Coleman is a power-winger. He's a very average skater though once he gets going he can develop decent top speed. He has played with the Prince Albert Raiders in a depth role and was still able to put up some decent points with limited ice-time.

Coleman is only an average skater especially in terms of agility. However, he does tend to work hard at getting his frame around the ice. Coleman can be a frustrating player, as he needs to learn how to follow up on his plays in the offensive zone. Often he will make a good initial play, especially if he got to the puck with speed and has a shooting lane open, but his efforts there tend to be one and done as he doesn't follow up on the play. He has the frame to be an engaging player and get loose pucks back, but that part of it has not yet developed. He is also a rather obvious player to defend against and can be pushed to the outside with the puck as he lacks creativity to make things happen.

Overall, Coleman has some interesting physical tools but is very raw at this point in time. His decision-making with the puck can be inconsistent and he can get into a sequence where he makes a series of mistakes. He has shown the ability to score and doesn't mind using his body. He will go to the scoring areas, work to protect the puck on the wall, but needs to follow it up better with a second effort if the first one doesn't accomplish its purpose. That has a good chance at coming together with maturity as he does exhibit a decent work-ethic in other aspects of the game like backchecking, getting his body in front of the net, and taking hits to make plays. With a good developmental year and a bigger role, his physical tools should allow him to take another step forward next year.

Colton, Ross
LW – Cedar Rapids RoughRiders (USHL) 6'00", 190
HockeyProspect.com Ranking: 161

Ross is a 96' Birthday and quickly got put on a lot of scout's radar due to his excellent play in the USHL Top Prospects game this past year (3G 2A). While we don't believe that any one game should tell the tale of a player, Ross's complete body of work in Cedar Rapids this year, as well as his steady progression in his development make him an interesting overage pick for this year's draft.

Ross was Cedar Rapids most prolific scorer all season long, ending the season 14 pts ahead of the next closest player, despite playing 5 less games. The Robbinsville N.J. native scored 35 goals in 55 games for the Rough Riders which was good for 2nd in the USHL. Ross is a smart and gifted offensive player, he continues to look for ways to improve and better his game. Ross is one of those players that doesn't need a lot of separation to score and is good at identifying holes and finding a way to get open for the puck. His hockey IQ in the offensive zone is off the Charts. Colton still needs to round out the rest of his game; his effort coming back into the play can be lacking and misses opportunities to apply back pressure and force turnovers. Colton is also susceptive to taking bad penalties, some out of frustration. There is no questioning Ross's offensive instincts and skill. There is a decent chance Ross Colton will hear his name called in this year's draft but we feel Ross is a prospect we would want to see how he progresses at the college level before making a decision on him, Colton will be off to The University of Vermont in the fall.

Quotable: "He's really smart, he's competitive, he's skilled and has a great shot. I think someone will draft him." - USHL Scout (April 2016)

Commisso, Domenic
RC - Oshawa Generals (OHL) 5'11" 178
HockeyProspect.com Ranking: 99

Commisso was selected in the 5th round of the 2014 OHL Priority Selection Draft by the Oshawa Generals out of the Don Mills Flyers Minor Midget program. After spending his 16 year old season with the Mississauga Jr. A Chargers of the OJHL, Commisso made the jump to the OHL this season. He played a big two-way role for a Generals team that saw a ton of turnover in all positions.

Commisso is a speedy, offensive two-way centre who has continually improved and impressed throughout the 2015-2016 season. Commisso's most noticeable attribute is his overwhelming speed. He plays with excellent pace, possesses strong edges along with an explosive first step and excellent straight line speed. He uses his edges to the utmost effectiveness as he displays strong change of pace and direction abilities along with the ability to spin and drive off of opponents in tight spaces. Extremely shifty and elusive in possession, Domenic's puck skills are impressive, displaying quick hands and strong puck control, the shifty centre shows an abundance of offensive creativity while remaining responsible with the puck, limiting his turnovers. Offensively speaking Commisso's shot and puck protection skills improved throughout the season as he continued to add strength to a slender frame. He is more of a playmaker than a scorer displaying strong vision and an ability to create chances for his linemates. Boasting an excellent compete level and willingness to engage physically, Commisso shows a tenaciousness in puck pursuit forcing turnovers consistently with his aggressive forecheck. He competes hard in all three zones. Under sustained pressure he looks like a third defenseman competing down low in the defensive zone.

Commisso had a very successful rookie season in the OHL. He has good offensive tools, he has the hands to deke the goaltender but also has the vision and passing to set up chances. His numbers should only improve this season. His defensive game is a huge part of what should help him get selected at the 2016 NHL Entry Draft. He competes incredibly hard in all three zones which should help him overcome his size, especially as he adds muscle to his frame.

Quotable: "I was really impressed with Commisso as a two-way player this year. Great vision and playmaking ability but a good defensive forward as well. I think when you look at the middle rounds he's a solid option" - HP Scout Ryan Yessie

Cormier, Evan
G - Saginaw Spirit (OHL) 6'02.75" 202
HockeyProspect.com Ranking: 107

Evan was selected in the 5th round of the 2013 OHL Priority Selection Draft by the North Bay Battalion. After spending a full year with the North Bay Trappers of the NOJHL, Cormier played his first full season starting out with the Battalion before being dealt to Saginaw for Nick Moutrey.

Cormier logged a ton of minutes this year, appearing in all but 10 games for the Saginaw Spirit this season. Evan displayed wild inconsistencies in his game, something we saw last season as well. He has excellent size and does a good job of aggressively taking away the shooting angles. He has quick reflexes and a good glove. With his size, he handles traffic well in the slot. When he's on his game, he does all of these things well proving to be one of the more difficult junior goaltenders to beat. However when he's off his game he fights the puck a lot and will let in some soft goals here and there. His vision and reaction time seems to vary widely on a game by game basis. He handles deflections, direction changes and one-timers fairly well when he's locked in.

Cormier is a goaltender who will only last so long due to his upside. If he can generate more consistency on a night by night basis, he has the upside to be one of the best goaltenders in this draft class. But the consistency is really his biggest concern. If taken in the right spot, Cormier provides low risk, with good upside.

Quotable: "Cormier reminds me of a lower end Mackenzie Blackwood. Good size, but you never know what you're gonna get on a night by night basis. He can steal games, but when he's off, he fights the puck all night long." - HP Scout Ryan Yessie

Quotable: "My top ranked goalie in the draft." NHL Scout (October 2015)

Quotable: "I don't think he did one bench press." - NHL Scout (Combine week)

Corneil, Johnny
RC - Niagara Ice Dogs (OHL) 5'10" 190
HockeyProspect.com Ranking: NR

Corneil is an NHL Draft re-entry player who was selected by the Niagara Ice Dogs in the 4th round of the 2013 OHL Priority Selection Draft out of the Central Ontario Wolves Minor Midget Program. Corneil surprised by making the OHL as a 16 year old and has spent all three seasons with the Ice Dogs. Despite never going above a third line role with the team on a regular basis, Johnny had 20 goals this season and was one of the most underrated players in the OHL this season.

Corneil plays with a ton of energy and speed. He pressures opponents hard and forces a ton of turnovers. He loves to hit and consistently finishes his checks whenever possible. No matter where he is on the ice he's battling for space and is surprisingly strong for a player his size. He works hard in all three zones and has good defensive awareness. He will block shots and quickly takes away passing and shooting lanes. Offensively he has taken his game up a notch. He has a powerful shot and gets into good scoring areas. He has the speed and the hands to beat defenders one on one and can get his shot off deceptively quick which has fooled some goaltenders.

Although he would be a late round pick or a free agent invite, this might be a buy low type of situation for a team looking at Corneil. With the massive player turnover expected by Niagara, Corneil is a top candidate to be one of their key offensive players next season. Being able to produce as much as he did in a third line role, Corneil is primed for a breakout season next year. If he continues to improve his offensive game, while maintaining his tremendous work ethic away from the puck, he could become a true sleeper prospect.

Cranford, Ryan
RW - Kingston Frontenacs (OHL) 6'00" 195
HockeyProspect.com Ranking: NR

Cranford was selected in the 10th round of the 2014 OHL Priority Selection Draft by the Kingston Frontenacs from the now inactive Eastern Ontario Wild Minor Midget Program. Cranford played for the Ottawa Jr. A Senators of the CCHL last season and made his OHL debut this year with Kingston.

Cranford was a consistent presence on the Frontenacs third line all season long playing all 68 games. Cranford plays with tenacity and aggression, consistently competing throughout the game. Cranford shields the puck well and works the cycle with effectiveness. He competes hard in all three zones and was consistently one of Kingston's best penalty killers. He scored 13 goals on the third line, many of which came from crashing the crease and jamming pucks home and rebounds. He does have a heavy shot but doesn't currently have the accuracy to pick apart goaltenders. Cranford's skating is a work in progress. While his stride is short and choppy, he does still manage to generate average to good straight speed, although his east/west mobility needs a lot of work.

Ryan is an ideal role player who is tough on the walls and is a good two-way winger competing in the defensive zone. He loves to play physical, he hits hard and is willing to drop the gloves. His offensive upside is limited but he has some value as an NHL prospect as he understands his role and excels within it. If he makes it, it will be as a bottom six forward, but as a junior player he will be a valuable role player who plays second line plus top penalty kill minutes and some power play.

Culina, Mario
G - Windsor Spitfires (OHL) 6'02" 174
HockeyProspect.com Ranking: 175

After being passed over two consecutive OHL Drafts, Culina was picked up by the Windsor Spitfires as a free Agent out of the SOO Thunderbirds Jr. A program. After spending more time with the SOO Thunderbirds to open the season, Culina eventually rejoined the Spitfires and even took over the starting job down the stretch.

Culina has a very low stance which supports his great quickness. He cuts down angles very well and does a great job of taking away net on shots down the middle. He has great reflexes and has made some outstanding saves because of this. Teams that were able to exploit him usually jumped on rebound opportunities or would spread him out across cross crease and force him to make difficult saves. He has decent vision through traffic but due to his style of game looks much smaller than your average 6'02" goaltender. He is average with the puck generally making the simple play with it.

Mario only has 20 games of OHL experience and is a re-entry player, but he proved in a short time to have a very intriguing level of potential. He has the size required to play at the NHL level and has handled top scorers well making impressive saves. With proper development and more action at the OHL level, Culina could turn out to be a real steal at the 2016 NHL Entry Draft.

Quotable:" He drops to early and makes himself too small in the net too often. I'll pass." - NHL Scout (February 2016)

Quotable:" I like how he competes. He's athletic, his legs are lightning quick." -NHL Scout (February 2016)

Quotable:" He was really good the first few times I saw him. Struggled a bit the last couple of viewings. Loved his quickness and his athleticism." - HP Scout Mark Edwards

Dahlen, Jonathan
LW – Timra IK (SHL-2) – 5'11.25", 176
HockeyProspect.com Ranking: 24

As a late '97 born, Dahlen didn't have the chance to showcase his progress on the international stage with his U18 national team. However, the kind of year he had while playing against men in the second best Swedish senior league could hardly go unnoticed. The son of former NHLer Ulf Dahlen managed to lead his team in goals and points, putting together a very productive second half of the season. In particular, he put on a show in the Allsvenskan playoff round, scoring 6 goals in 5 games, half of his entire team's post season output.

Dahlen is primarily a goal scorer, has a quick and accurate shot and really likes to be around the net, but also has a strong passing game inside the offensive zone. He has very good vision and is quick recognizing opportunities and maneuvering with his stick. He seems to turn it on when an opportunity arises and he looks better and quicker the closer he gets to the net. Drives to it consistently, is a threat on the wraparound and is quite creative in finding ways to be dangerous inside the offensive zone. Has impressive edge work and can skate sideways while shielding the puck away from the defenseman. His skating became more powerful as the season progressed, improving his game through the neutral zone as a result. He began to create chances for himself and even in transition, whereas he was used to be a threat only in the slot, like when we saw him at last year U18 Worlds in Zug (he still managed to be a PPG there despite that Swedish team's struggles).

Jonathan is a bit undersized, doesn't possess outstanding acceleration and even adding some mass won't be a power forward at the next level, but is a smart player who doesn't mind working along the boards and doesn't hesitate to battle through traffic. He shouldn't have many problems adapting to the smaller rinks and would have probably scored a lot of goals if playing major junior this year. He brings a pretty consistent effort and seems to elevate his game when it matters the most. He doesn't make many mistakes either, but he looks less alert when in the defensive zone.

Dahlen doesn't have the potential to carry a line offensively at the NHL level, but could develop into a great compliment to an offensive line. He is expected to spend another season in Allsvenskan with Timra, probably playing alongside mate Elias Pettersson.

Quotable:" Not a huge kid but he's skilled and smart. He's got some jitterbug in him and has scored some highlight reel goals. Showed some good vision too. Popular player with our Euro scouts." - HP Scout Mark Edwards

Quotable:" When he gets to the dangerous areas he gives me a 'shark smelling blood' feeling, that's something I've always liked with him." - HP Scout Mik Portoni

Danielsson, Hugo
LD – Skelleftea J20 (SWE) – 6'03", 187
HockeyProspect.com Ranking: NR

Danielsson is a defensive-defenseman who already boasts good size. His main strength would be the fact that he has a good positional sense in his own end. He isn't a high-end skater, so relying on his positioning is a must. Danielsson will almost always play a very conservative game that tries to minimize mistakes and provide a safety valve on the back-end. Offensively there is not much to speak about and it is not part of the game that Danielsson should be counted on.

At the junior level he doesn't overly struggle with getting pinned in his own end. When he has enough time he is capable of completing an outlet. However, when pressured, he doesn't' have the skill to get himself out of trouble on his own. While the offense will very likely never come, it would be important for Danielsson to add another defensive component to his game, whether that would be increased physicality, a better usage of his stick for pokechecks and control of space, or additional mobility. His decision-making on outlets will also need to get faster.

Davidson, Dawson
LD – Kamloops (WHL) 5'11", 181
HockeyProspect.com Ranking: 170

Showed steady improvement throughout the season for a surprise Kamloops team and by season's end he was staple all situations defenseman that was an essential part of the rush and their top puck mover. Missing a large portion of games in January Davidson managed 6G, 33A in just 59 games which was good enough to tie for the team lead in defensive scoring. Speed and skating are the strongest part of Davidson's game, he shows agile footwork and strong opening strides that explode from a standstill. Mobility is obvious and shifty, works up the ice with ease and uses sharp lateral cut to avoid traffic, reverse staking is quick, he track well and holds a tight gap staying with attackers and limiting their space. Not the most physically engaging player in front of the net, prefers to use his stick to pick pucks and tie up attackers. Physical stature limits his ability to compete below the goal line, has trouble pinning forwards on the boards and often gets over matched or knocked over down low. He is quite good at relieving pressure and starting transition through open ice.

Shows strong offensive instinct and isn't afraid to use his quick feet to jump into the rush, works the point with shifty hands and feet and makes smart passes. Can put a quick wrist shot on net. He needs to develop a stronger slapshot but does fire an accurate one-timer, especially if he's shooting from the circles.

Improvement throughout the season shouldn't go unnoticed, a strong skater with good smarts to start the transition and decent offensive instincts, he has also put up more than respectable point totals placing him fourth in scoring amount draft eligible defensemen from the WHL.

Day, Sean
LD - Mississuaga Steelheads (OHL) 6'02", 228
HockeyProspect.com Ranking: 103

Sean was selected first round, fourth overall at the 2013 OHL Priority Selection Draft as an exceptional status player by the Mississauga Steelheads out of the Detroit Compuware U16 program.

Day is an extremely mobile, speedy two-way defensemen with impressive physical attributes. He has excellent puck rushing ability and enjoys taking the puck up ice as frequently as possible, but after gaining the offensive zone, Day rarely shows the ability to create a play. Too often he is skating the puck into a corner, circling the net, or trying to force a play that isn't there. If he can play these rushes smarter, he would have much better overall results. His decision making ability is below average, which helps lead to hockey sense that is questionable at best in our opinion. He has a powerful shot from the point and can get it through, making him a threat to score, or create rebounds. That said, he had a whopping 6 goals and 16 assists this season while logging big minutes in 57 games. In the defensive zone, Day lacks a sense of urgency in possession and while it may look as though he shows poise/patience, his lack of awareness often leads to a questionable decisions. With that being said, Day did show improvements throughout the season, showing more of a willingness to take a hit to make a play, while also using his elite mobility to elude a forechecker with effectiveness. Day is also a physical player in his own zone. He has a huge frame and utilizes it along with his speed to land some crushing checks on the opposition. Day makes hard, accurate stretch passes, however he also has a tendency to see the #1 option, look it off, only to take on pressure and end up forcing a low quality play up the half boards. Day's mobility and foot speed should allow him to handle transition opportunities with success, however he often allows easy entry to the offensive zone. Day is at his best defensively when he keeps his feet moving and is engaged physically, using his large frame to bully the opposition in puck battles.

Day is one of the biggest boom or bust prospects available at the 2016 NHL Entry Draft. If he can get on track with his potential and upside he will become a player that would have been worthy of a first round selection. However that is a very risky expectation for him, as he has shown since joining the OHL that he has not been able to reach that ability, either physically or mentally for long stretches of time. His upside is of a top four, power play defenseman in the NHL, but his bust of never making the NHL is a very realistic concern.

Quotable: "He drives me crazy. So much talent wasted in far too many games. I think he has been better this year though." - NHL Scout (January 2016)

Quotable: "Where do you think he will get drafted? Because I have no idea." - NHL Scout (December 2015)

Quotable: "Not on my list." - NHL Scout (March 2016)

Quotable: "I told myself last summer that I was going to go into this season with a clean slate for him (Day). It didn't take long before he frustrated me. For me he is the classic case of 1st round talent but late round production. I will say he had some decent games in my viewings this year but for there are just too many red flags in his game to consider him in the early rounds." - Mark Edwards

Quotable: "He was fine." - NHL Scout (Combine week)

Quotable: "Not much chatter about Day this week." - HP Scout Mark Edwards (Combine week)

DeBrincat, Alex
LC - Erie Otters (OHL) 5'07.25" 163
HockeyProspect.com Ranking: 33

DeBrincat was passed over at the 2013 and 2014 OHL Priority Selection Drafts, ultimately being signed as a free agent by the Erie Otters out of Lake Forest Academy. He joined the Erie Otters where he played top minutes posting back to back 51 goal seasons.

DeBrincat is a very flashy, skilled forward who weaves through traffic. He gets his shot off, even when he has very little space and it possesses great velocity and accuracy. He knows how to slip into high percentage scoring areas. His scoring ability is among the best anywhere at the junior level. There are few opponents that have the skating ability to keep up with him. DeBrincat plays at a high rate of speed, which makes him difficult to contain. When you slow him down you can contain him, but it's not an easy task to achieve. He has a gritty edge to his game and likes to mix it up with opponents and get under their skin. Despite this, he takes very few penalties. Despite his size, he's capable of landing some solid hits. His playmaking ability doesn't matchup with his scoring ability. He is much more dangerous shooting than passing. His defensive play will also need to improve. as he can be very hit or miss in this area.

DeBrincat is quite possibly the biggest wildcard in this year's NHL Draft. He has the skill to be a top 10 pick, but possesses size that could prevent him from ever making an impact at the NHL level. It's that high risk high reward that makes his draft placement very difficult for us and unpredictable as far as when an NHL team will grab him as well.

Quotable: "Some nights he picked apart good defenders and goaltenders and he was convincing as a top prospect, but other nights his concerns weighed on me more than others. All it takes is one team to be confident in his upside, I think in the end he'll go off the board higher than I'd have him ranked." - Ryan Yessie

Quotable: "He was easily the best player on the ice last night." - NHL Scout (November 2015)

Quotable: "I wouldn't take him with our first rounder but I would consider him given where we pick in the second round. - NHL Scout (March 2015)

Quotable: "I wouldn't touch him in the first round but the second round is a different story." - NHL Scout (December 2015)

Quotable: "He is a faller for me. He hasn't been very good in recent games." - NHL Scout (March 2016)

Quotable: "I began the pre-season with him ranked 50th, his skating isn't bad but I like to see high-end skating from really tiny guys like him. Some early season viewings began to sway me because he just kept finding ways to score despite not being an elite skater. I had quite a few 'average at best' viewings of him after Christmas and his stock began to trend downward a bit." - Mark Edwards

Quotable: His interview was just ok. He thinks he is going to late first round. Maybe someone is telling him that..." - NHL Scout (Combine week)

Quotable: "His interview was fine. He thinks he is going in the first round but about 58 other players told us they were late first's or early seconds." -NHL Scout (Combine week)

De Jong, Brendan
LD – Portland (WHL) 6'05, 189
HockeyProspect.com Ranking: NR

De Jong is long and lean but looks thin on the ice and undersized when skating at full-stride. He hasn't been a point producer in either his rookie season or his draft year even with increased playing time. He does have some positive qualities, mostly related to his big frame. For instance, he does a lot of reaching with his long stick and has a decent pokecheck. However, he doesn't defend with his body very much and looks clumsy in his skating, especially in reverse. For a guy his size, he is quite weak in his own zone and is an underwhelming physical presence. His reach is good and he can be effective with his stick, but he needs to fill out and grow his game, as we don't feel he's a prospect with great potential for the 2016 draft.

De Mey, Vincent
C/W – Shattuck St. Mary's Prep (MN-HS) 6'01", 178
HockeyProspect.com Ranking: NR

Born in Los Angeles, Vincent De May is a Shattuck product through and through, he started at SSM in 11/12 as a Bantam and Graduated with the Prep Team in 2016. Vincent was always a solid player for each of his teams at Shattuck St. Mary's but saw his game really come together in his senior year (2016) where he averaged well over a PPG and played in all situations for his team.

Vincent plays a smart game in the offensive zone and can put the puck in the net in a number of different ways; he possesses a great shot off the rush and is good at using the defender as a screen and getting it through to the net. He can also lower his shoulder and drive the net with a power move as well as being extremely smart in finding the soft areas in the zone to get separation to get open for a pass.

De May still needs to add muscle to his frame, develop more stop and starts to his game and continue to work on his play in the defensive zone where he can be caught watching the play at times. He has gotten better in these areas this season but still needs to continue to improve going forward if he was to become a legitimate NHL prospect. His skating isn't his strong suit but hasn't held him back up to this point. De May looks to be off the Madison Capitols (USHL) in 16/17 after being chosen in the Phase 2 Draft and is committed to Ohio State in 17/18.

DeNoble, Logan
LC - Peterborough Petes (OHL) 5'10" 189
HockeyProspect.com Ranking: NR

DeNoble was drafted in the 13th round of the 2013 OHL Priority Selection Draft by the Peterborough Petes out of the Peterborough Petes Minor Midget program. Logan spent much of the last two seasons with the Lindsay Jr. A Muskies of the OJHL and really boosted his offensive numbers in his second season before joining the Peterborough Petes on a more permanent basis playing 20 games last season. This has been his first full season in the OHL going from bottom six role to playing top line minutes by the end of the year.

DeNoble is an undersized, physical energy forward with some deceptive scoring ability. He possesses a high compete level and decent hockey sense, DeNoble was a consistent performer for the Petes this season. A capable two-way presence with the ability to create offense. DeNoble is the type of player who can be impactful without putting up offensive numbers. DeNoble shows the ability to find soft spot's in defensive zone coverage's and possesses a deceptively heavy shot. DeNoble gets his shot off quickly, while it packs a deceptive amount of velocity and accuracy. While his best offensive tool may be his shot, DeNoble can create off the cycle, showing strong puck protection skills and an ability to shield the puck with effectiveness on net drives. While his puck skills and playmaking ability is average, DeNoble effectively finds shooting lane and seams in coverage's exploiting them. Away fro the puck DeNoble is a reliable defender, with awareness and anticipation skills, often breaking up passes or at the very least getting a stick or body in the shooting/passing lanes.

DeNoble's development has been very impressive over the past few years. He went from a decent Minor Midget player, become a very productive OJHL player in his second year and has posted 20 goals and over 40 points as a rookie. This is an impressive feat for DeNoble but his size, lacking top six upside and a need to improve on his skating are all concerns when projecting him at the next level. There's no doubt the Petes' found themselves a local diamond in the rough and a very good junior player, but as an NHL prospect, he will have an uphill battle.

De Wit, Jeff
RC – Red Deer Rebels (WHL) 6'03", 185
HockeyProspect.com Ranking: 192

De Wit is a strong, physical center that shows glimpses of an offensive upside. De Wit played a limited bottom six role on a strong Red Deer Rebels team. He was effective at times in his role getting pucks deep and working hard on the forecheck to win possession. He is a good skater for a player his size and loved competing for loose pucks in the corners and along the wall. With that said in all our viewings he was often chasing the play. There was evidence of effort but not a lot of execution. De Wit lacked the confidence of his coach as he would go long periods of time without seeing any action. He struggles with the pace of the game at times and lacks top end offensive ability to earn more ice time. He is at his best when he is using his size and driving hard to the net and causing problems for defenders. We feel that he needs to be much more committed to playing a simple hard working two-way game if he will make the jump to the next level.

Dhillon, Stephen
G - Niagara Ice Dogs (OHL) 6'03.75", 182
HockeyProspect.com Ranking: NR

Stephen was selected in the third round of the 2014 OHL Draft by the Niagara Ice Dogs from the Buffalo Regals Minor Midget program. Dhillon has only 28 games of OHL experience playing behind veteran goaltenders, but has gained international experience playing for Team USA at the Ivan Hlinka U18 tournament.

Dhillon has the ideal size desired by NHL teams in net. He does a good job playing angles well but when the play is coming down the middle he can back up too far into his net giving shooters extra shooting angles. Giving this extra space has given good shooters more to shoot at. He didn't get tested very much in a lot of his appearances, as he was primarily playing against teams that don't have much firepower. He handles deflections very well utilizing his size and reflexes.

If Dhillon was born two days later, hew would be ineligible for the 2016 NHL Draft. This may have been a huge benefit for him as his action is limited and so is the number of appearances he's had in situations where he's really been tested. He's the favorite going into next season to be the starting goaltender for the Niagara Ice Dogs, which would have given him a better chance to show off his potential. As it stands, Dhillon could hear his name called late in the draft, but he may need to prove himself as a 2nd time eligible if he is not picked up late this June.

Quotable: "Not on my goalie list. He's a no draft for me." - NHL Scout (December 2015)

Quotable: "I can only judge him by the games I saw him and he wasn't great in those games." - H/P Scout Mark Edwards

Dineen, Cam
LD - North Bay Battalion (OHL) 5'11", 183
HockeyProspect.com Ranking: 87

Dineen was selected in the 11th round of the 2014 OHL Priority Selection Draft by the North Bay Battalion out of the New Jersey Rockets U19 program. He spent his first junior season winning the EHL rookie of the year and defensive scoring title with the New Jersey Rockets. After playing at the Ivan Hlinka U18 tournament for Team USA, he joined the Battalion where he had an outstanding rookie season posting 59 points in 68 games.

Dineen is an undersized, offensive minded defensemen who displays good skating abilities and impressive offensive zone puck skills. While he has made some good first passes up ice he had a history of being pressured into making costly defensive zone mistakes if he didn't have enough time in his own zone. When rushing the puck, Dineen effortlessly gains the offensive zone in possession and often looks to create upon entry to the zone. He also likes to jump up in the rush at will and will often go to the net without the puck, which resulted in some goals. A shifty and elusive skater, Dineen works his edges extremely well and can change his pace and direction without losing momentum. A player who boasts impressive straight line speed, Dineen's explosive first step allows him to create space for himself to operate. Offensively speaking Dineen consistently shows the ability to create from the blue line, a play who boasts impressive vision and playmaking skills, Dineen also shows a deceptively strong point shot, despite his pass first tendencies. Defensively speaking Dineen relies on strong positional play, anticipation and stick on puck defensive skills. While Defensively he struggled physically and made mistakes in his own end. He was at his best when getting his stick in passing lanes and preventing scoring chances through that style of defending. One on one he was hit or miss as he does a great job of skating with the opposition, but sometimes struggles against bigger puck protecting forwards or higher skilled forwards who could stickhandle around him.

Dineen has big upside, because if he makes the NHL, it will be as an offensively productive defenseman. The down side is a big risk as he lacks the size, the defensive ability and mental mistakes all add up to the risk of never playing in the NHL. A team may want to take that risk taking him off the board earlier rather than later, but the risk his carries may also scare some teams off.

Quotable: "I went up to see him again last week. Stats look good but He doesn't do anything for me." - NHL Scout (February 2016)

Quotable: "I don't see it. Just a good Junior player for me." - NHL Scout (March 2016)

Quotable: "How can NHL Central have him ranked way down there? (117th)" - NHL Scout (January 2016 - after mid term rankings release)

Quotable: "You see where NHL Central as him? He's not even on my list. - NHL Scout (January 2016 - after mid term rankings release)

Quotable: "I need to go see him again. I have a no draft grade but he's posting big numbers." - NHL Scout (January 2016)

Quotable: "I need to give him one more viewing." - NHL Scout (March 2016)

Quotable: "He just makes too many mistakes for me at the next level. He's got all the tools to continue to be a good junior player, he just doesn't think the game at the level a sub six foot defender needs to, in order to succeed as an offensive defenseman in the NHL." - HP Scout Ryan Yessie

Quotable: "I had quite a few conversations with NHL Scouts about Dineen. Only one scout I spoke to liked him in the top 60. A bunch of guys kept going back for more viewings to see if they were missing something. I would talk to Scouts again after they went to see him and they still had him as a no draft or a late pick. I was in the same boat as far as a bunch of late viewings, he never really did anything to wow me. He was quite weak on the defensive side of the puck in most of my viewings, so that didn't help his cause. One thing is for sure, he is one of the most interesting players as far as my conversations with scouts since I have been doing this. A much different narrative than the one I would read in various media sources. I'd be happy to be wrong about him." - HP Scout Mark Edwards

Dmytriw, Jared
RW - Victoria Royals (WHL) 5'11", 180
HockeyProspect.com Ranking: NR

Jared is a two-way forward that plays a smart responsible game. He is a physical player that focuses on the defensive side of the game first. He is not big in size and stature but is a force on the forecheck and likes to use his body to win battles. Jared is a positional player that is trusted to kill penalties.

He is best when he makes the simple plays as he struggled with the pace at times this season and can get himself in trouble when he tries to do too much. Jared will have an impact as a role player as he continues his career in the WHL but needs to take his game to the next level working on bringing an offensive side to his game. His upside is limited and will need to take a huge step if he is to play at the next level. We do not expect Jared to get selected at the 2016 NHL Entry Draft.

Dostie, Alex
C/LW – Gatineau Olympiques (QMJHL) 5'10", 170
HockeyProspect.com Ranking: NR

Alex was coming off a good full year in the QMJHL, but was passed over in the NHL draft. It looked like he had a chip on his shoulder all year, because he came out of the gates in the month of September putting up points and competing hard every game.

Alex is a speedy forward with a lot of skill and hockey smarts. He has tremendous acceleration with or without the puck and his first 2-3 steps are outstanding, when he gets into full stride and has his top speed he is a very hard player to control. He has real good agility and his stop and starts are good. Alex has a very good shot and is very accurate with it as well. There were times in our viewings that he picked corners of the net with no room at all and nowhere to see the net and the puck found the back of the net. He has a good release to his shot when he coming of the rush or cutting into the middle and gets the puck off quick and hard not giving the goalie much time to react. He can score many ways with his shot, whether it's his wrist shot, slap shot or going backhand. He is ok on faceoff, we would like to see him be harder on his stick and bare down too win more key faceoff. He has high hockey IQ, as his vision with or without the puck is good, and he has really good offensive instincts on where to put the puck or where his teammates will be or should in the zone. He is really good at anticipating the play in the offensive zone, and making smart decisions and understanding what his options are in the zone. His skill and smarts really show when he is on the power play from the way he moves the puck around too his teammates or finding the open spot for the one timer.

His defensive game is good; unfortunately he's a little undersize for a centermen, so he tends to get pushed around on the cycle or any physical play in the defensive zone. He uses his speed and hockey smarts to avoid the physical side and tends to come away with the puck most of the time. He is good at anticipating cross-ice passes and getting into the way of them. He seemed to be reliable in his defensive zone as his coach put him he key situations of the game and in our viewings he was effective. With his speed and smarts he could end up being very effective at the next level, we would like to see him get stronger on his feet and in his upper body, and with another year in the QMJHL, he could dominate it and should help him going forward.

Doudera, Lukas
LD – HC Trinec (CZE) – 5'11", 165
HockeyProspect.com Ranking: NR

Doudera is a puck-mover with a bit of a light frame that has appeared in 31 games for Trinec in the top Czech league. As a defenseman, he lacks size but utilizes skating well and isn't afraid of jumping up in the play. Doudera is a good passer and can make the first pass out of the zone. He also is a pretty good skater and moves well around the ice. Doudera likes to skate with the puck, displaying very good puck control, and will take upon himself the role of a defenseman that doesn't just make a quick outlet but can take several strides forward and join up in the play. He will need to be more careful about physical contact while he takes off, as we have seen him several times get punished physically while he was trying to make a play. Doudera will be active in the offensive zone and has the poise and the hands to make plays at the offensive blueline under pressure.

Defensively, Doudera isn't quite the most solid defender one can find. Although he has good mobility he doesn't tie up forwards well and plays a rather soft game. That isn't unusual for undersized defenseman, however a bigger problem is that a mobile blueliner like Doudera would need to defend better against zone entries. Unfortunately, Doudera tends to let forwards walk in too easily on zone-entries and hasn't developed a strong anticipation and zone-entry defense that an undersized defenseman like him would really need.

Doudera is a decent prospect, however at this point in time we don't think he has shown enough defensively to be able to take regular shifts in the NHL along the next few years; he'll need to make big strides in his play without the puck to earn the chance to use his skills at that level.

Dube, Dillon
LW/RW/C – Kelowna Rockets (WHL) 5'11, 182
HockeyProspect.com Ranking: 60

A product of the Notre Dame Bantam program, Dube was a first round pick of the Rockets in 2013. Despite more than doubling his point total from 2014/15, it has been an inconsistent season for the speedy forward. Slowed by an early season eye injury he never seemed to find his groove during the year. A likely contribution was constant position shuffling as he lined up at all three forward positions finishing the year mostly on LW a change from the RW & C he played in his rookie season.

Dube excels off the rush playing an up-tempo game and pushing the pace, when he's involved in transition he seems to gain a better flow of the offense and his instincts have a tendency to take over. Skating is quick and explosive has a strong ability to create space and break away from defenders at high speed. Speed changes are good and 4 way mobility looks light when changing directions, leg strength needs some work as strong checkers can throw his balance off, gets knocked down too easily at times.

A pure shooter, Dube poses a hard and heavy shot with a very good release, can shoot in stride and gets good power on it. At times accuracy can be an issue possibly due to wanting to shoot as hard as possible at all times. However shows versatility in his shooting ability with capable both of a quality one-timer and soft backhand that rises quickly in tight. Can use his body to guard of defenders his skating allows him to be slippery and protects the puck well, this is where his passing can be dangerous, as he can create space with his footwork and dish the puck to an open player.

Not afraid to play dirty and go to the tough arenas of ice, he has learned to embrace more of the grinding role and can absorb contact below the goal line. Shows a high compete level in all areas of the ice with a "buzzsaw" mentality, often goes after bigger forwards and lays big hits. Shows a temper and in-game frustration when he thinks a call is missed but has a great compete level, especially after making a mistake (loves to attack the puck, especially after giving up a turnover). He can also be prone to forcing plays that aren't there at times.

Dube has shown good upside as a versatile forward that can line up on different positions and can provide different dimensions of play. Although not the biggest, he is a strong skater and plays with a good compete level. He is a capable shooter, can make decisions on the fly and is a threat to score. He has good footwork on the cycle, buying time for himself with his skating and can make a tight cut to throw a checker off and open up space. Plays the type of game that can be used in a variety of different roles.

Dubois, Pierre-Luc
LW/LC/RW – Cape-Breton Screaming Eagles (QMJHL) 6'03", 202
HockeyProspect.com Ranking: 4

Dubois was the 5th overall pick in the 2014 QMJHL Draft coming out of the Collège Notre-Dame midget program in Rivière-du-Loup. He had a stellar rookie campaign last year with the Screaming Eagles and earned a spot as an underager on Team Canada at the World Under-18 Hockey Championship. After representing his country in April, Dubois suited up once again for Canada in August (this time at the Ivan Hlinka tournament) and won gold.

This season, Dubois has taken his offensive game to another level by being the 3rd best scorer in the league with 99 points. A natural left winger, Dubois has played center fairly often this year, but has also played at the right wing position with his team, showing his great versatility. Dubois' father has been coaching in the QMJHL for the past 10 years, either as a head coach or an assistant-coach and it has showed in the way Dubois understands the game. Dubois' hockey IQ is excellent, as he is capable of playing all three forward positions and he is able to thrive in any situation he's put in by his coaches. He has an excellent wrist shot, a real quick release and a lot of velocity on his shot. He's shooting the puck a lot more this year. He was previously looking to pass the puck more because of his great vision and patience with the puck. Dubois gained close to 20 pounds in the summer, making him tougher to contain for opposing defensemen along the boards. With that added mass, his puck protection has been very good. In December, he received an invitation for Canada's WJC camp, but was left off the final roster by the Hockey Canada brass. He was the youngest player at the camp and responded with a very strong 2nd half of the season. Dubois is a very complete player who seems to gets better every time we see him; he hasn't hit his peak yet, we love Dubois potential. He's been a favorite of ours all year long and will eventually make a strong power forward at the NHL level.

Quotable:" Even since his QMJHL draft year, he just kept getting better whenever I saw him. I don't think Gauthier and him were ever that close." -HP scout, Jérôme Bérubé

Quotable: "I don't see what you see in him. He's been very average for me when I've seen him." - NHL Scout (February 2016)

Quotable: "He was the best player on the ice." NHL Scout (October 2015)

Quotable: "I think he is one of the smartest players in the draft." - NHL Scout (October 2015)

Quotable: "He plays a pro game. He isn't as skilled as some people think he is though." - NHL Scout (November 2015)

Quotable: "It's tight between him and Tkachuk. I have Dubois ahead because I think he is a safer pick. The skating still scares me a bit for Tkachuk." NHL Scout (April 2016)

Quotable: "I don't like him in the middle. I think he's a winger." - NHL Scout (March 2016)

Quotable: "He's a winger in the NHL." - NHL Scout (February 2016)

Quotable: "Every year you have some players you love to watch. Dubois is one of those guys for me this year. I love how smart he is all over the ice. My last viewing of him was in the playoffs. He was always going to the proper spot and doing the right things. If his team had better Dmen, I think his numbers would have been even more impressive. So many times I saw he was the smart option but his defenseman didn't get him the puck. He also showed me even more scoring ability this year than I originally thought he had. I saw some pretty impressive goals and assists. I also watched tape of all his points over a 4 month period. It was impressive. Add on the fact that he has some nastiness in his game and it's just the icing on the cake. I think if he was physically stronger he could play in the NHL next season. His NHL coach will love his smarts right away." - HP Scout Mark Edwards

Quotable: "I had a quick one on one with him at the combine. I asked him about teams asking him about playing centre. He told me everyone asked him. In short he thinks he might be able to play centre in the NHL down the road. I also listened to his media scrum. Well spoken kid and his english is excellent if you're wondering." - HP Scout Mark Edwards (Combine week)

Duehr, Walker
RW – Tri-City Storm (USHL) 6'02", 206
HockeyProspect.com Ranking: NR

Duehr is a late 1997 in his first year of eligibility. He's a right winger who has played his second season of USHL hockey. Duehr is the type of forward that isn't particularly flashy, but does several things well. He missed some time after recovering from a bad knee injury, but had a good finish to the year. Duehr has good size but isn't physically intimidating, he uses his reach well to protect the puck while bringing the puck over the offensive blueline or circling around the offensive zone, but he doesn't play an overly aggressive style. Duehr's best asset are his reads and hockey IQ as he finds himself in the right positions offensively and although he won't wow you with his skill, he still finds ways to get on board. He has fluid movement but doesn't stand out as a particularly strong skater. His defensive reads are on-point but as he moves forward he could stand to use his size better to defend and win wall battles.

Duhaime, Brandon
LW – Tri-City Storm (USHL) 6'0.5", 198
HockeyProspect.com Ranking: 124

The Parkland, FL native had a solid season in the USHL, which saw him start the season with the Chicago Steel then traded to Tri-City. Duhaime has really hit a growth spurt and has grown close to 4 inches over the last 2 years and it has helped him be more effective in the tight areas where he doesn't get pushed around as much. Brandon is a fantastic skater and a very smart player. We feel his time spent playing as a smaller forward has helped his vision and he is able to identify and jump into holes that a lot of players his size don't see as an option. Duhaime is sound defensively and on the back check. Duhaime needs to continue to work on his scoring touch and develop specific aspects of his game like his body positioning both with the puck as well as in front of the net. Brandon physical attributes are not at an elite level but his hockey sense and all around game make him an intriguing overage prospect for this year's draft.

Quotable: "He's a second year eligible kid who might get selected in a late round. He can skate and he shoots the puck well. Not sure about the hockey smarts." - NHL Scout (May 2016)

Dunn, Sam
RD - Cobourg Cougars (OJHL) 6'02" 194
HockeyProspect.com Ranking: NR

Sam has appeared with the Cobourg Cougars over the last three seasons first as an underager who was also the captain of the Central Ontario Wolves Minor Midget, then as a 16 year old rookie, then this, his second full season where he was rewarded with an "A" as the Cougars assistant captain, wearing a letter at the age of 17.

Dunn plays a good two way game who can contribute at both ends of the ice. He has deceptive skating for his size and protects the puck well carrying it out of trouble in the defensive zone. Sam's big standout skill is his outstanding endurance. Going back to Minor Midget he played about 70% of the game whenever we watched him play. Now in the OJHL we see him get left out on the ice for two, two and a half minutes only resting between whistles playing top minutes in all game situations. The remarkable aspect is how fresh he looks and how good his decisions are 90-150 seconds into these shifts. He has a decent shot from the point, with good hands and usually makes the right play with the puck. While he's reliable in the defensive zone, Sam doesn't have a mean streak and only provides enough physicality required to adequately complete the play. He usually makes the right defensive play but can occasionally get out of position, or won't play an opponent tough enough preventing him from shutting down a play.

Dunn has good two way ability but will likely play more of a shutdown role as he doesn't possess enough offense for the next level. He would certainly benefit from playing a more physical game as he has the size and the frame to do it. Dunn was selected in the third round of the 2014 OHL Priority Selection Draft by the Barrie Colts.

Quotable: "I had time for him in his OHL Draft year and still like parts of his game. I'd really like to see him play with a bit more of a heartbeat and a lot more physicality." - HP Scout Mark Edwards

Eder, Tobias
RC – EC Bad Tolz (GER) – 6'00", 176
HockeyProspect.com Ranking: 65

Eder started turning heads at the 2015 U18 World Championships in Switzerland where his work ethic and compete in all three zones became the lone shining light on a German team that was lacking depth and spark.

Despite enquiries from North American junior teams, Eder opted to sign with DEL club, EHC Munich in the summer of 2015. EHC Munich loaned Eder to his hometown club in Bad Tolz that competes in the Oberliga (German professional third tier). Eder also found himself making appearances on three different clubs this season: Bad Tolz U19, EC Salzburg U20, and SC Riessersee (DEL2). The reasoning behind his appearances with multiple clubs is simply Munich getting him more experience.

Eder possesses great offensive instincts and exposes weaknesses in teams defense. His hands are crafty and puck skills are already at a professional level. Has a pro pass, flat, accurate, just enough speed at the right time and he can receive pucks with easy on backhand and forehand while in motion without losing a step. Loves to find neutral zone holes where he can receive a pass and streak in for a break away. Eder loves to get pucks on net and knows when he should shoot or pass. His shot is fast and deceptive to goaltenders, which can lead to awkward rebounds and more scoring opportunities for his linemates.

His speed and feet are developing and he looked faster in viewings compared to last season. Still slender frame and will need to add some bulk and power. He can take hits, but gets knocked around easily due to his light frame. Despite his frame, his mind and skills are an intriguing combination.

Quotable: "Had never heard of him until last April but sometimes players catch your eye on the first shift you see them. I've only seen Eder on tape this year, but he impressed me at the U18 in Switzerland last April. He was smart, competed hard, had the puck on his stick a lot and flashed some skill. He drove Germany's offense in my viewings. I haven't heard NHL Scouts talking about him at all, but he's a kid I'd have on my draft list if I was with a team." - HP Scout Mark Edwards

Quotable: "Doesn't have the exposure of other prospects, but any time you see a kid with his smarts and instincts for the game, you take notice. Have seen him line up against 2015 NHL draft picks Dzierkals and Balcers against Latvia and he compared favorably." - HP Scout Nik Funa

Egan, Taylor
LD - Erie Otters (OHL) 6'00", 184
HockeyProspect.com Ranking: NR

Egan was selected in the sixth round of the 2014 OHL Priority Selection Draft by the Erie Otters out of the Ottawa Valley Titans Minor Midget program. Egan spent most of last season with the Kanata Lasers of the CCHL before playing his first full season in the OHL this past season.

Egan is a two-way defender who played more of a defensive role, primarily seeing ice as Erie's sixth defenseman. He uses his body positioning well along the wall down low to win battles then quickly advances the puck, not trying to do too much. He has good positioning in his own zone and can break up passes and scoring chances with his stick. He is a decent skater and can skate the puck out of trouble when he has a lane but provided a high percentage of accurate first passes. Offensively he didn't get to use his shot very often. However when he did, he showed a low, accurate, deflectable shot from the point.

Egan played a minimal role and while he showed he is a very capable junior defenseman, he didn't really show enough NHL upside to warrant a selection at the 2016 NHL Entry Draft. As his ice increases and he gets to show more of what he can do, he will have an opportunity as a 2nd time eligible player.

Eisenmenger, Maximilian
LC – Djurgardens (SWE Jr.) – 6'04", 190
HockeyProspect.com Ranking: NR

Eisenmenger was born in Germany but grew up playing hockey in Sweden and appears eligible to play for both countries. He is still a raw one, but this season he has made enough progress to be now considered a legitimate prospect. His frame paired with his tendencies is what makes him interesting. Standing at 6-foot-4 Maximilian already makes his size matter on the ice even if he has yet to start filling out. He shows the will to be physical along the boards and to take full advantage of his remarkable reach without the puck. He can read the play and has the ability to get into lanes, using his long stick to disrupt plays on a consistent basis. Shows good compete, regularly pursue pucks and is able to win possession more often than not.

Eligible for the draft by less than one month and only playing his first full season at high level, Eisenmenger shows good awareness on the ice and quickly recognizes what's the most effective line to transition the puck up from the defensive blueline once he gets it in that area. Sometimes he struggles with his straight forward acceleration, but already not a bad skater once he's going despite his tall, lanky frame. It's going to be interesting seeing how much skating and other parts of his game will improve as he develops physically. Stickhandling may need some polishing, but there have been plays where he showed us some patience and ability to make plays inside the offensive zone. He usually finds a way to make a useful play, if not pretty. Eisenmenger is definitely a project player, but one that could eventually make life difficult for his opponents if he puts it all together.

Eliot, Mitchell
RD – Muskegon Lumberjacks (USHL) 5'11", 188
HockeyProspect.com Ranking: NR

While Eliot's physical stature isn't overwhelming, his style of play makes him seem a lot bigger. Eliot is a strong kid who is almost impossible to move off the puck. He brings a level of physicality to his game on almost every shift. Mitchell doesn't do any one thing at an elite level but plays a smart all around game that is effective and is willing to battle in all area's the ice. Eliot isn't afraid to drop the gloves and mix it up and held his own in those situations as well.

Eliot's strong lower body, good skating stride allows him to be quick to loose pucks and elude fore checkers on the breakout. He takes care of the puck and makes solid reads out of his own end. Mitchell is good with his offensive zone entries when he chooses to skate the puck up by either finding the open teammate or placing pucks away from the opposing team in the corners where his teammates have a shot at it.

Eliot's offensive numbers are never going to pop out at you but he does a good job getting pucks to the net and has a powerful shot from the point. His skating ability allows him to keep pucks in the zone and control the blue line and will usually make the simple and reliable play but doesn't possess a whole lot of creativity in his offensive game.

Mitchell will be off to Michigan State in the fall where he should continue to get stronger and develop his all around game. What Mitchell Eliot has going for him is he has a good understanding of what he does well and doesn't try to be a player he is not.

Quotable: "At 5'11" he's not a huge kid but he is a good skater and he competes hard but lacks having a puck game." - HP Scout Mark Edwards

Elynuik, Hudson
LC – Spokane Chiefs (WHL) 6'05", 201
HockeyProspect.com Ranking: 78

Elynuik is yet another prospect available in the 2016 NHL Entry Draft who has NHL bloodlines, as he's the son of Pat Elynuik. Hudson plays the game on the slower side and sometimes has difficulties catching up to his linemates on the breakout, but he's a big kid and his skating is improving. He had the opportunity to step up into a first line role with the Spokane Chiefs this season following an injury to the 2017-eligible Kailer Yamamoto and had a strong stretch of hockey with a nice scoring run. With increased role during Yamamoto's injury he has shown growing offensive confidence and the ability to make plays with the puck, while he is not an exceptional stickhandler, his hands and the sense for manufacturing offense with the puck both looked reasonably good for a kid his size.

Hudson is good at utilizing his size to crash the net or to provide screens in front of the opposition's goaltender. He has real good instincts in the low-slot area, has the timing and the feel to slip through coverage and present an open blade for a pass, and can also anticipate rebounds well. With that being said, he could become more balanced on his skates and stronger on the puck. He has some difficulties in the corners as he can be pushed around a bit too easily by smaller forwards who are also capable of outskating him. He supports the defensemen when coming out of his zone and opens up for an easy outlet well, has good passing vision and can move the puck up ice and into the offensive zone. Although not a pure set-up center, he gets involved in the play nicely and doesn't have much problem hitting open linemates or getting open himself.

We like the package Elynuik offers, as he shows upside with his hockey IQ, scoring instincts from in-close, and size. Skating continues to be the biggest problem, especially straight-line top speed as he can struggle to catch up to the play. If he's able to improve his footwork Elynuik will make a good prospect as he has good instincts and an NHL-sized frame. While not soft, for a player his size, he could also be a bit meaner

Eriksson, Filip
G – Sodertalje J20 (SWE) – 6'02", 187
HockeyProspect.com Ranking: NR

Eriksson is a very raw goaltender with decent size for the position and athleticism that gives him some upside. Eriksson has quick movement when dropping into the butterfly and fluid, compact lateral movement across the crease. He seals against the post well but has the tendency to both play too deep and not protect the crease from passing plays. Will need to do a better job not shrinking in too much on lateral passes and passes from behind the net. Eriksson is just three days removed from being a 2017 eligible and it definitely shows in his game as he is also inconsistent. When he's on his game he does a really good job making saves on the first shot and moving around the crease, but he suffers from a loss of focus and can give up some bad goals. His rebound control will also need to be better, specifically he will need to do a better job directing rebounds to the side if he can't outright stop them. Eriksson is a raw goalie but one that has shown some upside. With good development he might look fairly improved by this time next year.

Fabbro, Dante
RD – Penticton Vees (BCHL) 6'00", 189
HockeyProspect.com Ranking: 11

Fabbro is an intelligent two-way defender who has good mobility and excellent vision with the puck. Aided by advanced lower-body strength a naturally low centre of gravity, Fabbro is very difficult to knock off the puck, resulting in exceedingly low turnover numbers. He additionally benefits from remarkable stamina allowing him to complete long grinding shifts or to quarterback two powerplay units. Dante played in all situations this year, providing a key power play and penalty killing presence for his club in Penticton.

Although not explosive with his first few steps, Fabbro has great mobility in all directions, which gives him good control of his gaps when defending in reverse. Fabbro reads the on-coming play well and utilizes smart initial positioning, he doesn't have to make tons of adjustments when defending because his anticipation allows him to maintain proper position without overly-exerting himself. His defensive zone reads are on-point but he has average upper body strength and isn't quite the defenseman that would manhandle forwards, even though he displays good compete in fighting for his position in front of the net and in the corners.

Fabbro also has terrific reads on his first pass. He is comfortable passing on either side of his body whether forehand or backhand. Easily spots open forwards up the ice and can dish an accurate stretch-pass, although at times he can be a bit too ambitious in trying to complete a high-end pass. He also uses the boards well to rim the puck to an open teammate if it's necessary. Generally maintains his cool in the defensive zone and doesn't panic with the puck on his stick, has good ability to delay and re-group if needed. His zone entry ability is outstanding as he has a head's-up style of movement and consistently scans the ice for options with the puck on his stick. Fabbro can distribute the puck from the offensive blueline in and also boasts a strong slapshot that has good power and gets through, that he can also line up as a one-timer. That also makes him a dangerous PP player.

Fabbro played key minutes and piled up points on a powerhouse Vees club this year, but he also had strong international performances, elevating his game while looking like one of Canada's best defensive prospects, especially at the Ivan Hlinka tournament, and in April at the World Under-18 Hockey Championships.

Quotable: "He wasn't as good as my previous viewings at the Junior A Challenge but other than that he's really impressed me going back to last season. I think he has a chance to be a star. His feet are great, he's smart and he makes great reads, especially in the offensive zone. He finished off his draft year in style with a great performance at the U18 in Grand Forks." - HP Scout Mark Edwards

Quotable: "He passed Chychrun on my list after Grand Forks. At some point you forget the noise and just take the player that showed better over multiple games." - NHL Scout (April 2016)

Quotable: " If there was one player that helped his stock with me in Grand Forks it was Fabbro. I've liked him all year, but he is even better than I thought. - NHL Scout (April 2016)

Quotable: " Mark my words, someone is going to take one of the Major Junior guys ahead of him and Fabbro will be a better pro." - NHL Scout (May 2016)

Quotable: " A little bit more quiet and reserved than I guy like Jost but he knows what he is and what he needs to work on. He was good." - NHL Scout (combine week)

Quotable: " Had a little swagger to him which I liked. He knows what his strengths are and knows that he can execute those strengths." - NHL Scout (Combine week)

Quotable: " All positive feedback from his combine interviews." HP Scout Mark Edwards

Falkovsky, Stepan
LD - Ottawa 67's (OHL) 6'07" 224
HockeyProspect.com Ranking: 176

Falkovsky was selected 42nd Overall by the Ottawa 67's at the 2015 CHL Import Draft out of MHK Yunost Minsk of the MHL. Falkovsky adjusted to the smaller ice in North America, and posted impressive 32 points as a rookie defenseman this season.

At the start of the year, when you watched Falkovsky it looked like he was going to struggle with the speed of the game and the smaller rinks. Once he got his feet under him and understood how to play in smaller rinks and use his massive size, he ended the year as a very steady defensemen and played in every situation. He is a surprisingly good forward skater for a defenseman his size, however he struggled skating backwards and would sometimes even defend skating forwards until the very last moment. He has a decent hard first pass out the zone and is was consistent with his first pass; in our viewings it was rare for him to miss a pass. Stephan doesn't have a hard shot from the point, but he has a really good accurate wrist shot that seems to always get through to the net for tips or second chances. By halfway through the season, he ended up being a very consistent player and you knew what you were getting every night. He wasn't overly physical again for a player with his size, he is good at angling opponents to the boards and is really good at taking away their time and space. He also has good hands, which helped him in battles. Stepan is good at anticipating the play. We would like to see him be more engaging physically and making players pay for going into his corner or standing in front of the net. He is really good on the Penalty Kill by getting sticks in the lanes and taking away cross crease passes. He is good at moving players away from the net so his goalie can see the puck.

Stepan is a late bloomer, but because of his 6'07" size and the overall performance he had in the OHL this year, there is a very good chance that Falkovsky hears his name called at the 2016 NHL Entry Draft. He will need to improve on his backwards skating and continue to add muscle to his frame.

Quotable: " I didn't see Ottawa as often this year as years past, but our scout in Ottawa saw them a ton. I'll defer to him a bit on Stepan but one area where our viewings didn't align was moving the puck. Stepan struggled in this area in my viewings of him. I actually thought his 'hands' were on the weak side." - Mark Edwards

Fallstrom, William
RW - Omaha Lancers (USHL) 5'10", 161
HockeyProspect.com Ranking: NR

Fallstrom is a player we expected to have more success in his first year in the USHL after coming over from Djurgardens (SWE) Jr. League. The University of Minnesota commit never seemed to really get comfortable with his role in Omaha and there were nights where he went largely unnoticed.

Fallstrom is an excellent skater who brings a lot of pace and energy to his game. He won't cheat you on effort in any zone and was able to create turnovers and strip players with the puck. Fallstrom seemed to struggle with the smaller ice service in North America where you have less time to make plays with the puck and was susceptible to committing turnovers in the neutral zone and coming out of his own end. Fallstrom is a gifted offensive player and has good finishing ability around the net but needs to learn to process the game quicker and make better decisions with the puck.

Quotable: "I expected more offense out of him at the USHL level." - NHL Scout (March 2016)

Felhaber, Tye
LW - Saginaw Spirit (OHL) 5'10.75", 191
HockeyProspect.com Ranking: NR

Felhaber was taken in the first, round, 10th overall at the 2014 OHL Priority Selection Draft by the Saginaw Spirit out of the Ottawa Valley Titans Minor Midget program. Felhaber had a very good year statistically as a rookie and was expected to take his game to the next level as a 17 year old. However he struggled to do so and actually scored less in his second year than his first.

The first think you'll notice about Felhaber is his smooth, speedy skating ability. He accelerates well and has the speed to burn defenders. He is capable of beating defenders one on one, but will sometimes settle for low percentage perimeter shots. He has a tendency to try and do too much with the puck, which can get him into trouble. He's passing more frequently than past seasons, and has made some creative, skilled passes, but his ability to create offense for his linemates is very inconsistent. Felhaber tends to avoid the rough stuff, isn't known for his ability to stay on his feet and can be knocked around and neutralized when the game becomes too physical. Defensively speaking Felhaber was hit or miss on a shit by shift basis.

Tye showed both in Minor Midget and at times through his first two OHL seasons that he has some offensive upside that will draw interest from some NHL teams. However, while we expect him to be a good junior player and may warrant a later round selection at the 2016 NHL Entry Draft, he simply doesn't play the style of game, nor does he have the skill to project well at the NHL level.

Quotable: "I actually crossed him off my list after three bad games." - NHL Scout (December 2015)

Quotable: "I wasn't impressed last season so you can probably guess what I think this season." - NHL Scout (November 2015)

Quotable: "I was not a big fan of Felhaber in his OHL Draft year, but he gave me some reason to watch him closer after posting some numbers in his OHL rookie season. This year he wasn't good when I saw Saginaw. I thought he was lazy away from the puck. - Mark Edwards

Felixson, Oliver
LD – Saint John Sea Dogs (QMJHL) – 6'05", 213
HockeyProspect.com Ranking: NR

We go a long way back with Felixson, as we first saw him as a 15 year old in Châteauguay for a hockey tournament versus the Quebec U-16 team. Felixson made the move to North America this season after being selected by the Sea Dogs in the CHL Import Draft (25th overall). The Helsinki native is huge, standing at 6'5", 213 lbs., and still growing. He does his best work in his own zone where he can use his size and reach to his advantage. He does a good job on the PK unit, clearing the front of the net and blocking passing lanes with his long stick. There's not a whole lot of upside offensively with Felixson, as his decision-making is slow with the puck on his stick and he doesn't have a lot of creativity in the offensive zone. His footwork is average at best. Because of this, he always plays a safe game to avoid getting caught by speedy forwards. He's huge and can be physical when need be, but we didn't see a mean streak out of him this season (his 15 PIM on the season is a good indication of that). It will be surprise for us to see him get drafted in June.

Field, Sam
RW - Kingston Frontenacs (OHL) 6'01" 190
HockeyProspect.com Ranking: NR

Field was drafted in the 6th round of the 2014 OHL Priority Selection Draft by the Kingston Frontenacs out of Choate Rosemary Hall School. Field made the Frontenacs as a 16 year old and has played a limited role over 2 seasons.

Field struggled to stay in the Frontenacs roster throughout the season, however when he did find playing time he often skated in a fourth line role with the team. A big bodied winger with limited offensive upside, Field is at his best on the defensive side of the puck. Field shows good defensive zone awareness with the ability to limit the oppositions effectiveness. He gets his body in the shooting and passing lanes well. Field will block shots and effectively deflect/pick-off passes. Field often errors to much on the defensive side of the puck and is the last forward to leave the zone. His skating would be considered average at best, due to a short and choppy stride that doesn't allow him to generate much speed. Field's lack of speed coupled with him often playing as a third defensemen of sorts, leaves him unable to join the offensive attack, trailing the play by a large gap. Field may turn into a decent third line, checking winger in the future, but his upside is very limited at the next level.

Filipe, Matt
LW – Cedar Rapids Rough Riders (USHL) 6'1.5", 196
HockeyProspect.com Ranking: 128

Matt is a late 97 Birthday who started the season in a bottom six role with Cedar Rapids and it took some time for him to adjust to the size and speed of the USHL but eventually saw himself playing a top six role for the Rough Riders and was a key point producer to their team down the stretch.

Filipe is a fast skating power forward with a solid base, is strong on his skates and can make power moves toward the net with the puck. Filipe has good hands and can make some slick moves with the puck in traffic and doesn't need a lot of room to get his shot off. Matt can bring a physical and nasty style to his game and won't cheat you on effort at either end of the ice.

The drawback to Matt's game at the moment is he doesn't think the game at a high level and makes some decisions with the puck that don't match his skill set or style of play. Filipe struggles understanding the player he needs to be in order to be successful and can try to play too much of a finesse game at times. The simpler Filipe keeps his game the more of an impact he makes.

Quotable: "He can really skate for a guy his size, big kid with athletic ability. I think he has limited hockey sense and I don't think he can make it as a skill guy so that obviously drops his stock on my list." - HP Scout Mark Edwards

Finoro, Giordano
RC - Barrie Colts (OHL) 5'11" 172
HockeyProspect.com Ranking: NR

Finoro was selected in the 8th round of the 2014 OHL Priority Selection Draft by the Barrie Colts out of the Guelph Jr. Gryphons Minor Midget Program. Finoro spent his 16 year old season with the Guelph Jr. B Hurricanes developing his game. He made his OHL debut this season and while he appeared in most games, he was utilized primarily as a fourth line centre.

While Finoro didn't get a ton of ice time he was fairly effective in a checking role. He is defensively responsible and was rewarded at times with some shifts on the penalty kill. He is not a very physical player but he possesses good speed and drive. This allowed him to win his fair share of puck battles and out race opponents to loose pucks. Finoro is at his best when he makes quick decisions with the puck and plays with pace. He doesn't look for contact but he doesn't play scared and tends to get a good portion of his shots around the paint as a result. He's a little more of a shoot first player, and prefers to put pucks on net than pass to his linemates. Finoro projects as a defensive forward at the next level and lacks enough skill to progress beyond that. With that said we don't expect him to be selected at the 2016 NHL Entry Draft.

Fitzgerald, Casey
RD – Boston College (Hockey East-NCAA) 5'11" 185
HockeyProspect.com Ranking: 200

He is a Dman that was given opportunity to play his game as a freshman at BC under Head Coach, Jerry York. While previous playing at NTDP, not sure he was given the situation to display his skill sets and hockey IQ during his draft year. He skates well and handles the puck with poise, even though he is not the biggest blue liner. He makes good puck decisions with the first pass and distributes well on the PP. His shot is more accurate than heavy and he does a good job at finding shooting lanes and the open seam to set-up scoring opportunities. He also isn't shy from the physical side and plays tough defensively. He has a good head on his shoulder and with added strength he will only continue to improve. He produced well in 39 games as a true frosh with 4-23-27 and solid +27. With his dad having a long, successful NHL career and older brother Ryan (BC) a draft pick of the Boston Bruins, a mid-late round selection could be a reality.

Quotable: "I only saw him a few times this year but he was pretty good. I liked the way he passed the puck. I'd call him an agile skater more than a pure speed guy. I think he'll get drafted." - NHL Scout (May 2016)

Fitzpatrick, Evan
Goaltender – Sherbrooke Phoenix (QMJHL) – 6'04", 206
HockeyProspect.com Ranking: 54

Fitzpatrick was the 4th overall pick in the 2014 QMJHL Draft coming out of the Newbridge Academy program in the Nova Scotia Major Midget Hockey League. In his second season with the Sherbrooke Phoenix, he was able to win the starting job and played in 54 games on a disappointing Sherbrooke team. Fitzpatrick is big and covers a lot of space in his net, he's very calm and he's a good athlete. He does a good job with his rebound control on most nights and has a good glove. At his best, Fitzpatrick could be a candidate to be the number one goaltender chosen in the draft and he could also be a top

40 pick in the draft. The big problem with him has been his lack of consistency from game to game over the last two seasons. During one game, he looks like a high-end goalie prospect and the next he will give up soft goals. He did, however, play his best hockey in the playoffs, highlighted by a 73-save performance against Shawinigan in game 5 of the first round. He looked really good in the playoffs, like a goaltender who took the next step in his development playing real focused hockey. He was also very good at the World Under-18 Hockey Championship, playing for Canada until the semi-finals vs. Sweden. He still needs to work on consistency issues in the next couple of years and being dominant for a long stretch during the season. He has the potential to be a good goaltender at the next level with that size and athleticism, but consistency will be the key for him to achieve success moving forward.

Quotable: "Interview was fine, seemed a little bit more immature than some other kids." - NHL Scout (Combine week)

Fontaine, Gabriel
Center - Rouyn-Noranda Huskies (QMJHL) – 6'01", 185
HockeyProspect.com Ranking: 163

Fontaine was not drafted in the 2015 NHL Draft and was also traded from his hometown team, the Sherbrooke Phoenix, to the Rouyn-Noranda Huskies during the summer. He did take part in the St. Louis Blues' rookie camp last September but was not signed. The move to Rouyn-Noranda was a good one for Fontaine. With the Huskies, he got the chance to play in a top-6 role on the top team in the league, whereas in Sherbrooke, he was at best playing on a 3rd line and destined to be a depth defensive forward with them. This year, he was a jack-of-all-trades, playing in every situation possible for the Huskies: PP, PK, against the top line of the opposition, and lead-protection in the final minutes of periods and games. He was a key member of the Huskies' PK unit: good on faceoffs, shot-blocking and with a good active stick to block passing lanes. He's a very smart player with excellent hockey sense; he pays attention to the little details at both ends of the ice. He's a good skater with a good burst of speed who can carry the puck into the offensive zone. He's strong on his skates; he's not an overly physical player but does very well along the boards with good body positioning to win his puck battles. His offensive production made big strides this year following his increase in responsibilities, but this is not a player who we expect to score big points at the pro level. His bread and butter will be his smarts and defensive game at the pro level.

Quotable: "One of the most under-rated trades of the off-season last summer was Rouyn-Noranda getting Fontaine out of Sherbrooke. He does everything on the ice. He's like having a coach on the ice, super smart and pays attention to all the little details. Wish he would score more, though." - HP Scout Jérôme Bérubé

Quotable: "Fontaine is one of my sleepers but he's about to play in the memorial cup so he might not be a sleeper much longer. I think you win with guys like Fontaine. He's a guy I would've loved on my teams back when I coached, he's a player coaches can trust. He is a warrior on the PK and the guy you have hopping the boards when you have the one goal lead. I saw him create some offense as well. I think he will get drafted." - HP Scout Mark Edwards

Fonteyne, Matt
LC/LW – Everett Silvertips (WHL) 5'10", 180
HockeyProspect.com Ranking: NR

Fonteyne is a playmaking center that is neither too big or too fast but has some feistiness to him. Fonteyne is a late 97' and has played his third season for Everett, more than doubling his production from last year. Fonteyne is a decent playmaker who sees the ice well. His game starts off-the-puck as he is useful as a forechecker, reads the ice well and can cause turnovers. He has good vision and can make plays off breakdowns. Since he is neither the biggest or the fastest, it is a bit more challenging for him to control possession with any consistency. He is more of a quick-strike forward. He will go to the scoring areas both with and without the puck and works for his offense. He will try to play bigger than his size on the wall, but with mixed success. Competes well defensively too, but it is unlikely to be a strong point of his at the pro-level. One issue is that he sometimes wants things to happen too quickly and will try to force plays on offense when even a slight delay would open up another option for him. This can sometimes result in him losing the puck as fast as he gained it, as he could show more patience for his linemates to catch up. The positive side is that he has good work-ethic and works to win pucks for his team all over the ice.

Fortier, Maxime
RW – Halifax Mooseheads (QMJHL) – 5'10", 178
HockeyProspect.com Ranking: 104

Fortier had a really good second season in the league, finishing with 77 points on a very mediocre Halifax team. One good thing about Fortier's season was that he kept producing and got better in the 2nd half of the season, even after Halifax traded away key players during the trade period. Fortier is a good skater. He can give opposing teams headaches with his speed while entering the zone, and he has the ability to blow past defenders. Ever since joining the Mooseheads, Fortier has improved his playmaking abilities. He still has a shooter's mentality, but now makes better use of his linemates than he did in Midget AAA with the Lac St-Louis Lions. When projecting Fortier at the NHL, he would have to be an offensive winger, as he's primarily an offensive player. He does have some attributes that could make him a good penalty killer, such as his anticipation and speed that make him a threat to score shorthanded. He was very good in Midget while shorthanded and scored many goals this way, but as of now, has not found that same success shorthanded at the junior level. His hockey sense is average, as he doesn't always make the right decision with the puck and his positional game could be better in the defensive zone. He has good puck skills and can score with his quick wrist shot, as he proved this past season by scoring 31 times. He has a good nose for the net and quick hands. He's not a physical player, though, and for the NHL level he's seen as a small player that will need to get stronger physically to compensate.

Fox, Adam
RD – USNTDP 5'10", 185
HockeyProspect.com Ranking: 67

Fox is an undersized and skilled right defenseman. Fox featured prominently on USNTDP's blueline and was its most consistent offensive weapon. Fox has some frame-size issues, but offers a solid offensive defenseman package.

Fox can be counted on to create offense both at even strength as well as on power-play. He's got a good ability to quarterback the offense from the back. Good skating ability, but not one that would knock our socks off for a defenseman his size. Has good puck-skills and creativity with puck. Adept at finding solutions in moving the puck out under forechecking pressure. Has confidence with puck and isn't shy about making a move to open up a lane and does so with good success most of the time. Will pinch and make good plays in offensive zone, isn't shy about pinching and taking the puck off the wall to make a creative play deeper in offensive zone. Good passing vision and can hit a stretch-pass out of his zone. Can also hit an open forward with a long piercing pass in the offensive zone. Great puck-distributor who can get shots on net and isn't stupid about his shot selection, but might not have huge point-shot threat from the offensive blueline.

Solid defensive positioning. Knows that he has to find forwards in uncomfortable situations to strip them of the puck as he doesn't have much chance of physically defending. Lack of size also limits his reach. Can pick up forwards with his skating but lacks the ability to control space with his stick as there is not enough reach in him, stick is good in-tight though. Can swat pucks off the forward's stick once he gets closer and quickly move it out once he has control of it. Fox is a good puck-mover, with good offensive hockey IQ and skills. The lack of size will make it an uphill battle for him to defend against bigger forwards.

Quotable: "He's pretty bigtime with the puck on his stick on the powerplay but I don't know how he's going to play 5 on 5 in the NHL at that size." - NHL Scout (April 2016)

Quotable: "Skating not great for a guy his size and he can be a little slow to move the puck up ice at times. I saw some hiccups retrieving pucks. I like his smarts and he looks good in the offensive zone. He just has a few issues that scare me off a bit. I'll say this, I heard a lot of varying opinions on him. NHL Scouts seem to either really like him or want no part of him." - HP Scout Mark Edwards

Fox, Trent
LW - Hamilton Bulldogs (OHL) 6'03", 199
HockeyProspect.com Ranking: NR

Fox is a 2nd time eligible prospect from the 2015 NHL Entry Draft. He was originally selected by the Erie Otters in the 5th round of the 2013 OHL Priority Selection Draft out of the London Jr. Knights program. He was invited to St. Louis Blues camp after going un-drafted.

Fox saw a solid increase in his offensive numbers this season and was constantly given opportunity on the top six lines. This resulted in him doubling his goal totals from last season. Fox is a big power winger who has a pretty hard shot, but sometimes doesn't have the best accuracy, not necessarily missing the net, but hitting the logo on the goaltenders chest quite a bit. He can be dangerous in the goal area and has the physical strength to fend off checkers. He flashed some offensive skill that has kept scouts interested. His skating is below average and will need continued improvements. He has also displayed a good physical edge to his game, but this part of his game is highly inconsistent, as he will sometimes look very disinterested. Trent's increase in production is appealing, but going back to Minor Midget he has always struggled greatly with consistency. He will look like a star one minute, disinterested the next. This will be his biggest obstacle to overcome in order to become a potential NHL prospect.

Quotable: "He scored the bulk of his goals in a handful of games. He's not on my list. NHL Scout (February 2016)

Frederic, Trent
LC – USNTDP 6'02", 203
HockeyProspect.com Ranking: 85

Frederic is a work-horse center that provides a diligent, blue-collar game down the middle. Frederic most often centered USNTDP's second line and didn't have the luxury of playing with the team's best offensive players in Keller and Bellows.

Frederic possesses good size and skating ability. Together they provide him with the framework to play his typical hard-nosed game. Frederic never stops moving his feet and will work his butt off to be involved on both ends of the ice. While Frederic's offensive game lacks high-end skill, he was able to produce through hard work and a honest approach, taking straight lines to high-percentage areas. He also has some playmaking ability as he can spot open forwards in the offensive zone, but his hands and deception might not be good enough to manufacture lanes on his own at the next level. Impressive is also his commitment to defense, as he can be an annoying presence when working to establish body contact with his size and the willingness to dig-in in battles.

Frederic has a well-rounded game and is the type of player that can consistently provide you with a honest shift full of effort. He knows his game inside and out and there is really no question mark as to what he will provide while he's out on the ice, he is a low-maintenance player for coaches. Ultimately, the biggest question mark is his offensive upside. Right now, he is capable of producing through sheer effort and while not lacking in smarts, his game has a certain lack of high-end skill and deception with the puck that would throw off defensive coverages.

Quotable: "He always seemed to score when the game was already out of hand. - NHL Scout (April 2016)

Quotable: "Pretty good player down the middle, was good on draws when I saw him and he is pretty smart defensively. I think he lacks on the offensive side of the puck and needs to get quicker. Upside is probably a 4th line centre in the NHL but I'm not sure he has the pace of play to get there. - HP Scout Mark Edwards

Friend, Jacob
RD - Owen Sound Attack (OHL) 6'02", 185
HockeyProspect.com Ranking: NR

Jacob Friend was passed over at the 2013 and 2014 OHL Priority Selection Draft. Jacob was signed by the Owen Sound Attack late last season after a strong season with the Cobourg Jr. A Cougars of the OJHL. Friend played his first full season in the OHL and made an impact with the Attack quickly being moved up to a top four role.

Friend is anything but Friendly when engaging with the opposition. He loves the physical game and always seems to crush multiple opponents every single game. He has a great mean streak and wins a ton of battles as a result of his edgy play. He also showed the ability to not only drop the gloves, but handle his opponents well. Away from the physical stuff, he's a very defensively minded. He does a good job one on one as his skating and his puck skills both saw steady development this season. He moved the puck up ice quickly and made smart decisions. He also has a pretty hard shot.

Friend is in his first re-entry year for the NHL Draft and could warrant a late round selection. If he is not picked, Jacob will likely get multiple camp invite offers where he'll have the opportunity to show his physical play against bigger and more talented opponents.

From, Mathias
RW – Rogle BK (SHL) – 6'01", 187
HockeyProspect.com Ranking: 86

From is a right winger that has good size and speed. He also has a competitive streak which along with his athletic tools has allowed him to already appear in 16 SHL games as well as to play with Denmark's men's team.

From is the type of winger that can drive the play in all three zones. He has good acceleration and top speed and a solidly built frame. He can be engaged in his own zone and skate pucks out. He is a player that is most successful when he keeps moving his feet, this allows him to be involved in bringing the puck through neutral and into the offensive zone with a straight-ahead effort. From has decent hands and good stickhandling ability but won't necessarily beat defensemen with his puck skills, instead he is better when using his size and skating to gain separation and protect the puck. He can be dangerous on counter attacks and has good enough offensive zone instincts to chip in with offense.

Overall, he is a player that has a good combination of physical tools and enough smarts and skills to make him a decent prospect. There are enough dimensions to his game that he could play a variety roles and special teams in his future and could easily be projected either as a checking winger that can drive the play forward or someone who could legitimately be a complementary wing on a scoring line. This will depend on how his offense keeps developing and how much he will improve his play without the puck.

Galipeau, Olivier
LD – Val D'Or Foreurs (QMJHL) – 6'01", 200
HockeyProspect.com Ranking: NR

Galipeau is in his 2nd year of eligibility for the NHL Draft; he has been the Foreurs' captain since the 2014-2015 season. He has become, in his 3rd season, a very dependable two-way defenseman in the QMJHL. After the regular season was over, he was one of three finalists for the Kevin Lowe Award (awarded to the QMJHL's top defensive defenseman). Galipeau is a big boy and loves to play a physical game. He has good anticipation to step up and deliver hard hits. Even by playing a physical game, he's able to stay disciplined. On the penalty killing unit, he often blocks shots, not hesitating to clear the front of the net when necessary. He was the defenseman with the most ice time for the Foreurs this year; he played in every situation and was often the lone defenseman on the first power play unit. He has improved his play with the puck since coming into the QMJHL, but his decision-making is still slow and he got a lot of points just by playing alongside a very good group of forwards on Val-d'Or's power play. This season, 6 of his 9 goals came on the power play. His improvements are still not enough for him to be considered as a natural puck mover and an offensive defenseman. Galipeau's bread and butter remain his defensive and physical play when trying to project him at the pro level. He could get a look late in the draft after his strong season, but more than likely will get a try-out for an NHL rookie camp in the summer.

Gambrell, Dylan
RC – University of Denver (NCHC - NCAA) 5'11.75", 175
HockeyProspect.com Ranking: 138

Gambrell is another overage prospect for this year's draft that we though had a shot at getting drafted last season after having a terrific year with Dubuque (USHL). Gambrell plays a solid game in all 3 zones, he understand assignments and works hard all over the ice. He possesses and excellent shot, the puck rips off his tape quickly and catches goalies off guard. Over the course of this season we saw Gambrell gain more confidence and started to make an impact on a nightly basis in the second half of the season and was key to Denver returning to the Frozen Four in Tampa.

Gambrell's skating has improved but still needs some work, his foot speed is ok but not where it needs to be yet and needs to work on moving the puck quicker. Gambrell gets into position and finds the open ice well but can take too long to get the puck off his tape and see's his time and space disappear quickly. We feel these are issues in his game he can certainly work out in his time at Denver; Dylan has a strong work ethic, very coachable and has a desire to improve.

Quotable: "I think his numbers got inflated a bit this year because he played with two of the best players on college hockey." - NHL Scout (April 2016)

Gardiner, Reid
RW/RC – Prince Albert Raiders (WHL) 5'11", 193
HockeyProspect.com Ranking: NR

Gardiner is a third time draft eligible scoring forward. Gardiner's game mostly centers around his shot. He can play both wing and center positions, has a reasonably stocky frame, decent skating ability, but when it comes down to it, it's really his shot that sets him apart. Gardiner has made improvements to his overall game as he got older, his skating improved and he put on some muscle, which is to be expected as he is already 20 years old. Gardiner at his best is a player that looks for his shot in the offensive zone and competes when without the puck. Gardiner won't cheat you on effort but can struggle to get involved at a consistent level. He's a solid if unspectacular defensive player and when he's not getting opportunities for his shot, he is just passable overall. Gardiner's shot is high-end, he has a great wrister that he can both get off quickly from up close or load it up and release it from distance beating goalies clean. He reads the offensive gaps well, but might not have the vision or the skill to create offense at the next level. While Gardiner's shot is clearly a projectable trait and his game has improved overall, he is a also a 20 year old in his fourth WHL season and still doesn't truly stand out as a dominant force on ice, which raises some question-marks about his upside at higher levels.

Gauthier, Julien
RW – Val D'Or Foreurs (QMJHL) – 6'04", 224
HockeyProspect.com Ranking: 25

This season was Gauthier's 3rd season in the league after being drafted 6th overall in the 2013 QMJHL Draft by the Foreurs. Gauthier was red-hot in the first half of the season, averaging a goal a game and earning a spot on Team Canada's World Junior team in December. At the WJC, he didn't get much ice time and was not able to have much of an impact in the tournament. Back with Val-d'Or, he struggled in the 2nd half, as he was not scoring like he did in the first half and averaged under a point a game, which was a bit worrisome playing on the 2nd best team in the league. Gauthier has a lot of tools to make him a successful NHLer one day: NHL size, speed, shot, and hands, but we're concerned about his ability to think the game and make players around him better. His low total of assists was a real concern for us all year long; he's not the most creative player with the puck as he usually uses his strength and speed to create scoring chances for himself. He's very good to protect the puck in the offensive zone, using his size and long reach well. Sometimes, you could see him with one hand on his stick but still managing to keep control of the puck because of his pure strength. On the power play, he was the guy screening the opposing goaltender - he did a terrific job, without having to take penalties. Gauthier can score from many different ways: with speed off the rush, using his shot in the slot or in front of the net by jumping on rebounds, or by tipping pucks in front of the opposing goaltender. Defensively, Gauthier has made some strides since coming into the QMJHL. He's strong along the wall and is able to get the puck out and has used his long stick better to block passing lanes. Gauthier won't ever be known as a penalty-killing specialist, but he has improved enough to not be a liability in his own zone at even-strength. Even if Gauthier is one of the most physically imposing forwards in this draft class, his physical game is very inconsistent at this point, as he doesn't play like a power forward every game and in some games he prefers playing a soft, skilled game. There's still a lot of immaturity in his game. Gauthier's bread and butter will remain his offense, even with an average hockey sense there's still tools that he possesses that could make him an NHL'er one day.

Quotable: "Other than a game at Team Canada camp in December, Gauthier wasn't all that graet in my viewings. He could barely complete a pass at times. He is a huge kid with great tools, but I seldom saw him make use of them. I question his hockey sense and at times he seemed to have selective hustle. Just not a player that overly impressed me this season." - HP Scout Mark Edwards

Quotable: "For me the most over hyped player in the 1st round is Gauthier. I wouldn't touch him in the 1st round." - NHL Scout (October 2015)

Quotable: "I'm not a big fan." - NHL Scout (December 2015)

Quotable: "He didn't do anything to impress me at World Juniors." - NHL Scout (January 2016)

Quotable: "I like him but not in the top 15." - NHL Scout (October 2015)

Quotable: "He was a funny kid and he is ripped. His arms are unbelievable. He was a really easy kid to talk to." - NHL Scout (Combine week)

Quotable: "I got great feedback from teams on their interviews with Gauthier. Several mentioned that he was an easy going or funny kid." - HP Scout Mark Edwards (Combine week)

Gerlach, Max
RC – Medicine Hat Tigers (WHL) 5'09", 163
HockeyProspect.com Ranking: NR

Gerlach is a small but mobile sniper who completed his first year of WHL hockey. Gerlach displays really good speed off the rush and high-end offensive instincts past the blueline.
He has unpredictable movement with good hockey sense. Still undersized, he'll become more useful as an F-1 forechecker with added size and strength. Away from the puck, Gerlach manages to sneak into high-opportunity scoring areas seemingly unnoticed. From there, he hoists a full toolbox of shooting options, highlighted by a strong and accurate wristshot from anywhere in the offensive zone.

Aside from his lack of size and strength, there are several other question marks that surround Max's game. Gerlach's defensive game and defensive effort both leave something to be desired. Furthermore, his compete level disappears when the score seems out of his reach. He can also look a bit reluctant when it comes to battling in the tough areas of the ice.

Gettinger, Tim
LW - Sault Ste. Marie Greyhounds (OHL) 6'05.25", 200
HockeyProspect.com Ranking: 52

Gettinger was selected in the third round of the 2014 OHL Priority Selection Draft by the Sault Ste. Marie Greyhounds out of the Cleveland Barons U16 program. Gettinger played in the bottom six as a

16 year old rookie last season and put up some good numbers with 25 points. However, those totals only increased to 39 despite playing a top six role with plenty of power play action.

Gettinger is a huge winger who has extremely skilled hands. He does a great job stickhandling around defenders despite lacking great skating ability to evade defenders. When he can combine this with good body positioning it makes it nearly impossible to get the puck off him. He has improved in this area, as he was too easy to knock off the puck early in the season. He has good positioning in the slot on the power play and has contributed to some goals here because of quick hands and the goaltenders inability to see past him. Despite the big frame, Gettinger lacks much strength. This affected him with his ability to finish his check, as lacked the power someone his size should and looked awkward when trying. He will take the puck to the net but has a habit of shooting at the goalie's logo.

His skating will also need work and his hockey sense is a little questionable at times, but he has the size and puck skills to give him value in this draft. Gettinger would be considered a project, as he has a lot of room to add muscle, improve skating and improve his awareness of the play. All of these will take time. His upside would be as a secondary offensive winger who is in the higher end when it comes to size, but he will need to be a little more nasty to play against to get the full value out of his size.

Quotable: "Because of his size he will get drafted long before I'd be willing to take him." NHL Scout - (December 2015)

Quotable: "I saw him quite a bit this year and he had some flashes but in general I left thinking he could be much better. I think he struggles to keep up with the play at times, I really noticed it in the playoffs. Really like his hands but in the end I didn't like that I had to make an effort to find him on the ice too often." - Mark Edwards

Gignac, Brandon
LC – Shawinigan Cataractes (QMJHL) – 5'11", 173
HockeyProspect.com Ranking: 93

The name of the game for Gignac is his speed. He is one of, if not the best skater in the entire QMJHL. When he can hit his top speed in the neutral zone, not many defenders in the league can contain him, as we saw him beat several of them wide numerous times with ease. He's not the biggest player on the ice, but he has grown at least three inches since being drafted in the QMJHL, and has gotten stronger physically. There's still a concern with his strength for the next level. Gignac can play all three forward positions, but we really liked his work down the middle. He's a smart player who plays very well at both ends of the ice. He makes good use of his speed on the backcheck, and is always there deep in the defensive zone to support his defense. He also loves to start rushing the puck from his own zone. He's a strong player on the PK unit; using his speed and anticipation very well. Offensively, he was never put into a leading role with Shawinigan. He was always featured primarily in a supporting role (2nd or 3rd line). It was only in December, with Beauvillier away at the World Juniors', where he filled the role of top center and had great success, with 14 points in 9 games. His offensive production had always been underwhelming since coming into the league. Gignac is not a natural finisher around the net and tends to play on the perimeter too often while in the offensive zone. A lot of the time, instead of taking the puck to the net on a rush, he will try a wrap-around attempt, shying away from the physical play. Overall, Gignac is a player we like because of his smarts and speed, but we worry about his offensive production and size for the next level.

Girard, Samuel
LD – Shawinigan Cataractes (QMJHL) – 5'09", 165
HockeyProspect.com Ranking: 70

Girard came into the QMJHL after being selected 3rd overall in the 2014 QMJHL Draft and had a stellar rookie season with the Cataractes: amassing 43 points in 64 games. Girard also played internationally at the U17 Hockey Challenge and the Ivan Hlinka U18 tournament last August.

Girard had a strong season offensively this year, leading all defensemen in the CHL in scoring with 74 points. Girard's 7 of 10 goals this year came on the power play and overall he racked up 38 points on the man-advantage, good for 6th overall in the QMJHL and 1st among defensemen. Girard has great footwork; he gets around the ice very well and controls the pace of the game. He loves to rush the puck in the offensive zone, either on the power play or at even-strength. He sees the ice very well and won't hesitate to rush the puck if the opposing team gives him free space on the ice. He's at his best on the power play; he possesses elite vision and can find his teammates on the ice with ease. He makes quick decisions on the ice and he's always in movement on the man-advantage. He can play a bit of a rover style on the power play by not standing still at the blueline. He's a terrific power play playmaker and can make plays that few players can execute. He doesn't possess a big shot from the point; it lacks velocity behind it, but it has good accuracy. With some added strength, his shot should improve, which would help him camouflage his current preference of being a passer on the play and be more diversified. His size is a major issue when trying to project him at the NHL level; defensively he does encounter some trouble versus bigger forwards along the boards and in front of the net. He's not afraid to dish some good hits here and there, but his size will limit him in what he can do. It's tough for him to battle in front of the net against big forwards, he needs to use his smarts and stick to win those battles. He also needs to play smarter in the defensive zone, keep his game simple and strong positional play. Girard has the offensive tools to one day quarterback a power play in the NHL, his size and defensive play are concerns we have when trying to project him at the next level. He had outstanding playoff with 22 points helping Shawinigan reach the QMJHL final.

Quotable: "Toughest to rank and project of any player in the QMJHL. His puck skills and vision are high-end, but his size is an issue. I believe he will find a way to become a PP specialist at some point in the NHL. On skills alone, he's a top-10 talent in this draft." - HP scout Jérôme Bérubé

Quotable: "It's not often that our Montreal based scout (Jérôme) and I disagree on a player but we did on Girard. I don't see Girard as often, but when I did, I didn't see a high pick for the NHL Draft. He was awful defensively, he kept turning away from the puck and it was driving me crazy. He did create some offense but his shot was nothing spectacular. His skating wasn't even as good as I expected. For me, when you are a 5'9" defenseman you need to be more impressive than Girard was when I saw him. - Mark Edwards

Quotable: "He hasn't done anything here today to make me think he can be an NHL'er" - NHL Scout - (November 2015)

Quotable: "I might end up having him (Girard) ranked higher than I thought. I'm struggling to find enough players I like enough to put on my list." NHL Scout (December 2015)

Quotable: "I really like him. I think he is a special player." NHL Scout (January 2016)

Gleason, Benjamin
LD - Hamilton Bulldogs (OHL) 6'00", 168
HockeyProspect.com Ranking: 90

Gleason was selected in the second round of the 2014 OHL Priority Selection Draft by the London Knights out of the Detroit Honeybaked U18 program.

Gleason has excellent skating ability and can get pretty fancy with the puck. Unfortunately sometimes he'll get a little too fancy and won't complete the play he's attempting to make. Gleason is at his best when using his quick hands and feet to exploit lanes, as he is very capable of completing an end to end rush. His passing ability is inconsistent. Over the course of the year he's made plenty of high end passing plays well across two lines and set up some big breakout plays. He has also missed some of these passes by a mile resulting in either risky turnovers or icings. Gleason lacks strength and sometimes his reaction time isn't great in the defensive zone, causing him to get exposed defensively. In the opponents end he creates offense and has a great shot, helping create scoring chances for his team.

Gleason is one of the tougher players to rank. He has a lot of skill to his game, but he is extremely inconsistent from shift to shift. We fully expect Gleason to hear his name called at the 2016 NHL Entry Draft and he projects as an offensive defenseman. He will be a project, but one who has the tools and the upside to possibly make the NHL one day.

Quotable: " I saw him in London's main camp and noticed how much bigger he got over last summer, he looked like a much improved player. He had some flashes of brilliance and played with more confidence this year but also had some ugly mixed in."
- Mark Edwards

Gosiewski, Matt
LC – Cedar Rapids Rough Riders (USHL) 6'3.75", 220
HockeyProspect.com Ranking: NR

Gosiewski only played 39 games for Cedar Rapids this season due to injury. Also because of the depth the Rough Rider's had down the middle, Matt mostly played a bottom six role but was very effective. Gosiewski can skate well and plays a very responsible game at both ends of the ice. Matt showed an active stick in the defensive zone and uses his size well in the faceoff circle. Gosiewski can really shoot the puck and has the skills going forward to be more than just a shut down center who can win draws. Matt still needs to add muscle and lower body strength so he can play a stronger game along the wall and control possession efficiently. Because of his lack of offensive production, limited playing time and injury Gosiewski may be a long shot to be drafted in June but we will follow Gosiewski closely next season as he will likely see a more significant role with Cedar Rapids.

Graham, Michael
RC – Eden Prairie (MN-HS) 6'1.5", 193
HockeyProspect.com Ranking: 202

Graham is yet another Minnesota High School player who opted to split his time between the USHL (Fargo) and Minnesota High School in 15/16. Graham de-committed from Minnesota Duluth and will likely return to the USHL next season and is committed to Notre Dame for 17/18. Graham was largely overshadowed throughout the season by fellow Minnesota H.S. Draft prospects Riley Tufte (Blaine) and Mitchell Mattson (Grand Rapids); however Graham had an impressive season for Eden Prairie H.S. and outplayed Mitchell Mattson in the Class 2A Semi Final game.

Graham plays a very balanced game down the middle, he is good at identifying his options and has the skill set to make the correct play with the puck. Graham comes away with the puck out of the corners more often than not and can do damage setting up players from behind the goal line and on the half wall. Graham played on a line with 2017 NHL Draft prospect Casey Mittelstadt and their line was dominant all season long, they had great chemistry and were able to read off each other well. Graham is a good skater and likes to come into the zone with speed to create his own space, cut to the middle of the ice and use his quick release to snap pucks on the net. It is possible Graham ends up being one of the top NHL Draft Prospects to come out of Minnesota High School hockey in this Draft Class.

Quotable: "He is a smart player who has a knack for making plays in traffic, it may take some time for him to get there but he could turn out to be the best player in this class of Minnesota High School players, he doesn't get a lot of the pub, but goes about his business." *HP Scout Dusten Braaksma*

Quotable: "Big kid who plays down the middle and is able to make plays. Like his skill and hockey IQ. He is a solid skater as well. That's that good. The bad is that he lacks some compete in his game, his motor doesn't run at top speed. He loses too many puck battles." - *HP Scout Mark Edwards*

Grametbauer, Mark
G – Gatineau Olympiques (QMJHL) – 6'01", 178
HockeyProspect.com Ranking: NR

Grametbauer started his rookie season with the Blainville-Boisbriand Armada, who selected him 41st overall in the 2014 QMJHL Draft. After playing backup to Florida Panthers' prospect Samuel Montembeault, he was traded during the QMJHL trade period to Gatineau. There, he shared the workload with fellow draft-eligible goaltender Mathieu Bellemarre. Grametbauer won 12 of his 15 games and posted great numbers, playing with one of the top defensive squads in the league. The Halifax native is an excellent competitor. He never quits on any pucks and made numerous saves on 2nd and 3rd rebounds. He's extremely athletic in his net; covering the lower part very well. He has excellent reflexes which help on deflections in front or on rebounds. His glove side has improved nicely since his midget days with the the Cole Harbour Wolfpack in the NSMMHL. We like his compete level. He might give bad goals here and there, but he always bounces back and stays focused on the game. With his size and athletic ability, we feel Grametbauer could be a nice option for an NHL team looking for a young goaltender late in the draft.

Grannary, Colin
RC – Merritt Centennials (BCHL) 6'00", 170
HockeyProspect.com Ranking: 156

Colin Grannary of the Merritt Centennials slowly became one of our favourite players to watch this year in the BCHL. Not overtly big or physical, Grannary finished the season eighth in league scoring, getting by on his maneuverability, his stickwork, and his intelligence. While his club struggled in the BCHL standings throughout most of the year, Grannary shined individually. He was also named Team MVP at the CJHL Top Prospects Game in Surrey, putting out one of the best performances in the showcase.

Equipped with really strong puck work and a knack for finding the key scoring areas, this University of Nebraska-Omaha commit stands out as the type of player who manufactures excellent plays out of seemingly nothing. Away from the play, Grannary is a dangerous offensive presence, as he likes to sneak his way into open scoring areas and has decent hands from in tight. With the biscuit on his stick, he frustrates opposition players in the offensive zone by playing keepaway with the puck. Furthermore, he's equally strong along the boards or in open-space, making him extraordinarily difficult to contain.

Definitely more of an offensive player, Grannary will have to work on becoming bigger and becoming more dependable in all situations. He's a good passer, but his shot could be a bit stronger and more accurate. His first-steps and acceleration speed will also have to undergo some improvement if he expects to take his game to the next level.

Grant, Owen
RD – Carleton Place Canadians (CCHL) 5'11" 165
HockeyProspect.com Ranking: NR

Owen was highly touted player coming out of his minor midget year playing for the Ottawa Valley Titans, he ended up playing half the year with Carleton Place last year as a 16 year old and played well. He is a commit to the University of Vermont in 2017-2018 season. Owen had a very solid year helping lead his team to a CCHL Championship. He didn't put up a lot of points this year, but was very solid in both ends of the ice.

Owen is a good skating puck moving defensemen that shows flashes of his skill as well as being a solid defender in his own zone. He is mobile defensemen that is good on his edges and can go forward to backwards effortlessly. His first 2 steps with the puck can be good, but would like to see him get quicker so he could pull away from defenders. He isn't an overly big defensemen so he does tend to get knocked around a bit, we would like to see him get stronger on his feet. He has a really good first pass out of his zone; he always tends to find the open man and always hitting him on his stick. Owen is really good and smart and reading plays and watching plays develop in front of him and reacting to the situations. He is good at carrying the puck up the ice and finding the open man and if there is no option, he doesn't panic with the puck, he will either go glass and out or regroup in his zone and find the open man. He doesn't have a hard shot from the point, but he has a very accurate shot that always hits the net, he is also really good at getting the puck through traffic looking for tips in front of the net.

Owen is good in his defensive zone and takes pride in his defensive game. Again not the biggest D so he's not going to hurt you physically, but he's really good at angling forwards into the corner, he has an active stick in the slot, and is good at anticipating where the puck is going to go in the defensive zone. Owen has a really good work ethic and competes every night and it shows, as he was an Alternate captain for his team this year at 17. Owen needs to get bigger and stronger in his frame and work on his quickness, with the right amount of time and development could turn out to be a good player at next level.

Quotable: " Owen is an undersized defensemen, but plays in all situations during a game and is excellent at reading the play and reacting to every situation." - HP Scout, Justin Sproule

Quotable: " Owen moves the puck very effectively and sees the ice really well. He makes the right decision on where to move the puck." - NHL Scout (April 2016)

Quotable: " Owen has a strong work ethic, and competes hard every shift and wants to win every battle." - HP Scout, Justin Sproule

Quotable: " He was a very steady and solid defensemen for Carleton Place and was a key player for that defense core all year long." - NHL Scout (April 2016)

Green, Luke
RD – Saint John Sea Dogs (QMJHL) – 6'01", 186
HockeyProspect.com Ranking: 71

Green was the top pick in the 2014 QMJHL Draft by the Sea Dogs, coming out of the Newbridge Academy Gladiators in the Nova Scotia Midget League. He had immediate success at the QMJHL level in 2014-2015, scoring 36 points and playing internationally at the U-17 Hockey Challenge.

This year, he repeated his offensive production with 35 points, but improved his defensive game under new head coach Danny Flynn. The name of the game for Green is his skating ability. He is one of the best skaters in the QMJHL, with an ability to rush the puck with ease and an effortless stride that makes it hard for players to keep up with him when he gets going. He saw ice time on the power play a lot this season, whether it was on the first or 2nd PP unit. Saint John is deep on the back end with the likes of Thomas Chabot, Jakub Zboril and Matt Murphy as capable point producers on the man-advantage. At even strength, in our viewings, Green played often with Murphy. The veteran, like Green, has good speed but is not the best in his zone and his decision-making is poor. We feel that if Green had played with a better defensive partner it might have helped him out a bit more. Green is strong physically, enough to handle players down low. He didn't show much desire to play physical in his own zone. At times, he was too easy to play against whilst in his zone. His decision-making has improved, as he was a bit of a mess in his own zone in Midget. He has made great strides since joining the Sea Dogs and playing under Danny Flynn sure didn't hurt him this season. Offensively, he creates a lot of chances with his feet, is a strong puck-rusher and is also active in the offensive zone at even-strength or on the power play. Right now, he's a purely offensive defenseman, always thinking offense and playing a high-risk game. Green has great puck skills, soft hands and moves the puck well out of his zone. His decision-making still needs work; as he needs to pick his spots better offensively. Next season, we would like to see him take the next step offensively and become one of the league's best offensive defensemen like Samuel Girard did this season.

Greenway, James
LD – USNTDP 6'05", 213
HockeyProspect.com Ranking: 82

The first thing that jumps out at you with Greenway is the large body. In addition to his frame-size, Greenway also has one or two flashes of brilliance per game that immediately put him on the radar, but lacks the consistency to make a shift-by-shift impact.

Greenway doesn't have the best acceleration in his first few steps, but still moves reasonably well for his size. There isn't a lot of explosiveness in his game, but he does possess a reasonable amount of fluidity to his movement. Greenway's game overall can be quite inconsistent as he is as prone to making a glaring mistake as he is to making a quality play. His defensive zone game is just average, he has a body that allows him to compete physically, but he's not really what we would classify as a punishing defenseman nor a defenseman that plays with a lot of energy. His positioning and control of space are also average. Offensively, Greenway isn't a consistent force, but he has several times in our viewings surprised by high-end moves whether it was deking someone out, or making a high-end stretch pass. In that sense, he seems to have some creativity and natural ability to see and execute plays.

Greenway is a big defenseman, that will need to continue to work on his footspeed and work harder to define himself as a player. The tools are there, but the shift-by-shift impact and the identity of his game are something that he will still need to establish. Often, we would walk away thinking that there is more to his game than what he bothered to show on a shift-by-shift basis.

Quotable: " I like him a lot at times but he can be a frustrating player. One example of how he will flash was his fantastic goal at the U18. The problem I have is he *seems to find a way to flash the bad as well. He's one of those guys who seems to make costly mistakes. He has some great tools but he scares me a bit." - HP Scout Mark Edwards*

Gregor, Noah
LW/C – Moose Jaw Warriors (WHL) 5'11", 175
HockeyProspect.com Ranking: 56

Noah was known as a pure scorer in his bantam year, a reputation that remains intact after a great seventeen-year-old season with the Moose Jaw Warriors. Gregor is a quick-footed and offensively gifted player who can be slotted into both wing and center positions.

Gregor has fantastic skating ability, both in his acceleration and top-speed as well as edgework and he uses this to his advantage with and without the puck. Gregor can protect the puck well utilizing his skating to put separation between himself and the player checking him, he can weave around the offensive zone with ease and will make plays off that. Gregor can dish the puck and shows decent vision in making plays with his linemates, however he is primarily a shooter. He's got an excellent release on his wrister, that he gets off quickly. He needs little room to shoot and can snap it even in crowded areas with bodies around him. He had a lot of success scoring goals as a power-play trigger-man. That said, this also ties into the fact that we would like him to become more of an even-strength presence. Gregor can at times be guilty of having too many "quiet" shifts in a game.

Gregor could definitely be more physical but he's well balanced for a player of his physical proportions and is difficult to knock off the puck as he has strong balance with the puck on his stick. Gregor has also shown a decent compete level, however his skating ability should allow for him to become a bigger checking presence than he is at this moment.

Gregor is a high-end skater with a fantastic release on his shot and the hockey IQ to find his way into high-percentage scoring areas. He is a very good power-play scorer. Going forward, we would like to see a more consistent impact at even strength. This year, he also had the benefit of playing alongside some great forwards like Brayden Point, Dryden Hunt, and Brett Howden.

Grundstrom, Carl
LW/RW – MODO (SHL) – 6'00", 194
HockeyProspect.com Ranking: 36

Grundstrom logged a full season with MODO in SHL, putting up a respectable 16 points in 49 games and also appeared for the Swedish U20 squad internationally. Coming in at 6 feet and 194 pounds, Grundstrom already has a fairly strong build which helps him compete against men. He has a strong compete level which is apparent in his will to drive the net with and without the puck. Once he gets going he shows above average skating ability, which helps him arrive to the net with speed and cause havoc. He likes to play a power-game at a high pace that when working continually drags the defense out of position and causes coverage break-downs as the defense will need to continually re-assess their position.

Grundstrom also likes to play a physical game, throwing his body around on the forecheck, in fact we have seen him make some borderline dangerous hits which resulted in penalties. His physicality and compete along with speed allow him to play an up-tempo game full of energy, but he also has enough puck skills to play with more skilled players.

That said, we have also seen Grundstrom make some rather questionable decisions with the puck. He has at times struggled to let the play develop. Instead of making a smart play, he would be stuck in his up-tempo mindset and force passes that weren't there or take himself out of play. For Grundstrom to project as a player that could play with skilled players at the NHL level, he will need to iron out those decision-making qualities and add some polish to the way he processes the game.

Quotable: "Was really high on him going into the year but ended up gradually cooling down on him with each passing month. I like the compete but he's tried forcing plays that weren't there too often in my viewings, made me question his offensive upside. Really like his will to drive the net, causes havoc in other team's defense and that will be something that should translate well to North American hockey." - HP Scout Nik Funa

Gustavsson, Filip
G – Lulea HF J20 (SWE) – 6'02", 184
HockeyProspect.com Ranking: 35

Gustavsson is a decently sized goaltending prospect that has strong positioning, fluid movement and an inherent calmness in his game.

Filip relies on his excellent positioning above anything else. He gets around fluidly in his crease and has an economy of motion to his movement. His size is legit and he uses it well to fill out the net. Has very solid fundamentals and sticks to his approach under pressure. He has a disposition of a calm, panic-free goalie which has a calming effect on his defense. While he doesn't rely on his athleticism, Gustavsson is capable of a quick burst and has a strong initial push. Athletic ability isn't a big weakness of his, especially as he doesn't particularly rely on it, however it's not quite high-end. Gustavsson tracks the play well and has good focus. Plays relatively conservative in his crease-area, more likely to retreat back than to wander too far out. Could maybe display a bit more authority over his crease on jam plays. Rebound control is good, doesn't give up a lot but when he does, he'll occasionally let one bounce right back out instead of to the side, which is a minor issue.

A positional goalie with solid technique, Gustavsson offers the size, the fundamentals, and the calmness in a package that makes him one of the better goalie prospects in this draft.

Quotable: "Clearly the best Euro goalie in this draft out of what is for me a rather underwhelming year for European goalies" - HP Scout Nik Funa

Quotable: "A goalie a few of our guys liked going back to last year. I just saw him again in Grand Forks and he is a notch above most of the goalies in this draft on tools alone. I've got him and Parsons in London as my top two goalies." - HP Scout Mark Edwards

Hall, Connor
LD - Kitchener Rangers (OHL) 6'02.5", 190
HockeyProspect.com Ranking: 40

Hall was selected in the third round of the 2014 OHL Priority Selection Draft by the Kitchener Rangers out of the Cambridge Hawks Minor Midget Program. He played a valuable role helping the Elmira Sugar Kings to the Jr. B provincial championship Sutherland Cup semi-final series, all while playing a handful of games with the Rangers. He started this season with Elmira, dealt with a jaw injury and then went from healthy scratch to a top minute defenseman for the Kitchener Rangers.

Hall is a big defenseman who loves to play physical. He finishes his checks every chance he gets. He will get in the face of the opposition and will battle hard for pucks down low. He is very strong for his size, but unlike a lot of big physical defensemen, Hall is actually a very good skater. He does a great job keeping up with his man one on one and closes the gap quickly. His reach and strength helps make him very tough to beat defensively. He is also capable of carrying the puck up ice and evading checkers. When in the offensive zone, he moves his feet well on the point making himself available as an option.

Hall has two-way ability but projects very well as a defensive first defenseman. His combination of skills and smarts is hard to find is a tough defender, which will raise his value that much more with NHL teams. He has also proven over the last three years to be on a continual sharp incline when it comes to improving and development which means the sky is the limit for Connor.

Quotable: "Connor is one of my favourite prospects in the entire draft. He's big, he loves to get involved physically, but he can also skate and has underrated puck moving ability. Someone's going to get a steal in this kid." - HP Scout Ryan Yessie

Quotable: "I thought he was great in the playoffs." - NHL Scout (April 2016)

Quotable: "Hall is the only reason I'm at this game." - NHL Scout (March 2016)

Quotable: "I really like Hall's game. He's a hard nosed player who often plays like it may be his last shift he ever plays. He impressed me playing well with big minutes versus the other teams top lines. One of the things that made a big impression on me was his blend of toughness matched with good puck moving ability." - HP scout Mark Edwards

Hagel, Brandon
RW – Red Deer Rebels (WHL) 6'00, 165
HockeyProspect.com Ranking: 180

Brandon played his first full season with the Rebels after having a strong Midget AAA campaign in 2015. He is an undersized yet very skilled forward who is always around the puck. When it comes to skating Hagel has good edges and agility and moves well laterally. His acceleration and top end speed is something that could improve however.

Hagel is a competitor, for a smaller forward he competes at a high level and does not allow his size to be a hindrance. He has shown the ability to produce offensively and has good hands around the net. He has good vision and is strong at protecting the puck, combined with his quick hands; he can easily slip past his check and use his quickness to gain space to create scoring chances. Hagel is a pass first type player but has the ability to score goals and we would like to see him use his shot more.
Hagel is a late developer that is still finding his way at the junior level, if he keeps on his current development path he could be a decent pick-up for a team

Hajek, Libor
LD – Saskatoon Blades (WHL) 6'02", 196
HockeyProspect.com Ranking: 32

In his first season in the WHL Libor was a bright spot in a rather disappointing season for the young Saskatoon Blades. Libor stands out as a strong, smooth skating defenseman who impacts the game on both sides of the puck. He he has very good acceleration and can explode off a stand-still. His first couple steps are very good as is his edge control and this allows him to have great escape ability in his own end as well to be a threat offensively as he can get up ice and join the rush. Hajek can also surprise with a move in the offensive zone where his quick feet allow him to quickly gain some space forward and try to make a play with the puck on his stick before the defense sets up into position again. Hajek is capable of getting his shots on the net but isn't a big threat there, his mobility and offense that springs from transition is more impressive than his offense from the point.

Hajek is a strong player that has great balance and agility and uses this to win puck battles along the wall, although he still needs to add some polish to his physicality as he can be prone to chasing the play a bit and losing his positioning in the process. Hajek is a strong defenseman in transition as he uses his size and skating to keep opponents to outside. He can also be the defenseman that recovers in time if his team turns the puck over in a dangerous position. Hajek is very hard to beat one on one and is very steady on odd man opportunities. If the forward dumps the puck past him, he also has the skating ability and size to win the race, get it back under control and start the transition the other way.

Libor needs to work on being more consistent from shift to shift if he is going to make the jump to the next level. We found that at times he would get caught chasing the play. He projects as a mobile two-way defenseman with size that will probably lean more towards the defensive side of it at the pro-level. That said, Hajek not only already is more than a defensive defenseman, he also has enough offensive tools to develop the offensive part of his game further as he moves forward.

Quotable: "He has a chance to be a first rounder. He really impressed me with his feet. This kid is mobile." - HP Scout Mark Edwards

Haman Aktell, Hardy
LD – Skelleftea J18 (SWE) – 6'03", 198
HockeyProspect.com Ranking: NR

Haman Aktell is a big defenseman who has spent the majority of the year playing for Skelleftea in the J18 league. For a big guy, he had quite impressive numbers putting up a point per game. The thing that stands out for Haman Aktell was the fact that despite his rather large frame, he still shows upside with his passing, vision, and surprisingly even offensive instincts. We have seen him line up on PP and he didn't look out of place at all, his sense for the game is quite good as he reads the play well and makes natural plays with the puck. Aktell will have to however improve on his footwork, especially in reverse as he tends to get beat wide by forwards with speed. There he often has to turn his feet to catch up. We've also seen him step up and lay a hit on a forward with his head down and he might become a more consistent physical presence once his skating improves and he becomes a bit more agile in all directions.

Hancock, Kevin
LW - Owen Sound Attack (OHL) 5'11", 180
HockeyProspect.com Ranking: NR

Kevin was selected in the fifth round of the 2014 OHL Priority Selection Draft by the Owen Sound Attack out of the Toronto Jr. Canadiens Minor Midget program. After a fairly successful year with the Jr. A Toronto Jr. Canadiens in his first junior season, Kevin joined the Attack full time, mostly in a third line role.

Hancock got off to a bit of a slow start in the OHL but progressed well this season finishing the year strong and showing some clear improvements from September. Hancock does a good job battling along the wing. He has a good compete level and can create chances from winning puck battles. He has a decent release on his wrist shot, and when in question he will shoot first. His skating ability is average, but he has good instincts, which help make up for his lack of higher end skating. Hancock may have improved enough to warrant a late round pick but at sub six feet with average skating and not projecting to have top six skill, we don't think he's a likely candidate to go at the 2016 NHL Entry Draft.

Hanley, Jack
LD - Hamilton Bulldogs (OHL) 5'10", 209
HockeyProspect.com Ranking: NR

Hanley was selected in the fourth round of the 2014 OHL Priority Selection Draft by the Belleville Bulls out of the Whitby Wildcats Minor Midget program. Hanley made the Bulls out of camp but has struggled to take his game to the next level in his second junior season.

Hanley is a good skating defender. He has excellent strength for his size. He landed some good hits and won more than his share of battles on the wall for his size. He can rush the puck up ice on occasion, but his puck skills are below average. One on one he's a little hit or miss. He can skate with players but he can still get walked. His reaction time is also a little off in the defensive zone.

Hanley's strength for his size has really helped him consistently receive ice as a 5'10" defensive defenseman. However he simply lacks the skill, consistency and upside to be a player that we would consider a prospect for the 2016 NHL Entry Draft.

Hannoun, Dante
RC – Victoria (WHL) 5'05, 154
HockeyProspect.com Ranking: NR

A highly touted player in the 2013 WHL bantam draft going eleventh overall, Hannoun has shown some flashes of strong offense but hasn't quite lived up to his high draft selection, despite increasing his point totals from 11 in his rookie season to 58 in his draft year. Plays the game hot and cold and sometimes looks difficult to find on the ice as he can get pushed around a lot. Despite his size he does show flashes of a powerful game and can shield pucks to make plays when he asserts himself. Plays in the slot on the power play and battles bigger forwards when it suits him, but doesn't show consistent push back physically and his game regresses when he takes heavy contact.

More of distributor than a shooter holds his stick in tight and uses small openings to distribute in a variety of directions; awareness of the players around him is very good. Makes strong plays off the rush and finds small spaces that others would miss, will drive the net but not consistently. Has a decent shot with a good release but telegraphs that he's more often looking to set up his line mates. Skates pretty well, showing decent acceleration and above average top end speed however has difficulty separating himself from defenders and opening himself up for plays, in turn limiting his skill set at times. His lack of size will make the transition to higher levels of hockey difficult and there is likely not enough offense to make up for it.

Harrogate, Brendan
RW - Mississauga Steelheads (OHL) 6'01", 174
HockeyProspect.com Ranking: 150

Harrogate was taken in the 7th round of the 2014 OHL Priority Selection Draft by the Mississauga Steelheads out of the Chatham-Kent Cyclones Minor Midget program. Harrogate played with the LaSalle Jr. B Vipers as a 16 year old playing a big offensive role for the team. He gained the opportunity to play in the Sutherland Cup, usually big roles are reserved for 19-21 year olds, Harrogate scored 9 goals in 13 games of the Sutherland Cup. He made the jump to the OHL this season and hasn't looked back.

Harrogate is an offensive forward who has adapted to a bottom six role with the Steelheads. He consistently shows great work ethic and competes for the puck. He battles hard and although he needs to add strength, his speed and determination helps him with a fair amount of battles. He has underrated offensive ability. He is capable of creating offense for himself and others and has done so with his speed. He is equally capable of finishing and setting up linemates.

Harrogate is a very well rounded talent who's offensive upside is untapped up to this point of his career. He has grown 4-5 inches and has the size once he fills out. He has the skating and the mindset to be an effective player in all game situations. A team may take a shot at Harrogate at the 2016 NHL Entry Draft. However, if he does go unselected, he will be a re-entry player to watch going into his second OHL season.

Quotable: "I believe Brendan was about 5'08", maybe 5'09" when he entered the OHL Draft. He's grown a ton. In Minor Midget he was known for his skill and offensive creativity and talent. I think you'll see a lot more of that as he gets more offensive opportunities. This kid is a sleeper with his skill and newly acquired size." - Ryan Yessie

Quotable: " If there is such thing as a sleeper these days, Harrogate is one of mine for a later round. He rarely got on the ice but I liked him more than many of the Steelheads players. Brendan managed to catch my eye flashing some skill and doing some smart things despite getting very few shifts in my viewings." - Mark Edwards

Hart, Carter
G – Everett (WHL) 6'01", 180
HockeyProspect.com Ranking: 43

It has been a big calendar year for Hart leading up to the draft as he managed an Ivan Hlinka gold medal, selections to the CHL Top Prospects game and the WHL/Russia series, and winning the Del Wilson trophy as the WHL's best goaltender while playing all but 9 of his teams regular season games. High praise for a goalie that was selected in the eight round of the WHL bantam draft and who received very little offensive support playing behind the 2nd lowest scoring team in the WHL and lowest of any team to make the playoffs.

He plays a compact game that shows very few holes to shooters both under his arms and at the five hole. Lateral movement is very quick and he plants and changes directions in a fluid manner and moves from his knees to his feet in the butterfly as quick as any goalie in the league. Hart is very sound in his positioning, efficient in his movements, both quick and flexible. He has a natural ability to read the flow of play and remain square to shooters showing patience and not over reacting to the attack. Fairly conservative by nature, he plays deep in his net and plants himself in the blue ice, although it would be more beneficial to challenge shooters and step outside the crease at times. This can lead to larger openings in the top of the net, something better shooters at pro levels will be able to take advantage of more so than in the WHL.

Hart will need to work on swallowing rebounds better as pucks do seem to bounce off him with some pop, although he does use good angles to direct pucks away from the slot and into the corners to keep high quality secondary chances to a minimum. Not the biggest frame by NHL goalie standards, Hart will need to bulk up to withstand the rigors of pro hockey but at 17 years old he likely hasn't finished growing. Some will attribute his success to the heavily defensive system played in Everett, but structure is something he'll find at pro levels as well, all in all Hart is one of the top goalie prospects for the 2016 draft.

Quotable: "He's in my top five goalies. I have Woll, Parsons, Gustavsson and Lafontaine with him." - NHL Scout (May 2016)

Quotable: "A goalie I really like but another one in this draft class who isn't that 6'4" that the NHL teams seek these days." - HP Scout Mark Edwards

Harvey, Samuel
G – Rouyn-Noranda Huskies (QMJHL) – 6'00", 190
HockeyProspect.com Ranking: NR

Harvey shared the workload with overager Chase Marchand in Rouyn-Noranda crease this season, playing in 35 games and winning 25. The Huskies selected Harvey in the 2nd round of the 2014 QMJHL Draft (39th overall). He's not the biggest goaltender, and would be well-suited to playing bigger in his net. He currently tends to play a bit deep in his crease and challenges shooters more aggressively. Harvey is a goaltender who won't get rattled by much on the ice, is always calm in his crease and focuses on the action. He does a good job covering the lower part of the net and tracks the puck well, even with traffic in front of him. Not the best athlete, but is very sound technically and doesn't make unnecessary movements in his crease. His puckhandling still needs some improvement, as he could help his defensemen out more this way. He had a bit of a slow start to the season but found his groove later on. He did well in the 2nd half when he got the call. Next season, he will be the Huskies' #1 goaltender with Marchand graduating, leading to a lot more playing time. The Huskies will still be a very good team next season, featuring a lot of returning players.

Hawerchuk, Ben
LW - Barrie Colts (OHL) 5'10", 182
HockeyProspect.com Ranking: NR

Hawerchuk was selected in the sixth round of the 2014 OHL Priority Selection Draft by the Barrie Colts out of the Toronto Titans Minor Midget program. Hawerchuk made the jump to the OHL as a 16 year old and provided an excellent work ethic in a reduced fourth line role to give his team a boost of energy. Hawerchuk moved up to the third line this season and saw a boost in his offensive numbers and his gritty game.

Ben may be a little undersized but he plays a lot bigger than his stature. He is at his best when he finishes his checks, is aggressive on the forecheck and is engaged physically. Hawerchuk won't hesitate to go to the dirty areas of the ice and will fight to stand up for teammates if necessary. With the puck Hawerchuk is a mixed bag. He does possess some playmaking skills but at times he tends to try and to do too much and that often doesn't go well. He needs to clean up his decision-making with the puck, especially in the defensive zone. Hawerchuk's shot lacks power and he hasn't shown a consistent ability to capitalize on chances when they come about, even in high-danger areas. Hawerchuk also struggles to create his own shot and can be prone to shooting it into opponent's shin pads. His top speed isn't overly high and he lacks explosiveness in his first three steps.

Ben lacks the offensive upside to be projected as a top six prospect. His style of game, toughness, ability to get under the skin of opponents, or simply outwork them projects very well to a bottom six role at the NHL level. However he lacks the desirable size at definitively under six feet tall to thrive in such a role.

Quotable: "Odds might be against him getting drafted but I'll say one thing, he's improved a lot since his OHL Draft year." - HP Scout Mark Edwards

Hebig, Cameron
RC – Saskatoon Blades (WHL) 5'11", 191
HockeyProspect.com Ranking: NR

Hebig is a strong skater with good speed and agility. He has great core strength and balance and is very hard to separate from the puck. Cameron played on a weak Blades team this year and was one of the few bright spots. In his third season in the WHL he has shown very steady progression during this time finishing with 69 points this season. He was relied upon to lead a younger group and was a great example in how he was always well prepared and brought an energy and compete to every game.

Hebig was always noticeable whether he was scoring a goal, laying a huge hit or blocking a shot. Cameron plays a fast, high paced game and loves to engage physically on the fore check by using his speed to force turnovers and play the body. He played both on the power play and the penalty kill and other important situations. Hebig played 59 games and had his best offensive output of his career. He is a solid, two way forward that can impact the game in many different ways. He wears his heart on his sleeve and competes hard every shift. He consistently does the little things very well and keeps his game simple and it has paid off for him.

Hellickson, Matthew
LD – USNTDP 6'00", 177
HockeyProspect.com Ranking: NR

Hellickson played more of a depth role on USNTDP's blueline as he was further down the depth chart than several more high-profile prospects. Hellickson is a mobile blueliner with good smarts. He makes good defensive reads and generally keeps up with his man well, his positioning is on-point but he tends to lack strength to really be effective. His overall mobility is well above-average and that helps him out as he is good on puck-retrievals and can get first to loose pucks. He's an easy player to play with as he always makes sure he's open up for an easy D to D pass. He has good vision with the puck and can spring forwards with stretch-passes. However, Helickson has just average size and hasn't shown himself to be much of a offensive producer. He is a fundamentally solid defenseman but hasn't distinguished himself as having NHL upside. He would either need to grow bigger and stronger or add more offensive punch to his game.

Helvig, Jeremy
G - Kingston Frontenacs (OHL) 6'03.25", 195
HockeyProspect.com Ranking: 183

Jeremy Helvig is an athletic, hybrid style goaltender that boasts ideal physical attributes. A goaltender who began to excel with the Frontenacs this season as his confidence continued to rise, Helvig showed impressive composure and a strong compete level throughout the season. Helvig is goaltender who takes up a lot of net, He uses his size to his advantage, getting to the top of his crease to challenge shooters. Helvig is positionally sound as he remains square to the shooter and under control as he moves from post to post. He plays his angles extremely well and displays a quick glove hand and strong lower body movements. This allows him to drive from post to post quickly and effectively. Helvig uses his size to battle/see through and around screens effectively. While Helvig has improved his consistency throughout his OHL career, he does struggle with rebound control. His consistency has improved in that facet of his game, however it is still a work in progress. Second and third chance opportunities often arise from his inability to control rebounds and have proved costly so far in his OHL career.

Quotable: "There was a ton of buzz on him the last couple months this season and then the playoffs hit and just like that the buzz wasn't quite as loud. Another kid who played for my friend in Junior A. I know he liked the kid." - HP Scout Mark Edwards

Henderson, Eric
LW - Oshawa Generals (OHL) 6'01", 182
HockeyProspect.com Ranking: 148

Henderson was drafted in the third round of the 2014 OHL Priority Selection Draft by the London Knights out of the Sun County Panthers Minor Midget program. Henderson spent his 16 year old season playing a big role for the Leamington Flyers Jr. B team, while receiving a handful of games with the Knights. Henderson posted a point and a half per game with the St. Thomas Jr. B Stars to open this season while caught behind the depth of the Knights. He was eventually dealt to the Oshawa Generals after playing sparingly for the Knights where he posted 22 points in the final 35 games of the season.

Henderson is a big bodied, two-way forward who boasts strong hockey sense and an intriguing offensive skill set. Henderson battles hard down low in the offensive zone possessing decent size and great positioning to win more than his share of battles. The left winger can dominate off the rush and on the cycle, however tends to be a non factor towards the tail end of his shifts, looking gassed and ineffective. A player who protects the puck well and works the cycle effectively, Henderson has an uncanny ability to find soft spots in defensive zone coverage. Henderson used to be more of a shoot first type of player with an accurate and hard shot, but has developed into a more well rounded offensive player. He displays both a nose for the net along with deceptive vision and playmaking abilities. Henderson is most effective when dropping his shoulder and driving the net, as he can be tough to contain when reaching his top speed. While the 6'1 winger gets around the ice well, he does lack an explosiveness to his first stride and would benefit from lengthening his stride as his overall speed is average at best.

Eric has intriguing upside at the next level. He has some untapped offensive ability that started showing through late in the season for the first time at the OHL level. So he has an outside shot at being a secondary power winger if he can add muscle and be a little meaner. He also has attributes that would make him a solid bottom six forward, with better offensive upside than a lot of the bottom six projected forwards in this draft. The 2016 NHL Entry Draft should be an unpredictable experience for Henderson.

Quotable: "Watching Henderson a lot in Minor Midget I've always been really intrigued with his upside. He always seemed to come up big when the game mattered the most. He hasn't had a chance to show that side of his game yet in the OHL. I think there is definitely some value in Henderson as a prospect." - HP Scout, Ryan Yessie

Quotable: "He needs to get much stronger and get himself in shape." - NHL Scout (February 2016)

Quotable: "I think he has some upside. If nothing else, I think he is going to put a lot of points on the board in the OHL. - HP Scout Mark Edwards

Henrikson, Arvid
RD – AIK J18 (SWE) – 6'03", 176
HockeyProspect.com Ranking: NR

Henriksson is a defenseman that played most of the season at the J18 level, while getting a shorter stint of 6 games against J20 competition and 1 game in Allsvenskan. Henriksson has good size and gets around the ice reasonably well for his frame. We liked his competitiveness and the physical game in his own zone. His positioning in front of his own net is quite good as he consistently looks to clear the crease-area. He knows how to position his body to push and keep forwards to the outside and is good at tying up their sticks. He tracks the play well and keeps good gaps in his own zone. He has played well on PK utilizing those same assets and also clears the zone with authority, making himself quite useful there. In our limited viewings his first pass was rather average and he didn't exhibit a lot of offensive upside. Although, he has shown some upside, we also didn't see him truly pulling away from the pack while playing against J18 competition.

Hirano, Yushiroh
RW – Youngstown Phantoms (USHL) 6'1", 198
HockeyProspect.com Ranking: NR

Hirano is a 95' Birth Year but being his first season in North America is NHL Draft Eligible and has put together an impressive first season with the Phantoms. Hirano played last season for Tingsryds AIF in Sweden's Top Junior League and was invited to the Chicago Blackhawks summer prospect camp.
Hirano is a sniper who possesses an excellent wrist shot with great velocity and accuracy and doesn't need a lot of time to get it on net. Hirano is hard working player who won't cheat you on effort in any zone. He is very strong on his skates and difficult to move off the puck. Yushiroh's foot speed and overall straight line speed limit the impact he can have on a game, he doesn't play at a high pace and is slow to get to loose pucks. Hirano has good hockey sense and knows where he needs to get to but at times just doesn't get there fast enough due to his lack of foot speed.

Quotable: "The kid can shoot the puck but he lacks in the hockey IQ department and doesn't share the puck enough. His skating is weak and he doesn't play a very hard game. To me he's a bit of a one trick pony." - HP Scout Mark Edwards

Hotchkiss, Matthew
LW - Guelph Storm (OHL) 6'01", 195
HockeyProspect.com Ranking: NR

After being drafted in the first round of the 2014 OHL Priority Selection Draft out of the Whitby Wildcats program, Matthew has struggled to play up to his first round selection. His game picked up midway through the season, showing flashes of the player he could become.

Matthew is a big bodied forward who started using his size to go to the net as this season progressed, and he began seeing some success. He is good at deflecting the puck, so when he takes up space in the slot he's a threat to score or create a rebound leading to a goal. When he's not going to the net he has a tendency to throw low percentage shots on goal. He is a positional player who played well on the penalty kill. He puts pressure on the puck carrier and can force mistakes. Matthew got some opportunities in all game situations this year on the young Guelph Storm team. His skating is below average and needs improvement.

Hotchkiss has some upside, which is why the Storm took him in the first round, however he doesn't play a physical enough style of game to be a power forward and doesn't produce enough offense to be a scoring forward. He provides a moderate amount of energy on the wing and is willing to work in all three zones. All in all he is not a player we expect to get selected at the 2016 NHL Entry Draft.

Howden, Brett
LC – Moose Jaw Warriors (WHL) 6'02", 193
HockeyProspect.com Ranking: 27

The younger brother of NHL prospect Quinton Howden, Brett is clearly cut from the same cloth. Like his older brother, Quinton is tall and lanky and benefits from a strong elongated straight-ahead skating stride. He doesn't shy away from contact and isn't afraid to go to the dirty areas of the ice. Finally, perhaps most excitingly, Howden is a fantastic two-way player who proved extremely valuable to his club in all three zones and in all situations.

Despite looking a bit underdeveloped in terms of lower-body strength, Howden's first-step explosiveness is definitely above-average. He wins the majority of his short-area races through a combination of size, speed, and superior body positioning along the boards. When left in open space, meanwhile, Brett hoists a really underrated wristshot that is both decently powerful and very accurate. He has a good shooting repertoire as he has a good slapshot, too, and is capable of making some outstanding deflections and providing screens in front of the opposition goaltender. His stickhandling through small areas is yet another underrated quality to his game.

Able to play at all three forward positions, Howden looks most natural playing at centre. He's very good in the faceoff circle, using his size to gain leverage and his strength to overpower opponents in the dots. His playmaking off of the rush could be better, as he has a tendency to dish the puck off to teammates in low-percentage areas instead of taking advantage of his excellent wristshot. Adding muscle to a lanky frame and becoming more selfish with the puck are two areas of improvement, but otherwise, this is a very complete prospect.

Quotable: "A wide range of opinions on this kid amongst our scouts." – HP Staff Mark Edwards

Quotable: "His interview was good. Steady." – NHL Scout (Combine week)

Howdeshell, Keeghan
LW/LC – USNTDP 6'00", 201
HockeyProspect.com Ranking: NR

Howdeshell is a competitive forward who has played an energy role on USNTDP's U18 team. Howdeshell is a player that provides effort on his every shift and plays a physically engaging game. He's useful on the forecheck and competes in all three zones. He protects the puck well on the wall and will push back in one on one battles. Although he won't make mistakes, his puck-skills are below average and he doesn't have much vision in the offensive zone. His skating also doesn't stand out as a strength. While a likeable player, we don't see much NHL upside in Howdeshell's game.

Hrenak, David
G – Slovakia U20/U18 (SVK) – 6'01", 176
HockeyProspect.com Ranking: NR

Hrenak is an athletic goaltender that has a calm demeanor. He is an intriguing prospect with potential to become a good stopper at a high level. The immediate area of weakness is his mental game and being consistently ready for the first 20 minutes. He has shown an inability to be mentally sharp early on. However, despite the slow starts, he has shown tremendous resiliency by bouncing back and playing strong.

Taking away that weakness, Hrenak has strong footwork and can read threats very well. A great communicator in the crease always ensuring his defenders know where threats are forming. Had injury problems in the past that slowed his development, but Hrenak works hard off the ice and truly enjoys being on the ice. His lateral power is developing well and he has shown the ability to make key saves to change the games momentum. Hrenak may join the consistent stream of Slovakian goaltenders making their way to the USHL as he was drafted by the Green Bay Gamblers in the 2016 USHL Phase 2 draft.

Hronek, Filip
RD – HK Hradec Kralove (CZE) – 6'00", 163
HockeyProspect.com Ranking: 68

Hronek is an offensive defenseman who is also strong at starting transition. He's not terribly short, but his frame is very light and will need considerable filling out. Last year, Hronek was physically even weaker but we have seen progression from him this year, even though it is clearly still an area that will need to improve. Nevertheless, Hronek has spent the majority of the year playing against men in the top Czech league.

Despite the light frame, one thing that Hronek never lacks is energy and a competitive spirit in his game. He engages players much bigger than him and shows nothing that would hold him back from going at it, but at times he can look quite comical as he simply bounces off big bodies, despite his best attempts. Hronek's play with the puck is already an area of strength. He gets around the ice well, and has a good head for the game. Checks off both boxes as far as his passing game goes as well as skating with the puck, although his skating is better with the puck than without. One thing he does quite well is scanning the ice for options while still being aware of what the opposition is doing. In this respect, he uses his peripheral vision well as he might be looking at a teammate but easily adjusts to an oncoming forechecker and buys himself time, sometimes even outright surprises him and puts him out of the play with a fake.

Hronek is also a strong offensive player from the offensive blueline in. He can run the PP and can pass the puck around. His ability to get shots through is good and we like him as a shooter from the point. Hronek isn't shy about letting it rip from the blueline but he is also willing to slide up the ice on the weak-side and surprise the defensive coverage by sneaking in back-door if there is an opportunity. He is also willing to join the rush if there is a play to be made and won't hold back, quite an active player offensively.

Hronek has all the makings of a solid offensive defenseman prospect, however the lack of strength is still a real problem right now. While he is more than willing to engage and compete, he simply won't be able to play at the NHL level unless his strength improves significantly. From that perspective, he has quite a way to go. Once his strength is at least average, his chances of making it will improve considerably.

Quotable: "He's not too far off from having a pretty complete offensive and puck-moving game. Strength is still a major issue, even though there was some improvement there since last year" - HP Scout Nik Funa

Huber, Mario
RC – Victoriaville Tigres (QMJHL) – 6'02", 218
HockeyProspect.com Ranking: NR

Huber, a '96 born forward, came to the QMJHL this season after being selected 7th overall in the CHL Import Draft last summer. Before joining Victoriaville in August, Huber took part in the Montreal Canadiens' rookie camp in July, after going un-drafted in the 2015 NHL Draft. Huber is a big, two-way centerman who works hard at both ends of the ice. He's very tough to handle along the boards and competes hard there. He's capable of delivering big hits and loves to get engaged physically during games. This season, he was used mostly on the 2nd or 3rd line with the Tigres, playing on both their PP and PK units. His skating is an area of concern, as there is not a lot of speed or agility out of him. He can get by at the QMJHL level, but at the next level, he will need to work on it. He uses his size well along the boards. There is a real strong puck-protection game from him and he won't hesitate to take the puck to the net. He scored his goals this year using mainly two methods: his big slap shot and retrieving pucks in the slot. Huber is not expected to be back next season with Victoriaville. He could end up going back to Europe or, if drafted, could play pro hockey in North America.

Huether, Kenny
RW - Oshawa Generals (OHL) 5'09", 170
HockeyProspect.com Ranking: NR

Huether impressed us in his initial draft year with his work ethic and compete, but wasn't a big offensive player. Huether was selected in the 9th round of the 2013 OHL Priority Selection Draft by the Oshawa Generals out of the Huron-Perth Lakers Minor Midget program. He spent his 16 year old season with the Listowel Jr. B Cyclones before making the jump to the OHL's Oshawa Generals.

Huether is a smooth skating forward who is a little undersized but has a ton of quickness and tenacity going after the puck carrier. He is willing to finish his hits, but isn't overly physical. He can make opponents lives difficult with his forecheck pressure. He works hard in all three zones and is capable of playing a two-way role. Huether has developed his offensive game greatly over the last few years. He has a powerful shot which has good accuracy and can fool goaltenders with his release. He also has the hands to score when in alone and deke out goaltenders. He's a very shoot first forward and doesn't really seem to enjoy passing the puck, but has gotten better in this area. With the huge turnover in Oshawa after winning the memorial cup, Huether really stepped up his game and showed a level of offensive ability he's never really shown comparable to the different levels he's played at. His size and re-entry status could combine to prevent him from being selected, but at worst he will be a free agent invite who gets interest from multiple teams.

Hultstrand, Tim
G – Malmo Redhawks J20 (SWE) – 6'00", 176
HockeyProspect.com Ranking: NR

Hultstrand is a fundamentally sound if somewhat undersized goalie that has posted quality numbers for Malmo in J20 league-play. Hultstrand is a real fluid goalie with little wasted movements. He's reasonably quick but lacks the explosiveness that would help a smaller goalie like him. Nonetheless, he's got a very calm approach and sticks to his fundamentals. Hultstrand remains calm in traffic even with large bodies in front of him and never panics in any situation, in fact he can look almost too passive at times. He does well on initial shots and has good recovery. Despite the small size, he doesn't leave tons of room upstairs while in butterfly. Hultstrand is a good goalie at this level, but with his size and a rather passive if fundamentally sound game it will be an uphill battle to reach the NHL.

Ilomäki, Valtteri
RD – Ilves (Fin U20) – 6'03", 190
HockeyProspect.com Ranking: NR

Valtteri is draft eligible for the second time and has taken good development steps during the past seasons. In season 2013-14 he didn't earn a spot in Ilves' U18 team. He spent the following year in

USPHL in North America and returned to Finland this season where he had a strong junior season. He improved a lot and was one of the better d-men at the U20 level. He was also invited to Finland's U20 camp in February. Ilomäki is quite a big defenseman who plays a good game in his own zone. Plays with toughness and makes smart decisions with and without puck. Right-handed player who reads the game well and can give good short and long passes. He's got solid skating ability. He will need to improve his puck skills to improve his offensive game.

Ingram, Connor
G – Kamloops Blazers (WHL) 6'01", 212
HockeyProspect.com Ranking: 164

Connor Ingram is a second-time draft eligible goalie who continues to impress with his performances for Kamloops. Ingram was one of the key reasons Kamloops qualified for the playoffs and also had a strong showing there. Ingram isn't the biggest or most athletic goalie, but is one of those goalies who simply gets the job done. Ingram is strong down-low and plays a competitive game, he plays with confidence and seems to have the ability to get his body on the puck, even if in unorthodox ways. Him saving Kamloops defense's bacon was a common occurrence. Ingram also excels under a heavy workload and shows no signs of wear against high volume of shots. Ingram's size is just OK for a modern goalie, and he does show more weakness upstairs. While Ingram might not be the most technically or athletically proficient goalie prospect, we have liked his performance this year and he has built up a reputation of someone who can be relied upon in difficult situations and continue to perform at a high level. It would be fair to say that the mental part of goaltending might be Ingram's biggest strength.

Isokangas, Severi
G – Karpat U20 (FIN) – 6'00", 187
HockeyProspect.com Ranking: NR

Isokangas is a slightly undersized goalie with a strong positional game and rebound control. Isokangas's best asset is his calmness and the ability to suck up rebounds without giving up anything. With clear sight of the puck, it's hard to get second opportunities out of him as he rarely doesn't smother the shot. We have seen him even give up no rebound on clear grade A 1 on 1 scoring chances against. One weakness of Isokangas is that he tends to retreat deeper and deeper into his net under pressure and can make his calm game a bit passive to the point that it becomes a weakness. He would benefit from exhibiting more push-back in pressure situations. The lack of size is also quite a big problem. Isokangas is a sound goalie, but at his size we are concerned there isn't enough pop or unique abilities in his game to project him as an NHL goalie.

Ivanyuzhenkov, Artyom
LW – Team Russia U18 (MHL) – 6'03", 226
HockeyProspect.com Ranking: NR

Ivanyuzhenkov is a forward that has lined up both as left and right wing and possesses an intriguing combination of size and skating ability. When he is firing on all cylinders, Ivanyuzhenkov can be quite a force on the ice, but his game is very inconsistent and he can be a frustrating player, especially when considering his toolset.

Ivanyuzhenkov has the size and the speed to be a factor when he chooses to do so. When he is playing an engaging game, he gets first on pucks, uses his body to protect it and has enough skills left to execute plays. Unfortunately, in our viewings Ivanyuzhenkov only rarely displayed that combination of size, speed and skill. He is prone to periods of passive, un-inspired play and he is not quite skilled enough to afford not using his size. It seems that at times he himself doesn't understand what makes him successful.

Ivanyzuhenkov is an intriguing blend of physical tools, but one that simply doesn't show up with enough consistency. He will need to improve his willingness to engage and put those tools to work on a shift by shift basis in order to become a better prospect.

Quotable: "He looks like a legit prospect when he's actually using his size, but far too often he has shifts with no impact whatsoever. I had some hopes for him in the beginning of the year but he did nothing to back it up in my later viewings" - HP Scout Nik Funa

Jääskä, Juha
LW/RW – HIFK (Fin U20) – 6'00", 185
HockeyProspect.com Ranking: NR

Jääskä was a big part of HIFK's U20 team and he also made his debut in the Finnish elite league. He's a versatile kid who played both wings and centre during the season but he's more valuable as a winger. Jääskä is a hard-working kid who is a perfect player for a bottom 6 role. He is always ready to get his nose dirty. Likes to battle in the corners and he's an effective player along the boards and in front of the net. Wins rebounds and can re-direct pucks into the goal. Juha also has decent puck skills and vision. Jääskä is a committed penalty killer and plays a decent two-way game. Versatility is his biggest asset and you can put him into any role on the ice, but he doesn't seem to possess the hands and skills required to become a legit offensive player at the next level.

Järvinen, Ville
LD – Ilves (U20) – 6'04", 203
HockeyProspect.com Ranking: NR

Second year eligible Järvinen missed the majority of last year due to an ACL injury. He finally came back in the fall and had a decent season in the U20 league, recording 15 points in 26 games. He also made his Finnish elite league debut in winter, playing against men. Ville is a tall defenseman who plays a strong game in all three zones. Has good mobility and vision which makes him a valuable player in the offensive zone. However he could improve his shot. He's got solid positioning but the whole season he missed last year impacted his physical development. He has never been that physical to begin with and has some problems from time to time in front of the net and in the corners. He hasn't bulked up that much and he still struggles when the game gets more physical. If he stays healthy in the summer he could jump to the professional level next season.

Jensen, Robin
G – Djurgardens IF J20 (SWE) - 6'02", 209
HockeyProspect.com Ranking: NR

With a January 1996 birth-date Jensen is in his third year of NHL draft eligibility. A goalie with good size, Jensen is a calm and collected presence in his crease. He uses his size well and plays a bit deeper back in his crease. He doesn't waste movement, but moves around his crease smoothly and with no excess motion. Jensen is the type of goalie that will stick to his fundamentals and make the saves he needs to make. He is a good fit with responsible defensemen in front of him that will let him see shots and protect the middle of ice and in turn he can be a calming influence on them.

Jerry, William (Billy)
C – St. Thomas Academy (MN-HS) 6'2.75", 188
HockeyProspect.com Ranking: NR

Jerry is a Hudson, WI native but played his High School Hockey in the Minnesota Prep Ranks at nearby St. Thomas Academy for the last two seasons where he has excelled, Jerry was also really good for Team Southeast this past fall in the Minnesota Elite League where he averaged over a PPG. Jerry finished the season with the Madison Capitols (USHL) where he didn't look at all out of place and made their team better for the final 9 games.

Jerry has good offensive instincts and skills, he seems to always be in the right place and the puck finds his stick in the offensive zone and can really shoot the puck. The puck gets off his tape quickly for both shots and passes. Jerry's skating and foot speed need improvement but there is no reason to think that won't improve as he gets stronger and adds muscle to his lanky frame. Jerry plays a good 200 foot game; he provides great back pressure and tracks back into the play well, using his long reach to disrupt passing lanes. Jerry shows good fundamentals along the wall, uses body positioning to shield the opponent and battles to keep pucks alive. As previously noted Jerry's skating needs some work, while he has decent straight line speed and decent edge work, he has short choppy strides for a person with long legs, once he learns to smooth out his stride and add some strength; his skating could turn out to become a positive in the end.

Quotable: "Needs to really get stronger in the lower body but has good offensive instincts and skill." NHL Scout (March 2016)

Jette, Tyler
LD – Farmington (MN-HS) 6'03", 209
HockeyProspect.com Ranking: NR

Jette is a big, physical defenseman who plays a steady game in his own end but can also chip in offensively. Jette was a Finalist for the Minnesota Mr. Hockey's award this year and committed to attend to Boston University. Jette displayed excellent footwork and a solid powerful skating ability. He is able to control the offensive blue line, has the footwork to open up shooting lanes and does a good job getting pucks through traffic. While we don't think Jette projects as an elite point producing defenseman at the pro level, he can be a reliable depth piece that can skate and move the puck efficiently if his game continues to progress.

Johansen, Lucas
LD – Kelowna (WHL) – 6'02", 176
HockeyProspect.com Ranking: 38

After being pick 119th overall in the WHL Bantam draft, Johansen slid into the Rockets organization under his older brother (Ryan) shadow, amassing only 8 points (1G 7A) in 65 games during his rookie year. In that rookie season the Kelowna blue line was stacked and in turn his playing time was limited. However in the 2015 post season he managed 5 points in 19 games (1G 4A) and started to flash his strong rushing ability and offensive instincts which earned him a spot as the top offensive option on the Rockets backend in 2015/16 garnering first unit power play and top pair status as a go-to two way defender.

Although he doesn't posses explosive starts, Johansen does show good jump in his opening strides and overall has strong top end speed. This benefits his ability to jump into the zone off the rush as a trailer and to either get a shot off or overload the middle of ice making transition difficult to defend. Has good strength from the lower body, doesn't get muscled off pucks easily and stays on his feet during battles and after throwing hits. Showed improvement through the course of the year on his mobility, stays with attackers and doesn't get beat to the outside very often. Edge work and leg power show a consistent ability to drive attackers to the boards and away from high scoring areas. Needs some improvement in reverse skating, doesn't always appear fluid and can get closed on by speedy forward ending in him up losing his gap or gets turned around chasing.

The offensive game is where Johansen shines he reads the rush exceptionally well and has a knack for finding the soft ice with timely pinches. This allows him to get his quick and accurate snap shot off that doesn't require his feet to be planted to be effective. Works the point as the only defenseman on the power play and moves well laterally to fire through traffic and often gets pucks cleanly on net. Has developed a strong look off move from the point to feed either winger on the half boards with accurate and quick passing. Has poise at the blue line and shows good puck protection and strong use of space to assist on zone entries, uses soft hands in tight spaces to create time for a pass or a shot.

On the defensive side of the puck Johansen has shown noticeable improvements from the beginning of the season. Early play was erratic and often resulted in him chasing players out of position to lay a hit or battle for a puck. His demeanor has grown calm while defending, not overly physical but uses stick checks and angles to tie up players and efficiently clear the space in high traffic areas. Decision making looked slow coming out of the zone, was plagued by turnovers early on but managed to clean up his zone exits with solid one touch passes and supported play up ice.

Could stand to play with a little more emotion and fire, looked a little over whelmed early in the year with his expanded role but grew into it over the course of the season, will need to gain more strength, but is certainly trending upwards in that regard.

Quotable: "I saw a lot of flaws in early viewings, really lacked confidence with the puck especially in the defensive zone, having seen him play a lot he really ended up winning me over, I would have avoided him on draft day before Christmas, not since" - HP Scout Andy Levangie

Johnson, Kenny
LD – Shattuck St. Mary's Prep (MN-HS) 6'2.25", 220
HockeyProspect.com Ranking: NR

Kenny is a physical defenseman who prides his game on taking care of things in his own end first and being difficult to play against. Johnson has done a good job this year in playing a smarter physical game where he doesn't take as many penalties or take himself out of the play in an attempt to deliver a big hit. Johnson does take some risks at his own blue line.
Kenny doesn't project as an offensive contributor from the back end at the next level. He struggles to handle pucks. He does have a decent shot from the point that gets through to the net.

Johnson will follow his Brother Jack Johnson's footsteps and head to the University of Michigan in the fall where he can continue to round out his complete game.

Quotable: "I can't see him being drafted, but you never know. His puck skills are lacking and his pivots are very weak, his mobility is sub par." HP Scout Mark Edwards (May 2016)

Quotable: "He was built to play in the seventies but it's 2016." NHL Scout (April 2016)

Quotable: " I don't see a lot of offensive upside to his game down the road, however he still has plenty of time to develop that area of the game, but has a mean streak in him and he could turn into that defenseman that is a nightmare to go up against."
- HP Scout Dusten Braaksma

Johnson, Will
LW – University of Wisconsin (BIG-NCAA) 5'10", 175
HockeyProspect.com Ranking: NR

Johnson is in his 2nd Draft Eligible year and had he not gotten injured last year with the Madison Capitols (USHL) he may have gotten drafted last season. He was leading the USHL in scoring with 9 Goals and 36 points in 30 Games before his season was cut short. This year Johnson played on a struggling Wisconsin team who had a hard time scoring goals but managed to chip in offensively with 6 goals and 9 points but we saw significant gains in his complete game in his freshman year at Wisconsin. Johnson's skating allows him to close on defenders quickly on the fore check and create turnovers. He was more physical in his puck battles as well. While we don't expect Johnson to gather a lot of attention at this year's draft, he is a talented prospect to track as his college career progresses and a new coaching staff takes over at Wisconsin.

Jonsson, Joseph
LC – HV71 J20 (SWE) – 6'03", 183
HockeyProspect.com Ranking: NR

Jonsson is a raw center with a lanky frame-size that has room to be filled out. Although he is tall, there's quite some room for physical development. Jonsson is still building his game but has certain skills that stand out as positives for him. He shows upside with the puck, skating looks somewhat underwhelming at this point but with room to improve once he adds some strength. Can pull off moves with the puck but is limited sometimes by his skating. Gives off the feel of being low-energy at times and can struggle to bring the puck into scoring areas, even though he seems smart enough to keep possession. Not someone who would endlessly hound the opposition and limit their time with the puck, but is willing to throw the body if he has position on the player. Shot shows upside with wrist-shot release. Raw center that shows upside with tools but will need to develop plenty before he starts looking like a legit player. Has room for growth.

Jonsson Fjallby, Axel
LW/RW – Djurgardens IF J20 (SWE) – 6'00", 170
HockeyProspect.com Ranking: 179

Jonsson Fjallby is a right winger coming out of the Djurgardens program who has also appeared internationally for the Swedish U18 team this season. He is a competitive forward that plays with good energy and sees the ice well.
Jonsson Fjallby has good speed and he knows how to use it to be a factor on the ice. He uses it less to dictate the play with the puck, but finds ways to get involved through short bursts that can cause havoc on the forecheck or by beating a defenseman into the slot, either opening himself up on the weak-side of the ice for a pass or looking to get involved in traffic. Jonsson-Fjallby can be a dangerous player when the defense is on their heels trying to re-group. In those situations he processes the play quickly and can make a good play with a burst of energy. Playing against defense that is already set-up and in position is a bit more challenging for him. Jonsson Fjallby has decent hands and some skill to him, which aids him in creating offense. He is a good playmaker and will find ways to extend possession for his team.

He does a good job playing to his strengths which also includes the forecheck. Jonsson-Fjallby is a useful checker and uses his energy to cause turnovers. He also has a pretty good feel for how the other team is going to move the puck which allows him to intercept passes or quickly pressure the puck-carrier and force him into errors.

Johnstone, Dane
RW - Flint Firebirds (OHL) 5'11", 186
HockeyProspect.com Ranking: NR

Johnstone was selected in the 9th round of the 2014 OHL Priority Selection Draft out of the Elgin-Middlesex Chiefs program. After spending a year in Jr. B with the St. Thomas Stars, Johnstone made the jump to the OHL this season.

Johnstone is a player who earned every second of ice he received this year. After starting out the year as a healthy scratch, he found himself playing on the second line by February. His relentless style of play has played a huge part in his movement up the Firebirds depth chart. Dane plays with a ton of energy. He puts pressure on the puck carrier and is a great forechecker. He constantly forces turnovers and takes away time and space very well, making his opponents misplay the puck. He plays a strong two-way game and is all over the puck. His skating is average and his offensive skills are below average, which limited his offensive potential. However, he can get involved offensively primarily through winning battles in the offensive zone.

Johnstone is the type of player who has the compete and physical nature of a player who could be effective in a top six role, but he doesn't appear to have enough skill to project as an NHLer. He should serve as an excellent two-way junior player over the next few years.

Jones, Max
LW - London Knights (OHL) 6'02.5", 203
HockeyProspect.com Ranking: 20

Jones was selected in the first round, 18th overall at the 2014 OHL Priority Selection Draft by the London Knights out of the Detroit Honeybaked U18 program. Jones spent his first junior season at the U.S. National Team Development Program Under-17 Team. At this event he won a silver medal at the World Under 17 Championship and really put his power forward potential on display for NHL scouts. He made the jump to the OHL this season where he had a very respectable first year.

Jones is a big power forward and is at his best when taking the body crushing opponents. He was one of the most punishing checkers in the OHL this past season. Jones has a good compete level and can be an imposing figure with his size bearing down on opponents. He protects the puck well and is very tough to knock off the puck. When he wants to, he is capable of plowing through some of the toughest and most physical defenders the league has to offer. Offensively he has a very heavy shot, but his accuracy is very inconsistent. He has very deceptive skating. At first when you see him move around he doesn't look that quick, but he utilizes this to catch defenders flat footed then will blow by them before they can react. His puck skills at speed are effective when coming in on goaltenders and he is capable of deking out the goaltender.
Jones is an effective player in all game situations, proving he can succeed 5 on 5. He can go to the net or open up for his shot on the power play, but work hard, force turnovers and apply pressure on the penalty kill. Jones projects as a top six power forward who can play in all game situations.

Quotable: "He's one of my favourite prospects in the entire draft. His combination of power, skill and deceptive skating make him a very intriguing prospect at the next level."
- HP Scout Ryan Yessie

Quotable: "He was good in my interview with him. He was a likable kid and when I asked him what his weakness were, he was very self aware." – NHL Scout (November 2015)

Quotable: "Skill wins. Having Jones ranked ahead of guys like Nylander is setting yourself up for failure." – NHL Scout (November 2015)

Quotable: "There's parts of his game I like but he's a simple player. He is a one speed, one mindset player." – NHL Scout (October 2015)

Quotable "Only got feedback from two teams about his combine interviews, one liked him and one noted him as one of their weakest interviews. I personally never ended up speaking to him this season." – HP Scout Mark Edwards (Combine week)

Jordan, Zachary
RW – Des Moines Buccaneers (USHL) 6'03", 213
HockeyProspect.com Ranking: 211

A November 1996 born, Jordan is in his second year of eligibility. Jordan is a big winger who gets around the ice quite well for his size and has good scoring instincts. Jordan spent his third year of USHL with Des Moines and put up an impressive 32 goals in 60 games. Jordan was trusted by the coach to be used in all situations and key moments. Jordan can be a hard player to stop as he moves forward with his large frame and reach. He also boasts above-average hands and a good wrist-shot which has allowed him to produce offense off the rush, including shorthanded. In the offensive zone he could use his size better to generate zone time, however he makes good reads off-the-puck and looks for his shot. Jordan likes to anticipate turnovers and spring himself for breakaway chances but that at times leads to him leaving the defensive zone too early. In general, he could use his size more in his own end and be more engaging than he is. Another area of improvement for Jordan would be him using his linemates better.

All in all, although he is in his second year of eligibility Jordan has shown good instincts, possesses a big frame, above-average skating, and decent hands with a dangerous shot. There are certainly areas left to improve, but he does offer some upside in the 2016 NHL draft.

Jost, Tyson
LC – Penticton Vees (BCHL) 5'11, 191
HockeyProspect.com Ranking: 10

Tyson is a talented center that brings a high level of skill and smarts to his game which makes himself and the players around him better. He is a quick agile center that competes at a truly high-end level and can impact the game on both sides of the puck in all situations. He possesses a very good set of hands and is always a threat offensively. He tends to be more of a playmaker than outright goal scorer but can put the puck into the net with ease. Tyson was named MVP of the BCHL finishing with 42 goals and 62 assists for 104 points in only 48 games.
His skill set is anchored by his high hockey IQ and his excellent ability to make plays at a high pace. He has great vision and sees the ice very well, which allows him to make plays before the defense can react. Tyson has very good acceleration which allows him to pull away from defenders. He is a very mobile skater with good edge control and has great balance that he uses to protect the puck. He possesses a heavy, accurate wrist shot with a fast release that he can get off at full speed. Jost has a very quick, smooth set of hands which allows him to handle the puck at top speed and in small areas like along the boards and in the corner.

Not only does Jost possess very good skills he also brings tremendous work ethic and compete level. He is very responsible on the defensive side of the puck and when he doesn't have the puck he works hard to get it back. Jost is a very versatile player that can kill penalties or run your power play. Jost is not an overly big player but plays much bigger than he looks. He is strong on the puck and is very powerful down low and can grind it out with anyone.

Even though he played tier two junior, he has proven himself to be a high-end player at every level. He has represented Canada at many different international events and has excelled and raised his level of play. Jost has the combination of skill along with the character and compete level that is needed to play at the NHL level. He has committed to the University of North Dakota for the 2016-17 season.

Quotable: "Certainly wouldn't classify him as big forward, but his compete level against larger defenders was impressive in every viewing. Always impressed by his body position when protecting pucks, it's a big part of his dynamic offensive game" - HP scout Andy Levangie

Quotable: "Not sure he's quite as highly skilled as some think but I love the way Jost plays the game. He's smart and he just finds a way to get things done. My background work on the kid was all extremely positive. I haven't seen him play a bad game for quite some time." - HP Scout Mark Edwards

Quotable: "The kid that you just know is going to be a big timer after interviewing him is Jost." - NHL Scout (Combine week)

Quotable: "He was a great interview. He's one of those kids you trade up to get because you know he's going to impact your roster." - NHL Scout (Combine week)

Quotable: "A tight race because I got feedback that a lot of prospects had great interviews this year but I'd say Jost would probably edge out as the favorite overall by scouts I spoke to." - HP Scout Mark Edwards (Combine week)

Quotable: "I heard all week how impressive Jost was in interviews, I witnessed it myself when I got to the combine." HP Scout Mark Edwards

Jozefek, Grant
RW/LW – Lincoln Stars (USHL) 5'10", 170
HockeyProspect.com Ranking: NR

Jozefek is a late 1997 born who has enjoyed a successful season with the Lincoln Stars. Jozefek has hovered around point per game pace in regular season and post-season and has also appeared internationally for Team USA at the World Junior A Challenge where he put up 4 points in 5 games. Jozefek is a skilled playmaking winger that relies on his quick footwork and hands to create offense. He shows good offensive zone instincts and it is hard for defensemen to get a good handle on him. He can handle the puck well at speed and can make plays at high pace. Jozefek has good playmaking vision and can make a high-end pass. While capable of finishing on plays, he could stand to work harder at being a shooting presence on the ice. Jozefek has solid off-the-puck reads and that translates to his defensive game as he can steal pucks. However in our viewings he wasn't the most engaged defensive player and that will have to improve.

Juolevi, Olli
LD - London Knights (OHL) 6'02", 182
HockeyProspect.com Ranking: 6

Juolevi was selected first round, 45th overall at the 2015 CHL Import Draft by the London Knights out of the Jokerit U20 program in Finland. Juolevi got off to a great start for the Knights adjusting quickly to the North American game and has quickly become their best defenseman.

Although Juolevi didn't quite put up the same numbers this season that we saw out of a player like Sergachev in Windsor, he may have more long term offensive upside because of the high level of hockey sense he's blessed with. Juolevi is smooth skater and does a great job choosing lanes to skate. When he has an option up ice he responds quickly and accurately setting up his teammates on odd man rushes. He loves to pinch in from the point during sustained pressure and does an excellent job doing so. Defensively he struggled at times early in the season. We also saw that happen with Olli Maatta early on when he was a London Knight. Juolevi really developed his defensive game throughout the season. He got better with his defensive zone positioning and handling opponents better one on one off the rush. He will still make the odd defensive miscue but the point here is that he has shown good progression in this area this season.

We think Juolevi has a chance to be a top pairing offensive defenseman at the NHL level. His biggest weakness right now is just strength. He needs to get stronger as he can get banged around at times and lose the odd one on one battle to big strong forwards. His offensive skills and hockey sense are what will lead him to becoming successful at the NHL level. Juolevi is a candidate to be the first defenseman taken at the 2016 NHL Entry Draft, we fully expect that he will be.

Quotable: "He seems to get a lot of comparisons to Olli Maatta. From the time he arrived in London in September through May, I've always felt he's been ahead of Maatta's development at the same age." - Ryan Yessie

Quotable: "One of my favourite players in this draft. From my first viewing this season in the Knights pre-season, right through to some outstanding performances in the playoffs, Olli impressed me. He's so smart and so poised, those tools along with his great feet and vision make him my number one defenseman in this draft. It was tight between Olli and Sergachev for me earlier this season but Juolevi pulled away the last few months and became my clear cut top Dman. - Mark Edwards

Quotable: "He's a stud. I think it's interesting when I see all this Chychrun is the top D stuff...it's not even close. Juolevi is in a class by himself this season." - NHL Scout (November 2015)

Quotable: "When I think about how much better this kid is going to be in a few years it makes it easy to rank him in the top five prospects for me." - NHL Scout (December 2015)

Quotable: "His body is still miles from where it will end up. When he's in his early twenties and has man strength he will be phenomenal." - NHL Scout (March 2016)

Quotable: "Juolevi was the best player on the ice tonight." - NHL Scout (April 2016)

Quotable: "Imagine if Dubois had a guy like Juolevi getting him pucks. His point totals would've been scary." - NHL Scout (March 2016)

Quotable: "One of the smartest players in the last few years." - NHL Scout (March 2016)

Quotable: "Outstanding interview." - NHL Scout (Combine week)

Quotable: "His interview was excellent. He's heading home after the combine and won't be back until the draft. I don't blame him." - NHL Scout (Combine week)

Quotable: "Multiple teams raved about his combine interview being not just one of the best this year but over multiple years." - HP Scout Mark Edwards (Combine week)

Jurusik, Matthew
G – University of Wisconsin 6'00", 194
HockeyProspect.com Ranking: NR

Jurusik is a perfect example of where the numbers don't tell the story. Jurusik saw himself quickly earn the #1 job in Madison after being brought in from Janesville (NAHL) after previous Goaltending recruit Luke Opilka (15' St. Louis) de-committed and went to the OHL. For a last minute desperation addition, we don't think Wisconsin could have done much better. Jurusik was under siege most nights and certainly looked overwhelmed early in the season, with a struggling team in front of him that didn't offer him much goal support, Jurusik continued to improve as the season progressed and kept Wisconsin in a lot of games. He managed to steal some games along the way for his team; the most impressive was on the Road in Grand Forks against #1 Ranked and eventual National champion North Dakota.

Jurusik is an athletic goalie who stays big in the net and has excellent lateral movement. He takes away the lower portion of the net very well and is good at tracking pucks in traffic. Because he only stands at 6 feet tall, Jurusik is aggressive to shooters, staying on the top of his crease and sometimes beyond to try to shut down the angle and make himself bigger. There is a certain level of risk he takes in playing such an aggressive style, however Matt has the athletic ability to get himself back into position quickly. He needs to add a bit more structure and sound positioning to his game. We view Jurusik as a long term project, probably someone that won't get drafted this year but has shown enough to be worth keeping an eye on as his College career progresses.

Kachyna, Ondrej
LD - Hamilton Bulldogs (OHL) 6'03.5", 192
HockeyProspect.com Ranking: NR

Ondrej was selected in the first round, 21st overall at the 2015 CHL Import Draft out of Ceske Budejovice. Ondrej had a very up and down season and started his career in Hamilton strong. He displayed intriguing tools as a potential NHL prospect. He has great size at 6'03" and skates surprisingly well for his size. He likes to shoot from the point and is confident with walking in from the point, or firing it from the point and regularly gets his shot through.

He has a habit of making mental and positional misplays. Not taking the extra stride before the redline when dumping the puck, not having the proper defensive positioning in a defensive situation are among the concerns in his game. He's all over the place on a regular basis and one shift he could be right where he needs to be, then nowhere to be found the next. This inconsistency can be found in his puck moving ability, one on one situations and physicality.

Kachyna has all the tools you're looking for out of an NHL prospect. He has size, he can skate and has flashes of skill, but he doesn't think the game well at all and this is a critical ability in order to handle the game at the next level. He'll need to get coached up big time but if he ever "gets it" Kachyna could emerge as a true NHL prospect.

Quotable: "I love the size and potential Kachyna has, but he's the first prospect I've ever used the term 'positional incompetence' with." - HP scout, Ryan Yessie

Kalapudas, Antti
LC/W – Kärpät (FEL) – 6'00", 178
HockeyProspect.com Ranking: NR

Antti was part of the Finland's U20 team which won gold at the WJC and he had a good tournament. He started the tourney as a 13th forward but was quickly promoted to higher lines. However, his season as a whole was a bit of disappointment. After being a top rookie in the Mestis (Finnish second highest pro league) there were big expectations for him but he spent almost the whole year on the fourth line playing 10 minutes or less per game. He was also loaned to Mestis and assigned to juniors during the season. Antti is a smart centerman whose strengths are in the offensive zone. He reads the game well, competes and has good playmaking ability. Earlier his skating has been a concern but that has improved and his quickness is now average. The skating technique still needs to get better so there is still room for improvement.

Karafiat, Jiri
RW/RC – HC Zlin U20 (CZE) – 6'02", 169
HockeyProspect.com Ranking: 178

Karafiat is a competitive centre. Strong in the face-off circle, very tough to beat. Coach loved to use him a lot - power play, penalty kill, empty net, etc. It was not uncommon to see him log the most ice time on his team in our viewings this season. Has been used on the wing, but looks more confident at centre where he can be in the middle of everything. Likes playing in pressure situations and was a workhorse for Zlin this season. With his size, he is very strong on the puck, hard to knock off. Works hard in all three zones - doesn't quit on the back check and can fill in as defenseman if coverage is lost. Doesn't have a fluid stride or a high gear, will need to develop this area. But he thinks the game at a high speed in the offensive zone and is still figuring out how to not overcompensate for his teammates in the defensive zone. Possesses a great one-timer that is utilized on the power play and hard wrist shot. Strength is not a weak area for Karafiat.

Karlstrom, Fredrik
LC – AIK J20 (SWE) – 6'02", 185
HockeyProspect.com Ranking: 109

Fredrik Karlstrom has all the makings of a smart two-way center with size. The 2015-2016 season was the first one Karlstrom played at the J20 level and he turned in a good showing for the year, he also managed to end the season on a high-note, contributing on a very productive line with Max Lindholm in the playoffs.

The game comes naturally to Karlstrom in all three zones. He is a heads-up center who can anticipate where the play is going a step ahead and position himself accordingly. His top-speed is decent, however it takes him a bit longer to get up to speed. His first few steps will need additional explosiveness and he will have to improve his footwork to allow him to come out of turns with a bit more speed.

Karlstrom has the size that all the teams covet down the middle. More importantly, his reads are very intelligent. He knows how to skate into open lanes instead of getting there too early or too late. He knows where to take the puck to open up a passing lane. He understands when he has to go to the slot to come up with an opportunity, he doesn't skate head-first into coverage nor does he avoid the high-scoring areas, but has good timing and reads where the open space is and can take advantage of it with his shot or passing ability.. Defensively, he uses the same hockey sense to support his defensemen and will make everyone's job easier on the break-out.

Karlstrom isn't supremely skilled nor does he have a lot of dynamic ability with his footwork. However, he is an intelligent center with size that can contribute in all three zones.

Karrer , Roger
RD – ZSC Lions (NLA) – 5'11", 170
HockeyProspect.com Ranking: NR

Karrer is a smallish Swiss defenseman who has the vision and skills to become a good right-handed puck-mover. Has a good handle on the puck and can make plays with it both in the defensive zone and at the offensive blueline. Can find lanes, shows instincts and will to join the rush and has good understanding of his opportunities. Has pretty good playmaking ability and can hit long range passes. His skating is adequate and has room to improve as he gets stronger in his lower body, something he will probably need to do in order to be able to fully take advantage of his skills at the next level.

Despite some injury problems this season he played 14 games at the NLA level and didn't look out of place in our viewings. However, he seems to still lack the confidence to make 'his' plays with the puck at high level, was it WJC or NLA. Moving forward he will need to stay consistently healthy while playing against men to make the expected improvements. Roger doesn't mind initiating contact and can actually deliver legit hits along the boards despite his limited stature, he also has an active stick defensively. As an undersized European defenseman who went un-drafted last year Karrer may not be very likely to be selected, but his talent level would be worthy of a draft pick.

Katchouk, Boris
LW - Sault Ste. Marie Greyhounds (OHL) 6'01.25", 192
HockeyProspect.com Ranking: 22

Katchouk was selected in the second round in the OHL Draft by the Sault Ste. Marie Greyhounds. Part of Katchouk's OHL Draft decline came from his four goals in 14 playoff/OHL Cup games after posting nearly a goal per game during the season. Katchouk posted big numbers in the NOJHL for the SOO Thunderbirds last season.

Katchouk played a huge role for the Greyhounds this season. His contributions progressed from a third line role to playing top minutes in all situations.In the playoff series against Sarnia, he was the most tenacious forechecker on either team. He competes very hard for the puck and has a great frame and strength to win battles. His body positioning down low is excellent which also helps him. This work ethic extends to the defensive side of the game as he competes very hard in his own zone, blocks shots and will win battles defensively. Katchouk has deceptive skating where he can look a little sluggish, but then turn it on and has burned defenders who are not prepared for it. Offensively he has a dangerous shot which is both powerful and accurate. He has the ability to protect and drive the net and the ability to finish. He also possesses the hands to make a move on the defender and walk in alone. His offensive zone positioning is excellent, he knows where to go and it has opened him up for scoring chances.

Katchouk has offensive upside and his gritty style of play gives him more value than other prospects. As long as he continues to put the work in, Katchouk is up with safest prospects you'll find outside of the top 10 in the 2016 NHL Entry Draft. He projects as a multi-faceted winger who can grind it out, kill penalties, but possesses the offense to put points on the board.

Quotable: "I love his upside, he's a first round talent. One of my favourite prospects this year. His combination of hockey sense, compete and skill is very exciting for the NHL level." - HP Scout Ryan Yessie

Quotable: "I interviewed him last week. Let's just say it wasn't the best interview I've ever had." - NHL Scout

Quotable: "I've got him as a late first rounder." NHL Scout (January 2015)

Quotable: "This kid just helped himself tonight." NHL Scout (April 2016)

Quotable: "He didn't play many games in the OHL last season and I didn't see him much in AAA, but right from when I saw him in the Soo's third game this season versus Guelph, he put himself on my radar. I ended up seeing him a lot and by the time December rolled around, I was sold on him as a high pick. Numerous late viewings did nothing but help his stock. He was outstanding in the Sarnia series. He can play on my team anytime." - Mark Edwards

Quotable: "He was good. He's a what you see is what you're going to get because he wants to make it. He doesn't want the other option." - NHL Scout (Combine week)

Quotable: "He was exactly what I expected after seeing him interviewed during an intermission once. He was good." - NHL Scout (Combine week)

Kayumov, Artur
LW – Team Russia U18 (MHL) – 5'11", 176
HockeyProspect.com Ranking: 75

Kayumov is the type of forward who can carry the puck for long stretches without even looking in danger of losing possession, occasionally making an opponent look bad in the process. That's been the case on the big ice at the junior level, the question is whether he'll be able to do anything like that with less room against pros, or at least be able to remain effective while learning to play a bit of a different game. Kayumov doesn't have legit size on his side, but has a few other things going for him. His little stick, short stride and quick feet allow him to react promptly and look comfortable in tight spaces. He can also complete plays in the blink of an eye when lanes open up. He is a very shifty and elusive player whose trademark is his tremendous puck control. He can zoom around the ice with the puck attached on his stick, attrack opponents to himself and then hand the puck to an open linemate. He can sense opponents, makes quick decisions and is smart using support once he gets it. Uses his body well to protect the puck, finds ways to create room for himself and is fast getting his shot off. In juniors he can also be effective on the cycle and is used regularly on the penalty kill, but those elements shouldn't be expected to be relevant parts of his game at the next level. He doesn't mind throwing his body around sometimes and has a strong balance, but he doesn't bring a physical element.

Kayumov usually does a pretty good job defensively, as he stays alert in his zone, uses his quick stick to steal pucks from opponents when he gets in tight and puts in the effort on the backcheck. There are however some concerns when projecting his game to the top level. His short legs get him up to speed in little time, but as of now he doesn't seem to possess the acceleration to really create separation from his opponents. When he starts making fast turns with the puck inside the offensive zone, sometimes he seems to lose his focus on making an offensive play and ends up just showcasing his great hands and agility to no real avail. The worry is at the NHL level he may not be able to avoid physical punishment, getting pushed to the margins of the game as a result. Artur is probably the player who has improved the most from last season among the members of his U18 national team and his progression is definitely encouraging, but he could be among the Russians suffering the most from missing the U18 Worlds.

Kaspick, Tanner
LC – Brandon Wheat Kings (WHL) 6'00", 200
HockeyProspect.com Ranking: 89

Tanner Kaspick isn't as celebrated as many of his teammates on the powerhouse Brandon Wheat Kings and perhaps that's because he plays a less flashy, more dependable and more mistake-free game than most. Kaspick plays a forechecking game in which he crashes and bangs to create turnovers and space for his linemates.

Kaspick is the type of player coaches really covet. His skating is very good and he has decent size and power. He backchecks hard and doesn't forget his defensive responsibilities, he will also support his team's puck-movement coming out of his zone. Kaspick plays in all situations, although he played more of a depth role this year in Brandon. As an added bonus, he generates a lot of power plays himself by playing with an agitating style and by getting underneath the opposition's skin.

The most exciting aspect to Kaspick's game might be his physical game. He surprises the opposition when he bowls them over, and can do it with the puck on his stick. His passing game might require some work next year, but he has a good wristshot from the prime scoring area. Additionally, Kaspick does a great job getting the body position against defensemen on the wall and winning battles for puck-possession. Key graduations from the Wheat Kings to the NHL and AHL will open up a lot of icetime for Kaspick in the next few years, allowing him to blossom alongside Nolan Patrick, Stelio Mattheos and other prospects.

Kehler, Cole
G – Merritt Centennials (BCHL) 6'03", 201
HockeyProspect.com Ranking: NR

Cole Kehler is a really intriguing goaltender who is already NHL-sized and has the perfect physical dimensions for the modern pro game. He was the victim of unfortunate circumstances this year, being deferred to a starter role in Merritt instead of playing adjacent to Connor Ingram as a backup for the Kamloops Blazers, who own his rights. As a whole, Merritt had some struggles early in the season, which reflected Kehler's individual skills a bit unfairly.

His fundamentals are good and he possesses the trio of strength, agility and size. Fast and nimble in terms of his movement even though he's already very tall. Kehler generally plays a conservative game in the paint. He got caught scrambling for pucks in one early season viewing when he got lit-up, although we liked his commitment to tracking pucks. We found he looked his best when playing calmly in his butterfly and taking full advantage of his size.

Kehler proved invaluable in a late season run and ranked as the only goalie in the BCHL to have beaten the powerhouse Penticton Vees twice in the regular season. He's spoken highly of in terms of character and attitude. He comes up big when the game really counts and he has all the necessary prerequisites for a prospective NHL goaltender prospect in terms of having size, skill and the intangibles. He could prove to be a decent prospect despite the ugly statline and some early season struggles.

Keller, Clayton
LC – USNTDP 5'10", 168
HockeyProspect.com Ranking: 9

Keller is one of the more offensively gifted players in the draft, dominating both on home turf as well as internationally while putting up high-end numbers. Keller provides a fantastic blend of skill and hockey IQ and was the engine behind this year's USNTDP team.

The game comes easy for him as he easily turns whatever situation he is presented with into his favor. Keller has high-end hands which in combination with his elusive skating allow him to avoid getting rubbed out of the game. Instead, he is the one that puts players on their heels and makes them guess what he is going to do. But it is not just the skating and skill, his anticipation and the ability to see plays develop two steps ahead also stand-out. He does an excellent job manufacturing open lanes with subtle movements that throw the player checking him off, he sees the ice very well and is an excellent playmaker in all three zones. We have seen Keller make fantastic reads with the puck on his stick in his own zone, in the neutral zone, and in the offensive zone. Keller can do anything from an intelligent pass that kills the other team's forechecking pressure, to a neutral-zone pass that hits the weak-side wing with speed, to gift-wrapping his linemate a goal in the offensive zone. While primarily a playmaker, Keller can also finish on his own with ease, however he is slightly more picky about his shot-selection than pure shoot-first players are.

Keller has also shown good effort on the backcheck and keeps his feet moving, his hockey IQ isn't just limited to offensive play but he is also an intelligent defensive player. While he lacks the size to truly compete in a physical sense, he still works to get his body involved and especially has a sneaky defensive stick that can cause turnovers. He often uses his ability to quickly control bouncy pucks to his advantage defensively.

His biggest question-mark going forward remains his size. As defenses get up to NHL level, and the game becomes faster and tighter, this will pose some challenges for Keller to find the time with puck, especially if he gets pushed to the wall or forced into physical one on and battles. Containing some of the bigger players on the defensive side of the puck might also be a problem. However, size aside, Keller ticks off all the boxes of a top 6 NHL forward.

Quotable: "At the Five Nations in Switzerland he was just on a different level than the competition. Speedy, creative and effective, he dominated that tourney" - HP Scout Mik Portoni

Quotable: "He always seems to play well in my viewings. Imagine how much more you would've heard his name this season if he was 6'1". That U18 team would've been in big trouble without him." - HP Scout Mark Edwards

Khaira, Sahvan
RD – Swift Current Broncos (WHL) 6'04", 218
HockeyProspect.com Ranking: NR

Sahvan Khaira, yet another product of the Okanagan Hockey Academy developmental pipeline, is a big bodied defenseman who plied his trade with the Seattle Thunderbirds before a midseason trade to the Swift Current Broncos. A bit of a bone rattler, Khaira stands out as a strong defensive presence whose offensive game remains fairly limited at this point.

At this point, he's not a great puck mover or a great puck rusher, so he's a bit limited in his breakout options. Coaches get the best out of him when he's defending the space in front of his goaltender, as he has a good meanness to him and doesn't back down from intimidating situations. For a defensive defenseman he will need to get better at his positioning.

Savhan is the younger brother of Edmonton Oilers prospect Jujhar Khaira. Like his older brother, Savhan comes equipped with a good strong frame and a high compete level. Indeed, Khaira is a big kid who can hit and fight with the best of them, but he has significant improvements to make in many areas, including his mobility, passing, stickhandling, and shooting skills as well as his positional sense.

Kiersted, Matt
LD - Chicago Steel (USHL) 6'00", 180
HockeyProspect.com Ranking: NR

Kiersted has been well known for his puck moving ability and willingness to jump into the play and generate offense. In our viewings of him in Chicago this year we saw tremendous gains in his complete game and saw a more mature player who understood assignments better and was trusted more by his coaching staff as the season progressed. Kiersted has excellent vision of the ice and moves the puck efficiently in all 3 zones. He has really improved his positioning and gab control this season with Chicago. Matt still needs to continue to improve his stick work and physicality to be as effective as he could be. He is good at defending the rush by using good awareness and positioning, where Kiersted sometimes struggles is when his team is hemmed into his own end, he lacks the physicality and ability to win a battle and clear the puck, certainly as he gets stronger this is an area that can improve over time and we see Kiersted as a legitimate NHL prospect down the road. Kiersted will be off to the University of North Dakota in the fall to further progress his development.

Kirwan, Luke
LW - Flint Firebirds (OHL) 6'02", 230
HockeyProspect.com Ranking: NR

Kirwan was a highly touted American prospect entering the 2013 OHL Draft where he was selected in the second round by the Guelph Storm. Kirwan's rights were traded to Windsor before suiting up for Guelph and he was dealt yet again this season to the Flint Firebirds for New Jersey Devils prospect Connor Chatham along with 2nd and 4th round picks.

Kirwan has never reached the lofty expectations placed on him prior to him coming to the OHL. He has excellent size but has struggled with conditioning. His skating has improved a bit, but he isn't physically at a point where he has been able to create much offense. His strongest asset is his puck protection ability. He is capable of carrying it to the net where he has been able to create some chances. He also has landed some pretty big hits throughout the season. He has a decent shot and can get it on net. However his playmaking ability is well below average and has trouble completing passes, often resulting in turnovers. He is at his best when keeping the game simple. Using his body to drive the net and dumping the puck deep and chasing it down with his big frame.

Kirwan may hear his name called due to the high potential he possessed as a younger player, but his performance thus far has not warranted a pick and is not a player we would select or expect to be selected at the 2016 NHL Entry Draft.

Kislinger, Max
LW - North Bay Battalion (OHL) 6'02", 201
HockeyProspect.com Ranking: NR

Kislinger was selected 48th overall by the North Bay Battalion at the 2015 CHL Import Draft out of EC Salzburg U18 program. Kislinger actually played his Minor Midget hockey for the Peterborough Petes Minor Midget program before spending a season with EC Salsburg.

Max Kislinger is a competitive, two-way winger who possesses intriguing size. Kislinger played in a depth role for the Battalion this season but started to develop his offensive game a bit near the end of the year. Kislinger shows a strong compete level and takes direct routes to pucks, although he isn't very physical for his size. Max forechecks under control, and his anticipation abilities allow him to pick off outlet passes, creating turnovers with good positional play. While he can be tenacious in puck pursuit and display a quick an active stick, which allows him to separate player from puck, he needs to be more willing to engage with his physical play. Kislinger's offensive repertoire is limited, as he lacks offensive creativity and vision. He does make good reads in possession, limiting his turnovers, protects the puck well and packs a deceptively strong shot.

Kislinger has size and work ethic on his size. He also has a good shot which helped him start to rack up points. However he needs to be more aggressive in order to maximize his potential. He is not a prospect we would consider selecting in the 2016 NHL Entry Draft.

Klavins, Erlends
LC – HK Riga (MHL) - 6'02", 176
HockeyProspect.com Ranking: NR

Klavins is a forward prospect that caught our eye at the U18s in Grand Rapids in North Dakota. Klavins had a strong tournament putting up 6 points, including 4 goals in 7 games. He's got a good frame that has room to fill out, a quick wrist-shot that gets quickly off the stick. He can get it up top and doesn't need a big wind-up or a lot of time to release it. Klavins is a good stickhandler through traffic as he can retain possession of the puck and shows good creativity with it. Has been able to show a nifty move or two while deking out a player. Klavins is also a player that competes and works without the puck on his stick as well.

Knierim, William
RW – Dubuque Fighting Saints (USHL) 6'2.75", 210
HockeyProspect.com Ranking: 201

William Knierim was a player we were expecting big things from this year in Dubuque and while by no means did he have a bad season, given his size and skill set we expected more production and consistency. The Chicago Mission product played in 53 Regular Season games and scored 14 Goals and 13 assists; when he's on he is really on but can disappear for long stretches of a game as well.
William is a big bodied winger who can get up and down the ice well for his size but still has room for improvement in his overall skating. William has grown a lot over the last couple years and his skating stride has yet to catch up to that but we think it will continue to improve going forward and isn't a huge concern at this stage. His first few strides could be quicker but once he gets going he can be difficult to handle and can take the puck to the net. Knierim does his best work in front of the net where he can be almost impossible to move or get position on, he has good hand eye coordination and can deflect pucks in front, has a quick stick and hands and can bang home rebounds and loose pucks. Has a good shot and good one- timing ability. He can bring a nasty physical element at times and showed the willingness to drop the glove on occasion. William showed good vision of the ice and can make crisp plays with the puck and is good at threading passes from the wall, below the goal line and shows good effort at both ends of the ice. Knierim has a good understanding of his game and

what he needs to do to become the player he needs to be to reach his full potential, it may take some time but William has the size and skill set to be an effective power forward at the next level. He will be off to Miami (OH) this fall to continue his progression.

Quotable: "Saw him back at the beginning of the year at Hlinka, he had some good shifts alongside Mittelstadt and Yamamoto when he got bumped up to their line, seemed like he could contribute in a power-winger role with two skilled players, but was less effective when he was relied upon to create offense" - HP Scout Nik Funa

Quotable: "His game is solid around the net and in the scoring areas and brings a good physical edge to his game, needs to show the same puck hounding ability in his own end that he shows in the offensive end." HP Scout Dusten Braaksma

Koch, Davis
RW – Edmonton Oil Kings (WHL) 6'00, 157
HockeyProspect.com Ranking: NR

Davis is a gritty player who competes hard in the offensive zone. He likes to get in on the fore check and the majority of his goals came off the rush going hard to the net. He also has a good small-space game and can make plays in-tight. He is not an overly physical player and needs to work on the defensive side of his game. While he shows glimpses of a player that could play as a bottom six forward he needs to bring more compete on a shift by shift basis and must work to gain weight and find another gear when it comes to skating. He will need more time to develop in order to improve his status as a prospect.

Kodytek, Petr
LC – HC Plzen U18/U20 (CZE) – 5'06", 146
HockeyProspect.com Ranking: NR

Kodytek brings a lot of energy every time he steps on the ice. His feet never stop moving. Despite a small frame, he generates enough power and speed to be effective in every zone. He showed that he has playmaker abilities at the Ivan Hlinka tournament this year, but his line mates lacked the finishing touch. During the Czech season he put up 38 points (17 games) at the U18 level and 32 points (19 games) at the U20 level. He has an effective shot and he is trusted to log key minutes – end of games, power-play and penalty kill. What is really noticeable about him is his character. He is always talking to his teammates and giving a pat when they come to the bench after a good or bad play.

Kodytek could benefit from shooting more. He is the type of player that prefers to set up a teammate than take a shot. He has some areas in the defensive zone that need correcting and learning, but his work ethic is great and helps make up for his mistakes. He doesn't shy away from physical play and likes to hit. Very versatile player that is effective in a shutdown role or creating offensive chances. Unfortunately, his size is an apparent issue as he has a tiny frame, and his skills might not be enough to make up for it.

Koivula, Otto
LW – Ilves (Fin U20) – 6'04", 219
HockeyProspect.com Ranking: 193

Big winger whose offensive instincts are quite good. Koivula is a really smart kid who can create scoring opportunities for his linemates and for himself too. Good puck handling skills and he can operate with the puck in small places. He's a raw talent who doesn't use his physical tools as well as he could.

On top of using his size more consistently, his skating will need a lot of improvement in both technique and quickness. At the moment he's a pure offensive player but he reads the game well and if he can improve his skating he could be an effective player in all three zones. His strengths work at the junior level and he finished this season 49 games with 58 points. He made his Finnish elite league debut also but he's not ready to become a full-time pro yet.

Quotable: " Here's a player with significant upside, the way he finished the season I'm pretty sure someone will take a chance on him, no matter how raw he is" - HP Scout Mik Portoni

Kopacka, Jack
LW - Sault Ste. Marie Greyhounds (OHL) 6'02", 185
HockeyProspect.com Ranking: 120

Kopacka was selected in the 8th round of the 2014 OHL Priority Selection Draft by the Sault Ste. Marie Greyhounds out of the Detroit Compuware U16 program. He spent last season primarily with the Detroit Compuware U18 team while making a handful of appearances with the Greyhounds. He played primarily on the third line for the Hounds in his first full OHL season seeing a little special teams action here and there as well.

Kopacka is a big winger with a great frame. He does an excellent job protecting the puck and is at his best when protecting and driving the net using his frame and strength to create scoring chances. He's effective picking up the garbage goals banging home rebounds and going hard to the net. His play was highly inconsistent this season, sometimes getting very involved physically and offensively, other times playing a very passive game, not utilizing his strengths. His skating is below average and this will need to improve before taking his game to the next level. He isn't a great passer and gained a pretty large percentage of his assists through rebounds. When playing physical he makes an impact and gets good power in his checks. He needs to play this style more consistently in order to be successful.

Kopacka projects as a big power winger who's offensive upside is borderline for a secondary role and may max out as a third line winger if he reaches his potential. He will need to be tougher to play against defensively, improve his skating, play a more consistent physical game. With that said when he does play his game, finish his checks and drive the net he can be a very effective player.

Quotable: " He's so soft." - NHL Scout (November 2015)

Quotable: " Kopacka was actually really good last night." - NHL Scout (February 2016)

Quotable: " I saw a few games early that made me want to keep watching. He flashed skill at times, but in the end I just had too many viewings of him where he was just average or invisible. - Mark Edwards

Koppanen, Joona
LC – Ilves (Fin U20) – 6'04", 192
HockeyProspect.com Ranking: NR

In 2014-15 Joona scored 57 points in 38 games in the Finnish U18 league. After jumping to U20 level he couldn't replicate the success. In U18 league he produced taking advantage of his size but this year this wasn't enough anymore. Joona's role was smaller and that affected his game, but he managed to play well in a bottom 6 role and had a decent season. His skating ability is decent for his size and he's a pretty smart kid. Likes to use his size and hits heavy. He is also good in front of the net. Has decent hockey sense and plays a good two way game, but his offensive ability is questionable. Versatile player that struggles with the puck once the pace of the game picks up.

Korenar, Josef
G – HC Dukla Jihlava U20 (CZE) – 6'02", 172
HockeyProspect.com Ranking: 143

Korenar is a true competitor in the crease with tremendous feet. On a team that was young and lacking depth, Korenar ensured his club had a chance to win every night with big saves and confident play. His footwork in the crease is impressive as he can generate terrific bursts of power from his inside edges. He moves effortlessly around the crease showing his strong core and agile feet. Because of his strong skating abilities and fast legs, he seals up the ice quick and efficiently. Can make tremendous cross-crease saves sealing up the backdoor or taking away a two-on-one pass. When he rotates and slides into his butterfly, his chest and shoulders remain square and in control.

Tracking pucks high is an area that he will need to continue to improve upon. While he fills the net well, he needs to utilize his elbows on high shots and get on-top of pucks in tight. Puck handling is a major concern for Korenar as he consistently struggles to make the right pass or decision when he ventures out of the crease.

Korenar was in the net for 69% of his teams wins this season and averaged 32 shots against. He was selected 43rd overall in the 2016 USHL Phase 2 draft by the Lincoln Stars.

Korshkov, Yegor
RW – Lokomotiv Yaroslav (KHL) – 6'04", 180
HockeyProspect.com Ranking: 118

Korshkov is a forward prospect eligible for the third time for the NHL Entry Draft. Last year he split time between MHL and KHL, while this year he doubled his KHL appearances, logging 45 games and scoring 12 points before going back to his junior team for the playoffs, leading it to the title. Korshkov also made Russia's WJC squad and was one of their better performers in that tournament.

Korshkov is a skilled winger who however excels playing a grinding game that can wear the opposition down. He has developed terrific puck protection skills and he can keep possession in the corners using his large frame to shield it. His ability to pin the play into other teams' end is something that can be valuable and he could fit on any team that likes to play a puck-possession game and focus on keeping it in the offensive zone. Yegor has also shown he can drive the puck to the net from down low, with the ability to score from up close in scrambles. But he has poise as well and can wait for the play to develop before hitting teammates with accurate passes. He has improved his physical game, but as of now Korshkov is not the kind of forward that grinds down defensemen by regularly finishing his checks, he does that by keeping possession for extended periods of time instead.

Korshkov can be a dangerous player in transition as well if given room, and has been a threat on the penalty kill at the junior level for that reason. He is a good skater with good top speed and at 6-foot-4 he can carry the puck up through the ice using his very good puck control, reach and puck protection to find a way through the opposite blueline. The big ice definitely helps his game in the neutral zone and on North American rinks he would need to become quicker in his executions and even more so in his reactions to plays. Yegor has clearly improved his compete level over the last couple of seasons, but will still need to become smarter and more effective in puck battles, he can't rely on puck protection until he does get full possession. He has good power on his wrist shot but we would have liked to see him capitalize more often on his chances.

Korshkov brings intriguing tools and the way his game has been evolving he might as well become an option for a bottom six role. That, along with his performance at the WJC, should give him better chances on the draft table this time around.

Quotable:" I've never been a fan of his, but you gotta give him credit, he's been improving and he put together a solid season" - HP Scout Mik Portoni

Kosorenkov, Ivan
RW – Team Russia U18 (MHL) – 6'00", 183
HockeyProspect.com Ranking: NR

Kosorenkov is a left-shooting right winger who has shown upside with his goal-scoring prowess. Although not the flashiest player, Kosorenkov works hard for each of his goals and will get his nose dirty looking to pounce on any loose puck he can find.
He was added to the Russian U18 team mid-season, and had a solid season potting 13 goals in 22 games for the Russian U18 squad after scoring 5 goals in 11 games for Spartak Moscow junior team. Kosorenkov is a shooter and his goal-scoring style is less of the high-skill variety and more about his work-ethic and the ability to find space for himself in prime scoring areas. Kosorenkov has decent acceleration and even if he isn't the fastest, or the biggest player around, he can be quite a pesky presence on the ice. He doesn't mind skating head-first into traffic, he doesn't mind pushing and shoving to find his space and there are some elements of a goal-scoring agitator to his game. Kosorenkov puts the effort in backchecking hard through the neutral zone but his defensive zone game could improve, as well as his play in transition. While his all-around game and skillset will need to continue to improve, Kosorenkov has an interesting foundation to build his game around as he develops.

Krag Christensen, Nikolaj
RC/LW – Rodovre (DEN) – 6'03", 201
HockeyProspect.com Ranking: 149

Krag Christensen is a pro-sized right shot center that gets around the ice well. He looks good darting through the ice at top speed as he is a challenge to stop and can drive the play forward. First few steps and pivots still have some room for improvement but his straight-line top speed is quite good and he can handle the puck while coming down the ice with jump in his step. Does a good job creating space with his frame and speed and then looking to dish a pass to an open linemate. Also has a nice off-foot wrist-shot. Krag Christensen has played in the Danish top league but also appeared for Denmark internationally, he has logged significant minutes both at the U20 World Junior Championships as well as the U18 World Championships.

Krassey, Evan
RW - Hamilton Bulldogs (OHL) 6'03", 194
HockeyProspect.com Ranking: NR

Krassey was drafted in the 8th round of the 2014 OHL Priority Selection Draft by the Niagara Ice Dogs out of the Thunder Bay Kings Minor Midget program. After playing for the St. Mary's Jr. B Lincolns last year, Krassey started the season out with the Ice Dogs. He was later traded to the Hamilton Bulldogs before the trade deadline.

Krassey is a big bodied forward who loves the physical game. He crushes opponents and provides an intimidating physical presence. He isn't afraid to drop the gloves and has faired pretty well in these situations over the last two seasons. Krassey is your prototypical checking forward who will drop the gloves. His skating isn't very good and he doesn't have a great deal of offensive ability. While he has the size to be an intimidating presence in junior and in some pro levels, he lacks NHL upside and will have to show some skill along with his tenacious physical play in order to be considered a legitimate NHL prospect.

Krempasky, Martin
RD – Team Slovakia U18 (SVK) – 6'02", 212
HockeyProspect.com Ranking: NR

Krempasky is a pro-sized defenseman that has both the height and the filled out frame to compete in his own zone. Primarily a defensive defenseman, Krempasky will play an engaging defensive game while looking to get the puck to a safe place (usually with a simple pass) once he obtains it. Protects the middle of the ice and the crease area well. Krempasky doesn't have a lot of skill with the puck but does show inklings of offensive utility. He can pinch up the wall and has the physical tools to hold the blueline or to send the puck back deep into offensive zone. He has a rather simple shooting game, won't be the guy that walks the line or fakes the shot-blockers out, but he will get it quickly on net if he finds a seam.

Krikunenko, Roman
LW – Loko Yaroslavl (MHL) – 5'10", 165
HockeyProspect.com Ranking: NR

Roman is a late '97 born forward that finished the regular season at the top of his junior team scoring ranks. He possesses good technical skills and puck control, but makes efficient use of those qualities, rarely tries to do to much and usually doesn't hold onto the puck for too long. That doesn't mean he doesn't have the confidence to carry it. In fact, he has good poise with puck and moves it with his head up, showing good playmaking abilities. Still, in our viewings his best passes have come in situations where the puck was off his stick right after getting it, quickly recognizing a better positioned linemate and setting him up. Even at junior level Krikunenko is not someone who can take over shifts, more like someone who can effectively combine with linemates and look for soft spots in the defensive coverage. He plays a fairly disciplined game and likes to position himself around the slot, he can pick spots with his wrist shot and his ability to find angles to shoot from that area is appreciable. Despite his size he is surprisingly capable of delivering and absorbing legit hits, even if he's far from a physical player.
Roman is a well balanced and agile skater, but will probably never have the acceleration to separate himself from opponents. He is fairly quick, but especially as a small player his chances would benefit from becoming more explosive and from adding another gear at top speed. Either way, with his small frame he will have to make it a powerful one to define his identity at the next level.

Krys, Chad
LD – USNTDP 5'11", 185
HockeyProspect.com Ranking: 126

Krys is a puck-moving defenseman that can use his skating to move pucks and also has good enough vision to pass the puck around. Krys also does a good job using his skating offensively, he can keep control of the point on PP and does a good job walking the blueline. While a good puck-distributor, we wish Krys would display a bit more decisiveness in manufacturing offense from the offensive blueline, but he often settles for the basic play and doesn't overly exert himself.

His mobility is also a big part of his defensive game. At his best, Krys does a good job getting into position quickly to recover pucks or win foot-races, this is especially the case on the defensive blueline and in neutral zone as Krys has the mobility that allows him to retrieve pucks and start a quick regroup. Krys is undersized for a defenseman, so defending deeper in his own zone and around the net poses some challenges to him. This is magnified by the fact that he is not the most engaging defensive zone player.

Right now, Krys does a good job playing his game, but additional improvement will be needed either in defensive zone or in becoming a bigger offensive threat from the offensive blueline in. Krys has a solid framework with his mobile puck-movement game to build upon, but becoming a full time NHL defenseman without improvement in those two areas will be quite hard, especially at his size.

Quotable: "He's two hundred and eleventh on my list." NHL Scout (September 2015) (responding to our pre-season ranking of Chad Krys)

Quotable: "He has NHL feet, love the skating but I think he's slow moving pucks. I'm not a big fan of him. He's a bit undersized and I'm not sure he thinks the game fast enough right now to make it to the NHL. When he was younger he could just skate his way out of problems but now that the game has caught up to him, it's causing him a lot of grief. Not a guy that NHL Scouts raved to me about." - HP Scout Mark Edwards

Kryski, Jake
LW/LC – Kamloops Blazers (WHL) 5'11", 175
HockeyProspect.com Ranking: NR

Kryski is a forward that has good skating ability, competes well and has decent smarts. Kryski had a decently productive rookie season for Kamloops last year, he also appeared for Canada at the U17s and put up 5 points in 5 games. This season Kryski put in just an OK season from a production standpoint as he had 39 points in 67 games and only a point in Kamloops' 7 playoff games. With that said, Kryski is a rather likable forward prospect. He competes well in all zones. Though we wouldn't classify him as a very aggressive player as he won't seek out contact on his own, he still exhibits good effort level in races for loose pucks. He will battle against the opposition and will sacrifice his body when needed.

Kryski has good speed out of his zone and through the neutral zone and can be an involved player on the rush. We like his offensive zone smarts. He's a player that does a good job coming off the cycle and taking the puck to the middle, where he will often dish a pass and find an open linemate in the slot. Kryski isn't the biggest player, but has shown good smarts and the will to work in all three zones. He's a good skater and an adept playmaker, but not a dynamic player with the puck on his stick. The fact that his production was just average, was a bit of a let-down as well. Overall, Kryski is a likable forward prospect, but will need to show a bigger offensive impact on a consistent level.

Kunin, Luke
RC/W – University of Wisconsin (BIG-NCAA) 5'11", 190
HockeyProspect.com Ranking: 17

Luke Kunin is a late 97' birthday and was able to escalate his schooling to be able to attend Wisconsin in his draft year and instantly stepped into a struggling team and was able to make a contribution right away. Kunin is a mature young man both on and off the ice and showed good leadership qualities despite being one of the younger players on the team. Kunin was close to a Point Per Game with 32 points in 34 games, ended the season with 9 Goals in the final 10 games and started to dominate games down the stretch. Kunin spent most of the season playing left wing but did spend some time at center and was effective at either and good in the faceoff circle.

Kunin likes to play a scrappy game and brings a good work ethic and physicality along with the ability to get under the opponents skin and draw penalties. Luke has an elite hockey IQ which allows him to anticipate and disrupt plays in his own end as well as be in the right position to find loose pucks in the offensive zone. If there is a weakness in his 200 foot game it is in the neutral zone where he showed the tendency to not engage in as many puck battles and gets caught on the high side of the puck at times. Kunin is a player who likes to play with pace through neutral zone which can cause issues if his team doesn't win possession and the play goes the other way.

Kunin's skating balance, agility and acceleration allows him to cover a lot of ice, win a lot of races to loose pucks as well as pressure the puck carrier on the fore check. When Kunin has the puck on his stick in the offensive zone he has a shoot first mentality and can get the puck off his tape quickly and accurately. He possesses an accurate one-timer with decent velocity. While Kunin's playmaking ability isn't as high end as his finishing ability he is an accurate passer of the puck and knows how to move the puck quickly in all 3 zones. Kunin played in all situations for Wisconsin and his anticipation and ability to read the play allows him to be a dangerous penalty killer. He picks his spots to challenge and can be a threat to create scoring chances shorthanded.
Certainly Kunin needs some more seasoning and success at the NCAA level before making the jump to pro hockey but we believe he projects as a solid top 9 forward at the professional level.

Quotable: "I'm a big fan of him, could turn out to be an elite scorer at the next level." NHL Scout (November 2015)

Quotable: "You can tell this kid thinks the game at an Elite level, he always knows where he needs to be to find the puck on his stick and has the finishing ability to convert on his chances." HP Scout Dusten Braaksma

Quotable: "Even with not a lot of help around him, he started to dominate games in the second half of the season." NHL Scout (February 2016)

Quotable: "He has that rare ability to get under the opponents skin, both on the scoreboard as well as between and after whistles." NHL Scout (February 2016)

Quotable: "Multiple Scouts rated his combine interviews from very good to outstanding." - HP Scout Mark Edwards (NHL Combine week

Kuokkanen, Janne
LC – Kärpät (Fin U20) – 6'01", 175
HockeyProspect.com Ranking: 57

Janne had a strong season playing the majority of the year in juniors, as he recorded 53 points in 47 games. He also made his debut in Mestis (2nd highest pro league) and in the Finnish elite league. He should be ready to jump to the pro level soon, he scored two goals in his only FEL game. Janne is a really smart forward with good mobility and skating technique. He plays a mature two way game and doesn't have any big flaws, has good hands and can protect the puck from opponents to keep possession going when he doesn't quickly dish it off to linemates. He has strong vision and he is a playmaker first but has also shown upside in the goal scoring department. While playmaking is his main strength, we have seen an improvement in his willingness to shoot and he can also be a useful player on the forecheck as he is willing to compete off-the-puck. Kuokkanen is a really versatile and can play both center and wing.

As he moves forward, he would benefit from filling out his frame and maintaining a good shoot-pass balance, as early in the season he looked prone to over-passing.

Quotable: "This is a kid who made a very positive impression on me at the U18 in Grand Forks. A big riser for me." - HP Scout Mark Edwards

Kurovsky, Daniel
LW – HC Vitkovice U20 (CZE) – 6'04", 198
HockeyProspect.com Ranking: NR

Big kid who spent most of the year on a loan from AZ Havirov, playing for Vitkovice in the U20 league. Kurovsky's a raw power forward who plays a simple offensive zone game. He can generate some speed but will need to further improve in that respect. Stride doesn't look too awful and has potential for improvement. Has good upper body strength and likes to get in on loose pucks. Handful to handle for defensemen when playing against him in corners. Can be a presence on the forecheck. Shows signs of decent hockey IQ and smarts. Puck skills could be better, needs to control the puck quicker and smoother. Understands how offense is developed and can anticipate plays, goes to net when puck is passed to the point to be a net presence, makes good guesses when to drive to the middle from the weak side anticipating a pass. He is a player that will battle but even though he's a handful and has good strength, his balance on skates will need to improve, can look a bit awkward while engaged in a shoving match.

Kutkevicius, Luke
LC - Hamilton Bulldogs (OHL) 6'00", 163
HockeyProspect.com Ranking: NR

Kutkevicius was selected in the second round of the 2014 OHL Priority Selection Draft by the Mississauga Steelheads out of the North York Rangers Minor Midget program. Midway through his first OHL season he was traded to the Hamilton Bulldogs after spending last season in the OJHL with the North York Rangers.

Luke has played effectively in a depth role for both the Steelheads and the Bulldogs this season. He provides a good two-way game where he does a lot of the little things well. He gets pucks deep, pressures the puck carrier and works hard for pucks. He has had some moments this season where he's shown some flashes of skill on the third line creating some offense, but didn't do this on a consistent basis. He projects as a solid two-way forward in the OHL, but currently doesn't project as an NHL pick for us in the 2016 NHL Entry Draft.

Kuznetsov, Vladimir
LW – Acadie-Bathurst Titan (QMJHL) – 6'02", 214
HockeyProspect.com Ranking: 101

Kuznetsov is a tank. He's big, strong, and tough to knock down or take the puck away from. He was the first overall selection in the CHL Import Draft last summer, and coming over to the Titan and getting a lot of ice time was a key in his development this season. His skating will need a lot of work over the next couple of years, as he lacks explosiveness and agility. He's very strong down low, doing a lot of work below the hash marks. Small defensemen in the QMJHL are often overmatched against Kuznetsov's pure strength. He can score with his big and heavy shot. He has good positioning in the offensive zone and knows where to go to receive passes, getting his nose dirty in front of the net if there's a rebound there. Kuznetsov needs a playmaking center to be successful; when placed with Antoine Morand, both had great success, due to Morand's playmaking abilities. When not paired with a playmaking center, he had more difficulty. We would like to see him more involved in the play and more active in puck battles instead of waiting to get the puck from one of his linemates. We kept knocking him due to his skating, but his offensive tools were tough to ignore. He can score, but his playmaking abilities are underrated. He has good poise with the puck in the offensive zone and can wait at the last second to make a pass to a teammate in a scoring area, especially on the power play. We love his offensive tools, but he does worry us with his below-average speed and the fact that he has seemingly already reached his peak in his physical maturation process, compared to other draft-eligible players.

Kyrou, Jordan
RW - Sarnia Sting (OHL) 6'00.25", 175
HockeyProspect.com Ranking: 69

Kyrou was selected in the 2nd round of the 2014 OHL Priority Selection Draft by the Sarnia Sting out of the Mississauga Senators Minor Midget program. Kyrou had a solid rookie season as a 16 year old with a strong finish to his season.

Kyrou got off to a bit of a slow start again this season, but much like his first season he improved as the year went along. He had trouble early on holding on to the puck too much and trying to do too much himself. This got him into trouble and resulted in him getting him more than he needed to for a smaller forward. As the season progressed, Kyrou started moving the puck more to his teammates. This in turn made him that much more dangerous with the puck on his stick when deciding to shoot. He has great speed and excellent hands. He can stickhandle around defenders and goaltenders effectively. Multiple goals this season for Kyrou were of the highlight reel material and he displayed good vision with some excellent passes resulting in goals. He lacks strength and can get overwhelmed in tight spaces when he doesn't have the puck on his stick. He will need to get stronger and improve his ability to battle. Defensively he is average at this point.

Kyrou has intriguing offensive upside and we fully expect his name being called at the 2016 NHL Entry Draft. He has hands and puck skills and generally thrives when setting up his linemates. He needs to improve on his strength and ability to win battles in order to make the jump to the pro level.

Quotable: "This Kyrou kid is a tough one to figure out." - NHL Scout (November 2015)

Quotable: "He is going to fool some scouts this season and be selected higher than he should be." - NHL Scout (January 2016)

Quotable: "I'm not a big fan,. One game stands out to sum up why he would probably be selected before I'd be willing to pick him. It was a game in Guelph late in the year. I had just watched Givani Smith drive the net hard right in front of me. Later that period Kyrou had an opening to drive the net but wanted no part of it. He just continued wide and the play died on his stick. He can look good against bad teams that give him room, but when things tighten up..." - Mark Edwards

Laberge, Pascal
RW– Victoriaville Tigres (QMJHL) – 6'01", 173
HockeyProspect.com Ranking: 48

Laberge was the 2nd overall pick in the 2014 QMJHL Draft by the Gatineau Olympiques. He only played for half the year with them before he was dealt to Victoriaville. That trade reunited him with his

Midget AAA coach Bruce Richardson, with whom he went all the way to the Telus Cup final in 2013-2014 with the Grenadiers de Châteauguay.

It took until December this season to see Laberge to start playing some great hockey, the kind that you expect from a top prospect. At that time, he started playing on the wing full-time, which seemed to click for him offensively, with less responsibility and more freedom to create offense. He went on a great run in December before breaking a bone in his hand, but made it back for the Top Prospects' Game where he was named MVP, playing great alongside fellow Quebecer Pierre-Luc Dubois. Overall this season, Laberge had 45 of his 68 points after December 1st, showing great progression through the season. The St-Martine native skates well and is a good scorer. We like his scoring potential more, even if he had a lot of assists this season. He has a good shot and can score from anywhere in the offensive zone, but his decision-making will need to improve. He has great puck skills, great one-on-one moves and can make defenders playing the puck instead of the man regret that decision.

Physically, he will need to get bigger and stronger, as he is not a physical player and doesn't win enough one-on-one battles. Laberge is an exciting player on the ice with his speed and hands that grant him the ability to make highlight-reel plays, but he's still searching for that consistency that could make him an elite player. He's not involved in the play enough; in some viewings he barely touched the puck and was on the perimeter too often. At this level, he still can get by, due to his superior skill level. But once he reaches the pros, this tendency could hurt him. Another area he will need to improve on is his defensive game. Moving him to the wing was a way of giving him less defensive responsibilities compared to a center. He still needs to be more focused in the defensive zone, leaning towards making the smart play instead of cheating to go on offense.

Laberge progressed well this year; after a tough rookie season and an up-and-down first half he took a major step from December onwards and was one of the top players in the league in this portion. He has areas in his game that he needs to improve on, but you can't deny his offensive upside and skill level. At the U-18s, he scored twice on the power play in the tournament but his decision-making and complete game was lacking.

Quotable: "Much better on the wing than at center, but he still remains a frustrating player on the ice in terms of his decision-making, most notably in passing situations." - HP scout Jérôme Bérubé

Laberge, Samuel
LW – Rimouski Océanic (QMJHL) - 6'02", 218
HockeyProspect.com Ranking: NR

Laberge, who went un-drafted last season, made nice progress this year while playing a much bigger role offensively with the Océanic. He improved his offensive output and kept playing his solid all-around game. Once again this year, he was a key player on the Océanic PK unit which finished 3rd in the league. He was also one of the best shot-blockers in the league, showing no fear while getting in front of pucks. He's a big kid who does good work along the boards and in front of the net. His physical game is good, as he loves to finish his hits on the forecheck and is capable of dropping the gloves here and there. He lacks vision with the puck, though. He is not a good playmaker and gets a lot of assists from his hard work down low. He can score, he has a big, powerful slapshots, and on the power play he can do some good work in front of the net. He's an above-average skater and makes good use of his speed on the forecheck and in puck-pursuit situations. An NHL team could take a gamble on Laberge late in the draft; he attended Los Angeles' rookie camp this past year and had a great showing, earning himself a spot on the main camp roster in September. He's a big kid who can score some goals, can be an asset on both special units, and has NHL size.

Laczynski, Tanner
RC – Lincoln Stars (USHL) 6'0.5", 190
HockeyProspect.com Ranking: 139

The Chicago Mission product was eligible for the 2015 NHL draft and had a solid rookie season in the USHL but a lack of consistency from night to night contributed to him being passed over on draft day. Upon completion of the 14/15 season, Laczyski worked hard in the gym and tacked on 15 lbs to his frame and it showed in his play this season where he was among the USHL points leaders all season long and was able to extend plays and stay on the puck better. Laczynski saw himself get traded from Chicago to Lincoln midway through the season but had no trouble continuing his PPG pace with his new team.

Laczynski is a silky handed center that see's the offensive zone extremely well and has a knack for finding the open man. Tanner is a good skater to uses his speed well, seems to have another gear when entering the offensive zone and can get around defenders and takes it to the net. He possesses solid finishing ability with an accurate shot and willingness to battle in front for rebounds and garbage goals.

Tanner shows a decent 200 foot game where he tracks back into the play well, produces good back pressure and uses his stick well to clog up passing lanes. Laczynski will be off to Ohio State in the fall where more seasoning to his all around game is needed but Tanner possesses a good skill set and work ethic that could see him not getting passed over in this draft.

Quotable: "I like his skill, he has NHL hands. I like him below the dots. I think he excels there." NHL Scout (April 2016)

Quotable: "Skating would be the concern for me." - HP Scout Mark Edwards

LaFontaine, Jack
G – Janesville Jets (NAHL) 6'03", 197
HockeyProspect.com Ranking: 96

Jack Lafontaine is a Mississauga, ON native who was drafted and tendered by the Fargo Force but Fargo wanted to go with 2 more experienced goalies this year. La Fontaine found himself being the #1 goalie for Janesville and getting a lot more starts than if had he won one of the spots in Fargo.

The University of Michigan commit is an athletic goaltender at 6'3" but is pretty sound positionally as well, he stays square to the shot and you will rarely find him swimming around in the crease. He doesn't make a lot of acrobatic saves but he makes the saves he's supposed to make and keeps his rebounds under control. The Jets were an Up and Down team this season, so there were some nights that he was left hung out to dry a bit. There are a few warts in Lafontaine's game but he was pretty solid in our viewings. He dos need to get better with his recovery for 2nd and 3rd shots and get a bit tracking anticipating plays. While his playing of the puck isn't bad, he certainly could improve on that aspect of his game. There were a couple games where after a poor start either for his team or himself, he didn't rebound in the 2nd or 3rd periods and things usually went from bad to worse, we would like to see more compete out of him when the chips are down.

Laine, Patrik
LW – Tappara (Liiga) – 6'04", 206
HockeyProspect.com Ranking: 2

Already well known for his scoring prowess at the junior levels as a 15 year old winger, Laine's development was temporarily interrupted when he suffered a serious knee injury early in 2014. Patrik underwent knee surgery in March and after an off-season spent rehabilitating his knee he played most of last season in the second highest Finnish pro league, showing glimpses of his immense potential despite struggling with his skating. He showed us to be on the right track in Zug at the U18 Worlds where his improvements were already apparent. Fast forward another year, his game has reached a completely different level, allowing him to make a big impact already in top level competitions. Patrik was a key part of Finland winning gold at WJC on home soil, was voted MVP of Liiga playoffs after winning the title with Tappara and was among the best forwards at the World Championships at the end of a season where he played a crazy amount of demanding games for such a young player. His skating has been improving leaps and bounds over the last 18 months, to the point he now shows above average top speed and his limited agility has become way less of a concern. His first few steps still need to further improve to keep up with the play in the most intense games when he is forced to make numerous starts and stops, but even if that never becomes a strength of his, it is clearly trending in the right direction.

Laine has great offensive instincts and is one of the most dangerous shooters we have witnessed. He is a threat to score with all kinds of shots, his devastating right-handed one-timer will be a problem NHL goaltenders will have to deal with for years to come and that laser will make him a key factor on the powerplay right from the start of his NHL career. His wrist shot has a fast release, impressive velocity and is fairly accurate. He likes to pick corners and he has proven he can regularly beat goalies. Patrik works well without the puck to make his stick available and ready to shoot. His less than ideal footwork often leads to not being perfectly positioned for the shot, but he has the ability to adjust with his body and still release threatening shots from unorthodox positions.

Laine has outstanding reach paired with impressive hands and puck control. He can also effectively use his big body to protect the puck and take advantage of those traits to slow down the play when he needs to put his playmaking ability to work. He can carry the puck inside the offensive zone, use his vision to detect defensive breakdowns and exploit them executing accurate passes. On the powerplay he loves to use his reach to create passing lanes for his backhand. On North American rinks he will have less room to maneuver and will be interesting to see him adapt his play with the puck. Another area where Laine has made obvious improvements during the last year is with his defensive game. He consistently puts his long stride to work on the backcheck and has managed to not be considered the defensive liability he had been not all that long ago. His longer sticks helps in that department and paired with his good reads makes his ability to create turnovers an underrated part of his game.

Laine can play both wings but is more of a one on one threat on his off side. Coming down the left side he is a threat with his forehand shot, but depending on the gap left by the defenseman he can move the puck through his legs and go to his backhand instead. When challenging the defenseman he could actually do a better job deciding whether to shoot or try to stickhandle through. He should go for the shot more often, even more so at the NHL level.

The big Finn is able to deliver legit hits when the right opportunity arises, battles around the corners and as he hopefully adds a bit more quickness and adds more power to his frame moving forward, he should be able to do a better job at cycling the puck down low.

As his game quickly matured over the season, Laine has managed to reduce turnovers and limit them more and more to the offensive zone. He has been playing with impressive confidence and has thrived under pressure, proving to be a clutch performer. He is the kind of player that can be a difference maker even on his bad days. He doesn't need to be on top of his game to be a threat to score whenever he is on the ice. Those are traits of a special player who projects to be a future NHL star.

Quotable: "They are both great (Laine vs Puljujärvi) but I like Puljujärvi better because he is better defensively." - NHL Scout (September 2015)

Quotable: "I'm a Puljujärvi guy. Laine is great but I think Puljujärvi makes players around him better." - NHL Scout (October 2015)

Quotable: "Puljujärvi is ahead of Laine for me." - NHL Scout (November 2015)

Quotable: "It's close. I wake up one day and have Puljujärvi ahead and then wake up the next day and have Laine ahead." - NHL Scout (January 2016)

Quotable: "It's tighter between them now, Laine has proven to me that he is one of the most dangerous scorers in the draft." NHL Scout (January 2016)

Quotable: "It's not a slam dunk that Matthews is number one." - NHL Scout (April 2016)

Quotable: "I think what gets underrated about Laine is the fact that he has that healthy doze of cockiness in him, he really believes he can make a difference at any level." - HP Scout Nik Funa

Quotable: "With the tools he has and with how much better his skating looked after the summer, for me he has been the clear cut #2 since September." - HP Scout Mik Portoni

Quotable: "It's been enjoyable scouting both these big Finnish players the past few years. We first saw Laine at the Macs Midget Tournament in Calgary. Laine made big strides to improve some weaknesses in his game this season. They were a large factor for him moving ahead of Puljujärvi on many scouts lists. For me personally, Laine moved ahead of Puljujärvi on my list last April after the U18 in Switzerland. I thought he was outstanding there. Then one of our scouts saw both Finns in Lake Placid later that summer and he moved Laine ahead of Puljujärvi on his list. These were factors that led to our pre-season ranking of Laine at 3rd overall and Puljujärvi 4th. In November both players moved ahead of Chychrun on our list and have not budged since. I did a lot of polling NHL scouts on their ranking of two big Finns all season long. It was interesting that while most said it was close, not one scout I asked had Laine ahead of Puljujärvi until after World Juniors, a couple still have Puljujärvi ahead." - HP Scout Mark Edwards

Lajoie, Maxime
LD – Swift Current Broncos (WHL) 6'01", 183
HockeyProspect.com Ranking: 64

Maxime Lajoie is a smooth skating defenseman who has been an important contributor to the Broncos blue line for a couple seasons now. Lajoie has decent size and is a good skater. He is very good at producing offense from the point, specifically he has an excellent sense for walking the blueline, distributing the puck and is very good at getting his wrist-shot through to the net.

Lajoie's hockey IQ is above-average and he does a good job with his defensive positioning. Lajoie typically plays an engaging game and is decent at protecting the front of the net, although he is not going to quite pass for a shutdown defenseman. He does a good job on puck-retrievals and has shown some ability to also break up plays on the wall. Lajoie who is typically a strong first-pass defenseman had a somewhat inconsistent season, his start was quite slow and he was making uncharacteristically poor choices on his outlets, he also took a lot of physical contact while moving the puck, getting battered by the forecheck, but his played picked up significantly later on in season and he was back to his usual self. Lajoie hoists a really dangerous seeing-eye wristshot from the blueline that he consistently gets through and on net, it produces dangerous rebounds and allows for tips. He's also a great passer and playmaker who has a few years of quarterbacking experience on his resume.

Lajoie plays the game at a calm pace and is the architect of many good plays through smart first passes and good reads. Lajoie has experience playing in a full-time role playing in all situations for two seasons with the Broncos. He's not terribly big or imposing in the difficult areas, but we expect him to improve in those areas as he adds needed size. He had some hiccups this season, but still tracks favorably as a puck-mover with a nice game from the offensive blueline and point-shot ability.

Lakatos, Dominik
LC/W – Bili Tygri Liberec (CZE) – 6'00", 178
HockeyProspect.com Ranking: 209

Lakatos is a versatile center that can also line up on the wing. He is a second time eligible who has had a fantastic progression in his game since last year. Lakatos was a below PPG player at the U20 level in his draft year, but now only a year later he is a mainstay in the top Czech league, playing against men and having good success there. Lakatos put up 11 points in 36 games in regular season and scored additional 5 in 12 playoff games. He also had a solid showing for the Czech U20 squad at the WJC.

Lakatos is a forward who keeps his feet moving and makes quality reads with and without the puck. His size isn't too bad, but will still need some additional filling out. His compete level is good in all three zones and in all situations. The foundation of smarts, compete and the will to move his feet allow him to play both center and wing positions with equal success. Lakatos is a smart offensive player, he anticipates plays and can beat his coverage to the slot for a scoring chance. Presents his stick well to receive a pass or line up for a shot, he is an easy player to play with. Not the biggest but gets good body position against other players, knows how to keep his body between the puck and the checking player and will push back. Skating is just OK and could get better especially for a lighter player like him. Can fire a quick snap-shot from the slot and has some scoring ability. Good playmaker, finds open men and when he makes the pass he doesn't watch and follow his own puck, but keeps moving to open up and looks to get puck back. Works well with equally smart players who think the game at a similar level.

Lakatos has done a lot to improve his stock after going un-drafted last year. While he will still need to get stronger, he has shown enough upside as a smart versatile forward to be noticed as a second time draft eligible.

Larsson, Filip
G – Djurgarden J20 (SWE) - 6'02", 180
HockeyProspect.com Ranking: NR

It was a bit of a challenging season for Larsson who hasn't had the best year either in his domestic league or internationally. Larsson is a goalie with decent size, that likes to play a calm controlled game in his crease. He communicates with his defense well and usually does a good job on initial shots that he can clearly see. One issue in our viewings was that he failed to come up with that big save that would change the momentum into his team's favor. His strength is that he makes the saves he is supposed to make, but this year even that part of it wasn't consistent as higher-quality accurate shots were beating him a touch too often. He has also struggled to re-focus in his bad games. Larsson also struggled against up-close plays with traffic and jam-plays around the net where he struggled to make himself big and protect his crease area. He has shown good rebound control especially on shots up high but tends to leave rebounds off his pads that can bounce right back into the slot. Larsson still offers some upside as a goalie, but he will have to bounce back with a stronger year next season.

Lauzon, Felix
LC – Victoriaville Tigres (QMJHL) – 5'08", 174
HockeyProspect.com Ranking: NR

Lauzon was selected in the 2nd round of the 2014 QMJHL Draft by Victoriaville after playing two seasons with Magog in Midget AAA (one as an underager). Lauzon doesn't have the ideal size or speed to play at the next level. What makes Lauzon attractive is his hockey sense and attention to details. He is already a premiere defensive player with his team and a key member of the Tigres' PK unit. Lauzon is the player who will take key faceoffs in the defensive zone for the Tigres most of the time. He often acted like a 3rd defenseman for his team; he is usually the first to backcheck and gives good support to his defensemen deep in the defensive zone. His offensive production was not as high as expected this season (38 points in 64 games), but with his smarts and additional responsibilities offensively we expect it to improve next season. Offensively, he has nice vision and is a talented playmaker. We don't expect him to get drafted, but he could be a nice candidate to get try-outs in NHL camps during the summer and in September.

Lazarev, Maxim
RW – Cape Breton Screaming Eagles (QMJHL) – 5'10", 175
HockeyProspect.com Ranking: NR

Lazarev is in his third year of being draft eligible after going un-drafted in 2014 and 2015. He was originally drafted 3rd overall in the 2013 CHL import draft. He had his best year this year with 75 points and playing in one of the top line in the QMJHL with his countryman Evgeny Svechnikov and Pierre-Luc Dubois. He also played for Russia at the World Junior this year finishing the event with 6 points in 7 games. This year was where we felt Lazarev was the most comfortable on the ice in his junior career and was a difference maker on the ice. He can play either wing and is primarily a playmaker, real good vision and passing ability. He's good at slowing down the play in the offensive zone. He also possesses a good wrist shot with fast release. He's a good enough skaters at this level but for a small player we would like to see improved his top speed and acceleration. As said he's on the small side and still lack strength to win battles along the wall and to play consistently good defense in his own zone. He's a bit risky as far his NHL projection goes but we could see a team take a flyer on him due to his offensive upside.

Leskinen, Otto
LD – KalPa (Fin U20) – 5'11", 170
HockeyProspect.com Ranking: NR

After a good first season at the U20 level Leskinen has shown further improvement and was one of the better defensemen in that league. He played 28 games and scored 31 points but it was not just his production to be impressive, he showed a strong all-round game. As a result he spent time with KalPa's pro team and played 19 Liiga games, but didn't got a fair chance to show his skills as his average ice time was around 5-10 minutes. Otto is a smart d-man with solid all-round ability. His positioning is good, he likes to join the offense and does well there. Has decent puck skills and good mobility. He sees the ice well and is an adept puck-distributor. He's not the biggest kid on ice but he's quite strong and plays with passion.

Lestan, Filip
LW – HV71 J20 (SWE) – 6'05", 191
HockeyProspect.com Ranking: 197

From a purely physical perspective, Lestan could line up for any professional team tomorrow if needed. Thus, it is not a surprise that he logged 11 games in SHL with HV71 squad even though he only put up 7 points in 25 games at the J20 level.

Lestan's game is mostly about two factors. Size and speed. Lestan is a manchild with tremendous skating ability for his 6'5 191 frame. He's got good acceleration, top speed, solid technique, turns with no problems, no agility issues. If Lestan was 5 inches smaller, we would still classify him as a good skater. Adding to that is his strength. Lestan can already compete with men because his physical development is frankly already that of a man. When playing against kids his age, he can flat out rag-doll them without much problem. Lestan also is a competitive player, plays with good energy and finishes his checks on the forecheck.

When playing against juniors, his size and speed allow him to just skate forward and not lose the puck, although he doesn't know yet what to do with it once he gets to the offensive zone. Lestan isn't quite lacking in hockey IQ, but there is too much reliance on his physical tools at this point in time. He hasn't quite learned how to create offense nor are his general playmaking skills very developed, he needs to get better at using his linemates as well.

While he is mature physically, he is very raw in that sense. It will be interesting to see to what extent those skills can develop, but even with minimal development there, Lestan's size and skating package still offers some upside as a fourth line checking forward. It helps that he is competitive and plays an up-tempo game with energy. In order to be projected above that role, Lestan will need patient development in his play with the puck, in learning how to utilize his linemates better, and in processing the ice and being more aware of his options.

Quotable: "His play with the puck needs work, but it's rare to find his combination of size and skating ability. Helps that he competes hard, too." – HP Scout Nik Funa

Lindgren, Ryan
LD – USNTDP 6'00", 198
HockeyProspect.com Ranking: 80

Lindgren is a mid-sized left defenseman, the captain and one of more heavily relied upon players on USNTDP's blueline. Lindgren has average height for a defenseman but a reasonably sturdy frame. Lindgren has always been a player with solid tools, but one that was at times overly shy about using them for offensive play.

The development of Lindgren's confidence on the offensive side of the puck was one of the things that we hoped to see throughout the 2015-2016 season and Lindgren's best answer to that question perhaps came at the U18 World Championships, where he consistently played with confidence while the puck was on his stick.

Lindgren always displayed a solid positional sense, calmness with the puck and in his decision-making and a solid first pass. He is an engaging player in his own zone and while you might see him throw his body around on the occasion and line someone up, he's not really a punishing defenseman on a regular basis. Lindgren's offensive game is somewhat inconsistent, at times he seems to prefer playing a game that is solid defensively and solid from a puck-moving perspective but lacking in offensive firepower. He would lay back and opt to make good passes out of his zone but not really join the play much up front. However, Lindgren also had games where he showed us a more complete effort with the puck as well and that was culminated by a long-stretch of confident hockey at the U18s. There, Lindgren confidently skated with the puck, activated himself more often by pinching, and displayed solid offensive sense when joining the rush or making an extra stickhandle through neutral zone or in the offensive zone.

While Lindgren is a solid defensive prospect even when he tends to play a more conservative game, his finish to the season might suggest that he has found the confidence to be a more active player. That would certainly be a big improvement in his game as he moves forward and allow him to be more of a two-way threat.

Quotable: "Opinions from scouts I spoke to about him but varied. Personally I think he's a good skater and he's smart, but he's not an overly big kid and I just don't see his game translating all that well to the NHL." - HP Scout Mark Edwards

Lindholm, Max
LC – AIK J20 (SWE) – 6'01", 187
HockeyProspect.com Ranking: NR

While Lindholm appeared in only 10 J20-league games last season, he has turned in a full season this year and has been quite productive putting up near a point per game and finishing the season with a very strong performance in playoffs as he and his linemate Fredrik Karlstrom tore through opposition. Lindholm also put in 12 Allsvenskan games at the senior level, so his success and progression through different age-groups was quite rapid in a span of one year.

Lindholm continues to show that he is a strong playmaker. He has good vision, puck-skills and the ability to hit teammates with either his forehand or backhand passing. Lindholm is good at dragging a checker to himself and still finding ways to throw an accurate dish to an open linemate. He has some elusiveness and deceptive footwork, but his stride at full straight-ahead speed could still improve.

Overall, Lindholm has nice hands, good offensive zone instincts and the ability to hit players with accurate passes on either side of his body. Though not very physical, he pays attention to what is happening in his own end. As a second-time eligible, he offers some offensive upside, however it remains to be seen whether his offense will translate against men as his skating could still get better and he doesn't excel against physical play.

Lindstrom, Linus
LC – Skelleftea J20 (SWE) – 5'11", 164
HockeyProspect.com Ranking: 63

Lindstrom is a player who kept coming up in our notes as a center that didn't take any shortcuts in the way he plays the game on both ends of the ice. Lindstrom had a strong season at the J20 level, putting up over a point per game for Skelleftea and finishing with a strong playoff performance.

While he was rather impressive in our viewings of J20 league play, he was a bit more average internationally. Despite that, we have continued to like his commitment to a team game and compete. For example, he would always go back to help out his defensemen, whether it was tying up guys on the wall and helping out in battles or going back deep to offer another lane for an outlet. Offensively, Lindstrom won't stand out with his hands, but has a good understanding of space and how the holes develop in the offensive zone. This allows him to find his way to scoring areas, and he also has a good compete level around the net. Lindstrom can also quickly find an open linemate in the offensive zone, but lacks the physical tools to play a puck-possession game on a consistent level, thus his playmaking tends to be more based on quick passes rather than a controlled approach with a lot of time on his stick.

While his skating and strength has improved, it remains the single biggest issue that holds him back. It is by far his biggest hole and improvement there will be necessary. Additionally, Lindstrom can be prone to getting into a bit of a chasing game on the forecheck, as he tends to take straight lines towards the puck-carrier in order to hound him. This is admirable from a compete standpoint, but requires him to utilize a lot of stop and starts as the puck gets moved and isn't as useful in closing off passing lanes. Considering the improvement needed in his skating, it can put him a half a step behind the game action, especially against teams that move the puck quickly. This was apparent against some of the top international competition but was less of an issue at the J20 league level.

Quotable: "I like his game a lot. I think of him as one of the guys that makes a big leap in development once he gets stronger and faster after an additional year or two of gym-time and physical maturity." - HP Scout Nik Funa

Quotable: "Been on our radar for a while and I like him a lot. I think he's a smart player who will really emerge when he gets stronger. He has skill to go along with the great hockey IQ." - HP Scout Mark Edwards

Lochead, William
LD - Niagara Ice Dogs (OHL) 6'00", 195
HockeyProspect.com Ranking: NR

After going un-drafted at the 2014 and 2015 OHL Priority Selection Drafts, the former London Jr. Knight was picked up as a free agent by the Niagara Ice Dogs. Lochead started out as a healthy scratch behind other drafted prospects but his hard work and determination helped him become a durable player who played both defense and left wing.

Lochead has decent size and good strength and played very well in one on one situations as a rookie. He is tough down low, loves to finish his checks and packs a fair amount of power into it. Defensively he shows good awareness and will play the opposition tough but will be careful not to run out of position when doing so. He has good skating ability and can carry the puck out of trouble and will generally make the smart simple play with the puck. He makes effective first passes. He spent some time as a forward and provided an excellent forecheck in a bottom six role. Whatever role he was given he worked hard and forced the opposition to make mistakes.

Lochead was one of the most improved Minor Midget defenders in the Alliance in his OHL Draft year but was ultimately un-drafted. It appears he will likely be passed over at the 2016 NHL Draft as well. With that said, Lochead has surprised and impressed in his first OHL season and has a track record of being able to succeed taking the longer route.

Lockwood, William
RW - USNTDP (USHL) 5'11.25", 172
HockeyProspect.com Ranking: 151

While his production isn't eye-popping, Lockwood has emerged as a quite interesting offensive player. He has very good skating ability, quick and light first few steps that generate good top-speed and has the ability to change angles on defensemen. Lockwood has a soft touch with the puck and can handle it at his top speed. He is especially dangerous when he has a step or two of advantage on defensemen. Lockwood plays an up-tempo offensive game and has also shown some physicality as we have seen him finish checks on the forecheck. Lockwood has good offensive zone instincts and can finish plays. He shows the ability to buy himself time with the puck through his skating but is still learning how to utilize his tools to generate extended offensive zone time. He will also need to learn to engage and win his battles and become a better defensive zone player. His game right now is mostly about his skating ability and soft hands with some finishing touch thrown into the mix, but he will need to improve his all-around ability.

Quotable: "I love the speed and he competes hard." -NHL Scout (April 2016)

Quotable: "He has NHL speed but I see him as just a speedy energy guy. I'm not that high on him. I think he lacks some hockey sense." - HP Scout Mark Edwards

Luce, Griffin
LD – USNTDP 6'03", 217
HockeyProspect.com Ranking: 173

Luce is a towering physical defenseman. Luce's skillset is best fit for a shutdown defenseman and he does play that way. He is a physical presence on the ice as he has good strength and looks to finish his checks. Strong in the corners and in front of the net, Luce can crunch forwards with his physicality. His footwork isn't the best, but he does show some upside in getting around for a big guy. Although, still more improvement will be needed there. Luce's puck-moving instincts aren't bad and he is capable of executing basic plays. Although not the most natural skater with the puck on his stick, he will take a stride or two forward if given a chance instead of immediately getting rid of the puck. Luce clearly projects as a physical shutdown defenseman with size but will need further work on his skating and will have to make sure he executes faster. His decision-making can be a bit on the slower side.

Luff, Matt
RW - Hamilton Bulldogs (OHL) 6'02.5", 188
HockeyProspect.com Ranking: NR

Luff was prospect for the 2015 NHL Entry Draft. He was originally selected by the Belleville Bulls in the 7th round of the 2013 OHL Priority Selection Draft from the Oakville Rangers program.

Luff has excellent size and good puck protection ability. He has also done a good job using his shot and his net presence to triple his goal scoring numbers from last season. He has a great frame and is tough to control in the goal area. He does a decent job down low and wins his share of battles. What will really hold Luff back is that he doesn't have a great deal of skill with the puck. He has a good shot, but he isn't a very skilled player with the puck. His skating also needs a lot of improvements before he will be able to make the jump to the next level.

Lyszczarczyk, Alan
LW - Sudbury Wolves (OHL) 5'10.25" 184
HockeyProspect.com Ranking: 144

Alan is a speedy skilled forward for the Sudbury Wolves. Lyszczarczyk was picked up as a free agent by the Sudbury Wolves and made an immediate impact this season.

Alan has good speed and can carry the puck up ice. He likes to rush the puck and can beat defenders one on one, leading to scoring chances. He has good offensive tools, including an accurate shot and good passing ability. He has the vision to find his linemates and create chances for his team. He is well positioned in the offensive zone, which has lead to scoring chances, but will need to finish more frequently when he has the opportunity in order to maximize his offensive output.

Lyszczarczyk will need to improve on his play away from the puck and improve on his defensive play. He had a great first season of junior hockey in North America and was a solid junior pick up for the Sudbury Wolves. Projecting as a pro, he possesses the skill to warrant a selection at the 2016 NHL Entry Draft, but has some room to develop in other areas.

Magwood, Zachary
RC - Barrie Colts (OHL) 5'10", 184
HockeyProspect.com Ranking: NR

Magwood was selected in the sixth round of the 2014 OHL Priority Selection Draft by the Barrie Colts out of the Cambridge Hawks Minor Midget program. In his first junior season Zachary put up respectable numbers for a 16 year old with the Cambridge Jr. B Winterhawks. Magwood had a pretty good start to his first OHL season playing in a bottom six role but he often found himself scratched in the 2nd half as a result of added depth up front.
He has above average speed and is a quick, agile player and that allows him to play with good pace in his game. Magwood regularly showed the ability to navigate his way through the neutral zone and gain the opposing line with possession of the puck. Magwood is quick to get in on the forecheck and can be tough to break out against because of his positioning and good stick. He showed good awareness throughout the year sitting on stretch passes in the neutral zone and jumping up to intercept them and take play the other way. Magwood possesses good vision, which allows him to quickly find open teammates and keep the game flow high. He doesn't have a plus-shot and is a pass-first guy. While he is not a physically assertive player he did land some big hits throughout the season and won't avoid contact.

Magwood only played in about half the games this season and while he showed flashes of his offensive ability he doesn't currently possess the upside for a team to take a shot at him at the 2016 NHL Entry Draft. He is a bit undersized but has good tools in the skating, puck skills and compete departments that should at the very least make him a very effective junior player.

Maher, Jordan
RC/RW – Acadie-Bathurst Titans (QMJHL) – 5'11", 171
HockeyProspect.com Ranking: NR

Maher was the 6th overall pick in the 2014 QMJHL Draft. The Gander, Newfoundland native had a decent first year in the league in 2014-2015, but his development stalled this year. Maher, who can play both down the middle and on the wing, had trouble finding the back of the net this season, scoring only 15 times after scoring 13 as a rookie. Maher has a real good shot with a quick release, but has trouble with his positioning on the ice. Sometimes, he took himself out of good scoring opportunities due to his lack of hockey IQ and improper positioning. Multiple times during our viewings this season, we came away with the note "not noticeable today", as he was not involved enough in the action. He has good speed, can make some interesting plays off the rush, and give opposing defensemen nightmares with his speed. He has a good two-way game, can play on both special teams and always supports his defensemen well in his own zone.

Mahura, Josh
LD – Red Deer Rebels (WHL) 6'00", 170
HockeyProspect.com Ranking: 62

Josh is a very polarizing player as he suffered a season ending knee injury in the first game of the year vs the Calgary Hitmen. His injury has given us limit viewings of this player, that being said he has returned from injury and played 16 games in the playoffs, not missing a beat. Josh combines quick, agile skating with strong puck skills and good offensive and defensive awareness. He has a heavy wrist shot that is accurate and he gets off quickly. He defends the rush well and does a great job at maintaining a good gap with an active stick which helps him to hold the blueline and force errant passes or off-sides. He is a smooth, quick skater with good acceleration and great edge control that he uses to elude checkers. Overall Josh is a good defender that can move the puck and shows a high offensive upside. He could stand to put on more weight on his frame which will give him more balance and strength in one on one battles. Josh has a good ceiling, but has injury problem will play a roll on draft day.

Makeev, Nikita
RD – Team Russia U18 (MHL) – 5'09", 165
HockeyProspect.com Ranking: NR

A mobile, competitive undersized defenseman, Makeev is the type of player that is really hurt by the lack of size considering the type of game he plays. Makeev is a good skater and plays with a certain amount of authority on ice. His balance and mobility in all directions is more impressive than his pure speed or first few steps, which while not lacking are not too impressive for his size. He makes good passes when he has time and space but can be prone to blindly rimming the puck around the wall when pressured. He is also willing to take hits to move the puck. . Despite the smaller stature, he manages to complete what he set out to do even with bigger forecheckers strapped on his back.

Makeev doesn't force plays offensively and usually makes intelligent choices, however the lack of high-end offensive upside at his size is a real concern. Makeev can run the PP and displays good offensive qualities on the point, especially with his ability to walk the blueline and distribute the puck from one end to the other. But he is quite conservative and picky about creating offense at even strength. Defensively, he competes very well and is more than willing to engage physically. However, here too, his lack of size is a severely limiting factor. He has a low center of gravity and a wide base which allows him to battle bigger players his age, but it is hard to imagine him being physically in the same league against pro-players, no matter how hard he tries to outplay his lack of size.

While a likable player, Makeev plays the type of game that makes it really hard to succeed if the defenseman doesn't possess at least average size. Unless his offensive game develops further or his skating improves to better than just passable, it will be really hard for him to project to an NHL role.

Quotable: "He's one of those really likable defensive prospects who takes an absolute beating on his projection due to lack of size. He was good in most of my viewings, but it's just very hard seeing him play his game when he lacks the size to be effective at it against men." - HP Scout Nik Funa

Mäkinen, Otto
LC – Tappara (Fin U20) – 6'01", 178
HockeyProspect.com Ranking: 140

Mäkinen played his third season at the U20 level. He had a promising year in 2014-15 but this season was a bit of a disappointment. He's a mature and reliable center but his quickness and agility are probably the main reasons why he hasn't been that productive. He has however looked better in most of his international games than in the U20 domestic league this season.

Otto is strong on the penalty kill and on faceoffs. A technically sound and smart center overall, has a deceptive shot he should use more as he often prefers to distribute the puck even when he could try to score himself. Can be limited in his effectiveness in games played at the highest pace. Has a nice side-step when carrying the puck but overall his skating will need to improve further to become an effective player at the next level. That might come naturally if moving forward he manages to add more power and energy, right now Makinen can look somewhat lethargic at times and slow to react. He will always provide a honest effort in all three zones and reliable play along the boards but will have to learn to play regularly at a higher pace and intensity level to become more of a consistent threat offensively and to dictate the play more often rather than getting caught observing it or chasing.

Quotable: "In my viewings he became much less effective when the pace and intensity picked up. Some of it can be attributed to skating, but I wonder whether he's just not somewhat a passive player overall." - HP Scout Nik Funa

Quotable: "I have a hard time ranking this guy" - HP Scout Mik Portoni

Maksimovich, Kyle
LW - Erie Otters (OHL) 5'08.5", 172
HockeyProspect.com Ranking: 155

Maksimovich was selected in the 5th round of the 2014 OHL Priority Selection Draft by the Erie Otters out of the Toronto Marlboros Minor Midget program. Maksimovich played a minimal role for the Otters last season, but still found a way to put up respectable numbers as a 16 year old. He really took off this season putting up great numbers for a second year player.

Maksimovich is an undersized forward with excellent speed. He is extremely shifty and very difficult to contain. He is small with a tiny frame so he need to stay at top speed, as he can get physically overpowered and dominated at times when he slows down or goes into corner battles. He has good puck skills and handles the puck through traffic well. Kyle is capable of both creating offense and has above average vision and good passing ability. He also has some underrated goal scoring ability and will take the puck to the net fearlessly when he has a seam. He is great when carrying the puck up ice, but he can get pressured into mistakes in his own zone if he doesn't have a lane to use his speed.

Maksimovich is a boom or bust prospect. His skill level warrants top six upside if he can reach his potential and overcome his size. However, for someone his size he will have a real uphill battle to fight to make the NHL. He has the potential to grow, as his brother Quentin is 6'03", but he was already 6'01" at 15. If nothing else, his skillset and progression is very intriguing.

Quotable: "There are shifts when he looks like the most productive forward on his team." - NHL Scout (December 2015)

Quotable: "What do you know about the Maksimovich kid? He's been better than Debrincat my last two viewings." NHL Scout (November 2015)

Malenstyn, Beck
LW – Calgary Hitmen (WHL) 6'02", 191
HockeyProspect.com Ranking: 136

Beck is an impactful player that brings a lot on both sides of the puck. He is a player that shows a tenacious work ethic and compete in all three zones. He is strong and loves to pressure the puck carrier and while doing so he wins a lot of one on one battles for the puck. The very noticeable thing about Malenstyn is he works extremely hard to always be first to the puck. He is a strong and powerful skater who has great balance and uses this to be very effective in one on one and board battles.

He did not put up high offensive numbers and needs to work on having more poise with the puck and making better decisions. He does have a quick and deceptive release along with a heavy shot and needs to find ways to get more pucks on net. With the compete and work ethic that he brings to his game and the willingness to do whatever it takes to win, he will be a valuable asset to any team that looks at drafting him. He will need to develop more of an offensive skill set if he looks to continue to be an impact player at the next level.

Maltsev, Artem
RD – Chicoutimi Saguenéens (QMJHL) – 6'02", 181
HockeyProspect.com Ranking: NR

Maltsev came over this season from Russia after being drafted in the CHL Import Draft by the Saguenéens (70th overall) last June. In his first season in North America, the Russian defenseman didn't take long to adjust to the physical game, throwing his weight around numerous times. He has shown good timing in his hits and has delivered some good hipchecks during the season. He even dropped his gloves a couple of times this season; he has some sandpaper to his game. Maltsev has decent mobility but an awkward skating stance and will need to work on his skating technique. He did, however, make progress with his backwards skating this season. In the 2nd half, he started to show flashes offensively, making more plays with the puck and showing more confidence with the puck on his stick. He has a good, hard slapshot from the point and was not shy to use it on the power play. He got to play on the 2nd power play unit in the 2nd half of the season. When on the power play, he was not shy to throw pucks on net was decent at puck distribution. He's an interesting defenseman in this draft that could get picked late in the draft. He showed a good level of improvement throughout the year while playing on a young Chicoutimi team. There's some similarities between him and another Russian defenseman in the QMJHL, Sergei Boikov (Colorado draft pick), as both like to play a physical game. However, we see a lot more puck skills and offensive potential in Maltsev at the same age.

Maltsev, Mikhail
LC – Team Russia U18 (MHL) – 6'03", 198
HockeyProspect.com Ranking: 131

Maltsev is a pro-sized center, once he gets his large frame moving and working for pucks he can be difficult to handle. He had a productive season for Team Russia U18, where he usually lined up as the second line center behind German Rubtsov, but can also play left wing.

Maltsev has good top speed and his first few steps are better than average for his size despite an unorthodox stride. He may not have enough skills and vision to dictate the offense on his own, but adding his physical tools to the mix makes for an intriguing package. Mikhail is still a raw prospect and he gets mixed results when he tries to be a difference maker on offense, he has very good hands but he is prone to making some odd decisions with the puck. As of now he is more effective when he keeps his game simple instead of trying to be a playmaker. He has the ability to keep the puck in a shooting position while he carries it towards the slot and has a good reach too. Another strength of his appears to be in the faceoff circle, as he has been terrific there at the MHL level. However, there are shifts where his game starts losing purpose and he looks like a big man going through motions without contributing much offensively or defensively. It's not a common occurrence but it's something that will have to be eliminated.

With his size and speed he can be a useful forechecker, but needs to develop better consistency as a physical presence. He can be physical along the boards, but he could stand to become more engaging in defensive zone where his size and skating could be a bigger asset than they are at this point in time. This will have to improve especially since he is unlikely to make it on skills or offensive game alone. If Maltsev focuses on his strengths and makes sure he impacts every shift with his physical tools then he could have a bright future going forward.

Marmenlind, Daniel
G – Orebro HK J20 (SWE) – 6'01", 191
HockeyProspect.com Ranking: 153

A late 1997 birth, Marmenlind is a technically sound goaltender with strong footwork and a terrific butterfly. He moves with great ease around the crease and like most high-end Swedish goaltenders, his butterfly and post-play technique is at a veteran status despite his age. Laterally, he pushes with ease and proper direction nearly every time. He seals up the ice terrifically making it very hard to beat him down low. Showed great patience on breakaways in viewings, knows when to break to post, squaring his shoulders as he pivots and brings his drag leg in - sealing up the ice.

Marmenlind has a lot of strengths in his game but there are some weaknesses. In viewings, goals tend to be scored low blocker and high glove. His hands are an area that he really needs to work on. On chances that come from low to high, he tends to drift out too far to challenge the shooter and loses his angle in the process.

Despite all his terrific technique, Marmenlind lacks some creativity in the crease and needs to adapt better to scramble situations. Sometimes, there is no proper technique besides throwing any body part in front of the puck on broken plays. Marmenlind is showing tendencies of being a 'hot' goaltender. Meaning, he thrives in games where his club is outshot, but struggles with mental focus in games that he sees significant lulls in action.

He spent the majority of the season on Orebro's J20 team, but also made appearances at the HockeyEttan level (Swedish third tier) with Arlanda and Arboga. Marmenlind made his SHL debut this season on February 23 against Lulea. He replaced Henrik Lundberg in the second period and made six saves on eight shots.

Mascherin, Adam
LW - Kitchener Rangers (OHL) 5'09.5", 206
HockeyProspect.com Ranking: 44

Mascherin was selected first round, second overall at the 2014 OHL Priority Selection Draft by the Kitchener Rangers out of the Vaughan Kings Minor Midget program. Adam jumped into the OHL as a 16 year old playing third line plus power play in his rookie season putting up respectable numbers. This season he nearly tripled his goal totals and saw a 279% increase in points playing top power play minutes and a top six role with the Rangers. Surprisingly only 9 of Mascherin's 35 goals came on the power play scoring the rest in 5 on 5 situations.

Adam lacks height but is skilled winger who has an excellent shot. In fact, Mascherin has one of the hardest shots in junior hockey and utilizes it with good positioning. His accuracy will need a little improvement as he's fired the puck over the net point blank, but receives a remarkable amount of scoring chances per game, because he knows where to go in the offensive zone to get open. As the season progressed, Mascherin started to show off some playmaking ability, proving that he can not only score goals, but also create offense for his linemates. Although he is an undersized forward height wise, Adam has a great wide, strong frame, which allows him to protect the puck against bigger opponents. His speed is probably just above average overall and not where you'd like it to be for a forward his size. This could negatively affect him on draft day. He will need to get his skating and speed up to where it needs to be at the next level before being able to make that jump successfully. Defensively he will need to improve on his positioning and consistency in which he engages in the play.

Mascherin has some tools to become a scoring forward at the NHL level. The shot, the positional awareness and the creativity all add up to a winger who is dangerous every time he touches the puck. He will need to improve on his skating though.

Quotable: "If his skating is better, Mascherin is a first round talent. He's going to score 50+ in juniors and if he gets his accuracy down, he could put up some big numbers in the NHL as well. He's a better passer than he gets credit for." - HP Scout Ryan Yessie

Quotable: "His weight scares me." - NHL Scout (October 2015)

Quotable: "Who do you do, take the safe route with Katchouk or the possible homerun with a guy like Mascherin?" - NHL Scout (March 2016)

Quotable: "This kid is climbing up my rankings. At the end of the day, he has proven that he can score." - NHL Scout (January 2016)

Mattinen, Nicolas
RD - London Knights (OHL) 6'04.5", 220
HockeyProspect.com Ranking: 66

Mattinen was selected in the 6th round of the 2014 OHL Priority Selection Draft by the London Knights out of the Eastern Ontario Wild Minor Midget Program. Mattinen spent his 16 year old season with the Cumberland Grads of the CCHL. This first season saw him caught behind a mix of skilled and veteran blueliners which saw him as a healthy scratch in about half of the games this season. He would fill in at forward on occasion.

Mattinen is a big bodied defender with an excellent frame and NHL ready size. He is a physical defender who loves to take the body and crush the opposition. He does a good job of keeping himself a powerful physical opponent while keeping it pretty clean as well. He uses his body and stick well to defend, but he can be a little clumsy at times as his coordination is catching up to his body still. He is a little hit or miss with the puck but is at his best when making simple decisions. Unlike a lot of big physical shutdown defenders, Mattinen has an offensive weapon which can help him contribute at the other end of the ice; a NHL level slap shot. Mattinen is a threat to either score or create a rebound whenever he touches the puck on the offensive blueline. He has a low, powerful blast which has hit the back of the net, but can also be very difficult for goaltenders to control let alone contain and has resulted in second chances in the slot.

Mattinen projects as a simple, physical shutdown defender who needs to keep it simple when looking to pass the puck. He will be able to chip in offensively from the point because that shot will be a weapon at whatever level he plays at. He has intriguing upside and may emerge from this draft as a sleeper as he has great NHL upside, but spent a lot of time in the stands this season, which will change next year.

Quotable: "I know the kid is getting scratched a lot, but he's on a very deep blueline. He's shown me enough this season to tell me he's a very good prospect." - HP Scout Ryan Yessie

Quotable: "It's pretty hard for me to put him on my list when He's scratched all the time." - NHL Scout (March 2016)

Quotable: "I like Mattinen. I don't know if I can sell him to the boss though." - NHL Scout (February 2016)

Quotable: "Considering how many times he's been scratched, I'd say Mattinen is my biggest sleeper this year. That said, I'd wager big money that he gets drafted. This kid has a bomb of a shot and looked great in December when the Knights lost players to World Juniors. Those viewings in December were very productive for me, I really like his upside. It will be interesting, I know several scouts who have barely seen him. I can't wait to see if he gets drafted, who gets him and which round they get him in." - HP Scout Mark Edwards

Matthews, Auston
LC – ZSC Lions (NLA) – 6'02.5", 210
HockeyProspect.com Ranking: 1

Auston made the decision to take an unusual path and play his draft season in Switzerland. The move to Zurich was a success even if the end was disappointing, as the #1 seed ZSC was swept in the 1st round by eventual NLA champions SC Bern. Throughout the season Matthews proved to be ready to compete against men on a regular basis and posted the best goal per game ratio in the league, while developing his two-way game under Marc Crawford's guidance. He was not able to convert his chances in his four playoff games, but his finishing ability is not in question. His play at the World Championships in May only confirmed he is ready to be an impact player in the NHL as soon as he steps in next fall.

Matthews is a smooth and powerful skater, without the puck in the offensive zone he keeps his feet moving, making himself a moving target that the defense struggles to keep track of. Especially if paired with players who can play and think an up-tempo game, defenders struggle to catch him, as he quickly combines with linemates and jumps on opportunities. In those circumstances he seems consistently one step ahead of the play, makes snap decisions time after time and he has no problems executing quickly. He can change gears and directions while he reads the play, shares the puck and makes himself available in high-scoring areas.

Matthews has tremendous puck skills but doesn't need to have the puck on his stick a lot to be effective and dangerous offensively, which bodes well for his transition to the NHL. He is the complete package offensively, has the skills to beat defenseman one on one, the vision to set up linemates and a dangerous shot that takes very little time (or space for that matter) to get off. He has good size, doesn't play a big physical game but he uses his size along the boards and is very effective on the cycle. A favourite move of his is bouncing the puck against the boards (or even the base of the net) to turn and escape the defender while keeping possession. He likes to be around the net and is a big threat down low.

He can still remain effective when slowing down the game, relying on his playmaking ability. He's committed to playing a sound defensive game and is a very complete and versatile player. He is a high-end talent who already plays a mature game as a 18 year old, it's difficult to find flaws in his skillset.

In most of our viewings he has not been able to play with maximum intensity throughout the whole game and usually showed less jump through the second leg of back to back games, but that's nitpicking considering it's not always been the case. It's not a big stretch to say an 18 year old will improve his endurance.

Surefire star two-way centers rarely come around and it's going to be really difficult for the Leafs to pass on him. You seldom find prospects that project to the next level as safely as this kid does.

Quotable: " I would've taken him ahead of Eichel if he was eligible in last seasons draft." - NHL Scout (November 2015)

Quotable: " He's number one. It's not close." - NHL Scout (March 2016)

Quotable: " He's my number one guy. Laine did tighten the gap between them quite a bit but I still go with Matthews." - NHL Scout (May 2016)

Quotable: " Aside from going deep in the playoffs, he has met pretty much every expectation I had for him going into the NLA season." - HP Scout Mik Portoni

Mattson, Mitchell
LC – Grand Rapids H.S. (MN-HS) 6'04", 186
HockeyProspect.com Ranking: 147

Mattson was another Minnesota Prep player who started to season in the USHL (Bloomington) but returned to his High School team before finishing the season back with Bloomington. Mattson is a player that we expected to dominate at the Minnesota High School level and while was really good at times; he didn't have the type of season we were expecting given his size advantage and skill set he possesses. There were nights where he left you expecting more. Another red flag for us is Mattson struggled to contribute offensively at the USHL level (2 goals in 21 games). He didn't bring a lot of physicality and got moved off the puck too easily for a kid with his frame and lacked the nose for the net mentality you like to see in a big power centers.

Once Mattson fills out his frame, learns to use his size more effectively and on a more consistent basis, he projects as a solid 2-way player down the middle of the ice. Mitchell can win face-offs and control puck possession down low. Mitchell has excellent hands both along the wall and in the open ice, good playmaking ability and is a threat to score with his shot if given time in the offensive zone. While his skating isn't considered at an elite level he gets around the ice well, has decent edges and a powerful stride. Mattson showed great anticipation and hockey sense in our viewings, which translates into a solid 200 foot game but struggles to put the whole package together some nights. Mattson will spend next season in the USHL before heading to North Dakota in 17/18.

Quotable: " He is one of the most overrated players in this year's draft in my opinion." NHL Scout (April 2016)

Quotable: "I love his size and his skill, just too many nights he doesn't show he wants it enough." USHL Scout (May 2016)

Quotable: "His struggle to make any impact in the USHL is a big red flag for me, too many games he went largely unnoticed. All the skill and size is there to be an effective 2-way center down the road, but he will be a long term project for the team that drafts him." HP Scout Dusten Braaksma

Quotable: "He's 6'4", he can skate and he's smart, but I don't think he will make it. He lacks a heartbeat far too often. Just no compete. That could change but it seldom seems to in my experience both coaching and scouting. Just not competitive enough for me." - HP Scout Mark Edwards

MacNab, Jack
RW – Culver Academy (IN-HS) 6'05", 203
HockeyProspect.com Ranking: NR

MacNab is a big, strong power winger with a shoot first mentality and an elite shot. It can take Jack a while to get to top speed but once he gets going north he can be a nightmare for defenseman to handle one on one. He needs to continue to improve his foot speed and first couple strides. MacNab likes to lower his shoulder, use his reach and drive to the net or below the goal line where he is very good at making plays from and finding the open man. His size and understanding of his skill set as a player make him an intriguing prospect for this Draft but he will have to sort out his skating before he can reach his full potential. We would not be shocked to see a team use a pick on the hulking winger as a long term project.

McAvoy, Charles
RD - Boston University (Hockey East) 6'00.25" 208
HockeyProspect.com Ranking: 13

He is a good skating D-man that covers the ice well defensively and makes intelligent plays all-around the ice. On a lot of nights, he will not jump off the roster at you, though he consistently makes good puck decisions with outlets and shows a strong, steady presence on the blue line. He has good agility, handles the puck well, and can fire the puck from the point. There are a lot of good qualities with McAvoy. He makes good outlets and puck decisions. Defensively he will close gaps and be physical effectively. He excelled in his freshman season at Boston University and also a member of USA bronze medal WJC team in January. He will use his mobility and reads on the plays to jump up on the rush and add offensively. Many scouts have the junior level defenseman from the CHL and BCHL ahead of McAvoy, yet in the end, the Long Island native might be the one of the best. He projects to have a long career.

Quotable: "He's been outstanding in my last few viewings of him. Up with the best Dmen and a top fifteen prospect for me." - NHL Scout (March 2016)

Quotable: "He's not tall at just 6'0" but he's a big thick strong kid. He's a great skater and a solid two-way guy. His gaps are good and I like the way he competes. I'm not sure his power play skills translate to him being a stud in that department at the NHL level. i don't see a high end PP guy in him. He's not in a class of a guy like Werenski, who is much bigger and is dynamic at the offensive blueline. That said, I *really like McAvoy's game off the rush. In the viewings where he struggled a bit it was usually just a case of him trying to do to much and playing too much of a high risk game. I like this kid a lot though." - HP Scout Mark Edwards*

McDonald, Kody
RW – Prince George Cougars (WHL) 6'01", 200
HockeyProspect.com Ranking: NR

Kody McDonald is an interesting depth player who made a bit of a name for himself with the Prince George Cougars this season. McDonald is one of those coveted and unique players who is easily capable of scoring, making a big hit, and winning a fight all in the same game. The only problem is that he can't do it consistently.

A fairly good skater who isn't terribly agile, McDonald is a strong forechecker who's a hound on the puck when it goes below the goal line. He's a good hitter and establishes strong body positioning when fighting for pucks along the boards. Passes tend to be rather simple. When left in open-space, meanwhile, McDonald can make you pay with an excellent one-timer shot from beyond the hash-marks.

His offensive is still a work in progress. And his defensive game can wane at times too. Yet there's still some potential here. Increased ice-time will be good for his development next year, as there will be some key graduations that open opportunities for promotion within the lineup. If McDonald can put it all together on a more nightly basis, he could be considered a legit NHL prospect.

McEwan, James
LC - Guelph Storm (OHL) 5'11.5", 190
HockeyProspect.com Ranking: NR

McEwan is a 2nd time eligible prospect for the 2016 NHL Entry Draft after leading the last place Storm in both goals and points this season. He was selected 172nd overall at the 2013 OHL Priority Selection Draft. He played a few games as a 16 year old despite going in the 9th round of the draft.

James is a hard working two-way forward who likes to shoot and has showed some hands with the puck. McEwan has always been known for his defensive ability first and he was arguably the best penalty killer for the Storm this season. He has quick reaction time and gets into opponents lanes very well. He can pressure the point and force turnovers and turn them into scoring chances. Proof of this is in the stats where James has more short-handed goals than power play goals. He has good work ethic and competes down low. When in the offensive zone he has good positioning and a dangerous shot. He can beat defenders one on one and has some good moves when going to the net. He also shows good work ethic in all three zones.

James has a little trouble with the pace of the game when it picks up. He is also an average skater, which needs to improve. James absolutely has an outside shot at being selected at the 2016 NHL Entry Draft, but if he is passed over he's a pretty good bet secure a free agent invite from an NHL team.

McGing, Hugh
LC/W - Cedar Rapids Rough Riders (USHL) 5'08", 185
HockeyProspect.com Ranking: NR

We were big fans of Hugh McGing in last year's Black Book 2016 Section, where we spoke to McGing's overall game and work ethic and he did nothing this season to disappoint us. As expected, McGing saw a big jump in his offensive output this season going from 19 Points in 54 games last season to 51 points in 60 games in 15/16.

McGing is a lead by example player who was relied upon in every situation for a very deep Cedar Rapids team. He is an excellent skater which allows him to jump into holes you don't even notice are there, he is slippery with the puck and it seems to be on a string at times. Hugh played with a lot of jump in our viewings, keeps good pace through the neutral zone and executes smart dump in's away from the defense where he or his teammates have a shot at getting possession. He just simply makes smart plays all over the ice. His shot isn't the hardest, he isn't the most physical player but he worked hard on every shift and made the players on the ice with him better.

The only things that may hold McGing back in this draft is his lack of size for the position he plays down the middle of the ice. If a team feels he can be as effective playing the Wing, a team could jump up and use a pick on him. We are of the belief that no matter what position you play McGing at he can have a positive impact on your team, both on and off the ice.

Quotable: "We had McGing on our 2016 watch list in last year's Black Book and he has done nothing this year to change my opinion of him. He fly's under the radar, mostly due to his lack of size and the emergence of teammate Matt Filipe, but he is a smart player that gets the job done in any situation you put him in. He makes a lot of small plays that go unnoticed but help his team win games." HP Scout Dusten Braaksma

McInnis, Luke
LD – Youngstown Phantoms (USHL) 5'9.5", 167
HockeyProspect.com Ranking: 162

McInnis had a good start to his draft year when he was the MVP of the American Prospects game this past fall. Luke is an undersized defenseman by today's standards; however that is about the only real knock we can find with his game. While McInnis's offensive numbers don't jump off the page at you (6 goals, 22 assists in 58 games) McInnis is a smart defenseman who moves the puck very well in all 3 zones and makes a lot of little plays that won't necessarily show up on the score sheet. Luke is able to skate the puck up quickly and with ease, makes smart plays with the puck in the neutral zone. You won't see McInnis committing a lot of turnovers at either blue line, has his head up at all times and is reliable with the puck on his stick. He can QB a power play effectively and move the puck around the zone well. Possesses a good shot and does a good job getting pucks through traffic and into the scoring areas and has solid one timing ability.

McInnis has done a good job this season improving his play in his own end, while he will never be the most physical defender, he does battle hard in the corners and in front of his own net and uses smarts and stick work to win puck battles. McInnis's excellent skating ability allows him to be aggressive in challenging plays at his own blue line and not giving opposing forwards a lot of room entering the zone. Luke will be off to Boston College where his Dad Marty played.

Quotable: "Has some good offense in his game, he's really competitive as well. He was great in prep last year." - NHL Scout (April 2016)

McKenzie, Brett
LC - North Bay Battalion (OHL) 6'02", 188
HockeyProspect.com Ranking: NR

McKenzie is a prospect from the North Bay Battalion. He was drafted 10th overall at the 2013 OHL Priority Selection Draft out of the Oakville Rangers Minor Midget program and is re-eligible this season. McKenzie had a solid rookie season for a first year player, but if anything looked like he took a step back last year. In his third season in the league he showed the two-way upside he possessed in Minor Midget.

McKenzie is a big-bodied centre who plays hard at both ends of the ice. He more than doubled his goal total from last season and stepped up his offensive game in a big way. He has a powerful shot and good positioning in the offensive zone, which has contributed to his improved numbers. He is a physical player along the wall and while he could stand to add more muscle, he does a good job winning his share of battles. Defensively he competes, works hard to get into passing lanes and blocks shots on a consistent basis. This has allowed him to play in all game situations. He also score five short handed goals, as he was a threat while killing penalties. He has a little trouble with consistency and while this has improved, he still needs to work on it. His skating is a little awkward and he would benefit from cleaning it up. McKenzie may be more suited as a free agent invite, but with the big increase in points along with his ability to play a variety of roles, McKenzie could bring some interest at the 2016 NHL Entry Draft.

McKinstry, Ryely
LD – Vancouver Giants (WHL) 6'01", 199
HockeyProspect.com Ranking: NR

McKinstry is a big smooth kid playing the left side of the blueline. Part of the Canadian U17 team last year, McKinstry also logged 30 games with 4 points on last season's Giants team. This year, McKinstry only appeared in 11 games with a goal and an assist to his name. McKinstry already has quite a filled out frame as he moves his 200 pound frame around the ice with a fluid stride. McKinstry won't burn anyone anytime soon, but his skating ability shows decent upside, especially at his size. He's got a long stick that he gets good reach out of and uses it well when defending. Provides a big body with a long stick on defensive blueline that makes it challenging to get around him. Has solid positioning but could use a bit more snarl around the net and in the corners.

McKinstry can start the transition and actually has looked reasonably good when joining the play as a late man. He also shows upside in skating the puck forward. Although a small sample size, in some of our viewings this year he made some questionable decisions with his first pass not connecting. With only 11 games in the book, it has been a challenging year to gauge McKinstry's progress, but he still offers some upside as a pro-sized defenseman who possesses mobility and reach. While his numbers aren't impressive, McKinstry does show small hints of upside on the offensive side of the puck and is already decent at starting transition.

McLeod, Michael
RC - Mississuaga Steelheads (OHL) 6'02.25", 188
HockeyProspect.com Ranking: 19

McLeod was selected in the 1st round, fifth overall of the 2014 OHL Priority Selection Draft by the Mississauga Steelheads out of the Toronto Marlboros Minor Midget Program. McLeod showed off his offensive ability right away entering the OHL with a strong rookie season. He followed that up with a successful second year where he more than doubled his points.

McLeod features high-end skating ability, which allows him to fly up and down the ice. At his size his speed can surprise some opponents who are unprepared for it and he utilizes it very well to create offense. Offensively McLeod has shown us some playmaking abilities. He is a player who can create offensively for both himself and his teammates. McLeod has shown good touch on his passes and can get them through a sea of bodies finding teammates in tight quarters. He also possesses a good shot, but it has not helped him translate into posting lofty goal totals thus far. This is one area that separates him from being ranked up with the big boys for us. We simply don't view McLeod as being a pure goal scorer. Too many good to great chances were not converted into goals. While we don't see him as a dumb player, we do think his decision making lacks at times.

McLeod has begun to improve the physical aspect of his game. Always aggressive on the forecheck, McLeod now engages physically on a consistent basis. This combined with his speed has allowed him to create turnovers as defensemen are unable to deal with the combination of speed an physicality that is coming at them. Defensively McLeod continues to improve his attention to detail, although he has puck watched at times and can completely lose his check. McLeod does everything at a high pace, to a fault in fact. He needs to watch his own linemate (Nylander) to see how to create gaps in the offensive zone by changing his pace. Too often, Mike is his own worst enemy.

We see McLeod as a player who doesn't get as much production out of his talent as we think he should. His skating is high end, he works hard, he has great size but just too many missed scoring chances and poor puck decisions for us to rank him higher.

Quotable: "I have him twelfth overall." - NHL Scout (January 2016)

Quotable: "I have him in the twenties." NHL Scout (March 2016)

Quotable: "I don't see him as top ten, not close for me." NHL Scout (February 2016)

Quotable: "I've seen McLeod a lot going back to his OHL Draft year. His skating is fantastic and he doesn't take shifts off. I think he's at his best along the walls. He is a tireless worker who wins puck battles. He's always seemed to struggle off the rush though. Too often he skates himself out of options. More than once I've seen Dmen back off because they couldn't handle his speed, but he would close the gap on himself by skating with speed into them. He needs to vary his attack. He needs to understand creating time and space for himself. He gains the offensive zone with ease, but it's after he enters where he shows some weaknesses. I think it's a case where too often his brain can't catch up with his feet. Early this year I thought I saw signs of him making some progress but it didn't happen. If this was my first year watching him, I'd probably have a more positive outlook on him making some progression, but I've seen the same thing for three years now. I think he will play in the NHL but I don't see the huge upside that some seem to see. - HP Scout Mark Edwards

Quotable: "Our worst interview. I don't know how a kid with that much energy on the ice can have so little energy off the ice. - NHL Scout (combine week)

Quotable: "Overall the feedback scouts gave me on combine interviews this year might be the best ever. That said, I had a few teams tell me McLeod's interview was either their weakest or of one of them." - Mark Edwards (Combine week)

McPhee, Graham
LW – USNTDP 5'11", 176
HockeyProspect.com Ranking: 165

McPhee is a forward prospect who might have more upside than his numbers would suggest. The first impression of McPhee is that of a hard-working player who plays a smart game without a lot of flash. McPhee is an engaging three zone player and shows good work-ethic with and without the puck. Although he isn't the biggest or the fastest player at this moment, he makes sure he's always moving his feet and tries to play bigger than his size. In fact, McPhee is actually quite mature in his approach as he already excels at the less-heralded aspects of the game. McPhee works hard to get first on loose pucks, goes to the dirty areas and will work hard to beat defensemen to the slot looking for garbage around the net. While he keeps his feet moving, his stride is a bit choppy and he doesn't generate a lot of speed. Although he hasn't been a big offensive producer, McPhee ranks as better than average in his vision with the puck. His hands are better than his statline would imply as well. He makes smart plays with the puck and can extend possession for his team. McPhee's skating will need to improve but there is some upside there that might come to the forefront with a bigger role than the one he played for USNTDP this season.

Mendonca, Mitchell
LC - Hamilton Bulldogs (OHL) 5'11", 160
HockeyProspect.com Ranking: NR

Mendonca was selected in the 5th round of the 2014 OHL Priority Selection Draft by the Belleville Bulls out of the Southern Tier Admirals program. Mendonca did performed well for the Thorold Blackhawks between performances with the Belleville Bulls before making the full time jump to play with the Hamilton Bulldogs this season.

Mendonca spent the large majority of his time on the fourth line and didn't get a lot of action in special teams situations. This really kept Mendonca as a real under the radar talent. He has very good skating ability and used it in both directions. He provided a tenacious forecheck pressure using speed and good stick work to force turnovers. He was also excellent on the backcheck. He did a great job in transition when forcing a turnover to quickly push the play up ice. He is relentless with and without the puck. He showed several flashes of his skill creating offense on the fourth line for his linemates and created some chances himself as well. His explosive speed and good puck skills helped him along when in the offensive zone.

Mendonca was a very good offensive talent in Minor Midget and has adapted and utilized his skill set to become a good two-way player at the OHL level. He is the type of player who could surprise and have a real breakout season exposing himself as a re-entry player. However there is likely not enough exposure for Mendonca to this point for him to be selected at the 2016 NHL Entry Draft.

Mescheryakov, Mikhail
LC – Team Russia U18 (MHL) – 5'11", 152
HockeyProspect.com Ranking: NR

Mescheryakov is a left-shooting center with good straight line speed to his game. Mescheryakov has the tools to play a skilled center game but will need to improve his defensive game as well as find ways to utilize his skill in a more meaningful way. He also has a lanky frame that clearly lacks strength as of now.

Mescheryakov has the ability to handle the puck at speed, but he has the tendency to get too far ahead of the play, especially considering he is a center. He could support his defenseman better on the break-out, but that is not unusual for young centers. Where it becomes more problematic with

Mescheryakov is that he doesn't use the width of the ice as well as he could. This makes it hard for him to open up for plays and support the puck-movement up the ice as he rarely comes up in play under an angle that would allow him to receive the puck in a good spot. While he can look impressive handling the puck with speed and quickly gaining space forward, he also has a tendency to skate himself out of options instead of letting his teammates catch up.

Mescheryakov's skills and agility with the puck allow him to buy himself some time in the offensive zone as he does have the ability to control the defenseman's feet and make him react to his moves. He is particularly good at stickhandling off the right side to open up his forehand shot. However he will have to do a better job turning the space he gains into actual benefits for his team when that doesn't put him into a dangerous shooting position. A common occurrence is him making a good move but then not knowing what to do with the puck. This can be seen both with his ability to move up ice at speed and then not knowing how to delay the play or make a pass into the space he created. Or in the offensive zone where he will gain some separation between him and the defenseman but not have the awareness on when or how to take advantage of it.

This has been a rather disappointing year for Mescheryakov, who was a big part of an extremely successful U17 Russian national team last season. For whatever reason he didn't improve as expected, he will need to grow a lot physically and his game to mature in order to exploit his talent in the future.

Mete, Victor
LD - London Knights (OHL) 5'09.5", 174
HockeyProspect.com Ranking: 108

Mete was selected in the first round, eighth overall at the 2014 OHL Priority Selection Draft by the Owen Sound Attack. After a bit of a holdout, Mete was dealt to the London Knights. Mete got a lot of opportunities as a 16 year old for the Knights and put together impressive numbers. Mete improved on those numbers playing a bigger role for the Knights run.

Mete possesses elite level skating ability, which is the lifeblood of his talent. His ability to move laterally is probably faster than some players can skate forward. This creates unique opportunities for Mete, in partially open ice to exploit lanes and take the puck into the offensive zone. He will carry the puck deep into the offensive zone where he can be a little inconsistent with his decision making. On the point he does a better job moving the puck and always keeps his feet moving. Fortunately for Mete, even on turnovers he has the speed to hurry back in the defensive zone, even when he's way behind the play. This special ability helps keep him in good positioning. Unfortunately for Mete, he is undersized for the defensive position and lacks strength. Bigger puck protecting forwards have been able to exploit him and drive to the net. While good with his stick, he also struggles down low and gets dominated in battles.

Mete has some puck moving skills and he is an outstanding skater. However his size, strength and defensive deficiencies weaken his draft stock. He also lacks a big shot, although he does a decent job of getting pucks to the net.

Quotable: "Mete is a great junior player and should be a productive offensive defenseman at the junior level, but his lack of size and defensive struggles worry me too much for his NHL projection." - Ryan Yessie

Quotable: " I love him in the OHL but I think he needs to be much better offensively to consider him early in the draft at his size. He uses his stick effectively and contains well along the walls defensively, but really struggles to take pucks away from forwards. Very little as far as chatter with NHL scouts about him this season." - Mark Edwards

Middleton, Keaton
LD - Saginaw Spirit (OHL) 6'05.5", 233
HockeyProspect.com Ranking: 83

Keaton was selected in the third round of the 2014 OHL Priority Selection Draft by the Saginaw Spirit out of the Huron-Perth Lakers Minor Midget program. Middleton had trial by fire in the OHL almost instantaneously playing a big minute role for the Spirit. He went through a lot of growing pains, but has come out of it with good development for a big defender.

Middleton has huge size and a massive frame, which can make him tough to get around. He has a pretty good stick and loves the physical stuff in his own zone. His balance and skating need improvement, but they have come miles since his Minor Midget season. Keaton's puck play has also come along over the past couple years, he is often able to make the smart simple pass up ice. He still makes a fair amount of puck mistakes and can get stripped, but he has shown consistent improvement in this area. He is a relentless competitor along the wall and wins a ton of battles through his size, strength and a relative comfort in these types of situations. Middleton played top minutes 5 on 5 and on the penalty kill, and secondary minutes on the power play. He's relentless in the slot area, making life difficult for forwards and has the reach to take away passes shorthanded. He's not an over the top fighter, but he has good toughness and isn't afraid to drop the gloves when necessary.

Middleton still has plenty of room for improvement, but has been showing clear progression, which is very promising. He projects as a shutdown defender at the NHL level. He looks comfortable playing the big man's game that he will need to in order to be successful. Middleton may go off the board a little earlier than we would've expected this time last year.

Quotable: "It's kinda weird but I can only remember one scout even saying his name to me this year and it was after McLeod burned him with speed." - Mark Edwards

Mieritz, Christian
LD - Guelph Storm (OHL) 6'01", 204
HockeyProspect.com Ranking: NR

Mieritz is an import selection by the Hamilton Bulldogs, who was claimed off waivers by the Guelph Storm midway through the season. Before playing in the OHL he developed through the Rodovre system in Denmark playing in the men's top league the previous two seasons.

Christian is a big defenseman who showed some potential at both ends of the ice. He can land the big open ice hit, but he can also move the puck up ice. He has the vision to make plays with the puck in all three zones but can sometimes get pressured into making mistakes. He has decent one on one ability. Christian has some upside but showed it in flashes playing a minimal role on both the Bulldogs and the Storm this season. A team may roll the dice on Mieritz but we don't expect to see him selected at the 2016 NHL Entry Draft

Miranda, Marco
LW – GCK Lions (NLB) – 6'02.5", 194
HockeyProspect.com Ranking: NR

A big Swiss left winger, Miranda played most his games this season against men in NLB as a 17yrs old and his frame helped him holding up with opponents, as he could still protect the puck and not be too overwhelmed in plays along the boards like most of his peers would be. However, his compete level will need to improve significantly to be effective in puck battles moving forward and at his size he should be able to play a more physical brand of hockey. If anything, he should spend more time in the slot and engage more below the goal line.

At almost 6'3", Miranda is a smooth skater with a powerful stride and noteworthy top speed who possesses slick hands and goal scoring upside. Had more than a couple of beauties along the season and the aforementioned traits make for an intriguing package. He is still a raw player overall, however. His efforts and performances are inconsistent, he had a disappointing showing at the U18 Worlds and in our previous viewings has had troubles finishing his chances more than once despite his skills. Has a pretty good shot and release which he should work to make more of a consistent threat. Can make the odd impressive play that leaves the viewer wanting more, but at this stage usually struggles when games become more intense. There are days where he seems to be lacking in terms of agility and will need to become quicker reacting to plays. He can feed the puck but inside the offensive zone he is often too casual with his passes and that can happen on the powerplay too. Nonetheless, despite these flaws, Miranda is a talented lad with legit long term potential.

Miromanov, Daniil
RW – Acadie-Baturst Titan (QMJHL) – 6'03", 183
HockeyProspect.com Ranking: 191

Miromanov is a Russian winger who played his minor midget hockey in Ontario with the Toronto Jr. Canadiens and was drafted in the CHL Import Draft by the London Knights (112th overall) in 2014. He came to the Titan this season after not being able to make London last season and was a pleasant surprise, scoring 20+ goals and being a very responsible player defensively. He never blew us away with his offensive skills during our viewings, but he was impressive without the puck and paid attention to all the little details on the ice. On the PK, he has good anticipation and uses his long reach well to strip opponents of the puck and block passing lanes. He's a streaky scorer, scoring 10 of his 22 goals in the month of January. In the playoffs, he scored 6 times in 5 games, including a 4-goal game. He showed good hand-eye coordination to tip point shots in front of the net. He's often involved in the play and makes good use of his reach and size along the boards. He's very good in the neutral zone as well, with his anticipation and good stick he's capable of creating turnovers. A very nice surprise for us and the Titan this season, we expect him to improve his offensive production next season.

Mityakin, Yevgeni
RW/C – Avto Yekaterinburg (MHL) – 6'03", 202
HockeyProspect.com Ranking: 129

A late '97 born Russian forward, Mityakin didn't get any international exposure this year but with the size and skills he possesses he is a strong candidate to get selected at the upcoming NHL Draft. He played very limited minutes in 17 KHL games and spent most of the season leading the way for his junior team. Evgeny is an adequate skater who could improve further once he adds more power to the lower part of his very good frame. He has first-rate hands and stickhandling abilities, key assets of his game that give him poise with the puck and the ability to make plays in most situations. He is effective on the powerplay from the half side boards because of the combination of his passing and shooting abilities. Has good power on his left-handed shot, can score with his quick wrister and slap shot, but has a backhander as well. He has the vision and execution to be a quality passer and is able to easily distribute pucks with his backhand too. He's got the moves to beat goalies one on one in multiple ways. Takes advantage of his frame and good reach to protect the puck, but as of now he can't be described as a physical player. He is already a good defensive contributor in the neutral zone and can take the puck away from opponents.

Mityakin however didn't progress that much from last season. The main aspect where he is still lacking is probably his intensity level. To remain effective at higher levels he will need to get better when the pace of the game rises, he can look a tad slow in high-paced contests. So far he hasn't been productive in those situations and his game will have to become a bit quicker overall.

Mizzi, Joseph
RW - Hamilton Bulldogs (OHL) 5'09", 173
HockeyProspect.com Ranking: NR

Mizzi was selected in the 7th round of the 2014 OHL Priority Selection Draft by the Belleville Bulls out of the Toronto Marlboros Minor Midget program. He spent his first junior season with the Newmarket Hurricanes. He made the jump to the OHL full time this season with the Hamilton Bulldogs.

Mizzi is a bit undersized, but is a strong skater with good speed. He is capable of rushing the puck into the offensive zone and creating chances. He likes to good the puck and has good power in his shot, but would shoot from low percentage areas. He provided good energy on the forecheck but lacked size and strength to have the impact he otherwise could have if he was bigger. Mizzi isn't expected to be selected at the 2016 NHL Entry Draft, but if he starts making smarter plays in the offensive zone, has the skill to produce offense at the junior level.

Morrison, Cameron
LW – Youngstown Phantoms (USHL) 6'2.25", 200
HockeyProspect.com Ranking: 50

The Aurora, Ontario native finished the USHL regular season tied for 2nd in scoring (34-32-66PTS) and registered a league leading 8 Game winning goals in 15/16. Morrison was able to do a lot of his damage offensively around the front of the net where he was a force night in and night out. Morrison possesses quick stick and hands that allows him to win battles in front, stick handle in traffic and bang home rebounds and loose pucks.

Morrison has a nice quick accurate release on his shot and is good at shooting in stride off the rush or cycle then crashes the net looking for rebounds. Cameron did a good job finding a way to get the puck to a scoring area in our viewings. He has good poise with the puck on the power play and is able to buy himself time in order to open up passing lanes and find teammates. Morrison needs to continue to work on his initial foot speed and edge work in order to win more races to pucks. Would like to see Cameron play with a bit more of an edge and do more to have an effect in games where he may not contribute on the scoreboard, there are stretches of games where he seems to go through the motions and doesn't show the same compete level at both ends of the ice.

Morrison is off to Notre Dame in the fall where he should be able to step right into the lineup and have an instant impact to their team. Morrison has the skills to develop into an effective 2 way power forward who can contribute at both ends of the ice but needs to continue to work on his consistency and skating to reach his full potential.

Quotable: "Everyone I'v talked to about him loves his game and complete package but I just don't see him as an elite power winger yet. He might turn out to be one of those players that can put up decent numbers in the USHL and in NCAA but never gets over the hump and produces at that level as a pro." - HP Scout Dusten Braaksma

Quotable: "A player I remember from his OHL Draft days because of his unique skating style. A pretty smart player with good size. He can shoot the puck and it translated into points. Very little chatter from scouts on this kid considering his point totals. At the end of the day his pace of play scares me a bit. I'm guessing I'd have him ranked in a spot where he might be gone before I'd be willing to select him. We shall see." - HP Scout Mark Edwards

Moverare, Jacob
LD – HV71 (SWE Jr.) – 6'02.5", 198
HockeyProspect.com Ranking: 72

Moverare is a Swedish defenseman who plays a rather complete and mature game despite being eligible for the upcoming draft only by a couple of weeks. Not a dynamic player by any means, he can however be useful in all sorts of situations. He is a reliable player in the defensive zone. Not really physical but positions his good frame well along the boards to win pucks, has a good stick and does a pretty good job in puck battles. Could be a bit stronger in the slot and on rebounds, but is still effective on the penalty kill and a very good shot-blocker. Moverare has notable poise under pressure, a result of his good understanding of the game combined with quality hands. This allows him to often complete plays in tight spaces and effectively start up the play from the back-end. As a shifty player with good puck control he is capable of transitioning the puck up the ice even at a slower pace. He is a guy that can make some smart plays when he has possession and he is able to use his body to buy himself time and space. Usually makes good reads, is quick at recognizing lanes for the outlet pass and can consistently execute breakouts. Even if he would need to add more power to his slap shot, Moverare can also take advantage of his qualities on the powerplay, as he can work along the blueline to find lanes to put the puck on the net.

What is going to define Jacob's success at the next level will be his capability to improve his skating. He has pretty good mobility sideways and is a legit backwards skater, however he really struggles to accelerate, lacks push in his first few steps and his top speed is well below average as well. This means when forwards manage to pass by him he has basically no chance to recover, which is obviously a concern. It also hurts him when he needs to get first on loose pucks. Adding power and at least some explosiveness to his skating are the main things he will need to work on moving forward while he tries to establish himself as a regular SHL player, after appearing in 4 games for HV71 early on this season.

Quotable: "I don't see what other people see in him. Even skating issues aside, for me he is far too much of a vanilla defenseman that doesn't really stand out with any of his assets. When I think of him at the NHL level, I don't see a strong puck-mover, I don't see a lot of offense, nor a strong defensive presence. Don't see a strong PP or PK player, either. What I see is a decent career Euro-league player." - HP Scout Nik Funa

Quotable: "Had he improved his acceleration, he would have been a 1st rounder for me" - HP Scout Mik Portoni

Quotable: "I thought his skating had improved a bit when I saw him in April and that was a big concern for me. That said, it's far from great. Not a player I'd bang the table for..." - HP Scout Mark Edwards

Murdaca, Joseph
G - Mississauga Steelheads (OHL) 6'03.25", 195
HockeyProspect.com Ranking: NR

Murdaca started the season is Jr B but was traded from Saginaw to Mississauga during the season. He got most of his minutes coming into games in relief.
Joseph is a big goalie who is very raw at this point in his development. He showed flashes of having some potential going forward but it was very difficult for scouts to get a read on him this season. Much like the team scouts, we had a limited opportunity to view him. He moved pretty well for a big kid but struggled with his recovery skills after making first saves. We expect Mississauga to trade for an older goalie this summer and have Murdaca serve as his backup. While anything is possible, we don't expect Joseph to be selected this June.

Murphy, Liam
LW/C – Moncton Wildcats (QMJHL) - 6'01", 198
HockeyProspect.com Ranking: NR

Murphy was in his second season with the Wildcats and had a good first half of the season playing with the Klima twins, but once he moved out of that line, his production dropped off. After having 25 points in 37 games before January 1st, he only had 3 points the rest of the way in 21 games. Murphy is one of the few Americans who decided to report to the QMJHL. Moncton selected him 43rd overall in the 2014 QMJHL Draft. Murphy has size and uses it well along the boards. When he had success with the Klima brothers, he was doing a lot of their dirty work, retrieving pucks. Skills wise, he had trouble keeping up with them and eventually was dropped to the 4th line most of the 2nd half due to his poor play and the acquisition of Vaclav Karabacek from Baie-Comeau. He lacks hockey sense and is often a second late in his reaction time. These are his biggest question marks. He's solid on his skates and can do some good work on the forecheck, not backing down from the physical game. Murphy came into the league with some hype around him, but hasn't delivered anything yet and had players pass him in the Moncton depth chart in the 2nd half of the season.

Murray, Brett
LW – Carleton Place Canadians (CCHL) 6'05" 215
HockeyProspect.com Ranking: 115

Brett is another 1st year player that came into Carleton Place this year as a bit of an unknown, but quickly made his presence felt early in the year with his size on the ice. He started off really strong in the beginning of the season, then slowed down a bit in the middle of the season wasn't as effected but then pick up at end of year and into the playoffs.

Brett is a big bodied forward that at times could take over a game because of his size and reach. His skating is good for his size, he still hasn't grown into his body yet and with time he should be good with his stride and speed. Brett has a very good and hard wrist shot and his accuracy is good, he doesn't miss a lot of shots wide and is consistent at putting pucks on net. He is good at protecting the puck with his long reach and stick, and uses it really well when he is cycling the puck down low and driving hard to the net. We would like to see him get stronger on his stick as pucks tend to bounce of his stick a lot; he has good scoring touch around the net, as most of his goals this year were either in tight on the goalie or in the slot. Brett has good hockey sense; he reads plays well and understands systems and where to be on the ice. He is really good in his own zone along the boards getting the puck out, by either finding the open man or making the touch pass to the curling center. We would like to see Brett be way more physical with his size and strength, there were too many times he passed up finishing his check on the forecheck or along the boards in the neutral zone, with a player his size and ability we would like to see him be more engaging physically as well as using his size and going hard to the net to create offensive chances for himself.

Brett defensive zone was okay this year, he tended to get lost in his own zone on who to pick up in certain situations and again wasn't physical enough along the boards. He has a really good active stick in his own zone by getting it in the lanes and breaking up cross-ice passes. Brett needs to compete more every shift, there were times this year where he would dominate a game or a couple periods and then you wouldn't notice him the rest of game or even an entire game. Brett will be attending Penn State University in 2017-2018 season. With his size and ability right now and if he gets stronger, faster in the years to come he could be a good hockey player at the next level and be effective as well.

Quotable:" Brett has great size coming in at 6's but he isn't physical enough for his size, he tends to stay on the perimeter and doesn't like to engaged physically with or without the puck" - HP Scout, Justin Sproule

Quotable:" We would like to see Brett go to "the dirty areas" to create more offensive chances for himself and use his big frame to his advantage." - HP Scout Mark Edwards

Quotable:" Brett has really soft hands and has a good hard shot, but he needs to focus on hitting the net more, too many missed opportunities at the net for second chances" - HP Scout, Justin Sproule

Murray, Justin
LD - Barrie Colts (OHL) 6'00", 179
HockeyProspect.com Ranking: 174

Murray was selected in the eighth round of the 2014 OHL Priority Selection Draft by the Barrie Colts out of the London Jr. Knights Minor Midget program. Murray had a very successful season with the London Jr. B Nationals last season. He made a very strong debut in the OHL this season. Where he made an impact on a veteran Colts team eventually checking in as a top four defenseman playing consistently with Rasmus Andersson.

Murray has decent size but would certainly benefit from adding some muscle. This didn't prevent him from playing with an edge. He landed some big open ice hits throughout the season, was physical along the boards and didn't hesitate to fight when necessary. While physicality is an important part of his game he is patient in waiting for play to come to him. His gap control is good, too, and he rarely takes himself out of position by going for a big hit.

Murray is accurate with short passes but was a little hit or miss with long outlets and stretch passes at times. Murray is a good skater and has the ability to carry the puck up ice when plays break down and nobody is open. He really picks his spots when pinching but has shown the ability to keep plays alive along the wall and by holding the opposing line. In the event Murray gets caught jumping into the play he does possess the skating ability to get back defensively. He has a decent shot from the point and can provide a little offense.

Murray will need to continue to add muscle to his frame but he has very good upside heading into the 2016 NHL Entry Draft. He is a very well rounded prospect who has puck skills and skating ability that helps him on the offensive side, and smart positional play with an edge to help him succeed defensively. He projects as a two-way defender at the next level.

Quotable: "Watching Murray play since Bantam it's been interesting watching him evolve as a player. He used to be a small, flashy, speedy defenseman and he's developed from a real offensive defenseman into a well rounded defender who does a great job taking care of his defensive abilities as well. This is a kid who's learned and adapted every step of the way to be successful." - HP Scout Ryan Yessie

Najman, Ondrej
LC – HC Dukla Jihlava U20 (CZE) – 6'01", 187
HockeyProspect.com Ranking: 134

Najman is a cerebral center that was heavily relied upon for every key situation on his Jihlava U20 team. There wasn't a situation that Najman wasn't used in this season, showcasing his versatility and maturity. While he possesses an accurate, hard release, Najman's strength is his ability to see opportunities. With the puck on his stick, he can slow or speed up the game depending on what is required of the situation. Protects the puck well in corners and doesn't shy away from getting below the goal line. Creative with the puck and is a threat to defenders with his ability to pass through seams and find his linemates at key scoring moments. Logged heavy minutes on his club this season and was the key face-off man. Works hard away from the puck to ensure taking away scoring opportunities and knows when he should fill in for his defensemen or missed coverage by linemates.

Najman has a well-balanced, full stride, but needs to develop more power in it and is far from dynamic on his skates. Strength will be an area that he needs to continue to develop to transition to the North American physical style of hockey. Has some hockey bloodlines as his uncle was a Toronto Maple Leafs draft pick in 1992 and his grandfather was a legendary Dukla Jihlava player and former Czech national team coach.

Quotable: "I like this player, love how he sees the ice with the puck on his stick, but I'm not sure if he has enough dynamic qualities in him to be an NHL player. When I see him on the ice, I think NHL defensemen will have too easy of an time closing down on him as he isn't quite elusive enough" - HP Scout Nik Funa

Nassen, Linus
LD – Lulea HF J20 (SWE) – 6'00", 167
HockeyProspect.com Ranking: NR

Nassen is puck-moving defenseman that is more on the smaller side. He has played mostly for Lulea's J20 squad but also logged 10 games in SHL. Nassen makes a good first-pass and plays a heads-up game, scans the ice well and can play an up-tempo game. He is capable of running the PP and is a good puck-distributor. Defensively he is alert and likes to play with energy despite his lighter frame. He likes to keep his gaps tight and will play quite aggressively against the puck-carrier. He doesn't mind engaging physically and also has a good stick. Because he likes to keep his gap so tight in defensive zone, it requires really active footwork with a lot of pivots and changes of direction. Nassen is a decent prospect, but one we are not sure will translate to the NHL game. The frame-size is a concern and he might not quite possess the offensive punch he would need to make it.

Neuls, Donovan
RW – Seattle Thunderbirds (WHL) 5'10", 181
HockeyProspect.com Ranking: NR

Neuls was a solid depth player for the Seattle Thunderbirds this season. He's not big, but he's decently fast and is known for going on unexpected rushes with the puck. Neuls does everything high octane. Both a sparkplug energy player and a playmaker, he's known for whistling the puck off his stick very quickly and so his passing game tends to be a bit hit-and-miss. As such, we sometimes questioned his hockey sense. He's skilled in tight but lacks the size to dominate along the boards.

Whatever the case, Neuls can bring a lot of hustle and positive vibes to a team. He played well in Seattle this season on a long playoff run that took them to the WHL Finals. He seems to up the tempo of a game the moment he steps onto the ice. However, it's his game away from the puck that can be especially disconcerting as there are times when he looks completely lost away from the play.

Neveu, Jacob
RD – Rouyn-Noranda Huskies (QMJHL) – 6'02", 194
HockeyProspect.com Ranking: 142

Neveu played for the top team in the QMJHL (Rouyn-Noranda) which meant he played more of a depth role; featured mostly on the 3rd pairing and getting ice time on the penalty killing unit. Neveu is a big and physical stay-at-home defenseman who understands his role very well and knows how to play within his limits. With the puck, Neveu does a good job making the safe play, as he is not a good puck mover but will make a safe pass out of his zone if available or will just get the puck out by the boards. With the puck on his stick in the offensive zone, he's not very creative; he won't add much offense to the game. In our viewings this year, he didn't get to touch the puck a lot. Sometimes he was not noticeable on the ice because of his lack of exposure to the puck. Defensively, he's good one-on-one; he will play physical along the boards and clear the front of the net. He's disciplined as well, as he doesn't take a lot of penalties, but won't hesitate to come to a teammate's defense if needed. He doesn't take a lot of risks on the ice. He really made his mark this year on the penalty killing unit, where he became a top shot-blocker in front of his goaltender and really took pride in that. There are some concerns with Neveu in terms of his offensive upside at the next level; today's hockey is about speed and moving the puck and those are two areas he doesn't excel in.

Quotable: "Love what he brings to the table with his size and defensive game, but I'm not sure he has enough skill to be an NHLer, as hockey is becoming more of a game based on speed and puck moving." - HP scout Jérôme Bérubé

Niemelainen, Markus
LD - Saginaw Spirit (OHL) 6'04.5", 198
HockeyProspect.com Ranking: 42

Niemelainen was drafted 18th Overall at the 2015 CHL Import Draft out of HPK in Finland. Niemelainen adjusted well to the smaller ice, as his ice time fluctuated throughout the first two thirds of the season from third pairing minutes to playing 75% of his teams' power play. After Greg Gilbert was fired, Markus steadily saw big minutes in all situations. Sadly for him, it was very late in the season.

Niemelainen has excellent size and on occasion has done well defensively utilizing it. He landed some solid hits, but doesn't really have much of a mean streak. One on one he has a decent stick but his average footwork can get him into trouble against more skilled opponents. With the puck Niemelainen was very hit and miss all season long. He is stronger in the offensive zone, especially when he gets a little time and space, such as on the power play. He doesn't have a great shot from the point. Outlet passes were hit and miss as he has shown some consistency in some games, other games he's missed by a mile for icings and turnovers. He can be a little soft on the puck when clearing the zone, resulting in sustained defensive zone pressure. He is capable of taking the puck up ice and getting pucks deep.

Markus has good upside as a defenseman who can contribute at both ends, but will likely take a while to develop. He needs to grow into his size and also gain more consistency, as he would have his good nights and his bad nights. Playing a consistent role with consistent ice should help him adjust and improve.

Quotable: "This team has some of the worst defensemen in the league and he is in the 3rd pairing. It's crazy." - NHL Scout - (November 2015)

Quotable: "I think he's their best defenseman and he can't buy a shift. That's why Saginaw is Saginaw." - NHL Scout (October 2015)

Quotable: "Why doesn't he play? I thought he looked like a 1st rounder coming into this season. - NHL Scout (November 2015)

Quotable: "So now he's fighting for minutes with Rocky Kaura?" - NHL Scout (January 2016)

Quotable: "He's sold me. He's in my first round." - NHL Scout (April 2016)

Quotable: "You have a better chance of winning powerball than predicting his icetime." - NHL Scout (November 2015)

Quotable: "I drove 2.5 hours to Sarnia to see him one night. When I left with 5 minutes remaining he had played three shifts, his last one being midway in the 2nd period. Apparently he got one more shift as the extra attacker when Saginaw pulled the goalie. Luckily he got more ice as the season progressed. He played his best hockey in a Finland jersey for me." - Mark Edwards

Quotable "Not a great interview at the combine. Interesting he mentioned that Saginaw's first two picks aren't coming and he doesn't know if he's going back." - NHL Scout (Combine week)

Noel, Nathan
RC – Saint John Sea Dogs (QMJHL) – 6'00", 178
HockeyProspect.com Ranking: NR

Noel was one of the biggest stories following the 2015 NHL Draft, after being ranked high by many and still not hearing his name called. Back in the QMJHL for his 3rd season in the league, he improved his defensive game under new head coach Danny Flynn. Offensively, he didn't take the next step, as his numbers were similar to last season. He did, however, play a much more complete game than last year. Noel had two excellent months at the beginning of 2016 where he put a lot of points on the board. More than half of his total points were created during those two months. Noel can create a lot of things offensively with his speed; he has quick, explosive feet and a great burst of speed – he can be tough to handle off the rush. He has a solid shot, but he tends to hold onto the puck way too long in the offensive zone and would be way more effective offensively if he used his teammates more. As a center, he's more of a shooter than a passer. He's stronger on his skates and played with a lot more grit and with a higher compete level in our viewings this year. He makes good use of his speed on the forecheck and in puck-pursuit situations. Overall, Noel is a good junior hockey player, but there are some questions about his smarts and how his game will transfer over to the next level.

Nother, Tyler
RD - Windsor Spitfires (OHL) 6'04.25", 198
HockeyProspect.com Ranking: NR

Nother was selected in the third round of the 2014 OHL Priority Selection Draft by the London Knights out of the Halton Hurricanes Minor Midget program. After spending a year in and out of the line-up as a 16 year old, Nother was dealt to the Windsor Spitfires early in the 2015-2016 season. This allowed him to establish a role on their third pairing with partial penalty killing duty.

Nother is a simple stay at home defender who is at his best when making the smart, basic play at both ends of the ice. He has great size as a defenseman but needs to add more muscle to his frame. His conservative game makes him very positionally reliable and his reach combined with a safe demeanor makes him difficult to work around and can keep opponents to the outside. Tyler has limited puck skills and can get himself in trouble when trying to do too much. He did however develop the ability to skate up ice with the puck and put it deep when the option was there, rather than resorting only to passing as he had in the past. His skating has shown improvements this year but still has room for development.

Nother would benefit from developing more of a mean streak accompanied by some added muscle. Teams know they'd be getting a low risk, low reward defenseman with Nother, but chances are he won't to be drafted this year.

Nurmi, Markus
RW – TPS U20 (FIN) – 6'04", 176
HockeyProspect.com Ranking: 185

Nurmi is a right wing with an intriguing frame and a good compete level to his game. He has a decent skating stride that should become more effective as he fills out and adds some power. Nurmi plays a straight-line game and can be useful on both ends of the ice. He battles well physically and also uses his stick well to win pucks. Nurmi is already a responsible defensive player and can also be used on the PK. Has smart reads and plays his position well, with a long active stick that clogs lanes and also allows him to pokecheck pucks away. He is useful as a F1 that gets in on pucks and uses his physical tools to cause turnovers. If he can create a turnover, he has enough smarts to play the puck to his linemate. Will go to the net in the offensive zone. Nurmi is still quite raw and is still a bit slow executing plays with the puck but has good smarts and compete. Probably not skilled enough to be a regular offensive contributor at the next level, but has upside as a checking forward.

Nylander, Alex
LW - Mississuaga Steelheads (OHL) 6'00.5", 180
HockeyProspect.com Ranking: 12

Nylander was selected 12th Overall in the 2015 CHL Import Draft by the Mississauga Steelheads out of AIK J20 team in Sweden. Nylander immediately became a game breaker for the Mississauga Steelheads and was a key part of their offense all season long.
Alex Nylander is a highly skilled, versatile offensive threat, who is equally smart as he is skilled. A player who is effective as both a goal scorer and a playmaker, Nylander is at his best with possession of the puck. He controls the pace of play in possession, Nylander possesses elite vision and playmaking abilities, anticipating the play a step ahead of his peers. Alex shows tremendous creativity in the offensive zone. Nylander's elite puck skills along with his quick feet and strong mobility make him difficult to contain both in tight spaces and off the rush. Possessing an explosive first step and high end straight line speed, Nylander has the ability to create separation. While Nylander is successful as a playmaker and has the abilities to make those around him better, he also possesses an excellent shot. Displaying a lightning quick release, Nylander's shot packs velocity and pin point accuracy, making him lethal in the scoring areas. He also has an excellent one-timer. Nylander exudes confidence.

Away from the puck, Nylander has been hit or miss. When utilizing his speed and shiftiness he will track down the puck carrier quickly and force turnovers taking away time and space. However, in other situations he can go several shifts at a time showing laziness and an unwillingness to work for pucks, even when the carrier is nearby.

Nylander has his highs and lows, but at the end of the day he's one of the most talented players available for the 2016 NHL Entry Draft. He has the upside of a first line forward who creates offense for his linemates, while having the finishing ability both on the breakaway and with a big shot. He will need to work on his consistency and at times, his work ethic away from the puck, but his skating, awareness and skill will see him selected very high in the draft.

Quotable: "I've been conflicted about Nylander all season long. I love the playmaking and the offensive upside as a whole. I hate the long stretches where he won't compete. I get the comparisons of his brother William, but I think Alexander is more of a playmaker than William." - HP Scout Ryan Yessie

Quotable: "He is exactly like his brother." - NHL Scout (October 2015)

Quotable: "Some guys have told me they have McLeod ahead of him. What are they watching?" - NHL Agent (not Nylander's) (March 2015)

Quotable: "It's tight between Nylander and McLeod for me." - NHL Scout (October 2015)

Quotable: "Nylander is way ahead of McLeod on my list." - Same NHL Scout as above (January 2016)

Quotable: "I think he's the most skilled and one of the safest picks in the whole draft. I love him. He's in my top six overall." - NHL Scout (February 2016)

Quotable: "I'm not as high on him as others, I see the skill but he's not my kind of player. Too many shifts off and too many viewings where he did nothing." - NHL Scout (March 2015)

Quotable: "I know he will probably go top ten but he's not even top twenty guy for me. You see those games last night? You're not winning in the playoffs with guys like him. Someone else can have him." - NHL Scout (April 2016)

Quotable: "I loved his game at the U17 in Sarnia. He reminded me of his brother but I thought he moved the puck better than William did at the same age. Our Euros didn't love him quite as much at the Hlinka. We had him ranked in the teens on our pre-season list. He rose up our list as I gained viewings in Mississauga. I cooled on him slightly the last 3 months. He had a lot more games where I barely noticed him. When he is on, he is as dangerous as anyone but when he is off he is really off. Slow start in Grand Forks but I thought he got much better as games progressed. Huge upside. - Mark Edwards

O'Brien, Brogan
LW/LC – Prince George Cougars (WHL) 6'02", 189

HockeyProspect.com Ranking: NR

Brogan O'Brien came to the Prince George Cougars this season from the BCHL's Spruce Kings looking like a new and improved version of himself. We had the pleasure of scouting O'Brien during his time in Junior A, identifying him as a lanky centre who was talented and hardworking, but a bit clumsy and rough around the edges. This year, playing in major junior, he's added new power, explosiveness and consistency to his game.

O'Brien is now looking like a slightly above-average skater with the Cougars as he begins settling into his large frame and acquiring more hand-eye and lower-body coordination. Significant improvements were made most notably to his backchecking speed, as he's a far more complete player than he was a year ago. He's good in the face off circle and has great range with or without without puck thanks to long arms and adept anticipation. Despite being so big, he also a knack for being slippery and hard to read at times.

His offensive game really came together this year, as he improved his shot and started burying his chances after amassing a ton of opportunities when he first debuted in the Dub. He was a good player last year with the Spruce Kings, but now he does everything with the Cougars a little better and with more skill than he did a year before. He received more ice-time, more assignments, and buried more chances as this last season wore on. We like his upwards trajectory as a prospect.

O'Leary, Michael
LC/W – Dubuque Fighting Saints (USHL) 6'01", 191
HockeyProspect.com Ranking: NR

O'Leary is a Halifax, Nova Scotia native who played his Prep hockey at Salisbury Prep School in CT prior to joining the Fighting Saints this season. Michael recently de-committed from Cornell University and has sense committed to Notre Dame for the 17/18 season.

O'Leary possesses excellent vision and playmaking ability, plays with a pass first mentality in the offensive zone, likes to play a give and go game out of the corner and supports the play well. He has a good set of hands that come in handy to stick handle in tight areas and deflect pucks in the slot. Michael plays a very sound 200 foot game and sacrifices some offense for his defensive positioning. He doesn't need to touch the puck on a shift to have a positive impact in the game. He plays in all situations for the Fighting Saints. O'Leary's skating has made significant improvement as he has gotten stronger.

Olischefski, Kohen
LW – Chilliwack Chiefs (BCHL) 6'01", 165
HockeyProspect.com Ranking: NR

Olischefski isn't a flashy player, but he's a dependable two-way forward. Committed to the University of Denver, after having previously committed to Wisconsin, Olischefski is a player equipped with high hockey IQ who plays a simple game in which he delivers pucks to and shoots from the prime scoring area. His skating could be better, but he gravitates towards the high percentage areas, backchecks hard according to his ability, and doesn't forgo his responsibilities on defense.

He can play at centre or at wing and saw ice-time in all situations this year with the Chilliwack Chiefs. Olischefski showed a willingness this year to block shots and to become involved in the more competitive battles along the wall. He's a decent passer and has a really nice wristshot with a good quick release.

Before arriving to the Chilliwack Chiefs, Olischefski was already a two time CSSHL MVP with the Yale Hockey Academy. Known as a complete player in the CSSHL, Olischefski has cemented that reputation with his strong two-way play in the BCHL. He's a strong penalty killer and a disruptive force in his own end. He needs to become faster and bigger, but he'll get some good years of development out of the Denver program.

O'Neil, Kevin
RW – Albany Academy (NE Prep) 5'11" 170
HockeyProspect.com Ranking: NR

O'Neil is an intriguing and interesting prospect as he shows good puck control as his stick skills are strong and shoots well in stride. He will quarterback the power play with good puck distribution although his size is average and he plays in the New England prep league so tough gauge. He has good offensive instincts and is committed to Yale. In 33 games played, he amassed 21 goals and 44 assists.

Olsson, Oliver
LC – Malmo Redhawks J20 (SWE) – 5'10", 176
HockeyProspect.com Ranking: NR

Olsson is a center prospect that combines both hockey IQ and compete level. His physical tools are very raw as he is neither the fastest, the strongest, or the biggest. Olsson's best asset is easily his hockey IQ, as he reads the play very well. Has got great off-the-puck movement in all three zones that opens up space for his linemates. Innate understanding of how his own movement changes the other team's coverage. Has good vision with the puck and is a playmaker. Hands and puck-skills are average but he makes deceptive plays that throw his checkers off. Good puck-placement on his passes, changes speed and direction of passing so that his teammates can skate into it with ease. Competes without the puck. Will throw his rather unimpressive frame around and hounds the puck-carrier. Pays attention in defensive zone. Ultimately Olsson has the smarts and the compete, but even if he already made his debut at the SHL level as a 17yrs old, he has a long way to go in the physical tools department. Needs to get faster, stronger and bigger to have a chance. He is a bit of a project.

Osmanski, Austin
LD - Mississauga Steelheads (OHL) 6'03.25", 196
HockeyProspect.com Ranking: NR

Osmanski was selected in the sixth round of the 2014 OHL Priority Selection Draft by the Mississauga Steelheads out of the Buffalo Regals Minor Midget program. Osmanski joined the Buffalo Jr. Sabres U16 and U18 programs posting great numbers as a defenseman before making the jump to the OHL for his first full season with the Mississauga Steelheads.

Osmanski is a big bodied stay at home defenseman. He boasts intriguing physical attributes with a big frame and a physical mindset. His upside beyond the defensive zone is a bit limited. Osmanski is at his best when he keeps it simple. He is a decent skater and provides decent mobility. He does a good job one on one using his stick and has improved his gap control. His long stick also helped in passing lanes breaking up chances effectively. Osmanski can struggle with contain in transition once he get his hips turned, as he lacks any recovery speed. At times Osmanski showed awareness in the defensive zone, showing an ability to contain along with an ability to clear the front of the net and a strong compete level. He effectively clogged shooting lanes and was an effective shot blocker. He lacks puck skills and has very limited offensive upside. Both his goals this season were fired from the point and found their way through a screen from the point. He has struggled greatly with the puck, fanning on the puck both in shooting and passing situations resulting in turnovers. He struggled to elude the forecheck and would often be forced to simply rim the puck around the boards.

Osmanski is a very raw defender. He would provide a team with size and a defensive, shutdown mindset. However he is a project and his upside is pretty low. He needs to get better with the puck to the point where he is consistently able to make the simple play. All his negatives may very well keep him out of the 2016 NHL Entry Draft.

Quotable: "What do you think of Osmanski? Anyone talking to you about him?" - NHL Scout (March 2016)

Quotable: "You're the first Scout to ask me about him. If I was with a team he would not be on my list." - Mark Edwards (answering question from scout above)

Ottenbreit, Turner
LD – Seattle Thunderbirds (WHL) 6'03", 190
HockeyProspect.com Ranking: NR

Returning to eligibility after being passed over in last year's NHL Draft, Turner Ottenbreit is a big-bodied loose-cannon who intimidates the opposition from the back end of the Seattle Thunderbirds. Both tall and very strong in his upper-body, Ottenbreit excels when jostling for space in either the corners or in front of his goaltender. Good defensive reach makes up for some of his skating problems. Ottenbreit can also let it rip from the point on occasion, but is overall fairly limited in his offensive upside.

His skating requires a great deal of work and he can be highly undisciplined at times taking far too many needless penalties. He will need to clean up his game a bit and become faster with his feet and his head in order to have a chance.

Paquette, Christopher
RC - Niagara Ice Dogs (OHL) 6'01.25", 207
HockeyProspect.com Ranking: NR

Paquette was selected in the second round of the 2014 OHL Priority Selection by the Niagara Ice Dogs out of the Kingston Jr. Frontenacs Minor Midget program. Paquette played a limited role as a rookie and while he gained more ice in his second season, his numbers stayed nearly identical.

Paquette has a very good size and skating combination. For a 6'02" forward, he skates extremely well. He skates a lot of miles but isn't overly engaging. With the puck on his stick he will stay on the perimeter and carry and hold the puck for long stretches of time before making a play. Without the puck he'll cut into the slot with good timing, but usually didn't result in much. He has trouble beating defenders one on one and can get outmuscled too much in key areas for a forward his size. He cycles the puck well when picking up the puck low in the zone. Defensively he's shown average ability to get into passing lanes and take away time and space on the point.

Paquette could hear his name called at the 2016 NHL Entry Draft. He has the size and skating that scouts like to see. However, his lack of aggression makes him a questionable choice as a bottom six forward and lack of top six offensive upside really doesn't leave him with much when projecting him as an NHL talent. If he can learn how to play a tougher, more physically imposing style of game, or develop his offensive game he would make a legitimate prospect. At this point we can't rationalize a selection for Paquette outside of the upside of his size/skating combination.

Parsons, Tyler
G - London Knights (OHL) 6'01.25", 184
HockeyProspect.com Ranking: 31

After being passed over at the 2013 and 2014 OHL Priority Selection Drafts, Parsons was picked up by the London Knights as a free agent out of the Detroit Little Caesars U18 program. Parsons adjusted surprisingly fast to the OHL game, taking the starting job away from the over-ager Giugovaz. This season Parsons handled even more games and really showed himself to be one of the best goaltenders in the league this season.

Parsons is exceptionally fast with both his reflexes and his lateral movement, making him very tough to beat. He is a very resilient goaltender who is never completely out of a play due to his competitiveness and quickness. Parsons is smooth moving around in his crease and has a good glove hand. He has some puck playing ability and generally won't try to do too much with the puck. He is good on breakaways and tough to beat in alone because of his excellent reflexes. The area of improvement for Parsons would be his rebound control. He has improved at directing them away from the crease, but he needs to continue to work on it, as it will usually be rebounds in the slot area that result in goals against him.

Parsons is one of the top goaltenders entering the 2016 NHL Entry Draft. He was rated a second round prospect in our September release and if anything, has impressed us more since that time. We like his chances that he eventually becomes an NHL netminder. It's not often you see a goaltender with his quickness and competitiveness.

Quotable: "Are the scouts talking up this kid watching the NHL playoffs? They might want to check the height of some of those goalies." - NHL Scout (April 2016)

Quotable: "I think the fact he's 6'1" slides him to the 3rd round. It shouldn't, but I think it will. - NHL Scout (April 2016)

Quotable: "It's laughable. If he's an inch taller he gets taken a round earlier. - OHL Coach

Quotable: "I actually saw Parsons at the Knights rookie camp as he tried to make the team. He showed his athleticism and stood out like a sore thumb. I'm not a big fan of the 'robot like' goalies. I like the guys that have structure but mix in their athleticism like Parsons does. When you mix those factors with his quickness, his legs are lightning quick, you get a great package. If Parson's was 6'3" or 6'4", you would've heard his name a lot more this season. NHL teams like their monster size goalies. I think this kid can buck the trend." - Mark Edwards

Quotable: "He reminds me of Jonathan Quick." - NHL Scout (April 2016)

Quotable: "After getting feedback all week from scouts at the combine, a lot of scouts raved about his interview and made a point of telling me it was up with their best interviews this year." - HP Scout Mark Edwards (Combine week)

Pasichnuk, Brinson
LD – Bonnyville Pontiacs (AJHL) 5'10", 190
HockeyProspect.com Ranking: 177

Pasichnuk joined the Bonnyville Pontiacs last season as a rookie where he posted only 29 points in 56 games. He took a huge step this season finishing with 65 points and winning the AJHL Most Outstanding Defenseman Award. He also won a Gold Medal with Team Canada West at the 2015 World Junior A Challenge. Brinson is a very smart, aggressive defenseman who plays with a high compete level and likes to play at a high pace. He is also a very physical, rugged player who will drop the gloves at anytime.

Brinson is not an overly fast skater but is very deceptive as he likes to get up ice and has great balance and footwork that allow him to make plays both offensively and defensively. He is not afraid to shoot the puck and has a very heavy wrist shot and slap shot that he can get off. One of the areas that he will need to work on is getting more pucks on net. Pasichnuk has an innate ability to handle the puck at high speeds always protecting it and making moves in traffic. He loves to attack the shooting lanes with and without the puck which causes him to always be a threat offensively. He has very good hockey sense and always gets in a good position to accept a pass or take a shot on net. When he rushes the puck, which happens a lot in a game, he is able to find open ice and easily find good scoring opportunities. Sometimes he would benefit by letting the play come to him instead of forcing plays that aren't there.

One of the great improvements in his game over the past two seasons has be his defensive play. He plays very aggressive and won't shy away from punishing opponents physically. He is good in front of his own net and is always willing to sacrifice his body and get in shooting lanes. He is a player that is a late developer but has shown high end offensive skill and solid defensive skills and positioning. He is committed to the University of Arizona for the 2016-17 season.

Quotable: "He's small but super competitive. I could see him getting drafted." - NHL Scout (April 2016)

Pastujov, Nick
LW/LC – USNTDP 6'00", 200
HockeyProspect.com Ranking: 189

Pastujov is a forward who has played both center and wing positions. He already has a decently filled-out frame and a knack for creating offense. With that said, we were disappointed with his consistency. Pastujov shows above-average puck-skills, decent skating and good offensive vision but it only comes in flashes. He can make plays with the puck, sees the ice well, is capable of setting up linemates and also showed good finishing ability. However, in our viewings he has struggled to put together a full game where he would be effective on majority of his shifts. While his tools do give him some upside, he will have to work harder at being a factor when he steps on ice. If he can find that consistency, he will look like a decent prospect. At this point in time, we haven't seen enough indications of that happening as he was roughly the same player at the end of the year as he was early on.

Peeke, Andrew
RD – Green Bay Gamblers (USHL) 6'2.75", 205
HockeyProspect.com Ranking: 61

Peeke was an effective defenseman for Team USA at the Ivan Hlinka tournament as well as the Junior B Challenge this past season in addition to being a reliable defenseman for Green Bay all season long. Despite being listed on the 3rd pairing for most of the season, Peeke saw a fair amount of ice time, as he was usually on the ice in crucial parts of the game, penalty kill situations and saw a decent amount of Power play time. Andrew is a smooth skating shutdown defenseman who plays a real steady and responsible game at both ends of the ice. He isn't going to do a lot to dazzle you but has an imposing presents on the ice and uses his size to his advantage. Peeke has good hockey instincts and great vision of the ice which translates into quick puck movement and few turnovers. Peeke has a great understanding of the game in his own end and is able to force plays out of the middle of ice and use his size and reach to turn pucks over and clear them out of his own end effectively.

Peeke isn't overly physical in the sense of trying to put guys through the boards or step up on players at the blue line but he uses enough physicality to get the job done and separate players from the puck. His foot speed with the puck on the breakout still needs improvement and needs to get the puck off his stick quickly on the breakout when pressured by speedy forwards. Peeke is a strong passer of the puck, makes solid tape to tap passes on the breakout as well as on the point on the Power Play. Peeke possesses a big shot and can be a great weapon from the point but simply doesn't use it enough. Peeke certainly has the tools to be more effective in the offensive zone but is still very effective with his current style of play.

Andrew Peeke joins a very solid recruiting class at Notre Dame in the fall where his game will have no trouble translating to the NCAA level.

Quotable: "He's not going to blow you away with his offensive skill but he is as steady as they come on the backend for that age. He needs to learn to use his shot a bit more." HP Scout Dusten Braaksma

Quotable: "He's reliable in all situations, plays a simple game but needs to learn to be more physical." NHL Scout (January 2016)

Quotable: "I like him. He's big and a smart kid and I like his poise with the puck. His feet need to get better and they would be the stopper if something is going to hold him back. He could play with a bit more pop at times." - HP Scout Mark Edwards

Pelton-Byce, Ty
C – Des Moines Buccaneers (USHL) 6'02", 185
HockeyProspect.com Ranking: NR

Pelton-Byce was a player we thought had a chance to be drafted last season in his first draft year, however due to him coming out of the Wisconsin High School Ranks we feel scouts needed to see more against a higher level of competition in order to use a draft pick on him. Pelton Byce has done a lot to improve his stock in his USHL rookie season where a lot of nights he was the best player on his team and putting up solid offensive numbers for a struggling Des Moines team (15G 28A in 60 games)

Ty covers a lot of ice with his skating and size, has good anticipation and hockey sense to read the play. He makes good tape to tape passes and makes solid simple plays in the neutral zone. Pelton-Byce showed great poise and playmaking ability in the offensive zone in our viewings this year. He wasn't afraid to go to the net and mix things up either. Can bring a physical element and win key puck battles for his team. Pelton-Byce has continued to progress and be an effective player at each level he has played at and projects as a center who can be effective in all 3 zones.

Pethrus, William
RD – Mora IK J20 (SWE) – 6'02", 183
HockeyProspect.com Ranking: NR

Pethrus is an offensive defenseman who has put up an impressive point per game campaign for Mora J20. He has also gotten a cup of coffee in Allsvenskan, playing 11 games against men. Pethrus is a defenseman that likes to play an active game, he will pinch and make sure he is involved offensively, sometimes almost to a fault. His puck skills are very good and he handles the puck with ease and control. He has good vision with the puck on his stick and will hit open teammates without much problem. He's got decent size but will need to fill out quite a bit. He shows some will to play physical in his zone but it's not always very effective. He doesn't seem mind taking a hit to make a play either.

Pethrus will really need to improve his defensive game, though. He has trouble anticipating the point of entry into the defensive zone and consistently blows gaps on zone entry plays, often setting himself way too wide with him scrambling to get back to the middle. His defense in neutral zone also needs work as he is prone to getting out of position way too far up the ice to pressure the other team, almost as if he were a forward which blows his team's structure leaving large gaps on the blueline. We like Pethrus's offensive ability, puck skills and vision with the puck, and his frame, but he has a long road ahead of him on the defensive side of the puck.

Pezzetta, Michael
RC - Sudbury Wolves (OHL) 6'01" 204
HockeyProspect.com Ranking: 106

Pezzetta is a former OHL Draft first round selection from the Mississauga Senators and has spent the past two seasons with the Sudbury Wolves.

Pezzetta is a physical forward who loves to punish the opposition. Consistently game after game he is noted for finishing his checks hard all game long. He can play on the edge and sometimes doesn't really have the mentality to let up when an opponent has turned which results in some pretty questionable hits from time to time. He is the assistant captain of the Wolves and leads with his physical play and his aggressive nature. He provided a good two-way game working hard on the penalty kill and will block shots. Offensively his numbers do not impress, but he has some offensive ability and has shown a couple flashes of skill which we saw much more of in his Minor Midget days.

Michael has limited upside, but if he can continue to improve on his skills, he could become a depth player at the NHL level, getting some action in the bottom six. His skills are very well suited for a checking/two-way role as he does both very well already. However, he does not possess the skill to project as a top six forward at the NHL level and thus his stock should drop a little going into the 2016 NHL Entry Draft.

Quotable: "Hidden away up in Sudbury but a kid I have some time for. In a draft that falls off a cliff a bit earlier than other years, I wouldn't be surprised to see Pezzetta get selected. - Mark Edwards

Quotable: "Pezzetta or Givani, who you take?" - NHL Scout (March 2016)

Quotable: "Givani and it's really close for me." - Mark Edwards (answering question above)

Philips, Brock
RW/D - Guelph Storm (OHL) 6'05", 205
HockeyProspect.com Ranking: 207

Brock is a defenseman who converted to forward due to the depth on the back end for the Guelph Storm. He switched back and forth based on injuries. He was selected in the 5th round of the 2014 OHL Priority Selection Draft out of the Waterloo Wolves Minor Midget program.

Brock is an extremely physical imposing defender for the Guelph Storm. He has a great edge to his game and loves the physical contact. He is capable of crushing opponents and looks for any situation where he might be able to land a hit. He has a nasty mean streak down low in his own end as a defenseman, or in the corners of the offensive zone as a forward. He will punish opponents and we've seen some players take the long route to the puck when Philips is baring down on them in a race. Brock regularly challenges opponents physically and is fearless against any opponent. His skating isn't bad and usually comes along a little later in development for players of his size. Defensively he has pretty good positioning in one on one match-up's and is very tough to get around.

Brock projects as a shutdown defender with a nasty mean streak that players dread going up against. His upside is limited but he's a decent prospect as a depth defenseman at the NHL level after a few years of development. For this reason, we tend to think that Philips won't get passed over all seven rounds. We tend to see teams take flyers on these big guys who show they have something to bring to the next level. Philips has done a pretty good job to show off his strengths.

Phillips, Matthew
RC - Victoria Royals (WHL) 5'07", 140
HockeyProspect.com Ranking: 204

In his first full season in the WHL, Phillips took his game to the next level. He finished the year with 37 goals and 76 points winning the WHL Rookie of the Year award and finished first in the league with 10 game winning goals. Matthew is a dynamic offensive player who can impact the game with his vision, compete and puck skills. Although he is not overly big and will need time to mature physically, he plays with a high level of compete and does not back down in the high traffic areas.

Phillips is not an overly fast skater but possesses great balance and very good mobility. He has very quick feet and is a deceptive skater with a great ability to change directions on a dime. Along with his strong skating ability are his terrific puck skills. He can handle the puck at full speed as well controlling the puck along the wall and in the corners. Phillips is a very competitive player who has a great work ethic. However, when it comes to size and strength and the ability to win battles in the corner and on the wall, Phillips struggles at times and needs to work on this aspect of his game.

Phillips is a gifted playmaker; he has great vision and hockey IQ. He can read and react and see the play developing at a high level. He plays with his head on a swivel and can see all options and makes hard accurate passes. Phillips has always been a smaller player at every level and to his credit that has never stopped him from being a dominant player. He does need to work at putting more weight onto his frame and getting stronger in the offseason in order to improve his chances of making it at the next level.

Quotable: "Certainly shows the drive to get better and battle bigger players, I always liked his consistency, didn't have to many dry spells throughout the season, if he learns to be more slippery he has a lot of potential, I like that he's has scored at every level, carrying that into the WHL was big for me" - HP Scout Andy Levangie

Picard, Miguel
LC – Blainville-Boisbriand Armada (QMJHL) – 6'00", 175
HockeyProspect.com Ranking: NR

Picard didn't have the season that he had hoped for after taking part in the U-18 Canada summer camp in August. The St-Gabriel-de-Kamouraska native couldn't take the next step offensively and had a very limited impact points-wise with the Armada this season. His offensive production regressed from his rookie season and he started the year with zero goals in his first 31 games. The Armada were challenged offensively all season long and Picard had his chances, but never delivered offensively. His skating abilities have not improved enough, he's a smart player but he's not quick enough to take advantage of holes in the defensive zone. His shot is just average and he is often too slow to release it, which gives time for the opposing defense to react. He's good on the forecheck, protects the puck well and has a good work ethic. Defensively, he became a go-to guy for Joel Bouchard; who made him a key member of the Armada PK unit and always used him in key situations, including late in periods and games. He does a decent job in the faceoff circle and he's good at blocking shots and using his stick to block passing lanes.

Pickard, Reilly
Goaltender – Acadie-Bathurst Titans (QMJHL) – 5'11", 174
HockeyProspect.com Ranking: NR

Pickard was Acadie-Bathurst's #1 goalie this season, playing in 58 games during the regular season and all their playoff games. In our early viewings this season, he had a lot of problems with his rebound control and it cost him some bad goals. He made some nice improvements in the 2nd half of the season in this aspect. Pickard is a sound positional goaltender who is not often out of position and is calm in his crease. He does a fine job tracking pucks, but at his size, it could be an issue when teams crash the net or put a big forward in front of him on the power play. The Halifax native is a strong skater for a goaltender; he is agile in his crease and moves from post to post well. The big question mark with Pickard will be about his size for the next level. Generally, goaltenders fewer than six feet tall are not very popular with NHL teams, if recent history is anything to go by. His lack of size will probably hurt him for the draft; he will need to prove that he's a top goalie in the QMJHL for an NHL team to take a chance with him. This is just part of the reality that average-sized and small goaltenders have to deal with in this day and age.

Pilon, Garrett
RC – Kamloops Blazers (WHL) 5'10", 175
HockeyProspect.com Ranking: 205

The family bloodline runs deep for the 7th round 133rd overall pick in the WHL bantam draft. He has been a big part of the resurgence of a young Blazers team and will be going forward. The smallish frame that Pilon has is easily pushed around and he tends to avoid contact by staying in safer areas of the ice. Makes good cuts and is elusive on his edges but lacks a high-end speed and a separation gear to open up space, which would be a big asset for his above average offense.

Shot release is quick and has a fast snap to it making it difficult read with surprising quickness. Flat and accurate passer utilizes soft hands and good hockey IQ to set up teammates, often ends up playing the point on the powerplay to utilize the combination of quick shot and good passing when given open space around the top of offensive zone. Increased compete level and more physical push back would really help Pilon evolve at a scorer, has the hands and the IQ, but needs to work harder to attack the high percentage scoring areas.

Pitlick, Rem
LC – Muskegon Lumberjacks (USHL) 5'9.25", 196
HockeyProspect.com Ranking: 121

The Shattuck St. Mary's Product is in his 2nd Draft Eligible year after being passed over last season where he struggled in his USHL rookie season with Waterloo. Sometimes it takes a player an extra year to come into his own as a player and Rem Pitlick is a great example of that type of player. Pitlick who was traded to Muskegon, started the season playing on the Wing, then Muskegon Head Coach, Todd Krygier decided to move him to Center in an effort to get the puck on his stick more often and Pitlick's offensive production took off and he ended up running away with the USHL Scoring Title despite missing parts of the season for the U.S. Junior Select Team and the Top Prospect Game.

Rem isn't the biggest or most physical player on the ice but has very good hockey sense and is very skilled with the puck on his stick. His Vision of the ice allows him to move the puck quickly, he can take some risks with the puck in the neutral zone and coming out of his own end and going forward he will need to learn to simplify his game in those areas. While most Power Play's are ran from the point, in Muskegon the power play was ran through Pitlick on the half wall, he is extremely good at threading passes through the slot and creating space for himself and has a powerful and accurate release and isn't shy to drive the net.

Pitlick added close to 25 LBS to his frame since last season, which has allowed him to develop a more powerful skating stride that has added more pace to his game and allowed him to be stronger in the corners both with and without the puck. While Pitlick doesn't have the size of today's prototypical Centers at the professional level, we feel Pitlick's hockey sense, work ethic on and off the ice, skating ability and high end offensive skill provide a package that will be appealing to a lot NHL scouts.

Quotable: "He will get drafted for sure. He's a real thick strong heavy kid. Very strong on the puck for his size." - NHL Scout (February 2016)

Quotable: "I like his hockey sense. I know a lot of teams were going to see him, especially late in the season." - NHL Scout (April 2016)

Point, Colton
G - Carleton Place Canadians (CCHL) 6'03" 215
HockeyProspect.com Ranking: 113

Coming into the start of this year Colton was signed to come in as a backup goalie, and too compete with the starting goalie for the last 2 years for playing time. Colton quickly made his presence felt as the team traded away there starting goalie early in the season, anointing Colton as there #1 goalie and he didn't disappoint. He ended the year with a 23 wins 6 loses and a 2.16GAA and 0.915 SV%, with an impressive 12 wins in the playoffs and a 1.82 GAA average, which led to Carleton Place winning the league championship this year. Colton also suited up for team Canada East at the recent Jr.A challenge in Toronto this year.

Colton has very good size for a goaltender standing 6'3 215 lbs. He is very good with his angles and doesn't give opponents much room to shoot at, he covers the net really well if he's out to challenge the forward or on he's on his knees in the crease. He has good rebound control, he doesn't give any chances to opponents and if he did it was cleared by his defense, We would classified Colton as a positional goaltender which means there isn't a lot of movement in his crease, as he is always squared to the puck and allows the puck to hit him. Colton has a very calm and relaxed demeanor to him when in the nets; there isn't a whole lot panic in his game. He tracks the puck well and has good reflexes on tip shots or screened shots. We would like to see him be quicker with his feet down low as he can be a little slow at going post to post. We would like seeing more battle from him fighting through screens and tracking pucks from the point.

Colton will be attending Colgate University in 2017-2018 season, and with more coaching and more time developing i.e. getting stronger and quicker, he could develop into being a solid goaltender at the next level and having a good pro career.

Quotable:" Colton is a very calm and relaxed goaltender with no panic in his game, whether he needs to make a big save to keep the lead, or if its big save to keep his team in the game and give them a chance to win." HP Scout, Justin Sproule

Quotable:" He has really good size for a goaltender and covers most of the net, which gives opposition very little room to shoot at." - Mark Edwards

Quotable:" Would like to see him battle in the crease to track pucks a little more as he tends to rely on his size and angles to stop the puck." - HP Scout, Justin Sproule

Poirier, Zach
RC - North Bay Battalion (OHL) 5'11", 191
HockeyProspect.com Ranking: NR

Poirier was selected in the first round, 14th overall by the North Bay Battalion at the 2014 OHL Priority Selection Draft out of the Upper Canada Cyclones Minor Midget program. Poirier has been caught behind veterans on the Battalion depth chart but has spent the majority of this season as the Battalion third line centre.

Poirier is a gritty, two-way centre with some flashes of offensive upside to his game. Thus far in the OHL he's been known more for his agitating presence on the ice, Poirier has a bit of a stiff skating stride which affects his speed. Despite this he is an aggressive forechecking taking direct paths to the puck carrier. He consistently engages physically and separates opponents from puck. Poirier is very effective on the penalty kill, possessing good anticipation skills along with an active stick and a willingness to clog the shooting lanes, blocking shots effectively. He brings a high compete level and a consistent work ethic, Poirier may be slightly undersized but he has a nastiness to his game. While Poirier projects as a bottom six forward, he does display some intriguing offensive traits that allowed him to score 15 goals this season. Poirier packs a deceptively good shot that boasts impressive accuracy and subtle velocity. Poirier lacks vision and playmaking abilities, but has good hands that allows him to create scoring chances for himself.

Poirier doesn't possess enough offensive upside to be considered a potential top six prospect. However, what he does well is play a defensive and penalty killing role. Within that role he can create some offensive opportunities for himself in 5 on 5 situations. Ultimately he has low end reward as a bottom six defensive forward at the NHL level.

Polunin, Alexander
LW – Lokomotiv Yaroslavl (KHL) – 5'08", 161
HockeyProspect.com Ranking: NR

Polunin is a small winger that after showing improvements at the end of last year junior campaign suddenly broke through this season at the KHL level. He scored 7 goals in 25 regular season games playing alongside junior mates Korshkov and Kraskovsky, providing spark and energy to their line.

Polunin plays the game at a fast pace and has a quick understanding of his options. He can combine with his linemates but in the offensive zone he is more often than not focused on getting lanes to the net. He seems constantly ready to shoot as he moves towards the slot and it doesn't take much time for his dangerous right-handed shot to get off. Consistently brings the effort and competes hard in puck battles, partially making up for size limitations. His a good skater and seems to fit in high intensity games, but may not possess the talent level needed to have more than marginal NHL potential at his size.

Popugayev, Nikita O.
RW – Team Russia U18 (MHL) – 5'08", 152
HockeyProspect.com Ranking: NR

Popugayev is an undersized wing with skill who doesn't dominate shifts but can make a high-end play out of nowhere. He has a good nose for the net and we have noted in our viewings his ability to come up with key offensive plays at key times, even if injuries (along with not being allowed to take part at the U18 World Championships) have significantly reduced the sample.

Popugayev is obviously not going to be able to do much physically at his size, but he has some shiftiness to him. Although he isn't the one to hold onto the puck forever, he can make a quick shifty play that will throw the defense off and open up ice. He is a good playmaker that can hit a linemate with an unexpected pass and he also has a good sense for reading holes and finishing plays himself. He has good timing on rush plays, often he will do a good job getting open immediately after the other team commits a turnover. Regardless of where that happens, Popugayev is ready to pounce on the opportunity.

The lack of size is definitely a big limitation for Popugayev. He is also not the type that would tirelessly hound the puck-carrier. He prefers to anticipate possible ways where he could quickly create offense out of a turnover, but isn't a player that often goes out of his way to take the puck away from the other team. This along with the fact that overall, despite his good speed, he isn't terribly dynamic or the most involved in each of his shifts means that his chances of making it as the next small NHL forward are not very good.

Priskie, Chase
RD – Quinnipiac (ECAC) – 6'00", 185
HockeyProspect.com Ranking: 187

Chase posted some bigtime numbers for a freshman defenseman. Priskie is a great skater, it's at the NHL level right now. He loves the puck on his stick and likes to lug it up ice, he's able to gain the offensive zone or join the rush. He skates hard everywhere but I'm not sure if he gets himself in the play enough for our liking. We'd like to see him block shots and compete harder in one on one battles. Not sure his hockey IQ is where we would like to see it. At the end of the day we think Chase might just wind up being a player that would add to your depth on defense in the organization. Height listing of 6'0" seems generous by our eyes.

Pu, Cliff
RC - London Knights (OHL) 6'01.5" 192
HockeyProspect.com Ranking: 84

Pu was selected in the first round, 16th Overall at the 2014 OHL Priority Selection Draft by the Oshawa Generals out of the Toronto Marlboros Minor Midget program. After struggling a little to get acclimated to the OHL, Cliff was dealt to the London Knights in the deal that sent Dakota Mermis and Michael McCarron to the Oshawa Generals. Pu struggled gaining icetime and then suffered an injury that may have set him back. When he returned to the Knights line up he got his speed to another level which really helped him move up the depth chart.

Pu has fantastic speed and great acceleration. If he has a little space when receiving the puck he will take off up the ice and can carry the puck end to end with ease. He seems to struggle with the confidence to take the puck to the net. There were times when we did see him take the puck to the net and he created some good scoring chances with an aggressive drive, but he doesn't do it often. Most of his offense gets created off the rush. We would like to see Pu play a little more aggressive style of game. He is very inconsistent when engaging in battles and generally will not use his size to win the battle and will rely on stick work.

The key to Pu's game is his speed. If he was able to utilize it more aggressively on the rush and was harder to play against, it could really help him get to the next level. The concern is his offensive inconsistencies that may keep him out of a top six role at the NHL level. The lack of grit and playing with an edge limits his effectiveness in a bottom six role. We've seen him play a lot. Pu is opportunistic and gets scoring chances, the problem is that too often he doesn't bury his chances. This hurts his top six value and his draft stock for us.

Quotable: "He's a late rounder." - NHL Scout (November 2015)

Quotable: "I like the speed but his hockey sense isn't there." - NHL Scout (February 2016)

Quotable: "He was actually good when I saw him last month but he's not good today." - NHL Scout (February 2016)

Quotable: "He's got some positives in his game. His speed is good and he forechecks hard. I can see him going in the late 2nd range." - NHL Scout (March 2016)

Quotable: "I'll give him credit. He's made progress in his game." - NHL Scout (March 2016)

Quotable: "I think he's Rico Fata. Rico was faster but both lack in the hockey sense department." - NHL Scout (March 2016)

Quotable: "He lacks some hockey sense and I don't think he's a good enough scorer for top six in the NHL and he isn't a bottom six type of player." - NHL Scout (May 2016)

Quotable: "What is all this first round talk about? I have him as mid rounder." - NHL Scout (May 2016)

Quotable: "I didn't think he was even draft worthy in November. Now he's on my list." - NHL Scout (May 2016)

Quotable: "I really liked Pu a lot early on in his OHL Draft year but liked him less as the season progressed. Since that time, Pu has improved and I like him as an OHL player. I don't personally see big NHL upside. Someone asked me if he was the next

Christian Dvorak, I don't think they are even close. Dvorak played 4th line and showed top six skill before he was sidelined by injury. Pu has got good icetime for months and is not in Dvorak's league as a scorer or a playmaker. We ranked Dvorak 32nd overall. Pu won't be that high on our list. As for NHL Scouts I spoke to about Pu, a couple guys told me he wasn't on their list, a few others had him as a mid rounder. - HP Scout Mark Edwards

Quotable: "His interview was really good. He's a smart kid and he knows his game. He knows he has a rep of being soft and is trying to play harder and thinks he's improving. He told us he knows it's important because he probably doesn't have enough scoring to be a top six guy in the NHL." - NHL Scout (Combine week)

Quotable: "Multiple scouts liked him in the interview process and gave me very similar feedback. I thought the info I got from Pu's interviews was interesting. He pretty much summed up how we see him. It's a good sign that he is self aware as it gives him a much better chance of succeeding. Big props to the kid." - HP Scout Mark Edwards

Puljujärvi, Jesse
RW – Kärpät (Liiga) – 6'03.5", 203
HockeyProspect.com Ranking: 3

Jesse was not very effective in the first part of his season in the top Finnish league and for a while it looked like his development was stalling, struggling to take another step forward after a very promising 2014-2015 season. The World Junior Championships played in his home country were the turning point of his season. He had a tremendous tournament on a line with S.Aho and Laine, was the top scorer and voted MVP of the competition on top of winning the gold medal with his team. Puljujarvi was much better along the rest of the Liiga, was one of the best players on his team and almost a point per game player in the playoffs.

This very talented Finn brings to the game a rare blend of power, skills and commitment. He is quick for a big kid and is an impressive skater who uses his speed to impact the play in different ways. He can be very effective on the forecheck, leaving defensemen little time to escape pressure. He can jump on loose pucks in high traffic areas and quickly recognize what's the best available play. He can be a one on one threat attacking the offensive blueline with the puck as he likes to challenge opponents. Jesse is not a pure goal scorer but he has a terrific shot. His wrister is fairly accurate and has a lot of zip, he also possesses a very powerful one-timer that he can put to work from the left side on the powerplay.

Puljujarvi has good hands and even if his puck control is not always flawless he comes away with it most of the time thanks to his very good instincts. He probably won't be too much of a puck carrier at the NHL level, but he is able to get his scoring chances in different ways. He is a competitive kid with very good vision and legit playmaking ability in the offensive zone. As a fast player who reads the game well and works hard in all three zones, he brings a two-way presence that is not often provided by young offensive wingers.

When he is on top of his game Jesse plays with high intensity and he'll probably need to do just that to be really effective at the NHL level. He has responded nicely in big games this season, but is not easy to consistently bring that kind of effort over an 82 games regular season. However, after Karpat playoff run was over Puljujarvi answered the call of his U18 national team even if reportedly not 100% and was still able to be as much of a difference maker as expected at the U18 Worlds, taking care of some unfinished business from last season and leading Finland to another gold medal after eliminating the US team in the semifinal.

Quotable: "All signs point to a very solid forward with a long NHL career. He's a work-horse. In some viewings, I thought he could finish a bit better in the offensive zone, but that's the only negative I had in my notes and that's nitpicking." - HP Scout Nik Funa

Quotable: "Almost feel like he's been the forgotten man of late and been beaten up a bit. This kid is a very good player." - HP Scout Mark Edwards

Quenneville, David
RD – Medicine Hat Tigers (WHL) 5'08", 182
HockeyProspect.com Ranking: 145

Quenneville is undersized, offensive defenseman who can put up very good offensive numbers. Quenneville finished the year with 14 goals and 41 assists for 55 points with the Medicine Hat Tigers this season. One of his strengths is his ability to get shots off and get shots on net. He is very poised on the offensive blue line with a great ability to sell the shot, fake out the defender and move to a better, open shooting lane. He loves to shoot the puck and uses his good stick handling abilities and lateral skating to elude defenders and get pucks to the net.

He makes a very good first pass because of his ability to handle the puck under pressure and escape ability as a defenseman. He has good vision which allows him to use his skating and puck handling skills to put him in a good position to move the puck. He also likes to engage offensively and likes to jump up in the rush. Quenneville does not shy away from the physical aspect of the game and likes to lay a big hit or throw a hip check on an unsuspecting forward when needed. When looking at him we feel that he needs to work on becoming stronger so that he can handle the one on one battles in his own zone at the next level.

We feel that David has decent potential but needs some time to continue to develop different aspects of his game. He brings good leadership and a high compete level and has high end offensive abilities but can be too aggressive at times which can lead to mistakes. His lack of size is also an apparent issue.

Raaymakers, Joseph
G - Sault Ste. Marie Greyhounds (OHL) 6'00.25", 185
HockeyProspect.com Ranking: 208

Raaymakers was selected in the second round of the 2014 OHL Priority Selection Draft by the Sault Ste. Marie Greyhounds out of the Chatham-Kent Cyclones Minor Midget Program. Despite being a 16 year old rookie drafted by a contending team, Raaymakers appeared in 27 games; one less than this season.

Raaymakers is on the lower spectrum of the desired size for an NHL goaltender. He has good reflexes and reacts quickly to chances in the offensive zone. Although he had a few mental lapses with the puck, he is active playing the puck and usually makes a good play. Joseph is the type of goaltender who can get off to a rough start but will get better as the game progresses. A lot of times we saw Raaymakers, the majority of goals allowed came in the first 10-15 minutes. He has a tendency to let in a bad goal a game but recovers from it and doesn't let it snowball on him. His glove hand is a little sporadic at times. Raaymakers was on NHL scouts watch lists this year, but isn't a goaltender that we are that high on. Goalies are generally later developing and although Raaymakers was highly touted coming out of Minor Midget, he will need to continue to progress and develop in order to reach that potential.

Quotable: "Hasn't been very good when I've seen him. Not on my list." - NHL Scout (February 2016)

Quotable: "I haven't spoken to many scouts about him this season but the ones I did speak to didn't have him on their lists. Small sample size but it meshes with my opinion." - Mark Edwards

Raddysh, Taylor
LC - Erie Otters (OHL) 6'02", 203
HockeyProspect.com Ranking: 46

Raddysh was selected 19th overall in the 2014 OHL Priority Selection Draft by the Erie Otters. Raddysh made a good impact on the Otters' third line as a 16 year old during their Western Conference Championship run providing good work ethic and a little offense to their bottom six.

Raddysh is a smart two-way winger who can contribute in a variety of ways without being dominant in any one area. Taylor has good hockey sense and can create offense for his linemates. He sees his linemates well and makes slick passes to help set up scoring chances. He does a good job getting into position to score, but doesn't have high-end finishing ability and will sometimes miss on his chances. He can put the puck in the net but sometimes lacks confidence in his shot and will pass off instead. He has a great awareness to get behind defenders, but lacks the skating ability to separate. If anything his skating seemed to take a step back this year as he added onto his frame from the previous season. He will need to get it to a place where he can separate and exploit the opposition with his awareness. He has a good sized frame and battles along the wall. He has a good work ethic and competes hard despite lacking ideal skating ability. Defensively he is very competitive and will do what it takes to win including blocking shots, taking the hit to make the play and getting into lanes to break up chances.

Raddysh could be a bit of a sleeper in this draft. His inability to finish on chances where he has had great opportunities to score and his skating have been the biggest concerns for us, but both could be developed over the next few years. What can't be developed is his hockey sense, awareness to exploit holes in the defense and his ability to get open in the offensive zone. He is a competitive player who could work his way into a lower end top six role, but has the two-way game and enough talent to make a solid third line forward at the next level.

Quotable: "I think he passes up way too many chances to finish his checks. His skating scares me too." - NHL Scout (November 2015)

Quotable: "I actually like the little guy Maksimovich more than him." - NHL Scout (November 2015)

Quotable: "I didn't like his numbers while his buddies were away at World Juniors." - NHL Scout (January 2016)

Quotable: "I liked what I saw last season but he slid a bit for me this year. He had quite a few games where I really had to look for him." - Mark Edwards

Rasanen, Aapeli
RC – Tappara U20 (FIN) – 6'00", 196
HockeyProspect.com Ranking: 135

In the 2014-15 season Rasanen made Tappara's U20 team and played in a defensive role. This season, Aapeli took a step forward and played a big role with significant minutes every game. Rasanen had a reasonably productive season putting up 39 points in 53 games. He was always a solid defensive player with a good compete level, but his offense has steadily come along as the season moved forward, culminating with his performance at the U18s in North Dakota where he was a big part of Finland's gold medal team.

Rasanen is a hard-working right-shot two-way center who plays a sound game in the defensive zone and doesn't mind sacrificing his body to make plays, as he is willing to engage in one and one battles. He's got an active defensive stick, can cause turnover and is a quite good penalty killer.

Rasanen's skating is only average, he can bring the puck up ice and has good enough vision to make plays. His puck skills are just OK and despite the improvement in his offensive game it is more realistic to project him as a checking forward at the next level, as he lacks a dynamic element to his game. Rasanen can however be dangerous around the net and possesses a variety of shots: has a good wrist-shot that he can get up high, a quick snap-shot or a one-timer which we've seen him score with on the PP.

Going back to the start of the year, we have liked Rasanen as a defensive player at the Hlinka Memorial Tournament in August, but in the second part of the season he has found ways to produce and has looked more confident with each passing month. While we are still a bit skeptical of his upside as an offensive player, that has certainly increased his chances on draft day.

Quotable: "I remember watching him back at Hlinka and liking his defensive game and two-way compete, but thinking there wasn't much there offensively. His offensive confidence then got better and better throughout the year and in watching some tape of U18s in North Dakota, it's clear he has come a long way" - HP Scout Nik Funa

Rathgeb, Yannick
RD – Fribourg-Gotteron (NLA) – 6'01", 200
HockeyProspect.com Ranking: NR

After two seasons spent in the OHL with the Plymouth Whalers, Rathgeb returned to Switzerland and enjoyed a breakthrough season of sort, finishing with 9 goals and 27 points in 50 NLA games, good enough to be the 4th best offensive producer on his team, recording more than twice the points of the next defenseman. A right-handed shooter, Yannick thrived on the powerplay, where he showcased his terrific shot and good puckhandling ability. He is able to move the puck along the offensive blueline to find lanes to the net. But his offensive contribution was noticeable at even strength as well. He plays a rather ambitious game, likes to anticipate the play in the neutral zone and join the offense, moving without the puck into open space towards the net, especially down the right side. He's been picking his spots better than during his North American seasons, but sometimes still gets caught out of position. Has a good passing game, often looks for long breakout passes from the defensive zone and is able to hit rushing forwards even from his goal line.

Rathgeb doesn't mind physical contact, but could be stronger on the puck and should rise his intensity in the defensive end. Comparing with the past he cut down on the number of unnecessary penalties, but it seems he's still looking for the right balance between discipline and physical game.

As a late '95 born who has already gone un-drafted twice coming off OHL seasons, it's hard to see him getting selected this time around, but Yannick took a big step this year and already played some games with the senior national team as a 20yrs old defenseman.

Reichel, Kristian
RC – HC Litvinov (CZE) – 6'01", 167
HockeyProspect.com Ranking: 186

Reichel is a diligent center who has a decent if lanky frame-size, a big shot and plays a mature game. Strong in the face-off circles. Reichel has shown a high IQ through his decisions. Most of his appearances this season were for Litvinov U20 but he also appeared in 20 games for the men's team in the top Czech league.

Reichel makes smart reads when opening up for pucks and can also distribute the puck well, while not being terribly flashy. He's got a nice frame-size that has some filling out to do, looks good when handling the puck at speed with his reach even if he doesn't possess high-end skills. Reichel likes to use his slapshot. On the PP he can let it rip from the left-circle with his right shot. He likes to use his slapper at even strength as well, and has show good power and accuracy behind it with a slowly rising shot that gets through. Compete level is not an issue but he could improve his ability to maintain possession in the offensive-zone and get his frame more involved on the cycle while establishing offensive zone control. Has some strong hockey bloodlines in him; father is IIHF Hockey Hall of Fame forward Robert Reichel.

Reichenbacher, Grant
RC – Edgewood H.S./Team Wisconsin U18 (WI-HS) 5'11", 165
HockeyProspect.com Ranking: NR

Grant is one of the youngest players eligible for this year's draft, with a birthday landing on 9/9/98, just a junior in High School; we feel Reichenbacher was the best player in Wisconsin Prep Hockey in 15/16 season and is starting to gather interest from a lot of D1 College Programs. Reichenbacher is a pure goal scorer and will take them however they come to him. He scored 36 Goals in 21 high School games in 15/16 and racked up 61 Points, In addition to 7 Goals and 7 Assists in 21 Games for Team Wisconsin U18. Grant is as smart as they come in the offensive zone, he knows where to be, he has a knack of finding the puck on his stick at the right time and has the shot and skill to finish more often than not. Displays good hands, good vision of the ice and the ability to know where his teammates are on the ice. Reichenbacher is far from a physical presents on the ice, and while he is elusive with the puck and does a good job avoiding contact, there are times where it was unavoidable and he was blown off the puck rather easily so there is a lot of strengthening and developing in that area of his game, but his offensive gifts and skating are very good. Grant was a recent draft pick of Lincoln (USHL) in the Phase 2 Draft and has a good shot at making that team this fall. While we don't expect Grant to be taken in this NHL draft, given his overall talent, He is a prospect we will be following close in the next couple years as a possible overage pick.

Quotable: "Was the most dominate player in Wisconsin High School hockey all season long, has a full arsenal in the offensive zone that allowed him to put up Monster numbers both for his prep team and Team Wisconsin, I don't expect him to be drafted but I will follow him close next season in the USHL." - HP Scout Dusten Braaksma

Repo, Sebastian
LW – Pelicans (FEL) – 6'02", 189
HockeyProspect.com Ranking: NR

Repo is a third time eligible who finally showed his potential this year. In 2014-15 he spent half of the season in the USHL playing 25 games and scoring 15 points. After returning to Finland he was ready to take the next step in his development. This season he had a big role on his Liiga team and played significant minutes every night. He scored 28 points in 50 games which is a great output for a 19 year old kid playing against men. Sebastian is a tall winger with adequate mobility. He isn't afraid of anything and likes to get his nose dirty. Plays a decent two way game and has some offensive potential. Possesses a hard and accurate shot which he likes to use. Good around corners and can really grind. He can play a variety of different roles and still be effective in all three zones, but his skill level doesn't seem high enough to have top 6 potential.

Reunanen, Tarmo
LD – TPS (Fin U20) – 6'00", 178
HockeyProspect.com Ranking: NR

During the season 2014-15, he was considered among the top defensive talents from Finland for the 2016 Draft. His rookie season in the U20 league was in fact remarkable and he was among the top of the class in the whole league. There were big expectations for Reunanen this season, but an early injury kept him out for almost 6 months. He played only 13 games but luckily returned for the post season. Ultimately he didn't receive an invite to the U18 WC camp even though he was healthy.

Despite the fact that this whole season was a big setback, Reunanen is still a solid defensive prospect. He's a d-man with good offensive tools and smooth skating with an average frame-size. He can be an effective player in all three zones since he got great hockey sense and reads the play well. Despite the smaller size he is quite sturdy and more than willing to engage physically. Before the season, he was named captain of his team at the age of 17, which tells how appreciated the kid is in Turku.

Reynolds, Keenan
LW - Flint Firebirds (OHL) 6'01", 205
HockeyProspect.com Ranking: NR

Keenan showed a lot of promise with the Ottawa Jr. 67's and was selected in the 4th round by the Owen Sound Attack at the 2014 OHL Priority Selection Draft. Reynolds made the Attack, but consistently being healthy scratched and playing very little didn't help him get better heading into this season. A mid season trade to the Flint Firebirds seemed to help him.

Reynolds has good size and a great frame. He has a good release on his shot, which has power and moderate accuracy. He has a good compete level and will battle for pucks. He will finish his check and played aggressive at times. During limited offensive opportunities he showed some creativity distributing the puck. He competes in all three zones. Defensively he showed good shot blocking ability, he also has a great stick, but needs to work on his ability to clear the defensive zone. Reynolds skating is below average and looks a little sluggish. It will need to improve before he can take the next step in his career.

Reynolds is still an intriguing prospect. He has desirable size, some offensive upside, and can be very tough to play against. He also showed signs of good two-way ability that could help him translate to the next level. While we don't expect to hear his name called at the 2016 NHL Entry Draft, he is a player with potential and could be primed for a breakout season in 2016-2017.

Quotable: "Went to Owen Sound, nothing there this year." - NHL Scout (October 2015)

Quotable: "A player that our scout Ryan Yessie liked a lot coming out of AAA, but probably hasn't quite had things go according to plan so far." - Mark Edwards

Riat, Damien
RW – Genève-Servette (NLA) – 6'00", 170
HockeyProspect.com Ranking: 182

Riat is a versatile forward who has been looking much stronger and consistent in his efforts than in his draft year, when he played a rather disappointing season in Sweden with Malmo J20 team. He did show some glimpses of his qualities in parts of Switzerland's games at the U18 World Championships in Zug, but some good moments there were not enough to earn consideration for the NHL draft. This season he returned to his Swiss club after three years and was able to produce at a 0.5 PPG pace at the NLA level. Damien took regular shifts on the powerplay where he showed the ability to cover different positions and to move the puck quickly. He is a good passer who can immediately spot the open linemate and execute through lanes to reach him even with a one-time pass. Sometimes he could use more patience on the powerplay, but he is calm enough to explore his options when he gets the puck in the neutral zone. In the offensive zone he tries not to leave the defense much time to adjust and is a good shooter.

Riat is a mobile player who can get open without the puck and likes to go to the front of the net. His strong skating also helps him being an effective backchecker. Considering he doesn't lack a physical dimension in his game and he finishes his checks regularly, the '97 born Swiss is projecting to become quite the complete player. Even if he looks much more mature than last season, sometimes he still looks green in puck battles, something that should obviously improve as he keeps gaining more experience at the pro level.

Riat may not possess top 6 offensive upside and his WJC national team ending up in the relegation round in what was his only chance to impress on the international stage probably didn't help his case, but he would be worthy of a draft selection.

Rifai, Marshall
LD - Hotchkiss School (HS Conn) 5'11.75, 180
HockeyProspect.com Ranking: 210

You want to talk speed? This kid has it. He is an elite skater in every category. Not overly big but a tough kid who competes hard. Like many players were not high on, he lacks hockey sense. That coupled with poor to average pucks skills is enough that he wouldn't be on our draft list. Rifai is a very competitive player with a high will to win. He will need to learn to channel his competitive nature at times to make others around him better. His best attribute is his skating as not only does he have quick feet, but also a long, powerful stride. He is able to break a puck out and lead the rush, and still be the first man back.

Quotable: "Multiple scouts noted his elite speed but his hockey sense is very poor. Very raw player with some upside." - HP Scout Mark Edwards

Rhodes, Kyle
RD - Guelph Storm (OHL) 6'02", 210
HockeyProspect.com Ranking: NR

Rhodes is a big physical defensive defenseman who provided depth to the Guelph Storm blueline this year.

Kyle is a big bodied defender and mixes it up in the corner. His best results this season came in physical situations either landing a big hit in open ice, or winning battles along the boards. His one on one play is hit or miss. He uses the body and the stick effectively, but got beat one on one a little too much for a shutdown defender. Although he's not much of an offensive defenseman, his puck skills are well below average and struggled to complete passes, often resulting in icings or turnovers. This combined with sporadic defensive play out weighed his good physical tools and mindset, thus he is not considered a prospect for us at the 2016 NHL Entry Draft.

Ronning, Ty
RW – Vancouver (WHL) 5'09", 163
HockeyProspect.com Ranking: 159

A high pick in the 2012 WHL bantam draft it took until the 2015/16 season for Ronning to be given an opportunity to shine as a front line player receiving prime minutes. With that being said, he's been an important energy player for the Vancouver Giants going back to the Don Hay era. Ronning was an injury addition to the CHL top prospects game and although it was one game he performed quite well there.

Ronning attacks the middle of ice and plays a fearless game despite his lack of size. His first three steps are fast smooth and bring him up to speed quickly. He weaves through traffic as an elusive skater using a wide stance for stability. Ronning has strong hands that show good puck control and he uses them effectively through speed changes. The pucks look like they stick to his blade highlighting his control.

Ronning fights well through high traffic areas and avoids getting rubbed out. He shoots the puck in stride with a quick wrist shot, which is his most effective shot. He has really soft hands in tight areas and both his backhand and forehand rise quickly when looking to score in tight. Finally, he's a clutch scorer who plays competitively regardless of the score. Size concerns effect Ronning's draft stock but his compete level is quite good, he looks consistently engaged in the game, is always involved the play and showed a lot of fire throughout a lost season in Vancouver.

Rossini, Samuel
LD – Waterloo Black Hawks (USHL) 6'03", 198
HockeyProspect.com Ranking: NR

He is a solid athletically built defenseman who can skate well and does a great job at winning battles and getting the puck out of his own end. Rossini is finishing up his 2nd season with the Waterloo Black Hawks, and while his offensive contribution has failed to progress, he has rounded out the other aspects of his game well.

Rossini does an excellent job with his stick at both blue lines and is able to use his reach to challenge plays without losing positioning. He is really strong on his skates and can deliver big hits both in the open ice and on the boards. Rossini skates well enough to bring the puck up the ice and elude fore checkers but at this stage lacks the creative playmaking ability and skill to be a real threat offensively, he does however possess a powerful shot from the point. Samuel can run your breakout effectively and provide good shut down minutes on the backend and is good on the Penalty Kill. Rossini will join a solid defensive core at The University of Minnesota in the fall.

Quotable: "I wish he played with some jam." – NHL Scout (April 2016)

Rubins, Kristians
LD – VIK Västerås (SWE Jr.) – 6'04", 216
HockeyProspect.com Ranking: NR

Rubins is a big Latvian defender who has been developing in the Swedish junior leagues over the past few years. He had some promising showings last season, but his draft year didn't go as well as hoped.

After missing a few months to injury to start the season, he had some disappointing performances at the U20 Div.1 World Championships in December, in fact he did better in the same competition the year before as a double underager. It's easy to see the potential in Rubins looking at how his huge frame can move with the puck, but the lack of pulse and progress in his game has been frustrating. Has moments where he shows he can make plays and remind you of his upside, but overall didn't show much drive in our viewings this year. His mobility becomes less impressive when he is not the one carrying the puck and needs to react to opponents instead. Even if he shows some spurts moving forward with the puck on his stick, his cut-short stride needs work and he gets beaten to pucks by quick forwards. Rubins has good balance and takes advantage of his size to punish forwards here and there, but his physical game and his efforts engaging in battles are inconsistent. He shows a willingness to join the rush along with some offensive instincts and can read the play in the offensive zone. His hands could use some further polishing to take full advantage of those attributes, but from the blueline he can execute good passes and owns a powerful slap shot.

A late '97 born, Rubins seems far from putting it together, but still possesses an intriguing toolset to work on. Positioning and gap control are among other things he could improve, but more than anything else he will have to show more competitiveness moving forward. An NHL team might very well take a chance on that given his overall package and two-way potential.

Rubtsov, German
LC – Team Russia U18 (MHL) – 6'0.5", 178
HockeyProspect.com Ranking: 16

As a 16yrs old Rubtsov had a secondary role at last year U18 Worlds and didn't shine offensively, but this season he was put on center stage as the leader of Russian national team and was able to thrive in the bigger role. Unfortunately, to prevent the risk of testing positive to meldonium him and his teammates were prevented from taking part at this year event, but the fact he had already been able to impress on North American soil at the WJAC may help his case.

Rubtsov improved in different areas this year, he has looked more dynamic in his skating and more comfortable on the powerplay, showing he can efficiently dictate the play with the man advantage as well. At this point, there aren't many flaws left in his game. He is the kind of player who seems to be always around the puck. His sense for the game paired with the work ethic he shows on the ice allows him to be consistently involved in the play, no matter if his team has possession or not. The way he pursues the puck time after time is impressive and his relentless backchecking through the neutral zone is often successful, when he targets and chases the puck carrier he is usually able to catch-up and engage sooner or later. He is a workhorse with an active stick that he uses to disrupt opponents' plays on a consistent basis in just about every area of the ice.

When his team has the puck, Rubtsov is always there to support his linemates and keep the play alive. He has the puck protection ability and the stickhandling to gain time and make plays. He can drive the net, play an up-tempo game with great intensity, or slow it down when he feels the need in the neutral zone or he looks for options in the offensive zone. He has very good hands and is a smart passer able to take advantage of his strong vision. His offensive numbers may not be overly impressive, but need to be put in the perspective of his all around work, he does the heavy lifting for his linemates making them better and plays a lot on the penalty kill as well.

German doesn't possess blazing acceleration, but is a strong overall skater, with nice balance and a powerful motor that can generate good speed. He has a legit shot that he should probably use more. We would have liked to see him finish a bigger percentage of the scoring chances he had in our viewings, but that doesn't seem enough not to consider him top-6 material. As a two-way center that projects to be relied in all situations he will probably need to improve in the faceoff circle, though. All in all, Rubtsov is a rare blend of skills, tenacity and hockey IQ, a prospect that has the likes of a terrific player in the making.

Quotable: "Loved his defensive game and work-ethic, but it took me half a year to be convinced on his offensive upside. Initially, I was very skeptical that he'd be anything more than just an ok #3 center, though I would still have liked to have him on my team. The more I watched and the more I thought about it, I realized that he's just a kid who gets it done against whatever opposition you put him up against. I have him as a #2 or a high-end 3rd center now." - HP Scout Nik Funa

Quotable: "It's rare to see a 17 year old skilled center play such a mature, all around game. Rubtsov just drives puck possession for his team." - HP Scout Mik Portoni

Quotable: "Even Don Cherry will like the way this Russian prospect plays the game." - HP Scout Mark Edwards

Quotable: "Interview was ok. Tough because it was through a translator and he gave a lot of one word answers." - NHL Scout (Combine week)

Rymsha, Drake
RC - Ottawa 67's (OHL) 5'11", 187
HockeyProspect.com Ranking: NR

Rymsha was selected in the 5th round by the London Knights. Rymsha played a good depth role for the London Knights. A smart defensive forward, Rymsha was able to provide a safe role for a young prospect in the bottom six for the Knights. As London began to see a bigger logjam in their line-up, Rymsha was dealt to the Ottawa 67's. Unfortunately he broke his femur and missed over half this season.

Rymsha is a solid, reliable two-way forward who works as hard in the defensive zone as he does anywhere else on the ice. He has good defensive zone positioning and knows when to pressure the opposition and has been able to force turnovers and clear the zone. He is a reliable penalty killer but doesn't possess much offensive upside. He makes good passes on the rush but can get himself into trouble when trying to do too much with the puck. He has a decent shot and decent passing ability but nothing above average offensively. He agitates the opposition very well getting under their skin and forcing them to take penalties. He is pretty good in the face-off circle winning the majority of his draws. Although Rymsha has been through a lot, he isn't a prospect we expect to be drafted at the 2016 NHL Entry Draft. He is a solid two-way forward at the junior level but doesn't project well for the NHL.

Quotable: "I admire his work ethic but he doesn't seem to have the hockey smarts I look for. He wouldn't be on my draft list." - Mark Edwards

Ryczek, Jake
RD - Waterloo (USHL) 5'10", 181
HockeyProspect.com Ranking: 194

Jake Ryczek is another undersized defenseman in this draft who possesses excellent hockey sense and puck moving ability. Jake is a product of the South Kent School and Selects Academy in New England and is committed to Providence College. Ryczek rarely makes mental errors or commits turnovers that cost his team. He has the ability to stretch the ice with excellent breakout passing ability and can find forwards in the neutral zone from his own end or can skate the puck up ice and into the offensive zone. He makes really good tape to tape passes on the breakout and in the offensive zone.

Ryczek is able to use his skating to always be in good defensive position; he is extremely difficult to get around the edge on because of his footwork and positioning, even against bigger power forwards. Jake will not deliver punishing open ice checks but uses his body well along the wall to separate players from the puck, then his first couple strides allow him to get the puck going North Quickly.

In the current climate of the game where hockey sense, foot speed and skating are at a paramount, we wouldn't be surprised to see a team use a pick on Ryczek.

Quotable: "Every time I watch him play, Jared Spurgeon comes to mind." - NHL Scout (April 2016)

Quotable: "He is near the top of my list when it comes to undersized defenseman in this draft, his hockey IQ and puck moving ability is fun to watch." - HP Scout Dusten Braaksma

Quotable: "Our scout in Wisconsin (Dusten) and I disagree on this player. I like his speed and he does a pretty good job on puck retrievals, but he's a smallish kid who lacks some strength. The biggest reason I slide him is I don't think he's a very smart player. Too many turnovers and I don't see structure to his game." - HP Scout Mark Edwards

Rykov, Yegor
LD – SKA St. Petersburg (KHL) – 6'02", 205
HockeyProspect.com Ranking: 181

Rykov is an agile Russian defenseman who was passed over at last year draft despite being a more than legit candidate. NHL teams may have not found a special quality in his game to make them forget about his passport, but a year later Rykov is still making a good case for himself. Appeared in 12 KHL games as an 18yrs old and was a reliable presence in the defensive zone for Russia at the WJC. Yegor was used in all situations and showed improvements in his game at the offensive blueline, making good reads and completing some nice passes.

Rykov is a very active player. He is really quick putting pressure on forwards along the boards, competes and engages even if he doesn't bring a punishing physical dimension. Has the wheels to keep up with skilled forwards, his stride could be better but overall skating is a strength. He can react quickly, is alert when covering the slot and has good timing when blocking shots. He is a player that works hard to gain possession and doesn't give it up easily, he can manage the puck under forecheckers' pressure and seems to have developed a strong passing game. He may need to add more power to be effective playing his game along the boards at the next level, but has a legit chance to develop into a dependable defenseman at the pro level.

Saigeon, Brandon
LC - Hamilton Bulldogs (OHL) 6'01", 197
HockeyProspect.com Ranking: 146

Saigeon was a highly touted player out of Minor Midget selected fourth overall by the Belleville Bulls out of the Hamilton Jr. Bulldogs. He had a decent rookie season in Belleville and looked primed to elevate his game following his first season. However, he struggled early on in the season and as he was gaining a little momentum in his play he suffered an injury.

Saigeon has good size and has quick hands. He shows off his skill on the rush making a lot of smart plays choosing the right lanes and dishing the puck off at appropriate times. He is effective in the neutral zone without the puck and will quickly transition up ice if he can force a turnover. He makes a lot of smart, low difficulty plays that helps advance the play and doesn't challenge the opposition often. Saigeon provides good two-way ability and competes hard in the defensive zone. He's also not afraid to get down and block shots. Brandon has good tools on his side, good hands, decent skating but hasn't really shown higher end offensive ability. He's not a player who makes a lot of mistakes, but he has struggled to finish on scoring chances and doesn't make higher end plays.

Brandon has some lower end upside at the next level. If he was to make the NHL it would be as a bottom six two-way forward who helps out in his own end and makes smart simple plays to higher skilled forwards. With that said, Brandon's lack of higher end skill may prevent him from hearing his name called at the 2016 NHL Entry Draft.

Salinitri, Anthony
LC - Sarnia Sting (OHL) 5'10.25", 168
HockeyProspect.com Ranking: NR

Salinitri was selected 17th overall by the Sault Ste. Marie Greyhounds at the 2014 OHL Priority Selection Draft out of the Windsor Jr. Spitfires Minor Midget program. Salinitri played a limited role on a contending Greyhounds team as a 16 year old before being dealt to Sarnia in a deal involving Anthony DeAngelo. Salinitri's ice fluctuated game by game, playing generally on the second or third line.

Salinitri is a smooth skating forward who has decent offensive ability. He does a good job of quickly getting to loose pucks and is an opportunistic forward who will jump on his chances and show flashes of skill. For the most part, Salinitri skates a lot of miles on a night by night basis, but will keep it in the centre of the ice appearing very disengaged with the play. On other nights, he was a little more tenacious and battled for pucks a more frequently. Adding strength will be necessary for Anthony before thinking about going the professional route. He has the tools to both score and set up scoring chances, but these have been shown in flashes, and have not been a consistent part of his game.

Salinitri was known for his offensive ability in Minor Midget but has shown a reluctance at the OHL level to do some of the dirty work and has been very inconsistent over numerous viewings. If Salinitri can consistently play an aggressive game and get involved in the offense on a more consistent basis he may be a player who still has some NHL upside in him. Right now he looks like a player who should develop into a decent, average sized junior player.

Salituro, Dante
RC - Ottawa 67's (OHL) 5'08.25", 175
HockeyProspect.com Ranking: NR

Dante was coming off his best season with the 67's last year, but was passed over in last year NHL Draft. This year he finished the year with 83 points, which led his team. He ended the year with 38 goals and 45 assists. He has been a very consistent point producer in his OHL career, Dante's biggest challenge is working away from the puck.

He is a decent skater who gets going fairly quickly, but lacks that separation speed he needs to pull away from defenders. He can create a lot of offense coming in of the rush or with his quick first 2 steps. He is good at stickhandling the puck at top speed and making plays at top speed. He has a good release to his shot and has good ability to shoot the puck without getting set, with good accuracy towards the net. He has ability to control the puck in tight corners or along the half-wall on the power play. Dante would be considered a shoot first player. He has decent hockey sense and understands the offensive side of the game. Through our viewings he needs to be quicker with his decisions making, as he sometimes takes too long to make a decisions and forces the puck into bad areas. He is good at reading plays and reacting to them to create turnovers and transition on offense. In our viewings Dante's work ethic sometimes came into question, too often we also saw bad body language going to the bench, or his overall effort wasn't there. Often if the score was out of hand he wouldn't compete. He needs to compete hard every shift; with his talent he could be an effective player for his size.

Because he is an undersized center, he tends to get pushed around in the defensive zone, and loses 1 on 1 battles, he needs to use his hockey smarts in the defensive zone to make it easier for him. He is 50% in the face-offs; we would like to see him get stronger on his stick to be able to win more draws. There were times in our viewings we saw no compete to get back into the play, or back checking hard to the man after a turnover.

Quotable: "Dante has a hard deceptive shot and catches goalies off guard with his quick release and accuracy." HP Scout, Justin Sproule

Quotable: "Dante needs better work ethic. There were too many nights he took off and wasn't effective at all." - NHL Scout (April 2016)

Quotable: "Only a certain number of players who come in at 5'08" and make the NHL, and they are dynamic, game-breaking player. Salituro is a very, very good junior player. But that's what I think he is." - HP Scout, Ryan Yessie

Sambrook, Jordan
RD - Erie Otters (OHL) 6'01.5", 187
HockeyProspect.com Ranking: 59

Sambrook was drafted in the 10th round of the 2014 OHL Draft by the Erie Otters. Sambrook made the move to the Toronto Nationals of the GTHL and played a big part in their Telus Cup Championship. He came to camp and impressed the Otters so much that he was signed and played a key role when defenders were missing. With a healthy line-up he was relegated to the third pairing.

Sambrook has decent skating ability and showed good intelligence on the rush. He chooses great lanes and has shown the ability to score goals going end to end. He does a lot of the little things right, like not jumping ahead of the play and supporting his defensive partner. He knows when to make the simple play and when to go for the big play. He has quick hips and a good stick which help him in one on one situations. He has good gap control and makes contact at the right times. He was able to shut down some skilled players, even early this season as a first year player. He has good body positioning in puck races and in battles along the board helping him win more than his share of battles. He has a hard, accurate shot and picks his spots well, which lead to him having one of the best shooting percentages among all defensemen in the OHL.

Sambrook has made his share of mistakes this season and didn't have a great playoff performance, but when looking at the big picture, Sambrook had a very successful first year playing hockey above the AAA level. He possess a great deal of potential and upside as a two-way defender who can contribute in all situations. Sambrook could end up being one of the biggest steals in the 2016 NHL Entry Draft if he slides past the third round.

Quotable: "I've been a big fan of Sambrook since watching him in the pre-season. He has that "it" factor despite being a little raw. I like his hockey sense and ability to impact the play at both ends as a rookie. That along with quickness in which he developed and improved all make Sambrook one of my favourite sleepers of this draft class." - HP Scout Ryan Yessie

Quotable: " He struggled a bit in my late season viewings but up until then, I really liked what I saw from him. He was great in my first four or five viewings and looked nothing like a rookie just getting his feet wet in the OHL." - HP Scout, Mark Edwards

Samuel, Antoine
G – Baie-Comeau Drakkar (QMJHL) – 6'02", 182
HockeyProspect.com Ranking: 105

Samuel, who missed being eligible for last year's draft by a mere two days, was traded early this season from Shawinigan to Baie-Comeau. It was a good trade for him, as things were not working out in Shawinigan with their three-goalie rotation. With the worst team in the league, he saw way more action, and played with more confidence than he did in Shawinigan. Samuel is big and athletic, traits that will make him attractive to NHL teams. He moves well in his crease, playing a butterfly style that helps him cover the lower part of the net well. His confidence is something that will need to be monitored; we have seen him get down on himself after a bad goal and lose confidence in his abilities in the past. This got better in Baie-Comeau, but he didn't play with any pressure there. His glove side was always a big concern with us going back to midget, it has improved over the last 2-3 years but he still does get beaten high-glove too often. He has worked hard in the past few years to improve his weaknesses. He did play for a small-market team that was last in the league (not known as a popular destination for scouts to visit), and this could affect him on draft day.

Sanchez, James
LW – USNTDP 6'01", 184
HockeyProspect.com Ranking: 166

Sanchez is a left wing with good size who can play a heavy game. First few steps could be better and he looks sluggish off pivots. His frame allows him to protect the puck with his body and reach. Gets open in the offensive zone and can be involved on the cycle. Capable of basic plays that extend possession but lacks creativity. He hasn't shown that he can create offense with the puck on his stick. His puck-handling is actually decent but his footwork isn't really challenging to defend. Defensemen don't have a hard time reading what he's going to do. His size helps him out there as he can try to bull his way through but that is unlikely to work against bigger defensemen. Sanchez does offer some upside as a bottom 6 option but will need to improve his skating going forward.

Sarthou, Evan
G – Tri-City Americans (WHL) 6'01", 186
HockeyProspect.com Ranking: 196

Like fellow 2016-eligible goaltender Carter Hart, Sarthou is only slightly above-average in terms of size, but he already has two years of starter experience under his belt at the WHL level. Unlike Hart, Sarthou is less calm in the paint, playing a more frenetic and entertaining style of game. His lateral quickness and side-to-side explosiveness is pretty good. While he's not the greatest at controlling rebounds and sometimes appears to lose track of the puck, we love his ability to steer away second and third chance opportunities. He's not terribly tall or strong, but his upper-body reflexes are fast.

His glove hand quickness, in particular, is a strong aspect of his game. Another quality of his, is his ability to make the flashy save to swing momentum for his club. He, however, isn't ideally sized for the modern NHL.

Evan Sarthou is the latest of several NHL goaltending prospects to have emerged from the Tri-City Americans pipeline. As an American born, in somewhat unusual fashion, he represented his country at the 2015 World Under-18s and won a gold medal despite not being a part of the National Development program throughout the year.

Sawchenko, Zachary
G – Moose Jaw Warriors (WHL) 6'01", 185
HockeyProspect.com Ranking: 130

Zack Sawchenko, a hybrid goaltender with quick lower-body reflexes and exceptional rebound control capability, has seen a ton of action over the last few seasons. He won a bronze medal for Canada at the 2015 World Under-18 Hockey Championships, a gold medal at the 2015 Ivan Hlinka Memorial Tournament, and made an appearance at the Canada-Russia Super Series (where he was unbeatable). He also led his Moose Jaw Warriors to their first playoff appearance in over three years.

Sawchenko is very good not only at limiting rebounds but also at controlling them. He plays fairly aggressively, often standing a foot or two beyond the paint when challenging a shooter. Luckily, his edgework is very good allowing him to move easily and to cut off angles quickly as the puck moves laterally in his own end despite playing so aggressively. Dramatic kick saves from his butterfly are one of his specialities, as he's able to effectively steer pucks into the corners and out of danger by these means. Advanced glove-hand save ability allows him to even further limit second-chance opportunities.

Sawchenko isn't terribly big by modern goalie standards, but he drops in and comes out of his butterfly very quickly and establishes good sightlines through traffic. He's a really good skater and he's very good at moving the puck up ice with an unexpected pass, which is one of his underrated qualities. He should get a few looks from Hockey Canada in preparation for next year's World Junior championships.

Sergachev, Mikhail
LD - Windsor Spitfires (OHL) 6'02.25", 208
HockeyProspect.com Ranking: 8

Sergachev was selected sixth overall at the 2016 CHL Import Draft after a successful MHL season with Irbis Kazan. He also made appearances in the World Under-17 Challenge and the IIHF U18 Championships. Sergachev immediately played a big role for the Spitfires earning top minutes in all game situations. He finished the season with nearly a point per game in his rookie season.

Sergachev is a big-bodied defenseman who skates very well. He carries the puck with confidence and with a combination of speed and protection ability rarely found in defensive prospects. Unlike some defensemen, he doesn't stop when entering the offensive zone. When possible he will challenge defenders one on one, winning a fair share of those match-up's. He possesses a lethal wrist shot which he has used to score some of his 17 goals this season on the rush. Sergachev also has a powerful slapshot from the point and unloads great one-timers. He puts the puck on net and can score, as well as create rebounds with that powerful point shot. He does a good job pinching to keep the play going in the offensive zone. Defensively he plays with a bit of an edge. He will take the body and has crushed some opponents. He has a good stick on one on one's and with his size and reach he has been tough to beat. He can sometimes lose his positioning during sustained zone pressure, which is not uncommon for OHL rookies.

Sergachev has all the makings of a top pairing offensive defenseman at the next level. He has to overcome defensive inconsistencies but has the hockey sense and skill to be very successful at the NHL level. Sergachev will be one of the first defensemen taken at the 2016 NHL Entry Draft.

Quotable: "He has his moments where he looks a bit lazy but aside from that he is a stud." – NHL Scout (October 2015)

Quotable: "I have him and Juolevi neck n neck." – NHL Scout (November 2015)

Quotable: "He's a stud, ahead of Chychrun but just behind Juolevi for me." – NHL Scout (December 2015)

Quotable: "Sergachev was a lot of fun to watch this season. He's so dangerous off the rush and has some of the best goal scoring ability we've seen in a defenseman over the past few years." – HP Scout, Ryan Yessie

Quotable: "He's talented but he was terrible in the playoffs versus Kitchener." – NHL Scout (April 2016)

Quotable: "He was a favourite of mine last season, you could see the offensive upside was there so it's been nice seeing how successful he has been in the OHL." – HP Scout Mik Portoni

Quotable: "There were games where he looked like he was about 27 years old and he could step into the NHL tomorrow. I love his poise, his toughness and his cannon shot. The best part is it's all packaged in a 6'3" frame that can skate." – Mark Edwards

Quotable: "His interview was good. He seemed pissed off about the U18's." – NHL Scout (Combine week)

Quotable: "The majority of the guys I spoke to liked his interview at the combine. One scout said it was just ok." – HP Scout Mark Edwards (Combine week)

Sevigny, Mathieu
LC/LW – Drummondville Voltigeurs (QMJHL) – 6'01", 172
HockeyProspect.com Ranking: 167

Sevigny was the 17th overall pick in the 2014 QMJHL Draft. His father is former pro hockey player Pierre Sevigny, who has been a coach with the Quebec Remparts since 2013-2014. He also played briefly for the Canadiens in the NHL, in the mid-90s.

The younger Sevigny is a very smart forward who understands how to play the game very well without the puck. As the center on his line, he always takes care of his own end first, always working hard on the backcheck and often supporting his defensemen deep in his defensive zone. He's a key member of the Voltigeurs' PK unit and is willing to block shots. He can play both at centre and on the wing, unafraid of getting engaged physically along the boards. He's good on the forecheck, taking good angles to pursue the puck-carrier. However, his lack of high-end speed and agility hurts him in that aspect of the game. This season, he's playing centre usually on the 3rd line, and he struggled to provide regular offense when used on an offensive line early in the season. He plays a pro style of game, a mature game, but has struggled to put in any considerable offense at the junior level as of yet. We had the same question mark coming out of midget; we liked the smarts and two-way game but we didn't see a lot of offense out of him. His hands are average at best; he gets in a good position to score and will take the puck to the net, but he's too slow sometime at releasing his shots, providing ample opportunity for the opposing defense to react. Sevigny will need to keep working on his offensive skills to achieve success at the next level as he's already strong in the defensive side of the game.

Shevchenko, Vyacheslav
LC – Team Russia U18 (MHL) – 5'09", 158
HockeyProspect.com Ranking: NR

A great skater with outstanding speed, Shevchenko has proven himself as a useful piece of the Russian U18 national team over the course of this past season. He has grown a bit physically from last year when he looked very weak and small, which is encouraging and gave him a better chance to compete, but he is still clearly undersized. His numbers are not enticing either, but are affected by the defensive role he played along the season. A centerman very effective in the faceoff circle, Shevchenko was a key contributor on the penalty kill. He has the ability to make plays at top speed and becomes a threat on counters in open ice. More frequently, he uses his speed without the puck. Can be a pest on the forecheck and is terrific on the backcheck. He is a committed player, gets first on loose pucks with impressive regularity and is not afraid to pay the price along the boards despite the size disadvantage.

Vyacheslav had some troubles finishing his chances this season and he will need to improve his shot moving forward. He still has ways to go physically as well, getting bigger would probably help him do a better job at protecting the puck. Shevchenko is a good little player, someone however who probably needed a very strong showing at the U18 Worlds to get drafted, an opportunity that was unfortunately taken away from him. He still has some distinctive attributes that give him a chance to develop into a valuable role player down the road.

Shoemaker, Mark
RD - North Bay Battalion (OHL) 6'02", 208
HockeyProspect.com Ranking: 188

Shoemaker was selected in the 11th round of the 2013 OHL Priority Selection Draft by the North Bay Battalion out of the Mississauga Reps Minor Midget program. Shoemaker spent his 16 year old season with the Brampton Jr. B Battalion of the GOJHL posting decent numbers for a first year player. Shoemaker surprised and made the Battalion despite being a late round flyer and earned his place on the roster. He moved up into second pairing duties and played second unit power play and penalty kill for the Battalion.

While Dineen has been getting all the attention in regards to NHL Draft eligible prospects on the Battalion, Shoemaker has quietly but effectively proven himself to be a very interesting prospect. Shoemaker has good size and provides a reliable, consistent effort at both ends. Defensively he has good size and a good stick making him difficult to get around. He finishes his checks, but isn't overly physical. He has good positional awareness where he sets himself up to intercept passes and take away potential scoring chances. He completes his first passes on a consistent basis and has even made some impressive breakout passes at times when the opportunity presents itself. He is a consistent puck mover who makes the smart play in relation to his options. On the powerplay he likes to shoot the puck. He has excellent accuracy with his shot and hits the net on a regular basis. He has decent power and his shot is deflectable.

Shoemaker has quietly developed into a solid two-way defender. He isn't flashy but he doesn't make a lot of mistakes. He doesn't have huge upside but has all the size and tools to become an NHL defender one day.

Quotable: "In my viewings of the Battalion I think Shoemaker has proven he deserves a look in the later rounds of this draft. He's not flashy but he's very consistent and does his job well at both ends of the ice." - HP Scout Ryan Yessie

Shvyrev, Igor
LC – Metallurg Magnitogorsk Jr. (MHL) – 6'01", 191
HockeyProspect.com Ranking: NR

Shvyrev is a forward that was part of the U18 Russian national team at the Hlinka tournament, but was underused there and spent the rest of the season with his club's junior team. He posted respectable numbers considering how green some aspects of his game looked in our limited viewings. The best part is when Igor has the puck, making the right play seems natural for him and he shows poise beyond his age. One of his best assets is his puck control. He can make plays with his head up, has good vision and can exploit holes in the defensive coverage executing accurate passes. Has good instincts in the offensive zone, making himself available in the right areas. He seems to focus on putting himself in a good shooting position, to then either go for passing lanes that may open up or for the net. He is not a player that uses his skills to try fancy stuff, he usually keeps it simple pursuing effective options. As of now he is not a very dynamic player though and is mainly a threat on the powerplay.

He'll need to bring a more consistent effort in his play without the puck, keep his feet moving and skate harder. He can win pucks with his hands when he gets in tight, but doesn't go out of his way to pursue them. Along the boards he's not bad at keeping possession but should engage more in battles. His defensive coverage can be inconsistent and his overall compete will need to improve as well. Shvyrev has long ways to go, but will still be 17 by the time the draft rolls around and the talent is there.

Sicoly, Nicolas
LW - Guelph Storm (OHL) 5'09", 165
HockeyProspect.com Ranking: NR

Sicoly is a hard working, energetic forward for the Guelph Storm. The Sault Ste. Marie native played his OHL Draft year in the GTHL for the Toronto Marlboros before being selected in the 4th round of the 2014 OHL Priority Selection Draft.

Nicolas is undersized but possesses a ton of speed. He is quick and shifty and uses this ability on the forecheck to frustrate the puck carrier. He is at his best when moving his feet and staying on the puck as aggressively as possible. Sicoly will do the little things to help his team like blocking shots on the penalty kill and taking the hit to make the play. He wins more than his share of battles considering his size. Sicoly was effective on the penalty kill getting in lanes, blocking shots and using his speed to create short handed opportunities. Almost half his goals this season came while short handed.

Unfortunately his point totals were not very impressive this year and he struggled to create much offensively. For a player of his size, without producing offensively it is tough to see a team pick him up at the 2016 NHL Entry Draft unless they either expect him to grow or see big potential in his future offensive upside. Sicoly projects to be a very solid junior hockey player, but is not considered a draftable prospect by us for the 2016 NHL Entry Draft.

Sissons, Colby
LD – Swift Current Broncos (WHL) 6'02", 172
HockeyProspect.com Ranking: 203

Sissons is a lanky defenseman that has shown real good progression throughout the season. He started off as a rather awkward kid that didn't exhibit much impact at all but has become a valuable piece on Swift Current's blueline by the season's end and could go up against most players in the league while holding his own.

Sissons has a good frame to build upon but will need to fill out and improve his strength. His legs look rather thin and he doesn't look the strongest on his skates. Still, while it's not the prettiest sight in the world, Sissons actually generates decent top speed and seems to get around the ice well enough. That's something that has looked noticeably better towards the end of the season as opposed to out early viewings. Sissons was a bit shy when making plays with the puck early on, but at the end of the year we saw a player that was making plays out of his own end, skating with the puck, and doing a good job on PP. Sissons reads the play well with and without the puck. He can pass the puck quickly but has also shown some ability to take off and gain space forward if given room. Sissons has also become more active from the offensive blueline in and has become a regular contributor there with his shot and passing. Defensively, Sissons reads the point of attack well and maintains his position, using his stick to strip forwards of the puck and quickly moving the puck back out. Though he will need to get stronger and fill out, we have seen him throw his body around on the wall and at least try to play a physically engaging game in his own zone.

Sissons is a player that put himself on map by his almost month-to-month improvement. By the end of the year we saw a defenseman that is quite raw but has started showing signs of upside as a two-way defenseman.

Sjolund, Nicklas
RD – AIK (Allsvenskan) – 6'02", 181
HockeyProspect.com Ranking: NR

A second time NHL draft eligible, Sjolund is primarily a defensive defenseman with good size and mobility. Sjolund's skating stride features a slightly hunched over upper-body, but nevertheless, Sjolund seems to get around the ice well and doesn't lack in the acceleration, top speed, or overall mobility department.

Sjolund does show some offensive upside, he is capable of skating the puck out of trouble or using his skating to quickly gain space forward, but it is unlikely that he will be much of a offensive producer at the next level. The appeal of Sjolund's game comes mostly through the combination of size, mobility and defensive play. That combination gives him some upside as a modern mobile defensive defenseman with a good frame-size. He has a big body that can quickly close-down attacking forwards and seal them off from creating anything productive and that is likely going to remain the foundation of his game as he moves forward.

Smith, Givani
RW - Guelph Storm (OHL) 6'01", 197
HockeyProspect.com Ranking: 41

Smith is a big power forward for the Guelph Storm. He was originally selected in the first round of the 2014 OHL Priority Selection Draft by the Barrie Colts but was traded to the Guelph Storm in his rookie season for Ben Harpur and Chad Bauman. Playing on the last place Storm gave Smith the opportunity to play a ton of minutes this season.

Givani has good size and loves to take the body. He's a very imposing figure on the forecheck and while he has slightly heavy feet, he does a good job of keeping them moving and always finishes his check. When opponents get after him, he shows a lot of pushback and he plays with a mean streak, especially if the opposition gets under his skin. His positioning is good in the offensive zone, which has resulted in plenty of good scoring chances throughout the season. He has a hard shot but accuracy is something that can be improved upon. He shows some skill here and there and has made some good plays to create chances for himself and others, but he would best described as more of a shoot first guy. He did miss capitalizing on some good scoring chances in our viewings.

Givani improved his skating throughout the season but his feet are still on the heavy side. He is a prospect who we think has a good chance to make the NHL one day. That said, we wouldn't bet on the likelihood of him contributing consistently in a top six role. He has the size, compete and physical mindset to succeed as a bottom six player and will create some space for more talented players. Givani has some intangibles that you can't teach.

Quotable:" He can't skate, I've seen him twice this year and he's done nothing." - NHL Scout (October 2015)

Quotable:" He doesn't have enough skill for the first round." - NHL Scout (October 2015)

Quotable:" I don't know what you see in him. I think he's barely draftable." - NHL Scout (October 2015)

Quotable:" He beat Kitchener all on his own when I saw him last week." - NHL Scout (January 2016)

Quotable:" I like that Givani kid. He's been great for me." - NHL Scout (December 2015)

Quotable:" The first time I saw him, I was actually coaching against him with Dale Hawerchuk in a one day prospects event before his OHL Draft season. I instantly liked him. Flash forward to this season and I haven't changed my opinion of him. His skating was slightly weaker than I remembered from last season but other than that, the kid is just a hockey player. He is hard to play against, plays with a ton of passion and can be an absolute SOB on the ice. He will go hard to the net, is a beast on the forecheck and can chip in on the score sheet." - Mark Edwards

Quotable:" Multiple scouts told me they thought he had a great interview." HP Scout Mark Edwards (Combine week)

Soderlund, Tim
LW – Skelleftea J20 (SWE) – 5'09", 163
HockeyProspect.com Ranking: NR

Soderlund is an undersized wing that has very good skating ability. Soderlund's edgework and top speed are both very good, which allows him to put some separation between himself and defensemen. In particular, his ability to take off with a puck and circle around the zone or cut to the middle is quite good

Soderlund's hands are good, though not quite amazing for a player his size. He handles the puck well at top speed and sees the ice well. He can handle the puck while rushing through space and makes solid decisions on the fly. However, he sometimes wants to gift-wrap a goal to his linemates. Instead of selecting the simple pass, he will at times look to hit a player through a maze of bodies and sticks just to set him up for a goal. This is great when it works, but can be frustrating when he had a simple option available that would work just as well. We have seen him pass up on some good shot opportunities in those situations.

Soderlund is also a competitive off-the-puck player and will use his speed on the forecheck looking to disrupt the puck-carrier, he doesn't have the physical ability to win battles but doesn't mind trying. Speed allows him to force puck-carriers into quick decisions and he can take away lanes.

Sokolov, Dmitry
LC - Sudbury Wolves (OHL) 6'00" 208
HockeyProspect.com Ranking: 117

Sokolov was the first round, third overall selection by the Sudbury Wolves in the 2015 CHL Import Draft. After an outstanding Under-17 and performing well as an under-ager at the Under-18 tournament, Sokolov had high expectations going into this draft, however his stock fell steadily throughout this season.

Sokolov's biggest strength is his goal scoring ability. He has an excellent shot and we saw him put the puck through some small holes that goalies gave him. He has one move in particular from the corner where he will cut out front, usually beating a defender in the process, then once the goaltender opens up a bit, finish on his scoring chance. We've seen this goal several times, unfortunately he sometimes had a habit of scoring a beautiful goal after the game was out of reach. He can take a little too long to get his shot off at times which is concerning at the next level. He moved the puck well in transition and is also willing to take the hit in order to make the play. Struggled one on one against good defenders, but was not afraid to challenge them, looking for a scoring chance. Sokolov's defensive game was all over the map this season. One shift he's floating around the red line, the next shift he's all over the puck carrier deep in the defensive zone. His skating is choppy and below average at this point of his development.

Anytime you have a player with a great shot like he has, but packaged with huge pitfalls, you're probably looking at a boom or bust prospect. If he can consistently improve on his deficiencies, while further impacting his team as an offensive threat, his upside would rise. Through weight, fitness and injury issues, Sokolov still found a way to score 30 goals this season.

Quotable: "The kid's numbers are good. I need to go back to Sudbury to see him again. I have time for him and our Euro Scouts love him." - NHL Scout (February 2016)

Quotable: "He might be the toughest player for me to predict as far as 'when' or possibly even 'if' he gets drafted. I heard everything from 'Beer League Player' to 'Gifted Scorer' from Scouts this season. In my viewings he didn't do much, but he did score a couple of beautiful goals on lasers to the short side. He has a lot of skill but I haven't seen him doing enough to contribute on nights when he can't get the laser shot away." - HP Scout Mark Edwards

Solensky, Samuel
LC/RW – Bili Tygri Liberec U20 (CZE) – 5'09", 167
HockeyProspect.com Ranking: NR

Solensky is an undersized forward who has good hockey sense, nice hands and decent skill. He has both the sense of someone who can find open holes for his shot as well as the vision to be an adept playmaker. Solensky is a good player in open space, but his lack of size becomes a challenge once pinned down on the boards or having to make wall plays despite his will to compete. His biggest problem is the lack of separation ability in his skating, at his size he simply isn't a fast or elusive enough skater. Strong player on the PP where with time and space his skill and vision shines through, but struggles more at even strength. An improvement in skating will be absolutely critical to his development.

Somppi, Otto
LC/LW – Halifax Mooseheads (QMJHL) - 6'01", 181
HockeyProspect.com Ranking: 112

Somppi came over from Finland, as the Mooseheads selected him in the CHL Import Draft (19th overall). The Helsinki native has played internationally, in both the U-17 Hockey Challenge and the U-18 Ivan Hlinka Tournament for his country. In his first season in the QMJHL, Somppi had to make adjustments to his game while playing on a smaller ice surface. He didn't produce enough offensively and had a tough time producing in the 2nd half with some of the best Halifax forwards gone. Somppi can play all three forward positions, as he is a smart hockey player without the puck and won't hurt you on the ice. He's responsible in his own end, showing good commitment to the defensive game and he's good on the PK. Offensively, he's more of a playmaker, a pass-first type of player and has not had a lot of success scoring goals at the QMJHL level just yet. He works hard all over the ice but his hands are just okay. There are some question marks with his upside at the next level. His skating is a big concern; it needs some serious work to improve his quickness, acceleration and grant him the ability to take advantage of space on the ice. To us, Somppi looks like a mid-to-late pick in this draft. We love his smarts – with an upgrade to his skating play, this combination could grant him a depth role at the NHL level, but there's a lot of work to be done here.

Soy, Tyler
C - Victoria Royals (WHL) 5'11", 179
HockeyProspect.com Ranking: NR

Tyler had a strong season picking up where he left off at the end of last year. He was 3rd in the WHL in goal scoring with 46 goals and finished the year with 85 points. Tyler has shown strong progression and improvement from year to year with 30 points in his rookie year following that with 63 points last season. He was given a much greater role on Victoria's top line and has continued to grow as a player.

One of the major things you will notice as you watch this player is he is very competitive and is willing to battle and pay the price by going hard to the net. He uses his size and puck skills to protect the puck and make plays as well getting into good shooting lanes. He has a quick, hard accurate shot wrist and snap shot that he likes to get off. He is a strong agile skater that has the ability to pull away from players with great acceleration. Tyler also possesses an understanding of how to be a deceptive skater by good edges and stopping and starting.

Along with being an offensive player you see the value in this player when you watch his play away from the puck. He is a 200 foot player that is very responsible defensively. He is very effective on the back check, communicating with the defensemen and tracking his man. He was also trusted with huge minutes on the penalty kill and finished the year with 6 short-handed goals.

All in all Tyler had a strong season. He has shown significant improvements year after year and may and has shown great growth in his game since he was first eligible last season. His consistent development and goal-scoring ability will put him on the radar.

Stadler, Livio
LD – EV Zug (NLA) – 5' 11.75", 163
HockeyProspect.com Ranking: NR

After a promising showing at home in last year U18 Worlds paired with Siegenthaler, Stadler raised expectations that he was not able to meet this season. He didn't grow physically and his game didn't look much improved either. Played a limited role for a bunch of NLA games with EV Zug early in the season (his father was a long time defenseman for the same team), but for the most looked a bit overwhelmed and was demoted to the junior team. On the international stage he didn't look mature enough to lead his U18 national team defense like he was asked to do as the team captain. He still has the qualities that made him an interesting prospect last season though. Even if he's been at fault for the odd turnover under pressure, he is quick to skate away from the forecheck and move the puck. He is an agile defenseman with a pretty smooth stride, good edges and he pivots well. Uses his mobility to quickly close in on opponents forwards. Makes good reads, has decent puck skills, keeps his head up and shows good composure when transitioning the puck up the ice. Can get passes off on his backhand and forehand accurately and with proper velocity. Can read the play well in the offensive zone and move the puck on the powerplay, does a good job at putting it on net with his quick wrister and already has a decent one-timer despite his slight frame.

Stadler projects as a defenseman able to play an up-tempo game, but will need to add strength and become tougher, at this point he is a rather soft smallish defenseman. Livio is expected to spend next season in Sweden with Lulea J20 team and we look forward to see him develop his game and become more consistent in his effort and man-on-man coverage over 60 minutes.

Stallard, Jordan
LC – Calgary Hitmen (WHL) 6'02", 188
HockeyProspect.com Ranking: 98

Jordy is a big skilled forward who had more of a secondary role on the Hitmen this year in which he proved his worth and value. He is very willing to engage in battles and used his size and speed numerous times to win possession for his team. Jordy is a two-way center that is very good on draws and plays a complete 200 foot game. He is responsible in his own and a strong player when he doesn't have the puck. Most of the time he is the first forward on the back check and does a great job tracking his man and taking pressure off of his defense on the rush. He is very strong in his own end and with his speed and anticipation is a great penalty killer.

We love his work ethic and competitiveness and as he matures and develops we feel he will be a solid two-way player that can impact the game in many different ways. He will need to continue to work on his offensive skill set if he wants to bring another dimension to his game.

Stal Lyrenas, Oskar
RW – MODO J20 (SWE) – 6'01", 194
HockeyProspect.com Ranking: NR

Stal Lyrenas is a right wing with good size and smarts. He is an average skater, he lacks slightly both in top speed as well as acceleration. He does have good hockey IQ, which allows him to play an intelligent game that isn't overly reliant on explosiveness. His game with the puck is rather simple and honest. He doesn't cheat in his own-end and is more than willing to involve himself into a 5-man unit type of game. Stal Lyrenas will support the puck out of his own end. However, when he does get the puck, he isn't very dangerous through neutral zone. He takes good lanes with the puck and can also pass, but doesn't have the speed to push the defense back. If he tries to bring it up the ice himself, he will be forced into a dump-in or a pass as his footwork isn't good enough to do much else.

Stal Lyrenas utilizes intelligent off-the-puck positioning in the offensive zone. While he is limited with what he can do with the puck, he does a good job following the play and looking for his shot. He has shown some ability to finish but getting the play to that point is a bigger problem as he isn't dynamic enough to create offense consistently. On the forecheck he will work to keep the puck in the offensive zone and he has good understanding of lanes and reading where the defenseman is trying to move the puck, but isn't a very physical player in terms of finishing his checks and the lack of speed is also a problem. Stal Lyrenas does many things decently well, but there is a lack of a true stand-out quality that would improve how he projects to the next level.

Stanley, Logan
LD - Windsor Spitfires (OHL) 6'07", 220
HockeyProspect.com Ranking: 30

Stanley was selected 12th overall at the 2014 OHL Priority Selection Draft by the Windsor Spitfires out of the Waterloo Wolves Minor Midget program. Stanley struggled in the majority of our viewings in his rookie season. This season was much different.

Stanley is an exceptionally big defenseman who has outstanding size that will make him appealing to NHL teams. His best ability is his shutdown game. He's pretty good one on one and has the long reach and plays with aggression that teams like. He's tough below the dots and completes hard for pucks. He is an imposing player in the puck battle and as he adds muscle this will also be the case at the NHL level. He will need to improve his coverage during sustained offensive pressure. He has improved his skating a great deal over the last 18 months. He still has a lot of room for improvement, but his development in this area is very promising. He has also developed his puck skills and has been pretty effective making the first pass and advancing the puck up ice. While he still has games where he struggles, as he did in the playoffs, overall he has improved in this area and should be effective if making the simple, advance the play type of puck decision.

As with any big defenseman who is just turning 18, Stanley still has some development to do and improve his game. He has the upside of a second pairing defenseman in a shutdown role and could be one of the biggest players in the NHL by the time he's done growing and filling out. He will need to further improve on his skating and puck movement along with small intricacies in his game.

Quotable: "He has really improved. I've been impressed with how well he's skating the puck compared to last season." - NHL Scout (November 2015)

Quotable: "I'm not as high on him as you guys. I probably have him 30-40 spots later than you do." - NHL Scout (December 2015)

Quotable: "I saw where you have Stanley, you're drunk, he's a 2nd rounder." - NHL Scout (April 2016)

Quotable: "Where do you have this Stanley kid?" (Answered 21st on our Feb 29th list) Scout laughs - NHL Scout (April 2016 in Grand Forks)

Quotable: "I think he goes top 15 like (Sam) Morin did." - NHL Scout (April 2016)

Quotable: " He wasn't my favourite interview." - NHL Scout (May 2016)

Quotable: "I think Stanley was a little inconsistent down the stretch, but considering how he's developed since Minor Midget I think there's still a lot of upside there." - HP Scout, Ryan Yessie

Quotable: " I was not a big fan of Stanley going into this season. I give him big props for how much he's improved, possibly the most improved player in the draft class. That said, he lost me a bit in the 2nd half of the season. I saw more turnovers and poor puck decisions. Based on my discussions with numerous scouts late in the season, I was not alone having him as a bit of a faller. Best way I could describe my conversations about him in the second half of the season is that Scouts seem to either love him or have very little time for him." - Mark Edwards

Quotable: " Feedback was interviews was ok. Nobody raved about him and no scouts said he was bad. One noted that he thought he seemed to be maturing." - HP Scout Mark Edwards (Combine week)

Staum, Casey
LD – Hill Murray (MN-HS) 6'01", 181
HockeyProspect.com Ranking: NR

Casey is a smooth skating Defenseman who can control the pace of the game with the puck on his stick. His hockey sense is probably just average but he can push the pace with his skating and quick puck moving ability or show good poise to slow things down. Staum can bring a physical element and uses his strong lower body to win battles and force the opponent off the puck. He possesses a good shot and his skating and footwork allows him to find lanes to get pucks to the net. Staum was impressive in the Minnesota Elite League last fall as well as in his games for Hill Murray and finished as a Mr. Hockey Finalist in the State of Minnesota. Casey Staum is committed to Nebraska Omaha but will likely spend next season in the USHL.

Quotable: " Had a bad leg injury. Probably a slam dunk to get drafted prior to the injury, could be a bit more in doubt now. His skating is high end but he has some other holes in his game." NHL Scout (May 2016)

Steel, Sam
LC – Regina Pats (WHL) 5'11", 178
HockeyProspect.com Ranking: 55

Steel is an intelligent playmaking center with good hands and good skating. Steel already had an impressive rookie season, putting up almost a point per game pace for Regina last year. This season, Steel didn't improve his pace by a lot, but had a rather productive playoffs and also appeared for Canada's U18 team at the Hlinka Memorial Tournament.

Steel is a center that plays with good hockey IQ and has been used in all situations and special teams for Regina. His reads allow him to always be near and involved in the play and he is quite good at being the player that supports puck-movement up the ice. Steel has a fluid, effortless stride and good speed. He gets around the ice with ease and can handle the puck at speed which allows him to be a good neutral zone player and someone who can be useful both in helping his defense exit the zone as well as on the offensive zone entry. Steel is an adept playmaker who easily spots open linemates and distributes the puck to them with accurate passes. He is already very good at making plays with speed and excels off rush plays where the defense isn't completely set up. He has a frame that is more on the light side and it is a bit more challenging for him to create offense against defense that is already set up in the defensive zone. In those situations, Steel is more likely to take what is given to him rather than challenge the defense. He will make good passes and can sneak into high-scoring areas if the defense isn't paying attention, but has a harder time establishing his presence, creating space for himself and controlling the possession.

Steel is primarily a playmaker but has shown the ability to finish. His shot isn't the hardest but he gets good accuracy on his wrist-shot and can get it off relatively quickly. Overall, he is a strong offensive player but can be prone to getting neutered and pushed to the perimeter. He will need to work on establishing his will more in the offensive zone and getting stronger. The latter is also an issue in the defensive zone. Steel has solid defensive smarts, but is simply not strong enough to win battles down low with any consistency.

Steel offers a good package of skating, skill, playmaking ability, and hockey IQ. As he moves up the ranks, he will have to work on finding ways to impose his will more in the middle of the ice as opposed to settling for what he is given by the defense. He will also need to get physically stronger in order to defend more effectively.

Steen, Oskar
RW/C – Farjestad (SHL) – 5'09", 186
HockeyProspect.com Ranking: 152

A small forward with good hands, Steen manages to contribute to the game in more ways than young players with those traits usually do. He likes to compete in puck battles and despite his size he is pretty effective because he is quite strong on his quick feet. He uses them to get inside position to the puck and beat out bigger opponents. Not a particularly impressive skater nor blessed with outstanding acceleration, but actually moves around effectively and is quick to get where he needs to be. In the offensive zone he likes to position himself around the net and that's where he is usually found on the powerplay. He has smart positioning in the slot or along the boards. Has a legit wrist shot and also uses it from outside high-scoring areas to generate rebounds usually going low far side. With the puck he seems to benefit from playing in a structured system, sometimes he fails to recognize when his standard play is not there.

Oskar is a pretty complete player that gets used on both special teams at the junior level. He is not a flashy player, but definitely effective at that level. It helps his case that in the last part of the season he joined Farjestad senior team and showed he can raise his intensity and still play his game against men. He has yet to record his first pro goal, but was effective on the forecheck and didn't struggle with the pace of the game. On the other hand, despite scoring a couple of goals he had a sub-par performance at the U18 Worlds and as a small player not showing his best game there might very well have hurt his draft stock. His ultimate upside is that of a versatile complementary player.

Steenbergen, Tyler
LC/LW – Swift Current Broncos (WHL) 5' 11", 178
HockeyProspect.com Ranking: NR

Steenbergen is a forward that is at his best when he keeps moving his feet and playing a high-energy game. He had a decently productive season for an otherwise underwhelming Swift Current team that lacked scoring depth. Steenbergen is the type of player that will create turnovers and be an annoying presence for the other team. When he keeps moving his feet he has the ability to push the pace and force other teams into mistakes, when he does get the puck he shows upside with his hands to make plays. Steenbergen likes to be active on the forecheck and likes to find soft spots in the slot. He's an active forechecker, but switches into a more sneaky look when his team has the puck, there he will look to set up shop and look for opportunities to pounce on, as he doesn't quite have the ability to manufacture scoring chances for himself. In our viewings, we saw him moved up to the top line a couple of times, playing with DeBrusk and he has not looked out of place there. Steenbergen isn't particularly strong but tries to play bigger than his size would suggest.

Stewart, Dean
RD – Portage Terriers (MJHL) 6'02", 170
HockeyProspect.com Ranking: 137

Stewart is a raw mobile blueliner that is developing into a two-way defenseman. Outside of his league appearances, he also played for Team Canada at the WJAC and in the CJHL Top Prospects Game. Stewart has good mobility in all directions. Although he will clearly need to fill out his frame, he gets good reach out of it and moves it around the ice well. Stewart can be quite inconsistent as his energy level can at times drop making him far less effective than he can be. When he is engaged he is using his skating and plays a competitive game, but with him that can change even from period to period let alone game to game. Nevertheless, Stewart makes a good first pass and skates well with the puck. He is useful in starting transition and is a plus player in zone exits. He reads the play well defensively and uses his stick well, he is effective at using his reach and mobility to quickly close down on forwards, but will need to become stronger and exhibit more push consistently around the net. Sometimes, you see outlines of his physicality but it's not consistent at this point as he has bouts of almost overly casual play. When he moves his feet he also shows upside offensively as he will join the rush and skate the puck into offensive zone on the occasion. His movement on the offensive blueline is good and he shows some instincts in pinching and sliding further up the ice while looking to unload his shot. His passing game is above-average both in his own end as well as in distributing the puck from the offensive blueline.

Stewart is a raw defenseman who certainly shows some upside but will need to develop consistency in his game. He is committed to University of Nebraska-Omaha

Stillman, Riley
D - Oshawa Generals (OHL) 6'0", 180
HockeyProspect.com Ranking: 81

Riley Stillman is an intelligent, two-way defensemen with intriguing upside. Stillman boasts impressive foot speed and strong mobility and played top pairing minutes with the Oshawa Generals down the stretch, thriving with the expanded opportunity. Stillman was versatile enough to play in a shutdown pairing or as a complimentary offensive minded defensemen. He consistently made strong contributions at both ends of the rink. He made strong decisions in possession, displays intriguing vision along with the ability to make a clean and crisp first pass. While Stillman's ability to make a clean first pass is noteworthy, the 6'0 defensemen also shows effectiveness as a puck carrying defensemen. Stillman shields the puck well on zone exits and can be tough to contain through the neutral zone, gaining the offense zone with relative ease. Offensively speaking, Stillman's vision is on display while plying his trade on the power play, consistently finding teammates in prime scoring position. While his strength as a passer is noteworthy, Stillman also possesses a potent shot from the blue line. Stillman shows strong awareness in transition as he appropriately joins the rush and makes smart/calculated pinches, keeping plays alive. Defensively speaking Stillman is an excellent open ice hitter, appropriately stepping up and separating a player from the puck. In transition Stillman controls the attack effectively, forcing the opposition to low percentage areas while showing excellent contain. Boasting an active stick and strong positional play, Stillman can be a smothering defender that is tough to play against. In a draft that lacks depth at the defensive position Stillman presents some qualities that make him a draft worthy prospect.

Stransky, Simon
LW – Prince Albert Raiders (WHL) 5'11", 178
HockeyProspect.com Ranking: 73

Simon Stransky is a winger with great puck-skills. His deking ability is high-end and he has good deception with the puck. On the powerplay, he uses his puck handling ability to create lanes before dishing off the perfect cross-crease pass to earn himself yet another assist. His shot isn't too bad either, making him a dual threat in the offensive zone.

Simon is an average skater who while not terribly dynamic on his feet, has the puck skills and deking ability to throw defensemen off their coverage. He likes to enter the zone and then stop-up quickly to open up space for his teammates. Both his shots and his passes are difficult to read. His wrist shot, in particular, can be challenging to stop as he's capable of shooting lasers while looking in a different direction or while in his mid-stride.
Stransky was a bit of a disappearing act when it came to defending his own end during the regular season but has done better in the playoffs. He also lacks some bite in the offensive zone as he can be rubbed out of the game against physical defense that doesn't give him any room and will need more push-back there. Stransky is a smart playmaker that can also finish and possesses good one on one moves, however he will need to improve both his compete as well as skating to have a chance at the NHL level.

Stukel, Jakob
LW – Calgary Hitmen (WHL) 6'00, 182
HockeyProspect.com Ranking: NR

Stukel really took a step forward this season as he was traded from the Vancouver Giants to the Calgary Hitmen. After only scoring 4 points in his first twelve games with Vancouver he joined the Hitmen and tallied 56 points in 57 games. Stukel is a skilled forward with good puck skills and a very quick and accurate shot. He is also a very smooth yet powerful skater with great balance which he uses to protect the puck. He likes to hold on to the puck and try and make plays one on one but sometimes fails to see open passing options. There is no question that Stukel posses a good offensive mind and the skills to be effective as an offensive producer, at least at the junior level.

Our main concern with this player is his play away from the puck. He sometimes seems complacent and waits to get engaged. He needs to work on competing away from the puck and becoming more of a 200 foot player.

Sukhachyov, Vladislav
G – Team Russia U18 (MHL) – 5'10", 181
HockeyProspect.com Ranking: NR

Sukhachyov is a smaller goalie with a somewhat acrobatic style to his netminding. He is a strong competitor and makes sure he gives his all on all saves. Sukhachyov works hard on second efforts and can be counted on to make a high-end save that he had a minimal chance of making. However, his style can make some routine saves look harder than they should.

Sukhachyov covers the lower portion of the net well and has strong side-to-side movement that however can lack in control. He leaves a bit more room up-top and that might be exploited by better shooters. He makes a strong initial push but can be prone to sliding out of position. He plays an active, energetic game in his crease and battles well down-low and with traffic, although he can sometimes overreact instead of keeping his calm. This season we have also seen him lose track of shots coming from the blueline more than once, something he can't afford as, at his size, he can't rely on making positional saves. He's got good ability with his glove. He communicates with his defensemen and stays focused on the play and on what the players on ice are doing.

Sukhachyov can wow you with a sprawling save or a fantastic second effort but for a smaller goalie like him there was simply not enough control in his movement in our viewings. His rebound control could also be better, which poses even more challenges.

Quotable: "Entertaining and competitive. I would be happy to have him on my team, but I don't think he's the next small goalie to make it to the NHL, there's just not enough control in his game" - HP Scout Nik Funa

Suter, Pius
LC – ZSC Lions (NLA) – 5'11", 170
HockeyProspect.com Ranking: NR

After being passed over again at last year NHL Draft despite scoring 43 goals in 61 OHL games, Pius returned to Switzerland this season and was able to show his qualities at the senior level while playing mostly 3rd line minutes. He had stretches of strong play where he confirmed to us he would have been a legit draft pick in the past.

Suter has a pretty good nose for the net and a rather dangerous wrist shot he can pick spots with. He is a fairly skilled player, but for the most makes a difference with the way he competes and think the game. He brings smart positioning, doesn't mind traffic, makes good reads without the puck and likes to engage in battles no matter the bigger size of opponents. He is the kind of player that always seems to find a way to contribute to his team success. His defensive efforts are consistent and is an effective penalty killer, a role he played all season long for ZSC. Doesn't possess the best looking skating stride, but when he is on top of his game he is an effective and elusive skater.

His offensive contribution at the WJC was limited to the relegation round where he scored three goals in less than 10 minutes at the start of the second game against Belarus, but for an undersized player it was probably more important to prove his value against men and the fact Suter did just that playing on the same team as Matthews may have helped his case. Still, for a small European prospect odds of getting eventually drafted after going back to their home country aren't that good. In any case, if this smart competitor will add more power to his body, he will have a legit chance to become a useful complementary player at any level.

Quotable: "Isn't he like 26 years old by now? Feels like we've been scouting him forever." - NHL Scout (May 2016)

Suthers, Keenan
LW – USNTDP 6'08", 223
HockeyProspect.com Ranking: NR

A behemoth forward, Suthers logs in at a towering 6'8. Most of the appeal with Suthers clearly lies in his size, but there have been small inklings that suggest he might have some decent hockey ability as well. While he would clearly not be much of a prospect if he were 8 inches shorter, Suthers actually shows decent hockey IQ on ice. He doesn't have a lot of finish but he generally reads and knows where he has to go on ice. He understands basic principles of offensive play and of puck-movement and can wind up with a scoring chance or two. His hands actually aren't outright terrible for a kid this big and he skate well enough to be involved. As he moves forward, he will obviously have to become more coordinated in that large body of his and make improvements pretty much everywhere, but the fact that he does look like a sensible hockey player at his size does suggest some upside.

Svetlakov, Andrei
LC – CSKA Moscow (KHL) – 6'00", 200
HockeyProspect.com Ranking: 199

Svetlakov is a 1996 birth who has had a rather productive first season in KHL, putting up 12 points in 38 games. Svetlakov also had a strong showing at the World Juniors tournament. He's a versatile center who can play also the wing position.

Svetlakov has quick feet and good edgework. At top speed in a straight line, his stride looks more of a shorter variety, but he gets to places in time with no issues. He has good deception in the offensive zone, utilizes good footwork and cuts to buy himself some time, can throw off his check and open up some space to make plays in. Svetlakov likes to play in scoring areas, he is not a perimeter player but will both take pucks to the slot as well as go there without the puck. Can tip pucks into the net and pounce rebounds home. Also utilizes a quick-release wristshot with good accuracy, doesn't have a big-wind up but can snap it quickly which makes it challenging to read. Has good offensive anticipation, without the puck has sneaky positioning coming just off the outskirts of the scoring area and sliding into high-slot and if there's room into low-slot area.

Svetlakov has a decent sturdy frame and can be a bit chippy both offensively in front of the net as well as defensively. He likes to get his body on players when checking and often gets enough contact to put them off-balance or slow them down without taking a penalty. Also uses his stick well to defend. Although a third time eligible who lacks the dynamic skills of some more talented countrymen, this Russian forward has built up his draft stock with a strong international and domestic KHL performance.

Sylvestre, Gabriel
RD – Shawinigan Cataractes (QMJHL) – 6'04", 186
HockeyProspect.com Ranking: 169

Sylvestre was drafted in the first round of the 2014 QMJHL Draft (18th overall) by the Shawinigan Cataractes out of the College Esther-Blondin midget program. After a promising rookie season in 2014-2015, Sylvestre took a step back this season with his play. He attended the Canada summer U-18 camp in August for the Ivan Hlinka camp but was one of the final cuts.

He really struggled in the first half of the season with his poor puck management, and had all sorts of difficulties moving the puck in the transition game. He was often paired with fellow draft-eligible player Samuel Girard. With him, Sylvestre could just pass the puck whenever he was in danger and Girard would make the smart play to get the puck out. Sylvestre has size that NHL teams covet and can bring a physical game to the table. Defensively, he can block shots on the PK unit and his long reach can also prove useful. There's no flash or creativity in his game offensively. He does possess a big shot from the point, which remains his main attribute in the offensive zone. With his struggles with the puck, his confidence was low and it seemed to affect the rest of his game. In our viewings, we saw him make bad reads, playing the puck instead of the man in one-on-one confrontations or just getting beat on the outside by speedy skaters. In the 2nd half, with less ice time because of new acquisitions, he kept his game more simple and seemed to regain some confidence that was lost in the first half, in the defensive zone. There is still a big question mark with him going forward : his play with the puck.

Quotable:" A big disappointment this season after a strong rookie year in 14-15, didn't look confident in most of my viewings this season and made a lot of dumb plays with the puck." - HP scout Jérôme Bérubé

Tetrault, Levi
LD - Guelph Storm (OHL) 6'01", 184
HockeyProspect.com Ranking: NR

Tetrault played a very simple shutdown role for the Guelph Storm, primarily playing on the third pairing. Levi was a fourth round pick out of the Chatham-Kent Cyclones program at the 2014 OHL Priority Selection Draft.

The native of Pain Court showed a little toughness to his game. He competes hard in the corners and won his share of battles. He's very effective when working below the goal line and has not only the size, but the proper body positioning to win a lot of battles. He was usually effective one on one but would occasionally mishandle the situation. which sometimes resulted in minor penalties. He plays a very defensive minded game and has limited puck skills. He is at his best when making the smart simple play with the puck and letting his teammates do the heavy lifting advancing the play. Tetrault has the size and played well within his role but projects as a limited, defensive first defenseman who is strong in battles in the corners.

Thompson, Tage
RW/C - U Conn (Hockey East) 6'05" 185
HockeyProspect.com Ranking: 28

Thompson, who is the son of former NHL defenseman Brent Thompson, posted good point totals as a freshman at U Conn this season after joining the Huskies from the USNTDP. He's a huge kid with soft hands who posted the bulk of his points on the power play. Thompson is a big raw talent who put himself on the map this season after making big strides in his development. After watching him you come away impressed with his defensive game and shooting ability. It was his shot that paid off big-time for him this past season. Despite his huge frame, Thompson is not an overly physical player but he will throw his share of hits. Tage is solid down low. He plays a good game below the hashmarks and is effective in the cycle game. Thompson's defensive game is stellar. He's smart and he understands defensive hockey. He's used on the PK where he even lined up as a defenseman.

Tage had a great development year and gave himself a chance to be a 1st round selection in this years draft. If he slides out of the 1st round he won't last long in the 2nd round before he gets selected. We don't see a top six scorer but he can chip in on offense and be relied upon to be a very responsible forward.

Quotable: "He's a first rounder for sure for me. I saw him twice recently and loved him in both games." - NHL Scout (February 2016)

Quotable: "The lack of scoring 5 on 5 scares me a bit. Obviously the size is great, but I like his smarts and his work ethic out on the ice. That work ethic really shows on the defensive side of the puck. He is a forward with a very responsible defensive game. Add in the ability to get production out of his shot and he brings a few things to the table." - HP Scout Mark Edwards

Thurkauf, Calvin
LW – Kelowna Rockets (WHL) 6'01", 197
HockeyProspect.com Ranking: NR

Calvin Thurkauf is a Swiss import who made an impact on the Kelowna Rockets this year playing in a physical depth role. A big hitter who never looks intimidated, Thurkauf plays a very Canadian game. He generates scoring opportunities and offensive zone possession time through being physically dominant along the walls and in the corners. He's got decent first-step acceleration and wins the majority of his short-area puck races.

Thurkauf attacks the net with fury and doesn't shy away from the hard-to-play areas. His playmaking skills and hockey IQ are both good, although he had some difficulty finding the net with his shot this season. His full-stride acceleration is only average and he needs to become better defensively.

Timleck, Adam
RW - Peterborough Petes (OHL) 5'09" 158
HockeyProspect.com Ranking: NR

The Peterborough Petes selected Timleck in the fourth round from the Toronto Jr. Canadiens Minor Midget program. Timleck made the Petes as a 16 year old and posted minimal numbers in a limited role. He had his role increased dramatically for his second season with the Petes and posted solid numbers.

Adam is an undersized forward who has decent skating ability. He has shown a little creativity in the offensive zone and has quick hands. His shot is average at best, but he has been able to capitalize on some chances around the goal area this season. Timleck's best asset is his great work ethic. He showed a good compete level and finishes his checks on bigger opponents. His hockey sense seems to be limited as he is generally at best making the lower percentage plays. He struggled in the defensive zone in our viewings, unable to help clear the zone or make quick decisions with forecheck pressure to help advance to play. Overall Timleck is shaping up to be a solid junior level player, but is not someone we consider drafting in the 2016 NHL Entry Draft.

Timms, Matthew
LD - Peterborough Petes (OHL) 5'09" 158
HockeyProspect.com Ranking: NR

Matthew was selected 22nd overall at the 2014 OHL Priority Selection Draft by the Peterborough Petes. Timms made the OHL as a 16 year old and played a limited role behind veteran defenders. In his second OHL season, Timms saw his role increase where he played a top four role on some nights along with power play action.

Timms is an undersized offensive defenseman with good skating ability. He shows agility and puck control, which has helped him on the rush. He struggles to make puck decisions in a timely fashion and will use his skating to backtrack and create more time. In the offensive zone he will make plays and move the puck effectively. His puck skills showed gradual improvements throughout the season. Matthew has some offensive upside at the junior level, which allowed him to get some action on the Petes' power play. He has a big shot for a small defenseman and gets a lot of power behind it. Defensively he has a lot of work to do. He is very strong for his size but still has trouble containing big puck protecting power forwards who drive the net. He lands hard hits for an undersized defender, but needs to get even bigger and stronger to experience more success in front of the net and down low. Although Timms showed good improvements throughout the season, he isn't a player we would draft in the 2016 NHL Entry Draft.

Timpano, Troy
G - Sudbury Wolves (OHL) 6'01" 184
HockeyProspect.com Ranking: NR

Troy was selected in the second round of the 2013 OHL Priority Selection Draft from the Toronto Titans program. He started out as the back-up for Sudbury before starting the majority of games for the Wolves over the past two seasons.

Timpano best asset is his great ability to read cross crease passes and getting over to stop them. It was consistently noted this season on his cross crease and ability to handle one-timers very effectively. He has a tendency to go down a little early, which has resulted in patient opponents being able to exploit the top shelf on Timpano. He has been noted for fighting the puck quite a bit, making the save but giving up lots of rebounds and not controlling where those rebounds go. He also has a little trouble with letting in some soft goals. This can sometimes affect goaltenders and snowball into a bigger issue. Troy handles the puck well for a goaltender and does a good job not trying to do too much with it and setting up his defensemen for quick transitions

Timpano was a very highly regarded goaltender coming out of Minor Midget for good reason. However he has struggled to really take that next step as a starting goaltender at the OHL level. He certainly has the upside to turn into one of the better junior goaltenders, but he has his work cut out for him.

Tkachuk, Matthew
LW - London Knights (OHL) 6'01.5", 200
HockeyProspect.com Ranking: 5

Tkachuk was taken in the 4th round of the 2014 OHL Draft from the St. Louis AAA Blues U16 program. Tkachuk opted to spend his first two junior seasons with the United States National Team Development Program. Due to a late birthdate, Tkachuk was able to make the jump to the OHL's London Knights for his NHL draft year. We were not surprised that Tkachuk made an immediate impact for the Knights and played a huge role in their offense and overall success. Twelve months ago we ranked him as the 4th best prospect for the upcoming NHL Draft.

One of the things that makes Tkachuk a high end prospect for this draft is his vision. His vision is on an elite level. He has a special ability to create offense when there doesn't seem to be a lane. He posted nearly two points per game and while he had great linemates to play with, they benefitted from him as much as he benefitted from them. Tkachuk stats would suggest he is more of a playmaker than a finisher, but he has proven that he has a good shot and can put the puck in the net. He's great at setting up his linemates and makes others around him better. Tkachuk will play a physically engaging game, he is one of those players who gets under his opponents skin. As far as a weakness, he's just an average skater and doesn't possess separation speed. Improving on his quickness and top speed would be beneficial but it hasn't held him back so far. He seems to find a way, there is nothing wrong with his compete level. Tkachuk has a thick frame, which he uses to protect the puck well. He chooses great lanes on the rush with and without the puck. One of things that we think will lead to him having great success in the NHL is his ability to play at an elite level in the dirty areas of the ice. He's fantastic from in tight, his ability to win pucks, fight off checks and score from inside is fantastic. His hand eye is great and his ability to anticipate possible scoring chances is impressive. We've seen him score numerous goals on deflections. He's ok defensively; he's had great nights and others where he could've been better. The quality of his back pressure was inconsistent from game to game.

Tkachuk projects to be a top line winger who makes his linemates better. His vision and passing ability is very high end and will translate very well at the NHL level. Don't sleep on his shot, he has buried some chances with impressive shots. His skating could be improved upon but we don't expect it to be a stopper as far as NHL success goes. He has the upside of a perennial all-star NHL forward.

Quotable: "He was great playing down the middle today." - NHL Scout (October 2015)

Quotable: "He's so good playing inside, that's the NHL game today and why I have him over Dubois." - NHL Scout (April 2016)

Quotable: "If we pick 4th it's the toughest decision in this draft. Dubois and Tkachuk is so tight." - NHL Scout (April 2016)

Quotable: "You have to take Dubois over Tkachuk. It's close, but Dubois is the safer pick because of Tkachuk's skating." - NHL Scout (April 2016)

Quotable: "Bloodlines." - NHL Scout (April 2016)

Quotable: "I was a huge fan of Tkachuk's game long before this season began so I'm not the least bit surprised at his success this season. He is a special player who seems to play even better when the stakes are higher. His ability to play at a high level inside the house is impressive. He always seems to be the guy who gets the better result out of 50/50 battles. He's scored both ugly goals through grinding in the dirty areas and he probably doesn't get enough credit for amount of high-end skilled goals he's scored. His hockey IQ is through the roof and his vision is up with the best in this draft class. The Oilers should have their choice of Tkachuk, his teammate Olli Juolevi (if they want to go the Dman route) or Pierre-Luc Dubois when they are on the clock with the 4th pick. I like their chances of landing a great player." - Mark Edwards

Quotable: "In my six years of scouting, there hasn't been more than one or two players who possess the type of vision Tkachuk has. He finds plays that a lot of hockey players in or out of the NHL simply can't. He took a lot of bad penalties in the playoffs, but it seemed like for every one bad penalty, he would rack up two points." - HP Scout, Ryan Yessie

Topping, Jordan
LW – Tri City Americans (WHL) 6'01", 196
HockeyProspect.com Ranking: NR

Topping is a second time NHL draft eligible who brings a blend of physical play and scoring ability. Topping had a great improvement from his rookie WHL year, putting up 66 points while he totaled just 18 last year. Topping is a competitive player in all three zones and can be a physical presence on the forecheck. He likes to finish his checks and was also involved in a couple of fights. Add to that the ability to score and you quickly get an interesting player. Not a bad playmaker, but his game is really about setting himself up in the middle or slightly to the weak-side looking for his wrist-shot that he can get off with minimal room. Topping can also come down on his off wing and let one go top corner, even finding a way to get it off with a defenseman in front or on him. Topping has shown good improvement in his second year of WHL hockey, but he will still need to improve his overall game. The physicality and scoring ability provide an interesting combination but he needs to do more to create his own chances and be involved on a shift-by-shift basis as someone who can make plays.

Tufte, Riley
LW – Blaine High School (MN-HS) 6'4.75", 205
HockeyProspect.com Ranking: 23

Tufte started the 15/16 season with the Fargo Force (USHL) but returned to his Minnesota High School team where he looked like a man among boys most nights in route to winning Minnesota's Mr. Hockey as the State's Top Player. Tufte finished the season back with the Fargo Force at the end of the year where he continued his impressive play.

Tufte gets around the ice well and his powerful lower body makes him a nightmare for opposing defenseman when he gets a head of steam. Tufte possesses excellent offensive skill and playmaking ability. He can get his shot off and stick handle in traffic with ease and once he learns to use his size to his advantage more he will be even more effective then he already is. In his return to Fargo later in the year we saw a more confident player who wasn't shy to take the puck to the net and use his size and reach more effectively. Tufte does lack some physicality and looses more puck battles then a player his size should and that is one area of his game that will need to improve going forward.

Riley is a smart player who understands the game and processes situations quickly, which makes him a solid 200 foot player. He rarely takes a shift off or misses an assignment in our viewings. We see Tufte as a high end prospect who has the skills when packaged together can be impactful playmaker at the professional level. Tufte will continue his progression at Minnesota-Duluth this fall.

Quotable: "At the Hlinka he was somewhat overshadowed by two 2017.5 in Mittelstadt and Yamamoto. His upside and ability were both apparent, but he struggled to show the impact you'd expect out of his tools." - HP Scout Nik Funa

Quotable: "He dominated every Minnesota High School game I saw him play, he was unstoppable and probably could have put in a couple more goals in a few of the games but he elected to pass." NHL Scout (March 2016)

Quotable: "Everyone loves his size and projection as a power winger, but his skill can be equally as impressive." - HP Scout Dusten Braaksma

Tuulola, Eetu
LW – HPK (Fin U20) – 6'02", 227
HockeyProspect.com Ranking: 88

Tuulola is a big, heavy winger with good potential. He likes to play a physical game, throwing hits and has a great quick-release on his wrist-shot. Tuulola could show more determination in front of the net, but likes to find the soft spots in the slot and wait for a pass. In one swift motion he can receive the puck and snap it out of his wrist, making it hard for goalies to react. He usually makes good decisions inside the offensive zone but his vision seems average. His biggest weakness is however his footspeed. It limits him in several ways. While he likes to be physical, as a forechecker he would often arrive to the puck-carrier and complete the hit when the puck was already safely passed. He can also be rather easily forced wide on zone-entries as defensemen tend to quickly close down on him. Making in-game adjustments to the puck changing direction is a bit of an issue.

However, to Tuulola's credit his skating already looked improved at the end of the year at the U18s as compared to the start of the season at the Hlinka Memorial Tournament. There might be some questions around his weight, the brother of Joni (Blackhawks' 6th round pick in the 2015 NHL Draft) is a naturally big kid but shedding a couple of pounds might help making him faster on skates. Tuulola is an intriguing package of size, shot and physicality, however the fact that his production hasn't really improved from last year in his domestic U20 league raises some questions.

Quotable: "His feet are the problem, although there's been some improvement there. Really like his combination of size and the release on his shot." - HP Scout Nik Funa

Quotable: "If this kid got in shape he could be dynamite." - NHL Scout (April 2016)

Quotable: "He always impresses me but his play back home in league play didn't match what I saw in International play. Fitness is an issue." - HP scout Mark Edwards

Twarynski, Carsen
LW – Calgary Hitmen (WHL) 6'02", 198
HockeyProspect.com Ranking: 133

Carsen is a big bodied kid that has very underrated skating ability. He is a strong powerful skater with a long reach that likes to throw his body around. He also prides himself on being first to the puck and if not will do whatever it takes to win possession for his team. He is relentless on the forecheck and creates space and scoring chances for his line mates with his physical play.

Carsen brings high energy when he is on the ice and he competes in all three zones. Carsen will sacrifice his body to make a play and help his team gain momentum. He leads by example and blocks shots and will do whatever it takes to help his team win. Along with all these intangibles he also can shoot the puck. He possesses the ability to use different types of shots and can get his shot off quickly. He has shown a lot of growth in the offensive side of his game from his rookie season and looks to continue to develop this area of his game.

He did not have huge offensive numbers, but consistently brought the effort and compete level that is required to be successful. He projects as a solid bottom six forward.

Vala, Ondrej
LD – Kamloops Blazers (WHL) 6'05", 207
HockeyProspect.com Ranking: 116

Ondrej Vala is a tall import defenseman from the Czech Republic who plied his trade with the Kamloops Blazers this season in the WHL. Vala is quite awkward on first impression, appearing like he's about to topple over at times. However, despite his ghastly appearance on skates, his stride undergoes slight improvements with each of our viewings.

Vala's first passes are decent as he has good straight-ahead vision out of his own end, but doesn't have the skating to get himself out of trouble under pressure and can be reduced to simply getting rid of the puck any way he can when he runs out of room. He saw some time on the powerplay this year, where he was able to display more of his distribution skills with the puck. He actually has some upside with his slapper but lacks the footwork and the ability to find seams to get it off in time, thus he does not use it as often as he could.

His gap control when defending will need to improve. Vala is a big kid who can play physical, so developing his gap and coverage is a must as he moves forward. He's got some reach in him, but isn't particularly good at steering the play to the outside or preventing controlled entries into his zone. His big frame allows him to block shots, but while he's willing to be physical he needs to maintain his slot coverage better when boxing forwards out of the slot and protecting the goalie. Too many times he loses his position and despite his tools, he is currently not a particularly strong defensive player. Vala is a raw kid with a frame and tools that show some upside, but he's really quite far off in terms of polishing his game. His positioning and gap needs work, his footwork will also need to improve.

Vehviläinen, Veini
G – JYP (FEL) – 6'01", 183
HockeyProspect.com Ranking: NR

Veini is a second-year eligible goaltender who has played two good seasons at the pro level. In season 2014-15 he had a strong year in second highest pro league in Finland and this season he continued with a good performance in the Finnish top league. He went un-drafted last summer which was a huge disappointment for him but he was invited to Anaheim Ducks' development camp in July. After an impressive first half of the season he had a disappointing showing at the World Juniors and was less effective in the second half. He still recorded a 2.04 GAA while saving 92.5% of the shots he faced in 28 Liiga games, but failing to impress on the international stage might hurt him on draft day. Overall he has improved especially from a physical standpoint. He's calm goalie who reads the game well and possesses sound technique, but he has to improve his stick handling and on rebounds. His size isn't ideal and he doesn't make himself look any bigger in the net.

Verbeek, Hayden
RC - Sault Ste. Marie Greyhounds (OHL) 5'09.25", 177
HockeyProspect.com Ranking: 160

Verbeek was picked in the fourth round of the 2013 OHL Draft by the Soo Greyhounds. Verbeek was a bit of a shoot first, control the puck style of player in Minor Midget, he seemed to adjust to more of a playmaking forward during his time with the Chatham Jr. B Maroons as a 16 year old. With a late birthdate he has two seasons with the Greyhounds under his belt going into his draft year.

Verbeek is a small, but highly energetic forward. His compete level is off the charts and is among the best in this draft class. He uses his excellent speed to ramp up the pace of the game and force turnovers. He is a very good two-way player who works equally hard in all three zones. He can play a bit of a chippy game, sometimes taking extra whacks on the opposition when he can. He has some ability to create offense. His speed in transition has lead to him both gaining chances via breakaways and setting up linemates on odd man rushes. He is one of the better penalty killers in this draft class and will block shots, get into passing lanes and take away time and space very effectively.

What stands in the way of Verbeek's NHL upside is the lack of size and lack of top six offensive upside. He is a fantastic junior player and will have great impact at this level, but will have an uphill battle making the NHL because of his size and a skill set, that projects towards a bottom six role. He has the speed, compete and drive to be part of the minority who can beat the odds, and thus may hear his name called at the 2016 NHL Entry Draft.

Volcan, Nolan
LW – Seattle Thunderbirds (WHL) 5'09", 195
HockeyProspect.com Ranking: NR

Volcan is a solid two-way winger who competes at a very high level. He is a versatile forward and can play in any situation. While not flashy offensively, he has decent offensive skills and can contribute on the scoresheet. The first thing that strikes you about this player is that he is an exceptionally hard worker and he never takes a shift off. His motor is always running and he never stops skating, he also plays a very physical game taking every opportunity to finish his check. He is great along the boards and in the corners and wins one on one battles.

Volcan plays much bigger than his 5'9" frame indicates. He is a very strong, powerful player that loves to throw his body around. He is not a fast skater but has great agility and balance. He possesses a hard and heavy wrist shot with a quick release, but could work on being more accurate. Volcan was used in all situations and was solid playing on the second unit power play for most of the season. He was also relied upon to kill penalties and was noticeable as he always is willing to sacrifice his body and block shots. He is a valuable player that every coach loves to have on his team and as he continues to develop the offensive side of his game he will get his opportunity to prove he can contribute at the next level.

Wahlgren, Tim
LW – MODO J20 (SWE) – 6'00", 178
HockeyProspect.com Ranking: NR

Tim Wahlgren is a forward with good scoring instincts around the net, the ability to hide himself from coverage and playmaking skills.

Wahlgren isn't the fastest skater which is quite problematic at his size, however he finds ways to produce through his instincts. Wahlgren isn't a powerful net-crasher, but does a good job operating around the posts and in front of the net. He has good finishing ability and can score in those situations, he is also good at avoiding too much physical contact as he finds his ways to the soft spots in high-percentage scoring areas.

Wahlgren is a also an intelligent passer and can set-up linemates for scoring chances. He has good hands in-tight and can operate in small, tight spaces, flipping a saucer to an open linemate even when he is under pressure. Even though Wahlgren has good vision and hands, he is severely limited by his skating. At his size, he simply doesn't get enough acceleration and especially top-speed, which limits what he can do in transition. His agility and balance isn't too bad and he does well in changing angles and being shifty in smaller space, but he lacks the speed when bringing the puck through neutral zone. This also limits him without the puck. He can't quickly catch up on the backcheck nor be particularly useful on the forecheck.

Wahlgren has some good offensive tools, but at this point in time his skating is simply too underwhelming. That is where he can make the single biggest improvement as he moves forward.

Wall, Tyler
G – Leamington (GOJHL) 6'03", 202
HockeyProspect.com Ranking: 195

Wall won 27 games and lost twice. We saw him both times he lost this season so he wouldn't have wanted us to watch him too often. Wall played on a strong Leamington team that didn't give up many shots. That along with playing in a weaker league makes things more difficult for scouts trying to assess him. Wall is a big kid who is still raw but has some upside. He will be heading to UMass Lowel as early as this fall. Wall moves pretty well in his net. He can get a bit scrambly when he is recovering to make second saves. He is a bit inconsistent when he sets up to a shooter. He anticipates the play pretty well and is solid at tracking pucks. Quickness is decent considering his size. It's not a great goalie crop this season so someone might want to take a stab at Wall as a project with good upside.

Quotable: " I saw him last night. He was ok, but my concern is that I think if he played the way he did last night in the OHL he would've let in seven. I won't have him on my list." - NHL Scout (February 2016)

Quotable: " I like the kid. I won't be shocked if he gets drafted." - NHL Scout (February 2016)

Walker, Jack
LW – Victoria Royals (WHL) 5'11", 179
HockeyProspect.com Ranking: 158

Walker is a third-time NHL draft eligible who has continued to improve his production for the third straight year, putting up a respectable season with over PPG numbers. With Walker his best asset is rather immediately obvious, it's his speed and skating.

Walker is a very high-end skater and most of his game is based just around that. Walker has both high-end acceleration as well as top speed. More importantly however, Walker has the ability to change directions, move his feet, and still handle the puck. In fact, he is quite an adept puck-handler with a rather soft pair of hands. The speed he generate pushes defenses off on its own, however Walker's ability to handle the puck and change directions allows him to be a dangerous offensive player as it's extremely difficult for the defending players to close down gaps on him, Walker can also easily beat his man to the slot looking for a pass or a rebound to finish on. He is also a decent defensive forward, though he could utilize his skating even more than he does to be a defensive presence. This is Walker's third year of eligibility and he certainly didn't hurt himself with his season, as the improved numbers and the speed factor clearly stood out in a positive way for him.

Walker, Zachary
RW – USNTDP 6'00", 200
HockeyProspect.com Ranking: NR

Walker is a winger who has played a checking game for the USNTDP this season in a limited role. Walker generates solid speed at his size which allows him to hound the opposition. He has some upside in bringing the puck up the ice but has only average puck-skills and isn't someone that would create much offense at the next level. His hockey IQ isn't bad but he has to rely mostly on his competitiveness to be a factor. He does have good footwork in the offensive zone and utilizes it accordingly on the wall and in the corners where he can back off his checker with tight cuts. Walker clearly projects as a role player at the next level, as his checking game and skating are likely to be his calling card.

Walli, Juuso
LD – Ässät (FEL) – 6'04", 227
HockeyProspect.com Ranking: NR

A 96-born d-man who's a pure stay-at-home type of player. Huge kid with decent mobility and hockey sense. He has improved a lot in past years and the development during this season was outstanding. Last year he was a third pair d-man in Ässät's U20 team and he started this season in juniors, but was promoted to the pro team in the fall. In the spring he was already an important player there, playing a safe game in the defensive zone. Always willing to play a physical game and can make a decent play with the puck on his stick as well.

Weissbach, Linus
LW/RW – Frolunda J20 (SWE) – 5'09", 156
HockeyProspect.com Ranking: NR

Weissbach is a skilled offensive forward with dizzying hands. His first three steps propel him around defenders allowing him to drive the net or create space for his linemates. He has the ability to attract defenders in and then find his line mates at opportune times, which contributed to the number of assists (31) he had at the J20 level. Versatile in the offensive zone, he was used at centre, wing and on the point during the power play. Possesses a quick release that he can get off while in motion.

Despite his diminutive size, he isn't afraid to throw his weight around. However, he can be reckless with his speed sometimes and find himself in vulnerable positions leading to big hits or injuries. Started the pre-season GK Feskarn tournament on Frolunda's J18 team, but was moved up quickly and found himself making his first and only SHL appearance on September 24. Was consistently partnered with Chicago Blackhawks draft pick John Dahlstrom this season and worked well with a smart forward who can finish. On February 6, against AIK J20, he suffered a an injury after trying to drive the puck to the net, losing his balance and slamming hard into the boards back first. Missed significant time after that including a tournament with the Swedish U18 team.

Weissbach brings a lot of energy when he is on the ice and it is rare to see him take a shift off. He generates a lot of shot attempts whether by himself or setting up his line mates, but he has been unable to finish his chances at the international level and there is some concern about his effectiveness when facing top competition. Linus has added some much needed strength since last season and will need to continue developing this area of his game. Needs to find his position better in the defensive zone and trust his teammates more, but will block shots when needed. Was selected by the Tri-City Storm in the USHL 2016 Phase 2 draft, 28th overall.

Wells, Dylan
G - Peterborough Petes (OHL) 6'02" 182
HockeyProspect.com Ranking: 97

Dylan was selected by Peterborough from the Niagara North Stars Minor Midget Program. Wells made the OHL as a 16 year old and had a respectable season playing behind Matthew Mancina. He spent his second season behind Mancina again and seemed to struggle to find his rhythm this year.

Despite struggling quite a bit this season, Dylan Wells is still an intriguing goaltending prospect for the 2016 NHL draft. A big bodied, goaltender who moves well in his crease, Wells possesses good size and mobility between the pipes. A goaltender who is at his best when he gets to the top of his crease and challenges shooters, Wells does an excellent job of battling through screens and tracking pucks in traffic. Dylan plays his angles well, however when he is struggling rebound control is one of his issues. A goaltender who possesses extremely quick reflexes, Wells can sometimes rely to much on his reflexes, playing deep in his net, which leads to struggles. Still, Wells is a goaltender who possesses an excellent compete level, battling through traffic to make second and third chance saves. Wells covers the lower half of the net well, showing quick lateral movements, while remaining under control. Wells effectively squares up shooters and does possess a fairly strong glove hand. While there is significant intrigue to Wells game, consistency was a big issue throughout the season.

Dylan will be an interesting prospect going into the 2016 NHL Entry Draft. He entered the season with a ton of expectations and was backed by an outstanding Minor Midget season entering the OHL. Wells has a lot of upside. He has the size and quickness to still become a top goaltending prospect, but concerns throughout the season will bring that potential into question.

Quotable: "So far he is one of the biggest disappointments for me this season. I had high hopes for him." - NHL Scout (November 2015)

Quotable: "He has all the tools, but I think he lacks mental toughness. Seems like once one gets past him, it can get ugly." - NHL Scout - (January 2016)

Quotable: "His numbers are ugly but he's still on my list. He has the tools." - NHL Scout (February 2016)

Werner, Adam
G – Farjestad BK J20 (SWE) – 6'05", 198
HockeyProspect.com Ranking: NR

Werner is a second-time NHL draft eligible goalie who has great size. Werner has improved his numbers this season being a starter for Farjestad at the J20 level. While Werner boasts tremendous size at 6'5, he still needs to learn how to fully use it to his advantage. He actually has decent athletic ability for that size, but needs to cut down on angles better. His movement across the crease is decent, but he doesn't make himself look big because he stays back on the goal-line at almost all times. This becomes a problem with lateral passes as he needs to anticipate them better instead of trying to get across the whole crease after over-committing to the possibility of a shot. His puck-handling and calmness in making plays from behind the net look good. Werner has some upside with his size and athletic ability but will need to find better ways to use that 6'5 frame to his advantage.

Westlund, Gustaf
LC - The Gunnery (HS Conn) - 6'00.25", 166
HockeyProspect.com Ranking: 168

Big kid who has some talent but we question his overall hockey smarts. Point production scares us a bit based on the league he plays in. That said, he can really skate, has skill and plays with some heart. One of those players that is always flying around but sometimes you start to wonder what he is accomplishing. He will be an interesting one to follow. He has talent but it's a bit of a red flag for us when you have the that much talent in that league but lack on the production.

Quotable: "He was a nice kid in the interview but his honesty hurt him a bit. Not sure if he's put a lot of work into his game." - NHL Scout (May 2016)

Wikman, William
LW/RW – Leksands IF (Allsvenskan) - 5'11", 194
HockeyProspect.com Ranking: NR

Wikman is a second-time draft eligible who has made good strides this season. He has improved from putting up just 7 points in 24 games at the J20 level last season, to being over PPG this year while also putting up 5 points in 18 Allsvenskan games. Wikman boasts a good combination of skating and ability with his hands. He has the ability to change the angle of attack and keep his speed while stick handling with precision. He has a decently sturdy frame and is an active checker in all three zones, he shows some upside with his ability to strip players of the puck and will also physically engage. Wikman can both finish as well as pass and he shows good finesse on his passes. He has a great soft-touch with the puck and distributes pucks that are flat on the ice, easy to handle, and on tape. We are not convinced that Wikman has done quite enough to warrant using a pick on him, but his progression from last year has been good and the type of game he plays is rather likable.

Woll, Joseph
G – USNTDP (USHL) 6'03", 198
HockeyProspect.com Ranking: 37

Woll is a big goalie that plays to his strengths, filling out the crease with his large size and has a will to compete. He moves well in the crease and looks quite controlled and fluid in his movements despite the heavy frame. Woll positions well on the initial shots and squares up to the shooter. With his size, it's hard to get pucks past him once he gets into position. He does a good job battling in the crease and will maintain his position on jam-plays, shows some good reaction time and agility when finding pucks laying around the crease and snatching them up before the opposition gets the stick on it.

He could track the puck a bit better through traffic, his size helps him as pucks will hit him regardless, but sometimes he could do a better job finding a clear sight-line on point shots with bodies in front of him. In those situations his rebound control can be better as well, as pucks can bounce right back into the slot. Overall, Woll offers solid potential for a team that is looking at a pro-sized goalie prospect with reasonably good movement and compete in his crease and that uses size to his advantage.

Yakovenko, Alexander
LD – Team Russia U18 (MHL) – 5'11", 172
HockeyProspect.com Ranking: NR

Yakovenko is a defenseman that shows most of his upside when the puck is on his stick and especially in offensive situations. He is a decent skater, he gets around well and will get to places in time, but at his size his speed isn't particularly impressive. He will find open lanes to move the puck but his top speed lacks that separation ability that would be expected of a defenseman his size.

Yakovenko shows good offensive ability from the point in the offensive zone and on power-play. He does a good job finding openings for his shot and also has a big slapshot in his arsenal. He gets his slapper off quickly and actually gets good power and accuracy on it. The fact that he is a shot threat along with a decent mobility and passing game gives him the ability to be useful as a trigger-man and someone who can play the point on PP.

Yakovenko understands his position and knows where he should be in defensive zone and how to cover his man. He is somewhat undersized which is an issue and compounded by the fact that he isn't a truly great skater. His compete level is decent but not something that would stand out either. At this point in time it is hard to classify Yakovenko as a strong defensive player.

Zachar, Marek
RW – Bili Tygri Liberec U20 (CZE) – 5'08", 146
HockeyProspect.com Ranking: NR

Zachar is a small left-shooting right wing who plays with plenty of bite and has tremendous speed. Zachar would be best described as fearless, as he certainly doesn't play like he would be afraid of bigger players. His skating is impressive, his acceleration, first few steps and edgework are great and he has fantastic top speed. He can push defenses back while penetrating the space forward and handling the puck. Despite the smaller size, Zachar will also drop the shoulder and drive to the net if the defenseman doesn't respect his speed. Zachar had some good showings in our viewings this season, but speed and competitiveness aside, he is really hurt by the lack of size and he is not overly skilled with the puck. He will need to add strength to his body and power to his shot. The speed gives him some upside and one possible way out of his size predicament, but at this point in time there is simply not enough evidence that he is someone who would project as the next greatly undersized NHL player.

Quotable: "More likely than not he will never make it to the NHL, but he's brave and I found myself cheering for this kid" - HP Scout Mik Portoni

Zelenak, Vojtech
LD – HC Sparta Praha U20 (CZE) – 6'06", 223
HockeyProspect.com Ranking: 119

Zelenak is a towering defenseman that plays with a lot of passion. He doesn't complicate his puck decisions and consistently chooses the simple play. He knows when to jump up in the play and when to hang back. Great shot on the point that finds seams. On the power play, he can quarterback from the point or place himself in front the goaltender creating a massive screen.

For his size, his footwork is relatively strong and his pivots are good. However, when facing forwards attacking with speed he gives too much gap allowing the forwards to get shots on net. But when his gaps are good, his reach makes it a nightmare for players to get around him. After making mistakes, he sometimes yells at himself on the bench and sulks, something that isn't a major concern but shows some lack of maturity.

Quotable: "When you first see him, you think he's just a defensive defenseman, but then you notice that he can actually generate some speed with the puck and even surprises with an offensive move or two. In my viewings, he was even utilized as a net-presence on the PP. Really big kid that at least has some tools to work with." - HP Scout Nik Funa

Zimmer, Max
LW – Chicago Steel (USHL) 5'11.75", 187
HockeyProspect.com Ranking: 95

The first thing that stands out about Zimmer's game in our viewings is his excellent skating ability. His straight line speed both with and without the puck is impressive and his first few strides and acceleration is among the best in the USHL. Zimmer likes to play with pace and use his speed to his advantage, especially through the neutral zone. Zimmer possesses good vision of the ice and creativity which allows him to create scoring chances out of nothing. Zimmer is still a player looking for a bit of an identity in the sense of being a playmaker or more of a shoot first guy and still needs to figure out how to best put his whole skill set together into a more consistent and effective package, however there are enough skills and intangibles there that make him an intriguing NHL prospect.

Zimmer's offensive skills are impressive and his 2 way game has come a long way this past season in Chicago. There is still room for improvement but Zimmer has found a way to use his speed and skating to contribute in his own end as well. He wins a lot more races to loose pucks and engages in puck battles more where as previously he would be the guy looking for the outlet pass. Zimmer is a very mature and coachable player who brings a team first mentality to his approach. He is a Wisconsin commit but likely returning to the Steel for the 16/17 season.

Quotable: "Probably the fastest skater in the USHL this past season, just hasn't figured out the best way to use it yet, however I am a big fan of this kids work ethic and commitment to improve his game." - HP scout Dusten Braaksma

Quotable: "Good skill, great speed and decent hockey sense but the issue for me is he isn't an overly big kid and there is no physical element to his game. He plays on the perimeter a bit too much for me." - NHL Scout (April 2016)

2017 NHL DRAFT TOP 30

2017 NHL DRAFT TOP 30

RANK	POS	PLAYER	HEIGHT	WEIGHT	TEAM
1	RC	PATRICK, NOLAN	6'02"	193	BRANDON WHEAT KINGS (WHL)
2	RD	LILJEGREN, TIMOTHY	6'00"	190	ROGLE J20 (SWE J20)
3	RC	VILARDI, GABRIEL	6'02"	193	WINDSOR SPITFIRES (OHL)
4	RW	TIPPETT, OWEN	6'01"	181	MISSISSAUGA STEELHEADS (OHL)
5	LW	COMTOIS, MAXIME	6'01"	192	VICTORIAVILLE TIGRES (QMJHL)
6	LC	MITTLESTADT, CASEY	5'11"	190	EDEN PRAIRIE HIGH (HS-MN)
7	LC	PETTERSSON, ELIAS	6'01"	152	TIMRA IK (ALLSVENSKAN)
8	LC	HISCHIER, NICO	6'00"	172	SC BERN (NLA)
9	LW	TOLVANEN, EELI	5'10"	172	SIOUX CITY MUSKETEERS (USHL)
10	RD	FOOTE, CALLAN	6'03"	198	KELOWNA ROCKETS (WHL)
11	LW	VESALAINEN, KRISTIAN	6'03"	203	FROLUNDA HC (SEL)
12	LD	PAQUETTE, JACOB	6'02"	203	KINGSTON FRONTENACS (OHL)
13	LD	HAGUE, NICOLAS	6'05"	207	MISSISSAUGA STEELHEADS (OHL)
14	RW	YAMAMOTO, KAILER	5'09"	160	SPOKANE CHIEFS (WHL)
15	RW	KOSTIN, KLIM	6'03"	190	HK MVD BALASHIKHA (MHL)
16	LC	MORAND, ANTOINE	5'09"	170	ACADIE-BATHURST TITAN (QMJHL)
17	RW	POPUGAEV, NIKITA A.	6'04"	204	MOOSE JAW WARRIORS (WHL)
18	LD	SAMORUKOV, DMITRI	6'00"	159	CSKA MOSKVA U17 (RUS U17)
19	LD	VAAKANAINEN, URHO	6'01"	187	BLUES (SM LIIGA)
20	LW	RATCLIFFE, ISAAC	6'04"	192	GUELPH STORM (OHL)
21	LC	DAVIDSSON, MARCUS	6'00"	185	DJURGARDEN J20 (SWE J20)
22	RC	REEDY, SCOTT	6'01"	187	USA NTDP U17 (USHL)
23	LC	ANDERSSON, LIAS	5'11"	198	HV71 (SEL)
24	LC	RASMUSSEN, MICHAEL	6'05"	200	TRI-CITY AMERICANS (WHL)
25	RC	STUDNICKA, JACK	6'00"	163	OSHAWA GENERALS (OHL)
26	LC	RUZICKA, ADAM	6'04"	209	HC PARDUBICE U18 (CZE U18)
27	LD	VALIMAKI, JUUSO	6'02"	200	TRI-CITY AMERICANS (WHL)
28	LD	BLACKER, IAN	6'03"	181	OAKVILLE BLADES (OJHL)
29	G	TARASOV, DANIIL	6'03"	154	TOLPAR UFA (MHL)
30	LD	HEISKANEN, MIRO	5'10"	154	HIFK U20 (FIN JR.)
HM	LW	BUCEK, SAMUEL	6'02"	192	CHICAGO STEEL (USHL)
HM	RW	MATTHEOS, STELIO	6'01"	194	BRANDON WHEAT KINGS (WHL)
HM	G	DIPIETRO, MIKE	6'00"	198	WINDSOR SPITFIRES (OHL)
HM	LC	MISMASH, GRANT	6'00"	183	USA NTDP U17 (USHL)
HM	RC	LODNIA, VANYA	5'09"	171	ERIE OTTERS (OHL)
HM	RD	FLEURY, CALE	6'01"	192	KOOTENAY ICE (WHL)
HM	RC	LIND, KOLE	6'05"	172	KELOWNA ROCKETS (WHL)
HM	LW	SAFIN, OSTAP	6'04"	198	HC SPARTA PRAHA U18 (CZE U18)
HM	LD	SALO, ROBIN	6'00"	181	SPORT (SM LIIGA)
HM	LD	GILDON, MAX	6'02"	179	USA NTDP U17 (USHL)
HM	RD	MARTIN, LUKE	6'02"	201	USA NTDP U18 (USHL)

2017 NHL DRAFT PROSPECTS

Abate, Joseph
RW – Chicago Mission U18 6'02", 169

Abate is an interesting prospect because he was easily good enough to play in the USHL last season but elected to return to Mission. Abate did see 3 games with Bloomington (USHL) toward the end of the season. Abate plays a power forward style who shows good speed down the wall and likes to use his size and strength to take pucks to the net and possesses a pretty good shot. Abate is a decent skater with good straight ahead speed but there is room for improvement with his footwork. Abate's hockey sense and playmaking ability isn't there yet but he is very good and knowing what he needs to do to be successful with his skill set and executing. Abate is a University of Wisconsin commit but will likely play next season in the USHL.

Alexeyev, Yaroslav
LW – MVD (MHL) – 5'10", 148

An undersized but dynamic Russian winger, Alexeyev spent pretty much the whole season on a line with Kostin and Bitsadze, for the most playing against older competition. That probably helped when the trio was forced by circumstances to become Russia 1st line at the U18 Worlds and the three underagers were able to hold their own.

Yaroslav seems the kind of forward able to put up fine offensive numbers even when he is not very noticeable. He is a smart player inside the offensive zone, he analyses the play quicker than most and can make something happen all of a sudden as he excels at taking advantage of defensive breakdowns. If defensemen make a mistake in coverage and leave the slot empty, Alexeyev recognizes it right away and is able to capitalize, he is in fact a dangerous passer in the offensive zone and is also good at sniffing out chances around the net, getting there at the right time.

Alexeyev's main feature is his tremendous agility. He has speed, he is shifty and can leave opponents behind with starts and turns. However, he only displays his skills in brief moments, as of now he is not the kind of player that dominates shifts or makes an impact on a shift by shift basis. He can often be invisible and he will need to get stronger and round up his game moving forward. To succeed at the next level in today's game he'll have to play with intensity on a more consistent basis and bring more of an all around effort.

Almeida, Justin
LW – Prince George Cougars (WHL) 5'09", 160

Almeida is a fifth overall pick of the Lethbridge Hurricanes going back to the 2014 WHL Bantam Draft. So far he's lived up to expectations, he's still fairly small, but he plays the game with a lot of drive and determination. Almeida is a decently quick forward who brings the puck through traffic with surprising velocity, power and ease. He has quick hands. He plays the game with a lot of hustle gets onto pucks with a lot of jump but could benefit from more patience and refinement in his decision-making. He had trouble playing a patient game with the puck this season. Although he's small, he's a good two-way presence and maintained his spot on the lineup by playing a complete game.

Anderson, Matt
LD – Holy Family H.S. (MN-HS) 6'00", 189

Anderson is an offensive defenseman with a solid base and excellent skating ability. Anderson plays a powerful game in every sense of the word; he possesses a powerful and strong skating stride. Plays in the corner with a bull in a china shop mentality, is physical and wills his way to winning puck battles. Matt has the ability to generate offense from the back end, is calm with the puck but knows where he is going with it and moves it up the ice quickly. Green Bay holds Anderson's USHL rights and is committed to attend University of Minnesota-Duluth.

Anderson, Mikey
LD – Waterloo Black Hawks (USHL) 5'11", 200

The younger brother of current USNTDP player Joey Anderson, Anderson is built like a tank and has the ability to play like it at times. Extremely strong lower body and skating stride, he is difficult to move off the puck in our viewings, even as a 99' year playing in the USHL. He can bring a physical presence and brings some nastiness to his game. He is reliable with the puck but in no way flashy or highly skilled. He will make safe reliable plays out of his own end but rarely jumps into the play past the center ice point. Committed to Minnesota Duluth, Anderson will be back in Waterloo next season to continue to develop.

Anderson-Dolan, Jaret
LC – Spokane Chiefs (WHL) 5'11", 181

A big scorer in Bantam, Anderson-Dolan was drafted in the first round into the WHL. He is on Hockey Canada's radar for future tournaments having played at the U17 and heading to camp for the U18.

A quick skater that shows another gear in his first three steps, he carries the puck with authority and is elusive when moving up the ice making him a threat for end-to-end rushes. He's quite good at entering the zone but can skate himself into less than ideal positions. He has a quick accurate wrist shot, with nifty hands that allow him to control pucks in tight spaces. He shows a willingness to battle for his space and attack the middle of the ice. Anderson-Dolan's compete level is one of his better assets as he will work tirelessly for his space on ice and is also a useful off-the-puck player. One issue that he has run into in our viewings is that he tries to force the play a touch too often. While we like his compete, he hasn't learned yet how to let the game come to him and opt for a simple play when nothing else is there. In those instances his instinct is to try to run his head through the wall and try to execute a difficult play that doesn't have a lot of chance of working. He will need to find a better balance there, although it is perhaps encouraging that he wants to create something everytime he is on ice.

His rookie numbers weren't staggering but he wasn't receiving prime minutes for the Spokane Chiefs. He should be a more focal point on the offense next season and should see an improvement in his production.

Andersson, Lias
LC/W – HV71 J20 (SWE) – 5'11", 198

Andersson is a sturdy center that can also line up at wing and likes to dominate with his combination of power and an up-tempo straight ahead game. Andersson already boasts a well-built frame at almost 200 pounds and it shows on the ice as he is good at obtaining body position against players and winning battles, his first few steps are good but he generates just slightly above-average top-speed. Andersson is a forward that is excellent at driving the play, he can take off from his own end and bring the puck into offensive zone, he is first on loose pucks, and he is aggressive in gaining space forward. Andersson is a player that will engage in all areas of the ice and make sure he is trying to win his battles. With the puck, he exhibits strong puck-protection qualities.

He is an adept playmaker and can easily play with other skilled players but stands out more as the engine of the team and a scoring threat. Andersson has a diverse shooting arsenal and can score in multiple ways. He can score from up-close and on his wristers, but also has a bomb of a one-timer that he likes to set up on the occasion. He was dominant against his age-group as he put up 61 points in 38 games against J20 competition and has also performed well internationally. Andersson is a well-rounded forward that can drive the play, as he moves forward and his physical advantages start waning, it will be interesting to see how much of his impact he can retain against men. If he adapts and succeeds he will have a chance at being a first round selection in the 2017 NHL Draft.

Quotable: "Liljegren aside, he might have had the single best game of a 2017 eligible I've seen this year in Europe. He kept coming in waves just driving the play and pinning the other team into their end endlessly. Had ridiculous energy. Really like how he drives the play. At his 200 pounds he can be a handful for junior defensemen, but I'll watch for whether he can produce offense against men." – HP Scout Nik Funa

Quotable: "I wrote a lot of notes on him in my viewings. Most of it was positive. Amongst what he showed scouts was a hard shot with a quick release." HP Scout Mark Edwards

Aucoin, Yan
LD – Baie-Comeau Drakkar (QMJHL) – 6'01", 212

Aucoin was the 31st overall pick in the 2015 QMJHL Draft. There's not much offensive upside with him, but he's strong in his own zone and plays a physical game. He had a dismal plus/minus rating while playing for the worst team in the league (-31 in 59 games). Aucoin is strong on his skates and will play a physical game along the boards, clearing the front of the net as well. He's big and strong but also moves around the ice pretty well for a defenseman of his stature. That mobility, mixed with that good stick, allows him to cover a lot of space in the defensive zone. His play with the puck is relatively simple. There is not much creativity to it and he makes the simple outlet pass out of his zone. He will need to make quicker decisions with the puck going forward. As it stands, he gets into trouble when he's under pressure. He won't ever be a mainstay on the power play, but his bread and butter will be his defensive game and play on the PK unit, as he is not afraid to block shots.

Auger, Kyle
RD - Windsor Spitfires (OHL) 5'09", 170

Auger was selected in the second round of the 2015 OHL Priority Selection Draft out of the Thunder Bay Kings Minor Midget program. Auger split this season between the OHL Spitfires and the Jr. B LaSalle Vipers. This proved to be a good balance for Auger getting him acclimated in the OHL but allowing him to get some ice playing his game in Jr. B.

Auger is an excellent skater and can rush the puck up ice. He has good quickness and agility in the neutral zone. In the offensive zone he moves the puck fairly well. On the defensive side he usually makes a good first pass and has good overall puck skills. He can get into trouble on occasion when bigger opponents put pressure on him, but this may change with more experience at the OHL level. Auger spent some time at forward and provided a pretty solid forecheck on the opposition. Auger will need to grow leading up to the 2017 NHL Entry Draft as he is quite undersized for the NHL level, but still has time to get bigger. He will also need to add muscle to his frame. He projects to be an offensive defenseman.

Ball, Jacob
LW - North Bay Battalion (OHL) 6'03", 181

Jacob was selected in the third round of the 2015 OHL Priority Selection Draft by the North Bay Battalion out of the Peterborough Petes Minor Midget program. Ball played a bottom six role for the Battalion but was able to get acclimated to the pace and size of the OHL.

Jacob is a big bodied, two-way player with a good shot and release. While Ball played predominately fourth line minutes for the Battalion this season, he was able to contribute in a limited role when he was in the lineup. Ball excelled off the rush, showing authoritative net drives and strong puck protection skills, Ball's ability to get his shot off in stride allowed him to thrive in tight spaces. He showed effectiveness along the half boards and cycle, displaying deceptively good hand and a heaviness on the puck. Most intriguing thing about Ball this season was the steady improvements he made from the start of the season through until the playoffs. He brought a relentless work ethic. Ball regularly engaged in puck battles, forced turnovers with his aggressiveness and was given the opportunity to play in numerous situations. Ball has the ability to become a complete two-way player with offensive upside a he boasts impressive hockey sense, an good shot and solid overall instincts. His size and frame are ideal for the NHL level as well as the way he uses it. If he can boost his offensive numbers and fill out that frame a little more, Jacob could have a very intriguing 2017 NHL Draft year.

Baribeau, Dereck
Goaltender – Val D'Or Foreurs (QMJHL) – 6'05", 184

Baribeau was the top goaltender selected in the 2015 QMJHL Draft (5th overall), and this season he was the backup with the Foreurs behind veteran Étienne Montpetit. This came as a bit of a surprise, but Baribeau was not selected for the U-17 Hockey Challenge in November by Hockey Canada. This season, Baribeau played in 16 games and was lucky enough to play in front of one the top teams in the QMJHL. He's a big and athletic goaltender with strong legs, and his pushes from side to side are powerful. He's already standing at 6'5", a size that NHL teams covet for goaltenders. There were a lot of adjustments to make in his jump from Midget AAA, notably the speed of the game and shots demanded a period of adjustment. He covers the lower part of the net well with his long pads and moves extremely well in his crease. He's comfortable with traffic in front of him thanks to his height and he has a calm demeanor. He can be dominant on the ice and intimidating for opposing shooters when he challenges them. A bit like the 2016-eligible Evan Fitzpatrick, he has a lot of great physical tools behind him, but consistency has been an issue. Next season should be a big one for him; it will be interesting to see how much playing time he gets with Montpetit back for his 19 year old season.

Barratt, Evan
LC – USNTDP U17 5'11", 170

Barratt is an elusive center with good offensive hockey IQ and puck skills. He isn't physically threatening as there isn't a lot of power in his game but he gets around the ice well enough and has the intelligence to get involved through smart short passing plays. He is a plus player in transition and has the smarts to bring the puck up ice. He has good stickhandling ability and it is difficult for defensemen to close down on him. Good playmaker that can set up linemates in the offensive zone. Barratt is committed to Penn State University for 2017-2018.

Bellerive, Jordy
LW/C – Lethbridge Hurricanes (WHL) 5'10", 190

Bellerive was a Lethbridge Hurricanes pick in the 2014 WHL Bantam Draft. Jordy is a speedy skater who likes to drive defenders wide with footspeed. He provided really good complementary offense along with a cast of quality players in Lethbridge on an unlikely run to a division title.

Jordy is a really quick forward who darts in and out of lanes rather unpredictably and has a good sense of timing, knowing when to position himself into the slot to do the most damage there. He's a good puck handler and has refined passing, delivering easy to receive pucks. His shots are well placed, and he passes the puck well from below the dots. He's also good at getting his nose dirty and providing screens or potting in the garbage, Bellerive does some of his best work up-close around the net and is overall a plus player from the dots to the end-boards area. However, he can get caught trying to force the play into scoring areas where more patience with the puck would produce better results.

Bishop, Joel
Center – Halifax Mooseheads (QMJHL) – 5'09", 170

Bishop was a late pick by the Mooseheads in the 6th round (95th overall) in last year's QMJHL Draft and was a pleasant surprise this season with his 21 points. He's the younger brother of Clark (Cape-Breton and Carolina draft pick). Like him, Joel can really skate and play with a lot of energy. He has a decent touch around the net, is a good stickhandler and creates a lot of chances with his speed and hustle. He's not a big player, but plays bigger than his size. At that size, he will need to overcome a lot at the pro level. A bit like his brother, he has good anticipation in the defensive game. With his speed, he can be a threat to take advantage of turnovers and on the PK. His decision-making and playmaking abilities are areas we think he should try to improve on in the next couple of years.

Bjugstad, Jesse
LD – Stillwater H.S. (MN-HS) 6'02", 180

Jesse Bjugstad, son of former NHLer Scott Bjugstad and cousin of Current Florida Panthers center Nick Bjugstad has some solid hockey lineage. Bjugstad plays a really solid all around game at both ends of the ice. Shows a good amount of creativity and hockey sense in the offensive zone makes some subtle mature plays like shooting wide of the net on purpose to get the puck down low, or attempt slap passes to forwards by the goal line. Very creative defenseman who isn't afraid to bring it into games. Has a great shot.

Bodak, Martin
RD – Tappara U20 (FIN) – 6'00", 185

Bodak is a fluid puck-moving defenseman who displays high hockey IQ in all three zones. Although he has not been a big offensive producer, we have liked his game in several different competitions and tournaments. Bodak makes a strong first pass and is a head's up player coming out of his zone. He can skate with the puck and move it through a puck-rushing game as well, but doesn't overextend himself, instead preferring to maintain his team's structure. He makes smart decisions in the offensive zone but isn't a big offensive threat. Bodak isn't the tallest defenseman but makes good use of his body and reads defensive coverage well. He is already a solid defensive zone player and also picks up forwards well through transition. If his offensive production can improve, he will look like a solid prospect next year.

Boqvist, Jesper
LW/C – Brynas (SHL) – 5'11", 174

Boqvist is a late '98 born Swedish forward who enjoyed a tremendous season at the J20 level, posting impressive offensive numbers for a 17yrs old. His success earned him a promotion to the SHL level late in the season and he had some good outings there, albeit not productive. Interestingly, he also failed to post significant production with the national junior team against his peers, perhaps a result of not being a central piece like for his club and of narrowed powerplay time.

Jesper is a terrific skater with outstanding speed, he is an obvious threat in open ice and can easily penetrate into the offensive zone. Watching him skate with the puck on his stick is a pleasure. The more transition play, the more opportunities for him to draw a penalty or create a scoring chance. An up-tempo game seems to benefit him. Once he is inside the offensive zone, that's where Boqvist will have to improve to become an effective offensive player at high levels. He doesn't always select the best option after his entry and doesn't help establishing and extending offensive zone possession time as well as he could. Perhaps more concerning is the fact he doesn't seem to like contact and as of now loses possession a bit too easily when defensemen are indeed able to make contact. He has the skills to work his way through some traffic, goes for the net when given the opportunity, but will need to become stronger on the puck. In our viewings his shot also looked like an asset he could improve on. But the main thing for him next season will be showing to scouts that he is not a soft player and has the compete to battle through more challenging opponents.

Boudrias, Shawn
RW – Charlottetown Islanders (QMJHL) – 6'03", 182

Boudrias was the Islanders' first pick in last summer's draft (13th overall) out of the Collège Esther-Blondin program. Boudrias has played in various international events for Hockey Canada, such as the Canada Winter Games last year and this year's U-17 Hockey Challenge. Boudrias is a smart forward, a bit in the mold of Frédérik Gauthier. He doesn't wow anyone with his offensive skills, but he's very smart at both ends of the ice. He's good on the forecheck, has a good active stick and really understands how to play without the puck. This year with the Islanders, he played mostly a depth role, but next year he should have more opportunities to make an impact offensively. He will need to learn how to be more patient with the puck (this goes back to his midget days), as he wouldn't keep possession of the puck too long. He protects it well using his big frame and also a very good stick. His long reach helps him keep possession of the puck in those situations. He uses his size well, but doesn't have a mean streak or play like a classic power forward. On the ice, he often acts like a 3rd defenseman, always backchecking hard and supporting his defensemen deep in the defensive zone. His skating will need an upgrade for him to be more effective offensively and take advantage of holes in the defensive zone.

Bowers, Shane
LC – Waterloo Black Hawks (USHL) 6'00", 170

The Halifax N.S. native had an impressive rookie campaign with Waterloo (USHL) putting up 15 Goals and 33 points in 56 games and was a key part of the Black Hawks success. Bowers is a playmaking 2-way center who has the ability to carry the play and make the players around him better. He has great vision of the ice and ability to create chances on a consistent basis. Even as one of the younger players in the USHL Bowers showed the ability to take over the game at both ends of the ice, at times it looks and feels like he is thinking the game faster than everyone else on the ice and is one step ahead, sometimes including his line mates. Bowers could use a little more selfishness in his game and shoot the puck more, as he possesses an accurate release that catches goalies off guard. At this stage there are few holes in his game on the ice. Shane needs to continue to fill out his frame and get stronger. Bowers is still keeping his NCAA options open and remains uncommitted which opens the door of him possibly heading to the QMJHL in 2016.

Brannstrom, Erik
LD – HV71 J20 (SWE) – 5'10", 170

Brannstrom is a high-octane offensive defenseman who processes the play quickly, excels on the offensive blueline and competes well despite having a slightly undersized frame.

Brannstrom is a defenseman that likes to push the pace coming out of his own end. The faster the pace of the game, the more comfortable he seems. He makes accurate fast outlets and takes little time to find an open lane for his pass. He is also adept at hitting forwards with on-point stretch-passes. Brannstrom's mobility is also at a very good level. He is a smooth skater that can skate in all directions, and has good top speed as well as acceleration. He excels on the offensive blueline as he has a very good shot, he can use both a slapshot as well as a wristshot. His ability to walk the blueline and change angles is also a positive. Brannstrom also has a good shot selection and will distribute the puck if he can't find an opening, he displays good patience there if needed.

Defensively, Brannstrom is a good competitor and his mobility certainly aids him in getting around. His lack of size poses challenges and he will absolutely need to bulk up going forward as despite his best efforts, he can get outmuscled by bigger forwards. Despite the lack of size, his compete level isn't an issue and we have even seen some feistiness out of him, from throwing hits to getting into shoving-matches, it doesn't seem like the physical play bothers him too much.

Brook, Josh
LD – Moose Jaw Warriors (WHL) 6'01", 177

Brook is a defenseman that has made good strides this season. At the beginning of the year we saw a solid if unspectacular defenseman that was just getting his feet wet and was a bit shy with the puck, opting to keep it safe and low-risk. Brook's confidence grew more and more throughout the year and he started becoming more active and adventurous in his play, allowing himself to dart forward with the puck and be involved all over up the ice.

His mobility makes him a very dependable defenseman in terms of both puck retrieval and puck rushing. His passing off the rush is very good too, making him a dangerous addition to breakout and transition plays. Once in the offensive zone, Brook hoists a really good wristshot and does a good job finding lanes for it. His slapshot is only average at this point. Like most defensemen his age, Brook will have to get bigger to be more effective in his own end, but he already displays solid reads and the willingness to engage. He makes the odd sixteen-year-old's mistakes, but generally his decision making his good, his growth throughout the year has been solid and he will be an interesting prospect to watch next year.

Bucek, Samuel
LW – Chicago Steel (USHL) 6'02", 192

Bucek is a power-winger that boasts some skill to his game. He has been a standout for Slovakia with his international play. He saw some time for HK Nitra playing against men in the Slovakian top league before crossing the pond and joining the Chicago Steel mid-season. There he produced a respectable 10 points in 18 games.

Bucek is a player that likes to be aggressive on the forecheck and finish his checks. He can be a physical presence there, but will need to be more intelligent in his choices. He is prone to taking bad angles that easily allows the other team to move the puck and doesn't really use his stick much to close off lanes. He also tends to arrive late on his hits. When he does get there in time, he is quite good at obtaining possession because his frame allows him to win the majority of battles and he has a quick stick. Bucek shows good puck-protection in the offensive zone and it's hard to strip the puck from him in the corners. He plays well against physical pressure and will push back out with his large body, giving himself more room. Bucek actually shows surprising vision with the puck and can catch defensemen off guard with a nifty pass to an open linemate. He has some skill with the puck which is nice to see at his size. Bucek has an accurate quick-release wrist-shot that he uses well, if he is given room he can pick corners.

Bucek offers good upside heading into the 2017 draft but he will need to polish out certain aspects of his game. His first few steps need to improve, his angles on the forecheck need to be more intelligent and he needs to eliminate the juvenile turnovers with the puck.

Burt, Robbie
RW - Oshawa Generals (OHL) 6'00", 209

Burt was selected in the first round, 10th Overall at the 2015 OHL Priority Selection Draft by the Kingston Frontenacs out of the Mississauga Rebels Minor Midget program. Burt was dealt to the Oshawa Generals in the deal that involved Michael Dal Colle going to Kingston. This deal allowed Burt to gain more ice and experience playing on a non contending team as a rookie.

Robbie Burt is a heavy two-way forward with power forward upside. While Burt displays strong physical attributes, he is still extremely raw as a prospect as there are several facets of his game that need improvement if the hulking winger hopes to be a high NHL draft pick in 2017. Burt shows intriguing bursts of speed, however his bulky frame seems to limit the amount of time he can continue to skate at an effective pace. Burt's straight line skating ability is adequate, however his north/south ability is hindered by a lack of mobility and foot speed. In possession, Burt needs to speed up his decision making process, because when the opposition closes on him, it often led to turnovers. Burt lacks high end vision and playmaking skills, however he does possesses a strong release and a heavy shot that. When Burt is able to get his shot off, it can catch goaltenders off guard. He does a good job going to the net and going after the garbage in the slot. Burt needs to work on his overall consistency as he slacks on the back check and is often caught flat footed and puck watching in his own end. Robbie has a few areas of improvement namely his skating and playmaking abilities, but he is built solid and has a great frame to protect the puck and play a physical game and a shot that should help him improve goal totals as he works towards the 2017 NHL Entry Draft.

Carson, Macauley
LW - Sudbury Wolves (OHL) 6'02", 209

Carson was taken in the second round of the 2015 OHL Priority Selection Draft from the Barrie Jr. Colts. Already possessing OHL ready size, Macauley made a pretty smooth transition to the junior game playing in the bottom six for Sudbury this season.

Carson is known for his edgy physical play. He never passes up an opportunity to finish his check and is a consistent physical presence. Despite being a 16 year old rookie, he showed no reservation when it comes to dropping the gloves, which is where the majority of his penalty minutes came from this year. He also destroyed his opponent in some of those fights. Macauley put up decent numbers considering he was in the bottom six of a non playoff team in his first year. Carson should be on the radar outside the first few rounds of the NHL draft as he is likely one of the toughest players to enter the 2017 NHL Entry Draft and has a little bit of offensive upside.

Caufield, Brock
RW – Stevens Point H.S./Team Wisconsin U16 (WI-HS) 5'07", 160

Brock Caufield is a speedy winger who likes to make plays off the rush. He possesses an excellent release on his shot and can really put up points. He was Team Wisconsin U16 best player throughout the Tier 1 playoffs and at the National Tournament in San Jose. He needs to add more stop and starts to his game and be more willing to engage in puck battles but there is no mistaking his offensive prowess. Caufield saw some time with Green Bay (USHL) at the end of the season and it looks like he will have a good shot at making that roster in the fall.

Chainey, Jocktan
LD – Halifax Mooseheads (QMJHL) – 6'01", 196

Chainey was acquired by Halifax during the QMJHL trade period in a blockbuster deal from Shawinigan. He was the 14th overall pick in last year's draft by Shawinigan, his hometown team. Chainey is mature physically; from the 2015 QMJHL Draft class he was one of the most physically-ready individuals to make the jump to major junior. He took part in November's U-17 Hockey Challenge and last year, he was a member of Team Quebec at the Canada Winter Games. Chainey moves the puck well, is poised with the puck with a strong first pass out of his zone. He doesn't play a flashy game but is very effective and smart. He has a great shot that he likes to use from the point and is a good puck distributor on the power play. His hockey sense is just okay, but he's able to get himself out of trouble with his skating ability and puck movement. His footwork (backward skating) will need some upgrades as he continue to progress, as he can get beaten on the outside due to his slow footwork. Look for him to be a key player on a rebuilding Mooseheads' team in the next couple of seasons.

Chmelevski, Sasha
RC - Ottawa 67's (OHL) 5'11", 172

Chmelevski was selected in the first round, tenth overall at the 2015 OHL Priority Selection Draft by the Sarnia Sting out of the Detroit Honeybaked U16 program. Chmelevski started out slow with the Sting as he got acclimated to the pace of the OHL. Sarnia started getting him involved in more offensive situations which seemed to boost his confidence as he began to show his offensive potential. Chmelevski was dealt to the Ottawa 67's in the deal involving Travis Konecny.

Sasha is a speedy forward who likes to have the puck on his stick. He is tough to contain and can beat defenders one on one. He has good offensive tools with a good release on his shot, but also smart playmaking ability capable of setting up his linemates for chances. With that said, Chmelevski will shoot first whenever there is any question and will occasionally force his hot from bad angles. He also possesses good hands. Chmelevski's areas of improvement generally come when the puck is not on his stick, competing for loose pucks, putting pressure on opponents and making life difficult for opponents. Chmelevski's time in Ottawa was cut short with a collarbone injury but is expected to be ready for the start of his 2017 NHL Draft season. Chmelevski is an offensively skilled, speedy forward but needs to be tougher to play against, get stronger, and improve his play without the puck.

Quotable: "He impressed me this past season. He's a reason my viewings of Ottawa will go up next season." HP Scout Mark Edwards

Clarke, C.J.
RW - Peterborough Petes (OHL) 6'00", 201

Clarke was selected in the second round, 29th overall at the 2015 OHL Priority Selection Draft by the Peterborough Petes out of the Toronto Marlboros Minor Midget program. Clarke played primarily on the fourth line all season long for the Petes registering only two points in 50 games played.

C.J. Clarke is an offensive minded forward with some grit and physicality to his game. Clarke struggled to adapt to a bottom six role and at times the pace of the OHL game after being such a key contributor and excelling as a minor midget player with the Toronto Marlboros. Clarke was ineffective in a depth/checking role with the Petes, however there were glimpses of his offensive skills. A player who handles the puck well, Clarke possesses a quality shot that combines a quick release and strong accuracy. He has good hands and decent speed. This season Clarke was at his best off the cycle as he had trouble finding open ice to operate in the same manor he did during his minor midget season. Clarke struggled with his consistency and his compete level. C.J played in spurts and showed a lack of effort away from the puck. Clarke has good top speed, but still needs to work on his first few steps, he has a powerful shot and good hands but is showing that he's the type of player who needs to play a top six role in order to be successful as he hasn't been able to embrace a checking role in his first year in the OHL. With several Petes forwards graduating, Clarke may have the opening he needs to re-establish himself as a prospect for the 2017 NHL Entry Draft, but will likely face the label of being a player who would need to be top six or nothing at the NHL level.

Quotable: "C.J was hit and miss when I saw him in AAA, this season he struggled in my viewings." - HP Scout Mark Edwards

Comtois, Maxime
LW/C – Victoriaville Tigres (QMJHL) – 6'01", 189

Comtois was the 3rd overall pick in the 2015 QMJHL Draft and had a stellar rookie season with 26 goals and 60 points. He did, however, get a concussion in January resulting from a bad hit from behind and struggled after his return to score at the same pace that he did in the first half of the season. Comtois can play all three forward positions; at age 16 he has already showed versatility for the Tigres by playing all of them as well as being featured on both special teams. On the power play, he was often used in front of the net, where he did a great job screening the opposing goaltender. He also has quick hands to get to loose pucks quickly in the slot. He was also used at time on the point on the power play, a position that he played for all of 2014-2015 in midget. On the penalty kill, he was used regularly, even during 5-on-3 situations. Comtois is very smart both offensively and defensively, with a great hockey sense. He makes players around him better and is an excellent playmaker. He can make some amazing passes on his backhand which not many players can do. He has a good shot, with good accuracy and won't hesitate to pay the price in front of the net to get a goal. His skating is average, and he gets by with his anticipation and hockey sense. He should work on improving his explosiveness to become even more dangerous in the offensive zone. After Victoriaville was eliminated in the first round of the playoffs, he did receive an invitation to Canada's U-18 World Championship camp as an underager and finished the tournament with two points in 7 games. Next season, Comtois should be one of the top players in this league and is expected to go high in the 2017 NHL Entry Draft.

Quotable: "I really liked him in my viewings this season. He's a player with big upside." – HP Scout Mark Edwards

Quotable: "Top talent for the QMJHL for 2017, can score and makes everyone around him better. Smart players and has a high compete level, skating is an area that will need to improve" – HP Scout Jérôme Bérubé

Coskey, Cole
RW - Saginaw Spirit (OHL) 6'00", 190

Coskey was selected in the third round of the 2015 OHL Priority Selection Draft by the Saginaw Spirit out of the Chicago Mission U16 program. Coskey generally played a third line role in his OHL rookie season providing decent productivity from within his role.

Cole is the type of player who will take the hit to make the play, but also land some big hits of his own. He provides excellent forecheck pressure and he has high end compete level which helps him force turnovers. Aside from being an excellent forechecker, Coskey has shown flashes of skill which were very prevalent in his previous season with the Chicago Mission. He is a good skater who can evade checkers and possesses the puck skills to create scoring chances for himself and others. Cole is a player we'll be watching closely leading into the 2017 NHL Entry Draft season, as he possesses a lot of upside going into his second junior season.

Côté, Louis-Philip
LW – Quebec Remparts (QMJHL) – 6'00", 174

Côté was the key player dealt to Quebec from Rouyn-Noranda at the QMJHL trade deadline for overage defenseman Nikolas Brouillard. Côté was drafted 8th overall by the Huskies, and this season was a tough one for him. He didn't get a lot of ice time in Rouyn-Noranda, and when he saw an increase in minutes following the trade, he didn't get a lot of results, playing on one of the worst teams in the league in the 2nd half of the season. Côté has a lot of skills; he has great on-ice vision and controls the play very well from the half boards. More of a playmaker than a shooter, he also has great skating technique. He has good top speed and is also very shifty, as he can change directions quickly and give the opposition a tough time. He has good hockey sense, which helps him in the defensive zone in his understanding of the game. He's more of a perimeter player and will need to get more involved in the tougher areas of the ice. Lacks strength for the QMJHL level right now, will need to get stronger and win more battles for the puck. With his skill level, we expect a serious amount of improvement on his play and production next season.

Crête-Belzile, Antoine
LD – Blainville-Boisbriand Armada (QMJHL) – 6'00", 176

Crête-Belzile was the 11th overall pick last summer, but slipped in the draft because he was leaning towards going to play south of the border to keep his NCAA options open. He eventually reported to the Armada, but was hurt at the beginning of the season and missed the first month. It affected him in terms of his adaptation to a new league, and his play all year was up and down as a result. He played his best hockey late in the season and in the playoffs. He also took part in the U-17 Hockey Challenge in November. Crête-Belzile is a smart defender; he has a good stick and good puck poise. He did, however, struggle this year with the speed of the game in the QMJHL and will need to work on his footspeed, as he had a tough time dealing with speedy forwards. He's calm with the puck and makes a good first pass, but he's not a flashy defender. This year, he kept his game simple and made the high-percentage play as much as possible to not get into trouble. He has some good tools to play on the power play. This season, he had to work hard to get his ice time on the man-advantage. By the end of the season, he was a regular on the power play. Crête-Belzile will need to stay healthy, as for a 2nd straight season he was plagued by injuries that cost him good chunks of those years. He will also need to get stronger physically to be more effective along the boards and in front of the net.

Quotable: "Got better as the season went on, did very well in round 1 vs Val D'Or in the playoff. The key for him will be to stay healthy as he had issues with injuries in the past two seasons. Good potential as a two-way defensemen but right now as the fragile tag attached to his name" - HP Scout Jérôme Bérubé

Davidsson, Marcus
LC – Djurgardens IF J20 (SWE) – 6'00", 185

Davidsson is a fluid skilled center that possesses the vision, skating ability and skill with the puck to be an offensive factor. He has good shiftiness to him and knows when to give up the puck before a defenseman closes down on him. He is a good playmaker and not only sees quality plays but has the skills to execute them. Davidsson uses his agility and anticipation to get first on loose pucks and is a multi-dimensional offensive threat. It is hard to defend him well because he can hurt you both with the puck as well as making intelligent off-the-puck reads. He can hit you with a pass but can also use his off-the-puck positioning to drag defensemen to him and open up space for his linemates that have the puck. Marcus has good hockey sense, doesn't force passes or shots, but selects whatever play is appropriate for any given situation and has all the makings of a good centerman. While he is not one of those classic big centers, he has shown enough smarts, compete and skills to be considered in the upper tier of prospects for the 2017 NHL draft.

Quotable: "He looked better in the 2nd half of the season than when I saw him at the 5 Nations in November. The more I watch, the more I like him and I struggle to find flaws in his game." - HP Scout Mik Portoni

Davis, Hayden
RD - Niagara Ice Dogs (OHL) 6'01", 194

Davis was selected in the first round, 13th overall at the 2015 OHL Priority Selection Draft by the Niagara Ice Dogs out of the Hamilton Huskies Minor Midget program. Davis played a very limited role for the Ice Dogs who for the most part had 5 NHL Drafted defensemen, and six 19 year olds on the blueline. With this situation Davis didn't see much action as the Ice Dogs were building for an OHL Championship and may have been better suited playing a big role at a lower level.

Last year we mentioned Davis has good offensive upside but defense is a work in progress. While he didn't get to show much of his offensive upside this past season, his defensive work in progress was on display. He struggled with body positioning against OHL forwards which made things more difficult for him than they needed to be in the defensive zone. His stick gets a little loose in one on one situations which has got him in some trouble when opponents are getting around him. He also struggled at times to hold the puck in the offensive zone. Fortunately for Davis the Ice Dogs will be graduating potentially all six of their starting defensemen, which leave Lochead who played some forward and Davis and his 40 games played as the two most experienced defensemen for Niagara. This will mean big minutes in all situations and a completely different situation for Hayden. He will be expected to play key power play minutes and will be trial by fire in the defensive zone. Davis skates well for a kid his size and has good puck rushing ability. He will be able to utilize his offensive tools and will be trial by fire in the defensive zone. Hayden will be able to put this season behind him and leading into the 2017 NHL Entry Draft he will have plenty of opportunities to show scouts what type of prospect he is.

DiPietro, Michael
G - Windsor Spitfires (OHL) 6'00", 191

DiPietro was selected in the second round, 23rd Overall at the 2015 OHL Priority Selection Draft by the Windsor Spitfires out of the Sun County Panthers Minor Midget program. DiPietro started the season as a back-up behind a few different options in net but for a stretch he took that role away which was a very impressive feat for a 16 year old. He appeared in almost half of the Spitfires games as a 16 year old and posted excellent numbers including a .667 win %.

DiPietro does an excellent job getting himself into position. He gets set very fast. He is great under pressure and maintains good calm and composure with traffic or heavy slot pressure with the puck in close. Michael has good strength in his legs and gets himself across well on cross crease passes. He maintains positioning well during sustained pressure, even when the defense is getting tired he still looks fresh and his positioning and movement doesn't drop off when his team is pinned. He has good reflexes but will need to continue to work on his rebound control. DiPietro has a ton of upside for the 2017 NHL Entry Draft and could very well be one of the first goaltenders off the board. He's just slightly below ideal size which could hurt him, but if he grows, even a little it should make teams a little more comfortable.

D'Orio, Alex
Goaltender – Magog Cantonniers (LHMAAAQ) – 6'02", 198

D'Orio spent the year in Midget AAA, as the Sea Dogs preferred to see him get ice time rather than spending most of the year on the bench. D'Orio was arguably the best goaltender in the Quebec Midget AAA league this season and led his team all the way to the final of the league. Last November, he took part in the U-17 Hockey Challenge, playing in two games during the tournament. The Sea Dogs drafted D'Orio 9th overall in last summer's QMJHL Draft; he's without a doubt their goalie of the future and could be as early as next season. He's big and athletic in his net and has great composure under pressure. He moves well in his crease and has powerful pushes from post to post. He challenges the shooters, tracks the puck well and covers a lot of space in his net. It will be a big year for him next season, as the Sea Dogs will be one of the top teams in the league and D'Orio could be their #1 goaltender going into the season.

Duchesne, Samuel
LD - Flint Firebirds (OHL) 6'02", 167

Duchesne was selected in the fourth round by the Flint Firebirds out of the Toronto Marlboros program at the 2015 OHL Priority Selection Draft. Duchesne developed well for the Firebirds, participating in most of their games as a 16 year old and began to show his potential as the season progressed.

Duchesne is a physical defensive first defender with some offensive touch. He is a decent skater for his size/age and can carry the puck up ice. His shot, while possessing power, needs to be more accurate as he can be a little all over the place with his slap shot, and can shoot at the logo when carrying into the offensive zone. Duchesne is a physical defender who takes enjoyment from delivering the big check. He likes to grind it out down low and already showed a bit of an edge to his game. One on one he was a little hit or miss this season making some good plays, but also making some rookie mistakes. Duchesne has a lot going for him with his size, style of play and ability to develop, next season will be an opportunity for him to take his game to the next level as he looks to be selected at the 2017 NHL Entry Draft.

Durandeau, Arnaud
LW – Halifax Mooseheads (QMJHL) – 5'11", 181

Durandeau is a pure sniper: he scored 12 times this season and added 17 assists for a respectable 29 points in his rookie season with the Mooseheads. They drafted him 7th overall last summer out of the Lac St-Louis Lions' program. It doesn't take many scoring chances for Durandeau to put the puck in the net, as he possesses a great wrist shot with a fast release. He's an opportunistic scorer, as you might not notice him during a game until he gets a scoring chance and it's in the back of the net. His speed will need to get better, as he is an average skater who will need to work on his quickness and acceleration. He's an average-sized player but will need to get stronger and more involved in the physical game. His work ethic is fine, but he will still need to work on his consistency. Durandeau is at his best when playing with skilled forwards and can finish really well; he had good chemistry with Joseph Veleno last season as Veleno would often be the one to feed him the puck in scoring areas. He has work to do to improve certain areas of his game, but you can't teach his talent to score goals. It will be very interesting to watch him next season and see how where he's at in his development.

Durocher, Jeffrey
C/LW – Gatineau Olympiques (QMJHL) – 5'11", 161

Durocher was Gatineau's 3rd-round pick in last year's QMJHL Draft and surprised a lot of people at their training camp by making the team. We had thought an extra season would have been good for Durocher in order for him to gain more confidence offensively, but kudos to him for making the big jump this season. His offensive upside remains a question mark for us, as we saw him at the junior level as an excellent third-liner, possibly a good second-liner. Durocher works his butt off for every shift and plays bigger than his listed size. He's good on the forecheck and will finish his hits. He can play down the middle and on the wing and will become a mainstay of the Olympiques' PK unit, with his good active stick and ability to block shots. He's a smart player; he keeps his game simple and efficient offensively instead of trying to be too fancy with the puck. For next season, he will need to improve his speed a bit and continue to work on his offensive game in order to make him a more valuable prospect for the NHL Draft.

Durzi, Sean
RD - Owen Sound Attack (OHL) 5'11", 185

Durzi was selected in the 12th round of the 2014 OHL Priority Selection Draft by the Owen Sound Attack out of the Mississauga Rebels Minor Midget program. Sean spent last season playing Major Midget and has transformed this season into a legitimate prospect for the 2017 NHL Entry Draft.

Durzi has average to below average size, but he a very good skater. He is fairly shifty moving up and down the ice with the puck and can beat defenders on the rush. He does a very good job activating on the rush and getting involved. He pinches from the point at intelligent times. Sean has an excellent shot and finds ways to get open and get it off. His shot also has great power to it. It's this combination of skills that helped him reach double digits in goals in his rookie season as a defender. Durzi has good strength for his size and showed a little toughness. He is effective defensively but has some room to improve in that area.

Entwistle, MacKenzie
RW - Hamilton Bulldogs (OHL) 6'02", 169

Entwistle was selected in the second round of the 2015 OHL Priority Selection Draft by the Hamilton Bulldogs out of the Toronto Marlboros program.

In Minor Midget he played a great two-way role, caught behind some talented players. While the situation was similar in his rookie season in Hamilton, as the season progressed he began to show some intriguing offensive upside. He showed good evasive ability in open ice for a big kid, and goes to the net without the puck resulting in some scoring chances. His skill appears to be developing at a promising rate. He also shows good hockey sense at both ends of the ice making him an intriguing prospect at the NHL level. He battles hard down low and although he needs to add some muscle, he did well for a 16 year old. Entwistle will be a player worth keeping a close eye on next season for the 2017 NHL Entry Draft.

Quotable: "He was their best rookie and on many shifts their best player in my viewings of the Bulldogs this season. - HP Scout Mark Edwards

Farrance, David
LD – USNTDP U17 5'10", 191

Farrance is a smooth skating offensive defenseman who already boasts a decent 190 pounds on his 5'10 frame. He has the ability to take off with the puck and skate it forward. He is an intelligent puck-distributor, sees the ice well and can find open teammates. Good puck-handler. His defensive positioning and commitment in his own end has been a question-mark, but we saw some improvement there. His game is becoming less risky and he is turning into a more well-rounded defenseman. He is committed to Boston University for 2017-2018.

Fleury, Cale
RD – Kootenay Ice (WHL) 6'01", 192

Fleury has been one of the few bright spots on a bad Kootenay squad and perhaps the biggest reason to watch them this year. Cale is the younger brother of Haydn Fleury and they do share some similarities. Cale isn't as big but has the same sturdiness in his frame and the ability to take off and bring the puck up the ice. This has been Cale's second season for Kootenay and he has roughly doubled his production from 13 points to 25 points while seeing quality minutes.

Fleury plays an engaging physical game in his own end and also likes to step up on his own blueline and establish contact right away against the forward. This can at times be a bit risky as he leaves room behind him, but results in quality physical play when executed properly. Fleury is hard to stop when he starts generating speed with the puck on his stick and has shown the ability to bring the puck up the ice. He also uses this skill well in his own end as he is capable of quickly taking the puck out of immediate danger. He relies more on his athleticism and physicality when defending as his reads can sometimes still be a bit shoddy and his positional play could still improve. Fleury also shows upside on the offensive side of the puck, he is capable of rushing the puck forward but can also be a threat with his shot. It has been a challenging year for Kootenay, however the one positive would be the fact that Fleury already saw plenty of ice time. We will look for him to take another step forward next year.

Foote, Cal
RD – Kelowna Rockets (WHL) 6'04", 198

The first thing you notice about Cal Foote is his size. He's only sixteen-years-old and he already boasts a big and heavy frame. That sizeable frame sometimes hurts the optics of his skating, but Cal is actually far quicker and more maneuverable than he looks on the first impression. His straight-ahead stride is a bit ugly, but he turns and pivots out of the corners with surprising ease. There's improvement to be made to his skating, but considering his age and where he is currently at, it doesn't look like something that will hold him back in the future as he gets older.

Foote understands that everything starts in his own end and will take care of the business there first. Foote has good defensive reads and defends well both around his net and on the wall as well as against zone entries. His defensive instincts already clearly project to a well-rounded defenseman with pro-size and mobility. He has good positional sense and rarely blows his coverage. When he does obtain the puck in his own zone, he displays above-average patience and vision in getting it out. While he is not a speedster, he can easily absorb contact and still make a play if needed. Foote also shows offensive ability and quickly rose to a top pairing role in a Kelowna Rockets organization that is known historically for producing top notch defensive prospect. Within months of debuting in the WHL Foote became a mainstay on Kelowna's power play unit. While he won't knock your socks off with his skill, the ability to see the ice and produce offense at his size and at his age is quite a good combination to have. He's a good puck-distributor but also shows upside with his slapper from the point.

Foote is already a freak of nature and he might not even be done growing. His body movements already look fluid with good balance and coordination and he displays solid poise for a kid his size. Overall, Foote clearly projects as one of the stronger prospects to come out of the WHL for the 2017 draft.

Fraser, Cole
RD - Peterborough Petes (OHL) 6'02", 191

Fraser was selected in the third round of the 2015 OHL Priority Selection Draft out of the Ottawa Valley Titans Minor Midget program. Fraser was caught behind several defensemen in Peterborough right off the bat but utilized his excellent physical game and his tenacious take no prisoners attitude and earn 50 games this season.

Fraser is a physical, defensive defensemen with a very nasty mean streak. He found ways to contribute in a limited role with the Peterborough Petes this season. While Fraser has some things to work on to improve into a quality NHL prospect, he did show some intriguing upside on the defensive side of the puck. Fraser is difficult to play against and showed a willingness to engage physically every chance he got. His defensive play is that much more impressive as this is only his third year playing the position. He was never rattled by a physical forecheck, rather handling it with poise. However, Fraser struggled at times with possession, as his puck skills are limited. Fraser's limited puck skills led to numerous unforced turnovers and affected his ability to make a clean outlet pass. Fraser contained well and handled an offensive attack very well for a rookie defensemen, his feet are a bit heavy and he lacks ideal mobility. While he didn't get much of a chance to shoot the puck this season he has a booming shot from the point, that may get utilized more as he moves up the depth chart. Fraser has a lot of upside as a physical shutdown defender, but will need to develop a consistent first pass. For a player his style, he doesn't need to have great puck skills, just be able to make the smart play consistently. Cole displayed good hockey sense, so if Fraser's skill set can catch up to the way he thinks the game, he could be an intriguing prospect for the 2017 NHL Entry Draft

Quotable: " Love the toughness of this kid." - HP Scout Mark Edwards

Frost, Morgan
LC - Sault Ste. Marie Greyhounds (OHL) 5'11", 160

Frost was selected in the fourth round of the 2015 OHL Priority Selection Draft by the Sault Ste. Marie Greyhounds out of the Barrie Jr. Colts Minor Midget program. Frost was the last pick of the fourth round but has been more successful this season in the OHL than some second round picks. He played a very effective game on the Hounds third line this season.

Frost has had a great season due to his strong hockey sense and good awareness of the play. He reads and reacts quickly, which allows him to get open. He has quick hands which helps him beat defenders and has the vision to make a play. He is more of a playmaker than a goal scorer but is capable of creating offense when necessary. He provided a decent two way role. He lacks the strength in order to outmuscle opponents but does apply pressure. Morgan has good skating ability and can accelerate quickly. He is a very intriguing prospect heading into the 2017 NHL Entry Draft. He will need to fill out and preferably grow more, but he has the natural hockey instincts and tools to help him succeed.

Quotable: " Based on what I saw from him in my viewings this season we had him ranked too low in his OHL Draft year. I liked what I saw from him." - HP Scout Mark Edwards

Fulcher, Kaden
G - Hamilton Bulldogs (OHL) 6'03", 186

Fulcher was selected in the 13th round of the 2014 OHL Priority Selection Draft by the Sarnia Sting out of the Lambton Jr. Sting Minor Midget Program. Fulcher played his 16 year old season with The Hill Academy U16 Prep team. He then made a splash in Sting training camp which resulted in him being signed and spending the first half of the season with the Sting, primarily on the bench. He was traded to the Hamilton Bulldogs at the trade deadline for Charlie Graham.

Fulcher has perfect size for a goaltender at 6'03" and he has good vision through traffic. He has good reflexes and is capable of making some impressive saves. He has good quickness for his size. He is pretty good at minimizing rebounds, but will need to improve on keeping the ones he gives up out of the crease area. Spending almost half the season sitting on the bench playing only three games, then playing 15 games in the final two months likely was a difficult adjustment for Fulcher. Next season will be a new opportunity to battle for the starting job with the Bulldogs. He will be one of the key goaltender to watch for the 2017 NHL Entry Draft out of the OHL.

Quotable: " I understand that Sarnia wanted a veteran goalie but I loved this trade by Hamilton. Fulcher was outstanding when I saw him. Big upside going forward." - HP Scout Mark Edwards

Gadjovich, Jonah
LW - Owen Sound Attack (OHL) 6'02", 201

Gadjovich was selected in the second round of the 2014 OHL Priority Selection Draft by the Owen Sound Attack out of the Whitby Wildcats Minor Midget program. Gadjovich had a solid rookie season playing a very limited role, but has moved up the depth chart this season and has been able to play more of an impact.

Jonah has great size and a good frame to protect the puck well. He drives the net with good puck possession ability and a dangerous backhand shot. He likes to take the puck to the net hard as much as possible and creates scoring chances and goals in this manner. He is more of a shooter than a passer. Jonah does a lot of the little things well, winning battles going to the right areas of the ice and forcing turnovers. He has good hockey sense and is willing to take the hit in order to make the play. Gadjovich has some very intriguing upside and could have a big year and increase his goal totals heading into his 2017 NHL Draft year.

Gagnon, Anthony
RW – Gatineau Olympiques (QMJHL) – 5'10", 164

Gagnon split this past season between the Olympiques and his Midget AAA team in Collège Charles-Lemoyne on the South Shore of Montreal. He was demoted back to Midget AAA after the trade period, when Gatineau made acquisitions and wanted him to get more ice time. Gagnon was picked in the 2nd round by the Olympiques in last year's QMJHL Draft. In his draft year, he was one of the players who was on the rise all year long and improved his stock a lot in the 2nd half of the season. This season, as a rookie, he didn't get a lot of ice time but he still found a way to impress us in our viewings with his versatility on the PP and PK. On the power play, he even played at the point on some occasions, as the coaching staff was trying to find ways for him to get ice time. He played this way on the PP last year in midget as well, as he has an excellent shot and can beat goaltenders from anywhere in the offensive zone. He skates well and has a good burst of speed. He can be dangerous if he can reach that top speed in the neutral zone. He did some good work on the PK with Gatineau as well, as his good stick and anticipation help him in those situations. Gagnon is not the biggest player and will need to get stronger to compete at the next level, but we liked his two-way game and scoring abilities.

Gallant, Zach
LC - Peterborough Petes (OHL) 6'01", 184

Gallant was selected in the first round, fifth overall at the 2015 OHL Priority Selection Draft by the Peterborough Petes out of the Mississauga Rebels Minor Midget program. Although Gallant doesn't possess the same offensive upside as most top five OHL Draft forward picks, Gallant plays an extremely well rounded, intelligent game.

Zach Gallant is a big-bodied player with budding power forward capabilities and a player who plays an in your face style of game. Gallant struggled to adjust to the pace of the OHL game throughout the majority of the 2015-2016 regular season. While he began to contribute in a minimal roll towards the end of the season and through the playoffs, Gallant's ability to be productive hinges on his ability to adapt to the pace of play along with his ability improve his speed and skating abilities. A slightly heavy footed forward with limited explosiveness and mobility, Gallant's inability to produce at the offensive end was a direct result of his inability to separate from a check. Gallant was arguably at his best at the defensive end of the rink, using good anticipation abilities to break up the oppositions attack, along with blocking shots and making strong decisions with possession. Offensively Gallant rarely made an impact, although he did show intriguing puck protection skills, working the cycle effectively, while showing little to no hesitation getting to the gritty areas of the ice. Gallant may lack the offensive upside desired, but he does a lot of the little things well, committed defensive forward who will check and do what it takes to win, which in it's own will hold plenty of value at the 2017 NHL Entry Draft.

Garreffa, Joseph
LC - Kitchener Rangers (OHL) 5'06", 157

Garreffa was selected in the third round of the 2015 OHL Priority Selection Draft by the Kitchener Rangers out of the Toronto Titans Minor Midget program. Garreffa made the Rangers out of camp and did a great job showing durability and flexibility playing a variety of roles in a variety of situations including playing both defense and forward.

Garreffa has high end skating ability and is capable of carrying the puck end to end. He is very shifty and evades checkers very well. He has good creativity when entering the offensive zone and can make his linemates better, creating scoring chances for them. He has more goal scoring ability than he has shown to this point of his OHL career and can beat goaltenders and defenders with quick hands and quick moves on the rush. He plays a two-way role well utilizing his speed in both directions which made him an ideal candidate to step onto the blueline when the Rangers experienced injuries at that position. There is very little question as to Garreffa's upside as a junior player. However due to his lack of size, strength he will have a real uphill battle for the NHL. Garreffa will have a shot to increase his role with the Rangers next season while taking a run at being selected at the 2017 NHL Entry Draft.

Gildon, Max
LD – USNTDP U17 6'02", 179

Gildon is a defenseman that has every tool at his disposal to be successful but has been plagued by inconsistent decision-making. He's got good size, puck skills and skating ability. He shows flashes of brilliance but just doesn't quite get the positive impact you would expect out of his tools on a consistent basis. His defensive coverage can be suspect but especially he can make some odd decisions with the puck on his stick. He doesn't always recognize his options or makes mistakes on his passes and he can be quite slow to execute. Gildon doesn't lack the upside but going forward he will certainly need to improve his decision-making and become the player that his physical tools should allow him to be on a consistent level. He is committed to University of Wisconsin for 2017-2018.

Quotable: " I had heard a lot about him prior to seeing him play for myself. I was a little underwhelmed with his play in my viewings." - HP Scout Mark Edwards

Gilmour, Brady
LC - Saginaw Spirit (OHL) 5'10", 170

Gilmour was selected sixth overall at the 2015 OHL Priority Selection Draft by the Saginaw Spirit out of the Quinte Red Devils Minor Midget Program. Gilmour came to Saginaw a very successful Minor Midget forward who had some areas of his game to work on.

Gilmour has good hockey sense and reads the play well. As his skating improves this will help him as there are times he reacts quickly enough, but lacks the higher end skating a player of his size requires in order to be highly successful. Despite a lack in speed, Gilmour is able to create plays for himself and his teammates. He is a pass first type of forward and does a good job beating defenders then finding his teammate once he draws the attention of the defense into him. He has good two-way ability and competes hard in all three zones. He has good awareness and gets into passing lane showing good defensive intelligence for a rookie. Gilmour will need to improve his pace, quickness, strength and hopefully grow a little in order to make the biggest impact possible leading into his 2017 NHL Draft year.

Glass, Cody
RC – Portland Winterhawks (WHL) 6'01", 168

A scoring center that shows good offensive instincts, he played on the third line in Portland and still managed 10G and 27 points while playing 65 games. Has a good reach and a quality stick that he uses to defend well with tie ups and takeaways. Showed improvement throughout the season and became more of a factor in the overall game. Smart player in all three zones, capable of making give and go plays and supporting the puck up the ice. Sneaks into scoring chances well and isn't afraid of the tougher parts of the ice. Shows good upside as a goal-scorer. Will need to put some weight on his thin frame to play bigger minutes but has a 6'1 frame to build upon. He has good reach uses it well to shields pucks. Moves his feet consistently but will need more power in his skating stride. Can be counted on to show up on every shift with his effort and has a good compete level that he uses as a forechecker and in his own end. Glass is a competitive center who reads the ice well and can score. He will need to physically mature and add strength to be more effective as he moves into his draft-year.

Gourley, Jarrod
LD - Brooks Bandits (AJHL) 6'01", 178

Gourley is a smooth-skating and intelligent two-way defenseman who's had a great year. First, he received a scholarship to play at Arizona State University beginning in 2018, then he won a gold medal at the World Under-17s and then he led his club to an AJHL championship. A proven winner, Jarrod is a competitive and maneuverable two-way defenseman with middling size who plays a well-paced game that is appropriate for all situations.

Gourley is a consistent workhorse with good skating ability and high hockey sense. He takes risks in the offensive zone but has excellent feet and recovery speed. He's one of those players who always seems to be thinking the game a couple steps ahead of everyone else. His anticipation along the blueline is beyond his years. This is just one reason Gourley was a fixture on the Bandits power play this season. He additionally has really good scoring ability thanks to a combination of his vision and a slick wristshot.

In his own end, Gourley is very competitive in all the important areas. That includes board battles, one-on-one races, fighting for space in the slot, and at reading the opposition's offensive game plan. His penalty killing work was almost as impressive as his power play work this year. Although he's committed to Arizona State, he was also selected by Brandon in the 2014 WHL Bantam Draft, so an eventual move to the powerhouse Wheat Kings isn't outside the realm of possibility.

Grima, Nick
RD - Peterborough Petes (OHL) 5'11", 188

Grima was selected in the second round, 25th overall at the 2015 OHL Priority Selection Draft by the Peterborough Petes out of the Toronto Titans Minor Midget program. Grima was caught behind some depth on the Petes' roster as a 16 year old but had a good season showing off his two-way ability.

Grima is a smooth skating, two-way defensemen with an impressive compete level and strong puck skills. Grima's most noteworthy attribute is his skating ability. As a player who transitions up ice extremely well, Grima can be an effective puck carrying defensemen, as his skating ability make him tough to contain at times. Despite being a strong skater, Grima occasionally lacked the confidence to rush the puck and would defer to his d-partner or make a limited skill set play. Not surprisingly, Grima displayed much more confidence in possession as the season went on, making an excellent first pass, while showing solid overall decision making. Grima brings an impressive compete level but does lack a real physical edge in his own zone. That said, he battles hard and shows impressive contain with an active and effective stick. Grima also relies on strong anticipation abilities and positional play, which only add to his effectiveness on both sides of the puck. While Grima may have been limited in his offensive contributions this season, the smooth skating defender does show good vision and ability to create offence from the back end, as his impressive foot speed allows him to open both shooting and passing lanes. Grima also shows impressive offensive instincts, as he consistently made smart and calculated pinches, looking to inject himself offensively. Although he's still sub six feet, he has good smarts, puck skills, skating and two-way upside that should all work to his benefit with the hope that he will grow.

Guay, Nicolas
RW/C – Chicoutimi Saguenéens (QMJHL) – 5'10", 163

Guay surprisingly made Chicoutimi out of training camp after being the 32nd overall pick in the QMJHL Draft last summer. He was not expected to make the team, but Chicoutimi really wanted to give their young rookies all the opportunities to make the team and have an impact this year. Although Guay only played 37 games this season and was a healthy scratch many times, another year in Midget AAA where he would have dominated offensively might have been better for his development. Guay has a quick active stick on the ice, always keeps his feet moving and is tough to handle for the opposing team. He plays with a lot of passion and plays a fearless game, even though he lacks the ideal strength to play that style. He's also versatile, as he can play both on the wing and down the middle. Defensively, at times he can be drawn to pucks, leaving his position in the defensive zone. Next season should be a big one for Guay. With some added offense, he could be viewed as an NHL prospect for the draft, whereas without it, he would be considered to be just your regular average-sized hard worker from the QMJHL.

Hamblin, James
LC - Medicine Hat Tigers (WHL) 5'09", 170

James Hamblin is a hard working two-way centre who contributes in all three zones. He's a fairly good skater with good jump who reacts quickly to the play. He comes equipped with a great knowledge of where to be and when to be there. He doesn't really dominate the offensive zone, but he creates turnovers by sliding into passing lanes or by using smart stick work.

Hamblin takes a real leadership role in other areas, meanwhile. He's extremely committed to winning the key defensive zone draws. He's fairly well positioned. He's good at disrupting the opposition's offense before it develops. He's a great shot blocker. He's defense-first oriented when circumstances require it. All in all, he's exactly the sort of player you want out on the ice when trying to defend a lead.

Hamblin's point totals probably weren't what he was looking for this season, scoring only three points (G, 2 A, 1) in 58 games with the Medicine Hat Tigers. He also needs to add a lot of size if he wants to be that type of player at the next level, but his leadership abilities speak for themselves. He captained Canada White to a gold medal at the World Under-17 Hockey Championships.

Hague, Nicolas
LD - Mississauga Steelheads (OHL) 6'05", 207

Hague was selected in the second round, 29th overall at the 2014 OHL Priority Selection Draft by the Mississauga Steelheads out of the Kitchener Jr. Rangers Minor Midget program. Hague was a favourite of ours in his OHL Draft year, but he developed very well with the Kitchener Jr. B Dutchmen in his first junior season. As a late birthdate Hague still had two seasons to go before his OHL Draft year and played his first full OHL season with the Mississauga Steelheads playing top minutes in all situations.

Hague is an impactful two-way defender that uses his high Hockey IQ to excel in all three zones. Hague skating is above average, which has come a long way since his Major Bantam season. He uses his long and lengthy strides to cover large portions of the ice. However his first few steps lack explosiveness. Hague close gaps well and shows impressive contain in his own zone, effortlessly separating players from puck in puck battles. There are times where he can look beat but can play the body perfectly, showing he's able to use both his stick and his body effectively. Hague's transition ability is impressive, as he gets himself involved into the offensive attack effectively and appropriately. Offensively, Hague possesses a heavy point shot that he is able to get through from blue line. He also has the ability to walk in from the point and fire a hard, accurate wrist shot on net. Hague has good vision in the offensive zone which is most notable on man advantage opportunities. Hague is solid off the rush, as he's hard to contain once he picks up speed. Hague showed physicality at the AAA and Jr. B level but it took him a little time to pick up his physical game at the OHL level. Once he did, he became even tougher to play against as he started asserting himself along the walls and in front of the net providing some nastiness.

Hague has excellent upside leading into the 2017 NHL Entry Draft. He has size, good top speed, a dangerous shot, but can also take care of his own end. He's a smart player who has tremendous upside and will be valued high in next year's draft.

Quotable: " I saw him a lot this season and he just kept getting better with every viewing. He skates with a little bit of a knock-knee style but it hasn't hindered his game." - HP Scout Mark Edwards

Harrison, Jake
LD - West Kelowna Warriors (BCHL) 5'10", 171

Harrison is a hometown kid and two-way defenseman who helped his West Kelowna Warriors club earn themselves their first ever BCHL Championship and RBC Cup. Scoring at a really decent pace (G, 6 A, 20) over 56 games, Harrison was a big part of his team's historic run in 2015-2016. Harrison does not, however, play a big or flashy game. Very average in terms of size, and only slightly above-average in terms of pure speed, Harrison plays a fairly quiet and relaxed game from the back end.

A really strong skater with good mechanics, Harrison is usually well positioned and doesn't take a lot of chances with or without the puck. He's one of those players who generally waits for the game to come to him. When defending in his own end, mind you, he's very reliable, competitive, and quick to react.

He's not huge, but he plays a chippy game and makes the game difficult for his opponents. As such, he's a highly reliable mid-pairing defenseman who can do a little bit of everything without blowing away anyone's expectations. If he feels like he's achieved all he can at the Junior A level, Harrison's WHL rights belong to the Spokane Chiefs.

Hawel, Liam
RC - Sault Ste. Marie Greyhounds (OHL) 6'04", 169

Hawel was selected in the first round, 22nd overall at the 2015 OHL Priority Selection Draft by the Sault Ste. Marie Greyhounds out of the Ottawa Valley Titans Minor Midget Program. Liam provided good effort in a bottom six role for the Greyhounds this season. He was not called upon often to provide much offense with plenty of veterans ahead of him.

Hawel is a big bodied forward with a lanky frame. He is a good skater, particularly for his size and he was able to utilize his speed through the neutral zone and got pucks deep. He was effective on the dump and chase and would grind it out on the Hounds third or fourth line. Hawel lacks strength and struggled at times in battle, though not for a lack of effort. He greatly needs to add muscle to fill out his frame. He showed great flashes here and there but never seemed to get things rolling offensively. He has good puck skills and can create offense for his linemates. He also has untapped goal scoring ability which has not been realized yet at the junior level. Hawel is a bit of a project at this point, but with his size, skating and untapped ability his ceiling is very high. He will need to add muscle to his frame in order to maximize his potential.

Hedberg, Tom
LD – Leksands IF (SHL-2) – 5'11", 161

Hedberg is a slightly undersized puck-moving defenseman prospect playing for Leksands. Although a 2017 NHL draft eligible, Hedberg has already played more than 30 games against men in Swedish's second best league and held his own there. Hedberg is a smart puck-mover who can bring the puck up ice with his skating and likes to get involved in the play. His offense from the point is just OK at this point and he hasn't been a big producer at the J20 level either as he only put up 5 points in 18 games there. While he is a smart offensive player, we would like to see more production out of him. Not surprisingly he will also have to get bigger and stronger.

Heiskanen, Miro
LD – HIFK U20 (FIN) – 5'10", 155

Heiskanen is an intriguing defenseman that has all the tools of a puck-mover but lacks in the size department at the moment, as he is quite light. Internationally, he had a very strong U17 WHC performance and another good showing at the U18s in Grand Forks.

More than a pure offensive defenseman, Heiskanen is a puck-mover that does a fantastic job of bringing the puck out of his own end and making sure his team has full control of the puck. He is a real smooth skater and has high hockey IQ, his decision-making is very good and he reads the play well, never forcing a pass that isn't there. Heiskanen is a big factor for any team's zone exits and zone entries as he continually tilts the ice into his team's favor with smooth, intelligent movement and quality passing. Heiskanen is also a good powerplay quarterback as he is very good at distributing the puck from the blueline as well as reading where and how the other team will attempt to clear the puck. He does a good job keeping the puck in the offensive zone but also knows when to ease back to get into position if a turnover occurs or simply to simply go back and collect a cleared puck.

He is a smart defensive player and thanks to his smarts he doesn't spend a lot of time in his own zone, but he will need to fill out quite a bit in order to be effective there at the next level. While his passing game and smarts are very impressive, his shot is less of a stand-out.

Quotable: "He's really light right now, but I love his smarts and how fluid he is on the ice. If he can add some weight to that frame and maybe show a bigger threat with his point-shot he'll start looking real good, real soon." – HP Scout Nik Funa

Quotable: "Not a big kid but I like his hockey IQ skating and the way he moved pucks. Good hands too." – HP Scout Mark Edwards

Hischier, Nico
LC – SC Bern (SUI Jr.) – 6'00", 172

After taking part at the U18 Worlds last year as a 16yrs old, this season Nico Hischier made the U20 team even before turning 17, giving himself the chance to potentially reach as many as four WJC participations in the future. That provides a good hint of where he stands in terms of prospects ranks for his country. He didn't look out of place this year in Finland even if he could only show glimpses of his remarkable talent and finished the season on a high note: he won the domestic title with four assists on his team's four goals in the decisive game of the U20 junior season and then impressed in North Dakota at the U18.

Nico has been posting outstanding numbers as an underager moving up through the Swiss junior leagues and not because his physical development was ahead of his age. He possesses top notch offensive instincts and soft hands, doesn't need much time or room to release his shot but he's more of a playmaker and likes to get into real scoring areas before shooting. Has poise, nice timing, impressive eye-hand coordination and smarts that are rarely seen in such a young player. Good things seem to happen pretty naturally with him, he thinks quickly and is just as quick moving his light feet and maneuvering the puck to separate himself from opponents. His decision making his flawless, he reads the game extremely well and is not bad defensively either, often taking away pucks from bigger opponents. He could pay more attention at protecting himself in battles along the boards and his chances for a high selection at next year Entry Draft may partially depend on how much he will grow physically over the course of next season, but Hischier is certainly among the most promising 17yrs old prospects in Europe .

Quotable:" To me Nico looks like the most promising 17 year old forward Switzerland has produced" - HP Scout Mik Portoni

Quotable:" He was impressive at the U18 in Grand Forks. He's smart, flashed a burst of speed and was willing to drive the net. Moved the puck well too." - HP Scout Mark Edwards

Hoefenmayer, Noel
LD - Ottawa 67's (OHL) 6'00", 183

Hoefenmayer was selected in the third round of the 2015 OHL Priority Selection Draft by the Ottawa 67's out of the Don Mills Flyers Minor Midget program. Noel played on a 67's blueline that boasted several veterans on the back end, so he played only about 60% of the time.

Hoefenmayer is a good two-way defender who breaks down his game well for a defender. When playing on his side of the red line he likes to keep it simple making smart, high percentage passes and gets pucks deep. When he's on the offensive side of the blueline he is a little more creative moving the puck well in the offensive zone and possessing a big shot which he can unload from the blueline. One timers are still a work in progress but if he can get them down he's a threat to score from the blueline. Defensively he has good anticipation and is capable of intercepting passes. He has good reaction time in the defensive zone which gives him an advantage chasing down pucks. Hoefenmayer has a well rounded game, he doesn't really have any glaring weaknesses to his game, but could stand to improve on his footwork and get stronger.

Hollowell, Mac
RD - Sault Ste. Marie Greyhounds (OHL) 5'10", 162

Hollowell was selected in the 12th round of the 2014 OHL Priority Selection Draft by the Sault Ste. Marie Greyhounds out of the new dissolved Niagara Falls Rivermen Minor Midget program. Hollowell spent his 16 year old season with the Niagara Falls Jr. B Canucks of the GOJHL while playing 11 games with Sault Ste. Marie posting an impressive 6 points in those games. He boosted his play and earned extra ice time in his first full season with the Hounds this year.

Hollowell is an excellent skater who leads the rush with quickness and agility. He protects the puck surprisingly well for a player his size and makes sure he gets it deep when he doesn't have a lane. Hollowell is an offensive minded defenseman, who doesn't try to put the puck on net too often. He tends to make smooth passes and set up his teammates under offensive zone pressure. Defensively he shows good compete and won his share of battles because of this. However, he often had trouble handling the size and strength of the opposition and had moments where he was getting dominated in the defensive zone by big strong power forwards. Mac has been a pleasant surprise for the Greyhounds. A 12th round pick and he has emerged as a very solid junior player. Looking towards the 2017 NHL Entry Draft, Hollowell is undersized for a defenseman and will need to grow and add muscle while not affecting his great skating. His skillset projects well as an offensive defenseman, but will give himself a better chance if he grows and gets stronger.

Hoyt, Peyton
RW – Cape Breton Screaming Eagles (QMJHL) – 5'09", 170

Hoyt plays with tremendous passion and energy on the ice. He's a really good skater with a great burst of speed and the ability to beat defenders wide and use his speed very well on the forecheck. Hoyt was the 6th overall pick in the 2015 QMJHL Draft, and this season he didn't get a lot of chances to play on an offensive line with the Screaming Eagles. He was more of a depth player who provided energy and speed on the 4th line for the majority of the season. At 5'9", Hoyt is not the biggest player, but plays as if he was a 6'3", 220-pound power-forward. Always involved in battles all over the ice, his speed helps him make a lot of good hits. He can score as he proved in his midget year, and he has great wrist shot with fast quick release. He controls the puck well at high speeds and has above-average vision and an above-average shot. Next season, with more ice time, his offensive production should improve by a lot. Hoyt can score and play with an edge and that should make him a favorite among NHL scouts.

Quotable: "Really love the way he plays, tons of speed and energy. I think his offensive production will make a big jump next season with more ice time with the Screaming Eagles. He's very noticeable on the ice even with limited ice time" - HP Scout Jérôme Bérubé

Hugg, Rickard
LC/LW – Leksands IF J20 (SWE) – 5'10", 179

Hugg is an intelligent forward that has good skill and playmaking vision. He is an engaging player on the wall and will battle for pucks. He has been used as both center and a winger. He turned in a successful campaign at the J20 level hovering around point per game, Hugg was also a mainstay for the Swedish national team, appearing both for the U17 as well as U18 squads. Hugg reads the ice well and positions himself accordingly. A player that understands puck-movement, he opens up for pucks and is a plus player in terms of establishing possession. He has the ability to find his way to the slot and get his shot off, but is more of a playmaker. However, Hugg will need to improve his skating and define himself as a player. He has an interesting toolset, but he hasn't really established himself as a consistent presence on the ice.

Hughes, Aidan
G - Sarnia Sting (OHL) 6'03", 242

Hughes was selected in the second round of the 2015 OHL Priority Selection Draft by the Sarnia Sting out of the London Jr. Knights Minor Midget program. Hughes spent the majority of his 16 year old season with the Sarnia Jr. B Legionnaires but got some regular season experience with the OHL Sting.

Hughes is a big goaltender who has excellent size. He has a great frame that makes him difficult to beat. He has good positioning and covers his angles well. When he drops into the butterfly he still covers most of the net which is an asset to his game. He has a good glove hand and decent side to side but would benefit from getting quicker. His rebound control is still a little hit or miss and will need to be improved upon. Hughes projects to be the back-up for the Sarnia Sting behind veteran Justin Fazio and appears ready to handle the OHL full time. Although he may not be one of the first goaltenders of the board at the 2017 NHL Entry Draft, he certainly looks like a goaltender who will make a solid NHL prospect.

Quotable: "He was one of my favorite goalies in his OHL Draft year. He gave the Sting the depth to trade Fulcher to the Hamilton Bulldogs." - HP Scout Mark Edwards

Ikonen, Joni
RC – Frolunda HC J18 (SWE) – 5'10", 168

Ikonen is a skilled center with nice wheels. He does a good job gaining the offensive zone and distributing the puck once he gets there. Has the ability to sniff out scoring chances and will pounce on the opportunity once he recognizes an opening. He has good hands and control of the puck. While not very big, he does a decent job at competing. He will play in the corners and is willing to go to the middle to get his scoring chances. Having to take physical contact doesn't turn him away from trying to win puck battles in the corners or getting to pucks in the slot.

One aspect we feel could improve is his shot selection on the powerplay, as he has a tendency to fire pucks with his lanes clearly blocked. This results in blocked shots and sometimes turnovers.

Isaacson, Nick
LW - Peterborough Petes (OHL) 6'02", 180

Nick is rangy two-way forward with impressive offensive instincts, a fantastic shot and a high compete level. While his time at the OHL level was very limited, Nick Isaacson excelled throughout his season with the Lindsay Muskies of the OJHL. Isaacson routinely showed an impressive level of hockey sense along with awareness in all three zones. This allows him not only be effective on both sides of the puck, but as well as in possession and away from the puck. While Isaacson does possess the intriguing combination of smarts and size, his skating is still a work in progress. Isaacson's possesses a long stride that allows him to cover a lot of ice, however he still lacks explosiveness, power and fluidity which somewhat hinder his overall mobility and effectiveness. With that being said, his skating did improve this season and when Isaacson reaches his top gear he can be tough to contain. Off the rush as he shows a willingness to drive the net with authority, displaying deceptively good hands and strong puck protection skills. Isaacson could stand to add more physicality to his game, as he often lets defensemen off the hook on the forecheck, however his tenaciousness in puck pursuit does allow him to force turnovers as he can show a relentlessness on loose pucks and in puck battles. A player who is arguably at his best in areas where he can use his size to his advantage, Isaacson works the cycle and half boards well. He shows deceptively quick hands in tight, excelling as a net front presence. Isaacson is a player who exudes confidence and should be an impactful presence with the Peterborough Petes next season.

Quotable: "I managed to catch a couple games. One early in the season before the coach gave him ice time and one later in the season. Even in the early season game I already saw signs of his skating improving. In the other game he was one of the best players on the ice." - HP Scout Mark Edwards

Ivanov, Georgi
LC - Team Russia U18 (MHL) – 6'00", 190

Although a 2017 eligible, Ivanov has already distinguished himself as a good contributor for Russia's U18 team in MHL league-play and in several international tournaments.

Ivanov already possesses legit strength and plays a pretty smart game down the middle. He follows the puck-movement easily and will present an open blade to receive pucks and move the puck forward. Ivanov keeps his feet moving in both directions and is a plus player in all three zones on the ice. He is a pretty good skater and does a good job at gaining the offensive zone entry. In the offensive zone he tries to dictate the play with the puck on his stick as he knows how to use his feet to force the defender to react and gain for himself that critical small moment to make a play. Georgi's wrist shot is a good asset, but sometimes he could use better shot selection and his playmaking ability will need to develop some more to be a valuable offensive center at the next level. He will also have to pay more attention at not getting caught with his head down.

Ivanov has enough skills, power and competitiveness to deserve close monitoring in his draft season even if, as a late '98 born, he won't be able to participate in U18 international events.

Jokiharju, Henri
RD – Tappara U20 (FIN) – 5'11", 165

Jokiharju is a defenseman that makes a good first pass out of his zone and is a strong skater. He has the ability to see the ice well and will make passes out of his zone. Despite being a smooth skater, he isn't someone who would rush the puck out of his own end a lot, let alone go off on rushes where he would get involved in spear-heading the rush. Instead, Jokiharju prefers the play to develop and come to him, rather than dictate the pace on his own, but is quick activating himself when he has a change to get involved.

Offensively he does a good job at getting his shots through, however at this point in time they tend to lack in power. He positions well defensively and will use his body when he has to, but is not a defenseman that seeks out physical contact on his own.

Quotable: "In my limited viewings I've been really impressed by this kid. The way he reads the game, how quickly he recognizes plays and moves the puck, makes him a promising defenseman despite his size." - HP Scout Mik Portoni

Joly, D'Artagnan
RW – Baie-Comeau Drakkar (QMJHL) – 6'02", 177

Joly was acquired by Baie-Comeau at the trade deadline from Gatineau in the Nicolas Meloche trade. Originally from Gatineau, Joly was a standout performer in Midget AAA this season, playing with Benoit-Olivier Groulx (top prospect for the 2016 QMJHL Draft) on their top line. Joly's older brother Michael has been one of the most prolific scorers in the QMJHL for the past three years, with Rimouski and Cape-Breton. The younger Joly is a different player than his older brother; he already has a good frame and is still growing into it. He has improved his skating abilities a lot in the past year and uses his long strides well when rushing the puck. A bit like his brother, he's also a good stickhandler, has quick hands and uses his long reach very well in one-on-one confrontations. After the trade, he joined Baie-Comeau right away. As they were the worst team in the league, he didn't have much success offensively, but he gained some experience and will be more ready for his NHL Draft year next season. Joly, even with a good frame, is not a physical player and will need to keep working on his strength. He scores a lot from the rush with his speed and skills, but we would like to see him be more successful in the tougher areas in the offensive zone, as he can be victim of playing too much on the perimeter.

Karow, Michael
LD – Notre Dame Academy/Team Wisconsin U18 (WI-HS) 6'02", 194

Karow, recently drafted by Youngstown (USHL) in the 2016 Phase 2 USHL draft is a steady Defenseman who can play a solid all around game and defends very well. His skating is good enough where he is rarely caught out of position. In our viewings both for Notre Dame H.S. and Team Wisconsin U18 Karow was impressive and controlled the game for his team from the back end. A strong skater who protects the puck on the breakout and has good vision of the ice. Karow is a defenseman that could probably put up more points but takes pride in being a reliable defender. He has good offensive instincts in the zone, moves along the blue line well and has good vision and passing ability. Karow fly's a little under the radar due to playing WI Prep hockey, not being drafted in the USHL Futures draft and still uncommitted to a NCAA school but is a player we will be following closely because of the mature game he possesses.

Keating, Austen
LW - Ottawa 67's (OHL) 5'11", 162

Keating was selected in the first round, 16th overall at the 2015 OHL Priority Selection Draft by the Ottawa 67's out of the Guelph Jr. Gryphons Minor Midget program. Keating started out a little slow but was given top six ice time fairly quickly afterwards into his OHL career. This has really helped him get acclimated and play with some skilled veteran players.

Austen is an offensive minded forward that on some nights showed his skill and put up some points, but then you wouldn't see him for a couple games. He needs to work on being a consistent player every night and if he's not scoring points to be more effective away from the puck. His skating is average at best, and at his size it needs to improve. Going forward Austen is going to have to work on his skating to maximize his efficiency and create more offensive chances. He was just under 50% in face-offs this year, we would like to see him get stronger on his stick and to use his frame to win more face-offs and also taking key face-offs. He has shown good hockey sense and a good shot with a quick release in our viewings of him. Defensively he needs to get stronger on his feet, he would get knocked around trying to take his man, or he was to slow to react on speed with the cycle. Keating has good scoring ability and offensive upside. However the key for him will be adding muscle to his frame, yet at the same time finding a way to get quicker and faster. At sub six feet, not having good speed is a killer when projecting for the NHL. Keating will also need to work harder and be a tougher player to play against away from the puck.

Quotable: "Skating will be the biggest issue for him as he enters his NHL Draft season. - HP Scout Mark Edwards

Keyser, Kyle
G - Flint Firebirds (OHL) 6'02", 182

Kyle was selected in the fourth round of the 2014 OHL Priority Selection Draft by the Flint Firebirds out of the Detroit Victory Honda U16 program. Keyser was a pleasant surprise showing the ability to handle a lot of rubber in the OHL very early into his career.

Keyser has great size and shows good, calm movement in his crease. He handled pressure situations well and showed good quickness and reflexes. He has great positioning on initial shots, but will sometimes over commit to shots which gets him into trouble from time to time. Kyle performed well in our viewings on a team that is still experiencing some growing pains. Next season could be a big opportunity for him to try to take on a bulk of the action. Already through one junior season in the OHL he has shown very intriguing and promising upside as a pro level goaltender.

Quotable: "Very solid in my viewings this past season." - HP Scout Mark Edwards

Kneen, Nolan
RD – Kamloops Blazers (WHL) 6'00", 170

Kneen is a two-way defender on the smaller side who struggled in terms of keeping up in speed and strength at the WHL level, but he has good skill with the puck and a really high compete-level. He was another standout at the World Under-17 Hockey Championships where, playing against smaller and younger opponents, he looked physically dominant. While he is not as physically effective against WHL competition, we really liked Kneen's willingness to step up and still try to be physically involved. He's a defenseman that likes to play with some snarl in his game, although getting bigger would improve the efficiency of his physical game.

Kneen's skating is fairly good, as he makes up for a lack of power with a large surplus of agility. He's a quite good open-ice hitter and was known as a punisher in bantam. He should start throwing his body around more and more in the WHL as he adds strength to his frame. He's small but as he fills out in stature we expect his game to settle in and become effective at the WHL level as well, as he will be able to utilize his abrasiveness and compete level more effectively.

Kofron, David
RW – HC Trinec U20 (CZE) – 5'10", 146

A late '98 birth year, Kofron likes to creep around the net looking for a weakness in the opposing teams defense. He demonstrated on separate occasions his ability to set up beautiful scoring opportunities, but his linemates were often unable to finish. He can be slippery down the wall and dodge out of checks easily. Strong on his feet and has a nice stride. Struggled early at the Hlinka Tournament against Canada, but was named player of the game against Switzerland with two great goals - both coming off of quick releases with pinpoint accuracy.

Has some mental lapses in games that leaves you wondering what he was thinking about. However, he works hard away from the puck and was used on his clubs power play and penalty kill when viewed. Unfortunately, he missed significant time for undisclosed reasons and only played 12 games in domestic leagues this season.

Kostin, Klim
RW – MVD (MHL) – 6'3", 190

Kostin already competed most of the season against older players at the MHL level and made some appearances as well with the U18 national team, so when the meldonium scandal happened the captain of the U17 national team was inevitably asked to lead the way in North Dakota. Even if he failed to score, he was able to carry the load and didn't disappoint, bringing leadership and a strong performance while playing in all situations. Something that certainly helped him is how physically strong he is for his age. Still 16 at the time of the tournament, he looked already more powerful than most of his opponents. He can protect the puck very well, using his reach to his advantage when he challenges defensemen. He can be physical along the boards, win pucks and help establishing the cycle in the offensive zone. At the junior level he is a winger that can drive his line and shows the rare ability to split defenses. He is strong on the puck, still has room to add muscles and could develop into a great skater. He is sturdy on his skates, with nice balance and a great lateral push while carrying the puck around the offensive zone.

Especially for a player that carries the puck so much through the fire, Klim maintains good awareness on the ice and has the vision to see plays develop and find the open linemate even when he appears to have his head down. His passing and shooting abilities don't let him down when he doesn't have the option to drive the net or challenge defensemen. He also works well to position himself without the puck. His efforts are fairly consistent and if anything he is at fault for trying to do too much. Kostin plays an ambitious and demanding game, it will be interesting to see how effective he'll be against men. Sometimes he forces plays and doesn't always make the right decision. Besides, he will have to pay attention not to expose himself to dangerous hits when facing more punishing defensemen at the next level.

Kousal, Pavel
RW - HC Dukla Jihlava U20 (CZE) 5'10", 148
Kousal, a late '98 birth year, brings a lot of excitement and creativity. Doesn't possess a large, strong frame, but his game is based off his speed and skill. His hand-eye coordination is nothing short of impressive, as it is common to see him bat pucks out of mid-air to score goals or intercept passes from defenders sending pucks midair through the neutral zone. Loves to try new moves and different techniques in every game. Great ability to get a one-timer off while in motion, has a nice scoring touch. His wrist shot isn't powerful, but it is accurate, well placed and released in stride. Could get a fuller stride and extend more, but skating is still a strength. Protects the puck well to get off passes while under pressure.

Krief, Alex
LD – Chicoutimi Sagueneens (QMJHL) – 6'03", 183
Krief is a big, mobile defenseman who was drafted in the first round by Chicoutimi last June at the QMJHL Draft. He skates like he's 5'10", using very smooth and powerful strides. He is dangerous when he rushes the puck in the offensive zone and can act like a 4th forward on the ice. This season, he saw ice time on the power play with Frédéric Allard, and usually played on the 3rd pair when he was in the lineup. With three '99-born defensemen on the team, all three rotated as healthy scratches at some point during the season. On the point, Krief possesses a big, heavy slapshot, and still needs to work on its accuracy but it has great velocity. There's a good amount of work to do with him in terms of his play in his own zone, as he often forgets his position and runs around his own zone too much. Despite his size, he's not known for his physical game and won't necessarily put fear in the minds of opposing forwards. He can get the puck out of his zone easily by skating it out or by using a good first pass. Krief will need to work on his decision-making and the mental sides of the game as he continues to progress into next season, but his physical tools are there.

Lapierre, Jacob
LW – Victoriaville Tigres (QMJHL) – 6'02", 225
Lapierre was in his rookie season with Victoriaville, after they selected him in the 3rd round of the 2015 QMJHL Draft. He has pro size already, standing at over 225 pounds, and moves around the ice pretty well for a young man of that stature. He has a powerful shot and decent hands. He scored seven times this season in 44 games getting 3rd-line ice time. He also saw some power play time, mostly in front of the net. At that size, he's tough to move from there. It's all about consistency for Lapierre, who looks like a legit NHL prospect at times, but all too often becomes invisible and floats around without making much of an impact. If the mental game can catch up to his physical tools, he could be a good player down the road.

Lauzon, Zachary
LD – Rouyn-Noranda Huskies (QMJHL) – 6'00", 189
Lauzon is the younger brother of Jérémy (Boston's 2nd round draft pick and current Huskies' defenseman) and, in his first full season in the QMJHL, was named to the QMJHL rookie team. A bit of a different player than his brother, Zachary is not as offensive as Jérémy, but he's a smart defender and

makes smart plays all over the ice. He has a good compete level, getting involved in the physical game. Once he gets stronger, he will win more battles along the boards and in front of the net. With the puck, he makes the high-percentage play most of the time, but lacks the vision and offensive upside of his brother. This year, he was often on the third pairing with Jacob Neveu, sometimes not getting a lot of ice time with Rouyn-Noranda's top-4 eating a lot of minutes. Defensively, he does a good job blocking shots and breaking up plays with his good stick. Next season, he should get more responsibility with Nikolas Brouillard leaving the team and more play on the special teams.

Quotable:" Love the way he competes every night and next year he will have more ice time and will play on Rouyn-Noranda top-4 with them losing 2 key LD (Brouillard and Caron)." - HP scout Jérôme Bérubé

Le Coultre, Simon
LC – SC Bern (SUI Jr.) – 5'11", 161

A very active puck moving defenseman, Le Coultre was part of the Swiss U18 national team all season long despite being eligible for next year draft by only one month. He didn't play a marginal role either and certainly didn't lack in personality, as he still tried to impact the game in all possible ways just like he likes to do with his club junior team. He brings enthusiasm and a pretty complete skillset for such a young player. Already possesses a legit slapshot, has adequate stickhandling for a defenseman and his very good wheels are the key element to his game. He can transition the puck up the ice and carry it to the offensive blueline if better options are not available. He is fast getting on dump-ins and trying to make a play with the puck. Sometimes he takes too many risks with his passes in the defensive zone though.

Le Coultre brings energy, likes to engage and doesn't mind getting physical along the boards. He has a lot of work to do defensively, however. The effort is there, but his coverage in the defensive zone is not consistently reliable. He tends to overplay situations, move around too much and get out of position. An even bigger problem is how often he gets caught up the ice, leading to odd men rushes. He will have to become smarter in picking his spots and play a bit more conservatively. Furthermore, Simon would be an undersized defenseman if he is done growing, something that would hurt his draft status next year.

Leschyshyn, Jake
LC – Regina Pats (WHL) 5'11", 176

Leschyshyn is a responsible two-way centre who was a fixture on the Regina Pats checking line this season, providing really strong play in all three zones and in all situations. The son of NHLer Curtis Leschyshyn, Jake clearly has good bloodlines. At only sixteen-year's-old, Leschyshyn is already fast enough, strong enough, and smart enough to be plugged anywhere on the Pats lineup.

Yet he still seems best suited to a checking role, as it plays to his strengths. Leschyshyn appears to be motored by both good feet and a high compete-level. His skating mechanics are very good, even though he's not necessarily blazing fast at this point. His backchecking speed is notably good, as he's very good at creating turnovers in transition. He reads plays very quickly and reacts to changes in direction almost clairvoyantly. Although he's still young, he looks physically mature when fighting for pucks in the tough areas. If left alone in the offensive zone, meanwhile, he can make you pay with either a quick shot or a smart-headed pass. He also sets up in front of the net and is willing to pay the price for his offense.

Leschyshyn is already good in the faceoff circle. He was a key member of Regina's number one penalty killing unit this season as he has great positioning and patience when defending the man advantage. He's also a very good shot blocker. His point totals won't blow anyone away at this point, but they don't do the rest of his game justice. Looking highly competitive even in the most futile situations, he's not likely to give up on a play or a games easily, already looking like a player who might be future captain material. He was behind Brooks and Steel on depth-chart but will have an opportunity to generate more production as he gets more prime minutes.

Liljegren, Timothy
RD – Rogle BK (SHL) – 6'00", 190

Liljegren is a mobile two-way puck-mover that shows tremendous upside as a 2017 defensive prospect. We have seen him excel at the U17 World Championships where he was in our opinion the best defenseman in the tournament if not the best player overall. He has shown a high level of play for Rogle in SHL against men and he also had a good showing at the U18s in Grand Forks, North Dakota. Liljegren has high-end mobility with a light fluid stride, he is an excellent distributor of the puck from the back-end. His ability to find lanes, execute delays and re-groups, and high-end vision allow him to control the pace of the game from the back-end. He is equally at home at skating the puck forward as well as dishing crisp passes. Liljegren is also a very good offensive zone player. He has an excellent feel for the game and makes very good decisions when deciding on whether to become more offensively active or to keep a more defensive position. This allows him to be a consistent offensive factor without overly exposing his team defensively. He has a high-end shot and a varied shot-selection. His slapshot is good and he gets it off quickly, but especially impressive is his ability to pick corners with his wristshot, often leaving goalies and defenses dumbfounded with the puck in the back of the net. Several times, we have seen Liljegren pick corners with a quick-release wrister that nobody saw coming.

While Liljegren isn't a huge defenseman at 6'0, he does boast a 190 pound frame. He's got a good compete level in his own zone and doesn't shy away. While he doesn't always seem like the strongest guy on the ice, it appears that he should at least be average if not better in the strength department when all is said and done. At this moment, his defensive game is probably the part that could use the most refinement, however, even at this point it is far from a weakness and there are no real red-flags going forward that would prevent Liljegren from projecting as a good defensive player at the next level.

Quotable: "He still needs to make some improvements defensively, but he has the rare ability to consistently manufacture offense from the back-end without being high-risk or exposing his team too much. He looks like a high pick next year." - HP Scout Nik Funa

Quotable: "Great Dman with a two way game. Great skater with a high hockey IQ. This kid can shoot the puck, he scored on a laser shot from a bad angle in one of my viewings. Should be a very high pick next year. - HP Scout Mark Edwards

Lind, Kole
RW – Kelowna Rockets (WHL) 6'00", 172

Came onto the scene during the 2015 playoffs getting into 7 games after only 6 in the regular season and started asserting himself with his skating and speed. Has good offensive instincts where he does a good job sniffing out spots for his shot. In his debut season he didn't receive favorable playing time often lining up in the bottom 6 and with little power play minutes, still managing a respectable 41 points (14G, 27A).

Has well-rounded game, skating is quick and shows good speed to open space with quick lateral cuts and has the strong and quick wrist shot to convert. Would like to see him assert himself more and taking the puck to the net consistently, when he does good things happen. At times he can get into a bit of a watching game where he waits for opportunities to come instead of working for his own and he can log several shifts without making things happen. Although he is quite good at reading offensive opportunities and getting into high scoring areas for his shot, his play with the puck as a playmaker is less impressive at this point and he can be kept to the outside. He should have an opportunity to rise as the season progresses if he is given minutes in an offensive role as he has good scoring instincts and is an intelligent player.

Lipanov, Alexei
LC - HK MVD Balashikha (MHL) – 6'00", 159

Lipanov is a center that plays a responsible two-way game and has good instincts. Especially impressive are his instincts away from the puck and defensively as he already plays a game that is mature beyond his years. He uses his stick well to cover lanes and takes intelligent angles to force the other team's puck-movement towards where he wants it go.

Lipanov is a smart offensive player, but could stand to show something more dynamic with the puck on his stick. He makes good high-percentage plays that don't hurt his team, but can at times leave you wanting more on the offensive side of the puck.

Lodnia, Vanya
RC - Erie Otters (OHL) 5'09", 171

Lodnia was selected in the first round, 20th Overall by the Erie Otters out of the Detroit Honeybaked U16 program. Lodnia played a wide range of roles everywhere from first line to third line over the course of this season for Erie. He adjusted to the OHL fairly quickly and was a consistent threat for the Otters offensively.

Lodnia is an undersized forward with good skating ability. He has a decent sized frame despite his size and controls the puck very well. He is a speedy forward who enters the zone with the puck and will challenge defenders going to the net. He has quick hands and a quick shot which makes him a threat to score, but he also possesses good vision in the offensive zone and can create offense for his linemates. Lodnia is fairly strong for his size which helps him fight off checkers but if he slows down he can be easy to contain, so gaining size would be valuable for Lodnia. He has a good compete level and will battle for pucks. However he does go through stretches where he disappears. Lodnia will need to hopefully grow leading towards his 2017 NHL Draft year as he does possess the offensive tools desired for a top six prospect but lacks the size.

Luukkonen, Ukko-Pekka
G – HPK U20 (FIN) – 6'03", 196

Big and calm goalie, Luukkonen played the 2014-15 season on the U16 team. This year he started in the U18 league but was promoted to HPK's U20 team during winter and performed well there. His development has been very fast which makes him a really interesting prospect. Internationally he backed up Lassi Lehtinen on Finland's WHC U17 squad and didn't look good in his lone game there. During the U18s in North Dakota he emerged as Finland's starting goaltender and won gold. Although, he looked shaky at times, he gave his team a chance in every game and even came up big a couple of times. At times he hangs too far back and hopes for the best with his size, instead of challenging shooters, his rebound control hasn't been the best either. He's still raw, however at his size, upside and the progression, he will be a goalie worth paying attention to next year.

Lyle, Brady
RD - North Bay Battalion (OHL) 6'02", 187

Lyle was selected in the first round, 18th Overall at the 2015 OHL Priority Selection Draft by the North Bay Battalion out of the Shattuck St. Mary's U16 program. Lyle got off to a rough start to his OHL career after breaking his collarbone. Because of this he was unable to make his OHL debut until late November. Once he did debut he played primarily third pairing minutes for the Battalion in his first OHL season.

Brady is a two-way defenseman with good size already. Lyle is a good skater who possesses good mobility, strong edge work and slightly above average speed. While Lyle does lack an explosive first step, once he gets going his fluid stride makes him hard to contain through the neutral zone. Lyle is at his best with the puck on his stick, as he has the ability to dictate the pace of the game in possession. The smooth skating defensemen uses his hockey sense, vision and on ice awareness to dissect the opposition on the breakout, making crisp, high quality outlet passes. While Lyle has the ability to skate the puck out of danger, he also shows an ability to make smart decisions in puck possession, and usually doesn't force plays that aren't there. However there are times where he will panic a little with pressure. Offensively Lyle has good power play capabilities, as his vision and decision making play a large role in his success. Blessed with solid point shot, Lyle is not going to wow you with incredible puck skills or highlight reel rushes, rather he takes what is given to him and plays a smart, calculated game. Defensively, Lyle isn't overly physical, generally using his mixture of body position an active stick contain and defend with some success. Lyle needs to add some muscle to his frame and limit mistakes further in order to maximize his potential.

MacIsaac, Keenan
LD – Chicoutimi Sagueneens (QMJHL) – 5'11", 172

MacIsaac is the defenseman with the best vision of all three '99-born defensemen in Chicoutimi. He sees the ice well and will make an excellent power-play quarterback in the QMJHL at some point. Coming out of the prep school system in Canada, MacIsaac made a big jump making the Saguenéens out of training camp and had to make quite a few adjustments in the defensive zone. He has great offensive instinct and saw his share of ice time on the man-advantage. Right now, he's more of a passer, as his shot lacks velocity and he should work on this in the offseason. He has good mobility and a good frame of footwork, but lacks strength right now and is not an explosive skater. By adding some strength, he will be much more comfortable in the defensive zone, battling along the wall and in front of the net. After getting his feet wet this season, look for him to be more of a contributor and have more of an impact offensively next season.

MacLean, Kyle
LW - Oshawa Generals (OHL) 5'11", 180

MacLean was selected in the fourth round of the 2015 OHL Priority Selection Draft by the Oshawa Generals out of the New Jersey Rockets U16 program. MacLean made the rebuilding Generals as a 16 year old and got the opportunity to play a third line role.

MacLean is a speedy, two-way winger with a strong compete level. He consistently rose up the Oshawa Generals depth chart as the season went on, Kyle MacLean brings a reliable two-way skill set to the table. A player who possesses an explosive first step along with high end straight line speed and a smooth, fluid stride, MacLean makes his way around the ice with ease. MacLean shows a tenaciousness to his game as he routinely gets to pucks first, engages in puck battles and shows a willingness to engage physically. MacLean's tenaciousness in puck pursuit often allows him to force turnovers, while his relentless fore checking becomes agitating to the opposition. In possession MacLean can be tough to contain as he combines strong puck skills with excellent change of pace and direction abilities. He finds seams and bursts through them effortlessly. MacLean's most notable offensive weapon is his shot. MacLean would benefit from slowing his game down some, dissecting the opposing teams defensive approach as he can force plays on occasion which lead to unforced turnovers. In his own zone MacLean is reliable as he shows strong on ice awareness, keeps his feet moving and shows an uncanny ability to break up pass attempts and shots with impressive anticipation skills. Kyle is a player that should see an expanded role in Oshawa next season.

Maksimov, Kirill
RW - Saginaw Spirit (OHL) 6'01", 190

Maksimov was selected in the second round of the 2015 OHL Priority Selection Draft by the Saginaw Spirit out of the Toronto Jr. Canadiens Minor Midget program. Maksimov is a very offensive minded forward who had to adjust to a third line role playing in the OHL this year, but still found a way to contribute fairly well for a second round pick playing bottom six.

Maksimov has good size and effective skating ability. He likes to have the puck on his stick and will challenge defenders regularly. He has good offensive tools and can both score goals and set up goals for his linemates. He will need to get stronger and improve on his two-way game in order to maximize his potential. Playing a bigger role next season should help him with his offensive side of the game leading into the 2017 NHL Entry Draft.

Maniscalco, Josh
RD – USNTDP U17 6'00", 208

Maniscalco stood out positively with his defensive ability. He doesn't have the most reach at 6 feet but already has a heavy frame with over 200 pounds and has good physical tools. Maniscalco has good initial positioning against rush plays which allows him to block or steer forwards off. He has some physicality to him too and will use that heavy frame. Good at lining up players and more than willing to engage. Can be a suffocating presence on the ice. Has shown some offensive upside and has a good shot from the point but offensive game hasn't looked like his forte yet at this point. Committed to University of Minnesota for 2017-2018.

Martin, Luke
RD – USNTDP 6'02", 201

Luke Martin is a late 1998 born defenseman with size, mobility, and smarts. Had he been born 5 days earlier, he'd be eligible for the 2016 NHL draft. Martin has established himself as part of the USNTDP U18 blueline, where he generally plays a rather low-maintenance game. Martin mostly played a rather low-risk game, he takes care of his own end and doesn't try to over-extend himself on the offensive side of the puck. He makes solid decisions on the first pass and can skate the puck out of trouble if needed but isn't consistently involved as an offensive threat. It's not a big hole in his game as he can get his shots on net and makes correct reads on the offensive blueline, but there hasn't yet distinguished himself as much of a threat from in the offensive zone. He's a solid defender that rarely blows his coverage and uses his size and stick well. As he moves forward, he will take upon a bigger role on the USNTDP blueline and will have a chance to progress from a solid if unspectacular defensemen into a bigger two-way presence on the ice

Mattheos, Stelio
RW/RC – Brandon Wheat Kings (WHL) 6'01", 194

Mattheos is a smooth skating scoring forward with good size who is yet another highly touted 2017 prospect from Brandon Wheat Kings. Mattheos already has more than a year of major junior experience and has been a part of two lengthy playoff runs. He's a good skater with pro size and well above-average puck skill.

Mattheos has a bevy of high-end qualities. His stickhandling and wristshot ability from tight space particularly stand out. The wristshot has a quick release and is accurate. On the playmaking side of things, he has good vision and makes some nice plays into the slot. He's definitely not afraid to truck the puck into the slot himself, either. In fact one thing we like about Mattheos is his ability to place his body between the checker and the puck. He has the natural sense of knowing where the checker is pressuring from and does a good job keeping the puck out of his reach. Mattheos won't necessarily punish you physically, but shows good upside in the grinding elements of the game. Considering that he also boasts good skill, this gives him the upside to provide a different, more heavy look when playing with other skill players.

Mattheos put up good point totals in Brandon this season, but was not quite a key player on a Brandon team that was stacked with quality older prospects. Mattheos will be a key benefactor of key graduations from the Brandon Wheat Kings lineup going into next season and will be expected to take upon a bigger role with more quality minutes.

McGregor, Ryan
LW - Sarnia Sting (OHL) 5'10", 148

McGregor was selected in the second round of the 2015 OHL Priority Selection Draft by the Sarnia Sting out of the Burlington Eagles Minor Midget program. McGregor got off to a slow start in his first season of the OHL getting acclimated to the pace and the size of the opposition. He settled in and had a very productive second half of the season which included some ice on the top two lines.

McGregor is a speedy forward who moves the puck very well in transition. He is capable of forcing turnovers on the forecheck at times but doesn't possess any physicality in order to pressure opponents to create turnovers. McGregor uses his speed when entering the offensive zone to beat defenders one on one and has a bit of a shoot first mentality. He is able to go to the net and has good positioning allowing him to get into these scoring areas despite lacking strength. His slot presence allowed him to get his quick shots past the goaltenders and resulted in a few goals. McGregor has great speed and good offensive tools leading into the 2017 NHL Draft year but lacks size and strength desired of him at this point. He will also need to be more consistent with his play when the opposition has the puck.

McHugh, Nick
LW - Kitchener Rangers (OHL) 5'10", 163

McHugh was selected in the 7th round of the 2015 OHL Priority Selection Draft by the Kitchener Rangers out of the Ottawa Jr. 67's Minor Midget program. It was originally expected that McHugh might need a season to prepare but he impressed at Rangers camp and made the team, who had plenty of veterans right out of camp and spent his 16 year old season in the OHL.

McHugh is a high energy player with good speed. He works hard in all three zones making him an effective forechecker. He received some time on the penalty kill this season where he used his speed and skating to play keep away and kill time off the clock. He's a player who is willing to do what it takes in the defensive zone to shut down the opposition. While he didn't get a lot of prime offensive opportunities, McHugh showed the speed and playmaking abilities that should help him advance. He does a good job setting up his linemates and has good hands. When he gets behind defenders using his speed he can be dangerous on the breakaway. McHugh will need to get stronger and hopefully a little taller as he is currently a little undersized for the NHL level.

McIndoe, Ethan
LW/C – Spokane Chiefs (WHL) 6'01", 175

McIndoe was a solid scorer in Bantam, however as a WHL rookie in the 2015/16 season he struggled to find consistency. He has good reach and a decent frame-size and shows good on ice awareness, keeping his head up. Plays a gritty game and uses his body to create space, isn't afraid to drop the gloves but this isn't the main focus of his game. Works hard in all 3 zones and plays a power game. His skating is just OK and needs improvement. Needs to attack the net with consistent purpose to create trouble for goaltenders, when he does he will make space for himself and his line mates. Needs to improve consistency and scoring ability to become a serious prospect for 2017, has some good tools but will need to take steps forward to distinguish himself in the 2017 class. We like his willingness to work and be involved in all three zones, but he needs to add some finish to what he creates with his compete.

Meireles, Greg
RC - Kitchener Rangers (OHL) 5'10", 163

Greg was selected in the first round, 12th Overall at the 2015 OHL Priority Selection Draft by the Kitchener Rangers out of the Ottawa Jr. 67's Minor Midget program. Meireles who had more than enough talent to spend the full season with the Rangers opted to play for the Ottawa Jr. Senators of the CCHL for the majority of the season. Meireles played 7 games with the Rangers posting nearly a point per game.

Meireles is a high energy forward who played at a very high pace. He has great speed and work ethic competing in all three zones. He is very defensively responsible and will battle relentlessly along the wall for pucks, winning more than his share of battles for his size. Meireles does a great job anticipating the opposition allowing him to intercept passes. He also has a bit of a physical side. Offensively he showed some creativity with the puck, capable of setting up linemates. He also uses his speed and has a decent shot to beat goaltenders. Meireles has some intriguing offensive upside, but it's his work ethic in all three zones and his compete level that jump out at you. Greg will need to add some muscle and hopefully get bigger; he is already pretty strong considering his size.

Quotable: "Was good for Kitchener in his limited games in the OHL this season. He has a chance to be a high pick next June." - HP Scout Mark Edwards

Mendel, Griffin
LD – Penticton Vees (BCHL) 6'03", 205

Mendel comes to the rink with all the things you look for in a defensive prospect: size, speed, and smarts. He's a really strong and agile skater for his size and is very dependable below the goal-line. He has solid hockey IQ and easily picks up his man. He reads the zone entries well and knows how to push the play to the outside but also easily picks up his guy on the cycle and protects the middle of the slot. Griffin is a tall dependable defenseman whose game is a bit unremarkable on the offensive side of the puck at this point in time.

Mendel served as a key penalty killer for the Vees this year. His speed allows him to win most of his puck races and he is good on puck-retrievals, his size lets him easily rub opponents out along the boards, and he plays pucks off the boards brilliantly. In fact, he has some of the best clearing ability in the BCHL.

Mendel had a strong performance at the World Under-17 Hockey Championships, where he took home a gold medal. As he moves forward, we would like to see him gain more confidence as a stick-handler and as someone who can get involved up the ice and on the offensive blueline.

Mersch, Dominick
F – Lincoln Stars (USHL) 6'01", 181

Mersch is not a flashy player; he plays a very straight ahead game, skates well and will go to tough areas and score dirty goals. He does possess decent vision and playmaking ability, he isn't going to score a lot of highlight real goals or make the prettiest setup plays but will out work a lot of other players and showed good hockey sense to know where he needs to go with the puck. Dominick needs to continue to develop more of a scoring touch around the net and find ways to get himself and his stick in the right area's to be available for more passes and plays in front of the net.

Messier, Simon
LD – Gatineau Olympiques (QMJHL) – 6'02", 176

Messier made the Olympiques straight out of Midget Espoir and played 28 games this season after being selected 74th overall in the 2015 QMJHL Draft. He didn't get to play a lot this year and in the games he eventually played, some were at forward. Looking back now, a strong year in Midget AAA might have been better suited for him. Nevertheless, Messier is an interesting package on the blueline with his size and mobility. He's clearly a long-term project and next year will be interesting to see where he's at in his development. Areas he will need to keep working on are his play with the puck and his decision-making. He has decent feet and won't shy away from playing a physical game along the boards and in front of the net.

Messner, Mick
LW – Madison Capitols (USHL) 5'11", 194

Messner had an interesting season in 15/16. He Split the season between the Madison Capitols AAA and Madison Capitols USHL teams. As expected Messner dominated his time in AAA but had a tough time in his 27 games in the USHL. Messner spent most of his time in the USHL on the 4th line and rarely with the same line mates. The first thing that stands out about Messner is his skating ability, he is a elite skater who will go to the dirty area's and battle and wins a lot of battles along the wall. Not a big player but plays a power forward style and has great finishing ability. Messner is a player we will follow closely next year as he will get more of a prominent role with the Capitols before heading to the University of Wisconsin in 2017.

Minulin, Artyom
RD – Swift Current Broncos (WHL) 6'02", 200

A big defenseman, Minulin has made big strides in his rookie WHL season and is looking like a prospect worth paying attention to for the 2017 NHL draft. Minulin actually saw some quality minutes for Swift Current and we have seen him take shifts both on PP as well as PK. His 33 points in 72 games is quite an impressive statline for a rookie defenseman.

Minulin looks upper-body heavy and a bit awkward on his skates. What's appealing about him is the fact that he displays solid hockey IQ. While he can look a touch awkward with that big body of his, he still makes intelligent reads and shows poise with the puck, often executing smart little passes and shows projectable puck skills. Sometimes Minulin will also surprise with a high-end offensive move that comes out of nowhere. Although not a consistent offensive presence, there are indications of untapped offensive potential in his game. Minulin is a big kid that shows good smarts and upside on both ends of the puck but is fairly raw. He will need to improve his in-tight quickness and agility. He could also use his frame more effectively in his own end at a consistent level. Nevertheless, Minulin has certainly shown that he has good upside despite being a very raw around the edges prospect.

Mismash, Grant
LW – USNTDP U17 6'00", 182

Mismash is a scoring winger that has had a successful season for the USNTDP u17 team. His game revolves around his will to score. He likes to shoot and while shooting is rarely a bad thing, Mismash has the tendency to take one low-percentage shot too many. He makes smart off the puck reads in order to get himself open, mostly again looking for his shot, but will need to find ways to develop as a playmaker and be more involved in the play consistently in all three zones. Mismash also likes to play with some power in his game and could develop into a scoring power-winger type forward. He is committed to University of North Dakota for 2018-2019.

Mitchell, Ian
RD – Spruce Grove Saints (AJHL) 5'10", 165

Mitchell is a puck-mover that still has some filling out to do but shows quality decision-making and some offensive upside to his game. Mitchell has spent the 2015-2016 season playing in the Alberta Junior Hockey League, but also had an appearance for Canada at the U17 WHC where he took home gold playing for Canada White. In fact, Mitchell was one of the more solid players on that team's blue-line and performed quite well in our viewings.

Mitchell is a player that has good mobility and vision with the puck. He can bring the puck up the ice with his skating but is also an adept passer. His first pass is good and he also distributes the puck well in the offensive zone. Mitchell is a player that can quarterback your powerplay. We really liked his wrist-shot from the point as it has a very quick release and gets through. It's a hard shot to read for goaltenders even if it doesn't have a lot of power to it and produces rebounds. Mitchell plays a controlled, smart game with quality puck-skills and keeps his head up to scan the ice. He is coming along nicely as a smart puck-mover although clearly he will need to add some pounds on his frame as he moves forward.

Mittelstadt, Casey
LC/LW – Eden Prairie High (USHS) 5'11", 195

Mittelstadt is a highly skilled forward who has proven himself to be one of the better prospects heading into the 2017 NHL draft. He had a successful 2015-2016 season at every level, but in particular his international performances against older players stand out as impressive. Mittelstadt already turned heads with a fantastic Hlinka Memorial Tournament performance where he was one of the better players on the ice each game. Mittelstadt is a natural center but can also line up on wing.

Mittelstadt offers a terrific combination of quick hands with high-end puck skills, vision with the puck and skating ability. Mittelstadt can buy time for himself with his hands but even more impressive is his ability to quickly scan the ice and make a high-end play out of nowhere. He's got great ability to deke defensemen out and to pull away from his check as he is a very hard player to read with the puck on his stick. Once he generates an extra half-step of space he will convert quickly on it either setting up a linemate for a goal or shooting himself. Mittelstadt is an impressive playmaker but can easily snipe on his own as he is good at disguising his wrist-shot into his stickhandling motion. There is not a lot of wind-up on his shot and he gets it off quickly with a snap, making it hard to read for goalies as they struggle to anticipate the point of release. Although not currently the tallest for a center, Mittelstadt already has a reasonably bulky frame at 195 pounds and he's quite strong on the puck. His defensive game doesn't stand out as a big asset for him right now but it's not subpar either and it should not be a hole in his game as he develops. He isn't soft either and will play in traffic and go to the net. Going into the 2017 draft, Mittelstadt projects as one of the more highly skilled and dangerous offensive players. With a good year he should have a chance to hear his name called in the upper half of the first round.

Morand, Antoine
LC – Acadie-Bathurst Titans (QMJHL) – 5'09", 169

The Titan made Morand the 2nd overall pick behind Joseph Veleno in the 2015 QMJHL Draft last June. Morand had a great first year with the Titan, averaging over a point per game and playing on a top line, often with Vladimir Kuznetsov, who is eligible for the 2016 Draft. After the playoffs were over, Morand also received an invitation to participate in the Hockey Canada U-18 camp as an underager, but was cut after the two exhibition games. He's not big, but Morand plays with a lot of heart and passion. He has game-breaking speed and can reach his top speed very quickly. He has great work ethic, a non-stop motor and plays hard in all three zones. However, his lack of strength does hurt him when fighting for space or for a puck along the wall. Defensively, he tries really hard, but his lack of size at this moment gives him some issues. With added strength, he should be fine, as he's committed to playing a good two-way game. Offensively, he wants pucks on his stick; makes players around him better and really hit it off with Kuznetsov on his line this season. He has great on-ice vision. If you're his winger, there is a good chance he will find you in the offensive zone if you're open in a scoring area. Offensively, the sky's the limit with Morand, whose vision, speed and smarts will ensure his status as a dominant player in this league as soon as next season. His lack of size will surely be a heavy topic of discussion next season when analyzing him for the 2017 NHL Draft.

Quotable: "If he was 2-3 inches taller he would be my #1 prospect from the Q for 2017, great skater with a non-stop motor and makes everyone better around him. A high end talent to watch out for next year draft" - HP Scout Jérôme Bérubé

Necas, Martin
RC - HC Kometa Brno U18 (CZE) – 5'11", 148

Necas has been a highly productive center in his domestic league as well as internationally. He has produced 45 points in 28 games for Brno's U18 team and has 19 points in 10 games for Czech's U17 squad. Necas has been highly successful at the U17 WHC tournament in Dawson Creek and Fort St. John where he was Czech Republic's most impressive player alongside 2018 eligible Filip Zadina. Necas will need to add a lot of strength as he moves forward, but he is a highly skilled player who has good acceleration and is fluid on his skates. Despite the lack of size, he is more than willing to get involved in traffic-dense areas and doesn't show any fear. His sense for sliding into holes and converting on pucks in the slot is very good. Necas has a soft pair of hands and great playmaking vision. Anticipates the play very well and will distribute the puck around, setting up his linemates and making them involved in the play. He projects well as a smart, fast, and skilled offensive threat, but will need to work on adding mass and strength to his frame as he moves into his draft year.

Neumann, Brett
RC - Erie Otters (OHL) 5'09", 165

Neumann was selected in the third round of the 2015 OHL Priority Selection Drafy by the Erie Otters out of the Don Mills Flyers Minor Midget program. Neumann was good value at the 52nd overall pick and joined the powerful Otters, starting out slowly getting comfortable with the OHL, but quickly became an efficient energetic forward, also chipping in with some offense.

Neumann is a speedy offensive forward who played primarily on the Otters bottom six this season. He adapted his role very well utilizing his speed to play a good two-way game, competing hard for pucks and pressuring the opposition. He is able to use his speed in both directions to compete for pucks but doesn't apply the body on the forecheck, primarily stick to using his stick to defend. Neumann is good in the offensive zone with the puck. He can make quick puck decisions deep in the offensive zone to keep the play moving on the cycle, or to set up a chance for his teammates. He has a decent shot and is capable of scoring some nice goals on the rush. Neumann is undersized for the NHL level and would benefit from growing a bit. He needs to add muscle to his frame as he is still pretty small.

Noel, David
LD – Blizzard du Seminaire St-Francois (LHMAAAQ) – 6'01", 172

If Noel was not drafted by Chicoutimi, the chances of him playing full-time in the QMJHL would have been much higher. Chicoutimi had been granted an exception from the league to play with five 16 year olds on their team this season. Noel was 6th on the list, and he eventually played two games with the big club, but he had a stellar season with his midget team, scoring 18 times in 45 games. His big weapon is his shot, which is one of the best in midget hockey. He scored many goals from the point with that big bomb. He's also strong in his own zone, plays a physical game and makes good use of his long reach to knock pucks away from his opponents. He has good footing, which helps him keep track of quick forwards on the rush. He has good patience with the puck, and makes good, simple breakouts. Chicoutimi already had three '99-borns on their back end this season, so ice time should be somewhat of a tricky situation with Noel in the mix next season. There's not a whole lot that we don't like from Noel, a solid prospect.

Oettinger, Jake
G – USNTDP 6'04", 201

Oettinger is yet another big kid between the pipes for the USNTDP U18 team splitting time with 2016 eligible Joseph Woll. Oettinger is a goalie that makes his size do the work for him. He moves around the crease well enough but hasn't shown particularly explosive qualities. He plays his angels well and lets the puck hit him. His rebound control has been pretty good, he directs shots to the side and out of dangerous areas. He is generally good on initial saves, although in our viewings we have seen him give up the odd bad goal on shots that should have been saved. Oettinger is looking like another positionally solid big goalie who gets around the crease well for his size. He is committed to Boston University for 2016-2017.

O'Grady, Reagan
RD - Sudbury Wolves (OHL) 6'02", 194

After being selected in the first round of the 2014 OHL Priority Selection Draft by the Kingston Frontenacs, Reagan was promptly dealt to the Sudbury Wolves in a midseason deal where he has spent the last year and a half.

O'Grady has shown some upside at both ends of the ice. His upside is more so as a defensive first player. He has good size and a decent stick, but will need to improve on his defensive consistency on a game by game basis. He has the size and the frame to win more battles along the wall and we would like to see a little more of a mean streak out of him. Offensively he had flashes of good passing with good reads which lead to Reagan being awarded with some power play ice last season. The upside is there and he has the physical size to become a legitimate prospect for the 2017 NHL Entry Draft, but will need to show steady progression and better use of these tools going into his third junior season.

Oksanen, Emil
RW – Blues U20 (FIN) – 6'00", 181

He took big development steps during past summer and he was definitely one of the better offensive players in U20 league this season. Oksanen is a skilled winger with a great shot. Accurate and quick release. His puck-handling skills and vision are above average and he has great skating technique. Emil is a raw talent and will need to improve is his all-around game. He's only a good offensive player at the moment. Oksanen is effective on the power-play and especially excels when maneuvering around the half-wall to goal-mouth area. All in all, Oksanen has good upside heading into the 2017 NHL Draft.

Paquette, Jacob
D - Kingston Frontenacs (OHL) 6'02", 203

Paquette was selected 2nd round, 31st overall at the 2015 OHL Priority Selection Draft by the Kingston Frontenacs out of the Ottawa Jr. 67's Minor Midget program. Paquette was the big sleeper for the HP staff ranked 15th Overall and the highest ranked player to fall out of the first round. Paquette adapted to the OHL rather quickly. Although he played on a team loaded with veterans , Paquette actually saw his ice time increase throughout the season. He spent the majority of the second half of the season with Toronto Maple Leafs prospect Stephen Desrochers on the second pairing.

Paquette has an idea mix of physical shutdown defender and highly intelligent puck moving defenseman. He skates well despite already possessing good size for an NHL prospect at 16 years old. Right from the start of his OHL career he was fearless playing physical against bigger veteran opponents. Paquette showed excellent poise and patience in possession, Paquette was able to defend at a high level throughout the season, as he combined an active stick with a physical edge and strong positional play. He contained both in his own zone and off the rush, holding the blue line effectively while also taking away the middle of the ice, forcing the opposition to low percentage areas before separating a player from puck. In possession, Paquette showed good vision with the ability to make a clean an crisp first pass, along with the ability to deal with an aggressive forecheck with composure, simply absorbing a hit to make a high quality play. While Paquette was a bright spot in the defensive zone, he also made contributions on the offensive side of the puck and showed intriguing upside as a two-way defender. Jacob transitions up ice well, makes smart and calculated pinches and will insert himself in the offensive attack at the appropriate times. He also showed the uncanny ability to get pucks on net from the point, doing a great job of creating shooting lanes with subtle stick and body movements. Paquette will need to continue development but doesn't have any glaring weaknesses as he handled every role extremely well as a rookie and has the size and the upside to be a high end defenseman at the 2017 NHL Entry Draft.

Quotable: " One of my fave players from last years OHL Draft. He had a fantastic year for the Fronts and should be a high pick in the 2017 NHL Draft." - HP Scout Mark Edwards

Paré, Cédric
LC – Commandeur de Levis (LHMAAAQ) – 6'02", 190

Paré was the surprise pick of the 2015 QMJHL Draft, going 10th overall to the Sea Dogs when he was projected to go in the 2nd or 3rd round. He went back to his midget team this season for his 2nd year, and averaged a point a game for the Commandeurs. He's a big center with a lot of smarts, who won't necessarily wow anyone with his offensive skill level but remains a very reliable player that plays a pretty complete game. He has good positioning in all three zones and has good qualities to be efficient on the PK. He's a player that coaches can trust in any situation, including key faceoffs and big minutes. At his size, we wish he played more of a physical game, but he's similar to Frédérik Gauthier in that aspect of the game. He's a fluid skater and uses that speed on both offensive and defensive situations. He uses his size well in puck-protection situations. Big questions for next season include: where does he fit in on the Sea Dogs' roster, and how much offensive production will he have at the QMJHL level?

Pastujov, Michael
F – USNTDP U17 6'00", 192

Decent frame with above-average skating although doesn't knock your socks off with his footwork. Good offensive zone instincts and sense for producing offense, he has good hands and can make crafty plays with the puck. Can take shifts off and will need to improve consistency in his game. Pastujov has good offensive potential but will still need to develop more consistency as he moves up the ranks in order to be a threat at higher levels. He is committed to University of Michigan for 2017-2018.

Pataki, Brady
RW - Sudbury Wolves (OHL) 6'01", 209

Pataki was the fourth round selection of the Sudbury Wolves at the 2014 OHL Priority Selection Draft out of the Chatham-Kent Cyclones program. Despite being a fourth round selection, Brady made the jump right into the OHL as a 16 year old.

Pataki is a big power winger with great size and excellent strength. He's the type of player who finishes every check he can with authority. He is very good in the corners and battles hard using his strength to win his share of battles. Shockingly, considering the type of player Pataki is, he is capable of staying out of the penalty box racking up only 8 penalty minutes last season. He has a heavy shot and goes to the net, proving to be a difficult player to move in the slot. He was caught behind several veteran forwards in his second OHL season and should get an opportunity going into his 2017 NHL Draft year to move up the depth chart and showcasing his style of play.

Patrick, Nolan
RC – Brandon Wheat Kings (WHL) 6'03", 195

Nolan Patrick is already one of the better WHL players and even as the youngest player on his club he was named his team's MVP on Brandon's run to the Memorial Cup. Patrick is a multifaceted center who has every tool to his disposable that he needs to be successful. His physical tools, skill, compete level, and hockey IQ all project as good or better. One aspect that can not be forgotten with Patrick is that he shows signs of leadership ability. While Brandon overall had a rather forgettable Memorial Cup performance, Patrick has several times shown us that he performs well under pressure in our other viewings and we have seen him make key plays that change the tide of the game into his team's favor.

Nolan is a great playmaker, but is also a very capable shooter who has a really powerful quick-release wristshot. He excels at creating offense off of the rush as he has exceptional vision and instincts which allows him to make quick decisions while at speed that other junior players have trouble keeping up with. He's also really good along the boards, using his big frame and puck handling skills to shield the puck and separate from defenders while maneuvering around the offensive zone. Patrick isn't shy about taking the puck off the boards and drive to the middle either and will get his nose dirty to create his offense. He is also a strong power-play player as he excels at distributing the puck around and finding openings.

Patrick isn't a stationary player and keeps himself moving with and without the puck putting defense into the position of having to react to his movement. He makes excellent reads on both sides of the puck. His hockey IQ stands out as a big strength, he immediately picks up on what both his teammates and the opposition are doing and is a step ahead of the game. He makes the subtle reads that make players successful at the next level. He understands how and when to pressure the opposing player in order to put him into a bad spot without taking himself out of position in the process, he anticipates turnovers well and gets back into position before others do if his team is the one that committed the turnover, or will take off and take advantage of a break-down when the other team commits a turnover. He understands when his teammates need support and offers an easy outlet to alleviate pressure. He sees the holes develop in the offensive zone and understands how his own movement on the ice changes the other team's coverage and utilizes it accordingly. He understands when there is an opportunity to force an offensive play or when to back off and make a simple play on the cycle or pass the puck back to the point. Overall, Patrick is already very good at making those quality reads.

Excellent in the face off circle and in his own end, there are no clear weaknesses in Patrick's game. He's the first guy over the boards in any situation. If we were to nitpick, we would say his skating stride could still improve, even though he already gets to places he needs to without a problem and it's not something that would hold him back in the future. He is the type of coveted multi-dimensional center with size that every club is looking for as he is a plus player in all three zones with and without the puck. He clearly projects as a very high pick for the 2017 NHL entry draft with a very realistic shot at going first overall.

Quotable: "He was impressive from last August in the Ivan Hlinka right through to the end of this season. He might be the first player pick next June in Chicago." - HP Scout Mark Edwards

Pettersson, Elias
LC/W – Timra (SHL-2) – 6'01", 152

Elias is a late '98 born but is physically greener than most other prospects eligible for next year's draft. He has grown up to 6-foot-1 and his body seems to have yet to catch up. Saying he will need to fill out is an understatement in his case. He struggled along the first couple of months of the season and as soon as he started finding his game was recalled by his senior team. Competed against men along the rest of the Allsvenskan season showing some flashes of brilliance and was then a PPG player for Sweden at the U18 Worlds. Has been playing on the wing on the international stage, but long term probably projects as a center.

Pettersson is a very skilled prospect with tremendous passing ability and high hockey IQ. He also has great puck skills and when playing with confidence he can complete some creative plays. He can make backwards turns with the puck and he could be a one on one threat but still lacks the power to really separate from his opponents most of the times. He is a bit of an awkward skater right now, his top speed is not bad but late in his shifts he can struggle with the acceleration.
Partially because of how well he thinks the game, Elias frequently finds ways to get possession after battles where he is physically overwhelmed. At this stage he finds himself down to the ice more often then not after engaging, but he doesn't seem to care. He reads plays well without the puck and takes useful positions along the boards to regain possession, duly provides support to his teammates and makes very good use of his body when protecting the puck, albeit with his current physical limitations. He is shifty with the puck along the boards and tries to gain a step to put his great playmaking ability to work. He is responsible on the backcheck, the effort is there, even if in busy shifts he gets tired soon. His compete level is definitely encouraging for such a talented player. He possesses a good, accurate shot, but he still takes a bit too long to load it up.

Pettersson is clearly a work in progress, but has significant long term potential and could be a difference maker once fully developed. How popular his name will be by the time next year's draft comes around will probably depend a lot on how much he will grow into his body along the next 12 months.

Quotable: "Because he's so behind in his physical development I think few realize how talented he is, he has more to offer than what he's shown so far at the international level." - HP Scout Mik Portoni

Quotable: "Wrote some positive notes on him in Grand Forks. He showed that has a good motor." - HP Scout Mark Edwards

Phillips, Markus
LD - Owen Sound Attack (OHL) 5'11", 203

Phillips was selected first round, ninth overall at the 2015 OHL Priority Selection Draft by the Owen Sound Attack out of the Toronto Titans Minor Midget program. Phillips immediately jumped into a promenant role with the Attack getting power play action right from the start of the season and often playing top four ice.

Phillips is an excellent skating defenseman who has a great frame and can protect the puck well at speed. He is an offensive minded defender who likes to get involved on the rush and create scoring chances. He moves the puck well on the power play and has a good shot from the point. Phillips has decent defensive zone ability, but will need to improve. He will also need to hopefully grow in order to maximize his potential at the 2017 NHL Entry Draft.

Quotable: "I really liked him in his OHL Draft year. I didn't see Owen Sound a ton this past year but Markus looked heavier and a bit slower. Regardless, he's very talented and is a player to watch next season." - HP Scout Mark Edwards

Plouffe, Dylan
LD – Vancouver Giants (WHL) 6'00", 189

Plouffe is a defenseman who was a standout at the Canada Winter Games for Team Alberta, but has struggled a bit on a Vancouver Giants club that has floundered as a whole over the last two seasons. Plouffe was a leading scorer in the AMBHL at the bantam level, but has rebranded himself as more of a defensive defenseman in the WHL. Plouffe's first passes are quite good and we expect his offensive game to develop with increased time on the man advantage. His shot is also very good, and powerful, but we would like to see him use that weapon more often.

He's a decent skater who manages his gaps well in reverse if he's already set up in good position. However, Plouffe requires those extra steps as he could be quicker in terms of his transition speed, his turns, and his pivots which makes it challenging for him to adjust to play. He was caught flat-footed too many times this season, resulting in far too many partial breakaways and goals against. He'll have to improve in terms of his overall mobility if he wants to jump into a consistent top four position in the lineup.

Poehling, Ryan
C – Lakeville North (MN-HS) 6'01", 185

Poehling had an excellent season for Lakeville North last year and was one of the top players in all of Minnesota Prep Hockey. He put up impressive numbers, 20 Goals, 54 PTS in 25 games. Ryan has the skill and playmaking ability of today's smaller skilled forwards but is a solid 185 LBS and sits at 6'1" and uses his size well. Poehling can beat you in a number of different ways, he has the skill to beat you 1 v1 but possesses great vision and playmaking ability to wait for numbers and spread out the ice. He still needs to develop more of a nose for the net and willingness to take the puck to the paint but he does show flashes of that at times. Ryan is an excellent skater with elite explosiveness that gets him to top speed quickly. He needs to continue to work on his 200 foot game where he can get caught watching the play instead of impacting it.

Poehling finished the season with the Lincoln Stars (USHL) where he didn't look at all out of place. While we believe 1 season in the USHL would certainly help Ryan get stronger and more prepared for playing against men in the NCAA, all indications are Ryan has escalated his schooling enough to where he will join his 2 brothers as Freshman at St. Cloud State in the fall.

Popugaev, Nikita A.
LW – Moose Jaw Warriors (WHL) 6'04", 204

Nikita Popugaev is a Russian import who made an immediate impression with the Moose Jaw Warriors. Popugaev is a big kid with a frame that's already up to 6'4 and 204 pounds. What's impressive is that he's still a good skater and in fact won MHL's fastest skater competition before coming to North America. Popugaev boasts an interesting combination of size and skill. He handles the puck well at top speed and it's challenging to stop him as he can go around you or through you. He has an above-average shot though his wristshot doesn't quite generate the power you would expect from his frame and that might improve in future. He does have good scoring instincts, though. Popugaev also has a soft pair of hands and shows the vision and to be a playmaker, he understands and can play with other skilled players and anticipates their intentions well. His offensive zone reads and the sense for making plays are well above-average for a player his size.

Popugaev came fast out of the gate impressing with 13 points in 8 games but has gradually cooled as the year progressed. There are still instances of him getting used to the North American game. While he looks like a tank on ice when he has speed, he can be easier to neuter in physical battles than he should be and can sometimes retreat into playing a skill-only game. He is still figuring out his identity as he isn't a consistent physical presence and depending on the game he can range from looking like a skilled power forward that can't be stopped to an uninspired forward with a big frame. His decision-making is not consistent and he doesn't always have a feel for when he should be aggressive or ease back. Through the neutral zone he can be prone to hanging on to the puck even when he will clearly lose it instead of opting for a dump and chase or making a simple pass. He has good upside as a forechecker as he can quickly close the gap with that big body of his, but right now he can be too focused on the puck instead of worrying about closing off passing lanes. This is also apparent in the defensive zone where he doesn't take full advantage of his reach and isn't closing off lanes consistently.

Popugaev will be one of the more prominent prospects to follow coming out of the WHL next season. He started off hot this year before cooling down. If he manages to have a consistent season and establishes a clear identity for himself, he has all the tools and skill to be selected high in the 2017 NHL Entry Draft.

Rasmussen, Michael
LC – Spokane Chiefs (WHL) 6'05", 200

Rasmussen is a big-bodied playmaking center who made a name for himself this year with the Spokane Chiefs and at the World Under-17 Hockey Championships. Rasmussen is a very good skater for his size, who uses his big frame to make plays in traffic. He's a lot more skilled than you would expect on first sight and has shown a surprisingly high offensive hockey IQ. He's been a big kid for a while now and physically dominated the competition while playing with the Okanagan Hockey Academy.

Rasmussen is beginning to show that type of physical domination at the major pro level, as he's very good along the boards and when fighting for pucks in open space. A natural centre, Rasmussen is already good in the faceoff circle where he uses size and leverage to his advantage. He can really punish guys in the corner with his hitting, but doesn't necessarily finish his checks consistently as much as he could. He's also not afraid to dust things up either, as he already has a few fights to his credit. Rasmussen is more than willing to use his body and does well in one on one battles but will still need to develop the ability to use his reach to keep the puck away from opponents on a consistent level. With his frame-size he should be able to keep the opponents to the outside and away from the puck more often than he does and learn to lean in against them while maintaining motion, instead of getting involved in a 50-50 battle.

All in all, there's a lot to like about Michael Rasmussen and very few glaring weaknesses. He's a good skater, can bring the puck up ice, gritty in the corners, and possesses surprisingly soft hands. His compete level is very high. He makes quality offensive zone reads with and without the puck which allows him to utilize his physical tools to produce offense. However, we saw him come into some games with a lot of hustle and then saw his energy decrease as he became gassed, so conserving his energy and playing with better pace are potential areas of improvement.

Ratcliffe, Isaac
LW - Guelph Storm (OHL) 6'04", 192

Although he missed about 20 games with an injury this season, Ratcliffe made his presence felt in the second half of the season. He was the first round selection of the Guelph Storm at the 2015 OHL Priority Selection Draft.

For a forward of his size, Ratcliffe is a deceptively strong skater. He can use his speed and size with the puck to take it to the net and has very good playmaking ability for a big power forward. By the end of the season he played secondary minutes 5 on 5 and on the power play. He is extremely difficult to move out front and when he takes up positioning he has the size, but also the hand/eye coordination to be a threat to deflect pucks in the slot. Unlike a lot of big wingers, Ratcliffe doesn't try to force a lot of shots, and likes to utilize his playmaking ability to make his linemates better. He doesn't play a very aggressive game, but he can handle a lot of punishment.

The sky is the limit for Ratcliffe. He has a lot of upside and potential going into next season on a Guelph team that should be much improved from this season. We would like to see him use his size a little more.

Quotable: "A player I was really high on in AAA and one we had ranked much higher than where Guelph selected him. He was great after he got his feet wet in the OHL." - HP Scout Mark Edwards

Reedy, Scott
RC/W – USNTDP U17 6'01", 187

Reedy is a center that can also line up on wing and has impressed with his hockey sense, size, shot, and playmaking ability. Reedy possesses a quality release and is a threat with his shot at all times as he can beat goalies clean. He doesn't have the most pop in his skating but gets around well. Considering his stride isn't deficient, he should be able to generate a bit more explosiveness as he gets older. Reedy uses his frame well to protect the puck along the wall and can keep possession in the offensive zone. He is adept at holding the puck away from checkers and distributing the puck under pressure. Although his shot is clearly a big threat, Reedy also has the ability to find open linemates and set them up. He's good at bringing the puck around the offensive zone and dishing a pass into the middle where he feeds an open teammate, he shows good patience with the puck on his stick and selects the right options without forcing passes that aren't there. Good reads off the rush. All in all, Reedy has been one of the more prominent prospects on the USNTDP U17 squad and has all the makings of a very solid NHL prospect as he heads into his NHL draft-year. He is committed to University of Minnesota for 2017/2018.

Quotable: "One of the players who caught my eye often when I saw the U17's this season." - HP Scout Mark Edwards

Reifenberger, Marko
C – Hill Murray (MN-HS) 6'01", 185

Marko is a big Powerful 2-way Center who has an excellent first few strides and doesn't take long for him to get a head of steam coming through the neutral zone. Plays a solid puck possession game as he protects the puck well and has a solid base. Marko averaged over a PPG with Hill Murray the last season and saw a couple of games with Bloomington (USHL) where he was the 8th overall pick in last year's USHL draft. We will be following Reifenberger's game close next season as he will likely be playing his Draft Year in the USHL with Bloomington.

Roberts, Elijah
LD - Kitchener Rangers (OHL) 5'08", 158

Roberts was selected in the second round of the 2015 OHL Priority Selection Draft by the Kitchener Rangers out of the Toronto Marlboros Minor Midget program. Roberts was able to find a spot on the Rangers' third pairing despite a veteran blueline to open the season for the Rangers.

Roberts is an offensive defenseman who possesses high end skating speed from the back end. He is capable of rushing the puck end to end and gives the Rangers a lot of speed off the rush gaining chances on offensive zone entries. Roberts has a good first pass when he doesn't have a lane to skate with and made quick decisions up ice. On the power play he did a good job moving the puck but would sometimes try to force his shot through from the point. Defensively Roberts is still a work in progress. He does a good job of getting into passing lanes and taking away an opponents stick, but he is too passive in one on one match-up's allowing forwards to back him up too far. He also gets dominated down low due to a lack of size and strength to handle bigger older forwards deep in the offensive zone. Roberts has intriguing offensive upside from the back end but greatly lacks size and will need to get stronger. His defensive game has seen some improvements but he will need to continue to get better in this area to maximize his potential.

Robertson, Jason
LW - Kingston Frontenacs (OHL) 6'02", 196

Robertson was selected in the fourth round of the 2015 OHL Priority Selection Draft by the Kingston Frontenacs out of the Don Mills Flyers Minor Midget program. He came into the season without being a lock to make the team as a 16 year old. However he impressed in camp and earned a spot on the roster. He quickly gained good ice time as he was put in the top six more often than not in the first half of the season. His ice reduced as the Frontenacs acquired some top end veterans for the run towards the playoffs, but Robertson adapted and remained a contributing player.

Jason is a big bodied, shoot first winger that displays impressive hockey sense and a strong compete level. Robertson's most noteworthy attribute offensively is his shot. Both heavy and accurate, Robertson displays a quick release with the ability to get his shot off in traffic. His ability to find soft spots in defensive zone coverage's allows Robertson to be lethal in the high percentage scoring areas. While Robertson is a shoot first forward he does display deceptively good puck skills, taking care of the puck and limiting his turnovers despite limited playmaking abilities. A player who protects the puck well, working the half boards and cycle with success, Robertson can be tough to contain off the rush as he drops his shoulder and drives the net with authority, shielding the puck before getting off a quick shot. However Robertson has below average skating with does affect his ability to exploit defenders as frequent as he could. A player with heavy feet and questionable mobility, Robertson often takes four or five strides before reaching ideal speed, which allows opponents to close gaps on him quickly. Robertson found a way to overcome his bad skating with good hockey sense, smart positional play and a great shot. He is without a doubt a prospect for the 2017 NHL Entry Draft, but improving that skating, even getting it to a point where it would be considered average would be huge for Robertson's development.

Rondbjerg, Jonas
RW/LW – Rungsted Seier Capital (DEN) – 6'00", 176

Rondbjerg is a player that has already put up an impressive 16 points in 39 games for his team in the top Danish division. He has appeared for Denmark both at the U18 as well as U20 level. In fact, he didn't look out of place at the World Junior Championships at all. Rondbjerg's reads and hockey IQ in all three zones are already at a quite high level. He gets around the ice well and exhibits smart positioning. His skating is above-average. Defensively, he doesn't have the physicality to compete but shows good ability to follow the play and maintain his coverage. While his smarts and skill appear to be decent, Rondbjerg will need to get stronger. He often has good ideas in the offensive zone but lacks the strength to execute them. Too often, he will get closed off by defensemen or rubbed out of the play under physicality. We will look for him to make some improvements there next season. In 2016-2017 he is projected to play for Vaxjo Lakers at the J20 level in the Swedish league.

Rule, Caleb
C/W – Shattuck St. Mary's Prep (MN-HS) 5'10", 165

Rule was a solid point producer for Shattuck St. Mary's U16 team this past season. Recently drafted by the Waterloo Black Hawks in the phase 2 USHL draft. Excellent skater who goes to the net and has a knack for scoring goals in the paint.

Ruzicka, Adam
LC/W – HC Pardubice U20 (CZE) – 6'04", 209

A pro-sized forward, Ruzicka has several quality physical tools to his disposal. He has the size, the power and the skating to be a factor on each shift. Those aspects are backed up by his skill with the puck as he is a good stickhandler. Ruzicka's ability to protect the puck, change angles of attack and skate through and around defenders is very good. He protects the puck well in open ice but less so on the wall where he could still do a better job with that big frame of his. Ruzicka has good hockey IQ and sees the ice well, although he could pass the puck a bit more often than he does. He is a dangerous shooter as he can walk into the slot and let it go quickly off his blade. Overall, Ruzicka is certainly a prospect to follow. He hasn't yet exhibited the high-end impact that he is capable of on a consistent level but his upside is very good. We expect him to become a more consistent shift-by-shift threat next year.

Salo, Robin
RD – Sport U20 (FIN) – 6'00", 181

Salo is a two-way defenseman that has several tools to his disposal. Defensively he has good positioning and compete, but lacks a bit in the footspeed department. He is a smart puck-mover and distributes the puck well. His hands are average, not a weakness but he's not someone who would impress with how he controls the puck. Despite the fact that neither his hands or feet are particularly impressive he still does a good job moving around with the puck and making plays, although at higher levels it would seem he will need to make those plays at a faster pace. The good thing is, he is dependable under pressure and still looks solid when facing a strong forecheck.

His best asset offensively is a big slapshot from the point, which is dangerous at even strength and powerplay. Salo has good potential and a combination of alluring tools, but will need to refine certain parts of his game for his game to work at higher levels of hockey. His skating and pace are the two main components that will need to improve going forward.

Samorukov, Dmitri
RD – CSKA Moskva U17 (RUS) – 6'00", 159

Samorukov is a strong defensive prospect heading into 2017. He was one of the players that tracked well the entire year and then managed to finish the year on an even higher note with an impressive U18 World Championship performance.

Samorukov is a very solid defensive zone defenseman. He has excellent reads and is always in the right position. Furthermore, he has a good compete level and already plays a mature type of defense where he can play a fairly controlled yet physical game. He competes on the wall and we have also seen him throw some open-ice hits despite his pretty lean frame. He has the ability to force the players trying to gain the zone into an uncomfortable position and rub them out of the play. When he gets the puck, he makes smart outlets and can also skate with the puck. His decision-making with the puck is already quite good as he doesn't try to be too fancy yet has the poise to delay and find a better option if needed.

Offensively, Samorukov has a good shot from the point and finds ways to get it through. When getting involved further up ice or pinching, he makes sure he's not exposing the back-side of the ice. Here too, he displays good hockey IQ and a mature approach to the position. Samorukov will be one of the defensemen to keep an eye on for the 2017 NHL draft.

Quotable: "Smart, good in his own end and can play physical. Big shot and good offensive ability. No real apparent weaknesses. Decision-making is far more mature than his age would suggest." - HP Scout Nik Funa

Sandhu, Jordan
C - Alberni Valley Bulldogs (BCHL) 5'06", 137

Sandhu is an underrated and undersized forward who plays for Alberni Valley Bulldogs in the BCHL. Sandhu is an aggressive but sneaky forward who finds ways to manufacture plays out of very little. He's not the world's most natural skater in terms of flat-out acceleration speed, but can jump on pucks and can dance through tight spaces with some good footwork.

His stickhandling is strong, as well, allowing him to dizzy opposing defenders with left-to-right dekes and head-fakes. He loves making the highlight reel. When he tries to do much, however, he can be a liability who costs his team.

He's a natural centre who makes good passes off the rush. He can be a bit of a perimeter player at times, which is justifiable given his size and how young he is. Not one to initiate contact, he doesn't run away from it either. His work in the defensive end could use some improvement. He doesn't always make the right decision with the puck, looking like too much of a gambler at times, but we like his creativity. Jordan is the younger brother of WHL journeyman Tyler Sandhu.

Semchuk, Brendan
RW – Vancouver Giants (WHL) 6'00", 167

A former first round pick in the WHL Bantam Draft, a bit more has been expected of him, as he struggled to stay in the Vancouver Giants line-up full time.

Semchuk is a darting winger who likes to drive wide on defenders with the puck and has good stickhandling ability at top speed. He can look a bit one-dimensional at times as he struggles to find secondary options but we like his raw skating speed. He's got a good wristshot which he can fire off while skating at top speed. He was a good playmaker at the bantam level. In the WHL, meanwhile, he needs to round out his game and make better use of his teammates. Semchuk has a good compete level and brings a honest effort to the ice. He uses his skating to get on pucks and will sacrifice himself to make plays on the wall but lacks the vision to make more elaborate offensive plays. His work ethic, and skating allow him to create some opportunities for himself but in our viewings he often lacked the touch to take advantage of them either as a scorer or a playmaker.

Shaw, Mason
LC – Medicine Hat Tigers (WHL) 5'09", 176

Shaw is an undersized center prospect who is a November 1998 born. Shaw had a productive season for Medicine Hat, falling just shy of point per game pace. He has also appeared internationally for Canada at the U18s where he played well and put up 7 points in 7 games.

Shaw was one of Medicine Hat's better offensive weapons, he displays good skill with the puck, excellent offensive instincts and plays bigger than his size would suggest without necessarily involving himself into more physical contact than is needed. Shaw's size prevents him from being a big presence on the ice or dominating the play on a consistent level, but his instincts are high-end and he has shown as much playing with equally skilled players at the U18s in North Dakota. Shaw has good vision and instantly recognizes opportunities where he can sting the opposition either with his shot or by making a high-end pass. He is a smart forechecker that can cause turnovers and will compete all over the ice. His reaction time to what is happening around the ice is very good and he has the quick hands and the vision to make dangerous quick-strike attacks in the offensive zone. Shaw has some feistiness to him and won't shy away, we have even seen him get into a fight. Not surprisingly he will have to answer the size question in his draft year, but he is projecting as a solid offensive talent coming out of WHL for next year.

Shore, Baker
RW – Colorado Thunderbirds U16 (T1EHL) 5'11", 170

Shore was a member for the USA U17 Select Team that won gold last fall. The youngest of the 4 Shore brothers, Baker brings a solid all around game with excellent skating fundamentals. He competes all over the ice, he showed the ability to take over games, as he did at the T1EHL National Tournament in San Jose where he lead the charge to bringing his team back from a 3-0 3rd period deficit to defeat and loaded Team Wisconsin U16 team. Baker's all around hockey IQ is impressive and makes a lot of little plays that all add up during the course of the game where even if he is left off the score sheet, he has had a positive effect on the game when it's all said and done. Baker saw some time with Chicago (USHL) at the end of last year and likely will spend next season.

Sillinger, Owen
LC – Penticton Vees (BCHL) 5'10", 170

If all goes according to plan, Owen Sillinger can continue the trend of BCHL players climbing into the top rounds of the NHL Draft. Sillinger arrives with really good hockey bloodlines, as his father Mike was a long-time pro and NHL journeyman. Fairly undersized, Owen is a really fearless and agile skater who gets around defenders with surprising ease.

Sillinger has a nose for the net and the skill to get there. Most of his goals came from within two feet of the blue paint. Away from the mouth of the goal, he competes very hard in getting on pucks and isn't afraid to bowl guys over in his pursuits. In fact, we saw Sillinger throw some of the biggest hits in the BCHL this season. Owen is a skilled and slippery player on the offensive end and a competitive defensive zone player. He's extremely dependable on the backcheck, usually being the first forward back in the transition. He also sacrifices and blocks shots on the penalty kill. We like his compete level and determination.

Sirota, Jakub
LD - HC Zlin U20 (CZE) 6'02", 179

Sirota is a December '98 birth with a pro looking frame. He moves his large frame smoothly and effortlessly around the ice. Lots of puck confidence and moves with his head up finding pockets to skate through and likes to jump in the rush. On most occasions, he can escape with the puck under pressure, get three quick steps and find his passing target accurately. Sometimes he tries to escape when it would be easier to chip the puck - needs to work on making more consistent decisions with the puck. Because of his strong skating, he can gap up well and pivots efficiently. Sirota was selected by Des Moines Buccaneers in this year's USHL Phase 2 Draft.

Skinner, Stuart
G – Lethbridge Hurricanes (WHL) 6'04", 197

Skinner is a highly regarded second-year starting goaltender for the Lethbridge Hurricanes. Skinner is a big goalie who has ideal dimensions for the modern pro game. Standing at 6-foot-4, and still possibly growing, he's able to utilize his size by cutting off angles and covering most of the net from either the standing or butterfly position.

Skinner plays a hybrid game for the most part and is neither overly conservative or aggressive in terms of his position. He shows strong upside with his pure athletic ability and also boasts quick reflexes that allow him to make high-end saves. His ability to move around the crease crisply at his size is very good. His rebound control is a bit of an issue, as he lets out too many second-chance opportunities but he is good at recovering and making the second save. He can frustrate the other team by making a high-end sprawling saves in chaotic traffic-dense conditions. Those tend to really deflate the other team's momentum.

He's getting better at steering shots wide and into less dangerous areas, but will need some work there as he moves forward. Skinner lacks a bit of polish but has all the tools to give himself a chance to be selected in the first round of the 2017 NHL Draft, which is quite a feat to achieve for a goaltender. He checks off all the boxes of a modern goaltender, as his size, agility, reflexes, and athleticism all project as above-average or better.

Smart, Jonathan
LD – Kelowna Rockets (WHL) 6'00", 172

It took Smart about a little past the halfway point of the season to really establish himself in the WHL. A bout of mono held him out during the early part of the season, but once he was back in playing regularly we noticed that he developed some confidence as he got back into the thick of things. A good skater with good mechanics his speed isn't top end yet but should get better as he continues to grow, his mobility in all directions is reasonably good though. Makes a great outlet pass from his own end and often contributes to efficient zone exits or starts a breakout. He isn't a flashy player with the puck but consistently executes safe, quality decisions that help his team move forward up the ice.

At times he can get over matched below the goal line, so he needs to get stronger. Shows good offensive instincts working the puck around the offensive zone with accurate passing. Although his shot needs to improve for him to be a bigger offensive threat. The accuracy is good, but needs to be heavier and get more power out of it. Smart should log heavier minutes on the Kelowna blueline next year.

Sparkes, Sullivan
LW - Oshawa Generals (OHL) 5'11", 180

Sparkes was selected in the 5th round of the 2015 OHL Priority Selection Draft by the Oshawa Generals out of the Waterloo Wolves Minor Midget program. Sparkes played a depth role for the rebuilding Generals getting good experience in the OHL without having a lot of pressure on him as a 16 year old. Sparkes is an aggressive two-way centre with an excellent compete level. He has quick feet and a bit of a deceptive first step, however his stride is short and somewhat choppy limiting his straight line speed, which is average at best. Given his stature and skating ability Sparkes was unable to create separation from the opponent off the rush which ultimately limited what he was able to do offensively. However Sullivan did do a very good job on the cycle and along the half boards as he possesses good strength for a sub six foot 16 year old, shielding the puck with effectiveness before making quality decisions with the puck. Sparkes has an ability to find soft spots in defensive zone coverage's, along with a quick strike ability in tight. He is not deterred by the gritty areas of the ice despite his size, Sparkes is aggressive on the fore check and tenacious in puck pursuit, even engage physically on a consistent bases. In his own zone Sparkes shows impressive understanding of positional play, keeps his feet moving and shows good overall awareness. Sullivan doesn't have huge offensive upside at the NHL level but a productive season in the OHL while playing a gritty two-way game should help him moving towards the 2017 NHL Entry Draft, he will need to improve his skating.

St. Cyr, Dylan
G – USNTDP U17 5'07", 163

St. Cyr is an undersized goaltender with good athletic ability. Despite the lack of size, he battles well through traffic. However, when he gets in too deep in the crease he gets beat. He has good lateral movement with quick-reflexes. St. Cyr is also a good puck-handler, he is good at making basic plays with the puck but can even hit some of the stretch-passes he attempts. St. Cyr lacks the size of a modern goalie but plays a likable game with plenty of compete. He is committed to University of Michigan for 2018-2019 where he will hope to hit a growth spurt. Dylan is the son of Manon Rheaume.

Stevens, Liam
LW - Guelph Storm (OHL) 5'08", 187

Stevens was selected in the second round of the 2015 OHL Priority Selection Draft by the Guelph Storm out of the Hamilton Jr. Bulldogs Minor Midget program.

Liam is an undersized but hard working winger for the Guelph Storm. He is a speedy, energetic forward who provided an excellent work ethic for the Storm this season. He started out in a very limited role, but by the new year he was seeing some ice in the top six and was able to chip in with a little offense. He is tough to play against in all three zones but has some offensive upside that could intrigue teams heading into the 2017 NHL Entry Draft. However he will need to add some size and some more strength in order to make some noise for next year's NHL Draft, as he certainly has the heart, drive and skill to succeed.

Strome, Matthew
LW - Hamilton Bulldogs (OHL) 6'03", 187

Strome was selected first round, eighth overall at the 2015 OHL Priority Selection Draft by the Hamilton Bulldogs out of the Toronto Marlboros Minor Midget program.

Strome took a little time to adjust this season but spent plenty of time on the first line and top power play unit playing with veteran players which gave him a ton of opportunities this season. Matthew does a good job playing a positionally sound game in all three zones. He goes to the net and knows how to get into scoring positions where linemates can find him for chances. He has decent playmaking ability and is willing to engage in battles down low. While he's a bit of a shoot first player, he wasn't forcing his shot in bad situations and was willing to pass off. He does a good job in the neutral zone forcing turnovers, but needs to be a little more consistent on the backcheck as he had some moments where he took his time which played a part in some goals against. Strome has great size and intriguing upside. He doesn't have highlight reel skill but he does a lot of things right and if he continues to get a ton of ice, his numbers should continue to improve leading towards the 2017 NHL Entry Draft.

Quotable:" It took quite a while to get adjusted to the OHL but he had a good finish. Smart player who gets a lot out of his tools." - HP Scout Mark Edwards

Studenic, Marian
RW – HK 36 Skalica (SVK) – 6'00", 163

Studenic is a scoring winger that has already put up 16 points in 36 games playing against men in Slovakia's top league. Studenic has been part of Slovakia's u18 team this season and has performed well there. Studenic isn't a huge kid but he skates really well and has a smooth stride. He has the ability to protect the puck well as he moves up the ice. Although he is capable of making plays, he has the instincts of a scorer as he looks for ways to create a scoring chance for himself. He is good at recognizing offensive opportunities and often reacts quicker than the man covering him does. Studenic has also shown a willingness to be involved in his own end and defensively. Although not an exceptional defensive player, he makes smart reads and can break up plays on the occasion. He also has good vision through transition and can move the puck up the ice out of his own end and through the neutral zone.

Studnicka, Jack
C - Oshawa Generals (OHL) 6'00", 163

Studnicka was selected in the first round, 21st overall at the 2015 OHL Priority Selection Draft by the Oshawa Generals out of the Detroit Belle Tire U16 program. Studnicka provided good skill and creativity to the Generals line-up and produced very well for a rookie forward.

Studnicka is an intelligent and highly skilled, offensive minded centre with a high-end compete level. Jack struggled at times early on with Oshawa as he adapted to the OHL style of game, but he came on strong throughout the second half of the OHL season. A strong skater with an explosive first step, Studnicka possesses good straight-line speed, strong edges and an ability to change direction without losing pace. He also possesses strong puck skills and has the ability to be shifty and elusive in possession, as he creates both time and space with his speed and puck skills. While Studnicka certainly isn't shy of the high traffic areas, his lack of strength was an issue but is not uncommon for players in their rookie season. Studnicka was easily knocked off pucks and despite engaging and being game in puck battles, he rarely came away with possession. With that being said, Studnicka is a gifted offensive player who thrives when he has the puck. He shows an impressive level of offensive creativity and Studnicka possesses intriguing vision and playmaking skills along with a deceptively good shot. Studnicka effectively find's soft spots in defensive zone coverage's and can be tough to contain both in tight and off the rush. As he adds strength and gets more confident Studnicka should begin to break out offensively.

Suzuki, Nick
RC - Owen Sound Attack (OHL) 5'10", 183

Suzuki was selected first round, 14th overall at the 2015 OHL Priority Selection Draft by the Owen Sound Attack out of the London Jr. Knights Minor Midget program. Suzuki got a great deal of ice in his rookie season and immediately saw action of the power play. This resulted in plenty of offensive opportunities for Suzuki who reached the 20 goal mark in his first season.

Suzuki is a speedy forward with good acceleration and mobility. He likes to have the puck on his stick and will challenge defenders regularly. He does a good job putting himself into position to jump on rebounds despite lacking the size to compete with big defenders. This was very noticeable down low in puck battles where it will be important for him to add muscle. Nick likes to get involved offensively when but the opposition has the puck he will need to improve on his compete level and backcheck in these particular situations. Improving defensively while continuing to improve offensively will help Suzuki going into the 2017 NHL Entry Draft.

Tarasov, Danil
G – Tolpar Ufa (MHL) – 6'03", 154

Tarasov has played his season mostly in the Russian U17 league where he put up very solid numbers. What's impressive about Tarasov is that he got a shot at playing some limited action in both MHL and for Russia's national team at the U18s and continued his strong performance. Tarasov hasn't skipped a beat in MHL action, but more importantly we really liked what he did against U18 competition in North Dakota. Tarasov put up some very solid performances and flashed his combination of athleticism, size, and solid fundamentals, often looking better than some of the older goalies he was going up against. He has firmly placed himself on the map as a goalie to watch for the 2017 NHL draft.

Teasdale, Joel
LW/C – Blainville-Boisbriand Armada (QMJHL) – 5'11", 197

Teasdale was the 12th overall selection in the 2015 QMJHL Draft out of the Antoine-Girouard midget program in Saint-Hyacinthe. He took part in the U-17 Hockey Challenge in November and did well, playing along Comtois and Morand like he did last year at the Canada Winter Games. He had a very impressive season with the Armada, winning the coaching staff's trust and playing in all kinds of situations for them this season. He played on both the PP and the PK. On the power play, at times he was used on the half wall, in front of the net or on the point. He's a smart player and was physically ready for the QMJHL this season. He's strong on his skates and did a great job along the boards and in front of the net all year long. He's not afraid to get his nose dirty in front of the net and scored many goals this year in front of the net or in the slot. He played both at centre and on the wing this year, showing good versatility, but this season he looked more comfortable on the wing. His skating is fine, though he's not a speedster and will need to add some explosiveness to his strides in the next couple of years. Still, it's not a weakness in his game. He competes hard all the time and showed a great level of commitment to his play away from the puck. He still has some work to do with his positional game in the defensive zone, but the effort is always there. Teasdale does a lot of things well on the ice and is already a favourite of Armada head coach Joel Bouchard. We will be curious to see how he handles next season, with more pressure on him to produce and as a go-to guy for the Armada.

Quotable: "One of the most impressive 99-born players in the league this season, he was very impressive playing on an offensively challenged team this season. Didn't look like a 16 years old on most night, very mature physically and helped his team different at both end of the ice" – HP scout Jérôme Bérubé

Teravainen, Eero
LD – Jokerit U18 (FIN) – 5'10", 159

Eero is a defenseman who displays good touch and finesse with the puck and makes a strong first pass. He is Teuvo's, the Chicago Blackhawks forward's brother and shows some of the same vision and craftiness with the puck. Teravainen's best asset is easily his outlet passing. Teravainen has great touch on his passes and finds ways to hit his teammates even through mazes of sticks and bodies and while under pressure. His passing is crisp, easy to handle and on-tape. He can hit forwards in motion with a pass into space or make a 10 foot on-tape pass to a linemate in vicinity to alleviate forechecking pressure.

Teravainen plays a heads-up game and never panics with the puck. In the offensive zone he does a good job distributing the puck, but at times passes up shots which is a weakness in his offensive game. Defensively, he has solid positioning but lacks strength. He reads and maintains his position against forwards but lacks the physical power to be effective if it evolves into a one on one battle.

Thilander, Adam
RD – Skelleftea J20 (SWE) – 6'00", 190

Thilander is a defensive prospect that uses his skills to try to be a steady presence in the defensive side of the rink. He isn't the tallest defenseman and doesn't have a big wingspan, but has good defensive instincts. He tracks the play well, when he doesn't have the puck he knows where the opposition is positioned and does a very good job at keeping proper inside body position against forwards. He isn't big or strong enough for that element to become a difference maker at the next level, but it is a good founding piece of his game. Thilander also has strong balance on his skates and moves well laterally going backwards. Straight forward he is however a bit slow and when he has to react to get first on pucks his mobility seems below average. He skates fine with the puck and has a good handle on it. When he has the time to set up the play from the back-end his first pass is usually accurate and he prefers quality simple decisions. On the contrary, when under pressure he loses his poise as soon as he doesn't have an easy way out to his defensive partner and incurs in way too many turnovers. On the other side of the rink it is unlikely that he will take chances unless he truly senses a good opportunity. In the offensive zone he can get shots on net with his wrister and always had good power on his slapshot.

Next year will be very important for Thilander to define himself as a player. He has a legit toolset, but as someone who doesn't bring dynamic qualities to the table he will really need to become more reliable in his own end in games where the intensity picks up. This season he was unable to keep up with the pace of the game and remain effective under those circumstances.

Thomas, Robert
RC - London Knights (OHL) 5'11", 177

Thomas was selected in the second round of the 2015 OHL Priority Selection Draft by the London Knights out of the York-Simcoe Express Minor Midget program. Thomas played a minimal role for the Knights for the majority of this season either skating on the fourth line or sitting in the stands. However Max Jones' suspension in the playoff opened the door for Thomas to play on the second line, where he performed quite well in Jones' absence.

Thomas is a speedy winger who likes to have the puck on his stick through the neutral zone and entering the offensive zone. He has a very pass first mentality and likes to set up his linemates. He makes quick decisions with the puck and can create scoring chances for his linemates, but also possesses a quick release that can surprise goaltenders at times, especially as he becomes known for his passing. Thomas has great acceleration and top speed. He needs to add more muscle to his frame and while he will compete in corners and backcheck it's something he will need to work on leading into next season. Thomas has the speed and the playmaking ability to help play an impact on the Knights next season as he looks to enter his 2017 NHL Draft year.

Tippett, Owen
RW - Mississuaga Steelheads (OHL) 6'01", 181

Tippett was selected in the first round, fourth overall at the 2015 OHL Priority Selection Draft by the Mississauga Steelheads out of the Toronto Red Wings Minor Midget program.

Tippett was our top ranked player in the 2015 OHL Draft and is an explosive goal scoring winger with high end potential. Tippett has an explosive first step and good straight line speed, he plays with excellent pace and possesses game breaking abilities. Tippett is difficult to contain when he has possession of the puck, as he boasts both strong change of pace and direction abilities, while also possessing elite puck control skills and the ability to beat a defender on speed alone. Tippett has a shoot first mentality and does an excellent job of getting his shot off both in stride and in traffic. Tippett's shot is both hard and accurate and comes off his stick with a lightning quick release. While Tippett is undoubtedly a shoot first winger, he does possess impressive vision and good playmaking abilities, making him a versatile threat in the offensive zone. He boasts strong hockey sense and impressive positional awareness away from the puck, Tippett shows an uncanny ability to find soft spots in defensive zone coverage's. He shows little hesitation getting to the high traffic areas of the ice, taking direct routes to pucks and engaging in puck battles, while also showing a tenaciousness on the forecheck and a willingness to engage physically. His physical game increased later on in the season and he became even tougher to play against. Tippett will need to work on getting even stronger and work on distributing the puck a little more as he is a good playmaker but can become predictable at times. He will also need to improve his attention to detail at times in his won zone. He sometimes get caught puckwatching and loses his man in coverage. He has a lot of upside for the 2017 NHL Entry Draft as potentially one of the best scoring forwards available in the draft.

Quotable:" My fave player and our number one ranked prospect for the 2015 OHL Draft. Tippett struggled to get consistent icetime in Mississauga but was able to show his stuff with a great performance at the U17 and then earned an invite to Grand Forks where he played 4th line minutes but gained experience heading into the Hlinka." - HP Scout Mark Edwards

Tolvanen, Eeli
LW/RW – Sioux City Musketeers (USHL) 5'10", 172

Tolvanen is a player whose game revolves mostly around his shot and scoring instincts. He was part of the Blues program in Finland before coming over and playing his 2015-2016 season for Sioux City Musketeers. Tolvanen had good success in the USHL, scoring 38 points in 49 games. He was even more impressive internationally as he has been a scoring machine at the U17 WHC as well as the U18s in North Dakota. In those two tournaments Tolvanen has played a combined 12 games and potted 16 goals. Tolvanen can release his shot from almost any position, immediately after receiving a pass giving goalies no time to react. His release is quick, he gets power on his shot and is accurate with it. More than that, Tolvanen has a full shooting arsenal as his wrist-shot, snapshot and slapshot are all good. He can score from a distance or from up-close. He has a good one-timer on the power-play and can be a shooting option there, although we have seen him force some shots that weren't there with the man advantage. He anticipates the play well and is very good at finding spots for his shot. Tolvanen also shows some upside without the puck as he will pressure the puck-carrier and generally reads the play at a high level enough to be in position defensively. He is an above-average skater and can handle the puck at speed. As he moves forward, we will look for Tolvanen to improve his all-around game. He is very reliant on his shooting at this point in time and we would like to see him develop more dimensions to his game.

Quotable:" This kid is a shooter and he's not afraid to show anyone how good his shot is. Very skilled player, I really like watching him play. - HP Scout Mark Edwards

Tortora, Jacob
LW – USNTDP U17 5'06", 151

Tortora is a competitive sparkplug who relies on his speed to produce. He is very dangerous when exploding with speed and catches defensemen in poor position. He can take turnovers and turn them into high-quality scoring chances out of a bat. He is a strong one on one forward and has the ability to burn defensemen both with his speed as well as dekes. Despite the small size he doesn't mind playing a physical game and will finish on his checks. Has a good shot and excellent first few steps to take off. He is a player that gives off a feel of a skilled and fast scorer that has some agitator qualities to him. While he excels off the rush and with speed, he will need to find ways to be involved on the cycle and find ways to be more involved with establishing offensive zone time. He is committed to Boston College for 2018-2019.

Trepanier, Maxim
LW/RW – Collège Charles-Lemoyne Riverains (LHMAAAQ) – 5'11", 171

Trepanier was one of the better players this year in the Quebec Midget AAA league, finishing 3rd in scoring with 63 points and as the best goal scorer, with 38 goals in 43 games. Trepanier was drafted by Rimouski in the 5th round (91st overall) after a tough QMJHL draft year where he only scored 11 points in 25 games. He was leaning toward going the NCAA route, but eventually signed with Rimouski mid-season and will make his official debut with them next season. Trepanier is a standout skater who loves to have the puck on his stick and was a man among boys in Midget AAA this season. His speed and puck control were just too good for this level. He has quick, soft hands and loves to be in one-on-one confrontations on the ice to show just how good his puck skills are. As previously mentioned, he loves to have the puck on his stick, but often kept possession for too long and could have used his linemates better. That will need to change at the major junior level. The same goes for his physical and defensive game. However, the fact remains that his puck skills and offensive upside are excellent. It remains to be seen how his complete game will follow next year.

Vaakanainen, Urho
LD – Blues (Liiga) – 6'01", 187

Vaakanainen is a toolsy defenseman who already logged 25 games against men in Finland's top league. Part of the reason for his appearance with the men's team might have been Blues' financial problems as they sold their best players to other teams. Nevertheless, Vaakanainen actually performed fairly well in his stint there.

Vaakanainen is a puck-mover with good offensive upside who also has a sturdy frame and can get engaged in a physical game. He's a good skater that gets around the ice well with the ability to bring the puck up the ice. His defensive zone footwork is good too and he can keep up with opposing forwards. Vaakanainen has a big shot from the point that he gets off quickly and it is a big threat of his. He is generally a smart player but tends to have moments where he makes some odd-decisions. His defensive coverage isn't always perfect and his puck-moving game can still be inconsistent. He sometimes waits too long to pass the puck or makes questionable decisions on his outlets. At the U17 WHC Heiskanen actually stood out as the smarter puck-mover of the two. Vaakanainen has big upside and if he manages to iron out some of those blemishes then he has all the tools at his disposal to project as an NHL defenseman.

Valimaki, Jusso
LD – Tri-City Americans (WHL) 6'02", 200

Valimaki is a big quick offensive defenseman who is difficult to shut down when he gets going at his full-flight speed. Few prospects of his physical proportions look so agile and so fast at his age. Exceptionally dangerous and especially fast going through the neutral zone he has quick hands as well as quick feet, and he makes really good passes off the rush using his peripheral vision. He can be a dangerous offensive player when he works up some speed and takes off. Can be involved off the rush but also boasts a decent shot from the point.

On the defensive side of the puck, his decision making can be a bit suspect, but he's passable on most nights. His compete level is high and he uses his big frame appropriately to win puck battles. He's got good feet and long range, so his play in reverse should improve with time. Defensively, he relies more on his size and speed and could stand to add a more controlled, structured approach to his defending, but that will likely come as he matures. Right now there's some guess-work involved with his coverage. His angles and gaps aren't completely polished out yet, but he's rarely outright burned as he has the skating and size to recover.

Valimaki already has a full resume of international experience, playing for Finland at the Ivan Hlinka tournament, the World Under-17 Hockey Championships, and numerous other events in Europe. When suiting up for his home country, he usually takes on a leadership role. More experience in North American rinks playing with Tri-City will also help his development.

Verity, Daniil
LW - North Bay Battalion (OHL) 6'00", 198

Verity was selected in the second round of the 2014 OHL Priority Selection Draft by the Windsor Spitfires out of the North York Rangers Minor Midget program. Verity made the OHL as a 16 year old playing 49 games. He started the year slow with the Spitfires posting just two points in 16 games. He was dealt to the North Bay Battalion where his offensive game picked up posting 24 points in the final 38 games of the season.

Verity got some top six minutes for the Battalion and seemed to put forward a more refreshed effort. He can be tough to play against when he wants to, but his overall effort can be very hit or miss. He has good offensive tools and will take the puck to the net to try and create offense. He has a pretty good sized frame which he uses effectively to protect the puck and take it to the net. Verity is capable of being a very effective player at the OHL level and is looking to prove he is an NHL prospect leading into the 2017 NHL Entry Draft. The late birthdate should certainly help him in his efforts as the change of scenery has helped him to this point.

Vesalainen, Kristian
LW – Frolunda HC (SHL) – 6'03", 203

Vesalainen is a big-bodied winger who plays a mature game, can be used in multiple situations including both special teams, and has already appeared in 19 games in the top Swedish league for Frolunda.

Vesalainen has very good size and relies primarily on his reach when skating with the puck, his offensive game is smart but not reliant on fancy stickhandling. Vesalainen is more than willing to use his size to his advantage, but is not a pure power forward. He doesn't force plays with his physical tools nor is he an intimidating physical presence. He will use his size to work in the corners, work for his own space and go to the front of the net, but one shouldn't expect huge amounts of aggressiveness out of him. He is also already a responsible defensive player, he doesn't cheat and reads the play well and makes sure he is helping his team in his own end before thinking of offense. When playing against his age-group, he often excels at making his linemates (who play a more junior-style game) better through his work and attention to detail.

Vesalainen is also a good PK player, where he tracks the opposition's puck-movement well and has the reach and compete to be a factor. He has shown the will to sacrifice his body to block shots and we have also seen him create some shorthanded scoring chances. Vesalainen can also be useful on the PP. One aspect that could improve is his awareness while skating the puck at top speed through open ice as he sometimes doesn't select the best decision on whether to pass the puck or continue skating with it.

Quotable:" Really mature player and already good defensively. Not flashy and in my viewings he really excelled doing some of the dirty work for Tolvanen and similar offensive players. The thing to watch for me next year is how much offense can he generate on his own." - HP Scout Nik Funa

Vilardi, Gabriel
RC - Windsor Spitfires (OHL) 6'02", 193

Vilardi was selected first round, second overall at the 2015 OHL Priority Selection Draft by the Windsor Spitfires out of the CIH Academy Minor Midget program. Vilardi joined the Spitfires and while he played a bottom six role this season, he found ways to make an impact for his team in a variety of ways.

Gabriel is a big bodied centreman who plays a solid two-way role. He has quick hands and creativity creating offense for himself and his linemates. He has a very quick release with power which make him a threat to score whenever he touches the puck in the offensive zone. He has an excellent net front presence where he displays high end hand/eye coordination deflecting pucks and reacting quickly to rebounds which accounted for several goals this season. Gabriel changes speeds well with the puck keeping the opposition guessing and gets up and down the ice decent for a 6'02" forward. This is notable as his skating in Minor Midget was below average, and we've already seen notable improvements. Vilardi does well with the puck down low, he knows how to protect it with his frame, and will cycle it effectively, occasionally when there is an opportunity he'll turn towards the net, protecting and drive with the puck. Vilardi is very defensively sound and takes care of his own end with good work ethic, smart positional play and stick placement.

Vilardi projects to be a high end prospect for the 2017 NHL Entry Draft. With the Spitfires earning a Memorial Cup berth by hosting the event in 2017, scouts will have all season long to keep an eye on Vilardi and watch his progression.

Quotable:" Played solid hockey in my viewings this year. Much like Tippett in Mississauga, Vilardi proved he was worth the high pick he was selected with." - HP Scout Mark Edwards

Voyer, Alex-Olivier
RC/RW – Rimouski Océanic (QMJHL) – 6'01", 174

Voyer was the Océanic's first round pick (15th overall) in last summer's QMJHL Draft, after playing his midget season with the Magog Cantonniers. This season he had some difficulty adapting to the speed of the game and often ended up playing on the 4th line. He also missed significant time with a knee injury and only played 38 games this season. He's versatile, as he can play both down the middle and on the wing. His skating and quickness will need to get upgraded in the next couple of years. He's a smart player at both ends of the rink; he understands how to play without the puck well and he's also good on the PK. He plays the role of a grinder well, showing some good work on the forecheck, and gets involved physically. His lack of speed and agility can hurt him in his puck pursuit on the forecheck, though. His offensive upside is a question mark. While we like his smarts and he is an underrated playmaker, his hands are just average. Going back to his midget days, he has still not proven that he can be a scorer. Next season will be huge for him, as he could answer some questions about his upside offensively and a full healthy season will also be good for him.

Walker, Samuel
C – Edina H.S. (MN-HS) 5'07", 155

Walker is a small but speedy forward who is shifty with the puck and uses his quick hands and excellent vision to create offense. Walker is an elusive skater and difficult to catch with the puck, he put up solid numbers both for Edina as well and in the Minnesota Elite League last fall. All signs are leaning toward the U. of Minnesota commit returning to Edina H.S. for his senior season next year but Lincoln (USHL) does own his rights, Walker has the offensive skills to put up points at either level next season.

Wejse, Christian
RC – Esbjerg Energy (DEN) – 6'01", 194

Wejse is a player that we liked at the U18s in North Dakota. He plays for Esbjerg in Denmark's top division and has been the captain of Denmark's U18 team. It would be fair to say that Wejse does indeed play like a captain as he exhibits high attention to detail and is a three zone player. Wejse already has a good sturdy frame and he generates decent speed with it. We like his hockey IQ in all three zones as he can be seen supporting his defensemen, making intelligent 10 foot passes as well as getting open to continue possession. He shows good ability to gain the offensive zone and then uses his body to protect the puck and extend zone time. He has shown some upside with his offensive instincts. He goes to the net and can convert on scoring chances but has also made nice passes from the perimeter into the slot. He can absorb physical contact and still make a quality pass to an open linemate. Defensively, he competes well and is a presence all over the ice. If he continues to develop well, he could look like an interesting player quite soon.

Walford, Scott
LD – Victoria Royals (WHL) 6'01", 188

A smooth skating defenseman with good size, Walford only played 36 regular season games for Victoria but has managed to establish himself on the team. He has played a full-time role in the playoffs even putting up 6 points in 13 games. Walford also appeared at the U17 WHC as part of Canada Black's team.

Walford's game is built around solid fundamentals. He has decent size but it's his mobility, defensive reads and quality if simple puck-movement that really make up the framework of his game. Walford's gaps when defending in transition are very good, he picks up forwards well and has an active stick. More importantly he has a good feel for when he can close down the gap and strip the player of the puck or simply protect the space and steer the forward into a low-percentage situation. He shows good agility and footwork and keeps up with changes of directions well, though his skating is more smooth than explosive. Walford is a smart defensive zone player but can sometimes be dragged a touch too far out of his position by following a forward back out as he checks him. Walford isn't a flashy offensive player but makes consistently correct decisions on his outlet and passes them on-tape. His offensive game is coming around as well and there might be more upside there. Walford won't be the flashiest player you've seen but he has shown a smart defensive game, good puck-movement and decent numbers for a rookie defenseman.

Welsh, Matthew
Goaltender – Charlottetown Islanders (QMJHL) – 5'10", 176

Welsh is the goalie of the future of the Islanders, with Mason McDonald moving to the pro level next season. The Islanders picked the Halifax product in the 2nd round of the QMJHL Draft (37th overall) last June. In his first season in the league, Welsh played in 26 games, which was probably a lot more than the team anticipated giving him at the beginning of the season. He also took part in the U-17 Hockey Challenge in November for Hockey Canada. Unfortunately, Welsh doesn't have the size that NHL teams are looking at these days. At 5'10", he will have to fight the odds to make it one day.

However, he's a good competitor; the best example of this was an October game in Rimouski where he made 38 saves (including 2 penalty shots), eventually losing in the 6th round of the shootout. In that game, Welsh showed a lot of composure playing on the road in a tough building and making a lot of key saves. Welsh is a good athlete, he moves well in his crease from post to post. Consistency is something he will need to get better at. When he's playing with confidence, even at 5'10", he can be an intimidating goaltender for opposing shooters. Next season, he will be the man in charge in Charlottetown. A very similar situation was Reilly Pickard in Acadie-Bathurst this season.

Williamson, Jagger
RW – Vernon Vipers (BCHL) 5'07", 150

Williamson is a BCHL prospect who we've noticed going back to the 2014 BCHL Showcase in Chilliwack when he debuted as a fifteen-year-old. Williamson is a smooth-footed head's-up skater who has provided a lot of secondary offense to the Vernon Vipers over the last two seasons. Playing a lot alongside playmaker Liam Finlay, Williamson has been able to develop his excellent shot, which has become something of a calling card for him.

Liam has a wide skating stance that makes him difficult to knock off the puck. He was more physical at the lower levels, but has been holding himself back playing against bigger and older opponents. He's able to compensate for that lack of physicality with really good imagination with the puck on his stick and tremendous vision from along the half-wall. He's also very good at finding advantageous open-space in the offensive zone, where he's got the time and space to let off his excellent shot. We expect his game to become more impactful as he adds size to his underdeveloped frame.

Yamamoto, Kailer
RW – Spokane Chiefs (WHL) 5'09", 160

Yamamoto is an undersized winger who has put himself on map for the 2017 NHL Draft with tremendous production in two seasons of WHL hockey. With his compete, hockey IQ, and skill, Yamamoto is coming along really well for next year's first round and should have a chance at hearing his name called early a year from now.

Kailer is a buzz saw player who plays a much bigger and tougher game than his height and weight listing suggests. He's not as fast as his statline might indicate, but he's incredibly agile in possession, can squeeze through tight spaces, and is incredibly difficult to contain or knock off the puck. He's an absolutely brilliant player below the goal-line who makes plays as though he has eyes in the back of his head and shows great passing instincts. He has great hockey IQ and consistently finds his way into quality scoring-chances. He has the ability to find a hole in the slot without taking physical punishment, but will not shy away from forcing his way to the net if contact is unavoidable. Additionally, Kailer is a competitive player and while he knows that as a smaller player he can't allow himself to get into stationary physical match-ups too often, he will still absolutely work his butt off when he senses an offensive opportunity.

Kailer is a smart player but lacks the tools to be effective in the defensive zone purely from a physical standpoint. Nonetheless, he is still a useful defensive player with his reads and shows some bite. In our viewings he has done a good job catching opposing players and causing turnovers. He has also played well on Spokane's PK. Like many of smaller players, Kailer too has the size issue going against him, but so far he has done everything he could to show that he will be able to play despite that limitation. He has also turned in strong international performances for Team USA.

Zablocki, Lane
RW – Regina Pats 6'00", 184

Zablocki has played right wing for Regina Pats putting up very respectable rookie numbers hitting almost 40 points in regular season and adding another 7 goals and 2 assists in 12 playoff games.

Zablocki is a winger that brings a combination of smarts and physicality to the table. He is an active forechecker and likes to finish hard on his checks, it could be said that he at times plays as a bit of an agitator as he likes to be involved in scrums and shoving matches and looks to annoy the opposition. Zablocki shows playmaking upside, especially from the right side of the ice. He's good at seeing the ice from the wall and hitting a linemate in the middle with an accurate pass. Even with traffic and under pressure he still maintains a soft touch on his passing. Zablocki generates above-average speed through neutral zone that he utilizes both offensively as well as to catch up on the backcheck. Although he is capable of being physical on the wall, he can still be caught flat-footed in the defensive zone and isn't as active and consistently engaged as he could be. Zablocki's skill level doesn't really stand out as a big asset for him, but he is a quite smart off-the-puck offensive player. He has good offensive zone reads and is very adept at finding space for himself. He recognizes the weak-spots in coverage and finds seams to get his shot off from up-close. He has the ability to sneak out of the defenseman's coverage and convert from up-close. Zablocki is a player that will be worth paying attention to next year as a prospect that has shown legitimate upside this year.

Zetterlund, Fabian
RW – Farjestad BK J20 (SWE) – 5'10", 194

Zetterlund is a forward with good hockey sense and offensive ability. He does a good job supporting the play when without the puck and makes sure he is open to receive a pass. Often presents an easy way out when the linemate who is carrying the puck is pressured. Zetterlund does a good job playing a puck-possession game, he skates well and has good hands. Makes good give-and-go plays and knows how to utilize his linemates.

When he plays with players who are smart and cerebral like he is, it can result in extended shifts of puck-possession for his team. At times, he can be prone to playing a bit of a perimeter game and not challenging the defenses enough. Zetterlund is a smart and skilled forward, but would benefit by adding a bit more purpose and bite to his game.

Zhukov, Maxim
G – Lokomotiv-2004 Yaroslavl U17 (RUS) – 6'03", 181

Zhukov is a goalie with good size that was one of the better performers at the U17 WHC. He is a goalie that thrives with bigger workloads and can become really frustrating for opposition if he gets into his groove. Has a confident body-language and doesn't quit on plays, he is capable of making high-end saves. He has good rebound control when he has clear sight of the puck but looks slightly less comfortable in traffic and when having to look around bodies for it. He isn't explosive but moves well for his stature and gets around the crease well. He has struggled at the U18s in North Dakota where he played below his usual standard, especially struggling blocker-side and was beat by clean high-quality shots. That aside, he is still projecting as an interesting goalie prospect for the 2017 draft.

2018 NHL DRAFT PROSPECTS

Addison, Calen
LD - Lethbridge Hurricanes (WHL) 5'09" 160

Addison is a smooth-skating two-way defenseman who lacks elite size but plays a smart and compact game. Selected second overall by the Lethbridge Hurricanes in the 2015 WHL bantam draft at only 5-foot-9 and 160 pounds, Addison fits within a larger trend of WHL teams coveting smaller offensively gifted defenseman. Although he isn't an imposing player physically speaking, Addison is dangerous coming out of his own zone as he makes a great first pass, has the speed to join the rush, and the hockey sense to take control of a game singlehandedly.

Addison's speciality is probably his high-end hockey sense. An excellent passer with superb vision, Addison loves tossing out a hard and direct hail-mary out of his own zone to spring the rush. He's not reluctant to join the rush, but is really smart about timing his pinches and being responsible defensively. He also has a very good shot from the point once he crosses into the offensive zone.

He obviously needs to get bigger, which is still a possibility given his age. He also needs to stay healthy. Addison would have likely seen more ice-time with the Lethbridge Hurricanes had it not been for a broken fibula and ligament tear near the bottom of his leg. The ailment eventually required surgery, cutting Addison's WHL tryout short.

Aucoin, Yan
LD – Albatros du College Notre Dame (LHMAAAQ) – 6'0" 202

Aucoin is a big defenseman with a fluid skating stride with good lateral mobility. This mobility allows him to cover a lot of ice and be quickly involved in one-on-one battles. At the beginning of the season, he lost the majority of his battles along the boards but made big improvements over the course of the season. He used his body and stick better and got his ice time increased from the mid-season. In past years he was always taller and bigger than his opponents, but this year he was forced to adapt, as for the first time, this was not the case for him. His transition game is good enough; he makes quick, accurate passes. He's capable of creating offensive scoring chances, he's quick at moving on the blue line and has a good wrist shot. He's good at finding shooting lanes and getting his shot through to the net. He was chosen to play for Team Quebec at the Canada Games and logged a ton of ice time. He was able to show off his consistently and reliability during the tournament, which gave the coaching staff the ability to trust him.

Alexeyev, Alexander
RD - Serebryanye Lvy St. Petersburg (MHL) – 6'03", 170

Though Alexeyev's game is quite raw as would be expected at his age, he has shown considerable upside as a 2018 eligible. Alexeyev has the size and mobility that every team covets in a blueliner. He already shows good compete, with the willingness to engage physically. Though not consistent offensively, we can see flashes of his offensive upside through his skating game, passing, and on occasion shots from the point. While he is at times still prone to wandering around in his own zone, it seems that is something that has a good chance of improving with age, as he doesn't show a deficiency in hockey IQ. Alexeyev will be a good defensive prospect to track for the 2018 NHL entry draft.

Antropov, Danil
RW - Toronto Marlboros (GTHL) 6'02", 165

Antropov was selected in the first round, sixth overall by the Oshawa Generals at the 2016 OHL Priority Selection Draft out of the Toronto Marlboros Minor Midget program. Danil is a big rangy forward with good agility and quickness. Danil has good awareness, a developing skillset and gets the majority of his goals in the goal crease area. Willing to go to the front of the net, Danil has great reach and a knack of skillfully deflecting shots from the point. Danil plays a strong give and go game with good offensive instincts, but would benefit from improving his shot to maximize his potential scoring ability at the OHL level. Earlier in the season, he was getting bumped off the puck a little, but recently he has started to use his size a little more to his advantage and as he fills out this will be an even greater advantage for him moving forward. Danil has good acceleration, but added strength will hopefully benefit Danil's stride length.

Bahl, Kevin
LD - Toronto Marlboros (GTHL) 6'03", 195

Bahl was selected in the 2nd round, 31st Overall by the Ottawa 67's at the 2016 OHL Priority Selection Draft out of the Toronto Marlboros Minor Midget program. Kevin is a rangy defenseman who has been heavily relied on in all situations this year for the Marlies. His first two steps still need some work, but once he's in stride he is a strong skater. Defensively, he uses his reach very will and maintains a very good gap in the neutral zone. Kevin reads the play in neutral zone well and plays a poised and confident game. He enjoys the contact and often looks to make an impact with a big hit. He has a very good stick and generally angles his man effectively. When given time, Kevin makes the simple exit pass as well as the stretch pass, but he does struggle a little when he feels the pressure. He skates the line well for a bigger guy and has a lethal slap shot that he keeps low and on net. As his feet continue to improve and he becomes more agile, we feel Kevin could be a solid contributor on an OHL power play.

Beaudin, Nicolas
LD – Drummondville Voltigeurs (QMJHL) – 5'10", 160

Beaudin split this season between his midget club in Châteauguay and the Voltigeurs who drafted him in the 3rd round of the 2015 QMJHL Draft. At the QMJHL level, he didn't get a ton of ice time and didn't even dress for every game but it was just enough to get his feet wet at the major junior level. He will become an important core player for the Voltigeurs in the next 2-3 years. Beaudin is an offensive defenseman with excellent on-ice vision who can do some damage on the power play. He's physically immature, hence why the Voltigeurs decided on taking their time with him and not rushing him into their lineup. He has decent footwork and agility, but will need to become more explosive on the ice at this level. He moves the puck well and has good tools to become a very good offensive defenseman in the QMJHL. Other areas of his game, such as his defensive game, strength and physical play will need to improve in order for him to become a solid prospect in his NHL Draft year.

Bernard, Xavier
LD – Châteauguay Grenadiers (LHMAAAQ) – 6'02", 187

Bernard is one of the best two-way blueliners in the QMJHL draft. This being his rookie season in the LHMAAAQ, he amassed 21 points in 46 games. He's got good size and reach; he's a smooth skater with solid strides and can keep up with fast forwards on the ice. He makes good decisions with the puck while playing a simple game. He's calm and composed on the ice. He still saw some solid power play minutes with Châteauguay this season, and this increased after the loss of Nicolas Beaudin to Drummondville. Bernard will need to continue to improve his confidence offensively, but his offensive upside is not as strong as other top-tier defensemen in this draft. He will also need to keep working on pushing his physical game up a notch, but there's no doubt that he projects as a strong all-around defenseman at the next level. Bernard took part in a lot of Hockey Quebec events this year, starting with the U-16 summer camp, Quebec Cup, and ending with the Gatorade Challenge at the end of April. At the Gatorade Challenge, he formed a pair with Xavier Bouchard - he was the defensive conscience on that pair. Finally, Bernard is not a flashy defender, but makes smart plays and is efficient on the ice.

Bouchard, Evan
RD - London Knights (OHL) 6'02", 178
Bouchard was selected in the first round, 17th Overall at the 2015 OHL Priority Selection Draft by the London Knights out of the Oakville Rangers Minor Midget program. Bouchard played about two thirds of the season due to several older players on the Knights blue line, but did a great job contributing.

Bouchard is an offensive defenseman for the London Knights, who began the first few weeks of his career as a 15 year old. Bouchard has great offensive tools His skating is decent, and his awareness of what is and isn't available to him helps him advance up ice. He doesn't have a quick few steps but he has good powerful strides at good size that helps him advance after a few steps. He consistently makes smart, accurate first pass up ice. Bouchard has a good shot from the point and finds ways to get it through. He makes smart shooting and passing decisions from the point. During the playoffs Bouchard slotted in at forward on a few occasions where he moved to defense on the power play, showing the Knights confidence in Bouchard's offensive tools. Bouchard is still a bit of a work in progress in the defensive zone. He gets beat one on one as his pivoting isn't very good. His positional play is usually good initially, but under sustained pressure he can chase the play a bit.

Evan's late birthdate should give him plenty of time to fine tune his game. Offensively he already shows flashes of a highly productive offensive defenseman at the OHL level. He has a great frame while will likely only get better. He will need to build muscle, play a little more aggressive and fine tune his skating and defensive zone coverage. The late birthdate will give him two years to refine these skills. He will likely play a more consistent role with the Knights next season.

Bouchard, Xavier
RD – Forestier D'Amos (LHMAAAQ) – 6'01", 160
Xavier is the son of the Rouyn-Noranda' Huskies head coach Gilles Bouchard and had a great year with Amos, even though they didn't have a lot of success as a team this season. He was by far the most talented player on the team. A tall and lanky right-handed defenseman, Bouchard has excellent potential as an offensive defenseman at the next level. He has active feet, good speed and is not shy to rush the puck in the offensive zone. He finished this past season with 22 points. With a better team, those totals would have been much better. He makes good, accurate passes to his forwards on the transition game, and often acted as a 4th forward on the ice. He can take some risks sometimes and try to do too much offensively, getting caught in the end. He will need to be more consistent and make better decisions, but his potential is still huge and one day he should be a quarterback in the QMJHL. Defensively, he will need to make simple plays and be better in his one-on-one battles. He will also need to get stronger physically to win more of those battles along the boards and in front of the net. Bouchard really impressed us last summer at the Hockey Quebec U-16 camp, as he was a standout and eventually played two more times for Hockey Quebec during the year. He was part of their team at the Quebec Cup in December and Gatorade Challenge in late April.

Bouthillier, Zachary
Goaltender – Gaulois Antoine Girouard (LHMAAAQ) – 6'01", 173
Bouthillier is the goalie of the future for the Shawinigan Cataractes, who drafted him in the 2nd round of the QMJHL Draft last June. Bouthillier a late 99-born played a second season in Midget AAA this year and helped his team win the CCM Challenge in December. Overall, he had the best save percentage in the league and the 5th-best goals against average. The Chambly native is now ready for the QMJHL after two strong seasons at the midget level, and next season he should share the Cataractes' workload with Mikhail Denisov. He has a tall and lanky frame and should continue to add mass to his frame in the next couple of years. He's calm in his crease; he follows the puck well even with traffic in front of him. He has great athleticism ability and can make some really nice desperate saves.

He will need to work on his rebound control that can be inconsistent and get better at handling the puck outside of his crease.

Bucheler, Jeremie
RD – Lac St-Louis Lions (LHMAAAQ) – 6'02", 180

Bucheler had an excellent season with the Lions, where he amassed 30 points in 40 games, good for 1st among 15 year old defensemen in the Quebec Midget AAA league. He's a defenseman with excellent hockey sense and a great first pass. He's great on the man-advantage, where he can show off his excellent vision. He has a good, low shot from the point, but will need to improve his velocity in the future. He's poised on the ice, nothing seems to stress him out, and he always seems to make the smart play under pressure. He also had an excellent postseason with the Lions, with 14 points in 16 games as his team won the Quebec league playoff championship, finishing in 3rd place at the TELUS Cup. Bucheler is already tall, closing in on 6'3", but will need to get stronger to be more comfortable when battling in front of the net or along the boards. Right now, it's one of his weaknesses, as he's not physical at all in his own zone and it's too easy for opposing forwards to play against him. His footwork is another area where he will need to improve, as he lacks fluidity in his movement and can get beaten wide by quick forwards. In those situations, he's still capable of getting by them by using his long stick to knock pucks away from them. Among defensemen from Quebec in this draft, we believe that Bucheler has the best potential, but it might take a little longer for him to achieve it fully. Bucheler could be tempted by the NCAA, as he was recently drafted by Chicago in the 3rd round during the first phase of the USHL Draft.

Burzan, Luka
LC – Moose Jaw Warriors (WHL) 6'00" 180

The sixth overall pick of the Moose Jaw Warriors in the 2015 WHL Bantam Draft, Burzan is a gifted offensive player who absolutely lit up the bantam leagues with the North Shore Winter Club scoring 131 points (G, 80 A, 51) in 62 games. That Burzan scored more than a goal-per-game should tell you everything you need to know about this prospect. Burzan has high-end hockey sense that takes him regularly to the prime scoring area, where he hoists a tremendous shot from between the hashmarks.

Excellent skating mechanics and a head's-up style of play underpin Burzan's game. His mobility allows him to elude checks and to create space for himself. He has a variety of shooting options: a lazer of a wristshot; a quick rising backhander; and a powerful one-timer slapshot. In addition to being a great shooter, Burzan is also a good passer, especially when given time with the puck along the half-wall. As a dual threat, he's very difficult to defend against when his club has the man advantage.

Burzan was a key forward for Team Canada on its silver medal run during the Youth Olympic Games. His seven points (G, A,) in six games was the best scoring total amongst all of his Canadian teammates. He's coming along nicely in terms of both his physical growth and his rounding out a complete game. Burzan was selected two spots after teammate Jett Woo in the 2015 WHL Bantam Draft, but there are a lot of onlookers who expect Burzan to be the more impactful player going forward.

Busby, Dennis
RD - Barrie Jr. Colts (ETA) 5'11", 176

Busby was selected second round, 23rd overall out of the Barrie Jr. Colts program by the Flint Firebirds at the 2016 OHL Priority Selection Draft. Dennis is a talented two-way defenseman with a high hockey IQ and high-end skating and skillset. Demonstrating good on-ice leadership qualities, Dennis is extremely capable in all three zones, but consistently pays a little extra attention to detail in his own end first. His defensive positioning is excellent. He maintains an excellent gap and he is one of the best stick on puck defenders in the draft. His first two steps are explosive which allows him to get to loose pucks quickly. He uses his strong lower half to win puck battles and promptly move the puck or skate it out of danger. When he chooses to jump up and be involved in the offence he is more than capable. He has scored some highlight reel goals this year from either leading the rush or joining the rush. Dennis has a very quick set of hands and handles the puck extremely well. He delivers strong crisp passes in all three zones, uses smart escape moves to find open ice and ha's the mobility to quickly change his shooting lane. Busby skates the line well, smartly gets a hard wrist shot through to the net and has the ability to spot the open man off to the side of the net. With the ability to control the pace of the game and thrive on defending against the oppositions top forwards.

Chisholm, Declan
LD - Don Mills Flyers (GTHL) 6'00", 163

Chisholm was selected in the second round, 24th Overall by the Peterborough Petes at the 2016 OHL Priority Selection Draft out of the Don Mills Flyers Minor Midget program. Declan has a very high hockey IQ and is one of the top two-way defenseman for his age group in the province. One of the most fluid skaters in the entire draft, he is tremendous on his edges and is effortless in his ability to change directions. Declan's strong positioning, active stick and excellent lateral mobiliy enables him to effectively defend through the neutral zone and in the defensive zone. While he does have the ability and willingness to throw a big hit, Declan is generally not the most physical player. He uses his body effectively and takes very good angles to the puck in order to win battles. In possession, Declan manages the puck extremely well and controls the tempo and pace of the game. He is at his best when he's consistently making quality exit passes both on the forehand and backhand and executing strong escape moves to find quite ice. Declan is an excellent puck carrier and skates the line very well. Comfortable with the puck on his stick, Declan's strong footwork enables him to create quality shooting lanes.

Corcoran, Connor
RW/RD – Barrie Jr. Colts (ETA), 6'00.25", 165

Corcoran was selected second round, 21st overall by the Windsor Spitfires at the 2016 OHL Priority Selection Draft out of the Barrie Jr. Colts Minor Midget program. Corcoran is a strong skating player who was quite possibly the most versatile player in the entire 2016 OHL Draft. Relied on heavily this year to play both forward and defense, often in the same game, Corcoran was nothing less than outstanding. In our viewings of Corcoran as a forward, he has demonstrated an outstanding work ethic and willingness to play a very physical game. His ability to quickly get in on the fore check and display a relentless work ethic while battling for pucks, has made Corcoran extremely valuable. His strength allows him to fight off checks as well as most. In possession, he is strong on the puck and is at his best when he's taking the puck wide and driving to the net. Corcoran also has a very hard accurate slap shot and a quick release on his snapshot which makes him a threat as a forward and a defenseman. He was also used to take important offensive zone face-offs. As a defenseman, Corcoran is responsible in his own zone and makes accurate crisp passes. He also skates the line well and gets his shot off quickly. Corcoran's versatility makes for a very compelling story leading into his OHL career.

Coxhead, Andrew
RW – Dartmouth Steel Subaru (NSMMHL) – 6'01", 180

The big right-winger is as a complete player as you will find in this draft class; he plays a strong 200-foot game with a high compete level. He has a tall and rangy frame but has skills in spades. He is perhaps described best as a power-forward, as he uses slick puck-handling and his big body and strength to get to scoring areas, although there have been many occasions where he could also be seen as a playmaker. He is a natural scorer, putting pucks in the net with a fast release and a hard net drive. His work ethic is top-class and he frequently empties the tank, only to repeat the performance on the next shift, thus showing a good physical fitness foundation. Coxhead's stock rose all season long, as he continued to push his abilities all year. This year, Coxhead played on an all 2000-born line with Evan MacKinnon and Luke Henman, and it was a very successful line as they led the Steel Subaru to the Nova Scotia playoff championship and earned a spot in the Telus Cup in the month of April. Coxhead is committed to play prep hockey with Salisbury (Connecticut) next season.

Dahlin, Rasmus
LD – Frolunda HC J18 (SWE) – 6'00", 165

Dahlin joined Frolunda this season and was soon moved up to the J18 level despite being a '00 born kid coming from a lower tier hockey program. It took him little time to become a central piece of the team and contributed to eventually winning the league title. What stands out with him is how fast and effective he is at reading the game. Dahlin immediately recognizes what needs to be done and usually will have the right pass completed before most other players would be done processing the play. He has the confidence to work with the puck to open up a lane when it's not available right away, can avoid opponents' pressure with a nice sidestep to the forehand and as a result of his qualities he is able to beat the forecheck and start up his team's transition most of the times.

Rasmus moves well in all four directions and can execute accurate passes in full motion as well. He makes very good use of his stick going backwards to cut down the space for the puck carrier. He doesn't mind making contact and playing hard along the boards. Without the puck he anticipates plays and activates in advance to gain a step on the opponent. He plays a very advanced game and it's difficult to identify specific weaknesses despite his tender age. He can quarterback the powerplay as a 15yrs old against players two years older than him and already displays a legit slapshot. Dahlin seems to have the makings of a special two-way defenseman and it's hard to temper expectations leading into next season.

Damiani, Riley
RC - Mississauga Rebels (GTHL) 5'08.5", 153

Damiani was selected in the 2nd round, 29th Overall by the Kitchener Rangers at the 2016 OHL Priority Selection Draft out of the Mississauga Rebels Minor Midget program. Riley was the Rebels captain and leader all season long and he found ways to contribute in every game. He doesn't possess to the slickest hands but he manages to be very effective at winning one on one battles and create space for his hard snap shot. His shot was more effective this season off the rush using the defenseman as a screen than it was from in tight as he had a tough time picking corners from the hash marks in. He has a very high hockey IQ which allows him to use a very good active stick in defensive zone to knock away loose pucks. He anticipates the play well and waits for lanes to open up before passing or deciding to rush the puck through the neutral zone. He doesn't distribute the puck very well on his backhand when rushing up the ice and it cause him to turn the puck over at the offensive blue line. His relentless play every game allows him to find ways to put himself in scoring position but he had a tough time finishing this season. Damiani looks like a future OHL captain one day but he may benefit from some time in the lower junior level to continue developing offensively. Damiani was one of the best two way forwards available in the 2016 OHL Draft.

Dellandrea, Ty
RC - Central Ontario Wolves (ETA) 5'11.25", 172

Dellandrea was selected first round, fifth overall out of the Central Ontario Wolves program by the Flint Firebirds at the 2016 OHL Priority Selection Draft. Ty is one of the strongest and most impressive open-ice skaters in his age group. He has the ability to carry the puck at top speed and effectively gain the offensive zone. Quality offensive instincts, with and without the puck, combined with slick one-on-one moves make him a constant offensive threat. Ty is one of a few players who can truly make something out of nothing and at the same time bring you out of your seat doing it. Very effective on the power-play, Ty has the skills to make a hard crisp pass, as well as, an accurate saucer pass. Ty transitions well and also does a very good job supporting the puck. Crafty on face-offs, Ty also has a nose for the net, an OHL shot and is extremely confident and skilled with the puck on his stick. At times his confidence with the puck may lead to him over handling the puck, but more often than not he is able to do something effective with it. Defensively, Ty is very responsible. He angles his man well, takes away passing lanes and willingly finishes checks often by throwing his full body weight at his opponent.

Der-Arguchintsev, Semen
C - CIH White (HEOAAA), 5'9", 145

Der-Argunchintsev was selected in the 2nd round, 27th Overall by the Peterborough Petes at the 2016 OHL Priority Selection Draft out of the CHI Academy. Semen is an all around excellent 200ft player. Semen finished the league 1st in scoring with 21 goals and 49 assist for 70 points. This is Semen 3rd year in Canada and all 3 years have been with CIH. Semen is a small extremely skilled and smart center. Semen's hockey IQ is outstanding and he knows where everyone else is on the ice, his vision on the ice is outstanding and there were a lot of times this year you wonder how he even found that player open. He is an exceptional playmaker and it shows it on the powerplay with 18 power play assist. He has the ability to control any game when he has the puck on his stick, the puck seems to always find him or follow him on the ice, and he has a good release on his shot, very deceptive. He is very good at not putting himself in bad situations to get hit hard based on his size. Semen is also very reliable in his defensive zone and has good body positions and understands the defensive side of the game. He was good on draws and was put in key situations to win important draws. Semen needs to get stronger and bigger to be a very dynamic and effective player at the next level.

Desgagnés, Mathieu
C/LW – Châteauguay Grenadiers (LHMAAAQ) – 5'08", 161

Desgagnés is a highly-skilled, smart, offensive forward. He skating strides could use some better mechanics, but he's still a decent skater who can get around defensemen at this level. He possesses good hockey sense and vision, and he's very good at finding his teammates, either on the man-advantage or at even-strength. Desgagnés was used in many situations this season: playing wing, center, on the point on the man-advantage and on the penalty kill. Desgagnés will need to adjust at the next level playing versus bigger players, but he definitely looks like a point-producer. In his first season in Midget AAA, Desgagnés had 49 points in 42 games, just two points shy of potential 1st-overall pick Benoit-Olivier Groulx. He was a regular playing for Team Quebec during the year, from the summer Hockey Quebec U-16 camp, Quebec Cup in December and Gatorade Challenge in April.

Dobson, Noah
RD – EC Red Bull Salzburg (RBHRC U18) – 6'00", 155

Dobson played this past season in Europe with the Red Bull Hockey Academy. The year before, he played prep hockey in Sherbrooke with the Bishop School in the PSHF. Originally from Prince Edward Island, he's the best prospect to come out of this province in quite some time. This season, because of him playing in Europe, we only saw him at the CCM Challenge in Gatineau and at the end of the year at the Gatorade Challenge. Dobson is a very good two-way defenseman with a good frame and will continue to add strength in the next couple of years. He has good footwork, good top speed and he's a good puck rusher. He's confident with the puck and can easily get it out of his zone with a pass, or skate it out by himself. He was more impressive defensively and physically later in the year, showing good improvement over the course of the season. He has a good shot from the point and has good upside offensively with his good one-ice vision. Dobson projects as a two-way defenseman who can play in all situations and should be a top pairing defenseman in the QMJHL

Dudas, Aidan
RC - North Central Predators (ETA) 5'07", 151

Dudas was selected first round, 10th overall at the 2016 OHL Priority Selection Draft by the Owen Sound Attack out of the North Central Predators Minor Midget Program. Aidan is a very dynamic player. He is an exceptional skater who accelerates very well from strong crossovers. Offensively, Aidan is very deceptive and he is often able to escape fore-checkers with a quick upper body fake. Consistently looking to receive the puck in the neutral zone with speed, Aidan is a constant threat to opposing defensemen. He is also very capable of handling pucks in his feet often without losing stride. One of Aidan's outstanding strengths is his ability to skate as fast with the puck as he does without it. While in possession he has the ability to instinctively find open ice. Aidan has a nifty set of hands and a hard snapshot that make him a consistent offensive threat. Despite being undersized, he has shown a resiliency throughout the season to be able to bounce back after a hard check. Aidan is an on-ice leader and the type of player who looks to make something happen every shift.

Dunkley, Nathan
LC - Quinte Red Devils (ETA), 5'09.75", 182

Dunkley was selected in the first round, 17th Overall by the Kingston Frontenacs at the 2016 OHL Priority Selection Draft out of the Quinte Red Devils Minor Midget program. In possession, Nathan's high hockey IQ and deceptiveness enables him to make quality no-look passes, thread the needle to find an open team mate or deliver a quality saucer pass. His core strength and his ability to absorb checks make it difficult for the opposing players to knock him off the puck. Always tenacious, his back pressure and speed allows him to strip pucks from opponents on a consistent basis. His overall work ethic is matched by few. Nathan rises to the challenge of often being matched up against the top defense pairing of the opposition. He times his zone exits extremely well, attempting to quickly gain speed as he receives the puck. Despite being slightly undersized, Nathan plays with some pushback and competes hard virtually every shift. Dunkley can get frustrated at times when a play doesn't go well and as an emotional player can sometimes let that snowball into a bigger issue.

Emberson, Ty
RD – Eau Claire Memorial/Team Wisconsin U16 (WI-HS) 6'01", 189

Ty is a smart player who makes safe and reliable plays with the puck. His fluid skating allows him to escape pressure and buy time, control the pace of the game and find the open man up the ice. Ty does have the tendency to hold on to the puck a bit too long in his own end, which against higher levels of competition can result in turnovers. Emberson isn't overly offensive in the sense of joining the rush and spending a lot of time deep in the offensive zone but picks his spots and has the offensive tools to generate offense when he does jump into the play. He is very sound in his positioning with his defensive play, brings a physical game but is smart about it and won't risk taking himself out of the play to deliver a big hit.

Emberson will be off to the USNTDP next season where we are eager to see him against elite competition. Emberson is still weighing his NCAA options and remains uncommitted at this stage.

Forhan, Rhys
RC - York-Simcoe Express (ETA) 5'11", 175

Forhan was selected in the 2nd round, 33rd overall of the 2016 OHL Priority Selection Draft by the North Bay Battalion out of the OHL Cup winning York-Simcoe Express Minor Midget program. Not only did Forhan win the OHL Cup, he scored both goals for his team including the double overtime winner in the championship game. A leader on his team, Rhys is a strong skater with good separation speed. He carries the puck with confidence and can be especially dangerous when he receives the puck in full flight. Excellent balance and strength on his skates combined with nifty puck skills, allow

Rhys to create time and space for himself in the offensive zone. His skillset, vision and patience with the puck in traffic enables him to consistently find the open man. He doesn't need a great deal of time to release a hard accurate shot. Rhys is at his best when he plays with an edge, consistently finishing his checks, winning battles and taking the puck hard to the net. Often leaving you wanting to see more, Rhys struggled over the course of the season to find a level of consistency. Rhys has the ability to impact the game in a variety of ways and as he matures, has the potential to be one of the more complete players from the OMHA.

Fortier, Gabriel
C – Lions du Lac St-Louis (LHMAAAQ) – 5'09", 164

Fortier is a forward with an amazing skating ability; he can reach his top speed in two or three strides. Whether it's in rushing the puck or on a backcheck, he uses his speed to the fullest. He is, without a doubt, the best skater in this draft class and the Quebec Midget AAA league. He's the younger brother of Maxime Fortier of the Halifax Mooseheads. Gabriel finished the year with 47 points in 41 games and added 18 more points in 17 playoff games. He also played for Canada at the Youth Olympics game in February, where he won silver. Fortier has a great work ethic, playing physical along the boards and also bringing offense to the table. He's a complete hockey player; he played on the point on the power play at the end of the season and in the playoffs. He was also on the penalty killing unit; he's useful there with his speed and anticipation. He can be a threat to score on the PK. Offensively, he creates a lot of scoring chances with his speed, quick shot and fierceness around the net. We would like to see a bit more creativity with him and see him slow down the play so that he can see play options more clearly. He's a low-risk player for the next level; he has great potential for the QMJHL and is one of the most complete players for the 2016 QMJHL Draft.

Foudy, Liam
LC - Markham Majors (GTHL) 5'11", 154

Foudy was selected in the first round, 18th Overall at the 2016 OHL Priority Selection Draft by the London Knights out of the Markham Majors Minor Midget program. Liam was one of the most elite skaters in the entire 2016 OHL Draft. His Markham Majors team relied on him a lot to carry the offensive load all season long. Foudy shows his elite skating ability while rushing the puck through the neutral zone. He never skates in a straight line and continues to pick up what seems like an endless amount of speed. His quick, shift hands along with his skating ability make him very difficult to contain when attempting to gain the offensive blue line. Foudy is also an elite track and field runner which means he needs to be light on his feet. This has caused him to be pushed off the puck quite easily and has been the one aspect of his game that has been holding back an even bigger offensive outburst. He played a lot of minutes all season long and late in the year it looked like it was wearing him down especially late in games. He plays more of an offensive playmaking game, but showed the ability to be a hard working two-way centre, especially in big games. Foudy seemed to play better against tougher competition all year and he was always the one to step up for his team when they needed it most. Foudy needs to get gets stronger and tougher to knock off the puck.

Gilhula, Owen
RC - Huron-Perth Lakers (MHAO) 5'09", 149

Owen was drafted second round, 34th overall out of the Huron-Perth Lakers program by the Sudbury Wolves at the 2016 OHL Priority Selection Draft. Owen has a tremendous amount of speed and can use it in both directions. With the puck he can evade checkers with his agility and also blow by them with his quick acceleration and good top speed. He has a very powerful shot which he gets on net and is accurate. He did a great job running the Lakers' powerplay moving the puck very well and getting his shot through. He has very good hockey sense and reaction time. He works just as hard defensively as he does offensively. Owen was one of Huron-Perth's best penalty killers putting a ton of pressure on the opposition forcing turnovers. He was also willing to block shots when necessary. Owen has the upside of a player who could play in a top six offensive role, while providing strong two-way play and contribute in all game situations. Gilhula suffered multiple injuries and will need to improve his strength as there is a little risk that comes with his upside.

Gogolev, Pavel
LW- CIH White (HEOAAA), 6'01, 170

Gogolev was selected in the first round, eighth overall by the Peterborough Petes at the 2016 OHL Priority Selection Draft out of the CHI Academy. Pavel is a high scoring winger and dynamic player for CIH Academy, this was Pavel first year in the AAA league, and he took the league by storm. He finished 2nd in the league in scoring with 38 goals and 30 assist for 68 points. He is a big forward with high-end skill and a very good skater, and can take over a game whenever he wants too. Pavel has a pro shot already, his accuracy is great and can pick any corner he wants in the net. His puck skills are outstanding, and his hands are exceptional. Pavel's skill really shows on the powerplay, whether its taking a one timer from the corner or in the slot, or making the smart pass to his teammate backdoor, Pavel is very good at finding open spots in the offensive zone and scoring his goals from there. He is not afraid to be physical with opponents and go too the dirty areas of the ice. Pavel needs to work on competing hard every shift and keep his feet moving and he can be a very dangerous all around player at the next level, Pavel needs to focus on improving his defensive game to be that much better at the next level.

Gravel, Alexis
Goaltender - Mississauga Senators (GTHL) – 6'01.5", 196

Gravel, who's originally from Asbestos, played the past two seasons in Ontario. This year, he played with the Mississauga Senators in the GTHL. He played for Team Canada in February at the Youth Olympic Games, where he won the starting job against Olivier Rodrigue. Gravel and Team Canada eventually lost in the final against Team U.S.A. Gravel is a big, athletic, southpaw goalie that has shown good consistency throughout the season. He is very poised in the crease and does a great job of putting himself in a good position to make saves off rebounds. That being said, his rebound-control is one of his strong points and has proven to be a key to his success this season. He makes himself look as big as possible with an upright crouch, but he has the ability to get low when fighting through traffic to see the puck. His quick, lateral movement and athletic ability make him tough to beat on breakaways where he, more often than not, is victorious. He was hands down the best goalie in the GTHL from game 1 this season and he will look to make an instant impact on a QMJHL team if given the opportunity.

Groleau, Jeremy
LD – Chicoutimi Saguéneens (QMJHL) – 6'02", 176

Groleau was the 17th overall selection in the 2015 QMJHL Draft and his father (François) was a former Calgary Flames draft pick, playing most of his career in Europe, now assistant-coach with the Saguenéens. The younger Groleau was part of a very young defensive squad in Chicoutimi this season, with two other 16 year olds on the team (Krief and MacIsaac). He didn't play in every game this season but also took part in the U-17 Hockey Challenge in November. He's not a flashy defenseman on the ice, more of the stay-at-home type who uses his smart to counter opposing forwards. He always seemed to be in the right position on the ice. He is not an overly physical player but always makes sure to have his body in good position to win puck battles and also use a good active stick in the defensive zone. He's capable of rushing and handling the puck but rarely does so; he can catch opposing teams by surprise by rushing the puck from his zone and has surprisingly good puck skills. This year, he saw important minutes on the ice when he played, mostly on the PK. He also was used in matchups at times.

The biggest thing he will need to improve on is his footwork (it is only average right now) but has a good work ethic and his NHL Draft year is only in two years.

Grondin, Maxim
LW - Vaughan Kings (GTHL) 6'01", 180

Grondin was selected second round, 37th overall at the 2016 OHL Priority Selection Draft by the Saginaw Spirit out of the Vaughan Kings Minor Midget program. Maxim is a big hard working winger who makes his presence known while on the ice. He was arguably the most physical forward in the GTHL all season long and he landed some of the biggest hits of the season. He is a strong skater with long powerful strides which helps him win puck battles and retrieve puck on dump ins. He play a more simple offensive game where he will go to the dirty areas and screen goalies while trying to tip point shots or pick up loose pucks off rebounds. Grondin has the ability to create offense by creating space with big hits and winning puck battles, but he doesn't yet have the skillset to make creative plays, although we did see improvement throughout the season. Grondin has great size and shows the willingness to be a very efficient power forward one day, but he will need to continue to improve his puck skills in order to become a more offensive threat off the rush.

Groulx, Benoit-Olivier
C – Intrépide de Gatineau (LHMAAAQ) – 6'00.25", 176

Groulx possesses a lot of interesting tools. He has a remarkable hockey sense. He understands the game very well at both ends of the ice. There are no major weaknesses in his game other than his skating, but it has improved a lot in the past year. Not only is he a good playmaker with the ability to make his linemates better, he possesses an amazing shot and quick hands. His physical game is also above-average and he doesn't mind getting involved in the rough stuff. He makes good use of his size to win battles along the boards and take over games. All of those traits make Groulx a very dangerous player on the ice and tough to play against. When Groulx is on the ice, the opposing team has no choice but to keep a close eye on him, as he can create scoring chances during most of his shifts. He was used in all kinds of situations this season: he was a regular shorthanded, and on the power play, he played on the point for most of the year. He was named to the U-16 Team Quebec roster at the Quebec Cup during the holidays and at the Gatorade Challenge. He was also named to Team Canada at the Youth Olympics in February and did well at this tournament in Norway. This season, he finished 10th in scoring in the league, 1st among 2000-born players with 21 goals and 51 points in 41 games.

Hayton, Barrett
LC - Toronto Red Wings (GTHL) 6'00", 176

Hayton was selected in the first round, ninth overall by the Sault Ste. Marie Greyhounds at the 2016 OHL Priority Selection Draft out of the Toronto Red Wings Minor Midget program. Barrett is a talented scoring forward with good hockey sense. His offensive skill set is highlighted by a rocket snap shot that makes him a constant threat anywhere in the offensive zone. When he's not shooting the puck, Barrett's uses his high-end vision to create chances for his line mates. Although he's been effective playing the point on the power play, we feel Barrett is more effective coming off the half wall where he has the awareness to spot an open teammate or release a quick hard shot. Not afraid to take the puck to traffic or drive the net, Barrett works for everything he gets. He is very patient in possession and his soft hands enable him to corral bouncing pucks and deliver a variety of quality forehand, backhand and crafty area passes. One of the most skilled players in his peer group, Barrett's skating has improved in this his second season of Minor Midget hockey and his long stride provides him with deceptive speed. While he does have a low panic threshold, at times Barrett might try to do a little too much with the puck and over handle it. Generally though, he is very good at knowing just when to move the puck. Barrett is also very disciplined, but will push back when needed either to defend himself or a teammate. Defensively, Barrett is responsible in all three zones and is perfectly willing to play a physical game. He is strong along the boards where he effectively uses his body and feet to protect the puck and win battles. Barrett also shows a willingness do whatever it takes to take away scoring chances by blocking shots.

Hillis, Cameron
RC – York-Simcoe Express (ETA), 5'09", 145

Hillis was selected 2nd round, 28th Overall by the Guelph Storm at the 2016 OHL Priority Selection Draft. Cameron is a cerebral and highly skilled forwards in the York-Simcoe Express. A high-end stick handler and playmaker, Cameron sees the ice extremely well, has the ability to control the pace and delivers quality passes of all types to his team mates. A 200-foot player, Cameron is willing to compete for the puck in all three zones. He possesses a variety of one-on-one moves and is smart enough to mix them up making him more difficult to defend him against. While he doesn't have an overpowering shot, he will surprise goalies with a quick release and an accurate shot. Despite being somewhat undersized, Cameron is shifty enough and avoids putting himself in vulnerable positions. His skating is good, but he does lose his edges at times when turning sharply. Being undersized, he does get knocked off the puck at times and will therefore need to get stronger to compete at the next level. Cameron is very effective on face-offs as well, often using his feet to free the puck for his forwards. Perhaps not given enough credit for his defensive game, Cameron is very aware in his own zone and his high hockey IQ makes him a threat to strip pucks from opponents, anticipate and break up passes. Cameron projects as a skilled top six forward at the OHL level.

Holmes, Hunter
LC - Niagara North Stars (SCTA) 6'00.5", 167

Holmes was selected second round, 22nd overall out of the Niagara North Stars program by the Flint Firebirds at the 2016 OHL Priority Selection Draft. Hunter is a big offensive centre for the Niagara North Stars. He has good offensive instincts with the puck on his stick and he was able to score on many of his high quality chances throughout the season. He has the ability to beat defenders one on one and he often does it by generating speed through the neutral zone and making a simple yet effective move to step around the defenseman. He showed at times the ability to play a good positional 200ft game but struggled to consistently chip in defensively. Holmes style of game heavily relies on his skill and skating ability which often limited his impact in games. He plays in the middle of the ice all game and rarely goes to work to win puck battles. He often played his best games when facing an opponent that didn't play a physical style of game, but once the game got more physical he would float around the ice and just wait for the puck to come to him. He reminds us of Jimmy Lodge because he has some very good offensive ability along with great size, but he will need to show more of a willingness to go into the dirty areas in order to reach his full potential at the OHL level.

Houde, Samuel
C - Phénix du Collège Esther-Blondin (LHMAAAQ) – 5'10", 140

Houde is two-way center that has a lot of tools offensively, including being a good skater with good hands. Defensively, he's responsible - his coach can trust him in different aspects of the game (such as faceoffs, at the end of games and in shorthanded situations, where he's very good at cutting passing lanes). He will need to get stronger over the course of the summer, which would help him win more puck battles in the corners. He also played the point on the power play, where he was good at moving the puck quickly thanks to his great vision and level of calmness while in puck possession. His speed allows him to rush the puck in the offensive zone. The biggest trait that separates him from other players is his smarts, which makes him a dangerous player in all aspects of the game. He also played the point on the power play with Team Quebec White at the Gatorade Challenge at the end of April. He had an outstanding tournament and won a lot of points with scouts at this event. He finished the season with 28 points in 45 games, which is good for a first year player in this league.

Hughes, Quinton
LD – USNTDP U17 5'08", 157

Quinton Hughes is a defenseman that was consistently impressive in our USNTDP U17 viewings. He's primarily a puck-mover that plays with high-end hockey IQ. Hughes has the ability to start the team's transition, be involved offensively and yet have the reads and mobility not to expose his team defensively. Hughes has crafty hands and easily maneuvers around the ice and around forecheckers. He has a soft touch on his passes and consistently hits his forwards with accurate on-tape passing. Hughes has the ability to get involved up the ice and offensively. That said, we feel he could stand to simplify his game. At times he will look to tread a perfect pass or try another move when he has already opened up a gap that he could take advantage of with a simpler play. That is likely to come with maturity.

Ingham, Jacob
G - Barrie Colts (ETA), 5'11.75", 152

Jacob was selected in the second round, 26th Overall by the Mississauga Steelheads at the 2016 OHL Priority Selection Draft out of the Barrie Jr. Colts Minor Midget program. Ingham is a very athletic and extremely poised goaltender. He has good size and does a very good job of staying big in the net. He moves well from post to post, has strong rebound control and his legs are quick enough to effectively cover the lower half of the net. Jacob reads the play effectively and has a solid positional foundation and knows how to use his size by moving less which allows him to get set to face the first shot with patience. Stable in his butterfly, he is able to angle pucks effectively. Jacob has a chance to emerge as one of top goaltenders from his peer group.

Jenkins, Blade
LC - Detroit Compuware U16 (HPHL) 5'11", 174

Blade was selected first round, fourth overall at the 2016 OHL Priority Selection Draft by the Saginaw Spirit out of the Detroit Compuware U16 program. Jenkins is a highly skilled forward who has excellent hands and vision which combine to create great scoring chances for his team. He is the offensive catalyst for his Minor Midget team and has the ability to make others around him look much better. His quick puck skills allow him to evade checkers and create time and options to make a play. He also has the ability to take the puck to the net, beat defenders and goaltending with highlight reel goal scoring potential. He has a good shot which has both power and accuracy which makes him dangerous in the goal area. He is a competitive forward who is effective playing a two-way game. Blade could be an impact player at the OHL level and should be highly regarded when the 2018 NHL Entry Draft rolls in.

King, D.J.
LD - Mississauga Rebels (GTHL) 6'00", 184

King was selected second round, 39th overall out of the Mississauga Rebels program by the Hamilton Bulldogs at the 2016 OHL Priority Selection Draft. He has also been selected to play for the USNTDP U17 team. D.J is a big defender who logged a lot of minutes for the Mississauga Rebels this season. He has good patience with puck as quarterback on power play and showed the ability to walk the line and open up seams. He has a good shot from the point whether he is winding up for the big slap shot or getting a quick hard snap shot through traffic. His improvement in his footwork throughout the year allowed him to be tougher to play against defensively and when he was playing physical he was able to get under the opposition's skin. Although he was at his best when playing physical, he had some bad penalties creep into his game all season long and some of them resulted in a power play goal for the opposition. He showed the ability to be a puck rusher and a puck mover but he struggled with his decision making when breaking out of his zone. King needs to continue to work on his skating and get quicker; this will allow him to be more effective when facing quicker more skilled forwards at the next level. U.S Development Program and he will look to be a high round pick in the 2016 OHL Priority Selection Draft.

Kovalenko, Nikolai
RW/LW – Loko-Yunior Yaroslavl (MHL B) – 5'09", 170

Kovalenko is a skilled shifty wing that has produced well in MHL B this season, putting up a point per game. He also appeared in 4 games at the MHL level and put up an impressive 4 goals and 1 assist, his international performance has also been good. He is a winger that has good hands and a very good small-space game. He operates in tight spaces with ease and avoids contact by utilizing his skating and hands to elude players. He is quite good at changing directions and throwing defensemen off just when they think they are closing in on him. Although he still has ways to go in order to exhibit a high-end impact on a regular shift, he still manages to make some high-end skill plays that speak of his upside. He also displays good compete on the forecheck and when battling for pucks.

Laferriere, Mathias
RW – Lions du Lac St-Louis (LHMAAAQ) – 5'11", 151

Laferriere had a tremendous progression this season with the Lions. He was outstanding in the 2nd half of the season, in the playoffs and at the Telus Cup. After he amassed 12 points in 31 games before the Christmas break, Laferriere exploded with 53 points in 38 games the rest of the year. He was named MVP at the Telus Cup, where the Lions finished in 3rd place. He started the season slowly by playing on a 3rd line and took some time to adjust to the Midget AAA level. Even with limited ice time, he was able to show some potential; a good understanding of the game, good puck-protection and good puck-control in tight areas. He had a good CCM Challenge in December in Gatineau and became a main contributor for the Lions the rest of the season. Laferriere possesses an excellent wrist shot that he can release in no time. He scored many times this season coming from his off wing. In the playoffs, he scored many goals and a lot of them where important ones, including the overtime game-winning goal in the Quebec Midget AAA final that sent the Lions to the national championship. He's first and foremost a natural goal scorer, but he sees the ice very well with his good hockey sense and is patient with the puck, which helps him find his linemates on the ice. His skating is not bad, but there's room for improvement which should come when he gets stronger physically. His acceleration and top speed should all improve. Laferriere is versatile; he can play down the middle or on the wing and can also be used on the penalty-killing unit.

Lalonde, Owen
RD - Windsor Jr. Spitfires (MHAO), 6'00", 171

Lalonde was drafted first round, second overall out of the Windsor Jr. Spitfires program by the Sudbury Wolves at the 2016 OHL Priority Selection Draft. Owen is an excellent two-way defenseman for the Windsor Jr. Spitfires. Offensively, Owen has an excellent shot. It isn't overpowering but it is very accurate. He can walk in from the point of find a shooting lane and does a great job of making sure his shot gets on net. He's been able to pick low corners which has lead to goals for himself, but is also deflectable leading to assists. Owen's ability to get his shot through lead to him scoring 13 goals during the regular season, without being one of those speedy high risk defenders who sacrifices the defensive game for offence. He is very smart with the puck and moves it successfully at a very high rate. He isn't flashy and can evade checkers smoothly while finding the best option available, rather than trying to do too much himself. 9 out of 10 times he will make the smart play. Defensively Owen is very difficult to beat one on one. He's calm and his reaction time is excellent. This allows him to shut down forwards at a high rate when he's in position. His hockey sense shows through in the defensive zone as he's constantly in ideal positioning. He won battles down low effectively despite needing to add muscle. Owen had a bit of a rough playoff during our viewings, misreading options and getting caught out of position. While his whole season needs to be taken into account, these struggles were a bit concerning. Owen has all the abilities to make the jump to the OHL next season. He won't blow you away with flashy skills, but he does everything well, has high hockey sense and can contribute at both ends of the ice.

Levin, David
LC - Sudbury Wolves (OHL) 5'10", 167

Levin was the first overall selection at the 2015 OHL Priority Selection Draft out of the Don Mills Flyers program. He had a successful rookie season where he overcame injury to still put up some solid points for his team.

David has excellent speed and likes to have the puck on his stick as much as possible. He has great hands and has the skill to beat defenders one on one. He has good playmaking ability and can create offense for his linemates. His vision is strong and he chooses good options on the power play and distributes the puck quickly. David gets himself into the most trouble when he tries to make a play look far more fancy than it needs to. At times he would beat a defender and would actually look to beat another rather than exploiting the lane he created with the initial play. He will sometimes choose the more difficult play, when a far more simple route would have a higher percentage of success. Hopefully Levin will learn that sometimes less is more as he matures as he has the skill to be one of the most dangerous players in the OHL.

Lundestrom, Isac
LC – Lulea HF J20 (SWE) – 6'00", 181

A late 1999 born, Lundestrom already plays a big role for Lulea's J20 squad. His 17 points in 34 games are quite impressive for a player who is still 2 years away from being draft eligible. Even more impressively, Lundestrom has already appeared for Lulea's SHL team playing 4 games against men. We have liked Lundestrom's international performances. First at the U17 WHC where Lundestrom was in our opinion the best forward on the Swedish team and later with the U18 team where he hardly missed a beat. Lundestrom already shows advanced hockey IQ as he easily gets involved in the play with players older than himself. His reads are good in all three zones and easily gets involved with the puck-movement game. Lundestrom has also shown a good skill-level with the puck and is capable of making a high-end move. An aspect that has stood out for Lundestrom is his vision as he is already an advanced playmaker, capable of both setting up zone time with give and go plays or hitting an open linemate with a high-end pass.

MacDonald, Anderson
LW – Saint-John Vitos (NBPEIMMHL) – 6'00", 204

What we got all season from MacDonald was a player that wants to be the dominant power-forward on the ice. He has a big-body presence, can skate right through several players with the puck, and score. He has well-developed skills and can handle a puck nicely at all speeds. He is one of the few players in this draft class that we can label as 'explosive,' as witnessed on a number of occasions. He can also be a bit of a game-breaker, playing better as the stakes increase. He showed some IQ and patience on power play sequences, where his team uses him extensively and where he loves to shine. He can beat you with his speed or power game. He's a big body and will learn with more experience to use it more efficiently, playing more like a true power-forward. There were some times early in the season where his body language was not the best, but he appeared more focused as time went on. We would like to see him battle more on the ice, as sometimes he has the tendency to wait to get the puck back instead of working to get it back. MacDonald was part of the U-16 Youth Olympics' Team Canada squad that won silver in Norway. After playing last season as an underager with the Vitos, MacDonald was among the league leaders in goals and points this season, scoring 18 goals and 36 points in 26 games. His team, the Vitos, had a remarkable season, eventually losing in the gold medal game of the Telus Cup. MacDonald was a big reason for their success.

McBain, Jack
LC - Don Mills Flyers (GTHL) 6'02", 173

McBain was selected in the first round, 20th Overall at the 2016 OHL Priority Selection Draft by the Barrie Colts out of the Don Mills Flyers Minor Midget program. Jack is a big rangy centre with excellent offensive instincts. He uses his size and reach extremely well allowing him to control the puck and create offence in a variety of ways. He possesses a soft set of hands and very good puck skills for a player his size and is at his best when he's challenging defensemen by carrying the puck wide and cutting into the slot to create scoring chances. Strong in possession down low, Jack has the ability to make quality tape-to-tape passes and take a hit to make a play. He is patient with the puck, but has had some trouble finishing when he gets the chance. Jack's tremendous reach allows him to make key takeaways in both the defensive and offensive zone. One of the strongest centres in the GTHL on the draw, he has the ability to adjust to the location and situation in order to win key face-offs. Despite his obvious talents, Jack is not the best skater. His stride noticeably weakens as he tires which in turn affects his ability to back check with consistency.

McIsaac, Jared
LD – Cole Harbour Wolfpack (NSMMHL) – 6'01", 203

McIsaac came into this season as the top Atlantic prospect and had his sights on being the number one overall pick in the QMJHL Draft. This was his second season of midget, having played last year as an underager. In the skills' department, it's clear that he has excellent skating ability and puck-control; everything he does can be done using speed, while in motion and while transitioning. McIsaac has the ability to explode from a stop and catch opponents flat. His first-pass vision borders on elite, and he sees plays developing before anyone else. Athletically, he can log tremendous amounts of ice time without fatigue, and is strong and physical when needed. Pegged as an offensive defenseman, he spent a lot of this season in a defensive posture, waiting to control the play and the puck from back to front. He really only jumped in when it was safe to do so. On the PP, he was the go-to guy and captained it well, moving the puck easily and getting a high percentage of his shots on net and scoring as well. McIsaac can transition into a contributing junior defenseman as early as next season, and has future top-pairing potential. He was the captain of Team Nova Scotia at the Gatorade Challenge at the end of April and was also drafted by Chicago in the USHL Draft in early May.

McMaster, Adam
LC – Niagara North Stars (SCTA) 5'09.25", 155

McMaster was selected in the first round, 13th overall by the North Bay Battalion at the 2016 OHL Priority Selection Draft out of the Niagara North Stars Minor Midget program. Adam is a skilled centre for the Niagara North Stars who led the SCTA in goals and points this season. He was an offensive threat every time he stepped on the ice no matter whom the opponent was. He possesses a lethal shot and can beat a goalie from anywhere in the offensive zone. His shiftiness, quick hands and ability to beat you with several different moves makes him very tough to contain when skating at a high pace. Despite his size McMaster showed the ability to bounce off checks while still maintaining control of the puck. Although he doesn't initiate contact very often he doesn't shy away from going into the corner or cutting through the middle of the ice. McMaster quarterbacked Niagara's power play from the point all season long and he proved to be very affective whether making passes through tight seams or using his hard accurate shot to pick the top corner through traffic. Early in the season he struggled to score consistently but as the season went on he got more creative and maintained his scoring at a high rate. McMaster shows the potential to be an elite scorer at the OHL level.

McLeod, Ryan
LC - Mississauga Steelheads (OHL) 6'01", 185

McLeod was selected first round, third overall at the 2015 OHL Priority Selection Draft by the Flint Firebirds out of the Toronto Marlboros Minor Midget program. After refusing to report to Flint, McLeod was eventually dealt to the Mississauga to join his brother with the Steelheads. Ryan generally played on the third line with second unit power play allowing him plenty of opportunity to create offense as a 16 year old rookie.

McLeod is a speedy, offensive minded centre who possesses a versatile offensive repertoire. Ryan struggled with consistency throughout the season and he was often paired with different linemates. McLeod showed effectiveness off the cycle throughout the season for the Steelheads while also displaying some vision and playmaking abilities. He has good power in his shot and is dangerous in the offensive zone due to a quick release. While McLeod took some time to adjust to the speed of the game, as the season progressed, he became more confident and more productive. While McLeod does possesses an intriguing offensive repertoire he does lack a physical element to his game and needs to become heavier on the puck. McLeod could also stand to show more poise in possession as he tended to force plays that weren't there leading to turnovers.

A lack of strength and consistency were the biggest issues that plagued McLeod through his rookie OHL season. Despite some struggles, there is a lot of upside to McLeod's game as his speed and skating are a great foundation to build on going into 2nd season in the OHL which is his draft season.

McShane, Allan
LC - Toronto Marlboros (GTHL) 5'10.5", 184

McShane was selected in the first round, 19th overall at the 2016 OHL Priority Selection Draft by the Erie Otters out of the Toronto Marlboros Minor Midget program. Allan is a very cerebral two-way pivot. With a strong, effortless stride, Allan has sneaky speed. He also possesses one of the hardest and most accurate shots in the GTHL which he is not afraid to use from anywhere in the offensive zone. Strong in possession, Allan is very good at releasing his shot off the stride which often fools goalies. At times, Allan tends to rely on his shot a little too much passing up opportunities to create alternative scoring chances. He has the ability to beat defenders in an almost effortless fashion either accelerating past them or using a nifty one-on-one move. With a shooter's first mentality, Allan passes the puck extremely well and his playmaking abilities are improving. Allan has a strong base and uses it to his advantage along the boards and in and around the net. His strength also comes in handy when he's relied upon to win both key defensive and offensive zone face-offs. Defensively, Allan anticipates very well and has the all the tools to shut down top opponents. McShane will need to improve on his consistency in order to experience the success at the OHL level that he has the potential to.

Merkley, Ryan
RD - Toronto Jr. Canadiens (GTHL) 5'09.75", 155

Merkley was drafted 1st round, 1st overall by the Guelph Storm at the 2016 OHL Priority Selection Draft. Ryan has been a big part of the Toronto Jr. Canadiens offence for the past two seasons and has also arguably been the GTHL best player the past two seasons. He played a year up in 2014/2015 and he was the offensively leader of his team as an underager. His vision with the puck is second to none and his ability to draw defenders to him then feed his teammate cross ice is a skill that is very difficult to teach. His patience and confidence with the puck allow him to make some plays that will make you jump out of your seat and wonder how he was able to pull that off. He can beat you by either moving slowly up the ice dodging defenders east to west or he can take on all five guys and beat you with speed or skill. He has a very good one timer from the point which he looks to get off on the power play but he also has a very good quick release from the point that he pretty much always gets through traffic. Merkley is one of those players that will help anybody on the ice with him put offensive numbers because of his ability to draw players to him then give him teammate the puck in open ice. He often makes passes that people in the stands didn't see were available and he has done it consistently the past two years. Defensively, Merkley is good when he is putting in the effort but quite often this season he did not show a high compete level in the defensive zone. That being said he was still effective when not giving his all which makes you frustrated at how good of a defender he can actually be. Merkley's biggest flaw is his body language towards his teammates or coaches. He is often being negative towards his teammate or ignoring a coach and doing his own thing during a timeout. While he is able to get away with this at the Minor Midget level he will learn the hard way next season in the OHL if he doesn't become more of a team player and buy into what it means to become a professional hockey player.

Nizhnikov, Kirill
RW - Toronto Jr. Canadiens (GTHL) 6'01", 190

Nizhnikov was selected in the first round, 7th Overall of the 2016 OHL Priority Selection Draft by the Mississauga Steelheads out of the Toronto Jr. Canadiens Minor Midget program. Kirill was our number one ranked prospect for the 2016 OHL Draft. He skates very well and demonstrates agility for a bigger forward which allows him to beat defenders of any size. He has very good edges which allows him to escape pressure quickly and his hockey sense allows him to read plays before they develop. Kirill's best attribute is his shot. It is one of if not the best in the draft and he very rarely passed up an opportunity to let it fly. He has a very good one timer whether he is winding up for the big slap shot from the point on the power play or setting up on the dot and one timing a quick release snap shot into the top shelf while dropping to a knee. He has slick hands and is able to beat defenders off the rush with many different moves. He uses the defender as a screen very often and he looks to find the top half of the net while doing so. He has a wide skating stance which makes him very difficult to knock off the puck and when his skill set isn't allowing him to create offense he will change his game to more of a hard-nosed style and start taking pucks to the net. He isn't an overly physical player but he does not shy away from contact. Kirill is a very offensive minded player which makes him forget about his role defensively at times. He gets caught flying out of the zone early at times, looking to stretch the offense and get a breakaway pass, but at times it proved to cost him as his open defenseman would get a shot on net. Kirill is very talented offensively and he will look to make an immediate impact on an OHL roster next season.

Nielsen, Tristen
LC - Calgary Hitmen (WHL) 5'09" 174

Tristen Nielsen, a quick-footed centre with good vision and high-end passing skill, was a first round pick of the Calgary Hitmen in the 2015 WHL Bantam Draft. He only played three games in the WHL (G, 1 A, 0), but had a great year at the prep level, scoring over a point-per-game over 22 contests (G, 9 A, 14). Nielsen is a smooth skater with slick hands who is quick on his edges and anticipates the play well. Because he's a good passer, a decent shooter, throws his body around a bit and plays a strong defensive game, he might be best described as an "all-around" type player who does a little bit of everything well.

He's not the biggest guy, but he plays a fairly mean rough-and-tussle game. Nielsen is a great backchecker who uses his stick well. Nielsen developed with the Edge School Prep program in the Canadian sports high school league. That's significant because 2015 top-end draft prospect Jake Bean is another Calgary Hitmen who came from Edge School, having made the team as an un-drafted tryout. Clearly, the brass in Calgary liked what they got out of Bean, and expect something similar from Nielsen.

Noel, Serron
C - Brockville Braves U18 (HEO) 6'03", 170

Noel was selected second round, 25th overall by the Oshawa Generals at the 2016 OHL Priority Selection Draft out of the Brockville Braves U18 program. Noel is a big kid and stands out every time he is on the ice because he's that much bigger than the other players. He is a really good skater for his size and can move really well laterally up and down the ice. He was awarded Top Prospect award for the HEO League this year. He gives you 100% effort every night he is on the ice and competes hard every shift. He was playing in the 2nd line this year but wasn't giving a whole lot of help and struggled to put up points. Noel some games showed some offensive skill and a good release to his shot, but then there were games where you didn't notice him. Noel needs to get meaner on the ice; with his size he should be physical on the forecheck and making them pay for going into the corner with him. He showed some good speed going wide on defensemen but he needs to go hard to the net with his size, he will open up so much more ice for him and offensive chances. He played well on the penalty kill and has a really good stick and uses it effectively. Noel could be one of those kids that hasn't hit potential yet, and if he does find it he will be a good hockey player at the next level with his size already and skating ability.

Poirier, William
LW – Drummondville Voltigeurs (QMJHL) – 6'01", 192

Poirier was drafted 18th overall by Drummondville last summer after playing his midget year with Châteauguay. He made the Voltigeurs out of training camp and played the full season in Drummondville. He didn't get a lot of playing time during the season, playing mostly on the 4th line, but he started getting promoted into their top line late in the season and we had some good viewings when he was paired with Carcone and Barré-Boulet. Poirier likes to play a physical game, will finish his hits on the forecheck and do the dirty work in front of the net and along the walls. He's not a natural goal scorer; he will need to work hard to get his goals in front of the net at even-strength and on the power play. He also will need to work on improving his speed, agility and explosiveness. His release on his shot will need some improvement as well, but it should be interesting to watch him next season with more ice time. There are not many players coming out of the province of Quebec with a certain skill level and a pro size.

Popov, Sergey
LW - Toronto Jr. Canadiens (GTHL) 5'09", 150

Popov was selected in the 2nd round, 38th overall at the 2016 OHL Priority Selection Draft by the Kingston Frontenacs out of the Toronto Jr. Canadiens Minor Midget Program. Sergey was often in on the offense in every game he played and he showed excellent play making ability. He has good vision in the offensive zone and he can thread the needle with passes just as good as anyone in the 2016 OHL Priority Selection Draft. He is a big undersized but he is very tough on his skates and hard to knock off the puck. He has slick hands and can makes quick moves to beat you out of traffic, or use smaller but more effective moves going east to west when given space in the neutral zone. He has a really good shot and can pick the top corner from anywhere in the offensive zone. He has a strong skating stride and is very quick on his edges which allows him to make quick turn or change direction quickly when in possession of the puck. While on the sideboard on the power play, Popov likes to look for a teammate sneaking into the back-door where he will make a skilled saucer pass over sticks to give his teammate a tap in goal. He protects the puck well on the boards and can kill off some important seconds on the penalty kill by holding puck deep in the offensive zone. Popov has a very high hockey IQ and he plays a 200ft game.

Popowich, Tyler
LC - Vancouver Giants (WHL) 6'04" 190

Popowich, the third overall pick in last year's bantam draft, is a big local kid from Surrey who plays a mean and physical game with some offensive skill sprinkled in. We had the opportunity to watch Popowich play for his Giants club during pre-season camp and during some tryout games this season. At least physically speaking, he already appears dominant out there. Consistency has been a bit of an issue, but that's not surprising given that he was the youngest player on the ice by a country mile. On the surface at least, he's exactly what the Vancouver Giants organization has been looking for since the graduation of Milan Lucic.

If all goes according to plan, we should see Popowich make his full-time debut with the Giants this season. The biggest knock on him at this point is his skating, which is understandable given his huge frame and obvious physical immaturity. There are definitely times when he looks a bit awkward and uncoordinated, but he's been plying his trade with the Okanagan Hockey Academy for a few years now and recently scored more than a point-per-game (G, 15 A, 27) in the highly competitive CSSHL league, so we know that he can find ways to put the puck in the net.

Popowich has a fairly good shot and sees the ice well. Because he's so big, he's also able to bully his way into high-opportunity areas and is very hard to move from the prime scoring zone. Perhaps his best skill, however, is his ability to wreak havoc along the boards or below the goal-line with his pure physicality. He's a really difficult player to combat with when he's forechecking as he throws big hits, is really competitive in the corners or along the walls, and can use his big frame and reach to block clearance attempts. Popowich can be a one man wrecking crew at times. He just needs to bring that night-in and night-out, especially if he wants to be a part of steering his Vancouver Giants organization onto the right track.

Rippon, Merrick
LD - Ottawa Jr. Senators (HEO) 6'01, 175

Rippon was selected in the second round, 36th Overall by the Kitchener Rangers at the 2016 OHL Priority Selection Draft out of the Ottawa Jr. Senators U18 program. Merrick is a good two way defensemen that plays for the Ottawa Jr.Sens of the new HEO AAA league and was named top defensemen in the league. He is a good size defensemen with really good skating ability, whether it's skating forward with the puck or transitioning backwards; he has a very good skating stride as well. Merrick has a very good and hard first pass coming out of the zone, he is also a very smart offensive defensemen which generated 29 pts in 43 games from the blue line, where he finished 3rd in the league in scoring for defense. He has a very good shot from the point as well where he scored 12 goals and 5 of those goals were on the power play. He is good in his defensive zone, very reliable defensemen and shows no panic in his game when faced with pressure. He can also play a physical game if needed and makes forwards pay when coming into his zone. Merrick just needs to get stronger in his upper body, and he will be a very effective defensemen and a player to watch at the next level.

Roberts, Connor
RW - Hamilton Jr. Bulldogs (SCTA) 6'00", 184

Roberts was selected first round, third overall out of the Grey-Bruce Highlanders program by the Hamilton Bulldogs at the 2015 OHL Priority Selection Draft. The first thing that jumps out at you is his size; the next thing is his powerful snap shot. He has one of the hardest, if not the hardest snap shot in his age group among OHL Drafted prospects and he looks to use it as much as possible. In many of our viewings Roberts would look to shoot as soon as he walked over the blue line. This resulted is a few goals but more often than not he struggled to hit the net. Consistency was also a big concern in our viewings, at times Roberts looked complacent or disinterested in the games and other times he looked like he could have been the top prospect in the entire draft. He has excellent size and is built like a prototypical power forward. However his game doesn't always relate to his physical stature. We would like to see Roberts play with more aggression and physicality at the next level; this will make him tougher to play against as well as create space for his line mates. Although he played center all year, we see him more suitable on the wing. This will allow him to get in on the fore check quicker, use his shot more effectively coming down the wing and have less responsibility in the defensive zone.

Robertson, Carter
LD - York-Simcoe Express (ETA), 6'01", 150

Robertson was selected in the second round, 30th overall by the Ottawa 67's at the 2016 OHL Priority Selection Draft. out of the York-Simcoe Express Minor Midget program. A tall, lanky rearguard, Robertson skates very well and possesses the skills and hockey sense to be succeed at the next level. Defending his own end, he uses his size and reach effectively and competes hard to win battles. Driven to defend his net, Robertson is also more than willing to get out and block point shots. Developing his ability to keep it simple in transition, Robertson can still be a bit of risk-taker which can work against him at times. He has the skills to play both sides of the ice and move the puck on his backhand effectively. His skating has improved and he is developing his ability to find open ice to escape oncoming checkers. Offensively, Robertson delivers one of the hardest point shots in the ETA. He is also willing to jump off the line when he sees an opportunity. In possession down low, he has used his reach effectively a few times this year surprising goalies with a crafty deke move. Robertson is one the top defense prospects in the ETA and is projected as a top four defenseman at the next level.

Rodrigue, Olivier
Goaltender – Élites de Jonquière (LHMAAAQ) - 6'00", 146

Rodrigue is the goaltender with the best potential coming out of the Quebec Midget AAA league. He was selected to be part of the U-16 Team Quebec roster, and also the Team Canada that played in the Youth Olympic Games in Norway. At this tournament, he was the backup behind fellow draft-eligible Alexis Gravel who won the starting job. With an excellent technique, Rodrigue is really quick in his movements and is always square to shooters. He's very solid in odd-man rushes or on breakaways. He tracks the puck very well, using good rebound-control, and is calm in his crease. He had some average games, most notably in the playoffs, but has the ability to bounce back after a bad performance or a bad goal. He's really focused in his crease and reads the play well in front of him. Finally, he's one of the rare 15 year old goaltenders to not go in the butterfly position too quickly. When he does use it, he's very efficient with his pads to redirect pucks out of the danger zone.

Roman, Milos
LC – HC Trinec U20 (CZE) – 5'11", 194

Milos Roman is a Slovakian center playing in the Czech U20 league with HC Trinec. Roman has produced slightly above the point per game pace there. He has also appeared with Slovakia's national u18 team. Roman is a cerebral center who reads the game well. Although he doesn't impress with an elite skill level, he plays the game mature beyond his years. He's an opportunistic scorer and has good playmaking skills. Most surprisingly for his age, his positioning without the puck and defensive reads are already quite good. He uses his stick well to break up plays. Although, his game isn't very defined yet, he is coming along nicely for the 2018 NHL draft as he shows quality reads, a decent skill level and a surprisingly mature approach to the game.

Schmidt, Colin
C – Wayzata H.S. (MN-HS) 6'04", 205

Colin is a power center who has good skills with the puck and soft hands for a big kid but prefers using power moves and using his size to push players around. Schmidt is hard to contain already and will only get better as his skating and footwork improve. His skating isn't poor by any means, but we feel once he gets stronger in the lower body is stride will smoothen out. Colin uses his size well in the faceoff circle, often just using brute force to win possession. The University of Minnesota commit has a couple of years until he finds himself on campus, his USHL rights are held by the Waterloo Black Hawks, who took him 10th overall in the 2016 Futures Draft, given his size and overall ability Schmidt could find himself playing in the USHL next season if he feels inclined, our feeling is he returns to Wayzata High School for at least one more season.

Skarek, Jakub
G – HC Dukla Jihlava (CZE 2) – 6'01", 165

Skarek is a agile goaltender with a calm demeanour. It's hard to believe when you first see him play that he is a '99 born playing professional hockey. He has great body awareness and moves with the maturity of a veteran. Great patience on his feet. Skarek needs to work on assessing game threats better, but that will come with more time and development. Lots of potential.

He spent most of the season with the men's team that competes in the second tier professional league. He also had an impressive playoff series where he was called upon in the final series and helped Dukla Jihlava win the playoff championship. Also saw game time in the promotion series where his club was unable to secure promotion to the Extraliga.

Smith, Ty
LD - Spokane Chiefs (WHL) 5'11" 170

After not only playing but thriving as the youngest member on a gold medal winning Team Alberta at the 2015 Canada Winter Games, Ty Smith went to the Spokane Chiefs 1st overall in that year's WHL Bantam Draft. Smith has yet to make much of a splash in the WHL, but he's a name worth keeping an eye on. He's a speedy and offensively charged defenseman with hockey IQ off the charts. Although he's not terribly big, he plays a powerful game, especially in the offensive zone.

Smith is very dangerous along the blueline thanks to great lateral mobility, excellent passing skills, and plenty of shooting options. He has a really great d-to-d sweeping pass that lies flat on the ice and is very easy to receive. He often initiates long passing plays in the offensive zone with that pass, as it seems to have a calming effect on his teammates. His shot is excellent, too, usually preceded by a quick head fake to keep opposition goaltenders guessing. He has he has that rare ability to control the pace of the game at his own will. His decision making with the puck is simply outstanding for his age.

He's a great stickhandler, a great passer, and is very creative, so he's almost able to buy himself some time and space or to find a unique way to get himself out of a jam. We're almost certain that the Spokane Chiefs were hoping Ty would get a lot bigger over the course of this season, but he still has plenty of time for one last spurt. Even when outsized, though, he finds ways to gain an advantage in body positioning. He led all fifteen-year-olds in WHL in plus-minus with a plus-five over just two games. It's really difficult to project guys at the bantam draft, but it looks like Spokane may have stumbled upon a winner.

Stratis, Peter
RD - Mississauga Rebels (GTHL) 5'11.25", 182

Stratis was selected in the first round, 11th overall by the Ottawa 67's at the 2016 OHL Priority Selection Draft out of the Mississauga Rebels Minor Midget program. Peter is a very mobile defender with excellent puck skills who consistently is able to move the puck out of dangerous areas by either making a solid pass or skillfully skating the puck to open ice. He always has his head up in possession and is able to make hard, accurate passes to teammates heading up ice with speed. He isn't overly physical defensively but he has thrown some big hits along the boards this season. Stratis makes his biggest impact in game while on the power play. He was the Rebels trigger man from the high slot and he looked to shoot the puck any chance he got. He has one of the best snap shots out of the defensemen in this draft and he was able to consistently score from start to finish. At time, especially when his team was trailing, Stratis would try to force shots through from the point and he was unsuccessful a lot of the time shooting it into shin pads. He needs to take his time more with the puck on the point and look over his options before deciding to shoot all the time. Stratis projects to be a very good two-way defender at the next level who will be a successful contributor on the power play and even strength play.

Struthers, Matthew
LC - Owen Sound Attack (OHL) 6'01", 180

Struthers was selected in the third round of the 2015 OHL Priority Selection Draft by the Owen Sound Attack out of the Halton Hurricanes Minor Midget program. Struthers had a solid opening season with the Attack playing a bottom six role. Struthers has good size and can protect the puck well. He has good skill with the puck and can be dangerous in the offensive zone. He skates well and can carry the puck confidently when necessary. Struthers got some action on the second power play unit but has some room for improvement in regards to some of his passing. Struthers has good offensive tools that will be on higher display with increased ice in offensive situations as older players move on and he can move up the depth chart. His late birthdate will also be helpful for his development with an extra year of exposure before becoming eligible for the 2018 NHL Entry Draft.

Svechnikov, Andrei
RW - Ak Bars Kazan U18 (RUS) – 6'02", 176

The younger brother of Evgeny has been dominating the Russian younger junior leagues with his superior power and skills for a couple of years. This season he's faced some tougher competition in international tournaments going up against older opponents and inevitably in those circumstances he has shown the need to polish his game a bit to adjust to the higher level. However, even at the U18 Worlds as the tournament progressed he had flashes where he displayed his impressive offensive arsenal as a double underager.

A left-shooting winger with every tool at his disposal to be a high pick in 2018, Svechnikov likes to power his way to the net with or without the puck. What stands out for him is his remarkable top speed paired with the capability to finish plays at such speed. He also already possesses a potent shot with a terrific release. Andrei certanly doesn't lack skills and creativity with the puck either. In our viewings he was not a consistent dominant force, but could make skill plays and see plays that are not teachable. Examples we have seen from him would include a pass off the boards to himself to beat a defenseman before deking towards the middle as well as a blind backhand pass from behind the net into the slot that his linemate didn't expect to receive.

Going forward, the challenge for Svechnikov will be remaining as effective while adjusting to having a smaller edge on his opponents in terms of power and speed. One aspect he will certainly have to improve on is bringing a more consistent effort shift-by-shift, where his high-end plays are supported by stronger play in between. As of now, he projects as a power forward with skills and great scoring ability.

Thomas, Akil
RC - Toronto Marlboros (GTHL) 5'09.75", 151

Thomas was selected in the first round, 12th overall by the Niagara Ice Dogs at the 2016 OHL Priority Selection Draft out of the Toronto Marlboros Minor Midget program. There is a lot to like about Akil's offensive skillset. He passes the puck with pinpoint accuracy and has one of the hardest wrist shots in the GTHL. Akil has a high hockey IQ and is at his best when he's entering the zone with speed and creating space by driving the defense back. He possesses elite puck skills and has the ability to elude defenders long enough for a passing lane to open up. A strong skater, Akil uses his strength to win corner battles and fight off checks to create offensive chances for himself and his line mates. His puck control, at top speed, both on the forehand and backhand is very good and his quick release often surprises goalies. Akil supports the puck very well and is a consistent threat with the puck on his stick. Defensively, Akil positions himself effectively in his own zone and has a very good stick. While he's not the biggest he uses his strength very well and does a good job of stripping pucks from opponents.

Tkachuk, Brady
LC – USNTDP U17 6'00", 176
The younger brother of Matthew Tkachuk, Brady has performed well for USNTDP's U17 team and brings certain qualities to the table that are quite similar to his brother. Although not entirely similar in style of play, Brady boasts some of that same stingy approach his brother possesses. Brady already shows signs of leadership ability and we have liked his willingness to work and change the tide into his team's favor. In key moments, Brady can put together a string of quality competitive shifts. He's a honest center who exhibits good hockey IQ and plays the game hard in the corners and in front of the net. He has also shown good vision with and without the puck as he reads the soft spots that develop in the slot and in front of the net well but can also distribute the puck.

Tucker, Tyler
LD - Toronto Titans (GTHL) 6'00", 201
Tucker was selected in the first round, 14th overall by the Barrie Colts at the 2016 OHL Priority Selection Draft out of the Toronto Titans Minor Midget program. Tyler was one of the most physical players in the entire 2016 OHL Draft which was a key reason he went off the board so early. He makes his impact in games by being very physical which makes him a tough defender to play against. After missing the first part of the season, it didn't take long for opposing player's to realize that they need to keep their heads up at all times while Tucker was on the ice. His biggest hits came against players skating through the neutral zone with speed. He has good skating ability which allows him to get into position quickly and lower his shoulder into the opposing player's chest. While playing this style every game, Tucker didn't take too many bad penalties as he more often than not kept his elbows down and go low enough to avoid the player's head. He has a good shot from the point and will rush the puck when given time and space but he rarely tries to force it. One aspect of Tucker's game that he will need to improve is his first pass out of the zone. He would at times try to force tough passes when he had a simpler option that would have been more effective. At the next level he will need to understand his role as a hard hitting defensive defenseman which will limit his mistakes and turnovers. Tucker's physical style of play could make him a real fan favorite has the capability to become a fan favourite for whichever team takes him at the 2016 OHL Draft.

Vallati, Giovanni
LD - Vaughan Kings (GTHL) 6'00.5", 186
Vallati was selected in the first round, 16th Overall by the Kitchener Rangers at the 2016 OHL Priority Selection Draft out of the Vaughan Kings Minor Midget program. Giovanni is a big, athletic defenseman who had a strong year for the Vaughan Kings. He is an excellent skater that looks to jump into the rush and create offense whenever possible. He does a good job of getting pucks through from the point and has shown the ability to make difficult passes through traffic. He has very good vision with puck which allows him to create some very nice plays for his teammates. Vallati has a very active stick when playing in the defensive zone which has made it difficult for the opposition to beat him one on one. He plays tough along the wall but not overly physical. Despite playing on the back end, Vallati

was the catalyst for his team offensively and was really the only player who was able to consistently generate offence for his team. Vallati struggled with injuries late in the season which didn't allow him to be as effective as he was throughout the regular season, but he is still one of the best defensemen to come out of this age group.

Veleno, Joseph
LC – Saint-John Sea Dogs (QMJHL) – 6'01", 177

The first-ever player to get exceptional status in the QMJHL, Veleno had a solid first year in the league, reaching the 40-point barrier while playing most of the year on a 3rd line. The former Lac St-Louis Lion saw ice time on the power play this year, mostly on the 2nd unit, and also played as an underager at the U-17 Hockey Challenge in November. What makes Veleno special is his hockey smarts. Even at 15 years old, he makes smart plays in his own zone and always works hard on the backcheck, creating turnovers by stealing pucks with his quick stick. He's very advanced at his age with his play away from the puck. He's a great skater with a great burst of speed and can beat defensemen wide that way. He has a good wrist shot, but could become more dangerous if he could add more velocity to it. His backhand shot is still very good, with good velocity; it is tough for goaltenders to track where the puck will go. He's willing to play a physical game and likes to compete, but at this point, he lacks enough strength to combat the physically stronger players in this league. As with many young centers, he will need to improve his faceoff game. Veleno will get more playing time next season, and we expect a big improvement in his production. The Sea Dogs will be a contender for the league championship next season.

Villeneuve, Gabriel
LD – Élites de Jonquière (LHMAAAQ) - 5'10", 173

Villeneuve is a skilled defenseman who can play well at both ends of the ice. He has a good, accurate shot, and varies his shot very well as both his wrist and slapshot are above-average. He played all year on Jonquière's first power play unit, and he's agile on his feet. On the power play, he's very active in the offensive zone, not standing still and making things happen. He communicates well with his teammates on the ice, and supports the play well by becoming a 4th forward on the ice. Defensively, he has good positioning, is efficient to clear the puck out of his zone and has a good first pass. He can at times make risky passes that can lead to turnovers, but his hockey sense helps him minimize those. He was a very good find by Jonquière in the off-season, as he's originally from Trois-Rivières and was playing in the LHPS the year before.

Wahlstrom, Oliver
C - Shattuck St. Mary's (MN-HS) 6'01", 174

Wahlstrom, from Yarmouth, Maine spent the 15/16 season with the Shattuck St. Mary's Prep team where he looked far from out of place despite in some cases playing against some players 3 years older than he was, putting up 26 goals and 52 points in 43 games. The Harvard Commit was one of SSM's most effective forwards throughout this season.

Wahlstrom is good at setting the table in the offensive zone, he thinks the game at a high pace and has great vision of the zone which allows him to move the puck quickly and thread passes through the slot. He also possesses excellent finishing ability with a powerful shot with a quick release. Wahlstrom needs to continue to work on the finer aspects of his skating but is far from a concern at this stage. Wahlstrom did tend to keep his game on the perimeter a bit too much in our viewings and will only become more effective the more he is willing to move the play to the middle of the ice and the front of the net. Because he spends a lot of the game playing a perimeter game he can go stretches without being noticed or making any impact on the game if he doesn't have the puck. Oliver has a solid frame at 6'1" and can already be difficult to separate from the puck, even against older and stronger players.

Wahlstrom possesses elite physical attributes with his skating, puck skills, shooting ability and hockey IQ but like many young players he needs be more consistent in finding a way to make an impact on a game when the puck isn't on his stick. Wahlstrom will be heading the USNTDP in 16/17 and is on pace to being one of the top prospects for the 2018 NHL Draft.

Wilde, Bode
RD - Chicago Mission U16 (HPHL) 6'02", 181

Wilde was selected second round, 35th Overall at the 2016 OHL Priority Selection Draft by the Saginaw Spirit out of the Chicago Mission U16 program. Bode is a big smooth skating defender who shows the ability to play an effective two-way game. He shows a lot of poise with the puck whether he is breaking out of the zone or manning the point on the power play. He has quick hands which allow him to beat opponents with quick east to west moves, or make quick backhand or forehand passes to set up a give and go for him to enter the neutral zone with speed. He has a very good stick in the defensive zone but he will need to become more aggressive along the walls and in front of the net in order the win more battles. Bode sits second overall on ranking list after leading the way all season long. While many of Wilde's tools are high-end, we felt that he could be slightly better in some of his decision making both with and without the puck. While we thought Bode might end up in the OHL with Guelph, it looks like the Montreal born Dman will play with the USNTDP next season.

Weiss, Tyler
LC - Don Mills Flyers (GTHL) 5'09.5", 140

Weiss was selected first round, 15th overall at the 2016 OHL Priority Selection Draft by the Sarnia Sting out of the Don Mills Flyers Minor Midget program. Tyler is a high-end talent and with blazing speed and an effortless stride is one of the most impactful players in the GTHL. Always a threat, Tyler has impressed with his ability to track down loose pucks and often make something out of nothing. His speed and puck handling skills often allow him to create his own zone entries. Tyler excels through the neutral zone, weaving through traffic and entering the zone. Upon entering the zone on his off wing, Tyler is most effective cutting back to the middle where he frequently surprises goalies by shooting back to his right with a strong hard wrist shot or making a quality no-look pass to an open teammate. Adding more stop and start to his tremendous skating ability would make Tyler even more effective. At times, recognizing when to move the puck has been a challenge for Tyler. Often it appears like he has enough speed to gain ice even deeper in the offensive zone, but he chooses to pass the puck to a teammate who may not be in a better position. Defensively, Tyler makes good reads picking up the trailer and takes away passing lanes. For Tyler to reach his full potential, he will need to add some strength to his frame and a physical element to his game. He is expected to play for the United States National Team Development Program next season.

Wismer, Jack
RW - Hamilton Jr. Bulldogs (SCTA) 6'00", 184

Wismer was selected second round, 41st overall out of the Hamilton Jr. Bulldogs program by the Flint Firebirds at the 2016 OHL Priority Selection Draft. Jack is a big power forward that was a consistent offensive threat every game this season. He has great size and he uses it to overpower his opponents and play his game in the dirty areas. His favourite move is taking the defenseman wide, lowering his inside shoulder and taking the puck hard to the net where he will either finish or create a rebound for one of his line mates to clean up. Although he isn't the quickest skater he is able to gain good body position on his opponents which allows him to consistently beat defenders without having to be too creative. He has a very hard, accurate snap shot that he likes to use in one on one situations where he will use the defender as a screen. His scored some big goals for his team this year and stepped up majority of the time when his team needed it most. Defensively, Wismer did his job getting pucks out and sticking to his point man. Wismer projects to be a very good power forward at the next level where he will look to be a consistent offensive producer. Adding some more separation speed will add an element to his game that will allow him to be more effective at playing his style. Wismer has very appealing upside due to his ability to play a pro style game reminiscent of a Remi Elie.

Woo, Jett
LD - Moose Jaw Warriors (WHL) 6'00" 153

Like Ty Smith, Jett Woo was one of only a handful of fourteen-year-olds to make an appearance at the Canada Winter Games as a fourteen-year-old, representing Team Manitoba. Woo is a strong-skating offensive defenseman who combines excellent footwork with soft slick hands. Blessed with strong skating mechanics and really natural edgework, Woo is able to elude all players in all three zones.

That type of advanced skating ability also allows Woo to track his checks like a hawk, quickly eliminating gaps or instinctively closing up passing lanes with a smart poke. For a defenseman who plays so well and so dependably on the back end, Woo has incredible instincts off the rush, especially in terms of his passing ability. We saw him make some really nice no-look and behind the back dishes this year that left goaltenders feeling silly.

Woo has his flaws. He can look a bit shellshocked when an opposition player gets past him with the puck. He suffers from a bit of a low panic threshold at this point and sometimes wanders out of position trying to make a big play. Therefore, his defensive game can be a bit erratic at times, so slowing things down and acquiring some on-ice maturity will probably be his goals going into next season.

Zabransky, Libor
RD - HC Kometa Brno U18/U20 (CZE) 6'00", 190

One of the youngest players on Brno's U20 team when he was called up, but consistently was on the first line and logged lots of ice time. Very smooth skating defenseman, that oozes confidence with the puck on his stick. Doesn't get rattled easily and shows lots of maturity for his age - especially playing against guys five years older than him. Was used regularly on first power play unit and first penalty kill unit. His first three steps backwards generates lots of power and speed allowing good gap control. Looks to make the simple pass but isn't afraid to carry the puck. Father, also named Libor and a defenseman, was a St. Louis Blues draft pick in 1995 and is currently head coach/general manager/owner for Kometa Brno. Zabransky helped lead his U18 team to a national championship this year, getting 11 points in 10 games.

Zadina, Filip
LW – HC Pardubice U20 (CZE) – 6'00", 187

Zadina is a winger that has had plenty of success domestically and internationally. He's already scoring at about 0.5 goals per game right for HC Pardubice U20 and has performed well for Czech Republic at the U17 and U18 level. Even at the U18s in North Dakota, Zadina looked entirely comfortable even being one of the better players on the ice against older competition. Zadina already has a reasonably sturdy frame and generates good speed with it. He's got good acceleration as well as top speed and uses it accordingly. Zadina boasts both above-average smarts as well as a good compete level. He has a good shot that he can score with from outside or get involved from up-close around the net. He makes good plays with the puck but has really distinguished himself as a scorer first. His game has certain power-forward qualities to it as he likes to challenge the defense. He looks like a player that should have the ability to be a high pick in 2018 if his development stays on track.

SCOUTS GAME REPORTS

Sweden vs Switzerland, Ivan Hlinka Memorial Tournament, August 10, 2015

Sweden

SWE #13 C Fallstrom, William (2016) - Looks like Fallstrom has added some weight since his last viewing in Swedish J20 playoffs. Strong skater with nice feet. Plants his feet well and can move up the ice with puck efficiently. Can see openings and find seams for passing. Has some tenacity too, likes to strip guys of pucks. Works hard on backcheck and away from the puck. Was complacent with the puck at times though. Scored on a 2v1, got pass at last second and put it in open net.

SWE #23 RW Weissback, Linus (2016) - Player that should have played more ice this game. He is dynamic and can be spark plug. See's the ice really well and can beat players with his speed. Good puck skills - passes, shoots well. Five shot attempts, three on net. Nice assist on second goal, showing puck composure on a 2v1 to dish it across to Fallstrom. Can beat guys 1v1 with his speed and quick hands. Blocked a big shot on PK, hard one-timer and got down in front using proper technique. Worked hard all over the ice. Impressive game for him tonight.

SWE #12 LW Bratt, Jesper (2016) - Good hands, crafty with the puck. Slightly awkward skater, can hunch and keeps legs wide, like he is riding a horse. But despite this, he is strong on his feet and can be fast, protecting puck well on wall. Nice release on shot - scored 3rd goal - wrister from slot.

SWE #28 C Lindstrom, Linus (2016) - Lindstrom was great in the faceoffs tonight – approximately won 75%. Really liked his work ethic – back checked hard. Has a good stride, but needs to get more power in his push. There isn't enough there. Lungs look short, runs out of gas early. Took a check to the knee in the third and left the game – late in game. But came out again.

SWE #26 RW Andersson, Lias (2017) - Good start for Andersson, putting five shots on net. Needs to work on accuracy and finish, but the potential is there. He can be slippery around the net; defenders have to make sure they always have an eye or stick on him, because he can get away easily. Blocked a big shot on a 5v3 tonight, really liked that.

SWE #10 RW Bokvist, Jesper (2017) - Struggled in all parts of the ice tonight and had some scary turnovers tonight – both while on the powerplay in the offensive zone. Needs to work on puck decisions.

SWE #18 C Davidsson, Marcus (2017) - Has grown since last viewing in J18 playoffs, filling out nice. Doesn't have the smooth skating as his older brother, but has a better mind. He works well when away from the puck and thinks the game. Doesn't shy away from the physical play and took a solid hit to make a good play and get the puck out tonight. Strong face-offs too, won over 70% of his draws tonight.

SWE #27 W Stal Lyrenas, Oskar (2016) - Got five shots on net tonight. Has some soft hands and a nice release. Dangerous turnover but made up for it working hard back. Not a pretty skater, labored out there tonight (injury?).

SWE #8 D Tilander, Adam (2017) - Probably played the 2nd most ice tonight (paired with Moverare) out of the defense and for good reason – he worked hard and kept it simple. Showed on the powerplay that he has puck confidence and can get pucks to the net. Nice stride with good power. Even in third period, he showed he had some endurance – outskating guys to lose pucks.

SWE #6 D Moverare, Jacob (2016) - Lots of ice for Moverare tonight. He was workhorse in all zones. His hands have improved since last viewing last season – softer, corals puck well and shields it. But, he over handled a little too much on the point tonight. Still, he got the shots off and showed he has a nice, hard release on net. Some fog on the brain tonight though, settling in to a new season. Couple questionable decisions, but he recovered well.

SWE #3 D Cederholm, Jacob (2016) - Cederholm was the 'big man on campus' tonight - exuding confidence. Knew what he was going to do before he did it. Physical presence and reliable in every end. Had some good jumps into the play tonight. Feet were moving well, getting power. Doesn't push off with his toes enough, in my opinion. Pushes off from back part of his foot. Beautiful goal tonight, game winner, seconds left on clock. Dangled in from the point, moved into the slot and release a well placed shot.

SWE #1 G Gustavsson, Filip (2016) - Gustavsson is a highly technical goaltender that needs to work on athleticism. Has great technique but lacked some initiative and creativity tonight. Had a shaky start, probably nerves, but his footwork was crisp and accurate. Didn't read some situations well – not recognizing a guy backdoor or a opportune moments for shots. He seemed to settle in better as the game went on. Got beat five-hole, and high glove.

Switzerland

SUI #17 W Miranda, Marco (2016) - Miranda's size makes him easy to notice right away. But his footwork is questionable. Doesn't seem like his feet have caught up to his large frame. Miranda reminds of me a 'lunch-pale' kind of guy. Nothing exceptionally special but works hard and grinds it out – forecheck, backcheck, paycheque. Used his frame once to drive the puck to the net.

SUI #13 C Hischier, Nico (2017) - Demonstrated his scoring ability early on the power play. Walked off the wall and let off a quick wrist shot that was destined to go in as soon the puck was off his stick. His first three steps aren't as explosive as they could be, but once he gets momentum going, it's hard to keep up to him. Had a nice breakaway and showed some soft touch.

SUI #11 W Volejnicek, Dominik (2016) - Offensive minded speedy winger that had seven shot attempts, five on net. He wasn't a huge factor tonight until the third period – then it was hard not to notice him. Scored two power play goals – within three minutes – in the third period. First one was a walk up the wall from behind the net - with speed - and got a shot off that I think Gustavsson is still wondering where it went (short side, high glove). The second was a rebound he snatched up off of a Stadler point shot and backhand roofed over a sprawling Gustavsson. Nice hands and good speed, but needs to play a little better with pressure.

SUI #14 D Stadler, Livio (2016) - Skilled puck moving defenseman. Has good poise with the puck and can move really well with it on his stuck. Nice footwork, effortless strides. Ice was really soft tonight (rink temperature was 25'C) and he seemed to get caught in some ruts, but otherwise he has good balance. Quarterbacked the powerplay and demonstrated his ability to get shots through to the net. Really impressed with his puck skills. Worth following more.

SUI #29 G Wuthrich, Philip (2016) - Busy night for Wuthrich as the Swedes has 56 total shot attempts and 40 getting on net. Technically, he knows what to do and execute the proper save selections. However, a weak glove was exposed tonight. He doesn't fully track the puck in to his glove and commits to early on shots. He also gave up some juicy rebounds off his chest, another indication of poor tracking. Is there potential? Definitely. He competes for all his shots and showed that he can make some big saves. But when stretching out for the big save he isn't pushing enough and relies on stretching himself out leaving some holes. He tends to drop his chest down when in the butterfly and this opens his legs, meaning any traffic shots can slip through his five-hole easily.

Final Score: Sweden 4:3 Switzerland

Czech Republic vs Canada, 2015 Ivan Hlinka Memorial Tournament, August 10, 2015

CAN #3 RD Fabbro, Dante (2016) - Fabbro was very impressive in his first viewing for me. His skill set and IQ stood out immediately. He was consistently making the right play and seeing the easy option. He was confident and composed every time the puck was on his stick tonight. Positional wise, he was sound as well and was able to cover for his partner if there was a mistake. He has a great shot – release – from the point. He has the intelligence to QB a powerplay and is usually called upon to kill a penalty kill (and there were plenty penalty kill's for Canada tonight). Good feet, really impressive footwork and hard to get knocked off the puck. Fabbro has a lot of potential; there wasn't a lot not to like in this game tonight.

CAN #29 C Steel, Sam (2016) - Good energy on the ice. He buzzes around and creates havoc for the opposing team when they have the puck. Tenacious is a good word to describe him. He has grit and strength. Moves with ease around the ice and overpowered some players easily tonight – stripping them of the puck. Center is a good position for him as he likes to roam and find his spots of attack. There is a lot to like about Steel and how he plays a hard, faced paced game. Sets the pace.

CAN #8 RW Dubois, Pierre-Luc (2016) - Dubois possesses some high-end puck skills. Displayed this by completing passes that made it look like he had eyes in the back of his head. Nifty playmaker that is hard to defend against. Good vision when the puck is on his stick; finds seams and shoots at opportune moments. Played on the wing with Patrick and Benson.

CAN #9 LW Dube, Dillion (2016) - Highlight real, short-handed goal to open up the scoring for Canada – right after the Czech's scored first. Took a pass on his backhand as he was streaking towards the net, deked the goalie and went backhand high. Great on the penalty kill tonight; aggressive, but smart; stick in lanes; filing lanes. Czech powerplay players will have nightmares about him. Fast, great three steps. Angles well and knows how to use his body. Playmaker as well, made some nice plays. Strong performance from him tonight

CAN #2 LD Bean, Jake (2016) - Had some good gaps tonight, showed ability to shutdown some attacks and had a nice assist on Malenstyn's goal. However, that was it for Bean tonight. Struggled to find momentum, fought the puck and cause some turnovers. Simple passes became complicated. Not a good night, but luckily it is early.

CAN #23 LD Girrard, Sam (2016) - Had a nervous first period; panicked with the puck a bit in his first two shifts. Settled down and in the third has some great escapes from pressure in his zone and was make good, crisp first passes. Had some good, hard, punishing hits tonight as well.

CAN #18 RD Quenneville, David (2016) - Showed some intelligence and grit tonight. Recognized threats and played conservative when required. Stopped a 3-on-1. Blocked two shots tonight as well.

CAN #19 C Patrick, Nolan (2017) - Patrick has speed and skill, but is young and it is noticeable at times. Some nervous situations for him early on in the game. Had a penalty shot in the third, but bobbled after trying to slow down and perform a move that reminded me of Patrick Kane.

CAN #5 LD Mahura, Josh (2016) - Lot of positives in his game tonight. Jumped up into rushes at right moments. Has good footwork and good gap control. Used his stick properly to stop attackers.

CAN #22 C McLeod, Mike (2016) - Worked really hard tonight. Got into a good groove and consistently had good shifts throughout the game. Showed his playmaking abilities and had clean crisp passes. Smart with his puck decisions and was smart away from the puck. Without the puck he was really fast, but a couple of times he struggled to move as fast with the puck. Good in the faceoff circle, was very dependable.

CAN #11 W Malenstyn, Beck (2016) - Not a lot to talk about in this game besides demonstrating that he can hit hard. Not afraid to through his weight around. Had a sneaky goal, took pass on his backhand from Bean and released quickly on Brizgala. Brizgala lost the puck after hitting him and Malenstyn kept his eye on puck and tapped it in – mid-air.

CAN #26 W Kaspick, Tanner (2016) - Demonstrated good puck control along the well. Was strong on his feet. Want to see him work back harder.

CAN #17 W Benson, Tyler (2016) - Primarily played on the wing tonight but in key offensive zone situations he would take the draw and usually win. Benson has soft hands, very very soft hands. He is crafty in tight and can dizzy a goaltender.

CAN #21 W Howden, Brett (2016) - Played a lot of PK minutes and was effective at anticipating weaknesses in the Czech powerplay. He plays a simple game but needs to work on his finish more. Even though the puck is on his stuck, he doesn't get it to the net enough. Want to see him be more crisp and execute better.

CAN #28 D W Mete, Victor (2016) - I like his effort and the way he can shutdown attacks. Nice hit tonight, felt it in stands. Strong, agile skater. He was little cavalier with the puck tonight. But overall, a good game from him.

CAN #7 C Jost, Tyson (2016) - Took time adjusting to the bigger ice. He is a smart hockey player that possesses some great wheels. He can move the puck very well, and skates well with the puck – agile and smooth. Wasn't his sharpest game though, but looking forward to seeing how he makes adjustments for the next game. Really like him centering Dube, paired well and fed off of each other.

CAN #14 RW Bitten, William (2016) - Really like how Bitten plays. A skillful playmaker with soft hands and gritty. Dizzied some defenders tonight with is magic hands. Great in the corners tonight, protecting the puck, fighting for lose pucks. A lot to like about his game tonight and how hard he works. Looking forward to seeing more of him.

CAN #31 G Hart, Carter (2016) - Nerves had the best of him in the first period as he bobbled rebounds. Could tell ice was soft around his crease, as he couldn't seem to get good footing. But once he settled in, he shutdown the Czechs. Didn't see a lot of action in the first period, but in third when his teammates let off the gas pedal, he was calm and made some key saves. One thing I noticed his when he pushes to his left side (glove side) he doesn't seal up his five-hole as quickly as he does when pushing to this right (blocker side). Leaves his stick behind him. In tight, this can pose a problem as puck can sneak through. Also needs to work on giving up fewer rebounds from his glove hand.

CZE #1 G Brizgala, Adam (2016) - Was really the lone shining light in this game. Without his effort tonight the score would have been a blowout. A very unique style that doesn't rely on proper technique and structure. Looks like his chest protector is three sizes too big for him. Relies on being positionally sound. When on his knees, generates lots of power – almost too much. He over pushed a few times tonight. Canada outshot Czechs 25-9 when the teams were 5on5. He is a great competitor and never gives up on a shots. Sinks really low in his stance, shrinking himself before a shot comes. Comes off his post too early sometimes. Athletic goaltender with lots of compete in him.

CZE #3 D Hajek, Libor (2016) - Jumps up in play well, he had a nice puck rush that lead to the lone goal. Good physical presence on the ice and showed a couple of times he can stop some quick attackers. Got some shots on net and showed he can rush the puck. Took a dirty penalty though in the game, I didn't like that.

CZE #27 W Kofron, David (2017) - Struggled with the pressure and pace of the game. Had a few turnovers, including two in one shift.

CZE #10 W Najman, Ondrej (2016) - Najman demonstrated he had some quick, soft hands when the puck was on his stick and could skate with the puck at a high speed.

CZE #18 W Kanter, Matyas (2016) - Nice frame on him, looks thick. Got the lone goal for the Czechs early in the first period by crashing the net on a shot and picking up the rebound.

CZE #9 D Budik, Vojtech (2016) - Has a pro ready frame but wasn't agile tonight. Lacked some speed and good pivots. Has a great shot that is hard and deceptive.

CZE # 22 C Reichel, Kristian (2016) - Struggled against Canada's top line to really produce much. But he didn't give up, and worked hard through out the night. Didn't show much finesse (didn't have much of a chance).

CZE #19 C Kodytek, Petr (2016) - Great effort, didn't quit at all tonight. Speedy little forward that is relentless. Rushed down the wing and got off a hard slap shot with pressure on him.
Final Score: Czech Republic 1:3 Canada

Finland vs USA, Hlinka Memorial Tournament, August 10th, 2015

FIN #6 LD Niemelainen, Markus (2016) - Looked stronger early on. He is a workhorse type of defenseman. Has shown ability in wall battles, sealing off forwards from puck. Had an active stick and broke up some plays with a pokecheck. Did not have tons of activity offensively, but has shown a decent if simple outlet throughout the game.

FIN #8 RD Reunanen, Tarmo (2016) - Had a solid game without much flash. Moves decently well and very engaging physically despite smaller stature. Doesn't take any nonsense from opposition and will respond to any type of yapping or questionable plays. Bites back physically. Didn't spend much time with the puck, but had quick accurate outlets and used his body well to block opposing forwards. Usually passed to first available option.

FIN #14 C Makinen, Otto (2016) - Played a responsible two-way game down the middle. Seemed sturdy on his skates even though he lacked in explosiveness as well as top-end speed. Showed good vision and intelligence for the game, and there were hints of some ability to execute a higher-end play, but it seems like his feet struggle to keep up with the rest of his game. Had a good game mostly utilizing his reads, good scoring instincts. Scored twice and added an assist. Wore an A.

FIN #18 LW Kuokkanen, Janne (2016) - Had some good wall plays both to win loose pucks as well as to extend the cycle. Energy level was good and moved his feet. Did not create much through skill plays. His center Makinen, was the main catalyst in this game, although Kuokkanen provided a nice complimentary role adding two assists.

FIN #19 RW Tuulola, Eetu (2016) - Feet need to improve quite a bit, but plays at a heavy weight for his age. Scored a goal with a wrister off a faceoff win and added an assist. Showed his shot throughout and was looking to get into holes where he could release it. Threw his body around quite a bit.

FIN #23 RD Salo, Robin (2017) - Excellent puck-movement, kept it simple yet made high-end decisions time after time. Defended well with his body as well as stick. Competed well. Tremendous intelligence both in offensive and defensive reads. Had a lot of puck-touches and controlled the flow of the game from the back. Skating was OK, could use improvement. Skill level is decent, but relies more on his reads than ability with the puck. Had a one-timer goal from the point.

FIN #24 C Somppi, Otto (2016) - Best player on the ice in the first period, slightly cooled off throughout the game. Played with high intensity, attacked and won loose pucks, puck distribution was effective and showed good reads in getting open. Controlled offensive zone in first period, even though he slowed down, he was never a liability in the game. Responsible defensively. Wore an A. Ended the game with a goal and an assist.

FIN #27 LD Valimaki, Juuso (2017) - Held his own on the first pairing. Had decent puck-movement, reads were OK but not high-end. Did not hurt you but did not show excellent decision-making either. Was impressive in some offensive rushes, has ability to penetrate forward and got involved offensively. Captained the team. Defensively he was fine, willing to use his body but he isn't very big.

FIN #28 RD Jokiharju, Henri (2017) - Had a quiet game, however not necessarily a bad one. Simple yet effective puck-movement. Defensively he is positionally solid, but not very physical. Had a fluid and intelligent game, but looked like he was capable of showing more authority on the ice than he has. Had an assist.

USA #3 RD Eliot, Mitch (2016) - Wore C for USA. Was up and down defensively, certainly competed but got outmatched physically on a couple of shifts. He was one of the few US defensemen who was trying to make something happen offensively. He was one of the few showing the will to play up to Finland's pace and try to create movement from the back-end, with mixed results.

USA #5 LD Gleason, Benjamin (2016) - He did a decent job with simple outlets. Held back offensively, didn't really try much, preferring a conservative style of game. Skating is fluid and uses it well in break-outs. He is a bit on the smaller side but despite that isn't too shy about physical contact. Did not have any notable mistakes, but also didn't contribute much.

USA #6 RD Peeke, Andrew (2016) - Similar to his partner Rossini, he had the size and was engaging enough to break up the Finnish cycle a couple of times but outside of some easy first-option outlets, he didn't show much on the offensive side here.

USA #8 LD Rossini, Samuel (2016) - Formed a big pairing with his partner Peeke (6'2, 6'3 respectively). Rossini showed good compete in defending against some of the bigger Finnish forwards, but struggled to get anything going on the offensive side of the puck.

USA #11 RW Gettinger, Tim (2016) - Looked a bit awkward on skates at his 6'5 200, but wasn't atrocious in overall mobility. Kept it simple, played to his strengths and scored by going to the net and deflecting a pass for the only US goal in the game.

USA #18 C Mittelstadt, Casey (2017) - Tough game for any American as they got thoroughly outplayed. Mittelstadt was one of the few who managed to get some sustained offensive zone time and flashed his playmaking ability, dissecting the offensive zone with his passes. He has decent size and does a good job protecting the puck with his back turned against the checker.

USA #22 RW Yamamoto, Kailer (2017) - Looked skilled and slick with a nice fluid stride. Outside of an early chance where he went to the net, he spent the rest of the game around the puck, looking for an opening he could pounce on, but never quite fully involved. Too much of a perimeter game today, his skill-level is obvious but didn't get any results in the game.

Slovakia vs Russia, Hlinka Memorial Tournament, August 10th, 2015

SVK #1 G Koziak, Jan (2016) - As a smaller goalie, he has struggled in his lateral movement often lacking in explosiveness and had lethargic recovery, also gave up several rebounds that ended up lying in front of him. Some of the goals he didn't have a chance on, but he didn't help his cause in this game.

SVK #15 RD Bodak, Martin (2017) - Not very big, but competed. Did well in moving the puck as a passer but also showed comfort in skating with the puck himself. Capable of moving it out of danger on his own. Had a secondary assist in the game.

SVK #17 LW Bucek, Samuel (2017) - He came ready to play. Moved his feet and was aggressive on the forecheck, he is adept at gaining inside body position and stealing pucks away in tight spaces. Showed some good puck protection and ability to sustain zone time for his team as well, had a primary assist on a 3 on 2 off the rush goal for his team.

SVK #19 RW Studenic, Marian (2017) - He isn't huge, but he knows how to turn his back against the player checking him to keep possession. Nice play stealing a puck on the wall in defensive zone, dishing it off for an outnumbered attack before getting it back and finishing the chance with a nice top corner wrister.

SVK #26 RD Zelenak, Vojtech (2016) - Competed defensively, has the size and the stick-length. Had some battles on the wall with mixed results but he was willing to get his nose dirty. Got a bit confused on some of the quicker passing plays in his zone. Did not show much offensively in this game.

RUS #8 RD Alekseev, Dmitrii (2016) - Had a solid defensive game with a good first pass. Also showed off some physicality by levelling two Slovaks in a span of 15 seconds. Despite a decent first pass and a solid outing in his own zone, he did not have much offense in his game.

RUS #10 LD Makeev, Nikita (2016) - Was Russia's best puck-mover. Showed excellent selection between knowing when to make a quick simple pass or delaying for a better option to open up. Once or twice his lack of size showed but not for lack of trying. Had a great PP sequence circling around the offensive zone with crossovers and handling the puck while looking for lanes.

RUS #15 C Ivanov, Georgii (2017) - Played a smart, puck-support type of game down the middle. Makes himself available for easy passes and has good recognition of his options when distributing the puck. Has shown ability to execute plays at higher speeds as well. Scored first goal of the game by jamming twice on a rebound in the slot.

RUS #17 C Rubtcov, German (2016) - Had a poor game. His compete level was apparent, but struggled to get into the flow of the game. Had several penalties. Only seemed to get going in the last 10-15 minutes when the Russian victory was already obvious.

RUS #28 LW Veriaev, Danil (2016) - Did a good job picking apart the defense by finding holes in their coverage. His goal came from going to the net and picking up a puck that bounced off a defenseman's skate ending it with a quick wrister. His assist came off a play where Veriaev again found a hole between both Slovak defensemen for a grade A scoring opportunity, his shot resulted in a rebound and an eventual goal by his linemate.

USA vs Russia, Hlinka Memorial Tournament, August 11th, 2015

USA #30 G Rasmussen, Dayton (2017) - Gave up several goals which were entirely saveable. A slapshot goal from the point with a clear lane to see the puck. Dropped a rebound in front of him from what should have been a routine save of a weak outside wristshot. Had trouble tracking the puck and routinely left chunks of his net exposed. Had a blind shot/pass end up in the corner of his net. Got scored on from an outside wristshot with no traffic. He did save the penalty shot, but tough game overall.

USA #2 LD Dineen, Cameron (2016) - Tried to keep it simple. His compete level was good but was stuck a play behind the entire game, kept his feet moving but often ended up chasing the play, seemed like the pace was too high for his comfort level.

USA #3 RD Eliot, Mitch (2016) - Had some offensive impact. Tried different moves to open up lanes or to create a rush out of his zone, sometimes had it broken up resulting in a turnover. Competed well, used his body defensively.

USA #4 RD Farmer, Ty (2016) - Had a couple of mishaps with his puck-movement. Played a stingy competitive game, even threw his body around on the occasion despite being a smaller defenseman.

USA #5 LD Gleason, Benjamin (2016) - Didn't overextend. Played a smart controlled game. Got better towards the end of the game when he started utilizing his skating to create more offensively.

USA #7 LD Perunovich, Scott (2016) - Limited impact overall, but has shown some ability in passing out of his zone and controlling the blue-line on PP.

USA #8 LD Rossini, Samuel (2016) - Was defensively solid, always willing to use his size to break up plays. Had some offensive zone time as well, can make simple offensive plays but doesn't have a lot of skill. Made a nice cross-ice pass for a goal.

USA #11 LW Gettinger, Tim (2016) - Played his typical heavy down-low game. Did well contributing as a net-presence and moving around the goal-mouth area. Skated well for his size. Took one penalty.

USA #12 LW Harper, Patrick (2016) - Tried to get involved with direct net-drives. Had some wristshots from the slot and did well in gaining offensive zone entry. Had a penalty shot saved.

USA #15 RW Leonard, John (2016) - Played a simple chip and chase game, not much there in terms of skill plays. Drew a penalty and competed well.

USA #18 C Mittelstadt, Casey (2017) - Had good offensive impact. Skated well, comfortable handling the puck at speed and while moving his feet. Showed his vision with passing plays several time including a spin pass into the slot for an assist.

USA # 20 C Tufte, Riley (2016) - Had a game where he showed his raw tools more than any sort of consistent impact. Big center, not a bad skater for his size but needs to grow into his frame. Showed some skill and ability to read the play but didn't have a consistent shift-by-shift performance.

USA #22 RW Yamamoto, Kailer (2017) - Had a couple of chances including sneaking in and scoring from the slot. Used his offensive-zone timing and reads along with his hands to contribute. Decent game, but felt like he could show a bit more bite and willingness to direct the play given his skill-level.

RUS #30 G Sukhachev, Vladislav (2016) - Good first period. Had some scrambles where he saved his defense. Saved penalty-shot as well. Competed well, second goal he gave up was tough but felt like he could have done a better job getting across laterally.

RUS #6 LD Gromov, Nikita (2016) - Moved the puck well and did a good job on puck-retrievals, had one hiccup but other than that a mistake-free game. Was good at picking up loose pucks and moving them out of his zone but less effective in neutral and offensive zone.

RUS #7 LD Ryzhenkov, Pavel (2016) - Had an OK game in a limited role. Saw some PK usage and broke up a couple of plays defensively. Had a nice hit along the wall to win the puck.

RUS #9 LD Iakovenko, Aleksandr (2016) - Was comfortable handling the puck and showed offensive upside along with a good first pass out of his zone. Was a shot threat from the point the entire game and scored 2 goals.

RUS #10 LD Makeev, Nikita (2016) - Had more of a quiet game. Not many mistakes but struggled a bit with his lack of size in some battles and his puck-movement was just OK, some simple passes but lacked the high-end poise. Had one chance on PP by the time the game was already decided.

RUS #12 RW Ivanyuzhenkov, Artem (2016) - Had one net drive and a penalty shot that he didn't score one. Overall, played too soft for his size. In third period he had one dominating offensive zone shift, once he actually decided to use his size. Skated well but needs to be more consistent.

RUS #13 RW Popugaev, Nikita (2016) - Started off invisible, playing soft perimeter hockey. Got significantly better later in the game.. Scored a breakaway goal and added an assist in the third period. Shift-to-shift impact could be better, but he found ways to get involved in the second half.

RUS #15 C Ivanov, Georgii (2017) - Scored and played smart hockey. Was not very noticeable but got better throughout the game. In third period he started to protect the puck better and got some more time handling it and making plays. Has shown willingness to sacrifice his body to be involved offensively.

RUS #17 C Rubtcov, German (2016) - Did a good job reading the play but failed to get going consistently. Some scrambles in offensive zone going to the dirty areas but not many results. Had one sequence where he showed off his tools by controlling the puck in the offensive zone for the entire shift.

RUS #18 LW Geraskin, Igor (2016) - Was buzzing with energy. He had several rush chances pushing the defense back with the pace of his play. Drove the net several times. Had one goal surprising the goalie with a half shot half pass that was directed into the corner of the net.

RUS #24 LW Kayumov, Artur (2016) - He was good on the forecheck, did a good job hounding the puck-carrier. Despite being mid-sized at best if not smaller, he knows how to protect the puck and elude being pinned down at the wall. Had one skilled net drive towards the end of the game that made US defense look silly.

Slovakia vs Finland, Hlinka Memorial Tournament, August 11th, 2015

SVK #30 G Durny, Roman (2016) - Mid-sized goalie. Seemed like he was lacking in the athleticism department. His movement looked unbalanced which often left him struggling to get into proper position on shots. Questionable reaction time. Looked slow to react.

SVK #8 C Roman, Milos (2018) - Only 15 years old at the time of this game. Shows good reads and seems to understand the flow of the game, but sometimes struggles in the execution department. His young age shows as he can look physically underdeveloped compared to his competition.

SVK #16 C Solensky, Samuel (2016) - Played well in open ice where he can use his stickhandling to create. Can contribute with his skill and knows how to take advantage of open space either with passing or positioning himself as a scorer. Lack of size limits him if he gets pushed into physical battles and away from open ice. Skating is just OK for his size, could stand to have more explosiveness.

SVK #17 LW Bucek, Samuel (2017) - Keeps his feet moving, had good plays both on the forecheck and backcheck. Drove the net a few times causing trouble to Finnish defense, but had nothing to show for it on the scoreboard.

SVK # 20 RW Galbavy, Matej (2017) - Didn't seem to have a big impact, not a very noticeable game but at the same time somehow finds ways to get involved in scoring opportunities. Had a goal from a relatively weak shot that trickled through Finland's goalie.

FIN #31 G Halonen, Niilo (2016) - He didn't have tons of grade A scoring opportunities against him. Let in a shot that he should have saved slowly trickle through him and otherwise seemed to play down to whatever the general level of play on the ice was, he made some routine saves but never one that would change momentum the odd time Slovakia pressured, or one that would say he's actively engaged in the game. Seemed passive.

FIN #4 RW Oksanen, Emil (2017) - Played a smart skilled game, had a few good passing plays. Was used on PP where he bounces back between half-wall and the goalmouth area where he is quite dangerous. Good jump to his game and consistent in applying pressure as a forechecker.

FIN #6 LD Niemelainen, Markus (2016) - Had a decent two-way minute eating game. Moved well on his skates and puts in the effort. Shows consistency in using his body and doesn't shy away from contact. Puck-movement was OK, but his partner seemed to have a bigger workload in that regard. Niemelainen recorded two assists in the game.

FIN #14 C Makinen, Otto (2016) - Had a goal, scoring on a one-timer from the blueline. Supported the play well as a center, but played more of a shoot-first type of game than a puck-distribution one. He doesn't have a lot of speed to his game, but he seemed to know how to pick his spots both offensively as well as defensively.

FIN #18 LW Kuokkanen, Janne (2016) - Has a grinding element to his game where he goes aggressively after loose pucks but combines that with quick passing plays into space. Stole the puck in the offensive zone stick-checking a Slovak player from behind and dished it off for an assist.

FIN #19 RW Tuulola, Eetu (2016) - Compete level is never in question with him but had a quieter game overall. Footspeed is not his forte, but looked a bit slower than usual in this game. Seemed to go wide on every zone-entry attempt and wasn't quite as impactful on the forecheck as he usually is.

FIN #22 C Rasanen, Aapeli (2016) - Played a two-way game. Has smarts both offensively and defensively and commits his body. Not a lot of creativity with the puck on his stick, hasn't shown a lot of offensive upside but played a responsible game in the third line role. Had an assist off a faceoff win.

FIN #23 RD Salo, Robin (2017) - Has an ease to his puck-movement game and good play-selection coming out of his zone. Scored from a one-timer blast from the point. In general, he was a threat offensively. Didn't show hesitation in shooting and had some dangerous accurate slapshots from the point.

FIN #26 RW Koivula, Otto (2016) - Plays a simple direct game. Big body and willing to be physical. He has a decent shot and he scored beating the goalie clean with a wristshot from the top of the circle. He isn't going to be a playmaker or make skill moves with the puck, but had a fairly good game for the type of game he plays and in the role he was cast.

Czech Republic vs Switzerland, Ivan Hlinka Memorial Tournament, August 11, 2015

CZE #6 LW Zachar, Marek (2016) - Zachar wasn't that noticeable last game but made some statements tonight. Scored a nice goal sneaking in backdoor recognizing the Swiss forward wasn't covering him. One-timed the puck in to give his club a big boost. At the end of the game, showed his speed buy blowing by the Swiss team to chase down a loose puck in the dying minutes. Still needs to work on his puck decisions though, had some questionable passes tonight. One instance he had one bad pass then complicated his mistake by getting the puck back and making another bad pass. Was on first power play unit tonight and showed that he can move the puck with little pressure on him.

CZE #22 C Reichel, Kristian (2016) - A hard working centre that loves to will himself through people. Strong in the faceoff and thinks the game at a high level, however, Reichel lacks some finishing touches. Sometimes can overcomplicate his game by trying to do too much. Good work ethic and leads by example on the ice. Has some strong hockey bloodlines in him. Moves around the ice well and has good leg power.

CZE #27 RW Kofron, David (2017) - Late 98 birth year, so will be 2017 draft, but put on a great performance tonight. Player of the game with two nice goal scorer goals – well placed, accurate. First one was quick release low shot and second (ended up being game winner) was shot high blocker, another quick release. Smooth skater that propels himself down the ice with ease. Showed he can be a playmaker as well, setting up his linemates with creative passes. Good work ethic/conditioning. He got stuck out on the ice for a long shift in the third but still rushed the puck at full speed getting the puck out his zone and deep into the Swiss zone.

CZE #19 C Kodytek, Petr (2016) - It is hard not to enjoy seeing him work hard every shift. I don't think he took one shift off tonight. I really liked him at center and on the second line. He is a good spark plug that turns momentum. Always moving his feet, finishes checks and not afraid to stir it up and get underneath some Swiss players skin – hard to play against. Possesses some crafty hands and can make timely passes at opportune moments. Set up his linemates with golden opportunities on multiple occasions tonight. Had a nice assist on 3rd goal of the night – while on the half wall, found Zachar streaking towards the net through the slot and sent him a perfect tape-to-tape pass. Scored the first goal (on the power play) of the game catching a costly Swiss turnover pass and releasing off his stick quickly. But once he scored, it looked like he wanted to share the goals instead of electing to shoot. He liked looking for the pass when he could have let off a shot. Great in the corners and digging out pucks. His small frame doesn't deter him from playing a big game. Generates lots of speed and power in each of his steps. He needs to work on trusting teammates in the defensive zone. He tends to jump in thinking he is helping out when instead he was complicating the dzone coverage.

CZE #10 LW Najman, Ondrej (2016) - Nice size with good hands. Can get off passes in tight situations and protects the well, using his body. Has a good brain and thinks the game well and sees opportune passing lanes. Shoots the puck accurately and hard. Footwork needs improving though. Needs to work on his stride and getting more power. Could add some strength in his legs this season.

CZE #13 C Psenicka, Tomas (2017) - Big forward that moves decently with his large frame. Has a good shot, with a quick release. Despite size, he doesn't finish his check enough. Needs to throw his weight around more.

CZE #16 RW Havelka, Martin (2016) - Fourth line tonight but consistently did the right things and found himself on the ice more regularly as game went on. Consistently worked hard tonight in all parts of the rink. Played regularly on penalty kill and was effective at filling lanes chasing down loose pucks. Had a really nice scoring chance in the second period getting to the front of net, just above the paint and letting go a one-timer. Swiss goalie made a big save. Had three nice shots on net tonight – quick releases and accurate. Had a nice hard hit in the third period and was good in the corners tonight.

CZE #5 D Hrdinka, Fratisek (2016)
I liked his game tonight. Was confident with the puck and picked good moments to rush it up the ice. Had first assist on a go-ahead goal right after Swiss scored to regain the lead. Passes were crisp, flat, and was seeing good seams. Had a really nice cross ice, neutral zone pass to send in one of his teammates on a good scoring chance. Recognizes when he should rush the puck and when not too. Was the top defenseman for Czechs tonight in my opinion. He handles the puck really well and has his head up when moving it. Nice, strong stride and can pick up momentum quickly when jumping up into play.

CZE #14 D Vala, Ondrej (2016) - Wasn't a strong game from Vala. Kept me wanting more from him this game. His gaps were questionable and he was not looking confident in his decisions with and without the puck. Couple of times he looked afraid to get hit. Wasn't gritty enough tonight. Had a bad pinch in the third that lead to a goal, he struggled to get back despite being pretty close to the guy that scored the goal.

CZE #3 D Hajek, Libor (2016) - Was on a lot against Swiss top line tonight. Played regularly on power play and penalty kill. Maybe showing some signs of fatigue as he wasn't as crisp. Really like his size, had a good presence on the ice. Used his body well to protect the puck and get passes off. Defensively he could have some better awareness tonight, but again, wasn't as crisp. Got some pucks to the net, he has a strong release. For his size, he moves very well and pivots properly – good agility.

CZE #30 G Korenar, Josef (2016) - Korenar has a solid foundation and plays with a lot of confidence. Despite the three goals he appeared to shake them off quickly and remained confident in the crease. Quick feet with good lateral pushes and recovers fast and in control. Chest is up when pushing and while in stance. Plays the puck well and made good decisions with it – albeit a little slow. Korenar's biggest struggles tonight were high shots. He doesn't track the puck all way in up high and he can drift easily losing his angle. These are big areas of concern.

SUI #13 C Hischier, Nico (2017) - Center man with good hands. Can skate fast really well with the puck and had some good looks at the net. Not eligible till 2017 NHL draft, so definitely worth tracking and seeing how he develops. Questionable effort away from the puck though, will need to develop a well rounded game and play in all zones. But has a good base in skill set. Could grow a little more be over 6'foot.

SUI #18 Lerch, Yannick (2016) - Small framed winger that likes to grind and push through tough checks. Works hard away from the puck, always moving his feet and relentless on the forecheck. Keeps his feet moving when the puck is on his stick. Good work ethic. Played significant time on PK and for good reason; gets in shooting lanes, stops/starts facing the puck, and recognizes threats. Get's his stick in the lane well. Scored a big goal tonight, when his club was down 4-2 late in 3rd period. Rushed puck up the wall and with pressure on him got a slapshot off that when high glove. Likes to crash the net.

SUI #14 D Stadler, Livio (2016) - Really good game for Stadler, top player for the club and was given player of the game. Offensively minded defenseman with nimble, soft hands. His passes were consistently flat and made to the right person. Can pass on his backhand as well; accurate and with velocity. His puck skills are very strong. Has a quick wrist shot that is accurate and also has a good one-timer. Plays PP, PK, and extra attacker. Scored 2nd goal of night on PP – quick release from point, high blocker. Reads the play well in the offensive zone and jumped into the play at right moments. One area he needs to work on his man-on-man. Couple times he lost man-on-man battles. Strong skater with good edges and pivots well. When he lunges to early, he usually makes it back in time to correct his mistake, but on a smaller ice surface he won't as much time to make up time and space. Late in the game, had a turn over when he was being pressured hard – trying to do too much on his own. Important player to track. Nice size and mobile.

SUI #30 G Ritz, Matteo (2016) - Athletic goaltender with a good frame. However, there are lot of areas of his game that need work. Struggles with tracking the puck – over commits on shots going wide, cheats off his post pushing too early. Good lateral pushes when his chest is up, but when his chest is pointing to the ice instead of at attacker, he cements himself and struggles with recovery. Really needs to work on playing the puck as he becomes a liability when he roams outside of his crease.. Some scary moments in tonight's game when he came out to play the puck.

Final Score: Czech Republic 5:3 Switzerland

Russia vs Finland, 2015 Hlinka Memorial Tournament, August 12th, 2015

RUS #29 G Kaliaev, Maksim (2016) - A smaller goaltender, he held his own in the first two periods. Did well stopping some wristers off half-breaks. Despite being of modest size, he battled well in traffic and stopped those opportunities as well. 1st goal he gave up came off a poor rebound that was cleaned up into his net. 2nd goal he had no chance on as it came off a breakdown and a quick cross ice pass in his zone. The final one came off an uncontested wrister from the slot. Overall, it's hard to place a lot of blame on him for the last two goals. He made the routine saves, but didn't show anything extra when Russia needed it. As a smaller goalie, he isn't teribly athletic or with perfect technique either.

RUS #3 RD Akhmetgaliev, Radik (2016) - Akhmetgaliev was paired with the smaller, mobile blueliner Makeev. Akhmetgaliev played the more conservative role on that pairing, leaving the majority of puck-movement aspects to his partner. In this game, he was largely a non factor. Did not have a lot of puck-touches but also didn't show much defensively or in bringing any sort of physical component to the game. Fumbled the puck at the blueline on PP which resulted in a turnover. Overall, was a passenger in this game.

RUS #6 RD Gromov, Nikita (2016) - Gromov was decent in the previous two games, playing a low-maintenance simple puck-movement game, while also being good at puck-retrievals off dump-ins. In this game, with Rhyzhenkov moving up to his pairing, they were ineffective. Gromov didn't have much going for him, offensively or defensively.

RUS #7 LD Ryzhenkov, Pavel (2016) - Rhyzhenkov got promoted after having a decent game the previous day where he saw some PK time and did a good job breaking up plays. Today, he was largely ineffective and was even worse than his partner. Struggled to establish a role for himself that he could contribute in. Had a tripping penalty in the 2nd.

RUS #8 RD Alekseev, Dmitrii (2016) - Alekseev had a pretty consistent tournament as a two-way defenseman. Although he, like most of team Russia was least effective against Finland. Still, it was decent performance. Continued to be a solid defensive presence and moved the puck in a simple manner. Not a fancy defenseman, but does his job. Wore an A.

RUS #9 LD Iakovenko, Aleksandr (2016) - Iakovenko got more comfortable with each game in the tournament and that continued today. After a bland 1st game, he is now comfortable handling the puck and looking for better passing options. Also started showing his shot from the point. Took a tripping penalty in the 3rd.

RUS #10 LD Makeev, Nikita (2016) - Makeev wore C for Russia. He is an undersized defenseman, however he has a fairly wide base and is willing to engage. Has been Russia's best defenseman today, again displaying poise, fluid skating stride, and ability to delay and find options as a puck-mover. Has high comfort level in all situations, good on puck-retrievals. Had a penalty but also drew one in 3rd with a nice move in the offensive zone. Comfortable walking the blueline and looking for openings. Also had some nice dekes deeper in offensive zone without exposing his team too much.

RUS #12 LW Ivanyuzhenkov, Artem (2016) - Ivanyuzhenkov is a big, heavy winger that moves decently well for his size. Can make a play or two with the puck. Biggest issue is consistency in approach. When he plays in an engaging manner and uses his body he is a force to be reckoned with, today he was largely uninterested in using his frame. As a skill player alone he has very little impact. Needs to use his body down low to be effective. Not much of that today against Finland.

RUS #13 RW Popugaev, Nikita (2016) - Popugaev is a smallish skilled winger with nice vision and nifty hands. Unfortunately, continued today in being too inconsistent. Strings together a shift or two where he flashes his skill, but he has been too passive in his approach, didn't do anything if somebody didn't get him the puck first.

RUS #14 RW Avramenko, Ilya (2016) - Avramenko had nothing going for him the entire game, his line was arguably Russia's worst. Didn't show much desire off the puck defensively, or even offensively, even just to get open. The odd time he did get the puck it didn't lead to anything.

RUS #15 C Ivanov, Georgii (2017) - Ivanov was Russia's best center throughout the tournament and continued that today with another solid performance. Plays hard on the puck, showed defensive effort and supported his teammates defensively, his feet are always moving. Opens himself up for a pass and is adept at dishing it off for give and go plays. Has gained entry into offensive zone consistently, but didn't get much help from his wings.

RUS #17 C Rubtcov, German (2016) - Rubtcov had quite an underwhelming tournament for his standards up to this point. The game today against Finland was his best one, although still mediocre. Competed and skated well, he is always cognizant of his defensive role. Had some dangerous passes and some looks in traffic offensively, but nothing serious. Even when he made a good play, he seemed to get his pass fumbled or broken up by an odd bounce. Effort was there, but couldn't quite break through and ended wirh an average game.

RUS #18 LW Geraskin, Igor (2016) - Geraskin was mostly outmatched and part of Russia's most ineffective line. Looked like he could do something with speed and skill if there was enough room given to him, but was mostly flushed out of the game against a big mobile Finnish defense. He was the smallest player on the ice.

RUS #19 RW Shvyrev, Igor (2016) - Shvyrev played a limited role, however thought he was underutilized. Competed well, one of the few Russians who could win battles against Finland. Played it simple and had a nice net drive that caused havoc. Showed good puck-protection ability on the wall.

RUS #23 C Shevchenko, Viacheslav (2016) - Shevchenko had a quiet performance until later in the game. Had a nice steal on PK that resulted in a breakaway and eventually a penalty shot that he did not convert on. Got better as the game progressed, culminating in a dominant offensive zone shift where he showed off his puck-distribution skills and positioned himself into holes for scoring opportunities. Too little shown throughout 60 minutes though.

RUS #24 LW Kayumov, Artur (2016) - More of a quiet game for Kayumov compared to his previous efforts. He is an intelligent player that has a good skill level and still provides a forechecking presence. Can also protect the puck on the cycle. Made some passes that extended possession but had nothing going in scoring areas.

RUS #25 C Mescheryakov, Mikhail (2016) - Meshcheryakov was the best player on his line, however he had a hard time doing anything with two struggling wingers. Played well in his own zone and showed effort defensively. Made passes but rarely got anything useful back. His line had little sustained offensive zone time. Mostly one and done efforts, although that was not fully his fault.

RUS #26 LW Bain, Maxim (2016) - Wore an A for Russia. Struggled to get involved. Not many puck touches, had a couple of isolated possession sequences, but mostly to the perimeter and not dangerous.

RUS #27 RW Verba, Mark (2016) - Verba has good size and likes to use his reach and body to protect the puck and bring it up ice or to cycle down low. He has used that skill and reach to gain entry for his team a couple of times but hasn't been to the dirty areas of the ice in front of the net much.

RUS #28 RW Veriaev, Danil (2016) - Veriaev had a couple of points in the first two games but his level of play has been dropping throughout the tournament. Played a 4th line role in this game and didn't have much to show for it. At his best he uses his feet well on the cycle to put the opposition a step behind with tight cuts. Has some skill as a puckhandler but not a good showing in this game. No real impact.

FIN #1 G Isokangas, Severi (2016) - Mid-sized goalie, Isokangas was one of the best players on ice for either team. Recorded a shutout in a remarkably calm performance. Seemed like he swallowed up rebounds on every single shot and had a calming influence on his defense. Showed controlled movement with no erratic motion. Had an impressive save on a clear breakaway, without giving up a rebound. Tracked the puck well the entire game and had no issues sorting out traffic.

FIN #4 RW Oksanen, Emil (2017) - Oksanen is a mid-sized wing. Played a sparkplug type game, was a hound on forecheck. One of his forechecking sequences resulted in a steal and a pass to Kuokkanen who gave it right back to him for a quick shot and a goal. Oksanen also continues to excel on PP in that half-wall to goal-mouth area.

FIN #5 RD Kotkansalo, Kasper (2017) - Kotkansalo had an up and down performance. Certainly competes well but hasn't managed to have a consistent offensive or defensive impact. He had a few erratic defensive plays where everything turned out fine for him due to his effort, he would benefit by having a more structured approach in his game.

FIN #6 LD Niemelainen, Markus (2016) - This was the first game where Niemelainen looked better than his partner Salo. Niemelainen is a big two-way defenseman with good mobility and he showed that tonight. Used his body to break up plays but also got offensively involved. With his skating and reach, he looks like a tank rushing the puck forward if he gets going. He did have a couple of hiccups, a high sticking penalty in the 2nd and a fumbled puck on PP that turned into a breakaway which he had to stop illegally resulting in a penalty shot.

FIN #8 LD Reunanen, Tarmo (2016) - Reunanen played another understated but solid game. He is sturdy and will use his body defensively, moves the puck well and plays with authority. He is a bit small for a defenseman and isn't a shutdown type nor particularly offensively gifted, so he falls a bit into that grey area.

FIN #10 LW Vesalainen, Kristian (2017) - Vesalainen played a sort of complimenatry role to the Somppi-Tuulola duo, to his credit he has excelled in it. Was used on PK where he had a nice shift stealing the puck from Russia. Played a simple north-south game on the 2nd line, using his size to protect the puck, drive the net and win battles.

FIN #11 LW Tolvanen, Eeli (2017) - Tolvanen played a simple competitive game, moving his feet and had one good chance in the slot in 3rd period. Played a hard game on the wall, even though he is mid-sized at best.

FIN #12 RW Moilanen, Sami (2017) - Moilanen was part of the Finnish 4th line. Kept his shifts short and at a high pace. Provided a forechecking presence and hounded the Russian defense. Had a good cycle sequence that pinned Russia down in their zone for a considerable amount of time.

FIN #13 LW Jaaska, Juha (2016) - Jaaska also was part of Finnish 4th line unit. He did well in that role, but also showed hints of vision and skill. Tried to take the puck from the wall to the inside, but didn't have much luck. Felt like he had more to show than he could do in a limited role.

FIN #14 C Makinen, Otto (2016) - Centered the top line, but might have had his worst game so far. Again showed off his scoring instincts by cleaning up a rebound for 1:0. His lack of foot speed might have finally caught up to him as his shift-by-shift impact was limited. Wore an A for team Finland.

FIN #15 C Koppanen, Joona (2016) - Koppanen is another member of Finland's aggressive, sizeable bottom 6. He won the majority of his battles and was a pesky presence on ice. Made a couple of plays to the middle, looking to cause havoc and trying to get a bounce to go his way. Looked solid in a checking role.

FIN #18 LW Kuokkanen, Janne (2016) - Kuokkanen continues to be one of Finland's better players. He was again excellent on the forecheck, played a high tempo game going to scoring areas and sacrificing his body. Excellent at winning battles on the wall but also has skill and ability to make plays. Made the first goal happen with a cut to the middle and a shot that would later be cleaned up by Makinen. Assisted on the 2nd goal with a nice cross-ice pass that froze the goalie.

FIN #19 RW Tuulola, Eetu (2016) - Tuulola had his best game of the tournament. Has a big heavy frame and established Finland's physical style by consistently finishing checks on the forecheck. His foot speed is an issue but he reads the play fairly well. Scored the 3:0 goal by sneaking into the slot and unloading a quick release shot. Continued to play like a physical power forward with scoring instincts and a heavy shot.

FIN #22 C Rasanen, Aapeli (2016) - Rasanen continues to excel as a two-way center on the 3rd line. Was defensively responsible, saw PK time and broke up some plays. Shows flashes offensively, he isn't terribly skilled but smart enough to make plays both ways. Had a nice pass into the slot for the 3rd goal.

FIN #23 RD Salo, Robin (2017) - Salo was the best blueliner in Bratislava for the first two days of the tournament. Today, he had a quieter game with his partner Niemelainen picking up the slack. Salo is a highly intelligent puck-mover that is solid defensively and has a bomb from the point. He wasn't an outlet puck-movement machine like he was in the first two days, but was still a threat with his shot from the point. Only weakness that he shows is just average footspeed, he also isn't a flashy stickhandler, but that doesn't hurt him. Should be a 1st round consideration for 2017 NHL draft. Wore an A.

FIN #24 C Somppi, Otto (2016) - Somppi is a skilled center that however still plays with considerable jam to his game. Had his hands and lateral agility on display again. Good speed and can handle the puck on either side of his body while skating. Didn't get a lot of traction in this game but had a few isolated dangerous shifts. He is quite competitive off the puck, might have overdone it in this game with 2 offensive zone penalties.

FIN #27 LD Valimaki, Juuso (2017) - Valimaki had another good game playing on the first pairing. He is an offensive defenseman that however doesn't struggle much in his own end. Shows a bit of flair and likes to try creative moves with the puck on the occasion. Compete level is good and he doesn't mind using his frame to battle. Wore C for Finland. Even though he has been solid on the whole as a minute eating defenseman, he does have the occasional fumble or a play where he doesn't select the best option.

FIN #28 RD Jokiharju, Henri (2017) - Jokiharju displayed his smooth skating motion as he effortlessly glides around the ice. He wasn't very physical but had solid positioning. Played a fairly controlled game. Had a couple of offensive rushes, he is also good at using his skating to move the puck out of immediate danger. Had some shots on PP. Solid if quiet performance.

Slovakia vs USA, Hlinka Memorial Tournament, August 12th, 2015

SVK #1 G Koziak, Jan (2016) - He started off scrambly before settling down into the game. Seemed to play too deep in net for his size. Around the mid-point of the game when Slovakia started pushing to tie the score, he had good control in his game and didn't give up much for US, controlled his rebounds well and did well with his glove. He broke down late in third period along with the rest of his team, giving up several goals in a short span.

SVK #7 LD Kmec, Dusan (2016) - Had a big hit that resulted in a penalty for kneeing. Got involved on the offensive side of a couple of times, but could be better in his own zone. Scored on a wristshot PP goal from poor US coverage of the slot.

SVK #8 C Roman, Milos (2018) - He shows good sense for the game and has some skill. Doesn't necessarily get a lot of time with the puck due to his lack of size and doesn't look very fast, but that might be due to him being younger than everyone else on the ice. When he does have the puck he makes smart plays, he had a nice assist on two goals showing off his vision.

SVK #17 LW Bucek, Samuel (2017) - Scored a goal by sniffing around the net, got a good pass where his initial shot got saved but he managed to jam it into the net. Had a good rush chance where he turned a US defenseman inside-out. Pressured hard when Slovakia closed the gap to 2 goals, drew a penalty on an offensive zone entry play.

SVK #24 C Solensky, Samuel (2016) - Slovakia had a lot of powerplays in this game and Solensky was one of the more notable players there. Orchestrated Slovakia's offense with the man advantage. Did well in seeing lanes and distributing the puck around the offensive zone and scored on the powerplay by sneaking in back-door.

SVK #26 RD Zelenak, Vojtech (2016) - Defended the cycle well, using his big frame to break-up plays. Vision in break-outs was OK, saw the lanes but sometimes struggled with execution, bobbled a pass out of his zone despite a clear lane. Sacrificed body to block shots. Showed some offensive jump to his game, moved well in offensive zone. On some occasions he was used to provide screens on PP. Had a couple of chances and a nice scoring chance by reading an offensive play and jumping into the slot.

USA #1 G Dhillon, Stephen (2016) - He's big and he competed well on all shots. He looks like he has a lot of room for improvement, his lateral movement, recovery, and angles aren't perfect, but he puts in the effort and tries to make himself look big. He takes care of his crease-area, looks alert. Did have a couple of rebounds that he left lying in front of him though. He does have some athleticism to him despite the big size as well.

USA #3 RD Eliot, Mitch (2016) - Had a key block on a rush chance against. Continued to compete well and use his body in being an engaging presence on ice. Took several penalties however and is prone to "overheating" and not letting the game come to him, like how engaging he is but could probably dial back his approach at times.

USA #4 RD Farmer, Ty (2016) - Did not have a lot going for him offensively, but played another stingy game on the back-end. Likes to stand up to forwards and use his body to block their way forward.

USA #5 LD Gleason, Benjamin (2016) - His top-end speed isn't exactly elite but he has a very fluid stride to him and mobility in all directions. Was consistently involved in the puck-movement aspect of the game and reads the play fairly well defensively. He also had a couple of mishaps. Had his slapshot blocked on PP which resulted in his tripping penalty and got turned badly by a Slovakian forward on one occasion.

USA #7 LD Perunovich, Scott (2016) - Had a mid-ice interception and drove the net recognizing the outnumbered attack. Had a nice play defending a 2 on 1 against him as well, but other than that didn't look the strongest in his own-end. He does well on offensive chances but could have been better overall. Not the strongest defensively.

USA #9 LW Berger, Christopher (2016) - Was not very noticeable in the game but doesn't cheat you on the effort part of it. He scored a goal by whacking away in traffic on his own effort, that was one of the late US goals that put the game away after Slovakia pressured hard.

USA #14 RW Knierim, William (2016) - Looked good early on when he got moved to the top line where he was focusing on doing the dirty work for Mittelstadt and Yamamoto. He scored the first goal of the game from in-close and added an assist for 2:0 before fading away a bit in the game.

USA #15 RW Leonard, John (2016) - He had a good play cutting from the boards to the middle and getting a good shot off that ended up resulting in an assist once his linemate scored on the rebound. Showed ability with his shot. Likes to drive from outside to the middle with his skating, however he sometimes got pushed outside and had the play die on his stick. Showed outlines of his shooting and skating ability in this game, despite his moves not always working out for him.

USA #18 C Mittelstadt, Casey (2017) - Another good offensive game for him in the tournament. He had a goal and two assists. His hands were on display again and he has no problem keeping his head up and looking for options while he handles the puck and changes angles to protect it.

USA #19 C Rymsha, Drake (2016) - He threw his body around on the forecheck. Had some drives towards the net. Did well on dump-ins and gained the zone for his team a couple of times, moved his feet with and without the puck. Scored a goal by driving the net and cleaning up a rebound. And added another assist off a battle he won before passing the puck for his linemate's one-timer. Also had a shorthanded chance that was saved by the Slovak goalie.

USA #20 C Tufte, Riley (2016) - Struggled to use his tools to get any offensive output, but had a couple of good plays defensively. His compete level didn't appear to be an issue but it seemed like he could use his size better offensively.

USA #22 RW Yamamoto, Kailer (2017) - He had a goal and two assists. He showed off some of his passing ability, does a good job hiding his passes making it hard to guess whether he's looking to shoot or pass. He had a very good feel for showing up in the right places on the ice, made good offensive reads and knows how to get into holes in perfect time to be a scoring option. He's slight and not physically developed, but continued to show his natural feel for the game.

Slovakia vs Switzerland, Hlinka Memorial Tournament, August 14th, 2015

SVK #30 G Durny, Roman (2016) - Got beat on a high-skill play off a breakaway where he should probably attempt a pokecheck. His lateral movement on a cross ice pass looked quite bad as well. He did OK on some initial saves, but his movement looked too slow often resulting in problems on rebounds or when he got challenged by any cross-ice movement of the puck.

SVK #7 LD Kmec, Dusan (2016) - Threw some hits, standing up forwards at the blueline. He did fine in those scenarios but was worse deeper in his own zone. Offensively, he had a couple of pinches chipping the puck up the wall to keep possession for his team.

SVK #8 C Roman, Milos (2018) - Had good reads off-the-puck, and did well defensively in breaking up plays with his stick and in being in the right places. He moved the puck well when he got it but didn't spend a lot of time skating with the puck.

SVK #15 RD Bodak, Martin (2017) - Was Slovakia's main puck-mover from the blueline. Had a couple of shots on net, two of which resulted in rebounds that his teammates scored on. He did a good job on the PP as well.

SVK #17 LW Bucek, Samuel (2017) - Scored a goal by beating a defenseman to the puck and finishing top corner on the breakaway. Had multiple chances in the game. Showed off a great saucer backhand pass to spring a linemate with speed. Had a big hit on the forecheck and continued to hound the puck. Sometimes tried to do too much on his own, had a bad PP shift where he lost possession 3 times and produced an offside to top it off. It was not a bad performance but he needed to distribute the puck more.

SVK #19 RW Studenic, Marian (2017) - Had some chances around the net, did well with cutting into traffic and looking to cause havoc. Had an assist on the PP passing into the slot from the side of goalmouth. Protected the puck well and played with energy off-the-puck, looking to put pressure on Switzerland's defense.

SVK #26 LD Zelenak, Vojtech (2016) - Had more of a two-way game and started distributing the puck more than in the past games. He had a bit of an erratic shift on PK, but otherwise had a good game overall. Scored a PP goal from in-close. Had another wrister on PP that hit the post. Showed a surprising level of mobility in utilizing his crossovers and moving laterally across the blueline considering his large frame.

SVK #27 LD Juriga, Matus (2016) - Had an understated but smart game. Made good outlets for most of the game, reads the play well and supported his partner. Had simple chips in the offensive zone, getting the puck back deep when needed, and joined the rush when it was smart to do so.

SUI #2 LD Gerber, Colin (2016) - Showed some of his physical tools, has good size and skated well. Had some odd decisions in coverage and defending his blueline. Has a pretty long stick, but could have been more active with it in taking up space and clogging lanes.

SUI #11 RW Volejnicek, Dominik (2016) - Had quick feet and looked skilled, but didn't get the results. Took almost every play wide and was prone to getting rubbed out against the wall and stripped of the puck.

SUI #13 C Hischier, Nico (2017) - Had a great shorthanded goal using his speed and hands to convert. Was dangerous on the half-wall in PP situations, including assisting on a goal. Very skilled player that was a threat both as a playmaker as well as a scorer and was Switzerland's best forward.

SUI #17 LW Miranda, Marco (2016) - Had two goals in the game. Good size, maybe not the strongest shift-by-shift impact but has scoring ability and finds soft spots on the ice to get his shot off.

SUI #20 LW Geisser, Tobias (2017) - Big kid, competed well but struggled to get much time with the puck. Looked a bit slow and was stuck behind the play quite a bit. His angles on the forecheck could have been better.

SUI #27 RD Riva, Elia (2016) - Was one of the better blueliners for Switzerland. Had one good offensive zone rush for a scoring chance. In transition, he was comfortable delaying and waiting for lanes to open up. Did well in board battles and protected the puck well when skating out of his zone.

Finland vs Sweden, Hlinka Memorial Tournament, August 14th, 2015

FIN #1 G Isokangas, Severi (2016) - Started off well with his usual calmness and rebound control. As Sweden started to gain more offensive zone time, he started becoming more unsettled and lost some of his composure. Rebound control got worse and he had a couple of awkward plays, a puck bouncing off his glove from a harmless shot and landing on top of his net and some second-guessing when playing the puck with his stick. First goal he gave up was a slapper from the blueline with traffic in front of him, second goal was a tip/redirection.

FIN #5 RD Kotkansalo, Kasper (2017) - Willing to play physical and competed well defensively. Had a good hit to block entry into defensive zone. Still looks overmatched with the pace, overcommitted on coverage at times with Swedish forwards shaking him off with cuts and changes of direction.

FIN #6 LD Niemelainen, Markus (2016) - Had some interesting offensive moves, using his skating and reach to sometimes move the puck out of his zone by himself. Got more active offensively as clock started winding down with his team trailing. Took a bad penalty in third period with 2:30 to go and his team down by one goal. Defensively, he was his usual physically engaging self.

FIN #8 LD Reunanen, Tarmo (2016) - He continues to be a stingy smaller defenseman. His decision-making with his passing is pretty good, he doesn't make high-end plays but sees lanes and will move the puck quickly when he spots a clear lane. Had some after the whistle scrums. Felt like his pairing with Kotkansalo struggled with pace at times in their own zone.

FIN #10 LW Vesalainen, Kristian (2017) - He played a pro-style game. Had a great shift circling offensive zone before making a drop pass for a scoring chance. Defensively used his size and reach to take puck out of immediate danger when required. Doesn't have a lot of flash, but his decision-making in this game was at a high level.

FIN #13 LW Jaaska, Juha (2016) - Saw limited minutes in fourth line role but played well when he was on the ice. Scored the lone Finnish goal in a shift where he cycled the puck well before going to the net and scoring in traffic.

FIN #14 C Makinen, Otto (2016) - Didn't think he had a lot of impact, he seems to read the play well enough, but played too passive and his lack of footspeed didn't help. Felt like he observed the game too much without getting involved.

FIN #20 RD Pylkkanen, Eetu (2016) - Saw very limited minutes. He did a good job on some simple outlets but was not much of a factor overall.

FIN #23 RD Salo, Robin (2017) - He started the game a bit slow but got up to pace in second period. Wasn't great but didn't hurt his team. He had some harmless shots, but was not a big threat to score.
FIN #24 C Somppi, Otto (2016) - He seemed to buzz around the play, looking for opportunities. Skill and compete level are not in question but he struggled a bit with establishing any sort of sustained pressure, most of his chances came through quick-strike efforts that often ended as one and done plays. Sacrificed his body on a very painful blocked shot, barely being able to skate back to the bench.

FIN #26 RW Koivula, Otto (2016) - Was a threat to score a couple of times with his shot, is willing to go to the net. Got caught up ice on a rush against his team. Lacks footspeed and took a penalty for hooking.

SWE #1 G Gustavsson, Filip (2016) - He had some juicy rebounds early on but settled into the game. The only goal he gave up was on a jam play in front of his net. After he settled into the game he made several impressive saves, and started playing more aggressively in coming further out of his net. Covered his net well, and seemed to be explosive enough without sliding out of position but retained control in his movement. He could have been better in directing where his rebounds go, but had a strong game overall.

SWE #3 RD Cederholm, Jacob (2016) - Moved well considering his rather large frame-size. Still looks a bit lanky though. Seemed to do ok in eating his minutes on the first pairing, but didn't feel he has shown any high-end quality tonight. He got a bit more active offensively later in game and did well in skating with the puck forward on a couple of occasions.

SWE #4 LD Deutsch, David (2016) - He had the goal that tied the game for Sweden by getting his shot through from the point with traffic in front of the Finnish goalie. Has shown ability in moving the puck out, he seemed to prefer direct quick passes, including some stretch-passes that connected.

SWE #8 RD Thilander, Adam (2017) - He had a good overall game with his puck-movement. Most of the time he was doing really well in seeing his options. Defensively he did well in protecting the middle of ice, he is engaging but at times struggled with the forward's back turned against him. Skated himself into trouble once on a break-out trying to do too much by himself. Had the assist on the winning goal with his shot being tipped by Fallstrom.

SWE #12 LW Bratt, Jesper (2016) - He played to his strengths. A skilled waterbug type of winger that did well when the pace was ramped up. Good edgework and was dangerous at times with his skill and speed.

SWE #13 C Fallstrom, William (2016) - With Bratt and Nylander flanking him, he did well playing a role where he held back a bit more and looked for openings where he could capitalize on an opportunity created by his wings. Scored the game winning goal with a tip by being in front of the net directly after his faceoff win. And put in the effort defensively as well, coming back deep to support his defense.

SWE #16 RW Nylander, Alexander (2016) - Showed off his edgework and hands. Has great elusiveness in open space, changing angles on defense to extend possession for himself. Has no issue at all with his stickhandling while skating in different directions. It didn't always lead to a positive result, but his ability as one of the top players on the ice was obvious.

SWE #28 C Lindstrom, Linus (2016) - Did all the things right on the ice. Had a good two-way showing, is willing to dig for pucks and has a good compete level. Felt he was limited offensively at times by his just average skill and especially lack of footspeed. Reads the play well though and can find ways to get involved.

Finland vs Russia, Bronze Medal Game, Hlinka Memorial Tournament, Aug. 15, 2015

FIN #1 G Isokangas, Severi (2016) - Played too deep in his net and seemed to shrink with pressure. His rebound control and technique remain solid, but the mental side with how he seems to shrink at times is a bit problematic. On the 3:2 goal for Russia he left an obvious cross ice pass go through his crease, just a hair in front of him without even attempting to block it. It was the passer's only option as he had no angle to shoot at all. Didn't think he responded well to Russia's pressure in the third period at all.

FIN #4 RW Oksanen, Emil (2017) - He was the one trying to make plays on the first line that was otherwise a bit cold. Didn't always succeed but the effort was there. Good jump, and is willing to play in traffic.

FIN #6 LD Niemelainen, Markus (2016) - He started utilizing his skating more to rush the puck forward throughout the tournament. That continued today in the bronze medal game. He was assuming more and more authority and tried to make things happen as a two-way presence. He can really use his reach to penetrate forward, but doesn't always have the vision to make plays off it.

FIN #10 LW Vesalainen, Kristian (2017) - Played a simple puck-possession game. Seems to have a good sense for the game and rarely tries a move extra but keeps it to simple effective decisions. Has good size and used his body to protect the puck.

FIN #13 LW Jaaska, Juuha (2016) - Might not have a lot of physical tools, but continues to find ways to contribute. Did a good job getting to loose pucks. Had a good offensive read sneaking into the slot to finish into wide open net.

FIN #23 RD Salo, Robin (2017) - With his partner taking more chances offensively, Salo played a more conservative game, settling for making the first pass and holding back a bit. Defensively, he sometimes looks like he lacks speed on puck-retrievals but is still willing to sacrifice his body to make a play.

FIN #24 C Somppi, Otto (2016) - He had a good game as a puck-distributor on the powerplay. He was good at opening up the blade on his stick and changing the angles to his movement to manipulate defensive coverage and open up lanes. Good skill with the puck.

FIN #27 LD Valimaki, Juuso (2017) - Had a great play on the first Finnish goal, skating through neutral zone, dishing it off to his winger, then going to the net and taking a Russian D with him allowing for space behind him to open up for a pass and eventual goal. Didn't have perfect decision-making, but showed some of his offensive upside. Scored a goal with a slapshot from the top of the circle, that the goalie should have probably saved.

RUS #29 G Kaliaev, Maksim (2016) - He looked shaky in the first period. Overplayed angles, had trouble with rebounds and seemed out of his comfort zone. The second goal he gave up was a slapshot close to the boards and from top of the circle with no traffic in front of him. He got pulled with Sukhachev starting the second period.

RUS #30 G Sukhachev, Vladislav (2016) - He started the second period after Kaliaev got pulled. He gave up one goal on a tip, but otherwise was more poised and made some saves that gave Russia confidence to complete the comeback and win the game. Seemed like Russia's defense played better in front of him. Was not exceptional, but made the saves he had to and was strong during late Finland push.

RUS #8 RD Alekseev, Dmitrii (2016) - Had a quiet yet smart game. He uses his body when he has to and is consistently solid in his own end. Although he isn't an offensive defenseman, he continued to move the puck well.

RUS #10 LD Makeev, Nikita (2016) - Became more involved in the second period, started making high-end outlets and was more active in an offensive role. Continued to show off his fluid stride and ability to find options in transition.

RUS #13 RW Popugaev, Nikita (2016) - Felt like he wasn't effective as he should be early on, but he was the key player in the third period, coming up with two goals to tie the game and then assisting on the game winning goal. Seemed to be in the right spots offensively and read the soft spots on the two goals of his, even if he wasn't the one that did the legwork on them. The assist was a terrific neutral zone pass to an open linemate that had speed.

RUS #17 C Rubtcov, German (2016) - Got more and more offensively involved. He is always solid as a two-way center, but became more active with his net drives and started mounting some real pressure in the offensive zone. Had two assists, including a drive to the middle of ice that was later capitalized on by Popugaev.

RUS #23 C Shevchenko, Viacheslav (2016) - He was ready to go from the first minute. Moved his feet, gained entry for his team, drove to the net, did well in handling the puck at speed and generally provided an up-tempo game for Russia. Scored the first goal of the game on the PP by going to the slot and finishing on a return pass.

RUS #24 LW Kayumov, Artur (2016) - He scored the final and game winning goal in third period, receiving a pass with speed, beating the Finnish defenseman and finishing with a wrist-shot.

RUS #28 RW Veriaev, Danil (2016) - He did well in using his frame to protect the puck. Didn't allow himself to get pinned down and did a good job circling the offensive zone looking for passing options. He had the primary assist on a give and go play with Shevchenko for the first goal of the game.

Brynas IF vs HV71 IF, GK Feskarn Trophy J20, August 22, 2015

BIF #1 G Dackell, Oliver (2016) – Consistent effort tonight and kept his team in the game with some timely saves. Dackell isn't a large goalie but keeps his chest up in his stance and doesn't shrink himself on saves – filling the net well. He was square all night with only traffic and deflections beating him. Very calm and focused in the crease; aware of threats around him. Has some exceptionally quick legs and moves efficiently and fluidly in the crease – good edge work. Dackell gave up a lot of rebounds tonight though, some very juicy. Rebounds were coming off him high and low in to some dangerous areas. However, his quick feet and lateral pushes allowed him to make a second and third save. The saves looked great and displayed his athleticism, but were unnecessary had he controlled his rebounds. Still looks raw in his develop and working on his coordination.

BIF #27 RW/LW Hirsch, Adam (2016) - Not a good showing for Hirsch tonight. He is a balanced skater with tight edgework but lacks some speed. Soft in the corners and didn't show he knew how to contain players in the corner, using two hands on his stick and allowed players to roll around him easily. Handles the puck easily, but he either doesn't like to share the puck or he isn't seeing the passing lanes ahead of him.

BIF #9 C Boqvist, Jesper (2017) – Boqvist had the puck on his stick a lot tonight – sometimes too long. There is no denying that Boqvist has some higher end puck skills and he can make a defenseman look like an old oak tree, he just try to do too much on his own. Has a good vision towards the net, but missed some passing lanes that would have created better scoring opportunities. Loves to shoot – which is nice to see in Sweden - but needs to work on getting a more powerful, accurate shot. Played on the penalty kill and powerplay tonight. He has a good stride and can get power out of it, but he hunches over too much with his chest pointing at the ice – needs to work on this.

BIF #16 D Deutsch, David (2016) – Works really hard in his defensive zone and doesn't quit on loose pucks. Gritty in the corners today and uses his stick well. Blocked a hard, heavy shot tonight – got low and used proper technique. Not a strong skater though, needs to get better balance and strength. Ankles look weak.

BIF #96 LW Palhom, Max (2014) – Nice work ethic tonight and got a few good shots on net. Had a hard, quick release. Played on penaltykill tonight and blocked a hard shot in his arm that made it numb and dropped his stick, but kept going and blocked another shot. Not a big frame on the ice, but is quick and made some good decisions.

HV #33 D Cederholm, Jacob (2016) – Continued to do the right things and show that he can control the pace of a game. Passes were crisp and he was escaping checks with ease. Used his stick really well, making it hard for attackers to do anything. Had a nice one-timer tonight, but goalie made nice save. Showed hesistation on a loose puck though tonight, didn't jump on it or try to outwork the attacker – gave up and let him half despite being a clear 50/50 puck race. Despite that one instance, this level looked almost too easy for him, wouldn't be surprised to see him get some more SHL games this year.

HV #71 C Andersson, Lias (2017) – Good showing for Andersson, a late '98 born. Not hard to see that he has picked up some his families skills. Dad is a Swedish hockey legend that played 165 NHL games and now scouts for LA Kings, his uncle played for Tampa Bay and has scouted for them since 2004. Good balance on his steel, hard to knock off of the puck. Gritty side to him. Battled in the corner and fought off an attacker to take out front of the net and got off a hard, quick backhand that forced the goalie to make a great leg extension – getting a toe on the puck. Had another scoring opportunity coming down the wing and shooting hard, accurately, to get a rebound to kick out in front but his linemate couldn't connect on it. Showed some physical play tonight as well. Delivered a hard hit at the end of the second period that caused some commotion on the ice.

HV #72 D Moverare, Jacob (2016) – Showed some good puck decisions tonight. Escaped well and got some passes off. Patience on the point as well, and got some shots on net, but the shots weren't well placed and easily smothered by goalie. Footwork is still a big concern and it was apparent tonight. He looked slow and sluggish in fast paced game. Was he tired from last night's game? Possibly, but his skating really needs to be improved.

HV #55 RG Johansson, Alexander (2015) – Solid game for Johannsson. Was only beat by a point shot that was deflected low blocker. Good patience on his post, doesn't leave it too early. Seals up the ice well and didn't leave any holes. Controlled his rebounds very well tonight. Looked mature and confident. Pushed across his crease cleanly and was square.

Final Score: BIF 1:2 HV

USHL Showcase, UPMC Lemieux Sports Complex (Pittsburgh), Sept. 18, 2015
USA NTDP-18

NTDP #18 LD Lindgren, Ryan (2016) – Lindgren looked average in this game and have seen in previous years as better Dman. He had one good rush in 2nd period with nice fake that created a nice scoring chance. It is early in the year, will see how he progresses in draft season.

NTDP #2 RD Martin, Luke (2016) – He is good size and played a steady game with no bells of whistles. He made the outlet passes and secure in his own end.

NTDP #25 LD Luce, Griffen (2016) – The foot speed definitely needs improvement. He's a good size kid with slow lateral mobility and also the processing of the game is behind too. Just doesn't act quick. With bigger body he should be finishing checks and playing the nasty streak.

NTDP #4 RD Krys, Chad (2016) – He played decent although not quite the standards of the past from Krys. He did make nice play on his off-side on offensive BL to quickly grabbed puck off wall and fire on net to create rebound goal by #7 Frederic. He skates well, yet again did not create offensively like expected. He showed bit more confidence with the puck than last month at NJEC.

NTDP #14 LD Greenway, JD (2016) – He is big, thick player who struggles with making quick puck decisions. Each game he seems to have some questionable puck decisions, yet then surprise you with nifty play as did in 3rd period on 3rd NTDP goal as made nice move and pass off the wall to set-up #16 Sanchez across ice.
NTDP #8 RD Fox, Adam (2016) – He always plays in control, as poised with the puck. Fox sees the ice very well as distributes the puck on PP very well and makes good outlets. The defensive game is improving with positioning, gaps, and stick.

NTDP #12 LW Bellows, Kieffer (2016) – There is no question he's a shooter but he also sees the ice to set-up plays. He was pretty quite throughout this game although made nice rush and move around defender in the 3rd period to show he hard shot for scoring chance. Will need to keep eye upon Bellows no doubt this season.

NTDP #18 C Keller, Clayton (2016) – He never seems to play a bad game in my viewings. He just has a knack for making plays in tight spaces when you think there is nothing, he makes something. He made beautiful play down half-wall in offensive zone, as stopped, curled, and toe-dragged defender then slid pass to #10 Lockwood going to net for easy re-direct goal. He is very crafty, elusive.

NTDP #10 RW Lockwood, William (2016) – He plays with speed and some nice offensive instincts as knows where to go. #19 Keller nicely set the table, although Lockwood went to the right space and finished the play for a goal.

NTDP #9 LW Pastujov, Nick (2016) – He was average in performance, you see the skill sets in flashes. Needs to bring that consistent play.

NTDP #13 C Khodorenko, Patrick (2017) – Just like his LW #9 Pastujov, he played well in spots, yet overall need to see more.

NTDP #17 RW Anderson, Joey (2016) – Anderson was decent in this game, although usually get a bit more offensively from Anderson. He did hit the post on 2-on-1 PK in 2nd period of #8 Fox pass. He is a player to monitor throughout the season.

NTDP #21 LW McPhee, Graham (2016) – He competes hard and gets in on pucks. McPhee uses his body well to protect puck and power to the net. He isn't the most crafty or gifted offensive player as question any pure finishing abilities. Example was he made nice move in the 2nd period in tight area and shot from high slot, but failed to score. He did make nice play behind the offensive net as side stepped a check to then find #16 Sanchez out front for NTDP's 4th goal.

NTDP #7 C Frederic, Trent (2016) – He is a good sized forward who works hard around the net and both ends of the ice. He might be a sleeper type in the draft from NTDP team. Frederic could develop into nice two-way centerman. He scored 2nd goal out front pouncing on rebound goal from point shot in the 2nd period.

NTDP #16 RW Sanchez James (2016) – He was one of the better NTDP forwards on the night as he used his size and strength knocking one player down while possessing the puck. He displayed some offensive thoughts here. Sanchez scored the 3rd goal receiving the pass in the slot with quick release over the glove – nice shot. He then scored the 4th goal out front making move and slamming rebound home – greasy style finish.

NTDP #27 LW Suthers, Keenan (2016) – He is big power winger with average stride and limited true offensive style.

NTDP #11 C Howdeshell, Keeghan (2016) – He plays very average game, not much to jot down.

NTDP #15 RW Walker, Zach (2016) – He didn't display much. He is a player coming back from injury.

Muskegon Lumberjacks

MUS #1 G Cooley, Devin (2016*) – He is a bigger size goalie. Does not look comfortable handling puck and techniques is a bit sloppy under pressure.

MUS #2 RD Eliot, Mitch (2016) – He is just a steady Dman that overall is solid yet doesn't really do anything dynamic to excite you. He did make nice stretch pass on the PK to create scoring chance. He will play physical and compete.

MUS #7 RD Green, Alex (2016) – For a rookie USHLer he did not back down from the physical play. He wasn't afraid to mix it up. He laid big hit late in 3rd period behind the net. He used a good active stick defensively and controlled gaps fairly well. He will need to add muscle and strength as frame is lanky and sometimes loses the battles. Question the hockey IQ a tad, as there were some plays he could have read the play better.

MUS #8 RD Berzolla, Zach (2016) – He really showed a physical side with a couple big hits and one in the open ice in the NZ on the bigger #27 Suthers.

MUS #16 LW Pitlick, Rem (2016*) – For someone who has seen Pitlick in the past from the early years, he has definitely added some pounds to the frame which is noticeable. He made a nice on the crafty #19 Keller picking his pocket at the defensive BL and then taking puck other way to set-up line mate #20 Paulovic in high slot for a goal. He scored his own goal on PP back-door play off the side of the net and then added another going to the net and picking up the rebound off #13 Adams shot. He competes hard and shows good hockey IQ. Scouts have been turned away with smaller size, although he finds a way to hit score sheet.

MUS #20 C Paulovic, Matej (DAL) – He showed some good size, reach, and strength to be involved offensively. He scored 1st goal receiving a pass in high slot and wiring quick shot high over the glove on 3-on-2 play. He then scored on the PP off the side of net using body and strength to win battle for puck on rebound. He also made nice back-door pass on the rd goal in 2nd period to #16 Pitlick. He completed the hat trick using his long reach out front to finish off rebound. You could see why Stars took 5th round flyer as shows some good offensive thoughts and could develop with body and strength.

MUS #13 LW Adams, Collin (2016) – He isn't blessed with size although he plays with good tempo/speed and grit. He will definitely fit the North Dakota mold. He actually scored a goal in the 2nd period with great puck movement with linemates #16 Pitlick and #20 Paulovic. He wasn't afraid to drive the puck to the net down his off-wing on the BH. He picked up assist on rebound shot to #16 Pitlick.

USHL Showcase, UPMC Lemieux Sports Complex (Pittsburgh), Sept. 18, 2015

USA NTDP-17

NTDP #33 G St. Cyr, Dylan (2017) – He struggled early on the first two goals against. He was beaten blocker side from top of circle with quick snap shot off the wall by #81 Hall and then misplayed puck behind net leaving puck for his Dman which was nowhere to be found and gave up easy open net goal to #12 Hirano. He can play the puck well although technique in stopping puck consistently needs work.

NTDP #32 LD Inamoto, Tyler (2017) – He is decent size and played overall decent game, although could move the puck quicker up ice in transition and breakouts.

NTDP #41 RD Maniscalo, Josh (2017) – He definitely plays with edge and likes the physical style. He was very tough in own zone as will mix it up. He took roughing penalty in the second period as got into it with #2 Petrie.

NTDP #45 LD Knoepke, Nate (2017) – He is big-sized Dman with slow feet. Nothing too impressive as handles puck very average too.

NTDP #43 LD Hughes, Quinn (2018) – Circled the late '99 born Dman name on scouting sheet as displayed as plays smart game and you like the skating ability. He can break away from pressure as mobility in all directions is very solid. Hughes handles the puck and can distribute as well. He made nice pass off the wall to create original play that lead to #37 Norris for the 3rd goal. He is very poised with the puck, makes good puck decisions, and has the smarts. Only thing going against is his smaller stature.

NTDP #56 LD Gildon, Max (2017) – It's funny how the hockey pyramid works as Gildon was one of the best players at USAH Select 15s in Summer of '14, yet watching here the hockey IQ is being questioned and the coordination/mobility isn't keeping up with the pace. Gildon handle with the puck and processing of the play looked below average as well. He did make one good play stepping up in NZ to pick pass and then head man up ice to create scoring opportunity. His stock though has definitely cooled off.

NTDP #55 RD Kemp, Phil (2017) – He was a top NE Prep player for his age, although here looks bit out of place keeping up with the pace. His foot speed is average here and lost in some gap control too. It may just be getting used to league.

NTDP #51 LD Farrance, David (2017) – Have watched Farrance through the years and still will need to improve defensive zone coverage and support without the puck to his partner. Offensively too hasn't really shown much. Again he is another player not used to the pace, even though strong skater. It's the mind set of now you're playing with the big boys, not public HS hockey.

NTDP #47 LW Cockerill, Logan (2017) – He is smaller sized forward yet plays with good tempo and offensive thoughts. He might have scored the 3rd goal for NTDP as he went to the right place and picked up #37 Tkachuk rebound off the side of the net, yet believe #39 Norris received credit. He sees the ice and has the ability to make plays.

NTDP #39 C Norris, Josh (2017) – He played with good offensive thoughts on the night as he created scoring chances. He isn't highly dynamic although plays a good two-way game. He scored the 3rd goal for NTDP as he went to the right place and picked up #37 Tkachuk rebound off the side of the net. He also was given a penalty shot late in game with 1:43 left down 5-4 yet attempt was mediocre with simple shot, hardly making goalie work. Perhaps fatigue at the end of game and shift.

NTDP #37 RW Tkachuk, Brady (2018) – He made good play on 3rd goal after taking #43 Hughes pass off offensive wall in 2nd period with quick snap shot not allowing goal to set that created rebound goal by #39 Norris. You can actually see the resemblance in his toughness and play around the net to his dad and older brother.

NTDP #34 LW Cassetti, Joey (2017) – He is good sized winger who skates fairly well with decent north-south speed and wasn't afraid to throw his body around. He scored the 4th goal on a breakaway taking #44 Hutsko pass in NZ and then firing 5-hole shot.

NTDP #57 C Reedy, Scott (2017) – Reedy continues to impress as he creates time and space, opens lanes that lead to scoring opportunities. He made a really nice set-up on 1st goal as he entered zone on his off-side and sold pass back to Dman on strong side, yet slide across ice pass through seam on his backhand right on the tape of #44 Hutsko going to net. He got his name circled at the end of the game.

NTDP #44 RW Hutsko, Logan (2017) – He is undersized winger that plays with speed and craftiness. He tallied the 1st goal driving to net and getting under Dman to then take #57 Reedy across ice pass and shelf it high over glove in one motion. He has good vision and set-up #57 Reedy from the behind the goal line in 2nd period for scoring chances.

NTDP #53 LW Barratt, Evan (2017) – He played average on the night. He actually struggled on 4th goal against as puck stuck early in the period on wet ice and then tipped the shot into his own net.
NTDP #38 C Slaggert, Graham (2017) – He is decent player with some speed although not sure if his hockey IQ is good enough to have success at the higher levels.

NTDP #49 RW Henandez, Randy (2017) – He is a hard worker the plays an honest up-n-down game on the wing. The skill sets and skating are decent yet nothing high-end.

NTDP #46 LW Mismash, Grant (2017) – He was one of the better NTDP forwards on the night as he sees the ice well to set-up plays, can handle the puck well, and has the smarts to make plays each shift. He scored a goal walking down the side slot, just shooting short-side block low. He shoots the puck well and shows good offensive thoughts.

NTDP #42 C Dhooghe, Sean (2017) – He certainly gets tons of ice time here for NTDP. He is quite small, yet plays hard with compete level and IQ all-around the ice. He plays the PK often. He will be a specialty player in the NCAA ranks. Once one of the top U12 players in USA, he just hasn't developed physically to keep pace.

NTDP #36 G Pastujov, Michael (2017) – He just seemed to play very inconsistent on this night. At times he made some plays, yet many shifts unnoticeable.

NTDP #52 RW Totora, Jacob (2017) – He was the designated extra forward on the night and was given very limited ice time. Not sure if dog house or because he was last roster add in the summer time. You like his up tempo, as plays with speed and likes to motor. He threw late hit in the 2nd period that caused stopped of play for injury.

Youngstown Phantoms

YNG #56 RD Farmer, Ty (2016) – He plays a poised game with the puck as handles and mobility is good. He makes good outlet passes and distributes puck well on the PP. There were times though in own zone he opted for the high risk play in pass or holding the puck too long.

YNG #3 LD McInnis, Luke (2016) – You could see the nerves early in game as made bad cross ice pass in own zone on 1st shift. He then took penalty early as well in game with late hit that was uncalled for on the play. After settling in he showed poise, handle, better puck decisions in making outlet passes. You would like to see that extra, quick step to break away from pressure.

YNG #28 RD Moore, Connor (2016*) – His game is steady at both ends of the ice, so you actually don't notice a whole lot. He plays a smart game with and without the puck. He actually did make an error on NTDP #39 Norris goal as he stepped up prematurely in the NZ to allow opponent to get by, yet overall makes the smart little plays around the ice to like making quick, touch pass or supporting partner or getting stick in passing lanes. He did end up scoring the 6th goal for Phantoms into empty net off face-off win on PK from other end of ice.

YNG #10 LW Conley, Kevin (2016*) – He scored a couple of couple on the night on two shots. The 1st he took pass off the wall from #3 McInnis in the high slot and fired it home and then scored the 5th goal for Y'town on broken play as puck popped out at the dot and Conley stepped in with a low slap shot quickly.

YNG #12 RD Hirano, Yushiroh (2016*) – He works hard all around the ice and was actually a nice surprise from Japanese native. He scored the 2nd goal after goalie misplayed and gave open net in 1st period. He then made nice play late in 1st period with hustle in beating out icing call and setting up #10 Conley for good scoring chance. His passes were little too predictable on the PP, yet he showed some compete and offensive thoughts.
YNG #7 RW Esposito, Eric (2016) – Esposito is making transition from NE Prep game to the USHL, and early on you could see he looked step behind the pace. As the game progressed he started to use his speed and competed for pucks more.

YNG #20 LW Craggs, Lukas (2016*) – Given 3rd line LW duties, he showed some decent thoughts throughout the game. He skates well with some speed and can handle the puck. Liked the skills and thought process.

Acadie-Bathurst Titan vs Moncton Wildcats, September 20th 2015

AB #88 C Morand, Antoine (2017) - Won some defensive zone faceoff which was nice to see coaching staff trusting him in those situations. He was more noticeable on the power play or 4 on 4 than at even strength. He showed good awareness in the defensive zone, with some good positioning. On the power play he was used mostly on the half wall where he can set up his teammate.

AB #16 RW, Maher Jordan (2016) - Not very noticeable today, made some smart plays in the defensive zone and supported his defense well by coming back deep. He showed an extra gear on one rush. Didn't generate much offense today.

AB #98 LW Kuznetsov, Vladimir (2016) - Big kid is the first impression I got watching the top pick in the import draft today. Didn't do a whole lot until the 3rd period to impress me, in the 3rd he made a sweet pass to #24 Simpson for a quality scoring chance after a zone entry. Skating will need some upgrade; he needs to improve his speed and explosiveness. He works a lot down low in the offensive zone using his size.

AB #62 RW Miromanov, Danill (2016) - He was one of the better Titan today, scored a really nice goal on the PK stealing the puck in the neutral zone and using a solid wrist shot to score the Titan first goal. All game he showed a good active stick on the PK. He was involve all game, using his smarts and size well.

AB #31 G Pickard, Reilly (2016) - He was pulled early in the 2nd period after allowing 3 goals which 2 he would probably like to have back. His rebound control was off during the game which lead to directly to Moncton 2nd and 3rd goal. He had no chance on Moncton 1st goal, he was beat high glove on a perfect shot by Leger from the faceoff circle.

AB #45 LD Francis, Elijah (2016) - He made some good reads in the offensive zone, getting open on the blueline to receive passes. Francis played on the 2nd power play unit. Some issues in his own end with the puck, fumbling it on one sequence that lead to a scoring chance for Moncton. Overall like his play in the offensive zone but need to work on his play in his own zone.

MON #19 RW Askew, Cam (2016) - Did a good job down low handling the puck and along the board overall in this game. Over the last two year he has become very good at handling the puck down low and finding linemates in the slot, and did again today for a great scoring chance for #21 Weiderer who hit the post after a quick shot from the slot. Askew used his long reach and body positioning in the offensive zone to protect the puck. He showed nice strength holding off two opponents while rushing the puck in the offensive zone, this lead to Moncton 5th goal of the game.

MON #14 LW Murphy, Liam (2016) - Played with the Klima twin, did a good job doing some of the dirty work for that line. Made a nice effort on the forecheck which created the 4th goal by the Wildcats.

MON #16 LD Glaessi, Maximilian (2016) - The German import played on the 1st power play during today's game, was effective when he made quick short passes on the power play. He tried to stretch the play with a 2 line pass on one sequence, it was not successful but I like that he tried to make things happen. In his zone his decision making was a bit slow at time, still adjusting to the QMJHL game.

MON #21 LW Weiderer, Manuel (2016) - The other German import on Moncton this year, he showed a willingness to shoot the puck from anywhere in the offensive zone. Hit the post in the first period after a great pass from Cam Askew. He played on a line with Askew and Leger tonight.

MON #6 RW Klima, Kelly (2016) - Strong game from Kelly, showed some good speed and very elusive as he was able to avoid checks. Liked his effort on the backcheck as well. At the start of the 3rd period he threw a big hit along the board but unfortunately was called for 2 minute but enjoyed to see him get his nose dirty.

MON #34 C Klima, Kevin (2016) - He was arguable the star of the game, scored 2 goals in the game. He was very dangerous in the offensive zone, showed a good & accurate wrist shot during the game. Not big but like his twin brother showed good energy during the game and was involved in all three zones.

Drummondville Voltigeurs vs Blainville-Boisbriand Armada, September 20th 2015

DRU #22 C Sevigny, Mathieu (2016) - Played centre today and was successful winning draws going 11/17. Scored Drummondville first goal from a good wrist shot from the faceoff circle. He was effective on the forecheck, showing good puck pursuit and throwing some good hits. He's strong on his skate; he did well along the board keeping possession of the puck. He was skating well, look to have improve speed since last season.

DRU #4 LD Gagne, Benjamin (2017) - Gagne played on both side today, showing good versatility. He had some iffy moments in his own zone in the game, almost scored in his own net after trying making a pass to his own goaltender. Later he turned the puck over in his zone which lead to BLB 2nd goal. He was used in different facets during the game; on the power play he was able to make zone entries without much trouble using his quick feet to rush the puck. He was quite active in the offensive zone on the power play giving different options to his teammates.

DRU #19 C Barre-Boulet, Alex (2016) - Un-Drafted last season, he was not a big factor for his team today. His best scoring chance came earlier in the game while on a breakaway where he lost control of the puck when tried to deke the goaltender. He was solid in the faceoff circle. Played on both PP and PK.

BLB #29 G Grametbauer, Mark (2016) - Solid game from the rookie goaltender, kept his team in the game all night long by making at 3-4 breakaway saves. His defense in front of him had a tough night. Good glove. Would likely like to have the 1st goal (Sevigny) back, and in overtime he was beat high blocker by a perfect shot by Bouchard.

BLB #11 C Poulin, Anthony (2017) - Called up for that game, Poulin showed good work ethic at both end of the ice in this game. For a 16yo rookie he did well in the faceoff circle, with his line they did a good job keeping the puck down low and cycling it. Often 1st on the puck in the corner, was a bit of sparkplug for his team. In one sequence, showed good acceleration when he was able to go between both defensemen for a good scoring chance.

BLB #18 RW Hylland, Tyler (2016) - Good work on the PK, used his speed and active stick in this situations really well. Work hard all over the ice. Offensively didn't do a whole lot outside of a nice pass to #17 Hamelin at the side of the net for a scoring chance.

BLB #24 LW Teasdale, Joel (2017) - Got hurt early in the game when he got hit in the face by a puck. With his line they did a really good job keeping the puck down low, for a 16yo rookie he's strong on his skate and does well along the board. He was used on the PK & PP, smart player.

BLB #89 C Picard, Miguel (2016) - Some good forecheck shifts from him with #18 Hylland. Played the game on a line with Hylland & #15 Sanche. Offensively didn't do much, had a good scoring chance early in the 3rd but that was it. Not very noticeable today.

BLB #96 LW Pospisil, Kristian (2016) - 96-born rookie Slovakian forward made a good impression today, use his size well along the board and handles the puck well in traffic. Good puck protection along the board, on the power play he's used in the half wall position and makes quick decisions in a playmaker role.

Regina Pats at Moose Jaw Warriors, September 24, 2015

WHL Regular Season

REG #38 LD Pouteau, Brady (2016) - Made some good one on one plays early on forcing outside or standing up opposing forward.

REG #23 C Steel, Sam (2016) - Lost puck battles against older/stronger opponents. Great play in offensive zone to steal puck and create 1-2 goal. Great speed.

REG #39 RW Zablocki, Lane (2017) - Good move to quickly score 1-2 goal.

MJW #2 RD Brook, Josh (2017) - Smart pinch to get quick hard shot off. Outstanding three line pass to set up 1-0 goal.

MJW #13 LW Smejkal, Jiri (2016*) - Beautiful first goal ran over defender then quick hands to beat the goaltender. Played a power forward game landing some huge hits. Great puck moving ability.

MJW #21 C Howden, Brett (2016) - A little slow to react at times. Excellent puck control on the wall. Slick pass then went to the net to score 2-0 goal on rebound. Drove net getting inside the defender drawing a power play. Good quick puck decisions, quick passing lead to 3-1 goal. Good position in the slot on the power play for scoring chance. Always makes himself an option. Calm with puck under pressure. Missed his target a few times with passes.

MJW #71 LW Popugayev, Nikita A. (2017) - Lacks skating, pace is a little weak but surprises with great hands in open ice. Undressed opponent one on one for great chance. Good work on the power play point followed by a good low shot resulted in a rebound which was directly put in for 2-0 goal. Leaps and gallops to generate speed. Great pass on the wall to the slot to create scoring chance.

MJW #31 G Sawchenko, Zach (2016) - Quite a bit of action early, extremely calm with pressure. Directs rebounds away well. Quick with pads. Only goal allowed, jammed in at the slot afer a turnover. Steady all game long for Moose Jaw.

Final Score: Moose Jaw Warriors: 3 - Regina Pats: 1

Baie-Comeau Drakkar vs. Gatineau Olympiques, QMJHL, Sep. 25, 2015

GAT #9 C Laplante, Yan Pavel (PHO) - 3 G +2, scored 1 even strength, 1 powerplay, 1 shorthanded goal, good speed, used his size well, hard on forecheck, finishes hits, stood in front of net on power play, generated a lot of chances down low in offensive zone, good balance on feet, didn't get knocked of the puck a lot, was good on draws.

GAT #11 LW Abramov, Vitalli (2016) – 1 G 3 A +2, great skating forward, great acceleration speed, broke away from defenders with his speed, was all over the ice tonight, every shift he generated something offensively, great skill with the puck, plays the point on power play, great vision on ice, worked hard every shift, has a hard shot, not physical at all, needs some work in the dzone, a fun player to watch.

GAT #13 C Dostie, Alex (2016) – 1 G 2 A +2, great skater, quick 2-3 steps, played really well on the power play, controlled the puck well along the side boards, good 2 way center, needs to be hard on his stick for faceoff's, has filled out more this year (body wise), he is more confident this year with the puck, doesn't like the rough stuff, set up a beautiful goal on the power play.

GAT #44 RD Bilodeau, Gabriel (2016) – Good size Defensemen, thick body frame, made a couple hard hits in his dzone, needs to be more intimidating, good first pass out the zone, made too many slow decision with the puck tonight coming out of his zone, played the point on power play good low hard right handed shot, gets pucks through to the net, good stick tonight.

BAI #11 RW Karabacek, Vaclav (BUF) – showed some skill tonight, stayed on the perimeter, created some chances on the power play, very comfortable with the puck on his stick, good speed burst with the puck on his stick.

BAI #71 LW Kabanov, Igor (2016) – Big body forward, wasn't engaged tonight physically, notice him on a couple shifts, good skater, needs to compete more, could be a power forward with his size and frame, has a good hard shot when he gets an opportunity to use it.

BAI #79 G Kiselev, Evgeny (2016) – Was outstanding tonight, his team in front on him didn't give him much help, face 25 shots in the 1st period and 50 shots total for the game, smaller size goalie, excellent laterally mobility, takes away the bottom on the net well, made some big saves in the 1st to try and keep his team in the game, rebound control was alright, gave up a couple rebounds that ended up in high quality scoring chances, tracks the puck well, positioned type goalie, does move around a lot in his crease.

Final Score: Baie-Comeau: 1   Gatineau: 7

Kingston Frontenacs at London Knights, September 26, 2015

OHL Regular Season

KGN #6 D Paquette, Jacob (2017) - Good pinch early on in this game. Finished checks on bigger forwards. Took the hit to make the play with the puck.

KGN #21 RW Cranford, Ryan (2016) - Finished checks hard and consistently. Jammed home the puck in the slot to score 1-3 goal. Played second unit powerplay and first unit penalty kill.

KGN #96 RW Watson, Spencer (Los Angeles) - Great compete throughout the game, landed some huge hits and used speed and put skills to create plenty of chances. Good shot to tie the game 4-4, then scored winner in overtime which was waved off after review due to offside.

LON #4 D Juolevi, Olli (2016) - Picked off clearing attempt, and fired it through a screen, deflected in for 2-0 goal. Blasted a bullet from the point to score 4-2 goal. Made an excellent play on the goal line to save a goal.

LON #7 C Tkachuk, Matthew (2016) - Battles in slot. Landed some great hits and played very physical throughout the game. Went to the net to score a bit of a soft 3-0 goal on a powerful shot. Only forward chosen to play 5 on 3 penalty kill. Smart passing to set up partial break. Used it to create offence throughout the game.

LON #23 C Rymsha, Drake (2016) - Good passes in transition. Was about 50% in the face-off circle tonight.

LON #49 LW Jones, Max (2016) - Dives at pucks he doesn't think he'll get to. Plays with a high level of determination. Took a bad penalty with 10 minutes left and a one goal lead.

LON #98 D Mete, Victor (2016) - Smart pass over on the power play lead to 4-2 goal on a one-timer. Took penalty down low in the defensive zone then argued with referee all the way to the box. Had some rough power play moments on line with puck. Was getting outmatched down low.

LON #1 G Parsons, Tyler (2016) - Taking away angles well early on and showed quickness. Dangerous puck play, missed and nearly lead to goal. Two of the first three goals allowed were cross crease passes that were tough to stop.

Final Score: Kingston Frontenacs: 6 - London Knights: 5 - OT/SO

USNTDP at Youngstown Phantoms, September 26th, 2015

USA #4 RD Krys, Chad (2016) - Krys played a key part in NTDP's second goal by making a nice move on the blueline throwing off his check and firing a shot on the net that Frederic would tip for the goal. Overall, Krys did a good job moving the puck around and displayed good skating ability. Could be a bit more engaged in his own zone though.

USA #7 C Frederic, Trent (2016) - Frederic scored by tipping a Krys point shot into the net. Good compete on both ends of the ice. Liked him breaking up a couple of plays in his own zone, doesn't shy away from battles. Very north-south game, he did not show much creativity or ability to delay and open up the play in the offensive end.

USA #8 RD Fox, Adam (2016) - Did a good job quarterbacking the powerplay. He also sneaked down the right side and made a great assist back to the middle for Keller's PP goal. Not the biggest player, it shows defensively, didn't see him use his stick much to control defensive space either, which made him look even smaller than he is.

USA #17 RW Anderson, Joey (2016) - He reads the play well in offensive zone but many shifts he just ends up deferring too much to Keller and Bellows. I liked seeing him read holes on the weak side or sliding into the slot from higher up in the offensive zone, but he needs to do more on his own.

USA #18 LD Lindgren, Ryan (2016) - There were a couple of quick plays around his net where he got a bit confused, should have tried harder to get firmer body contact on his player. First pass had mixed results. He opted for a delay once which resulted in him taking a bad hit. Did OK when he tried to make a pass right away though. Looked like he had the smarts but not necessarily the skills to pull off anything too elaborate with the puck.

USA #19 C Keller, Clayton (2016) - Was setting up plays for most of the game. Gift-wrapped Bellows two goals. One by drawing the defense to him before making a drop pass and another by a quick change of direction and a pass to the other side of the ice on PP. Great skills, vision, and skating ability. Avoids getting pinned down with ease, but saw some question marks in regard to what would happen if he played against a heavily structured physical defense that would push him to the wall.

USA #22 LW Bellows, Kieffer (2016) - Scored a hattrick in this game. Two PP goals one off a slick Keller pass, one on a rebound where he jammed the puck past the goalie. Third was another Keller set up, but to Bellows' credit he can really finish and he scored both from a quick outside shot as well as directly in front of the net. Had a couple of more shots, could have done a slightly better job in keeping the puck in the offensive zone though.

YNG #3 LD McInnis, Luke (2016) - Started off a bit shaky in his own zone, thought his first couple of shifts were a bit low energy and soft around the net but he picked it up later. Smart player with his passing and picked up two secondary assists, but didn't blow me away with his talent, especially considering the lack of size.

YNG #26 LW Morrison, Cameron (2016) - Morrison tied the game in second period with a backhand tip on a net drive. His feet look clunky but he does a good job setting up in the offensive zone and he had another good chance in third period by going to the net and opening up his blade for a pass. Showed good offensive zone sense and vision, a bit harder for him to make plays through neutral zone with speed as his feet need improvement.

Kingston Frontenacs at Sarnia Sting, September 27, 2015

OHL Regular Season

KGN #11 C Dorval, Zack (2016) - Good acceleration with the puck on his stick. Kept it simple on limited ice. Played second penalty killing unit.

KGN #13 Chernyuk, Konstantin (2016) - Good feet. A little rough on the long passes, made much better touch passes. Skating helps him stick with opponents. Quick to get down low from the front of the net. Showed some toughness down low, tough on the wall but needs to add more strength. Needs to improve on his positioning down low, but he does battle hard. Good rush but missed on the shot.

KGN #21 RW Cranford, Ryan (2016) - Consistently works hard. Finishes his checks. Was always well positioned on the rush. Played top power play minutes.

SAR #5 D Chychrun, Jakob (2016) - Great recovery to negate a scoring chance. Made some questionable decisions on the power play. Struggled with some puck misplays unbecoming of his usual play. Still has a massive NHL level point shot. Eventhough he didn't have a great game, he still has the skill set to potentially break the game open in one shift, and nearly did this a few times. Fell 3 on 3 but quickly recovered to make play. Great line holds on the offensive blue line in the last minute of regulation to keep the play going. Third shooter in the shootout for Sarnia, great stutter step to get goaltender to commit then nice backhand to score the winner.

SAR #10 C Salinitri, Anthony (2016) - Jumped up on power play rush and fired home a one-timer for goal. Played a bit on the perimeter, but won puck races. Made some excellent passes and puck decisions on the rush. Second shooter for Sarnia in he shootout, got mixed up by goaltender poke check and missed the net. Played top power play minutes and played sparingly on the penalty kill.

SAR #25 RW Kyrou, Jordan (2016) - Had two seconds left in the second period with the opposing goaltender down, but skated a wide circle killing the rest of the period instead of taking a shot on the partially wide open goal. Used his speed a bit but was very perimeter today. Had the puck on a three on one rush and fired from a very low percentage angle negating the odd man rush in the third period of a tie game.

Final Score: Sarnia Sting: 4 - Kingston Frontenacs: 3 - OT/SO

Flint Firebirds at Owen Sound Attack, September 30, 2015

FLT #41 C Bitten, Will (2016) - Good speed, went hard to the net with the puck. Fearless against bigger opponents. Finishing checks and competes for pucks. Does a great job using a variation of speeds to affect opponents trying to match up with him. Does a good job tracking where the puck is going to go, and gets there in a hurry. Accelerates well through traffic in the neutral zone.

FLT #38 G Keyser, Kyle (2018) - Entered game already down 0-3 with 6 minutes left in the first period for his OHL debut. Did well playing calm with smooth movement and looked very calm for his OHL debut. Allowed goal on a deflection shortly after getting run over, not much chance. Good cross crease save. Great quickness and reflexes. Quick pads but overcommitted sometimes to shots, which put him out of position on the second chance, which happened on 2-5 goal.

OS #2 D Friend, Jacob (2016*) - Landed some huge hits today. Good first pass. Had a great fight fairing well.

OS #9 C Szypula, Ethan (2016*) - Looks very much improved. Quicker first step, making decisions much quicker. Laser shot, one goal, one post.

OS #21 RW Gadjovich, Jonah (2017) - Protected the puck well driving the net and a backhander off the bar for 2-0 goal, which was a little soft.

OS #37 C Suzuki, Nick (2017) - Put the puck on goal, when the goalie couldn't find it his teammate tapped it in, Suzuki registered an assist. Scored 4-0 goal on door step, tapped into open net. Handles passes in skates well. Good three on two pass created scoring chance. Easily stripped down low offensive zone. Good release on his shot. Can give up on the play once the puck is lost.

Final Score: Owen Sound Attack: 5 - Flint Firebirds: 2

Charlottetown Islanders vs Victoriaville Tigres, October 1st, 2015

CHA #24 RW Balmas, Mitchell (2016): Got to play on the top line with Chlapik and Goulet but didn't get to play on the power play during the game. He had two great scoring chances in the game; he was robbed by the Victoriaville goaltender on both. He did a good job finding free space in the offensive zone on those two chances, though. Outside of those two chances, he didn't do a whole lot in this game. He was often the first guy on the forecheck on this line, but didn't have much impact with his hits or speed.

CHA #23 LW Boudrias, Shawn (2017): The big forward made a lot of smart plays in his zone and the neutral zone today. He was strong on his skates and used his long reach well to protect the puck in the defensive and neutral zones. Boudrias did a good job in the neutral zone, creating a turnover on the 3rd Islanders' goal.

CHA #2 RD Deschênes, Luc (2016): He did a good job on the Islanders' first goal, rushing the puck into the Victoriaville zone and taking a simple shot on net. The Islanders scored on the rebound. He was playing his former team and was playing them really hard even after whistles, trying to set the tone for his new team. He did, however, make numerous bad reads in the defensive zone and was a liability on the defensive side of the game. He played a lot today; even-strength, power play and penalty kill.

CHA #5 LD Smith, Andrew (2016): He had trouble handling the puck, taking too much time moving it out of his zone and getting in trouble for it. Smith is a huge kid who covers a lot of ice with his size and reach. Smith will definitely need to improve his quickness and decision-making with the puck. He was not overly physical in this game and was also on the receiving end of a good hit by Jacob Lapierre.

VIC #5 RD Lalonde, Bradley (2016): Lalonde did well on the PP, showing that he is capable of rushing the puck, and had some good shots on net. Outside of this, he struggled in his zone, was beat 4-5 times on the rush and made bad reads in his coverage. He was victim of a great one-on-one move by Alex Goulet on the OT goal, playing the puck instead of the man.

VIC #9 C Laberge, Pascal (2016): Laberge was strong in the faceoff circle, doing really well in the first period in that aspect. He didn't do a lot offensively in the game, though. I thought he was lacking jump and was playing too much on the perimeter. He scored in the 3rd period into an open cage at the side of the net after a great pass from Samuel Blais.

VIC #44 C Comtois, Maxime (2017): The young rookie played both down the middle and on the wing today. He played on the PP and PK; he showed great maturity with his play without the puck and on the PK. On the power play, he was used in front of the net to screen the opposing goaltender. He made some real nice cross-ice passes in the offensive zone, showing real good on-ice vision. He did some good work in retrieving the puck on the forecheck on the Mario Huber goal late in the game.

VIC #47 LW Lapierre, Jacob (2017): Big game from Lapierre today, who scored twice and was involved at both ends of the ice. His first goal was a good give-and-go between him and Lauzon and he finished it by going to the net. On the second goal, a long and juicy rebound was given up by the Victoriaville goaltender and he was able to score from the faceoff circle. He used his size well, throwing some good hits, including one on Andrew Smith. He did great work along the boards, showing good puck-protection and an ability to be strong on his skates.

VIC #48 C Lauzon, Felix (2016): Lauzon was a key player on the PK for the Tigres today. He often was on the ice in defensive situations. He had two to three solid blocked shots in his zone. He was always near the puck; a smart player who is good at avoiding hits. He made a really nice pass to Lapierre on Victoriaville's 2nd goal. Both of them did well together today.

VIC #96 C Huber, Mario (2016): The big Austrian forward was good today; working extremely hard at both ends of the ice. Not the best skater, but I really liked his compete level and how he never quit on backchecks. He threw his weight around many times in this game. He used his big frame well in the offensive zone along the boards to protect the puck. He scored a goal by going to the net in the 3rd period and also hit the post early in the game with a strong shot. On the PP, he was often playing on the point, where they would try to set him up for one-timers.

Erie Otters at Niagara Ice Dogs, October 1, 2015

OHL Regular Season

ERI #4 D Egan, Taylor (2016) - Low, deflectable point shot, created a chance when deflected in slot. Played a very simple game. Skates puck out of trouble. Good options on first pass.

ERI #6 D Sambrook, Jordan (2016) - Opens himself up for defensive partner as a passing option in the defensive zone. Smart first pass; makes decisions quickly. Great awareness to hold the line and keep the play going. Quick hips and a good stick to break up one on one plays. Made a puck mistake and quickly recovered to get the puck back then take it end to end then showed good patience to out wait the defenseman to fire a low shot to score 2-1 goal after video review. Good skater. Good body position and battle in puck races to win.

ERI #12 C DeBrincat, Alex (2016) - Great first step quickness. Good hands in close for early chance. Good pass to set up a partial break then went to the net to receive pass back and quickly fired puck home for 1-0 goal. Deceptive shot which got him close multiple times; hit posts. Good patience going to the net to out wait defenseman and fire home for 3-1 goal. Good position and quick release to score 5-1 goal and complete the hat trick. Shakes checkers well taking the puck to the net. Good release to score five hole 6-1, a little soft. Was excellent in face offs winning about 75% of his draws.

ERI #13 C Neumann, Brett (2017) - Made quick puck decisions down low to keep the play moving on the cycle. Competes for pucks with his stick, not body. Strong skating ability, showed some flashes of puck skills but also lost the puck in traffic.

ERI #17 RW Raddysh, Taylor (2016) - Good deflection in slot. Gets in great offensive zone positioning but couldn't convert early. Got puck off wing for a partial break but didn't have the angle so he made a nice pass back to set up Erie's 1-0 goal. Needs that extra gear on his skating that he just doesn't have at the moment. Takes away passing lanes on the back check very well. Quick read and good pass directly created 5-1 goal. Extremely good at deflecting shots. Would like to see his feet catch up to his hockey sense and ability to process game. Can generate speed over long distance and can still process the game very well at this speed.

ERI #24 D Raddysh, Darren (2016**) - Blocked a ton of shots tonight. Great defensive positioning. Difficult to beat one on one. Finished checks hard. Good first pass up ice. Does everything you can ask for in a defensive defenseman has just average size and average feet.

NIA #14 RW Paquette, Christopher (2016) - Kind of awkward skating but has good long strides. Drove wing and made a power move for scoring chance. Cycled the puck well down low protecting it with size along the wall.

Final Score: Erie Otters: 6 - Niagara Ice Dogs: 1

Sault Ste. Marie Greyhounds at Guelph Storm, October 2, 2015

OHL Regular Season

SSM #12 RW Katchouk, Boris (2016) - Good play in the slot to deflect home 1-0 goal on his first shift. Playing physical and mixing it up after the whistle. Good acceleration to split the defenders and create scoring chance. Came back around and put away his second goal of the game.

SSM #26 LW Gettinger, Tim (2016) - Picked off teammates breakaway pass, resulted in offside. Skating is awkward, gets some speed but doesn't handle sudden direction changes well. Doesn't engage enough in battles, especially for size. Decent power in shots but keeps firing at goalie chest. Had trouble with the pace at times. Easy to knock off balance down low with puck.

SSM #32 G Raaymakers, Joseph (2016) - Very active playing the puck, for the most part made good plays with the occasional mistake. Didn't face much action in the first period. Taunted opponent while holding the puck behind the net, who got back there quicker than anticipated, took the puck and nearly set up and open net goal. Happened more than once.

GUE #4 D Carroll, Noah (2016) - Gives a little too much time one on one. Made several excellent passes from his own zone tape to tape. Some where it didn't even look like he had an option. Bad turnover in his own zone on the power play under pressure lead to short handed chance against. Reads plays well and jumps up at good times.

GUE #7 D Phillips, Brock (2016) - Played very physical right off the start. Finished checks when team was down and tried to drop the gloves with some of the bigger Greyhound players.

GUE #19 LW Ratcliffe, Isaac (2017) - Tremendous speed for his size but needs to work on his turns. Has a good stick to break up possession on the forecheck, but doesn't use his size enough. Promoted to more ice due to his play and compete level. Uses speed on the back check hard to break up plays.

GUE #23 C Hotchkiss, Matthew (2016) - Good pressure on forecheck to force turnovers.

GUE #24 RW Smith, Givani (2016) - Powered through smaller opponents like they were nothing. Fanned on the puck in the slot but had the presence of mind to pass it cross crease to set up Guelph's 3-4 goal. Dropped the gloves with opponent requesting the fight, was initially declined but as he went to skate away the opponent quickly dropped the gloves, Smith responded well and won the fight. Finished his checks hard and landed a ton of them.

Final Score: Sault Ste. Marie Greyhounds: 8 - Guelph Storm: 4

Fargo Force at Cedar Rapids RoughRiders, October 2nd, 2015

FAR #25 C Graham, Michael (2016) - Didn't stand out much. Can't think of any good offensive zone looks that he was involved in. Took one bad offensive zone penalty tripping a defenseman from behind.

FAR #26 LW Tufte, Riley (2016) - Tufte started out a bit slow, only being dangerous on the powerplay. He did pick it up as the game progressed and showed off good hands and skating ability at his size. Gets nice power on his shot too, though no real high-end scoring chances to speak of in this game. I thought he read the play well, supported the puck and opened up but maybe could have done a bit more early on, his best shifts came when the game was already all but decided.

CED #11 C Burke, Cal (2016*) - Thought he was one of the better Cedar Rapids forwards but nothing in his game really jumped out and screamed that he's an NHL prospect in his second year of eligibility. Good game on both ends of the rink but nothing too impressive upside-wise.

CED #12 LW Filipe, Matt (2016) - Had some good offensive zone plays. Scored a goal dishing the puck in neutral zone and skating around the D before cutting inside and getting the puck back finishing on a nice backhand move. Picked up another goal on a Gosiewski shot where the puck might have touched him in front of the net before going in.

CED #16 LW McGing, Hugh (2016) - He was strong early on and especially on the PP with his playmaking from behind the net. One thing he was good at is arriving first to pucks and making quick passes with his peripheral vision to linemates skating into space.

CED #26 C Gosiewski, Matt (2016) - Slow start but had some good looks later in the game. Big body. He got credited with an assist on a nice top shelf shot after he found a loose puck in the slot, it might have touched Filipe before going in.

Niagara Ice Dogs at Peterborough Petes, October 3, 2015

OHL Regular Season

NIA #17 D Lochead, William(2016) - Landed excellent open ice hit. Good positioning on 2 on 2 rushes. Quiet but effective tonight.

NIA #30 G Dhillon, Stephen (2016) - Didn't face much in first but took away angles well on shots. Comes out to play the puck, missed his target but got back in net in time. Played too deep in his crease making things much more difficult for himself. Gave too much net to shoot at due to positioning on 0-2 goal. Handled deflections very well.

PET #2 D Fraser, Cole (2017) - Played a steady physical and defensively responsible game, especially for a rookie in one of his first games. Well positioned and reliable. Dropped the gloves with an 18 year old, landing several big punches and one the fight despite his opponents resiliency.

PET #3 D Lizotte, Cameron (2016*) - Played a very physical game off the start. Puck over glass early for penalty. Hit or miss on the rush had some great ones choosing good lanes but also had some where he tried to be too fancy. Good skater for size. Played a big 5 on 3 penalty kill. Willing to block shots.

PET #4 D Timms, Matthew (2016) - Good skating ability, undersized for defensive position. Takes too long to make passing decisions and will constantly retreat to gain more time. Good pinch with agility and puck control to create scoring chance. Constantly shouts or bangs stick for puck. Second power play unit.

PET #11 C Gallant, Zach (2017) - Provided a steady effective two-way game on the third line. Smart in all three zones and made good decisions with the puck.

PET #21 C Ang, Jonathan (2016) - Outstanding skater. Flies in ahead of the rush putting it offside multiple times. Great skating used it in both directions. Bad turnover in own zone lead to scoring chance. Over skates play in defensive zone sometimes hurting his positioning in the zone. Doesn't have the best vision on higher difficult passes, quickly and accurately completed easier shorter distance passes. Shot into screens on the power play. Played second unit both power play and penalty kill.

Final Score: Peterborough Petes: 3 - Niagara Ice Dogs: 2

Halifax Mooseheads vs Drummondville Voltigeurs, October 4th 2015

HFX #41 RW Fortier, Maxime (2016): Offensively, Fortier was quiet like the rest of his team playing a 3rd game in 3 days. He was able to show his good speed in some sequences during the game but nothing that ended up resulting in scoring chances. He was able to get on the scoresheet late in the 3rd after stealing the puck from #22 Sevigny inside the offensive zone and beating the Drummondville goaltender with a quick low shot from the faceoff circle.

HFX #17 C Crossley, Brett (2016): Did well winning some draws for his team, showed some good speed rushing the puck on some shifts. He was a key contributor to the penalty killing unit, saw him block a couple of shots. Centered the 3rd line with fellow 16-year-old Durandeau and veteran Brent.

HFX #89 LW Somppi, Otto (2016): He was very quiet in the first 2 periods, but was more active in the 3rd period, handling the puck more and trying to create more offense. I did like his effort on the backcheck to break up a 3-on-2 in the first period. He was able to create some offense on the power play in the 3rd period with more space and time, usually from the half wall.

HFX #40 G Resop, Kevin (2016): Gave up 5 goals but was the best Mooseheads' player today, without him, it would have been 8 or 9 goals. Halifax looked really bad in the first 2 periods and Resop had to make numerous amazing saves. He made 2-3 highlight reel saves by moving post to post, robbing Drummondville players of sure goals. He looks big in net and was able to track the puck well, even with traffic in front of him. Resop was un-drafted last season.

HFX #26 LD Ford, Taylor (2016): Un-Drafted last season, Ford was good today for the Mooseheads, showing a strong work ethic and no quit in his game. He competed well from start to finish. He is not an offensive defenseman, but played well in his own zone and on the PK. He was physical when he had to, taking his man out on the boards. He played most of the game with Fitzgerald as the top pair for Halifax.

HFX #2 RD Jones, Cooper (2016): An undersized American defenseman in his rookie season in the QMJHL. He didn't show much in the first period, but I started noticing him in the 2nd period. He started using his feet a bit more and trying to push the play in the offensive zone. He was not afraid to support the attack deep in the offensive zone. Good footwork.

HFX #11 LD Nauss, Morgan (2016): Nauss made some decent outlet passes to his forwards in the first period. He kind of disappeared after that first period, though. He had some power play shifts during the game, mostly on the 2nd unit. Footwork seems to be an area that will need some work.

HFX #3 LD Flower, Walter (2017): Liked his use of his stick in the defensive zone; he has a long reach. Footwork will need to improve, was beat wide by the small and quick Drummondville forwards.

DRU #4 LD Gagne, Benjamin (2017): He was used often during today's game, on both PP and PK units. Good active stick in the defensive zone, he's not the biggest defender but he used his smarts to defend well. Gagne finished the game with 3 points, scoring a goal by jumping on a rebound at the side of the net. He made a real nice play on Drummondville's 4th goal, making a quick pass in the slot to Girard (who was all alone) which resulted in Afanasyev's 1st goal of the day.

DRU #28 RD Aube, Frederic (2016): Un-Drafted '96-born defenseman who is off to a really strong beginning of the season. He's used in many facets of the game as a 3rd-year veteran with the Voltigeurs. He seemed to have improved his skating, as he made some impressive rushes with the puck, showing good acceleration as well. He was not afraid to get pucks on net in the offensive zone, although he will need to work on his one-timer, as he missed completely on 3 occasions. He looks very confident on the ice and is making more plays to contribute more in terms of offensive for his team (compared to the past 2 years).

DRU #8 LW Carcone, Michael (2016): A 2nd year player with Drummondville originally from Ontario, Carcone is off to a very strong start this season as well, and was good again today. He used his speed well and was successful beating HFX defensemen wide at times during the game. Always seems to know where to go in the offensive zone to get scoring chances, playing on a line with #19 Barre-Boulet and #11 Ratelle today. He was used on both PP and PK. He scored in the first period after tipping a Ratelle pass behind the HFX goaltender.

DRU #9 C Afanasyev, Kristian (2016): The 4th overall pick in the 2015 CHL Import Draft scored twice today (his first 2 goals in the league). He's a big boy and not afraid to play in the tough areas of the ice in the offensive zone. He did well in puck protection situations, using his back to shield opponents away. His two goals were scored 3 feet from the goaltender. The first one was a rebound at the side of the net and the 2nd one was a tip shot in front of the goaltender on the power play.

DRU #10 RW Gaumond, Samuel (2017): Undersized rookie forward who plays with a lot of energy and passion. Not afraid to get involved physically and was a pain to play against today. Really good speed; can get to top speed quickly and that helps him be a threat on the forecheck. However, his lack of strength does hurt him in puck battles in the corners or in front of the net.

DRU #19 C Barre-Boulet Alex (2016): Un-Drafted last season, Barre-Boulet is yet another Voltigeur off to a good start this season. He's a smart player and it showed today, as he was rarely in a bad position on the ice. His anticipation was very good too, as he seems to know where the puck will go before everyone else. He's more dangerous on the power play with more space on the ice; he controlled the puck well on the power play and created more plays with his playmaking abilities.

DRU #22 C Sevigny, Mathieu (2016): He did a good job with #10 Gaumond in the first period, making things happen in the offensive zone. Gaumond was winning puck races and Sevigny was finding holes in the offensive zone to receive passes from his linemate. He will need to get his shot faster on net, as his hesitation left the defense enough time to adjust. Did some good work along the boards. He's strong on his skates and protects the puck well. Fortier was able to steal the puck from him late in the 3rd just inside the Drummondville zone for the 3rd Halifax goal.

Kootenay Ice at Prince Albert Raiders, October 6th, 2015

KTN #2 LD Murray, Troy (2016*) - Played it simple and intelligent. Good, controlled defensive game. Had a shift on PK where he killed about 20 seconds by battling on the wall. Flashed his skating ability in moving the puck up the ice through neural zone a couple of times, but seemed to play a more defensive game without taking much risks.

KTN #4 RD Fleury, Cale (2017) - Was a two-way presence on the blue-line. Competed defensively, was physically engaging. Moved the puck well with passing. Can be hard to stop if he picks up speed with the puck on his stick. Skated it out of trouble by himself on a few occasions. Seemed confident throughout the game and was one of the better Kootenay players.

KTN #19 LW Legien, Jared (2016) - Had a couple of chip and chase plays. Compete level was there, he moved his feet with and without the puck. Not much there offensively, had some shot attempts but takes too long in wind-ups, too easy to block for a defenseman and too easy to stop if it gets to the goalie. Limited in impact overall.

KTN #22 RW Zborosky, Zak (2016*) - Simple, competitive game. Worked all game long. Reads puck-movement well and will cause some breakdowns where he can be dangerous. Not a lot of skill, size is average at best, and not very fast either. Easy to like in the way he plays the game, though.

KTN #24 RW Patterson, Max (2018) - Big body, especially for a kid his age. Got ejected early for a huge blindside hit on Gennaro. After the hit he got jumped and had to defend himself in a fight, looked like he wanted none of it.

PRI #6 LD Budik, Vojtech (2016) - Strong, mistake-free game. Good hands and skating ability that he uses really well in defensive situations. You can't dump the puck against him, excellent in puck-retrievals. Consistently first on loose pucks and has the ability to move it out. Had some good physical play blocking forwards when defending zone entry. Might have taken a total of 2 or 3 offensive chances in the entire game, didn't look to create offense unless he was 100% sure that it won't result in a turnover.

PRI #8 LD Paivarinta, Cody (2016) - Big, mobile defenseman. Early on that was just about the only thing he showed. Started to make some plays with the puck in second and third period, and started to become more engaging in moving up the ice. Despite lining up at LD, he seemed to have some odd sequences of movement to the right-side of the ice, despite his partner already being there.

PRI #19 RW Gardiner, Reid (2016**) - Decent but not great skating. Competes reasonably well. Fantastic release on the wrister and scored that way as well. Despite some upside and tools, it didn't look like he had a "draftable" performance once you account for his age and him being passed over twice already.

PRI #23 LW Stransky, Simon (2016) - Skilled wing, reads the flow of the play well. There is some compete and bite in him, but would have liked to see a touch more of that in this game. Showed off his vision and skill. While he did distribute the puck well, it felt like he should have looked for his shot more. He liked to come down off his off-wing (RW) and cut to the middle while looking to hit someone with a pass.

PRI #25 RW Montgomery, Sean (2016) - He's a fluid intelligent forward. Really made some good understated reads both offensive and defensive. Doesn't rely on his speed, but he is a good skater. Had a fantastic PK diving play to finally kill pressure. Not a lot of offensive impact, but seemed to be involved as a two-way presence, always supporting the play. Did well on the forecheck as well.

PRI #28 LW Coleman, Luke (2016) - Big body, top speed at his size and age is good. Can be hard to stop when he gets moving. Agility in-tight could be better. Good shot, scored first Prince Albert goal with a wrister top-corner. Can jump into holes and has the mentality of a scorer. Some power-forward features in him as well. Threw his body around a bit. Will compete.

PRI #33 G Scott, Ian (2017) - Struggled a bit in the first period when he didn't see a lot of action and gave up 2 goals despite Prince Albert dominating the period. Once he settled down, he started using his big size to play the angles better. Came up big a couple of times throughout the game, his rebound control in particular was quite good in this game. Also did a good job tracking the puck and being in position for second opportunities when needed.

Vancouver Giants at Moose Jaw Warriors, October 7th, 2015

VAN #7 RW Ronning, Ty (2016) - A smaller skilled wing. Has a low center of gravity and some lateral ability that allows him to protect the puck. Competed well and made some good plays in the offensive zone. He should have enough skill to produce at the junior level, but considering his lack of size, he hasn't separated himself from the pack enough in this game.

VAN #21 LD Mennel, Brennan (2016*) - Has done a good job of moving the puck around. Can skate, handle, and distribute the puck from the back-end. Not very big for a defenseman, and despite the solid puck-movement, he hasn't really shown anything dynamic.

VAN #24 LD Barberis, Matt (2016) - Was dangerous from offensive blueline. Has a good shot from the point. Scored top-shelf on the PP by unloading a wrister from top of the circle. His compete level was fine, he can move the puck and there is some bite in him defensively. Not a lot of size though. He likes to move the puck quickly, felt like he was forcing some of the passes that weren't there in break-outs.

VAN #28 RW Semchuk, Brendan (2017) - He played a competitive game up and down the wing. Moved his feet. Sacrificed body on the wall to make plays. He did a good job using his body to protect the puck. Was engaging both defensively and offensively, however didn't have a lot of offensive opportunities.

MJW #2 RD Brook, Josh (2017) - He played well in his own end. Competed, won battles and moved the puck out. Didn't try anything extra, just smart little plays. There was one instance where he lost coverage to Bondra on a quick play, and you could tell he was a bit overmatched in that match-up, but outside of that he was mostly fine. Played a pretty intelligent, steady game.

MJW #5 LD Paradis, Colin (2016) - He was better in the first half of the game. Was really engaging in his own zone, clearing bodies from the net and battling on the wall, later he faded in his performance. He was better using his body and battling in-tight than using his stick. Didn't do a lot with the puck.

MJW #16 RW Bargar, Blake (2016) - Had jump and tried to make things happen by going to the net. When he got the puck, he did well in skating it up the ice through the neutral zone. He had a couple of shots from outside. Competed well, but none of his efforts resulted in any real scoring chances.

MJW #18 C Quinney, Landon (2016) - Quiet game. He seems to read the play well enough to get into the action, but never had any tangible impact past a few easy passes in this game. He had one good shift cycling the puck in the third period, that resulted in an extended offensive zone shift, but was mostly a passenger outside of that.

MJW #21 LW Howden, Brett (2016) - Had good jump the entire game. Acceleration is quite good at his size. At top speed, he tends to have a shorter stride with a lot of foot movement, but not a lot of extension. He was digging in the corners and was taking the puck to the middle for most of the game.

If he managed to get some of the bounces to go his way, he could have put something more on board than a secondary assist. Was average in terms of making plays with the puck.

MJW #22 C Gregor, Noah (2016) - He has good speed and looked to get his shot on net. He has shown some offensive upside, but felt like he didn't really find a way to get fully involved in the game. He was a sporadic offensive threat with buzzing around the play and looking for his shot, but never really put a solid string of 3-4 shifts together.

MJW #31 G Sawchenko, Zach (2016) - He gave up several goals up over his shoulders, wasn't really late on any of the saves but seemed like he misjudged some of the angles or dropped down too quick. Towards the end of the second and in the third he took it up a notch and shut it down. Rebound control was good throughout and he seemed to have good technique in his movement in the crease. Calm goalie but in this game questionable focus on those early goals up-high.

MJW #71 LW Popugaev, Nikita (2017) - Popugaev was the best player on the ice. Big body, can skate, used his frame for puck-protection, was winning board battles, was taking it to the net, was distributing the puck with intelligent little passes… It was all there. A sequence that stood out was him firing a shot from the half-wall area, following it to the middle and converting on a second-effort with another quick-release shot.

Scout's Notes: Tyler Benson (Vancouver Giants) did not suit up for the game due to injury.

Peterborough Petes at Windsor Spitfires, October 8, 2015

OHL Regular Season

PET #7 D Grima, Nick (2017) - Great cross ice pass. Chooses good passing options.

PET #11 C Gallant, Zach (2017) - Outstanding two line pass to set up breakaway chance. Strong defensive positioning, even off an initial turnover. Good hit down low, engages in battles willingly.

PET #18 RW Timleck, Adam (2016) - Bad zone clearing attempt, not aware of the play. Made some good passes in offensive zone, one of which resulted in a scoring chance. Finished checks on bigger opponents.

WSR #17 D Stanley, Logan (2016) - Made several smart pinches to keep the play going. Stepped up and landed a big hit at the defensive line. Beat wide one on one resulting in 0-1 goal. Next shift redeemed himself with a great end to end rush which set up Windsor's 1-1 goal. Not a pretty skater but has the ability to get to where he needs to with long strides. Plays with a lot of toughness below the dots in the defensive zone and will get his extra shots in whenever possible. Good positioning on the penalty kill.

WSR #21 C Brown, Logan (2016) - Great pass through traffic set up big scoring chance. Made slick passes in small areas. Took holding penalty in third, could be heard yelling at referee from up in the stands, then received a very questionable call a few minutes later.

WSR #22 RW Carter, Cole (2016) - Speed is good, has agility but doesn't have that extra gear in races.

WSR #31 D Sergachev, Mikhail (2016) - Skates well for size. Excellent puck protection ability. Good puck decisions. Top power play unit. Pretty good stick in his own zone. Mishandled the puck in his own zone leading to chance.

WSR #44 LW Kirwan, Luke (2016) - Skating has improved quite a bit. Great puck protection to drive the net and create a big scoring chance. Landed some huge hits.

Final Score: Windsor Spitfires: 4 - Peterborough Petes: 1

Oshawa Generals vs Ottawa 67's, OHL, Oct 9, 2015

OSH #22 C Cierelli, Josh (2016) – Good 2 way forward, responsible in both ends of rink, smart hockey player, had a couple nice takeaways, smart on the PP, created some chances of the rush with his speed.

OSH #23 C Studnicka, Jack (2017) – skilled forward, one a couple players for Oshawa to show some flash of offense, couple nice rushes with puck, went inside out on a defenseman and made him look silly, works hard every shift, not afraid of the rough stuff, smart decisions with the puck, ok on draws.

OSH #30 G Devine, Liam (2016) – Played good tonight, team wasn't much help in front of him, very calm in nets, not a lot of movements, allows puck to hit him, rebounds were controlled good, plays a a lot like Herbst for the 67's, good size too, stop 2 breakaways in the 3rd to keep team in.

OSH #37 LD Desrocher, Stephen (TOR) – Steady defenseman, smart decisions with the puck, kept things simple tonight, good first pass out of the zone, Big body D, used his size well along boards in dzone, good body positioning, could use his stick better, scored a nice goal from point.

OTT #2 LD Hoefenmayer, Noel (2017) – Good size Defensemen, good first pass out the zone, kept everything simple with his play tonight, not a lot of panic in his game, needs to work on his quickness got beat a few times wide, played 2nd unit PP, needs to be quicker with his decisions, held on to puck to long.

OTT #9 C Keating, Austen (2017) – Notice him a couple shift, offensive forward, show some skill on half boards, not a great skater, looks a lot like Erik Bradford.

OTT #19 LW Baron, Travis (2016) – Was ok tonight, didn't notice him offensively tonight, was hard on forecheck, hits everything in sight, works hard every shift, good shifts on the Penalty Kill.

Final Score: Oshawa: 2   Ottawa: 5

Kärpät at Tappara, Oct 9th, 2015

TAP #27 LW Laine, Patrik (2016) – Injured in the first shift and didn't came back.

KAR #9 RW Puljujärvi, Jesse (2016 – Played fantastic game and scored one goal and an assist. His goal was amazing performance.. Showed his great skating which led to a one-on-one situation and he deked the d-man and the goalie. His puck skills are tremendous and he likes to go to the traffic. Great back and forechecking. Started the game in the third line, ended in the first line.

KAR #26 RW Ikonen, Juuso (2016) – His start of the season have been amazing but today he played his worst game so far. Great puck skills and hockey sense but couldn't do anything in the o-zone. He's more versatile player than before lacks of size which is a major issue. Good around corners for his size.

KAR #21 LW Kalapudas, Antti (2016) – Centerman who played as winger in the fourth line. Made couple of nice passes in the o-zone and worked hard. He truly have great hockey sense but can't do his best in this kind of role. Skating technique and the speed are still big problems.

KAR #51 C Aaltonen, Miro (Drafted by Anaheim Ducks 2013) – Showed his great hockey sense and created couple of good scoring opportunities for his line mates. Smooth skating and good puck skills but lacks of physicalness. Great weapon on powerplay.

KAR #8 RW Mäenalanen, Saku (Drafted by Nashville Predators 2013) – Hard-working winger with good scoring instincts. Likes to shoot a lot but his shot needs to improve. Fast player with good first steps. Made an assist.

KAR #16 LW Aho, Sebastian (Drafted by Carolina Hurricanes 2015) – Scored a goal but didn't show much in the o-zone. Played great two way game and battled hard. He never quits and he's really reliably player. Amazing player on short-handed.

KAR #11 LD Nutivaara, Markus (Drafted by Columbus Blue Jackets 2015) – Good size, good skating ability and good hockey sense but today he was lost. Wasn't reliable in the d-zone as usual and made couple of easy mistakes.

Victoria Royals at Kelowna Rockets, October 9th, 2015

VIC #4 LD Jarratt, Ralph (2016) - Big defenseman. In fact, thought he looked a touch too heavy on his skates. Has good active stick. Played a physical shutdown type of game. Several times did a good job clearing the front of the net and winning battles on the wall. Sacrificed his body. Took hits on the forecheck but moved the puck all the same. At times looked a bit slow in his decision-making and skating on breakouts.

VIC #10 C Peckford, Ryan (2017) - He did a good job on the forecheck, several times he had good jump in coming out of corners with the puck and establishing a cycle down low. Scored the first goal of the game in third period by planting himself in front of the net and redirecting a pass into the net.

VIC #11 LW Phillips, Matthew (2016) - He's very small, but had jump the entire game and got better as the game progressed. He was hounding the puck and was quite good at disrupting Kelowna's puck-movement up the ice. Less effective in defensive zone due to lack of size. Offensively, he was more than willing to drive the net and go to the middle. Scored a PP goal by throwing the puck from behind the net into the slot and having the puck bounce off Gatenby into the net.

VIC #17 C Soy, Tyler (2016*) - He reads the play well, competes, and has good vision with the puck and a nose for finding himself in the right places. Played a good game in all three zones. Projection-wise, thought the same thing plagued him as last year, for a smaller guy his skating is lacking.

VIC #19 C Hannoun, Dante (2016) - Very small at this point in time, still at top speed he can be dangerous. There was a play where he recklessly drove the net, full speed into traffic without much regard for his own safety. He has some skill with the puck and isn't shy about going to scoring areas, but size is going to be a big issue for him going forward.

VIC #24 LW Dmytriw, Jared (2016) - Has good speed through neutral zone. Worked well on the forecheck and did a good job of establishing the cycle. Worked his butt off, but didn't show any creativity with the puck. He was useful as a checker that can pin the opposition down in their end as well as compete off-the-puck. When he gets the puck, he can make some basic plays on the cycle but didn't find a way to turn the possession into an actual scoring chance.

KEL #7 LD Johansen, Lucas (2016) - He has a simple yet smart game. Decent size and battled well when engaging physically. Used his stick well for pokechecks. Skating is decent, struggled a bit in having to react to quick-movement when covering a forward in the slot and in changing directions. On the offensive blueline, he held the point very well and made quick passes that extended offensive zone time for his team. He played both PP and PK. While his passing is usually on-point, I thought he made some uncharacteristically poor decisions when making the first pass.

KEL #16 RW Lind, Kole (2017) - He was used on the PP and took regular shifts along some of the top Kelowna players, mostly on the Merkley line. Did not look out of place at all. Although he was not a huge contributor, he managed to follow the play and was jumping into holes where he was dangerous a couple of times with the puck on his stick.

KEL #19 C Dube, Dillon (2016) - He played a competitive game off-the-puck. Offensively, he did a good job and was dangerous both as a passer as well as a shooter. The thing that stood out was him using his skating and hands to weave through traffic and maintain possession in the offensive zone. He finds ways to get involved. While he had a strong start and a decent game overall, he tailed off towards the end, like the majority of his team, culminating in a 3:0 loss.

KEL #25 RD Foote, Cal (2017) - He showed good upside, but also had some mistakes in an otherwise quiet game. He fumbled the puck as the last defenseman, and sometimes seemed to struggle a bit with the puck. He saw PP time down 2:0 in the middle of the third period, where he did a good job. Showed off his one-timer and distributed the puck well there. Looked like a kid that is going through the process of adjusting his decision-making to the pace of the game at this level. He seems to be at the brink of getting it. Considering it was only his eight WHL game, he should be fine.

KEL #28 RD Gatenby, Joe (2016*) - Did a very good job reading the play defensively and being in the right positions. Had an unlucky bounce go off him into the net. Was a complete non-factor outside his own zone through 2 periods. With his team down in the third, he started being more active offensively. Big point shot, but not very accurate. Average when handling the puck and it's not something that's really part of his repertoire.

Calgary Hitmen at Red Deer Rebels, October 10th, 2015

CGY #2 RD Bean, Jake (2016) - Bean lined up at RD with Sanheim as his partner on the left. He was excellent on the powerplay and on the offensive blueline. Scored twice on the PP, first a quick shot that found a way through traffic, second goal was him changing the angle before the release to avoid getting his shot blocked. He was consistently dangerous from the point both on the powerplay as well as even-strength. On the flip side, his puck-movement was somewhat below-standard. He fumbled the puck more than once and made some questionable decisions. His skating backwards when defending zone entry is also a bit of a weak-point. Very good from the offensive blueline in, but his overall performance lacked polish in this game.

CGY #11 LW Malenstyn, Beck (2016) - He is a pretty smart player. Can really track the play, finds himself in proper positions and uses his skating well. Considering the type of player he is, he left me wanting more. Thought he should have been more engaging. Didn't really have any bad plays per-se, but too many flybys and being around the play instead of trying to make something happen, especially in the offensive zone.

CGY #17 C Stallard, Jordy (2016) - A somewhat quiet game until the third period where he was a key factor in Calgary starting to mount pressure. He played a pretty cerebral game, reading the ice and picking his spots. Scored a third period goal by skating into the slot just in time to pick up a loose rebound and convert on it.

CGY #24 LW Twarynski, Carsen (2016) - Good size, stick and mobility. Can use his skating and reach to be a factor off-the-puck. Supported the puck well by getting open through puck-movement up ice. Had one good chance sneaking into the slot.

CGY #31 G Petersen, Lasse (2016*) - He was just ok, he made some decent saves but seemed to be unable to come up with the big one when Calgary needed it. The second goal he gave up was a weak wristshot from the half-wall area with no traffic in front of him. Got yanked after the second period, it was probably partly due to the fact that Calgary needed a wake-up call, but he didn't do himself any favors.

CGY #33 G Dumba, Kyle (2016) - He started the third period. Didn't have a lot of work, he gave up the tying goal 30 seconds before the end on a shot off a quick cross-ice pass. He came up big in OT, making several big saves.

RDR #2 RD Strand, Austin (2016*) - He's big and he can skate decently well for his size. He logged quite a bit of minutes and did ok. Didn't think he brought any big-time value to the ice for his team. Looked like someone who can eat minutes at the junior level and not hurt you in the process, didn't flash many NHL assets though.

RDR #11 C de Wit, Jeff (2016) - Good size and compete level. Can skate reasonably well, although not high-end. He had some offensive chances early on purely on compete level. Really liked the consistency in his game on a shift-to-shift basis. Played the type of checking game that establishes that tough to play against look. Willing to go to the net and useful off-the-puck. Established the pressure that resulted in Red Deer's first goal.

RDR #14 RW Pratt, Austin (2017) - Already has good size and skating ability. Played with jump and has a bit of that power-winger type of game to him. Was useful on the wall, where he can play physically or use his skating to throw off the player checking him. Can protect the puck and is willing to go to the middle.

RDR #16 LW Pawlenchuk, Grayson (2016*) - Competed hard all game long. Hounds players, arrives first on loose pucks, sacrifices his body. Was rewarded by scoring a one timer goal to tie the game on the PP with 30 seconds to go. Question marks regarding NHL upside remain with average frame-size, just ok skating, and nothing too dynamic with the puck on his stick.

RDR #22 LW Hagel, Brandon (2016) - He did a real good job pressuring the point with his speed. Caused quite a few problems for defensemen who tried to hold the blueline against him. Had two or three chances just by exploding with speed out of his zone. He also did a decent job on the forecheck. Didn't have a lot going for him when he didn't have speed working for him though.

Ottawa 67's at Barrie Colts, October 10, 2015

Final score: 4-0 Ottawa

OTT #3 D Brown, William (2016) – Brown had a very quiet game. He pinched along the wall to keep a couple plays alive and made some smart plays with the puck but he was sparsely used throughout and wasn't overly noticeable.

OTT #19 LW Barron, Travis (2016) – Barron was one of Ottawa's better players in this game. He was defensively responsible, sound positionally in the defensive zone and his spacing was very good while killing penalties. He had a couple blocks and several clears on the PK. Barron won several battles along the wall and didn't shy away from contact, either. With the puck he struggled to create shooting lanes at times but did get a couple pucks towards the net. He picked up a primary assist on a drop pass that led to a goal and also drew a penalty by keeping his feet moving.

OTT #91 C Rymsha, Drake (2016) – Rymsha was very involved from start to finish. He played a very smart two-way game and was particularly effective on the penalty kill. He did a good job of pressuring the puck carrier and showed no hesitation while getting into the shooting lanes to block shots. Offensively he didn't generate a ton but he had a couple shots and gained the line with possession on several occasions.

BAR #8 LW Chiodo, Lucas (2016) – Chiodo had a couple controlled zone entries but was unable to gain a step around defenders and was sealed off rather easily at times. He was also pushed off the puck several times. Chiodo drew a penalty but didn't create a whole lot offensively and overall was rather ineffective.

BAR #10 D Murray, Justin (2016) – He looked as comfortable with the puck on his stick as I have seen this season. Murray wasn't afraid to try a skilled play or a stretch pass and looked less panicky than in prior viewings. Murray had a couple big hits and won his share of battles along the boards. His positioning wasn't perfect and he's still adjusting to the speed of the game at the OHL level but I thought he played pretty well.

Saskatoon Blades at Swift Current Broncos, October 11th, 2015

SAS #8 RW Hausinger, Cameron (2017) - Can really skate. Uses gear changes really well and doesn't stop moving his feet, rather adjusts speed to what is happening on ice. He read the play and was constantly working to make himself open. Supported the puck well and was buzzing for most of the night. Scored a goal by jamming it in, in front of the net.

SAS #9 C Hebig, Cameron (2016*) - Really moved his feet the entire game long. Dangerous coming into the slot with speed and looking to cause havoc. Changes of direction when possessing the puck, making him hard to pin down. Hit a post after he deked out a Swift Current defenseman and drove the net. Stripped DeBrusk of the puck on a backcheck, turned around and beat the goalie clean with a backhand top shelf.

SAS #23 RD Higson, Schael (2016) - For a guy listed at 6'0 210lbs he had surprisingly good mobility and utilized it to his advantage. Not very noticeable, but a lot of quality two-way play. Moved the puck well, and had a good pinch up the wall to keep offensive zone possession. He misread coverage on a rush chance against, overcommitting to his partner's side, leaving the slot open which resulted in a dangerous pass to the middle to a wide open Swift current forward.

SAS #25 LD Hajek, Libor (2016) - He played a more demure game than what I'm used to with him. Seemed to stay back a bit more and let the game come to him. Not many mistakes. Passed the puck when needed, and defended reasonably well. He had one or two odd pinches in the offensive zone, but seemed to recover well and none of them resulted in any chances against. On the point he kept it simple and did a good job getting wristshots through. There was a play where he got nailed by a hit when moving the puck behind his net, missed a shift but came back after that.

SAS #47 RD Reid, Nolan (2016) - His point shot lead to a rebound that Christensen cleaned up into the goal. Reid didn't see a lot of ice time, but didn't make any mistakes when on ice. Decent mobility and competed well. Didn't handle the puck a lot, but his outlets were accurate. He tried to throw a big hit on Gawdin entering his zone, only to bounce off and leave Gawdin with open ice.

SWI #2 LD Sissons, Colby (2016) - Great 3 vs 4 PK shift, blocked a shot twice and then intercepted a pass to clear it out of the zone. Can pass, skating needs work though both with and without the puck. Finished his checks on dump-ins into his corner.

SWI #5 RD Minulin, Artyom (2017) - Big kid. Was used on both PP and PK. Uses stick and body and competes physically. Skating needs a lot of work, legs look very thin. Despite the lack of skating ability, is quite decent with the puck. Can handle it and made several intelligent quick little passes, both on the PP as well as in moving the puck out of the zone. Despite looking somewhat awkward on his

SWI #10 RW Seidel, Owen (2016) - His positioning off-the-puck was decent, could track the play and be in right positions. Deferred to easy decisions with the puck, for example cleared the puck off glass and out of his zone despite having ample time to look for a pass to a linemate.

SWI #17 LW Steenbergen, Tyler (2016) - Started on the top line, battled well and played a high-energy game. Was going to the dirty areas and just looked to make himself useful playing with DeBrusk and Feser. Later in the game he moved down a line and got less minutes. He had less offensive zone time then and was not as consistently dangerous, but remained useful in a more defensive role by keeping his feet moving off-the-puck and trying to make turnovers happen.

SWI #27 LD Lajoie, Max (2016) - He got a lot of shots on net from the point, which resulted in a goal and two assists, all off them on PP. Did a lot of puck-moving on breakouts, with mixed results. One of his passes from behind the net resulted in a scoring chance against and while others weren't as erroneous, it wasn't the only time he made a questionable pass. Still, for the most part he did well in distributing the puck, considering the large amount of puck touches he had. Defensively, he did well in getting on loose pucks. He was better at splitting plays up on the wall than pushing forwards out of the slot. Body-language looked a bit too relaxed around the net.

Regina Pats at Lethbridge Hurricanes, October 14th, 2015

REG #4 LD Knyzhov, Nikolai (2016) - He did a good job boxing Lethbridge forwards out of the slot and protecting the front of the net. First few steps looked a bit on the slower side. Doesn't handle the puck a lot, but he fired a dangerous shot joining the rush as the late man. Was solid defensively.

REG #23 C Steel, Sam (2016) - Good skater. Read the play very well, always in right position. Only complaint would be that at times as a center he played a bit too high in the defensive zone for my taste. Drew a penalty by stealing the puck on PK and taking off, broke up several plays on PK. Has shown high comfort level in making plays at speed. Can receive passes in stride and has no problem making intelligent little passes that forward the play. Dangerous shot on a couple of occasions. Was better when having speed through open ice. While he competed well it was a bit harder for him to establish a presence in the corners and down-low. At times I felt frustrated that his linemates didn't read the play on the same level.

REG #38 LD Pouteau, Brady (2016) - Struggled for most of the game. Had trouble with picking up forwards, three times got beat clean by not being able to keep up laterally. Questionable positioning as well. Saw less minutes as the game progressed.

REG #39 RW Zablocki, Lane (2017) - He had a great game. Won the majority of his battles. He got his stick on a lot of pucks and had a lot of interceptions. Was good on the forecheck and also in the defensive zone when pressuring the point, seemed to arrive first on all the pucks and used his body as well. He had an excellent back-check on a 2 on 1 that eliminated Lethbridge's passing lane.

LET #15 LW Bellerive, Jordy (2017) - He saw some shifts on the first line with Estephan and Wong, where he did a good job playing an opportunistic high-pace game. Had some scoring chances early in the game just by jumping into holes and presenting himself as an option to the above mentioned duo. Had a dangerous play getting levelled by Zborovskiy by having his head down near the offensive zone blueline.

LET #19 LW Burke, Brayden (2016*) - He controlled the puck well along the perimeter and had several dangerous passes into the slot. Really likes making the "final" pass from the outside-in, looking for holes where someone can finish on his pass.

LET #22 LW Babenko, Egor (2016*) - Doesn't appear very fast, but elusive and sort of weaved in and out of play, lots of time sneaking behind the defense's back. Scored a goal that way by walking into the slot out of nowhere and unchecked. Quite shifty with the puck as well.

LET #74 G Skinner, Stuart (2017) - He gave up 4 goals but his tools were very obvious. He looked like a very strong goalie prospect for 2017. Has the size, the athleticism and the reflexes to build upon. He misplayed the fourth goal by overcommitting to the near-side post. In the third period, he came up big when needed. Battled well in the crease and was quite good on second opportunities.

Drummondville Voltigeurs at Shawinigan Cataractes, October 16, 2015

DRU #4 D Gagne, Benjamin (2017) - Slick skating with good mobility. Anticipates passes and opens up instead of chasing a puck he won't get to anyways.

DRU #16 D Patry-Gingras, Nicolas (2016) - Good play one on one to break up chance.

DRU #22 C Sevigny, Mathieu (2016) - Competes hard at both ends. Excellent work ethic down low in the defensive zone to fight for pucks. Quick hands moving up ice and advanced puck well. Second unit penalty kill. Good positioning, pressure and zone clears on the penalty kill. Excellent positioning in offensive zone, always making himself an option. Never took a shift off all game long, constantly working every second of every shift. Second power play unit. Very streaky in the face off circle and finished just below 50% on the night.

SHA #3 D Sylvestre, Gabriel (2016) - Gabriel has excellent size. Passing ability is below average. Mishandled puck on offensive line. Finished his checks. Beat one on one when he was looking for the hit at the defensive blue line. Played on second penalty killing unit. Made a smart slap pass, which initiated the sequence to Shawinigan's 1-2 goal. Dropped the gloves with an opponent two years older who he held a five inch advantage on, but got worked over pretty bad in the fight.

SHA #28 C Gignac, Brandon (2016) - Good speed. Won puck race. Great forecheck pressure. Good wrist shot for scoring chance, using his speed to get into open ice in order to get his shot off. Good speed and puck skill to rush the puck on the power play. Moved the puck well at high speed. Did great on face-off circle winning about 80% of his draws.

SHA #44 D Benoit, Simon (2017) - Good move to beat forechecker and take the puck end to end. Skates well for size. Good play on the line then followed up with a hard shot for scoring chance. Gets his shots through.

SHA #72 C Asselin, Samuel (2016) - Good compete to force turnovers.
SHA #91 C Beauvillier, Anthony (NY Islanders) - Jumped on rebound in the slot to score 1-2 goal. Great speed and puck skills. Drew three power plays tonight but will need to get stronger because none of them will be calls in the NHL, just pushed around and got the call.

SHA #94 D Girard, Samuel (2016) - Effortless skating. Will skate east-west to create lanes for himself. Has a small stick but does an excellent job both one on one or against puck possession down low to knock puck off the stick. On multiple occasions he made good plays on opponents going wide keeping them there and blocking the lane but then didn't follow up by getting back into position, or on one play turning away from the play, which lead to an open shooting lane on the 0-2 goal. Bullet shot post and in to score 2-2 goal. Great stick 2 on 2. Top power play unit.

SHA #35 G Samuel, Antoine (2016) - First goal against was beat by a one timer going cross crease, got a piece of it but didn't get enough; a little soft. Second goal allowed was very soft and was quickly pulled with 8 minutes left in the first period, two shots, two goals allowed.

Swift Current Broncos at Brandon Wheat Kings, October 16th, 2015

SWI #4 LD Jensen, Kade (2016*) - Played a pro-style game. Smart pinches, simple quick outlets, good defensive stick and steered the play to the outside, engaged physically without taking himself out of position and got his shots through from the point.

SWI #5 RD Minulin, Artyom (2017) - Decision-making was solid. He can move the puck and he can read the play and position himself properly. Sometimes a bit limited by agility and skating, especially in quick changes of direction. He had a fantastic third period goal with a burst of speed into the slot where he redirected the pass into the top corner.

SWI #17 LW Steenbergen, Tyler (2016) - He has good jump and moves his feet well. Stole puck on the forecheck and came out from below the goal-line with a backhand shot. Good pace through neutral zone but forced wide a lot. Likes to search for soft spots in the slot and get open. On the wall he was a bit too easy to strip of the puck. In defensive zone, he sometimes had trouble moving the puck and got pinned in by pinching defensemen. Good job skating on the forecheck and backcheck though.

SWI #27 LD Lajoie, Max (2016) - Better outlets than the previous time I saw him. Accurate passing, but took a lot of physical contact from the forecheck on break-outs. In one instance, he turned the puck over under physical duress and that play developed into a goal for Brandon. In the first period he had a good first pass that started a quick-break resulting in a goal. Almost never gets his point shots blocked, has accurate and quick-release.

BRA #10 RD Clague, Kale (2016) - Did a great job using his skating to find open lanes or to move the puck out of danger. Despite having great skating and puck-handling ability, he doesn't overdo it but uses it smartly. His pinching was smart, his shots are on the net and he constantly produced rebounds. Can fire both wrist-shots as well as accurate slapshots or one-timers that don't take a lot of time to wind-up. Did a good job with holding the blueline and in neutral zone re-groups to start the attack again. Once Brandon got a two goal lead early in the third, I thought he became a bit sloppy.

BRA #16 C Kaspick, Tanner (2016) - Supported his defensemen well, diligent two-way performance. Helped out with winning battles down-low. Did a good job driving the net without the puck to open up space for linemates. Finished his checks on the forecheck. Showed off some vision with a nice "blind" backdoor pass. Came out of the corners with the puck and made plays back to the point. Play with the puck was simple and to the point, not a lot of deception.

BRA #19 C Patrick, Nolan (2017) - Great puck-distribution on PP, weaving around the offensive zone, made a great cross-ice pass for the first goal of the game. Reads the play very well. For example he read a Quenneville (F1) steal on the forecheck and beat the D to the slot as a F2 resulting in a scoring chance. There's some sort of presence about him where it seems like the play revolves around him regardless of the situation on the ice and he always shows up in the right places.

BRA #26 LW McCorrister, Linden (2016) - Had good energy when digging for pucks on the wall. Fired a shot from his off-wing that Gutenberg would later clean up into the goal.

BRA #1 G Thompson, Logan (2016*) - He gave up a goal from a bit of a weak shot on a breakaway. Other than that he had a calm game, good size and can fill out the net. Did a good job playing the puck. Recovery can be a bit slow on some of his sprawling saves.

Portland Winterhawks at Tri-City Americans, October 17th, 2015

POR #18 C Abols, Rodrigo (2016**) - While he has good size and made some plays with the puck, it is hard to imagine him getting drafted after being passed over twice already. He's a decent player but not quite skilled enough to play the game he wants to play. His compete level was OK, but I don't think he packs enough punch or defensive smarts for a bottom 6 NHL role either.

POR #21 RD De Jong, Brendan (2016) - He looks like a legit 6'5 and can actually move at his size. Has that very long stick, but doesn't know how to fully use it yet in defensive situations. Can take off and skate with the puck using his reach to protect it. Defensive positioning and coverage in his slot were a bit lackadaisical. Not a lot there offensively, although he did a good job using his size on an offensive zone pinch up the wall to keep the puck in.

POR #43 LW McKenzie, Skyler (2016) - Small forward. Moves his feet well and is willing to hound the puck on the forecheck. Him going at it with Carlo battling for the puck on the wall was comical, as Carlo simply swatted him off his shoulder without even trying. McKenzie shows that he can read the play, can skate, and is willing to compete but as a smaller forward he will need something more dynamic on a consistent basis.

POR #44 LD Texeira, Keoni (2016*) - No glaring mistakes, but didn't really change my mind from last year with his performance. He's got some grit, some offensive ability, can move the puck in a basic manner, but simply lacks a tool that would set him apart beyond being a good junior defenseman. Lacks reach defensively and skating isn't quite good enough to be his saving grace. The feeling I got was that he played a decent junior game, however with limited upside projection-wise.

TRI #6 LD Valimaki, Juuso (2017) - Good puck-handling. He did make the occasional pass that put his teammate into a bad position. Can skate with the puck and has some creativity in using different angles and his puck skills to make plays offensively, sometimes a bit questionably close to committing a turnover.

TRI #10 RD Coghlan, Dylan (2016) - There was one instance where he should have cleared the net with more authority on PK. Outside of that he did a good job using his mobility, reach, and defensive anticipation to break up plays. Several good pokechecks and did a good job diffusing pressure by clearing pucks out of danger.

TRI #15 LW Rasmussen, Michael (2017) - A big, lanky kid. Seemed to fall down a lot, but he reads the play well and gets himself into position or at least tries to. Despite the somewhat lanky frame, he actually managed to protect the puck well on the wall. Scored a PP goal by tipping a Wotherspoon slapshot.

TRI #31 G Sarthou, Evan (2016) - He's 6'1 but covers a lot of net even when he drops down. Had quick controlled movement dropping down for saves and recovering for the next shot. The two goals he gave up were not really his fault. The first one went in after multiple whacks on a scramble in front of him. The second one he had 3 bodies covering his sight on a wrist-shot from up-close. In both of those instances, his defense did a poor job moving bodies out of the way.

Chicago Steel at Muskegon Lumberjacks, October 17th, 2015

CHI #2 LD Kiersted, Matt (2016) - Played the type of quiet yet effective game that you don't mind for defensemen. He rarely spent much time in his own zone and made accurate passing plays. However, he did not have much of an impact in the offensive zone.

CHI #6 LW Zimmer, Max (2016) - Had a nice steal on the backcheck. His best scoring chance came off a 2 on 1 where he opted for a shot but flubbed it. Thought he struggled a bit getting through a clogged neutral zone and there not being much space for him to make plays.

CHI #10 C Laczynski, Tanner (2016*) - One of the better forwards on the ice. Laczynski played a real good playmaking role, finding open players with ease in the slot and setting them up. Good vision with the puck.

MUS #2 RD Eliot, Mitch (2016) - Played like a defensive defenseman, though at his size he might have to show more offensively than he did. A physical chippy game, that got out of hand for him in the second period. Took two penalties there, the last one was a 2+10 for checking from behind. Chicago scored on the PP putting them up by another goal heading into third period. He also blew a tire that resulted in another Chicago goal in third, right after Muskegon managed to close the gap down to 2 goals.

MUS #3 RD Kallen, Nathaniel (2016) - Thought he had real good puck-movement in the first half of the game. Nearly every puck that made it into his corner or his side of the ice he would quickly and accurately dish out on heads-up plays. He cooled down as the game went on though.

MUS #13 C Adams, Collin (2016) - He scored both of Muskegon's goals both from up-close. First was him coming out from behind the net to backhand a loose puck for a goal. Second one was him setting up in front of the net for a quick snapshot off a pass from behind the goal.

MUS #15 LW Palecco, Dante (2016) - Thought he played a smart game all over the ice. He'd be involved in a lot of plays opening up and extending puck possession but never quite managed to get pucks into scoring areas.

MUS #16 LW Pitlick, Rem (2016) - He started the entire sequence in the Adams goal, by driving wide on a zone entry and firing a backhand shot that resulted in a rebound. Resulted in a couple of battles around the goalposts before Pitlick dished it off to Adams into the slot. Slow start but Pitlick got better once he started playing with more compete, getting onto loose pucks and sacrificing his body to make plays.

Saint John Sea Dogs at Gatineau Olympiques, October 18, 2015

QMJHL Regular Season

SJS #2 D Webster, Bailey (2016*) - Cleared zone well on penalty kill. When he was hit down low he put the puck over the glass for penalty. Top penalty killing unit.
SJS #9 C Veleno, Joseph (2018) - Good speed to initiate breakout. Takes passes at high speed well. Excellent skating through traffic with puck.

SJS #10 C Noel, Nathan (2016*) - Good positioning during a scramble on the power play opened him up for a big one timer to score 2-0 goal. Won some battles down low with quick stick and feet. Second unit on both power play and penalty kill. Took puck to the net with speed for scoring chance. Still has a very slender frame.

SJS #23 D Felixson, Olivier (2016) - Good size. Keeps his feet moving on the point. Everywhere he's not supposed to be on the power play, constantly out of position. Top penalty killing unit.

SJS #27 C Green, Matt (2016) - Blocks shots on the penalty kill. Decent skating ability. Second penalty killing unit.

GAT #11 RW Abramov, Vitaly (2016) - Great speed/skating. Put pressure on forecheck in neutral zone. Won races with skating and good body positioning. Will take the hit to make the play. Has excellent vision and on several occasions made some great passes to set up scoring chances for his team. Outstanding playmaking ability. Timed entry to slot well and made good move but stopped.

GAT #27 C Gagnon, Anthony (2017) - Excellent on the penalty kill for Gatineau. All over the opposition, took away time and forced numerous turnovers. Seemed to be everywhere at once sometimes.

GAT #44 D Bilodeau, Gabriel (2016) - Good patience on the point to get his shot through for scoring chance. Good puck decisions under pressure. Walked in from the point when he had the lane for good wrister. Good puck control. Good positioning one on one gets his stick in ideal position on rush to eliminate options for puck carrier. Won some puck races with average speed and a good stick lift. Made some smart simple plays, not rushing his decisions.

Final Score: Saint John Sea Dogs: 3 - Gatineau Olympiques: 2

Saint John Sea Dogs vs. Gatineau Olympiques, QMJHL, Oct 18, 2015

STJ #5 LD Chabot, Thomas (OTT) – Good Size Defensemen, great skater, moved the puck very well tonight, smooth skating, see's the ice very well, very smart Defensemen, he slows the game down when he has the puck on his stick no panic in his game, His dzone was better tonight, needs to be more physical in the Dzone, leader on the team as well, doesn't put himself in bad situations whether its offensively or defensively, a few times tonight he his gap control was not good, overall nice hockey player to watch.

STJ #10 RW Noel, Nathan (2016) – Good 2 way forward, scored a beautiful onetime goal tonight top corner, was involved physically tonight, good skater, wide strides, showed some offensive skill on PP and on the rush, has to be more consistent shift to shift, left the zone early a few times when his defence was trying to come up his wall with the puck.

STJ #31 G Bishop, Alex (2016) – Was outstanding tonight, 1st star of the game, faced 16 shots in the first period and definitely kept his team in the game, he tracked the puck really well tonight especially shots from the point with someone standing in front of him, good rebound control, didn't give much second chances to Gatineau forwards, he battled really well, very positional, didn't move around or scramble, let the puck hit him in the chest and covered it up. He's a big goalie but he needs to stand up and little better, went down to soon on a couple goals.

STJ #38 LD Zboril, Jacob – Played well tonight, was skating and moving his feet good tonight, good first passes out of the zone, nice skater when he has the puck on his stick, has some offensive skill, made a really nice soft cross crease pass for the PP goal in 2nd, doesn't like the physicality part of the game, but doesn't put himself in bad situations to get hit, needs to be more consistent in his dzone tends to follow the puck instead of the man.

GAT #8 RD Carrier, Nicolas (NSH) – Played really well tonight, was moving his feet a lot, was engaged in the game offensively tonight, join the rush a number of times creating chances, really good with his outlet passes tonight, was OK defensively tonight, got beat a few times with bad body positioning down low, QB on the PP, good low shot on the net allowing rebounds for his teammates, smart hockey player

GAT #9 LW Laplante, Yan (PHX) – competed tonight tonight, scored 2 easy goals tonight, on both his goals his teammates made really nice plays to him for easy passes, but what he's good at is finding those open places for goals and chances, really good skater, showed his speed a few times going wide on the D and then hard to net, got caught on the ice too long on a few shifts, but again the hardest worker on the ice for both teams tonight.

GAT #11 RW Abramov, Vitali (2016) – Played good tonight, had 1g and 1a made on very smart play and pass to Laplante for his second goal cross nice saucer pass goal, really good skater, very smart with and without the puck tonight, understands where to go and not to go with or without the puck, couple bad long cross ice passes that got turned over, needed o make the shorter pass coming out.

Final Score: Saint John: 3   Gatineau: 2

Sport U18 at S-Kiekko U18, October 21st, 2015

SPO #36 LD Manninen, Ville (2017) - He played decent game. Ville doesn't any showy moves on ice but he's reliable d-man in the d-zone. Gives safe first passes and reads the game well. Calm kid with good hockey sense.

SPO #8 LW Liljamo, Lassi (2018) - 99-born winger with great size and speed. His technique needs to improve but he can already be fast player. He got great puck handling skills and he's great player in o-zone. Need to improve his two way game.

Brandon Wheat Kings at Spokane Chiefs, October 21st, 2015

BRA #10 RD Clague, Kale (2016) - Great first few steps in all directions. Very good passing and did very well in moving the puck up the ice. Less impactful in offensive zone in this game. Gets into position quickly with his skating and blocks movement from forwards. Very good game in transition both offensively and defensively. Defense of slot and front of the net area not quite as good, especially obvious on a scoring chance by a 6'4 200lbs Curtis Miske. Faded again a bit in third period. Had a bad read in OT that resulted in a 2 on 1 against deep in his zone.

BRA #12 C Mattheos, Stelio (2017) - Uses his body well to protect the puck on the cycle. Good plays in-tight with bodies around him in the slot. Can make give and go plays and open up in holes for scoring opportunities. Did a really good job using his body and stick to lean into guys and obtain inside body position against them.

BRA #16 C Kaspick, Tanner (2016) - Excellent on wall battles, good at protecting the puck and coming out of the corners making plays back to the point and into the slot. Good at reading the play and coming in as a second guy to dig pucks out of the feet as well. Was solid defensively and intercepted several passes on forecheck. Not a flashy performance but brought a lot of structure to his team.

BRA #19 C Patrick, Nolan (2017) - Scored the opening goal on a weak wrister from the half-wall area. Uses the length of his stick well to move the puck away from his checker. There are some plays he makes where the size saves him from his average skating being exposed. Has a very good feel for the game's momentum and improved his level of play in key moments. Made a high-end pass for a Quenneville goal about a minute before the second period ended and just seconds after Spokane scored looking like they would pull away.

BRA #26 LW McCorrister, Linden (2016) - Did an ok job in limited minutes. Was decent on the cycle, looked to get pucks deep into offensive zone, competed well off-the-puck. Had a fight. He looked like he'd be better off quickly dumping the puck or making quick passes to his linemates. When handling the puck he got pushed to the outside rather easily.

SPO #7 RD Fiala, Evan (2016*) - Big, physical presence. Played a real no-nonsense type of game both defensively and offensively. The odd moment he got the puck in offensive zone, he did quickly get it on net. Passing was simple and quick, not really someone you want to handle the puck excessively. Sometimes was wondering about his awareness, can get a bit of a tunnel vision in what he wants to do. Lateral ability when skating looked mediocre.

SPO #11 C Anderson-Dolan, Jaret (2017) - Had good energy in the first, brought puck up ice but a lot of it was one and done as Brandon defense had an easy time closing him down. He got much better in the second period, focusing more on give and go plays as opposed to trying to do it by himself. Scored arriving to a pass with speed and snapping it into the net.

SPO #12 C Bechtold, Markson (2016**) - For someone who was passed over twice already he doesn't necessarily convince you that he has NHL qualities, but his compete was off the charts, especially in the first where he was effectively dragging the entire Spokane team to a tie. He worked his butt off the entire game, moved his feet and didn't even think twice about sacrificing his body to get things done.

SPO #17 RW Yamamoto, Kailer (2017) - Was used on PK quite a bit and did a great job. Stole the puck from Provorov, and later in OT from Clague, the latter resulting in a scoring chance that his linemate couldn't convert on. Great passing all-around. Had a slick pass into space for Dolan who scored the goal on the play. Even when he seems to have a quiet game, he finds ways to contribute through his ability to read the play and ends up on the scoreboard.

Flint Firebirds at Barrie Colts, October 22, 2015

FLI #10 RW Caamano, Nicholas (2016) – Caamano had a couple good chances and he certainly made the most of them potting a pair of goals. He scored one on a beautiful pass from Bitten on a 2-on-1 and scored his other around the net as well. He didn't hesitate to drive the net and he was rewarded for it.

FLI #18 RW Kantner, Matyas (2016) – Kantner wasn't very good in this game. He back checked hard on several occasions and was able to push guys off the puck but he couldn't accomplish much of anything with it. Kantner turned it over several times, struggled to gain the opposing line with possession and didn't register a shot or create any good chances throughout.

FLI #41 C Bitten, William (2016) – Bitten was one of the best players on the ice from start to finish. He showed good vision hitting teammates with passes all over the ice. He also showed good hands in tight on a beautiful breakaway goal in the 2nd period. Without the puck he was very involved in all three zones. He back checked hard, caused several turnovers in the neutral zone and was always back to support down low. On the penalty kill his positioning was excellent and he did a nice job pressuring the points and forcing bad passes. Bitten had a couple solid hits and won several puck battles against much bigger players. He also did not shy away from the dirty areas. Bitten accelerated quickly with the puck, was elusive in space and was able to carry it out of trouble when necessary. His speed forced defenders to back off and gave him extra space to gain the line with possession.

FLI #73 LW Collins, Jacob (2016) – Collins had a very quiet game. He was strong on the forecheck, played a very north-south game and did take a regular shift on the penalty kill. He didn't accomplish much with the puck, though, and was pretty quiet throughout.

BAR #10 D Murray, Justin (2016) – Murray had a bad defensive zone turnover early on as he through the puck up ice without looking and it led to a chance against. He seemed to settle in after that, though, as he battled hard for loose pucks, was physical when he could be and hit a couple stretch passes.

BAR #16 LW Hawerchuk, Ben (2016) – Hawerchuk probably played the best game of his OHL career. He made smart decisions with the puck, was effective in the cycle game and consistently finished his checks. Hawerchuk was able to get a ton of pucks on net and was rewarded for his efforts as he took a pass just outside the paint and finished in tight. He finished the game with a goal, an assist and five shots.

BAR #18 LW Magwood, Zachary (2016) – Magwood showed good vision early on as he had his head up while coming from behind Flint's net and was able to hit a streaking Cordell James for a goal. Magwood made some crisp passes in the neutral zone and did a nice job of helping drive play up ice. Without the puck he was good as he pick pocketed a couple Firebirds players and was always back down low to provide an easy outlet for the team's blue liners.

Kitchener Rangers at Sarnia Sting, October 22, 2015

KIT #10 RW Henderson, Jake (2016*) - Creative play with puck on rush set up 2 on 1 chance. Great forecheck pressure to force turnover. Good touch with puck to make quick, effective short distance pass. Second power play unit.

KIT #21 LW McHugh, Nick (2017) - Great speed and good hands. Good work on the penalty kill to evade checkers and keep puck away killing a lot of time. Second penalty kill unit.

KIT #23 RW Mascherin, Adam (2016) - Great power play positioning. Quickly gets open off the draw. Always in good position in the offensive zone. Reacts quickly to play, allows him to get loose pucks. Good pass lead to 3-0 power play goal.

KIT #74 LW Bunnaman, Connor (2016) - Awkward skating stride but gets good speed in his first few steps. Good puck protection ability down low. Didn't force decisions. Great down low winning a lot of battles. Quick puck decisions set up scoring chance. Good hands in slot to pick up loose pick and a good move, with poise under pressure to score 2-0 goal. Got his stick up in battle resulting in penalty. Gets puck out of the zone under sustained pressure without sending it down the ice.

SAR #5 D Chychrun, Jakob (2016) - Doesn't look like himself, not making some of the plays he usually does. Good line hold to keep the play going. Defensively he got his stick on shots. Good positioning one on one and uses his stick well. Flipped the puck over the glass under pressure in the third period for a penalty down 3-4 in the third period.

SAR #10 LW Salinitri, Anthony (2016) - Jumped ahead of play offside on numerous occasions tonight. Good positioning and a quick finish to score 3-4 goal. Using speed to put forecheck pressure on the opponents.

SAR #25 RW Kyrou, Jordan (2016) - Took a while to enter the zone at times throwing off the timing of his linemates. Bad giveaway in the offensive zone killed 30 seconds off the power play. Quick hands to control the puck and generally made good passes. Excellent deceptive play early third to create 3-4 goal.

SAR #26 RW Campbell, Chase (2016) - Good deflection in the slot to score 1-4 goal. Very small but quick.

Final Score: Kitchener Rangers: 6 - Sarnia Sting: 3

Owen Sound Attack at London Knights, October 23, 2015

OS #5 D Durzi, Sean (2017) - Good strength for his size. Hard point shot. Showed some hands. Second power play unit.

OS #15 LW Struthers, Matthew (2018) - Nice forehand/backhand move to score 1-3 goal and his first goal in the OHL. Pass too hard while defends was changing. Ending the power play chance; needed to float it in to give him enough time to get to the line. Second powerplay unit.

OS #37 C Suzuki, Nick (2017) - Worked hard down low but lost most battles; needs to get stronger. Cut through slot at smart time on power play to make things difficult for goaltender. Top powerplay unit.

LON #3 D Mattinen, Nicholas (2016) - Mishandled puck on the line but won race back to negate potential breakaway. Reaction time is a little slow. Has a big point shot.

LON #7 LW Tkachuk, Matthew (2016) - Slick puck movement on the rush. Made quick decisions in the offensive zone leading to scoring chances. Average skating affected him on a few occasions tonight.

LON #49 LW Jones, Max (2016) - Came out flying in this game. First shift landed huge hit down low, resulted in defenseman out of position and directly lead to London's 1-0 goal. Finished every check he could. Huge open ice hit in the offensive zone drew attention to himself and opened things up for his linemates. Takes up space in the slot on second power play unit. Stick in position and big defenders struggled to move him from the front. Made some slick plays with the puck in this spot to create some scoring chances. Good move on the rush to protect puck and drive wide beating defender then setting up chance.

LON #63 C Pu, Cliff (2016) - Picked up loose puck and made slick behind the back pass to set up scoring chance, then went to the net for the rebound but couldn't pull the trigger. Used his speed on multiple occasions to drive wide on the defender and centred the puck for chances with well timed passes. Can control puck down low but is quickly neutralized by contact. Good position in the slot and good deflection to score 4-1 goal.

LON #1 G Parsons, Tyler (2016) - Made some big saves early, particularly on back to back Owen Sound power plays utilizing his high end quickness. Sometimes kicks out too many rebounds. 1st goal against was a forehand/backhand move but one he probably should have had.

Final Score: London Knights: 5 - Owen Sound Attack: 1

Bloomington Thunder at Madison Capitols, October 24th 2015, USHL

MAD #31 G Ryan Edquist (2016) – Edquist was really good tonight. He controlled his rebounds well, was quick to cover loose pucks in traffic. Had quick lateral movement and solid positioning. He made some great saves on a couple breakaways to keep his team in the lead.

BLM #27 C Mitchell Mattson (2016) – Mattson displayed solid board play tonight, used his body and the wall to shield the defender. Executed well on the cycle down low but still needs to eventually try to get the puck to the net. Did well in the faceoff circle, uses his size to his advantage. Mattson was kept off the score sheet but played a solid 2-way game down the middle of the ice. Was slotted as the 3rd line center tonight but did see some decent Power Play time, mostly as a big body in front of the net.

Seattle Thunderbirds at Everett Silvertips, October 24th, 2015

SEA #5 LD Tyszka, Jarret (2017) - Has good size already. Mainly did a good job on PP where he held the point well, pinched up the wall when it was a smart thing to do to where he would send the puck back deep behind the net, and distributed the puck well. Some hard shots, but of slower release and with no traffic. The goalie didn't have any problem with them. Was not very noticeable even strength.

SEA #7 RD Khaira, Sahvan (2016) - Lost puck when pressured by forecheck that lead to a goal. He has good size and some mobility, long stick but doesn't use it to control space all that much. No real structure to his defending, in this game it seemed like he didn't quite know what to do in his own zone, often not being able to decide who he should pick up and often left in a vulnerable position not covering anyone in particular.

SEA #8 C Eansor, Scott (2016**) - He has good skating ability and pushed defense back when darting ahead. Skill was on display at times and he can handle the puck while skating at speed. Fought the much bigger Tristen Pfeifer. Reliant on quick strike attacks and struggled to establish extended offensive zone time.

SEA #26 LW Volcan, Nolan (2016) - He looked good in the first period when battling for pucks and looking to make things happen on the forecheck. Faded away considerably throughout the game and had limited impact. Stride looked a bit choppy, though he seemed to generate ok speed with it.

EVE #8 RW Bajkov, Patrick (2016) - Played a real intelligent game. Subtle little passes. Defensively involved as well, used his body to pin Barzal to the boards leaving his teammate to pick up the puck. Good situational awareness in covering for Juulsen's rush. Had a flashy third period play going through the whole team as well. Skating motion is fluid but not explosive. Likes to move around the ice, often ended up on his off-wing, seemed to be really aware of everyone's position on the ice.

EVE #17 C Fonteyne, Matt (2016) - Saw some minutes on PK and thought he did a decent job there. Has a bit of feistiness to him. Made a stupid pass 4 on 4 that got intercepted after his team already failed to exit the zone for three consecutive times. Drew a penalty when driving forward with his hustle. Thought he could have used his teammates better.

EVE #70 G Hart, Carter (2016) - Very quick to get into position when dropping down. Covers the lower portion of the net extremely well. He's battled at a high level with traffic in front of him as well and blocked a lot of pucks on second efforts. Real strong performance, was tested several times but ended the game picking up a shutout.

North Bay Battalion at Mississauga Steelheads, October 25, 2015

NBY #14 C Poirier, Zach (2016) - Used sparingly on the penalty kill. Took away time and space from puck carriers. Competes for pucks and wins battles. Good stick and cleared zone on penalty kill. Blocked shots. Quick hands, good reaction time.
NBY #19 LW Bratina, Zach (2016**) - Protects puck well. Powerful shot. Big body but has moves to beat defenders one on one. Drives net with skill and size. Good skater for his size. Good read to get open for breakaway but taken down. Received penalty shot but made a simple play and was stopped.

NBY #25 D Shoemaker, Mark (2016) - Likes to shoot on power play and was on target. Second unit on both the power play and penalty kill.

MIS #4 D Day, Sean (2016) - Made good first pass most of the time with the occasional misplay. Was out of position in transition plays and shouldn't be with his skating. Top powerplay unit. Used his frame fairly well to protect the puck. Outstanding end to end play on power play flying through two defenders but shot into the logo to negate chance. Second penalty killing unit.

MIS #9 C McLeod, Mike (2016) - Horrible point blank giveaway on power play directly resulted in North Bay's 1-1 goal. A little hesitant to go into corners. Made some slick passes that most players can't do so easily but didn't generate much in terms of chances in the first. Good positioning to go to the slot and was robbed on a good scoring chance. Later that shift he made a great pass to set up 2-1 goal. Top unit for both power play and penalty kill. Created scoring chance with speed and patience but linemate couldn't finish. Tried to do too much at times.

MIS #14 RW Bastian, Nathan (2016) - Doesn't get much out of his strides, below average skating. Finishes checks, good compete level, uses size down low but his feet definitely hurt his overall game. Top powerplay unit. Took puck down low and quick centrring pass to set up 3-1 goal. Lost races to the wall due to skating. Gets in position for chances. On 3 on 1 faked pass and shot it missing net and clearing zone. Next 3 on 1 chance he passed off setting up what should have been a sure goal.

MIS #36 D Osmanski, Austin (2016) - Keeps his stick in the passing lanes in defensive zone.

MIS #41 D Hague, Nic (2017) - Smart, quick first passes up ice. Good stick one on one. Consistently steady.

MIS #61 RW Harrogate, Brendan (2016) - Much bigger than minor midget. Good creativity down low for scoring chance. Great move to turn a nothing play into a chance. Consistently made scoring chances, impressive compared to ice time.

MIS #74 RW Tippett, Owen (2017) - Won battle in the slot against bigger defender, directly resulting in a scoring chance. Good moves one on one. Slows down and speeds up well to throw off defenders.

MIS #92 RW Nylander, Alexander (2016) - Put puck on net, rebound resulted in a 1-0 goal and an assist for Nylander. Slick hands and completed some difficult passes. Created a bunch of scoring chances with his high level passing ability. Had great chance to score in third but tried to get too fancy and lost a sure goal.

Final Score: Mississauga Steelheads: 4- North Bay Battalion: 2

Omaha Lancers at Madison Capitols, October 25th 2015, USHL

OMA #17 LW, McManus, Brandon (2017) – Showed good hands in traffic, good around the net in creating chances and showed good vision in the offensive zone in finding the open man. Good at finding the soft spots and getting open in the offensive zone. McManus did lack physicality and looked timid in a lot of 50/50 puck battles however and was casual in getting out to the point to block shots.

OMA #9 LW, Crone, Hank (2016) – Crone is known for a player with very high offensive skills with the puck and those skills were on display tonight, and can dazzle with the puck at times. However on too many occasions he tried to do too much on his own and didn't utilize his teammates very well and missed out on some scoring chances because of it. Crone used a couple unnecessary toe drags at times when the simpler play could have been to dump it into the offensive zone. Needs to learn to simplify and slow the game down, thought he played a fairly selfish game tonight, however there is no doubting his puck and skating ability.

OMA #61 RW, Fallstrom, William (2016) – Fallstrom displayed impressive speed through the neutral zone with the puck all night, has good vision of the ice and made some quick and decisive decisions with the puck in the neutral zone. Was very confident in his play, drove the net hard off the rush as well as made some good passes on the Power Play from behind the goal line and on the half wall. Impressive vision and passing ability all over the ice.

OMA #11 RW Wojiechowski, John (2016) – Showed good skating and ability to get up and down the ice well for a guy of his size.. Liked to drive the net and battle for positioning in front. Doesn't possess great skills with the puck on his stick but does have a decent shot and a quick release. His long reach made some good plays in the defensive zone, especially on the penalty kill.

Gatineau Olympiques vs Blainville-Boisbriand Armada, October 25th 2015

GAT #11 RW Abramov, Vitali (2016): Didn't generate much offense at 5-on-5 today, started generating a bit of offense on the power play in the 3rd period. On the power play he was playing at the half-wall position, where he created a couple of scoring chances in the 3rd period. At even-strength, he was not involved in the action, playing more of a perimeter game.

GAT #44 RD Bilodeau, Gabriel (2016): Liked his game today, he was not shy in terms of rushing the puck in the offensive zone. I noticed he rushed the puck 4-5 times during the game, but unfortunately, this didn't result in any scoring chances. He often tried a pass in the slot that was intercepted by an Armada defender. But I liked that he was active and trying to make things happen. He was solid defensively as well, as he didn't get beat and showed good hustle to get back in the defensive zone. He also had a good stick in one-on-one confrontations.

GAT #27 RW Gagnon, Anthony (2017): The 16 year old rookie played on the point on the power play during the game, which he also did last year with his midget team. He's still physically immature and it shows when battling for pucks in the corner. He had some good shifts with a good forecheck that annoyed the Armada defense. He missed a defensive-zone assignment on the Armada's first goal, giving Connor Bramwell too much room.

GAT #31 G Bellemarre, Mathieu (2016): A solid, yet unspectacular game from Bellemarre today, who made 21 saves. He was not tested heavily during the game, as the only goal came early in the first period when Bramwell was left all alone in front of the net and jumped on a rebound. Bellemarre is very undersized and has to work really hard to track pucks with traffic in front of the net; he can be caught out of position when he challenges shooters in an attempt to give them less room to shoot at.

GAT #91 C Alain, Alexandre (2016): Un-Drafted last season, Alain was centering Gatineau's 2nd line today. He supported his defense well by coming back deep in the defensive zone and acting like a 3rd defenseman at times. A smart player with decent speed, he was able to show off some of this speed during the game. He didn't have many quality scoring chances during the game, but had one where he was all alone in the slot but couldn't beat Grametbauer on the backhand.

BLB #29 G Grametbauer, Mark (2016): Gave up three goals on 21 shots and didn't seem comfortable in his crease today. He lost equilibrium in his lateral movements during the game including on Gatineau's 1st goal. His reaction speed was not good enough on some sequences. He was a bit better in the 3rd period and seemed to be more in control.

BLB #6 LD Crête-Belzile, Antoine LD (2017): Still adjusting to the QMJHL, Antoine showed good footwork, retrieving pucks in the defensive zone and showing more confidence at making plays in the offensive zone than in my last viewing (last week). He had a real good shift defending versus Vitali Abramov and not giving him much. Played on the power play and showed good poise at the point.

BLB #96 LW Pospisil, Kristian (2016): Looked way more confident and active on the ice this time around than in my last viewing. He showed good stickhandling when making zone entries and in the neutral zone. He's a big body and does a good job protecting the puck along the boards. Controls the puck well in tight spaces. He threw a couple of nice hits on the forecheck during the game.

BLB #89 C Picard, Miguel (2016): Not much offense out of Picard today again, but played sound defensive hockey and was used in defensive situations often during the game. He took defensive zone faceoffs during the game and on the PK. He showed good effort on the backcheck and used his stick well in terms of blocking passing lanes.

BLB #24 LW Teasdale, Joel (2017): Teasdale was very good today once again; his adaptation period to the QMJHL was a quick one. He's strong and wins a lot of battles along the boards and used his strength to get the puck to the net. He played on both special teams today. He did a good job in puck protection situations using his back to shield opponents away.

BLB #18 LW Hylland, Tyler (2016): Hylland had two to three good scoring chances during the game, as he was able to get open in the slot. He showed a good wrist shot with a quick release, although his accuracy will need some work. He used his speed well by putting pressure on the puck carrier on the forecheck. He also played on both special teams in today's game.

Prince George Cougars at Kamloops Blazers, October 28th, 2015

PGC #15 C O'Brien, Brogan (2016*) - Used his reach well defensively, including a steal on a D-to-D pass. Didn't get a lot done offensively in this game, some easy passes around the boards on a cycle but nothing to the middle. Was prone to gliding around and puck-watching when he didn't have the puck.

PGC #18 LW Bison, Bartek (2016) - Good size and was willing to throw his body around. He wanted to play a heavy game on the forecheck, but was stuck behind the play a lot, which resulted in him constantly playing chase up or establishing contact by the time the puck has already left.

PGC #26 RW McDonald, Kody (2016) - A disappointment of a game. He was barely noticeable outside one or two shifts in the second period where he was more decisive with the puck and was actually looking to make things happen by himself. Otherwise just another player on the long list of Prince George players that came out flat in this game.

PGC #28 LD Anderson, Josh (2016) - Decent on the point when moving the puck around. Defensively, his gap control was too relaxed, often gave up too much room for forwards to make plays in. Ended the game with a minus four.

KAM #12 LW Kryski, Jake (2016) - Played a good smart game. Doesn't have tons of speed or big size but keeps his feet moving and finds places on ice where he can contribute from. Good vision to find passing lanes. And didn't mind getting his nose dirty by going to the middle.
KAM #32 LW Loewen, Jermaine (2016) - Big, heavy wing and played that way as well. Finished his checks and used size to his advantage. Had a goal coming off the boards, cutting to the middle and then firing a wrister. Not a lot of skill, skating needs to improve.

KAM #38 LD Davidson, Dawson (2016) - He was just ok defensively but had a strong game from the point and as a powerplay quarterback. Good puck distribution and seems to be getting more comfortable handling the puck and getting involved offensively. Sneaked into the slot a couple of times firing a dangerous shot.

KAM #41 C Pilon, Garrett (2016) - Lacks a touch of top speed, especially at his size. Did a good job tracking the flow of the play and getting involved. Did well supporting the puck and making short 10 foot passes that move the play forward. Though he comes back defensively, might lack size to be effective as a pivot down-low.

KAM #42 LD Vala, Ondrej (2016) - He got beat once on a 1vs1 play due to lack of acceleration. Sometimes he struggles with agility in-tight and having to react to quick bounces. Overall an engaging defensive game though. His shot produced a rebound that would get cleaned up into the net. Had a couple of good pinches offensively and was also decent at getting his shots on net. Didn't handle the puck a lot, for the most part to his benefit.

Oshawa Generals at Hamilton Bulldogs, October 28, 2015

OHL Regular Season

HAM #17 C Saigeon, Brandon (2016) - Got into scoring areas but struggled to take advantage. Quick hands to create a chance on the power play under pressure. Above average skating, showed some moves carrying the puck up ice.

HAM #20 D Candella, Cole (2016) - Struggled moving puck on several occasions. Beat one on one not moving his feet. Showed above average speed on the rush carrying puck into zone and and made a good puck decision leading to 1-3 goal.

HAM #21 D Mieritz, Christian (2016) - Big open ice hit. Consistently effective passss in a three zones. Good vision to move the puck well. Played one on one decent. On the penalty kill tried to lift opponents stick with one hand on his stick. Got beat in the slot a few times tonight.

HAM #42 D Gleason, Benjamin (2016) - Great move to beat defender one on one walking in from point and get shot off. Top power play unit. Very hit or miss when moving the puck in three zones. Made some dangerous puck decisions. Skates well in all directions. Walked one on one in the third for chance.

Final Score: Oshawa Generals: 4 - Hamilton Bulldogs: 1

KalPa U20 at Sport U20, October 31st, 2015

SPO #61 RW Vähäkangas, Verneri (2016) - Played a great game and scored a one goal and two assists. Skilled winger with good speed who got amazing playmaking skills. Always doing great decisions in o-zone. He's not that straight forward and he should shoot more. He scored his goal with hard and accurate wrister. Undersized player who got huge problems around corners. Bad two way player.. Loses his battles and doesn't always read the situations right way.

SPO #33 RD Ahlmark, Eddie (2016) - Big stay-at-home d-man who's physically strong. Plays always tough game and doesn't lose one-on-one situations. Gives a easy first pass and nothing more. Sometimes his passing game is taking too much time and he should be more calm with puck. He's big kid but he's pretty good skater for his size. Not that fast but Eddie's technique is decent.

SPO #48 RD Kuoppala, Joni (2017) - Gifted d-man who's really calm and wise with puck. Joni isn't physically ready but he got amazing tools... Great mobility and great hockey sense. He's always calm with puck and make right decisions all the time. The way he reads the game is his biggest strength and and he can be effective in all three zones. His shot is still pretty weak but he's good blue liner because of his vision and passing game. Was one of the best players in this game.

KAL #25 LW Juusola, Mikko (2016) - Energetic forward with great speed. Mikko's skating is good.. great first steps and great top speed.. He challenged defenders with his skating but he's not always trying to go straight to the net. He's pretty good protecting the puck but loses battles because of his size. Decent puck skills and decent vision but he doesn't have any special feature in his game.

KAL #13 RD Torpström, Eetu (2016) - All-round d-man who can be great in all three zones. He got decent size and he can play tough game. Not a typical offensive defender but he's making lot of points with his calm puck moving game and good vision. He also got pretty tough and accurate slapshot. Played safe game and made couple of great decisions with puck and one of those led to a goal.

KAL #26 RD Ruuskanen, Waltteri (2016) - Played bad game. His passing game is too slow and his skating isn't improved. Huge d-man but doesn't use his size the right way. The opponent got their first goal because he lost the puck in front of his own net.

Barrie Colts at Mississauga Steelheads, November 1, 2015

OHL Regular Season

BAR #8 LW Chiodo, Lucas (2017) - Great passing leading line are to a good scoring chance going to the net. Extremely small but quick.

BAR #9 D Brassard, Matthew (2016) - Good puck protection and smart lanes to get to red line and put pucks deep. Got out of penalty box following coincidental penalty and went to the net with good positioning on the 2 on 1 chance to score 4-0 goal. Gets his feet moving on offensive line making himself an option. Good pinch. Read plays well in the neutral zone, and intercepted passes. Too far ahead in 3 on 2 coverage that opponent without puck got behind him too easily for chance. Good defensive stick.

BAR #16 LW Hawerchuk, Ben (2016) - Good compete level, finishes checks on bigger opponents. Skating is ok but needs an extra gear at his size. Dropped the gloves and faired alright.

BAR #18 C Magwood, Zachary (2016) - Great speed, quick feet, got to pucks in a hurry.

MIS #4 D Day, Sean (2016) - Tripped opponent going to the net on short handed chance, negating power play. Attempted to rush the puck deep a few times using his high level skating but was stopped. Afterwards showed no urgency to get back and allowed a forward to cover his position while coasting back. Took unnecessary penalty mid second which very quickly resulted in a power play goal for Barrie seconds later giving the Colts a 3-0 lead. Showed a little physicality in this game landing a few hits.

MIS #9 C McLeod, Mike (2016) - Landed multiple solid hits in this game. Has the size and a little strength. Handled puck in skates well without breaking stride leading to chance. Struggled to create much offensively in this game. Top power play unit.

MIS #14 RW Bastian, Nathan (2016) - Does a great job of regularly getting pucks deep. Dump and chase part struggled due to his skating. Doesn't get much out of his stride and almost looks like he's falling in slow motion when trying to win a race. Major refinements are necessary. Good position in offensive zone during sustained possession. Good defensive responsibility and competes equally in all three zones. Potentially had a few short handed chances but was too easily caught when carrying the puck.

MIS #92 RW Nylander, Alexander (2016) - Getting hit pretty hard when he stops moving his feet down low. Showed good speed on back check. Didn't get too much going offensively today.

Russia vs Sweden, U17 WHC, November 1st, 2015

RUS #4 LD Alexeev, Aleksander (2018) - Among the best Russian players on the ice, Alexeev already possesses considerable size and mobility. He logged heavy minutes and played a solid two-way game. Accurate outlets and didn't wilt under forechecking pressure. Played an engaging defensive zone game and showed offensive upside from the point as well.

RUS #6 LD Rubinchik, Mark (2017) - Rubinchik was a strong puck-mover for Russia throughout the game. He was dangerous on the powerplay and scored a PP goal by skating into the slot and wiring a wristshot past the Swedish goalie. He also made some solid reads, reading puck-movement through neutral zone and getting his stick on pucks or anticipating and immediately closing down Swedish forwards the moment they received the pass.

RUS #7 RW Svechnikov, Andrei (2018) - His natural ability as a forward is immediately obvious, that said he could have done more in this game. At times, too much of an observer. Felt like he was waiting for a high-end play to open up too much, as opposed to focusing on making small plays that would drive the play forward for his team. Though he didn't receive much help from his linemates at least offensively. He took a pretty bad hit into the boards in the middle of second period.

RUS #8 C Demin, Pavel (2017) - He played a competitive two-way game. He lacks the size to be a high-end defensive centre, but he worked and moved his feet for the most part. He was used on penalty kill and did a good job there, including blocking a shot and seeing key minutes on third period PK. Useful when hounding the puck-carrier as well.

RUS #9 C Bitsadze, Mikhail (2018) - Reads the play well and anticipated soft spots in coverage, though overall it was probably not his best game. He did better later in the game when he started being more active in racing for loose pucks. He was good in small space and has good balance on his skates, made passes even with a player leaning on him.

RUS #10 C Lipanov, Alexey (2017) - He was just OK, didn't do anything to tilt the ice to his team's favor for any extensive measure of time. Played a more mature game than most of the players on the ice. One of the few players who used his stick to cover lanes and dictate puck-movement, and made high-percentage though not flashy plays with the puck.

RUS #15 LW Zenchikov, Igor (2017) - Quite small. He scored the first Russia's goal. Anticipated well and likes to hide on the weak-side of the ice before coming into dangerous scoring areas. Faded considerably throughout the game.

RUS #17 RW Slepets, Kirill (2017) - He had a goal and an assist but that probably overstates his actual shift-to-shift impact in this game. He went unnoticed for chunks of the game, but seemed to find a way to activate himself and produce when he sensed an opportunity.

RUS #24 RW Kostin, Klim (2017) - He started out a bit slow but got going in the second half. Did a good job using his reach and skating ability to penetrate defenses and gain space, although he then often failed to make anything happen off it. Has a good base of skills and physical tools to work from though.

RUS #27 C Marushev, Maxim (2017) - First few steps didn't look too good, he also can stop moving his feet altogether, and at times looks lethargic with his body-language. Played on the fourth line and was interested in playing a responsible defensive game by coming back and being a safety valve down-low. He had a pair of offensive zone opportunities late in third period when Sweden was forced to take risks offensively in hopes of tying the game.

RUS #28 RD Osin, Aleksander (2017) - Looks a bit heavy on his skates. He scored a goal following up on a loose puck after the Swedish goalie pokechecked his teammate. Defensively doesn't take himself out of position, but could have used his size better to push forwards out and his stick to cover space.

RUS #30 G Zhukov, Maxim (2017) - Good size, not explosive but moved well for his stature. Solid through first two periods, though at times a bit shaky. Liljegren goal could have been played better. He was at his best in third period, especially when Sweden pressured. Doesn't seem to get flustered easily and has the physical tools to build upon.

SWE #1 G Eriksson Ek, Olle (2017) - He has decent size and movement in the crease. It's hard to really pin the goals on him, since he had a lot of traffic in front of him. Often the Swedish D had trouble keeping forwards out, be it with screens or second opportunities. Though, Eriksson Ek didn't really do anything to raise himself beyond an average at best performance. He did have a fantastic glove save in third period when Sweden was trying to get themselves back into the game.

SWE #4 LD Brannstrom, Erik (2017) - He scored the first Swedish goal with a blast on the PP. He is very dangerous when getting the puck on the offensive blue-line and can both distribute and shoot the puck. Good skating ability as well and plays an up-tempo, confident game. At times he got sloppy with his puckhandling. Attempted a horrible move in his zone that lead to a Russia goal.

SWE #6 RD Liljegren, Timothy (2017) - Best Swedish player in this game. Great puck-distribution and was a threat both in the offensive zone as well as when moving the puck out of his zone. He scored by skating the entire length of the ice before finishing on a wrist-shot from between the circles. Had a good balance between taking offensive opportunities and not exposing his team defensively.

SWE #11 LW Aterius, Erik (2017) - Didn't get a lot done with the puck, but was quite useful without it. Has skating that allows him to be a forechecking presence and to drive the net to cause havoc. He spent a lot of time setting screens, whacking on rebounds and generally causing trouble around the net. Screened the goalie on Brannstrom's PP goal. Took a penalty for running the goalie as well.

SWE #15 C Hugg, Rickard (2017) - He had a bit of an inconsistent game. Felt like his tools should allow him to do more than he did. Decent size and he does go to the right places and is willing to sacrifice his body to make plays be it offensively or defensively, but his line seemed to lose the puck a lot at even strength, leading to a lot of one and done efforts and shots based on hope more than any real scoring opportunities.

SWE #20 C Lundestrom, Isac (2018) - Probably the best Swedish forward, he was a key factor whenever Sweden had any push in second and third period. Battled well and was one of the few setting up offensive zone time for his team by winning battles, making intelligent short passes and getting back open. Good job moving the puck off the wall back to the point and going to the net to make something happen in traffic as well.
SWE #21 C Miketinac, Kalle (2017) - He was doing a good job evading pressure and using his skill to make plays. He was the guy driving most of the play in the early going for Sweden and was pushing the pace offensively. Got caught overhandling the puck in his own zone later in the game and faded down the stretch.

SWE #27 RW Sveningsson, Filip (2017) - His shot was his best asset. Especially on powerplay where he had enough room to find the lanes and set it up. Overall, he played a pretty straight-forward game and that of a scorer who is snooping around and looking for his shot. Doesn't mind getting physical either by dishing it out or absorbing hits.

Canada Red vs Finland, U17 WHC, November 1st, 2015

CAN #1 G DiPietro, Michael (2017) - Had a strong argument for being the best player in the game. Very good focus throughout, his performance never dropped. In fact he played even better against a strong Finland push in third period. A sequence where he blocked the puck from crossing the line while Finland was whacking away at it for a good 5-10 seconds really stood out for him. The only goal he gave up was a top shelf wrister after a turnover by his D.
CAN #2 RD Phillips, Markus (2017) - Covered a lot of ice with his skating. Moved the puck well and was the most engaging Canadian blueliner as far as offense went. Competed well defensively as well. He had one big mistake making a blind pass in his own zone that Tolvanen intercepted and roofed.

CAN #3 RD Brook, Josh (2017) - Very composed game, was a defensive presence. Protects the middle well and broke up plays. Made intelligent first passes, even if they were mostly very simple. Did a good job breaking up a two on one situation. Rather conservative offensively.

CAN #4 LD Smart, Jonathan (2017) - Found himself generally in the right positions and I liked his compete, but he seemed to lack in execution at times, as if the game was a little too fast for him. If he made his decisions a bit quicker he'd probably have a strong game, but he was just average tonight.

CAN #8 LD Watson, Nick (2017) - I liked him defensively and he played a decent if understated defensive game. He used his stick well. There was not much there for him offensively at all nor puck-movement wise.

CAN #14 LW Comtois, Maxime (2017) - Looked skilled and was dangerous. He made some good passes spotting forwards crashing the net, doesn't telegraph his moves either. Anticipated the play well, though at times you would wish for him to produce a dominant shift instead of relying on quick-strikes as much as he did in this game.

CAN #15 LW Bellerive, Jordan (2017) - One of the more active Canadian forwads in this game, Bellerive did a good job both as a passer as well as in finding holes where he could get his shot off. Had a good opportunity on a jam play in front of the net as well. One of the better forwards in producing offensive zone time in this game.

CAN #16 C Morand, Antoine (2017) - Thought he was just OK in this game, but he had the key goal to put Canada back up by two in third period which pretty much effectively ended the game. A real solid read by Morand on a turnover and a goal into the empty net after he received the puck on the far-side post.

CAN #17 C Studnicka, Jack (2017) - Just a hard-working game for him. He was constantly looking to get involved by going to the wall and winning battles and putting himself into traffic and around the net. He faded a bit down the stretch, but was one of the harder working players through two periods. A nice complement to Comtois' more skilled based game.

CAN #18 C Entwistle, MacKenzie (2017) - Part of the Canadian fourth line, came to life in second period and was a key factor in Canada going up 2:0. Continued to play well after that, using his reach and skating to move the puck up ice and kept it simple. Overall, exactly the type of game you'd want out of someone with more of a checking role on this team.

CAN #20 RW Teasdale, Joel (2017) - I liked his game a lot tonight. He played a very smart game, breaking up plays, being properly positioned be it offensive or defensive situations. Made everyone's job easier. Didn't hog the puck, but made something positive happen on most of his shifts.

CAN #21 RW Semchuk, Brendan (2017) - Useful on the forechek and has decent size and speed. Doesn't lack in hockey IQ either. He would produce opportunities but just didn't have the skill to capitalize. Decent game but slightly frustrating due to lack of execution on some of the skill plays.

CAN #22 RW Boudrias, Shawn (2017) - Good size and had jump to his step. Really used his size well to power over Finnish defensemen. Protected the puck well. Scored from up-close on a feed from behind the net.

FIN #3 LD Heiskanen, Miro (2017) - He moved the puck well, however never really felt he was dangerous in the offensive zone. Defensive game was OK, but he can struggle against size.

FIN #5 RD Jokiharju, Henri (2017) - Smooth skating and equally smooth passing out of his own end. Good anticipation when reading the play defensively, not much of a defensive force down-low. He gets his shots on net quite fast, but his snapshots and wristhots often tend to lack any sort of power.

FIN #8 LD Teravainen, Eero (2017) - Logged heavier minutes in third period with Finland trying to come back and tie the game. Good outlets and can play a smart game. Like his brother Teuvo, he seems to have a thinner frame and can get bounced around a bit.

FIN #11 LD Vaakanainen, Urho (2017) - Skating and size aren't too bad, he can also move the puck and can also fire it from the point. Decision-making was a bit inconsistent. Sometimes forced passing lanes that weren't there, some odd decisions on defensive zone coverage as well. His game was lacking polish although he has tools to work with.

FIN #13 C Ikonen, Joni (2017) - Undersized but was probably Finland's best center. He moves well and has the lateral ability to avoid contact, can handle the puck and make plays at speed as well. Circled the offensive zone a couple of times forcing coverage to change before making a play. Can bring the puck through neutral zone as well.

FIN #19 RW Moilanen, Sami (2017) - He was noticeable in the first period, having a couple of scoring chances. His performance fell off a cliff in the last two periods, stopped working for the puck, ended up observing the play too much and was largely a non-entity.

FIN #21 LW Tolvanen, Eeli (2017) - Quick decision-making, has good skill and skating. Very dangerous when he picks up the puck with speed. Good shot as well. Scored on a turnover by Canadian D, roofing it top shelf with no chance for DiPietro. After a mediocre first period, he ended up being the most dangerous Finnish forward.

FIN #22 C Virtanen, Santeri (2017) - He worked, but just struggled to get anything going. Although he was involved on the wall and defensively, his feet seemed to struggle to catch up with the pace of the game. Fell down a lot as well. Struggles to combine skating with handling the puck, and changes of direction. Had zero elusiveness and was too easy to strip of the puck for mobile defensemen.

FIN #23 LW Vesalainen, Kristian (2017) - Size and skating ability are both there. He's always defensively responsible and plays a very mature game. Good ability to move the puck up the ice. Can protect the puck with his size and makes smart plays. Not a huge amount of deception, just a honest game. Didn't have tons happening offensively, but his line as a whole never got going.

FIN #27 RD Rasanen, Eemeli (2017) - Legit huge kid. Skating will need to improve. His reads actually weren't too bad, and he even made some good first passes although nothing really advanced in that regard. Is willing to play physical and cleaned out quite a few Canadian forwards.

FIN #30 G Lehtinen, Lassi (2017) - Really undersized but quick movement and good technique. Quite controlled, doesn't slide out of position. The third goal he gave up could have been played better, didn't do the best job tracking the puck after the turnover which didn't give him enough time to react on a quick passing play.

Cobourg Cougars at Buffalo Junior Sabres, November 1, 2015

Harbor Center (Buffalo, NY)

COB #11 Dunn, Sam (2016) – He is decent size Dman with height and solid weight. He makes decent 1st pass and actually was involved in initial breakout on his team's 1st goal scored in the first period. He handles the puck decent and mobility is pretty good too although his speed and lateral foot speed is average. He plays physical style in spots and would be more effective using his strength more often, as sometimes plays bit lax on puck retrieval. In one goal against, he was beaten on the forecheck in the 2nd period. His tempo looks questionable for the next level.

Finland vs Russia, U17 WHC, November 2nd, 2015

FIN #1 G Luukkonen, Ukko-Pekka (2017) - Big goalie. He blocked a lot of shots, but his defense did a pretty good job cleaning up the rebounds in front of him. Though he didn't have a bad game, felt like his rebound control could be better. A lot of times it seemed like he was just trying to make himself big and hope the puck hits him, without much control over it.

FIN #3 LD Heiskanen, Miro (2017) - Solid quick puck-movement. Pinched quite a bit and it worked out for him most of the time. Active offensively in getting his shot on net. Good skating ability.

FIN #5 RD Jokiharju, Henri (2017) - A very consistent player as to what kind of game he brings. His usual self with skating and intelligent passing. He had a couple of good shots on the net, though he would at times be better off looking up and waiting a moment for some traffic to form instead of always quickly pulling the trigger.

FIN #8 LD Teravainen, Eeru (2017) - He lined up on the left side for this game. He did a good job making plays under pressure, one of the better defensemen on the ice at completing an accurate pass through sticks and bodies.

FIN #9 RW Viitasalo, Nuutti (2017) - Played D first game of the tournament, but lined up as 4th line RW in this game. Not very big, but a very engaging player. Finishes his checks a lot and moves his feet, didn't struggle at all playing a forward position and was an asset on the forecheck.

FIN #11 LD Vaakanainen, Urho (2017) - Used his physical tools well and played a solid two-way game. Kept his mistakes to a minimum and didn't try to do too much. Used his size well when moving the puck, was able to make plays even while absorbing physical contact.

FIN #12 C Koskenkorva, Jesse (2017) - He had two goals in this game, both times showing up in the right spot at the right time, but otherwise played a relatively quiet yet responsible game.

FIN #13 C Ikonen, Joni (2017) - Kept moving his feet and he played a bit reckless, but that in turn made him a factor on the ice. Was definitely willing to go to the front of the net and he used his speed well to pierce the Russian defense through the middle.

FIN #21 RW Tolvanen, Eeli (2017) - Promoted to the top line and once again the best Finnish forward. Scored two goals, has great anticipation and a quick release that doesn't allow goalies to react in time. Works hard, and is a threat from different situations, be it wristers from the slot or from up-close around the net. Could have easily scored 3-4 goals in this game.

FIN #22 C Virtanen, Santeri (2017) - He hit the crossbar by jumping into a hole in the slot after reading a turnover on the forecheck. He thinks the game at a high enough level, but the execution was problematic as he is often that extra moment behind the play due to his slow movement.

FIN #23 LW Vesalainen, Kristian (2017) - He had two shorthanded break-aways coming off his own effort. Several good defensive plays breaking up puck-movement and taking or passing the puck out of his zone. With Tolvanen on his line, a lot of his hard work got rewarded as he had a player on his line that could finish and make high-end skill plays.

RUS #1 G Akhmetov, Aresni (2017) - He got pulled about half-way through the game. Not all of the goals were his fault, but he looked somewhat shaky. The angles were off, the reaction time wasn't that quick, and you'd expect him to look bigger in net at his listed size of 6'2. Part of him getting pulled was also undoubtedly to wake up a Russia team that seemed to lack focus as a whole.

RUS #4 LD Alexeev, Aleksander (2018) - A quieter game, though he still appears the best Russian defenseman on the ice. Really used skating to his advantage both offensively and defensively. Defensively he's very quick to get into position and offensively he did a good job of controlling the point and the blueline.

RUS #5 RD Kazamanov, Vladislav (2017) - Consistent accurate first pass. He was a threat from the point, especially on PP and scored a goal there. Average defensively, but he was getting involved offensively in this game, mostly with his shot as he didn't handle the puck a lot.

RUS #12 LW Alekseev, Yaroslav (2017) - Smart plays for the most part, made accurate passes and was available as an outlet for puck-movement through neutral zone. Despite not being big, he did a good job driving the net and looking for those ugly goals, which was exactly what Russia lacked in this game.

RUS #14 RW Svechnikov, Andrei (2018) - Much more involved in the play than in his first game of the tournament. Worked to support the play more and kept himself available for short simple passes, good skill with the puck, was dangerous around the net a couple of times. Made a blind pass that his linemate didn't expect, his vision is obvious as well.

RUS #18 RD Samorukov, Dmitri (2017) - He was used on both PP and PK. Did a good job logging his minutes, very few mistakes and makes good decisions with the puck. Competed well, though he wasn't really a big offensive threat nor a shutdown force, just someone who provided solid minutes of two-way game.

RUS #24 RW Kostin, Klim (2017) - Very strong game. Used his skating and size to move the puck forward, can handle the puck on both sides of his body and can lean into the player checking him. Was hard to take the puck from him, showed his scoring ability as well.

RUS #30 G Zhukov, Maxim (2017) - He replaced Akhmetov. Did not have a lot of work, but one thing that's been consistent with him is that he does a good job when the momentum is turning either in his team's favor or when the other team is pressuring. There's a certain amount of confidence in his body language in those pressure situations.

Sweden vs Canada Red, U17 WHC, November 2nd, 2015

SWE #1 G Eriksson Ek, Olle (2017) - Started the second period with Sweden down 3:0. Thought he played well, although Canada seemed to ease back a bit going up by three. Played up to his size and had good rebound control.

SWE #4 LD Brannstrom, Erik (2017) - Not as offensively dangerous as he can be. He played more physical after Sweden started trailing and tried to get his team going. Had some pushes and shoves with Canadian forwards, dropped Comtois on a spin move as well.
SWE #6 RD Liljegren, Timothy (2017) - Good puck-movement. Was trying to make something happen out of nothing. Scored with a wrist shot from top of the circle. Saved a goal by blocking a wraparound attempt with his body. Not a perfect performance in his decision-making, but thought he was overworked trying to make things happen on an underperforming Swedish team.

SWE #9 LD Walfridsson, Sebastian (2017) - A decent game for him. He had some good pinches and held the blueline a couple of times resulting in the odd extended offensive zone shift.

SWE #15 C Hugg, Rickard (2017) - Played a two-way game, did a good job on a backcheck to strip Bellerive of the puck. He did an adequate job being at least involved in the puck battles and winning some of them, but received very little support from his wings.

SWE #21 C Miketinac, Kalle (2017) - He reads the play well and can make quick decisions, but also uses stickhandling to give himself some time and change angles, though there was never really any finish on his line. He has also competed well off-the-puck.

SWE #26 RW Zetterlund, Fabian (2017) - He has shown off good hockey sense, reading opportunities where he can jump into holes and receive a puck in a dangerous position. He also supported the play well in neutral zone. Would have liked to see more bite out of him.

SWE #27 RW Sveningsson, Filip (2017) - Struggled in the first period. Only looked dangerous on PP, but towards the end of the second he started being a bit more engaging and worked a bit harder to find lanes for his shot. He's got a nice release.

CAN #1 G DiPietro, Michael (2017) - He was very good throughout. Did a real good job making saves in traffic, really made himself big and pushed out and competed with bodies in front of him. Only question mark was him leaving some room upstairs.

CAN #2 RD Phillips, Markus (2017) - He had a couple of poor clearing attempts on PK, but otherwise used skating to his advantage. Moved the puck up ice quickly. Had some good stretch passes as well. Did a good job on PP and 4 on 4 situations, taking advantage of the excess room on the ice.

CAN #3 RD Brook, Josh (2017) - He was getting his shots on net, though he didn't use his stickhandling a lot, he was still involved offensively. Scored a goal from the point. Very solid defensively, thought he played a more polished defensive game than any other Canadian defenseman.

CAN #6 LD Paquette, Jacob (2017) - Used his size and was physical in blocking entries and pushing the play to the outside with his body. Decent job with the first pass but not very offensively involved.

CAN #9 LW Glass, Cody (2017) - Played a simple straight-line game. Very good compete level and was a factor on the forecheck. Drove the net and had a scoring chance. Most of his offensive zone play seemed reliant on work-ethic as opposed to creating anything with skill.

CAN #14 RW Comtois, Maxime (2017) - Made a good pass to Morand for the first goal of the game right after Canada killed a penalty. Did a good job of both distributing the puck as well as getting involved as a shooter. His line with Morand and Teasdale had several dominant shifts moving the puck in the offensive zone with give and go plays.

CAN #16 C Morand, Antoine (2017) - He didn't drive the play quite as much as Comtois on his line but had very good anticipation for showing up in the right spots. Scored off a Comtois pass picking top corner from the left circle and his second goal was him popping into the picture at the right time as well.

CAN #17 C Studnicka, Jack (2017) - Really used his reach and skating to circle the offensive zone and look for lanes where he can distribute the puck. I liked him dropping the shoulder and driving the net as well. He played an engaging game.

CAN #20 LW Teasdale, Joel (2017) - One of the smartest players on the ice. Had a backcheck where he stole the puck and drew a penalty. Very good off the puck and produced tons of turnovers. Had a goal as well.

CAN #22 RW Boudrias, Shawn (2017) - Used his body well on the forecheck and you could tell the Swedish defense wasn't comfortable at all with him on the ice. Protected the puck well with his frame as well.

Czech Republic at Canada Black, World U-17 Hockey Challenge, November 2, 2015

CZE #4 LD Kral, Filip (2017) - Just an average skater, but one with good vision who made really smart and dependable plays for his club tonight. A good passer who saw some time on the powerplay tonight. Played in all situations. Cleared his crease admirably. Additionally did a decent job making clearances in his own end. Very dependable in his one-on-one puck battles.

CZE #7 RD Bukac, Daniel (2017) - One of two defenseman who helped get the Czechs off to an impressive start with offense from the back-end. A simple low-lying shot from the blueline snuck its way past D'Orio to put the Czechs up 1-0 in the first period. Shot looked good and passing wasn't bad either. Finished the game with two points and was named his club's player of the game.

CZE #8 LD Galvas, Jakob (2017) - The second of two Czech defenseman to create offense from the back end. Captain for Team Czech Republic threw a shot on net from the right side for the second 2-0 goal on D'Orio from that part of the ice. Played good minutes at even-strength but also saw considerable time on the powerplay where he looked like a decent distributor and a strong shooter. Didn't do anything spectacular outside of his goal, but didn't do anything stupid either, and finished the affair with two points.

CZE #11 LC Kondelik, Jachym (2018) - Fifteen-years-old and already listed at six-foot-six on the line charts. Centred the Czechs' top line, which featured Zadina and Svoboda on his wings. Dependable in the faceoff circle. Also played on his club's top power play unit, where he did a good job of utilizing his size to create screens. Difficult to move. Strong in the faceoff circle. Knows his limitations and does a stand-up job of playing within them. An easy player to admire.

CZE #16 RW Svoboda, Matyas (2017) - Big Czech winger played on the top line alongside the offensively charged Filip Zadina and another big-bodied forward in Jachym Kondelik. Has really decent speed with the puck considering his large frame. Looks powerful but moves with sufficient speed. Provided some good screens in front of the net. Wasn't afraid to take a hit to make a play.

CZE #19 LW Zadina, Filip (2018) - A fairly fast-skating and trigger-happy shooter who came into the game advertised as one of the most dangerous Czech forwards. Lived up to his reputation when he got a couple wristers on net early. Was taken off the ice in the first period, however, after taking a series of big hits from Nolan Kneen. Skated through the slot with his head down and was absolutely crushed by a shoulder-first check from Kneen, taking him off his feet for a while. Returned to the game and got several more shots on net, including a 3-2 go ahead goal in the second period.

CZE #22 RW Kaut, Martin (2018) - One of four fifteen-year-olds on a decidedly young Czech club. Played energetically in all zones but just completely ran out of gas on one of his shifts, taking an icing call, resulting in a couple of chances for the Mattheos line against some tired Czech players.

BLK #3 LD Crete-Belzile, Antoine (2017) - More of the same, as his awareness continued to shine on the ice. Showed good hockey sense by trying to catch the Czechs on a line change with a smartly timed pinch. Picks his spots wisely on the offensive end. Got caught standing still once or twice in this game, as he could be a bit more active with his stick when he needs to be. Continued to win most of his one-on-one battles.

BLK #4 RD Kneen, Nolan (2017) - "Nolan Kneen was being mean," as one broadcaster put it. Looked like he ate his spinach this morning as he was all over the ice, closing gaps, pinching down low, making big hits, taking big-time chances wherever he could and usually cashing in. Received a major penalty near the end of the first period after the second of two crushing blows to Filip Zadina wiped him off his feet. Had some brain farts, but his energy level was off the charts in this one.

BLK #6 RD Davis, Hayden (2017) - A really good skater for his size who eats up a lot of minutes for Team Black. Advanced backwards skating ability is what makes Davis so attractive, but at times he advances back too quickly and loses his check. Didn't close the gap on Filip Zadina nearly fast enough resulting in two shot attempts and a go-ahead goal for the Czechs in the second period. Tightened up thereafter.

BLK #8 LC Leschyshyn, Jake (2017) - Looked extraordinarily engaged when playing in his own end, as he loves anticipating plays, identifying lanes, blocking shots, and disrupting passes. A really good penalty killer, but can also contribute here and there offensively. As an example, he broke into the offensive zone all by himself and connected with a quick wrister to tie the game 2-2. Showed good nerves scoring again in the shootout with a quick-release wristshot that snuck in five-hole.

BLK #9 LC Veleno, Joseph (2018) - Extraordinary edgework allows him to be very tricky and elusive with the puck. Initiates the breakout with some inspiring rushes. Saw a lot of ice time and was very dependable in the faceoff and offensive departments. Finished the game with one assist, but had more chances than the scorecard would immediately suggest. Strangely, he was only used once in the shootout, where he didn't score.

BLK #12 LW Mattheos, Stelio (2018) - Switches regularly between wing and centre, and seems to be one of those players who builds instant chemistry with whoever he's on the ice with. Excellent skating speed and body positioning allows him to win the vast majority of his puck races, even if he starts several steps behind. Threw some nice hits. Kept his feet moving in the offensive zone but can look a little uninterested in his own end. Had some long shifts in which he racked up scoring chances.

BLK #14 LW Rasmussen, Michael (2017) - A gritty effort from Rasmussen in this one, as he enjoyed breaking into the offensive zone and manufacturing some scoring chances. Made a disruption happen in front of the net that somehow deflected past the Czech goaltender to open the scoring 2-1 for Team Black. Seemed to tire out a bit as the game went on.

BLK #16 LW Bowers, Shane (2017) - Halifax-native wore the 'C' for Team Black but didn't really stand out too much for his club. Nerves seemed to get the best of him. He made some terrible fumbles of the puck near the blueline in the first half and looked like he was trying to do a bit too much.

BLK #17 RW Levin, David (2017) - Looks really big on the ice. Played on the first line energy and checking unit, which featured Dawson Holt at centre and Michael Rasmussen on the right wing. Took a checking from behind penalty on a borderline check into the boards putting his team in a five-on-three situation while down 2-0. He was ejected for twelve minutes and returned looking even more physical. Plays with a lot of grit.

BLK #20 LC Holt, Dawson (2017) - Skated with a ton of energy and put up some inspiring efforts in which he used his speed to skate fearlessly towards the net at full-pace. Did a really good job in a line-matching role that put him in a checking role against the big Matyas Svoboda. Excelled at working the puck down the middle between the hashmarks.

BLK #23 LW Durandeau, Arnaud (2017) - Came into the offensive zone with furious speed and really impressive stick skill when moving at full pace. On one entry, he zoomed past the opposition defence with good foot-speed and a toe-drag move that was just inches from being a goal. Saw considerable time on the power play, which is interesting as he was an injury replacement who arrived to northern B.C. as a last-minute call up. Was also used multiple times in the shootout, where he scored once.

Acadie-Bathurst Titan vs Blainville-Boisbriand Armada,, November 3rd, 2015

BLB #96 LW Pospisil, Kristian (2016): Scored a goal on the power play at the side of the net after taking a nice feed from defenseman Philippe Bureau-Blais. Once again tonight, the 19 year old Slovak did a good job along the boards and making use of his size to protect the puck. However, he took a bad penalty at the end of the game that could have been costly for his team.

BLB #18 LW Hylland, Tyler (2016): Scored a goal jumping on a rebound in front of the net. Worked hard in the offensive zone and used his speed well. Played on the PK. Threw a couple of good hits during the game.

BLB #29 G Grametbauer, Mark (2016): He was struggling in the first half with his rebound control but got better as the game went on. He gave up a weak first goal at the start of the game but won his team two points with a stellar 3rd period with some excellent saves late in the game, up by a goal. He was very active handling the puck in this game.

BLB #89 C Picard, Miguel (2016): Not much to say about his game offensively tonight, as it was very quiet. He does have good awareness without the puck and he's smart in the defensive zone. Played on both the PP and PK tonight and took important faceoffs for his team, going 11/18 in the faceoff circle.

BLB #93 C Boucher, Anthony (2016): The rookie forward is clearly still adjusting to the QMJHL, with a tough night in the faceoff circle (1/7). He was paired with Pospisil, but didn't generate much offense with him during the game. He missed some easy passes in the offensive zone.

AB #98 LW Kuznetsov, Vladimir (2016): The big Russian forward was one of the best Titan forwards tonight. He used his size well in the offensive zone to protect the puck. He could have scored 2-3 goals tonight, but was robbed by Grametbauer all night long. He's not a speedster and has average agility. He showed good vision with the puck, as he was able to find his linemates at times in the O-zone.

AB #16 RW Maher, Jordan (2016): Didn't generate much offense today. He is a good skater, but was barely noticeable offensively. He missed some easy passes on the power play. But late in the game, he made a very nice pass to Boivin, a very nice feed on the backhand to a striking Boivin who almost scored to tie the game.

AB #45 LD Francis, Elijah (2016): Showed good footing and good agility on the back end. He made some questionable decisions in his own end, though. Good compete level along the boards during the game.

AB #31 G Pickard, Reilly (2016): Not tested much by the Armada forwards today, he also struggled a bit with his rebound control during the game. He would probably like to have the 3rd BLB goal back, after giving up a bad rebound right in the slot from a routine shot which led to the Hylland goal. He's calm in his crease; he was working hard to track the puck when he had traffic in front of him, average size goaltender.

Sweden vs Finland, U17 WHC, November 3rd, 2015

SWE #1 G Eriksson Ek, Olle (2017) - He struggled with tracking the puck, especially on passes from behind the net and lateral passes which resulted in him not getting into position soon enough or just dropping down without being sure where the puck was. In combination with Sweden's awful ability to clear the slot it produced a lot of problems. He was a bit better early on and had a few bright spots, robbing Ikonen on a glove save and doing a good job on a scramble play.

SWE #4 LD Brannstrom, Erik (2017) - He played below his usual energy level and was not as engaging as I'm used to with him. While he did show off his offensive tools at times, I thought he was sloppy for most of the game. Mishandling the puck on the point and also got pinned down several times in his own end for being careless with the puck.

SWE #6 RD Liljegren, Timothy (2017) - Again the best Swedish player on the ice by a landslide. He uses his skating beautifully to move around opposing players and evade checks. His passing is accurate and he doesn't force plays. He has a fantastic shot. Dangerous slapshot, but especially flashed his high-end wristshot. He scored by picking up speed and wiring the puck into the top corner of the net.

SWE #9 LD Walfridsson, Sebastian (2017) - He did a decent job moving the puck and several times sacrificed his body blocking shots. He competed well and was willing to use his body both to make plays and to block opposing forwards. He is not huge, but it was something that was sorely missing from the rest of the Swedish defense.

SWE #11 LW Aterius, Erik (2017) - He was consistent with driving the net and he can be a bit of an agitating presence there. He needed to be better at extending offensive zone time and making plays with the puck though, for the type of game he plays to really be effective.

SWE #12 RW Elvenes, Lucas (2017) - Scored a goal crashing the net off a Liljegren pass. I thought he did a good job coming off the perimeter and finding ways to get involved in the middle. Was buzzing around the play and looking to receive a pass in the slot where he could be a scoring threat.

SWE #15 C Hugg, Rickard (2017) - He did a good job on the wall tonight. Winning footraces and obtaining inside body position against the defenseman, he was extending zone time for his team and made a couple of good passes into the slot for scoring chances. Had a late goal, that didn't mean much as the game was already decided long before that with a sizeable Finnish lead.

SWE #27 RW Sveningsson, Filip (2017) - As a scorer and someone whose got a pretty good shot, I thought he didn't find ways to get open which considerably limited his impact in this game. Not a lot of puck touches.

FIN #3 LD Heiskanen, Miro (2017) - Picked up two assists as a key player on a 1-3-1 PP setup that was destroying Sweden all game long. Good puck-handling and keeps his head up to see options. Not a standout defensively, but he didn't spend a lot of time in his own zone either.

FIN #5 RD Jokiharju, Henri (2017) - He had a goal that would put Finland up by one, quickly firing a point shot off a broken play. His positioning defensively was on-point, but can be pushed off by physically bigger players. He won't start physical contact unless he has to. His quick-release from the point helps him cause trouble with rebounds.

FIN #11 LD Vaakanainen, Urho (2017) - He's got some sturdiness to him that helps him with physical battles. Can skate as well. Sometimes wonder about his positioning defensively and his gap control. Has a very quick slapshot with quite a bit of power to it and was dangerous several times in that way.

FIN #13 C Ikonen, Joni (2017) - A competitve game. He's like a buzzsaw out there and works with and without the puck. He had a goal by going to the front of the net. Had another chance where he got robbed by Eriksson Ek's glove. His willingness to move his feet and hound players helps him on PK as well.

FIN #21 RW Tolvanen, Eeli (2017) - Best Finnish player on the ice. He's a left shot who was a huge threat on the PP from the right side, wiring one-timers and scored twice on PP. Has a very quick release on all shot types. Very good reads in finding spots where he can get it off. Intelligent play off-the-puck and defensively as well as he reads puck-movement lanes and gets his stick on careless passes. Can pressure the point defensively and stole the puck resulting in a turnover and hit the post as well. Ended the game with 4 goals.

FIN #22 C Virtanen, Santeri (2017) - Found a role by being useful on PK and by keeping close gaps and supporting the puck-movement. Had a couple of steals on PK and was quite good there. Skating continues to be an issue.

FIN #23 LW Vesalainen, Kristian (2017) - Him and Tolvanen had good chemistry. He had a nice assist on a give-and-go play with Tolvanen. Uses his stick well to cover lanes and break up plays. Sometimes he skates himself into a defenseman or out of room, due to the fact that he tends to utilize one consistent skating speed in a straight line. Solid defensively as always, but different gear changes would help him offensively.

FIN #27 LD Rasanen, Eemeli (2017) - The size and the stick-length are alluring but his skating is quite poor to the point that right now it's questionable whether the physicality and size he brings is worth a consistent shift at this level. Played limited minutes and can be beat wide by better skaters.

FIN #30 G Lehtinen, Lassi (2017) - Thought he played a calm controlled game. Good movement in his crease. Did a really good job making saves on PK, which helped Finland to regain momentum. He didn't have tons of hard saves to make but was consistent in saving the ones he had to.

Russia vs Canada Red, U17 WHC, November 3rd, 2015

RUS #6 RD Rubinchik, Mark (2017) - Good passing out of his zone and smart pinching moved the puck forward up ice and kept it in offensive zone several times taking hits to make plays. Had some bite in him and was willing to dish it back as well.

RUS #8 C Demin, Pavel (2017) - Had good compete level all game. Stripped several Canadians of the puck, was willing to play in traffic in the offensive zone and threw a nice hit on Morand.

RUS #12 LW Alekseev, Yaroslav (2017) - He did a good job working for his space where he could receive passes and then used his feet and body position well to protect the puck and make plays.

RUS #14 RW Svechnikov, Andrei (2018) - He simplified his game and made quicker decisions with the puck while still showing his high-end skill. Thought he was stronger on the wall as well. Had a nice spinorama move around Paquette on a zone entry.

RUS #19 LW Chekhovich, Ivan (2017) - He had a good shorthanded chance off a Brook mishandle. He has ended the night with a goal and an assist, though he looked like he mostly benefited from strong performances from Kostin and Lipanov.

RUS #24 RW Kostin, Klim (2017) - He scored from a Lipanov pass on a turnover just seconds after a previous Russia goal. Had several good driving plays using his body to shield the puck. His drive to the net resulted in a Chekhovich goal.

RUS #30 G Zhukov, Maxim (2017) - Was really good when making saves on unobstructed shots, often not giving up a rebound at all. Slightly less comfortable with traffic early on, but had a good performance overall.

CAN #4 LD Smart, Jonathan (2017) - He made good decisions with the puck and had good pace to his puck-movement. Can skate with the puck and did a good job utilizing that until he found an open lane for his passes.

CAN #4 LD Paquette, Jacob (2017) - He used his body well to absorb physical contact and still make plays. Didn't get involved offensively a lot but had smarts to make sure the play was going away from his own end and forwards.

CAN #9 LW Glass, Cody (2017) - He competed and had a couple of isolated chances. He can find open space in the middle and looks for his shot, but didn't get a lot of useful pucks back. Skating stride at top speed looks a bit clunky, a lot of foot movement but short stride that doesn't cover a lot of ice.

CAN #14 RW Comtois, Maxime (2017) - Created gaps with his foot movement and cuts, putting the player checking him behind the play. Had a nice backhand pass to Bellerive on the first goal. Scored in OT by redirecting a Flower point shot.

CAN #15 LW Bellerive, Jordan (2017) - Was a presence around the net and scored the first goal from up-close. Knows how to slide into lanes and get himself open. Thought he might at times be better off opting for a pass back to the point and then going to the net as opposed to forcing the direct net drive at all times.

CAN #19 LW Ratcliffe, Isaac (2017) - He did a good job using his size. Sacrificed his body and used his reach several times to move the puck past defensemen that were laying the body on him. Took physical contact on zone entries but still made plays and was willing to plant his big body in traffic.

Canada Black vs Canada Red, World Under-17 Hockey Challenge, November 5, 2015

BLK #3 LD Crete-Belzile, Antoine (2017) - Lost his man, Maxime Comtois, on one shift, but was able to recover and found himself draped all over his check at the last second, likely preventing a goal-against. Just looked average in terms of skating, but looks highly advanced in terms of his anticipation and hockey sense. To this point, he's led what has easily been the best and most dependable penalty killing squads in the tournament as of late. Did an excellent job on the first unit, while Kneen led an equally impressive second unit. Manages the puck really well along the boards or in the corners, and expertly clears the puck out of danger when he needs to. Was constantly standing guys up at his own blueline and denying entries.

BLK #4 RD Kneen, Nolan (2017) - Didn't impress me very much in a previous viewing during the Kamloops Blazers' preseason, but looks far more confident and imposing against players closer to his size listing. Received an assist after passing off a shot to Veleno who then passed off a shot to Durandeau for a game-opening goal to put Team Black up 1-0. Continued to look physical and aggressive. Has contributed at both ends of the ice thus far in this tournament.

BLK #9 LC Veleno, Joseph (2018) - Was an offensive force for Team Black in this one, as he simply dances around the ice when the puck is on his stick in the offensive zone. It looked impossible to strip him of the puck at times. Received an assist on Team Black's first goal. Fantastic wristshot struck the bar with a ton of force before ricocheting into the net to tie the game 2-2 for his club at the end of the third period.

BLK #11 LW Gilmour, Brady (2017) - A speedy player who looks dangerous in unexpected bursts. As an example, he used his speed to sharply cut in front of Team Red's net for a great chance in the third period.

BLK #12 LW Mattheos, Stelio (2018) - Struggled to be noticeable in a game that depended on Team Black playing a responsible defense-intensive style of game. Saw limited ice time as his offensive game is much better than his defensive game at this point in his development. After Team Black gave up a long-held lead, he fed Joseph Veleno for a third period wristshot and an emotional game tying goal.

BLK #14 RW Rasmussen, Michael (2017) - Continued to show good energy and compete-level, but wasn't quite his consistent, dependable self in this one. Showed decent hustle early on, but looked a bit gassed and sluggish in the second half. Took some bad penalties that ended up costing his team.

BLK #17 RW Levin, David (2017) - A fast and physical player who does a good job pressuring the opposition in the offensive zone. Hemmed Team Red in their own area on several shifts while playing alongside Rasmussen and Holt once again. Throws hits really well, but absorbs or dodges them as well as he throws them.

BLK #20 LC Holt, Dawson (2017) - A decent skater but one who drives through the ice with a lot of evenly distributed strength and body mass, with his head up and with his eye's open, making it hard to knock him off the puck. Comes off of the half wall and into open ice with a ton of skill. Surprisingly talented in his one-on-one open ice puck battles as his active stick and puck aptitude allows him to win almost all of them. Uses these skills most typically to hem the opposition in their own zone, and to wear the opposition down on long, winding shifts.

BLK #23 Durandeau, Arnaud (2017) - Continued to impress in yet another gutsy performance. Was trusted with key minutes thanks to his hustle in all three zones and a likeable consistency of effort. Scored the opening goal on a nice series of passes from Veleno and Kneen. Was then a part of a Joseph Veleno-Stelio Mattheos play for an emotional 2-2 game tying goal. Later took a dangerous looking spill on an awkward collision with Hayden Davis but returned to his bench and looked alright.

RED #2 Phillips, Markus (2017) - A smooth skater and confident puck handler who looked dejected and like he lost some confidence as this game wore on. Made some decent pinches that simply went nowhere thanks to poor efforts from his teammates. Looked really frustrated by Team Red's inability to score through two periods and exhibited some highly negative body language unbefitting of a team captain.

RED #3 RD Brook, Josh (2017) - Moose Jaw Warrior standout in previous viewings once again put up a great game. Can really fly up the ice quickly once the puck is on his stick. Showed good burst in his zone entries and wasn't afraid to stickhandle through bodies and oncoming bodychecks if he had to. Might benefit from stopping up with the puck and buying himself some more time, as he sometimes made mistakes trying to do much on a single quick rush through the middle. One-timer slapshot was extremely powerful and blasted itself into the goal for a 3-2 lead with just one minute left in the third.

RED #4 LD Smart, Jonathan (2017) - A patient if not slow-footed skating defenseman who lets the play come to him for the most part. Has good reach for his height listing and has a decently active stick that allows him to play a disciplined and relatively mistake-free game. Was beaten in a couple races but recovered and transitioned the puck to safety with fairly breezy looking efforts.

RED #7 Glass, Cody (2017) - Good size, decent speed. Did a good job handling the puck with good awareness, stopping up with it, absorbing checks, and then moving the puck to open-space. Played limited minutes. Most of his ice time was in the offensive zone, where he looked like he has some decent potential in the passing department.

RED #14 Comtois, Maxime (2017) - Has breakaway propulsion in his first steps. Broke free for a really nice breakaway opportunity in the first period that might have been successful had it not been for the last minute defensive effort from Antoine Crete-Belzile. Won a decent number of faceoffs. Got himself in front the opposition goaltender for some useful screens, including a screen that allowed Josh Brook to score the game winning goal with only a minute remaining in the third period. Was probably Team

Red's best player on the power play, continually trying to set up Studnicka for the goal--they were successful once, but had several more chances.

RED #17 LW Studnicka, Jack (2017) - Played on the point for his club's top powerplay unit and failed to handle the puck properly at the blueline several times. Played sloppy early on. Was a big component to a Team Red power play that failed to generate anything on three attempts. Redeemed himself, however, with a huge 2-1 go-ahead goal on Team Red's fourth opportunity in the final frame of play.

RED #21 RW Semchuk, Brendan (2017) - A fast player, but looked far more energized in the offensive zone than he did in his own end. Backchecking skill just didn't match his forechecking efforts. Played the body a bit, which was decently effective. Took some sloppy sharp-angle shots that were a bit questionable in terms of timing, as the puck transitioned quickly the other way. Saw his ice-time gradually decrease as the game went on, as he just wasn't his best in this one.

Final Score: Canada Black 2 - Canada Red 3

Sweden vs United States, Monthey (SUI) U18 Five Nations, November 5th 2015

SWE #1 G Gustavsson, Filip (2016) - Gustavsson struggled with his glove throughout this game, dropping a couple of pucks even on easy shots. The rebound that costed him the first goal against was however a pad rebound given up to the outside, just where Bellows was. On the 2nd goal he was beaten cleanly glove side by McPhee's nice wrister from the right faceoff circle on the powerplay. Was scrambling on a couple of other powerplay chances but fought through his struggles. He was however caught too deep in his net a couple of times and when he got sucked into his net instead of standing up to Frederic coming from a tough angle he allowed the GWG as a result.

SWE #3 RD Cederholm, Jacob (2016) - Cederholm displayed good awareness in his defensive zone coverage and used his big frame to make his physical presence felt up to the defensive blueline, but had an average game overall. His passing game was far from crisp, both on outlets and when forced to make plays at the offensive blueline. He struggled when used on the powerplay.

SWE #6 LD Moverare, Jacob (2016) - Used on both #1 special team units, Moverare was for the most reliable in all situations. Aware in the defensive zone like when made a nice read to deflect Keller's backdoor pass, also showed good composure with the puck. He had however two turnovers in his zone, one when he misfired a clearing attempt, one when failed to realize Bellows didn't follow him behind the net on the forecheck. Was a blocking shots machine throughout the game, had three in a row on a key PK in the 3rd period with the game on the line.

SWE #8 RD Thilander, Adam (2017) - Was paired with Moverare in almost all situations. In the 1st period got beaten one on one once and stripped of the puck under heavy pressure on another play. Had a tough time finding a way out when he was put in a bad spot by US forecheckers. Clearly the appointed shooter on the PP, his attempts were often blocked, also as a result of the Swedish powerplay being way too predictable.

SWE #12 RW Bratt, Jesper (2016) - Played on the 1st line but despite plenty of icetime he failed to make a positive impact on the game. Tried to engage physically. Was called for boarding while on the penalty kill giving team USA a 5 on 3 opportunity. When he had the chance he took too much time to shoot off the rush (slapper with huge wind-up).

SWE #20 LW Steen, Oskar (2016) - Was one of the most effective Swedes in this game, especially on special teams. He scored by deflecting a shot in front on a 5 on 3 situation. Was able to clear the defensive zone on the penalty kill more than once and with a good and smart wrist shot in transition generated the rebound that led to a shorthanded goal for his team. Also threw a solid bodycheck despite his small size. He did make a couple of mistakes though: put himself offside on a counter attack and misfired a one-timer from the slot on a good opportunity.

SWE #21 RW Pettersson, Elias (2017) - Had a very promising first shift as he stole the puck in the offensive zone and then twice set up chances in front. Drew a penalty by successfully challenging Greenway one on one coming down the right side, which led to a 5 on 3 and Sweden 2nd goal of the game. Provided good defensive coverage with his consistent backchecking in the neutral zone and sound positioning, but a couple of times could have made better use of his stick to intercept passes in the defensive zone. Was willing to block shots when needed. His skating got worse in the 3rd period.

SWE #23 RW Weissbach, Linus (2016) - Despite his small stature Weissbach showed some physical edge in his game. Drew a penalty attacking with speed, but was not effective in the scoring areas. Early in the 3rd period he crashed head first into the boards after inadvertently stumbling on an opponent's skate on the forecheck. It was a relief to see him get up on his skates and he was somehow allowed to get back into the game (note: he then missed the remaining two games of the tournament).

SWE #26 C Andersson, Lias (2017) - Andersson centered the 2nd line and displayed a pretty complete game. Showed a good active stick on the penalty kill and almost earned himself a breakaway. Was able to set up shots from the blueline after protecting the puck inside the offensive zone, but wasn't noticeable around the net.

SWE #28 C Lindstrom, Linus (2016) – Was the #1 center and regularly used in shorthanded situations, where he had good efforts and even scored a goal when he was ready to jump on a rebound. He was the guy taking the most important faceoffs for his team and did extremely well for that matter. Had a nice takeaway behind the net in the offensive zone, but looked slow late in his shifts.

USA #4 LD Krys, Chad (2016) - Chad overall played a pretty good game, but was not as good as the day before vs Czech R. His puck carrying inside the offensive zone was limited to the perimeter. Didn't take advantage when he had room to close in towards the net on the powerplay and his shooting selection got worse as the game progressed. Had a fearless blocked shot in the dying seconds of the game on a 3 vs 5.

USA #7 C Frederic, Trent (2016) – Scored a nice GWG late in the 2nd coming down the right side on 4-on-4 and driving the net hard, taking advantage of a smaller opponent. Clearly stepped up his game today, when it was needed. Looked stronger than opponents when going after pucks at the boards, consistently winning them. Had a nice steal low in offensive zone and was often effective on the forecheck. Wasted a scoring chance when he shot right into the goalie from the slot even if he had the time to prepare his wrister.

USA #8 RD Fox, Adam (2016) - Consistently made himself available for teammates by moving into the right place without the puck, showed nice poise on the offensive blueline. Made a couple of nice passes, one from behind opponents' net generated his team's first goal. Missed the net on two dangerous wrist shots. In one occasion got stripped of the puck down low in his zone while trying to play it cool under pressure.

USA #9 C Pastujov, Nick (2016) - Played a responsible game and had a couple of good moments, when he beat moverare off the rush but couldn't finish in front and later on with a good maneuver below the right faceoff circle to set up #27 in front with a backhand pass.

USA #14 LD Greenway, J.D. (2016) - Made some physical plays along the boards behind his net. Had a good shift in the 3rd applying and releasing pressure at the right time in the neutral zone, then adding a strong presence along the boards. His intensity level however looked a bit on-and-off, sometimes even during the same shift. Showed some lack of poise on the offensive blueline when he shot right into the defending forward when he could have easily waited.

USA #17 RW Anderson, Joey (2016) - Effective third wheel of the top line, jumped into the open slot at the right time to finish off nicely a Keller's set up and tie the game in the 1st. Showed nice timing & positioning in front of the net, with the hands to take advantage of opportunities. Was way less noticeable in the 2nd half of the game.

USA #19 C Keller, Clayton (2016) - Was not a dominant force like in other games of the tourney, but his playmaking abilities were on display and ended up with two assists. Had a pretty good one-timer attempt as well. Able to carry the puck into the offensive zone and make quick decisions with it. Took a stupid penalty with 1 minute left in a one-goal game.

USA #22 LW Bellows, Kiefer (2016) - Was deadly when he scored from a tough angle one-timing into the net Gustavsson's rebound. Didn't generate offense on his own. Showed some smart positioning in the offensive zone more than once.

USA #27 LW Suthers, Keenan (2016) - Attacked the end boards with speed to get first on pucks and was physical, but looked very raw with the puck.

USA #29 G Woll, Joseph (2016) - Beaten early in the game by a wraparound as he let the puck slips through his five-hole, but was not at fault on the other two goals he allowed. His best moments were a couple of nice glove saves on dangerous wrist shots.

Final Score: Sweden: 3 – United States: 4

Canada Black vs Canada Red, U17 WHC, November 5th, 2015

BLK #3 LD Crete-Belzile, Antoine (2017) - Good shot from the point, showed off accurate and powerful slapshot in third period. Made a decent first pass, but was at times prone to rushing his decisions under forechecking pressure.

BLK #4 RD Kneen, Nolan (2017) - Played an engaging game, physical at times as well. Had a couple of good delays to avoid the forecheck and make the first pass in a controlled manner. Struggled in the third when he tried to do too much at times and lost some of the composure.

BLK #6 RD Davis, Hayden (2017) - He was just ok throughout. Made some good passes and did a good job being positionally solid on defense, but felt like he could have done more at times. Seemed to settle for playing an average game.

BLK #8 LW Leschyshyn, Jake (2017) - He was good in the first period especially. He moves his feet well to arrive on loose pucks and competes well off the puck, but was not really an offensive threat.

BLK #9 C Veleno, Joseph (2018) - A real smooth skater. Showed off high skill level and vision to make plays. Was dangerous coming down the right side of the ice and then cutting to the middle. Both his assist and goal came from that similar move. Had quick release on his wrist-shot.

BLK #11 C Gilmour, Brady (2017) - Good reads off the puck both offensively and defensively. Was willing to support the defense in breakouts and makes himself available for an easy outlet. Dishes accurate passes that move the puck forward as well.

BLK #12 RW Mattheos, Stelio (2017) - He's done a good job playing more of a power game on Veleno's wing. Really gets physically involved, not with huge hits but with being in the middle of action and battling for position.

BLK #14 LW Rasmussen, Michael (2017) - Moved well for his size, though his balance doesn't strike me as very good quite yet. He did a good job in using the reach and speed to make plays. When he got pinned down at the boards, there wasn't much push back from him, he played it as if he were smaller than he is.

BLK #16 C Bowers, Shane (2017) - There was some compete to him but he never seemed to get quite fully going. Just when he'd make a good play getting the puck or going around one player he'd lose it the next second. Seems like the tools are there to do more than he did, but his entire line was underwhelming and probably the worst one for Canada Black.

BLK #17 LW Levin, David (2018) - Moved his feet and had good skill with the puck, though at times a bit too eager to make something happen which would result in a turnover. Had a nice backcheck and immediately hounded the opposition if his team lost the puck. Couldn't do much offensively due to limited minutes.

BLK #20 C Holt, Dawson (2017) - Solid puck-support and accurate passing but not a lot of bite in his game here. Thought he played too much to the outside and didn't get a lot done below the hashmarks.

BLK #22 RD Brahaney, Jakob (2017) - Probably the most defensively solid Canada Black blueliner in this game. Used his stick well and pushed the play to the boards. Tracked the players well and provided solid coverage deeper in his own zone as well.

BLK #23 LW Durandeau, Arnaud (2017) - He did a good job reading off Veleno and just finding the holes that Veleno would produce with his skill. Scored the first goal of the game off a quick release on a Veleno cross-ice pass.

BLK #30 G McGrath, Jacob (2017) - Strong through 2 periods, holding the 1:0 lead. Reacted quickly to what was happening around him and got himself in position in time, good recovery on a couple of sequences where he had two quick consecutive shots. His performance dipped a bit in the third as he struggled making himself big with traffic in front of him, but the goals were hardly his fault.

RED #1 G DiPietro, Michael (2017) - Thought he was a bit quick to drop on some shots where he could be a bit more patient. Was strong dow-low and in traffic. Gave up the tying goal after he didn't have a lot of work for a stretch of time. Thought he was good but didn't blow me away as in some other games of his.

RED #2 RD Phillips, Markus (2017) - I thought him and Brook were again the best two defensemen for Canada Red. Phillips was his usual skating and puck-moving self. On several plays he also found a way to get involved deeper in the offensive zone and made good plays there.

RED #3 RD Brook, Josh (2017) - He had a strong game on the point both even strength as well as on the powerplay. His defensive reads were solid as well. He'd fire several dangerous shots and scored the game winning goal to break the third period tie off a point slapshot with Morand providing the screen.

RED #4 LD Smart, Jonathan (2017) - Good game as a two-way minute munching defenseman. He broke up some plays and had a good first pass throughout the game. Although he wasn't a huge offensive threat, he'd still get involved in the play.

RED #7 RD Flower, Walter (2017) - He held back quite a bit. Although he didn't have a huge impact on the game, it seems he understood less was more for him. He competed well. Not a lot of time with the puck as he always makes the easy play though it is not necessarily poor.

RED #8 LD Watson, Nick (2017) - His strong point was cutting off play and then quickly making the first pass or skating it out of danger. Held the blueline well a couple of times by sending the puck back deep. Good ability to read the play.

RED #10 C Gallant, Zach (2017) - He was more noticeable in the first. Good defensive game in his own zone and pays attention to detail. Threw a big hit on Mattheos on the forecheck. Reliable though not much there offensively.

RED #14 RW Comtois, Maxime (2017) - Nice balance between utilizing his skill and his physical tools. Got into positions where he could be dangerous offensively. Good passing ability as well. There's a sense that he's always an offensive threat when he gets the puck.

RED #16 C Morand, Antoine (2017) - His offensive zone timing was very good, he doesn't need to have the puck on his stick to be dangerous. He provided the screen on the game winning goal. Really knew how to sniff out loose pucks or receive passes in front of the net area.

RED #17 C Studnicka, Jack (2017) - Came out of the gate ready to work. He was real solid in giving Canada Red a push when they needed it. Really liked his ability to turn momentum his team's way. He scored on the powerplay in the third period on a rebound off McGrath's pad.

RED #20 LW Teasdale, Joel (2017) - He works and he's smart and he's consistent in that. He's very good at coming up with chances off broken plays, whether he's reading a turnover as a F2 or F3 or creating it himself. He tied the game beating McGrath one on one.

Russia vs Canada Red, U17 WHC, November 6th, 2015

RUS #4 LD Alexeev, Aleksander (2018) - Received less minutes in this game than in his previous games in the tournament. He played an ok game, but not as noticeable as in other viewings. Used his skating well to get to pucks quickly and again displayed his shot from the point.

RUS #6 RD Rubinchik, Mark (2017) - Thought he struggled handling the puck early on which caused trouble with getting the puck out of the zone. He settled into the game later on, though he didn't get much done offensively he had a nice play late in the game using his body to separate Studnicka from the puck.

RUS #9 C Bitsadze, Mikhail (2018) - Flashed his wristshot firing several dangerous shots from the slot. I thought he could have worked harder to get second opportunities, something that improved late in third period and OT but was missing in his game prior to that.

RUS #10 C Lipanov, Alexey (2017) - He did a lot of the little things right that helped his linemate Kostin to dominate offensively, but he didn't convince me as someone that can create offense for himself. Engaging off the puck though.

RUS #14 RW Svechnikov, Andrei (2018) - As a 2000 born he doesn't dominate shift to shift but shows flashes of brilliance. One such instance was him banking the puck off the boards to himself then skating around a Canadian player to find himself open in the slot. He also scored on the PP tipping a Kazamanov shot into the net.

RUS #17 RW Slepets, Kirill (2017) - Tied the game by sneaking in backdoor and redirecting an Osin shot/pass into the net. Had a good opportunity in OT taking off in neutral zone and beating the Canadian D. He wasn't very useful when he wasn't finding those offensive opportunities.

RUS #18 LD Samorukov, Dmitri (2017) - He was probably the best Russian defenseman in this game. A lot of accurate quick passes that allowed for easy zone exits, good positioning defensively as well.

RUS #19 LW Chekovich, Ivan (2017) - He had a couple of chances early on just finding the soft spot for his shot. He did ok in his PK minutes as well.

RUS #24 RW Kostin, Klim (2017) - By far the most dangerous Russian forward. He was dominant taking off with his size and gaining offensive zone entry. He's also done a good job bringing the puck around the boards and controlling the offensive zone. At times he would just bull through players and nobody could really stop him from advancing.

RUS #25 RW Kovalenko, Nikolai (2018) - He didn't get a lot done but he's shown good balance on his skates. Top speed didn't look high-end but has good edgework and knows how to position himself to obtain position on the puck despite a smaller size. Thought he was smart in his movement as well.

RUS #27 C Marushev, Maxim (2017) - Thought he could have used his size more effectively for puck-protection. Had a harmless looking slapshot from the offensive blueline that hit the post almost giving Russia a late third period lead.
RUS #30 G Zhukov, Maxim (2017) - Outside of the first goal he was good throughout, but his third period and OT performance was absolutely outstanding. Russia was under siege for most of the third, but there was a sequence of about 5-10 minutes where he stopped every single grade A scoring chance and there were lots of them.

CAN #1 G DiPietro, Michael (2017) - He had a bit less work than his Russian counterpart but put in a quality performance himself. Made a save on Kostin 1 on 1 and he did a good job reading and reacting to second opportunities. His ability to make a quick save after the initial one even from close-range was very good.

CAN #2 RD Phillips, Markus (2017) - Very engaging both offensively and defensively and his skating helped him in both. Had a good wraparound attempt 4 on 4 after skating down the length of ice. His passes under pressure in defensive zone weren't always perfect, but that's just a by-product of having the most puck touches out of the Canadian defense. He also got beat wide pretty badly by Kostin resulting in a offensive chance for Russia.

CAN #3 RD Brook, Josh (2017) - Sneaked into the slot on PP for a Morand pass that he would finish on and give Canada the 2:0 lead. He wasn't as good defensively as in his previous games in the tournament. His slapshot from the point continued to be a positive for him.

CAN #6 LD Paquette, Jacob (2017) - He actually used his size to be effective even offensively. He had some good pinches and used the size to push the puck forward up the wall.
CAN #10 C Gallant, Zach (2017) - Thought he simplified the game for Canada when they were running around too much. He played a solid defensive game and had a good performance in that third period and OT stretch coming up with some simple offensive zone play getting the pucks in deep and taking the play to the Russian goalie.

CAN #14 RW Comtois, Maxime (2017) - He had a pretty consistent performance as one of the key Canadian offensive threats, but lacked the finishing touch. His skill and vision are apparent in how he sets up to receive pucks and the plays he makes with the puck. He is dangerous both in rush chances as well as off the cycle.

CAN #15 LW Bellerive, Jordan (2017) - He scored the first goal of the game just by throwing the puck on net from the halfwall area and having it go in. He had good jump early in the game and set the tone for Canada but faded later on. He did a good job being a net presence, screening the goalie and looking for rebounds on several Canadian opportunities.

CAN #16 C Morand, Antoine (2017) - He had a scoring opportunity reading a stretch pass after Russia dominated the play for a while. Had a good effort cutting to the middle and drawing a penalty as well. Good nose for the net and had scoring chances.

CAN #17 C Studnicka, Jack (2017) - He had a nice a toe-drag into a wristshot move on PP, and another chance on a backhand with Bellerive providing the traffic. He has found a way to make a contribution in game-breaking moments even if he wasn't on the scoreboard. With the game tied late, he has shown his effort to negate the icing and had a good blocked shot in OT as well.

CAN #18 C Entwistle, MacKenzie (2017) - He had a good game, found ways to get offensively involved. Had a golden scoring chance 5 feet from the net that Zhukov made a save on. He read the play well and used his reach and skating to drive the play forward in a simple manner.

CAN #20 LW Teasdale, Joel (2017) - A strong performance plagued by the fact that he was absolutely robbed by Zhukov several times. Teasdale probably had the most scoring opportunities out of anyone on the ice, but just couldn't finish against a very strong goaltending performance by Zhukov. However, his effort and reads to get those opportunities were very good.

CAN #21 RW Semchuk, Brendan (2017) - He was strong in the first period. Good as a forechecker and read puck-movement well which allowed him to get his body or stick on the puck. With the puck he was better off keeping things simple, his puck skills looked like they could be better.

Green Bay Gamblers at Youngstown Phantoms, November 6th, 2015

GBG #20 RD Peeke, Andrew (2016) - Good stick and body position in defensive zone. Showed good lateral skating ability while handling the puck, had patience with puck to find clear lanes. Not a flashy offensive zone game, made a nice diagonal pass on PP to Saliba who quickly got it across to Michaelis for the first GB goal.

YNG #3 LD McInnis, Luke (2016) - Good compete. Threw a good open ice hit, had a couple of good rushes bringing the puck up through the neutral zone. Showed good effort to make a one-handed pass to his linemate after getting his body pinned on the boards. Wanted to see more on the offensive blueline from him, wasn't a shot threat. Was caught too far up the ice on SH goal against, would have been better off staying deeper and supporting the play as his team didn't have full control on the break-out.

YNG #26 LW Morrison, Cameron (2016) - Had a couple of offensive zone looks by going to the net without the puck. He uses his size well there and does a good job getting the inside position on defensemen. Made some good passes in the offensive zone as well. Good compete on the wall but got mixed results, at his size he could have done better there.

Flint Firebirds at Sarnia Sting, November 6, 2015

OHL Regular Season

FLT #8 RW Johnstone, Dane (2016) - Great forechecking pressure. Forced Sarnia to make own zone mistakes. Takes away time and space effectively.

FLT #10 LW Caamano, Nicholas (2016) - Skating is extremely awkward, but can generate speed. Good pressure on forecheck and backcheck. Top power play unit but was pretty quiet.

FLT #41 RW Bitten, Will (2016) - Hooked on breakaway first shift. Received penalty shot and showed good patience and a quick release to fire a laser top shelf for an early 1-0 lead. Good pressure on backcheck. Went to the net with quick hands. Good speed to make plays, very explosive skater. Good forecheck pressure to force turnovers. Slips into scoring position very well. Top power play unit.

FLT #73 LW Collins, Jacob (2016) - Good skating, good compete level, hard shot. Competed but wasn't able to make a huge impact tonight.

SAR #5 D Chychrun, Jakob (2016) - Showed confidence early on rushing the puck end to end. Great skating and puck protection combination. Plenty of shots on top power play unit, very powerful. Quick decisions in offensive zone. Perfect position on the offensive line backing up enough to prepare for the defensive rush, but not too far that he can't hold the line if the situation calls for it. Pinches at the right time. Good stick one on one, lost position a couple times in own zone. Drives the net with great puck protection. Made solid first passes up ice. Does a great job of slowing down and speeding up, especially for a big defender.

SAR #25 RW Kyrou, Jordan (2016) - Good positioning in slot got puck with sure goal but froze up ending the chance. Moved puck well in offensive zone. Flashed a little puck skill but wasn't nearly as good as some previous viewings.

Final Score: Flint Firebirds: 3 - Sarnia Sting: 2 - OT

Saint-John Sea Dogs vs Drummondville Voltigeurs, November 6th 2015

SNB #55 RD Green, Luke (2016): Played on the 2nd pairing with Jakub Zboril and saw power play time as well during the game. Used his good footwork to skate the puck out and moved the puck well in the transition game. He was more active in the 2nd half of the game offensively, with two solid scoring chances late in the game to tie the game.

SNB #23 LD Felixson, Oliver (2016): Did a good job on the PK, using his reach and size to block shots and passing lanes. His decision-making with the puck was a bit slow, didn't get many chances to touch the puck, though.

SNB #10 C Noel, Nathan (2016): Played a solid game, working hard at both end of the ice. Got into a fight on his first shift of the game and made good use of his speed in puck pursuit. He rushed the puck in the offensive zone with good speed and took the puck to the net. He scored a nice goal at the end of the game.

SNB #7 RW Ward, Kyle (2016): Threw some good hits on the forecheck. Was strong on his skates. His skating stride is average. Worked hard and was used on the PK.

DRU #4 LD Gagne, Benjamin (2017): The left-shooting defenseman played on the right side tonight. Gagne has good footwork that helps him skate pucks out and get out of trouble. He got beaten easily one-on-one by Noel late in the 3rd period for Saint John's 2nd goal.

DRU #22 LW Sevigny, Mathieu (2016): He didn't do much offensively during the game, outside of a scoring chance in the first period where he was a bit slow releasing his shot which gave the goaltender the opportunity to move over to make the save. He played well on the PK and threw some good hits during the game.

Switzerland vs Czech Republic, Monthey (SUI) U18 Five Nations, November 7th 2015

CZE #3 LD Sirota, Jacub (2017) – This underager showed some personality, made himself available to skate the puck up from the defensive zone and made a nice physical play at the offensive blueline to keep the puck in. Was strong taking care of a dangerous rebound in front of his net.

CZE #5 LD Hrdinka, Frantisek (2016) – Made two solid defensive plays and was able to move the puck up the neutral zone. Looked better than last season, especially in terms of straight forward skating and passing game.

CZE #6 LW Zachar, Marek (2016) – One of the players that seemed to suffer more from playing the fourth game in four nights. The team captain was less explosive than usual on his skates and more than once when carrying the puck with speed didn't read well the opponents' defense.

CZE #10 C Najman, Ondrej (2016) – Made the most of his time on both special teams. He set up a shorthanded goal with a good backhand pass and his backhand to tap-in a rebound on the powerplay was the eventual game winner. Was not among the most dynamic players on the ice though.

CZE #18 C Davidek, Milan (2016) – If not for the suspect quality of the opponent, this could be seen as a revealing game for Davidek. If anything, Milan showed he is at least worth keeping an eye on. Looked taller than the 6'1" he was listed at and his raw skating showed some upside on a few plays. He was able to beat defenders with his reach and puck protection, and scored off the rush with a nice backhand to the far post. Played a strong game, was not limited to the perimeter and made a couple of good reads without the puck.

CZE #22 C Reichel, Kristian (2016) – Robert's son put up a good effort, still skating strong in the 3rd period even if it was the 4th game in as many nights for his team. Showcased his good right-handed shot and often tried to find the time and space to unload it, be it getting open without the puck or converging to the center from the left side after carrying it through the neutral zone. When he finally had the right opportunity to shoot from the high slot he scored with a beauty of a slapshot.

CZE #23 RD Doudera, Lukas (2016) – Played the point of the umbrella on the first powerplay unit, showing good poise and a decent shot too, even if he seemed to like more setting up teammates. Made more than a couple of good plays on the offensive blueline, be it to keep the puck in, entering the zone with full puck control or moving it to find a lane.

CZE #24 RW Smerha, Tomas (2016) – Showed a good shot off the rush coming down the left side. Small and a suspect skater, but looked better when he got the puck. He looks more involved inside the offensive zone and smart around the net.

CZE #28 RW Kousal, Pavel (2016) – Displayed good agility, his efforts culminated in two similar nice rushes with very good speed down the right side. He beat #15 (Steinmann) cleanly one on one.

CZE #29 LW Hrala, Krystof (2016) – Made a nice move on the offensive blueline to beat a Swiss defender one on one coming down the right side. Was close to complete the same move a second time and made a smart pass on the offensive blueline to keep the puck in. Saw some time on the penalty kill. He finished his checks but got called for boarding on one of them.

SUI #4 LD Le Coultre, Simon (2017) – Showed good mobility and was mostly effective quickly recovering pucks along the end boards to then beat the forecheck. Made a couple of mistakes at the offensive blueline and got caught.

SUI #7 C Suter, Kaj (2016) – An undersized center, Kaj was able to surprise when his weak body powered its way through the offensive blueline and defensemen to go to the net. Committed to the other side of the puck, made several good defensive plays in the neutral zone.

SUI #14 LD Stadler, Livio (2016) – Supposed to be the leader of the Swiss defense, Stadler struggled together with the rest of a porous defensive corp. Was able to execute a couple of quick and effective breakouts, but his game was not mistake-free and he was nowhere to be found on the rebound that generated the third goal against.

SUI #17 LW Miranda, Marco (2016) – Looked like a raw prospect and this was definitely not the best game he played at this tourney. He mishandled the puck on a good opportunity and had troubles finding lanes to shoot from his right side position on the powerplay. There was however a play where we was able to nicely create room for his shot on the left circle instead.

SUI #19 RW Simic, Axel (2017) – Invisible in the first half of the game other than when he was able to release a quick one-timer from in close while getting checked, almost scoring far post. Came alive in the 3rd period with his team already down by two. Was quick jumping on a couple of loose pucks on offense and quick moving the puck as soon as he got it on his stick.

Final Score: Switzerland: 2 - Czech Republic: 6

Finland vs Unites States, Monthey (SUI) U18 Five Nations, November 7th 2015

FIN #5 LW Kotkansalo, Kasper (2017) – Brought a physical presence in the defensive zone, delivering some good checks along the boards. Protected the puck well when he needed to carry it. His skates looked a bit heavier than in previous days, but he was clearly one of the very few Finns that were effective today.

FIN #14 C Makinen, Otto (2016) – Was flat early on, had a tough time getting going in his third game in three days. Worked hard in the defensive zone despite looking tired but took an unnecessary and obvious penalty. Made a very nice side-step move to get rid of a defender at the offensive blueline, achieving a clean entry.

FIN #18 RW Kuokkanen, Janne (2016) – He was invisible throughout the 1st period, but was much better in the 2nd. Manufactured Finland first goal when he generated a 2-on-1 by blocking a shot, then transitioned the puck and perfectly set-up his linemate Oksanen for an easy finish. Later on he hit the post one-timing from the right circle a pass he received from behind the net.

FIN #21 RW Nurmi, Markus (2016) – The effort was there, but struggled with his skating to keep up with the high pace of US players and looked like chasing the play all the time.

FIN #22 C Rasanen, Aapeli (2016) – Nothing more than responsible play, unable to get anything going offensively in this game. And mishandled the puck when he had a great chance open in the slot.

FIN #26 Koivula, Otto (2016) – This big-bodied forward had obvious troubles with his skating and just couldn't get his hands on the puck the few times he had the chance. Didn't look like he played after the 1st period.

USA #4 LD Krys, Chad (2016) – Chad seemed to have a lot of fun in this game, made several rushes with the puck and the most impressive one generated the first Keller's goal late in the 1st. Showed good playmaking abilities and completed a couple of remarkable passes, for example was able to launch Keller on a breakaway from behind his net while under pressure. Was very active and made a couple of mistakes, but was easily one of the best players on the ice.

USA #8 RD Fox, Adam (2016) – Fox was able to carry the puck up through opponents even at slow speed because of impressive puck control, consistently entered the offensive zone with ease on the powerplay and smartly put pucks on net. Made several nice passes in all three zones, had two primary assists and dominated this game from the back-end in similar fashion to what Keller did up front.

USA #17 RW Anderson, Joey (2016) – Opened the scoring after about 15 seconds with a quick forehand-to-backhand finish in the slot. Hit the post off a Keller's backdoor pass on his 2nd shift, had room to score. He did score his second goal with a deflection in front on the powerplay. Was less involved in the play as the game progressed.

USA #18 LD Lindgren, Ryan (2016) – Jump-started the transition from the defensive zone whenever he could and effectively contributed to make the Finns chase the play right from the start. Had a shot blocked at the offensive blueline that generated an odd men rush and the Finns' first goal.

USA #19 C Keller, Clayton (2016) – Drove the net more than once, scored on a rebound with 1 second left in the 1st and added an impressive shorthanded wraparound goal early in the 2nd, basically killing Finland hopes. Dominated the game, especially on the powerplay. Finished with four points, and going by the fact he didn't have a hattrick in this game one may say he could improve his shot.

USA #21 LW McPhee, Graham (2016) – Dynamic on his skates right from the get-go and was one of the most active players throughout the whole game. Nicely developed a beautiful counter attack passing play that generated his team's fifth goal.

USA #22 LW Bellows, Kiefer (2016) – Hit the post with a nice wrist-shot after intercepting the puck inside the offensive zone. Made a good rush through the middle showing some explosiveness in his skating. Had a couple of questionable passes at the offensive blueline, but his passing game was dangerous inside the offensive zone and he set up the first goal with a nice one-timing centering pass to the front of the net.

Final Score: Finland: 2 – Unites States: 5

Kamloops Blazers at Vancouver Giants, November 13, 2015

KAM #12 LC Kryski, Jake (2016) - Has the hockey IQ necessary to get himself to good areas, but doesn't always have the power and explosiveness necessary to break free on his own with the puck. Nonetheless, Kryski does a really good job of getting himself to the slot and getting a quick wrister on the net. Got a couple really nice backhand chances on net, as well.

KAM #15 LW Shirley, Collin (2016**) - Set the WHL record for most points in the Canada-Russia Super Series just a few days earlier while playing as a last-minute injury replacement. Came into this game looking highly energized and had some real standout shifts in the offensive zone. Looked like he was running low on gas in the second and third periods; witnessed a lowering in ice-time as the game continued.

KAM #22 RW Benjafield, Quinn (2016) - An average skater with a good build and strong positioning. Drove down the wing with good power and awareness. Isn't afraid to release the puck; shot comes off at a high velocity. A powerfully delivered high wristshot took a weird bounce off a teammate and found its way into the net to put Kamloops up 1-0. Had a couple more shots on net that created second chance opportunities for his teammates.

KAM #41 RC Pilon, Garrett (2016) - Looked like a good skater who has enough acceleration power to close the gap effectively and unexpectedly. Did a good job of pestering the opposition defenseman on the second penalty killing unit.

KAM #42 LD Vala, Ondrej (2016) - A giant body that appeared smoother on his feet than the last time I saw him. A much better defensive player than offensive in this one. Made some nice sweeps of the puck in his own zone and some good clearances on the penalty kill. Able to use his long stick to his advantage, as he's equipped with great pokechecking skills. Not overly physical. Wasn't where he needed to be in the offensive zone. Passes were jumping over his stick.

VAN #7 RW Ronning, Ty (2016) - Uses his foot-speed and agility to chase pucks down with remarkable hustle. Received a ton of ice-time playing on a line that also featured Carter Popoff and Radovan Bondra. Got himself between the hashmarks for some wonderful chances. Had two outstanding chances in the same two minute period of play but was robbed by Ingram on both opportunities. Later scored not once but twice in the last two minutes, before delivering a highlight reel pass to Trevor Cox for the game winner in overtime. Led his team to victory by being the centrepiece of a miraculous last-moment 3-1 comeback. An A+ performance.

VAN #14 LW Malm, James (2017) - Made some smart puck moves along the half-wall, as he did a good job of moving the puck from high-to-low or vice-versa and opening up space in the offensive zone. Net drive once again looked like a strength. It was hard to get a good read on his overall game, though, as he played limited minutes in this one.

VAN #17 LW Benson, Tyler (2016) - Made some headstrong plays with the puck while trying to break into the offensive zone. Hit the crossbar on a great opportunity while streaking down the left wing and cutting in towards the net. Set up Ty Ronning's game-tying goal in the last minute of the third period with a nice pass through the slot. Elsewhere, some weak passes in the offensive zone resulted in bad giveaways. Went the extra mile in finishing his checks.

VAN #19 RW Popowich, Tyler (2018) - Absolutely huge and, despite being the youngest player on the ice, carts around his large frame with an intimidating presence. Needs to add power and speed to his skating stride. Looked sturdy and decently balanced. Warded off physical pressure with surprisingly ease for a sixteen-year-old. Once again say fairly limited ice-time.

VAN #21 RD Menell, Brennan (2016*) - Continues to log a ton of minutes for the Giants, playing an important role in all situations. A smooth skater and very capable puck mover who navigates all three zones with a lot of confidence. Roved down deep on the umbrella power play, getting some good opportunities from below the hashmarks. Got a bit lost on one pinch during the power play, resulting in a two-on-situation and a Deven Sideroff goal to put the Giants down 3-1.

VAN #24 RD Barberis, Matt (2016) - Not terribly fast, but able to spin off checks and to protect the puck reasonably well. Did a great job of recognizing screens and getting his shots through traffic. A wrist shot from the blueline through multiple bodies tied the game 1-1, for example. Really active in terms of stick lifts and other defensive work in his own zone.

VAN #26 LD McKinstry, Ryely (2016) - Played the puck well when given time and space, but was overpowered once or twice for the puck in his own zone. Indeed, had some defensive fumbles that cost his team in this one. Put the puck in his own net when trying to block a pass down low, putting his club down 2-1 in the second period. Relegated to more of a depth role in this one and saw his ice-time limited as it went on.

Kärpät U20 at HIFK U20, November 13, 2015

HIF #5 C Borgström, Henrik (2016) - Man of the game. Scored 2 goals... First one by accurate wrister straight to the top shelf. He scored his second goal on a breakaway. He's fun player to watch because he can do fancy moves in every shift. Henrik got decent size and he's average skater what it comes to speed. Showed at this game his tremendous vision and pucks skills. He was also on good in faceoffes.

HIF #3 RW Jääskä, Juho (2016) - Juha had a bad game. He's hark-working winger who can be productive in the-zone but at this game he couldn't do nothing. Great mobility and great two way ability but the lack of puck skills is a major concern.

HIF #38 RD Heiskanen, Miro (2017) - He was his team best d-man at this game. Made lot of great decisions with puck... both long and short passes. He reads the game well and knows when to join the offense. Undersized kid but great in all three zones. Especially important penalty killer because of his ability to read the passing lines and block the shots.

KAR #22 C Kuokkanen, Janne (2016) - Scored an beautiful assist today but missed couple of great scoring chances. Especially one chance where he got an open net but the goalie made a incredible save. Janne played decent game today. Calm center who can create scoring opportunities for his line mates. Showed decent two way game at this game. Not that big and doesn't really play tough game. From time to time he was pretty lost around corners.

KAR #16 C Kuiri, Niko (2016) - Niko likes to play rough game and give big hits but doesn't always success so well. Good player in front of the net and he played in the first power play unit doing that role. Hard-working centerman with decent two way ability. He's bad with puck and doesn't really know what to do with that. Made bad choices at this game.

Saskatoon Blades at Prince Albert Raiders, November 13th, 2015

SAS #9 C Hebig, Cameron (2016*) - Took the puck to the net, several times sacrificing his body. He picked up an assist on a net drive effort around Warner. Good PK clear at the end of the period.
SAS #23 RD Higson, Schael (2016) - He took the body and cleared the zone a few times but had a disappointing game. Fumbled the puck, and turned the puck over several times. Outlets weren't very good.

SAS #25 LD Hajek, Libor (2016) - Good compete throughout, willing to use his size. Moved puck despite getting hit by forecheck. His skating was on display both in skating the puck forward as well as on puck-retrievals. After conservative start, he was getting more offensively involved throughout the game with point shots and was handling the puck on the blueline. Some of his angles when defending in his own zone were off, was prone to chasing the play a little bit. Primary assist on OT winner with a simple pass in offensive zone.

SAS #47 RD Reid, Nolan (2016) - Had a quiet game through two periods, though he didn't make many mistakes defensively. Two assists in third period. Joined the rush and a teammate of his cleaned up the rebound on a 3 on 1 play. His point shot late in the period was also the start of the sequence that tied the game.

SAS #61 C Paterson, Josh (2017) - Good interception in neutral zone, gained the zone and fired a shot. Thought he read the play well and got into the right positions to make plays.

PRI #8 LD Paivarinta, Cody (2016) - Made good if simple plays with the puck. Skated well for his size and used that on a couple of good pinches. Would have liked to see more effectivness in closing down defensively and using his size to be a factor on defense.

PRI #19 RW Gardiner, Reid (2016**) - Scored a third period goal coming into the zone with speed and firing his patented top corner wrist-shot. Thought his impact was very underwhelming outside of that.

PRI #23 LW Stransky, Simon (2016) - Had a good forehand-backhand deke scoring the first Prince Albert goal. Several dangerous passes from behind the net into the slot. Reads the play well and will find open ice where he can make plays from, can hide on the weak side of the ice. Left me wanting him to be just a touch more engaging and to show a bit more will to dictate the play.

PRI #25 C Montgomery, Sean (2016) - Played with two big bodies in Vanstone and Coleman and took advantage of their ability to gain the entry as he distributed the puck east-west in the offensive zone. Did well in the corners coming out with the puck even against bigger players. Good defensive reads and saw some PK time as well.

PRI #28 LW Coleman, Luke (2016) - Thought he did a good job gaining the zone but didn't do much with it. Often drove wide and fired a shot from the outside, no follow up on the rebound either. Not many second efforts.

Scout's notes: Vojtech Budik (Prince Albert) was not in the lineup.

Lethbridge Hurricanes at Brandon Wheat Kings, November 14th, 2015

LET #15 LW Bellerive, Jordan (2017) - He had some good offensive zone reads finding openings. Good centering pass from the boards to the middle recognizing traffic in front. Two or three isolated scoring chances but his line couldn't establish consistent pressure.

LET #22 LW Babenko, Egor (2016*) - Good on powerplay. Scored a goal coming off the boards losing his check and firing a wristshot. Had a good move beating Clague 1 on 1 later in the game. Thought he could have been more engaging in defensive zone with pressuring the points and battling on the wall.

LET #33 G Sittler, Jayden (2016*) - He saw lots of shots but not too many high-end scoring chances. Thought he did an ok job. There were a couple of hope saves lacking structure where he was lucky the puck hit him. A bit slow in his recovery.

BRA #10 RD Clague, Kale (2016) - A couple of good pinches sending the puck back deep. Good lateral ability in walking the blueline. Skating was good as always. He was average overall for a prospect of his stature. Wanted to see him take more authority over what is happening on ice but he tended to play down to the average level.

BRA #12 RW Mattheos, Stelio (2017) - Showed off his physical ability flat out outmuscling Andrew Nielsen on the wall. He wasn't much of an offensive threat in this game but did a good job bringing the puck up ice and not spending too much time in his own zone.

BRA #16 C Kaspick, Tanner (2016) - Started off strong, reading puck-movement and winning one on one battles to keep the play moving. Faded after the first period, though he had a diligent defensive effort.

BRA #19 C Patrick, Nolan (2017) - Not as much of a threat even strength as in my prior viewings. His ability to read the play helps him find pucks in dangerous areas even when he's not having a great game. He had a good backcheck breaking up a 3 on 1 situation. Was used both on PK and PP and did his job well on both.

Erie Otters at Kitchener Rangers, November 15, 2015

OHL Regular Season

ERI #6 D Sambrook, Jordan (2016) - Glass and out under pressure but put too much on it a couple times. Multiple great one on one plays. Uses his stick and body equally well and at appropriate times.

ERI #12 C DeBrincat, Alex (2016) - Landed massive hit in the offensive zone. Makes defenders look bad at times with his puck skills. Good pass and good finish on power play for 3-1 goal. Top power play minutes.

ERI #43 LW Lodnia, Vanya (2017) - Quick hands, good position in slot and quick shot to score 4-1 goal.

KIT #23 RW Mascherin, Adam (2016) - Three good chances in the first period, missed net twice, dropped on one. Speed is slightly above average, would like it better for his size.

KIT #98 D Roberts, Elijah (2017) - Shot into screen. Walked in on rush and fired hard writer off post, off goalie and in for first career OHL goal.

Final Score: Erie Otters: 6 - Kitchener Rangers: 2

Medicine Hat Tigers at Regina Pats, November 17th, 2015

MED #16 RW Gerlach, Max (2016) - His offensive reads are decent and he can make plays with the puck on his stick, though he didn't do much for me in this game. Had a good effort scoring a goal off a front of the net scramble, but lacked any consistent impact from shift to shift.

MED #18 C Shaw, Mason (2017) - Looks on the small side, but he competes. He was willing to be involved on both sides of the ice and fought Zablocki in second period, picking a good time to do it as his team had no momentum at all. He had an offensive zone steal off a careless pass that he converted into a goal.

MED #19 RD Quenneville, David (2016) - Surprisingly physically engaged, played bigger than his size would suggest in own zone. A couple of big shots from the point though none particularly close to being a goal. Good vision on outlets and tracks players well defensively.

REG #23 C Steel, Sam (2016) - Had a SH goal reading a turnover created by his linemate, finishing with a nice deke. Plays all situations and key third period minutes with faceoffs. Dangerous offensive zone passing, found teammates in scoring positions. Relied almost exclusively on stickwork when protecting the puck on the wall, would have liked him to show a bit more push-back there. Good skating ability and real smart seeing gaps that he can exploit with his passing, could use his footwork to manufacture some of the offensive zone gaps on his own more often. Smart off-the-puck reads, surprises players with his stick and can steal the puck.
REG #26 C Leschyshyn, Jake (2017) - Excellent on faceoffs. Played almost like a pest, engaging both offensively and defensively. Straight line game, favored shooting first and asking questions later. Scored a goal on a nice backhand from up-close.

REG #38 LD Pouteau, Brady (2016) - He used his size well defensively, more control in his game than the last time I saw him and wasn't getting beat as much laterally. Moved the puck in a simple manner when required.

Sudbury Wolves at Barrie Colts, November 19, 2015

SUD #11 C Lyszczarczyk, Alan (2016) – He was very hit and miss in this game. He displayed good speed through the neutral zone and gained the line with possession frequently. The problem is Lyszczarczyk turned it over several times after gaining the line and blindly gave it away on a couple occasions to try and avoid hits. He did put plenty of effort into regaining pucks, though, and broke up a couple solid chances with strong backchecking efforts.

SUD #13 RW Pezzetta, Michael (2016) – Pezzetta displayed good straight-line speed through the neutral zone. He did an excellent job of killing clock on the PK by skating around in the offensive zone before leaving the zone and giving it to a defenseman to dump it back in. He won several puck battles throughout and had some effective shifts in the cycle game. He didn't create much offensively but he was a big plus defensively.

SUD #71 LW Levin, David (2017) – Levin seemed a bit off from the get go. On the first or second shift he missed an open Dmitry Sokolov on what would have been a breakaway pass and he struggled to create offense on a shift-to-shift basis. He certainly wasn't a liability and the effort was there but the results were not.

SUD #98 RW Sokolov, Dmitry (2016) – Sokolov was held pointless and was a dash three on the night but he played better than the numbers show. One of the goals against when he was on the ice came on a play where he back checked hard and ended up putting it in his own net by reaching out to break up a cross-ice pass on what probably would have been a goal anyway. On the offensive side of things he was dishing out firm passes and created several chances for his teammates. He also had a couple pro caliber shots that gave Blackwood trouble and he rang one off the cross bar as well. At times he did try to do too much with the puck.

BAR #16 LW Hawerchuk, Ben (2016) – Hawerchuk got himself into the game early with a big hit on the forecheck. He was back regularly to support and came down low in the defensive zone several times to help win battles. On two separate occasions he slipped through the cracks of Sudbury's defense but he was unable to convert on his chances.

BAR #18 LW Magwood, Zachary (2016) – Magwood was positionally sound in his own zone and took several hits to make plays with the puck. Offensively he used defenders as a screen and did not hesitate to put pucks towards the net, although he missed a couple times. Magwood showed good vision from behind the net setting up teammates in the slot area, and he also made a nice pass on an odd-man rush to give a teammate a Grade A chance from just outside the paint.

AIK at Timra, Allsvenskan, November 19th 2015

AIK #98 LW Bratt, Jesper (2016) – Even if Jesper was not able to rush through the neutral zone like he was used to do at the J20 level, overall he was still effective offensively. Showed good patience with the puck more than once: attacking the offensive blueline he circled back as there was no opening, then was able to enter the zone with possession; after getting the puck on the left side in the offensive zone, he took full advantage of the big time and space given to move into a better shooting position and beat the goalie with a wrister short side. Bratt was used all game on the 1st PP unit, mostly on the left side boards. Had a nice one-time pass from the left corner to find a teammate completely open in the slot. The open lane was pretty obvious, but nice timing and execution on the play. He set up another scoring chance off a faceoff win by his centerman, as he quickly found an open linemate on the left side. He displayed his skills as a puck carrier when he got rid of an opponent on the offensive blueline with a quick turnaround and then cut to the inside with a strong move, but got his shot blocked. Had two turnovers entering the offensive zone, once he got stripped of the puck, another time he dumped the puck into the corner with no teammates coming. His contribution in the defensive zone was limited and we would have liked to see him more involved in puck battles, still Jesper received quite a lot of icetime in the 3rd period with his team down by two.

TIM #26 LW Pettersson, Elias (2017) – Recently called up from the junior team, in his 3rd career game at the senior level Pettersson started off making the safe plays at even strength, but was soon able to gain some confidence and display his talent when he had the opportunity to be out there on the powerplay. He set up Dahlen twice for grade A scoring chances from down low right side, and later on wasted no time when his pal found him completely open in the slot, recording his first career pro goal going high glove side with his wrister. In the 2nd period he made a great set-up play from behind the net, but Dahlen couldn't beat the goalie. Elias eventually added a primary assist: after carrying the puck through the offensive blueline on a 3 on 2 counter attack, his pass into the slot was nicely controlled and finalized by teammate Daniel Ohrn.

Pettersson was overall less effective in 2nd half of the game and with his team up in the score the time on ice of his line decreased. He had a nice block shot late in the game though, promptly diving into the shooting lane to defend a two goals lead. His age showed up when he tried an unnecessary stick-handling trick in the neutral zone despite an incoming opponent, which resulted in getting hit in an awkward position. Also, his lack of strength was apparent in the numerous puck battles where he ended up with his butt on the ice. However, overall he had an impressive performance and certainly confirmed to be a player to watch for next year draft.

TIM #54 RW Dahlen, Jonathan (2016) – Dahlen was usually the first forward in on the forecheck and was consistently positioned in the slot on the powerplay. Used on the 3rd line together with his junior mate Pettersson, the duo earned time on the first powerplay unit as the game progressed and was instrumental in last placed Timra's win against the second team in the league. Jonathan had a nice diving effort to set up Pettersson for his first career goal. He was however unable to finish his chances today, had at least three great opportunities in front where he was stopped by the goalie. Dahlen was dangerous in the offensive zone and also looked comfortable skating the puck up through the neutral zone. Had a strong entry with speed into the offensive zone while protecting the puck and never struggled with the pace of the game.

There was a play where he made good use of his skate to receive a pass and move towards the center to find a shooting lane. Was less alert when, in the 3rd period, a similar situation occurred in the defensive zone and he failed to connect with a pass in his feet, the turnover created a great scoring chance for the opposition.

Oshawa Generals at London Knights, November 19, 2015

OHL Regular Season

OSH #12 C Commisso, Domenic (2016) - Good two way forward competed down low in defensive zone. Smooth skater, good speed on rush and beat bigger D one on one leading to scoring chance. Excellent job winning virtually every draw he took. Pulled up on hit against bigger opponent.

OSH #16 D Stillman, Riley (2016) - Good compete one on one, likes to make contact in one on one match ups. Will look for any chance to make contact despite not being overly big. Good skater and rushed the puck effectively but lacks that separation speed.

OSH #56 G Brodeur, Jeremy (2016*) - Good vision and quickness to make some big saves early. Has a quick glove. No chance on first goal against, but second goal against he couldn't find the rebound quickly enough. Third goal allowed puck went off the back wall, off his skate and in. Shortly after he froze up and was beat for his fourth goal against.

LON #4 D Juolevi, Olli (2016) - Tried to do too much on power play rush eventually leading to icing. Has a lot of trouble containing opponents down low. Won races with good skating ability.

LON #7 LW Tkachuk, Matthew (2016) - Constantly around the puck, getting involved in scoring chances. Good pass set up 1-1 go. Creates chances for himself and his linemates. Skating still below average. Landed a big hit late in the first. Won race to puck and quick centring pass to set up 4-1 goal. Good body position and comfortable with contact helps him win races. Has a knack for forcing turnovers in neutral zone and quickly moves the puck up ice. Finished his checks all night long.

LON #63 C Pu, Cliff (2016) - Showed good compete working for pucks using his speed. Great moves on the rush to beat defender resulting in a scoring chance. Used to never go into battles but he looks a little thicker and coincidentally getting more involved in battles. Struggled in the faceoff circle tonight only winning about 20 percent of his draws.

LON #1 G Parsons, Tyler (2016) - After allowing a goal on his first shot, he wasn't tested much. When he was he made a couple sharp pad saves.

Final Score: London Knights: 5 - Oshawa Generals: 2

North Bay Battalion at Mississauga Steelheads, November 20, 2015

OHL Regular Season

NBY #4 D Dineen, Cam (2016) - Bad pinch resulted in scoring chance at the other end. A lot of smart passes playing on the top power play unit. Good point shot, gets it on net.

NBY #14 C Poirier, Zachary (2016) - Very stiff skating, affects his speed, needs to bend his knees. Good work ethic in all three zones. Top penalty killing unit and was chosen as the lone forward on a 5 on 3 kill. Second unit power play.

NBY #20 RW Ball, Jacob (2017) - Smart passing on the rush. Landing hits but not getting much power in them despite his size.

NBY #25 D Shoemaker, Mark (2016) - Stripped in defensive zone leading to chance. Willing to take body one on one. Made some very good defensive plays against some of Mississauga's top scorers. Played second unit special teams in all situations.

MIS #9 C McLeod, Michael (2016) - Takes the body effectively but doesn't have a mean streak. Had multiple good chances in the slot but couldn't convert. Great patience and excellent pass to set up 6-0 goal. Was outstanding in the face-off circle taking a ton of draws and either winning or splitting virtually every draw.

MIS #10 LW McLeod, Ryan (2018) - Will compete without puck but slides away when contact picks up. Jammed home 3-0 goal when ref didn't blow play down on covered puck. Good positioning in the slot and powerful shot top shelf for 7-0 goal.

MIS #14 RW Bastian, Nathan (2016) - Created chances in close using his size and good hands. Has a powerful shot. Top unit power play, second unit penalty kill. Skating still hurts him.

MIS #74 RW Tippett, Owen (2017) - Very shifty with puck. Good speed and good play to score 2-0 goal. Created chances all game. Fired an absolute rocket top shelf for 5-0 goal on breakaway.

MIS #92 LW Nylander, Alexander (2016) - Looked very complacent early on, several casual passes without looking lead to turnovers. Played the point on the top power play unit, on the first powerplay just seconds in fired a huge blast off the bar and in for 1-0 goal. His game picked up after that goal. Doesn't hesitate when he sees a good passing lane to exploit it. Made a lazy no look play with puck in his own zone resulted in an easy scoring chance against. Slap shot is high end. Gets hit hard. Showed off very good speed when choosing to use it. Drove net and was rewarded with 4-0 goal. Completed the hat trick with a nice tap in 2 on 1 for 6-0 goal. Has a lot of skill and a lot of negative tendencies.

MIS #98 C Kutkevicius, Luke (2016) - Showed a few flashes of skill tonight. Good speed in third, made good move on the defender followed by a great pass to set up 7-0 goal.

University of Denver at University of Wisconsin, November 20th 2015, NCAA

WIS #9 LW Kunin, Luke (2016) – Kunin showed great ability to read the play and anticipation all night, it was on full display on the PK to disrupt plays, he picks the right times to pressure a player and has a quick stick to get into lanes and create turnovers and wasn't scared to get in shooting lanes and block shots. Kunin also contributed in the offensive zone by scoring with a quick snap shot from the goalies right on a feed from #19 Cameron Hughes, beating the goalie over the shoulder on the short side.
Not all was terrific in Kunin's game tonight however, on a few too many occasions he didn't stop on pucks and tried to make a play on the move which resulted in turnovers or lost puck battles. He is very good in winning puck battles most nights but for some reason tonight he tried to do a lot on the move.

WIS #15 LW Freytag, Matthew (2016) – Scored a nice goal by driving the net after coming off the bench and received a nice backhand pass from #17 Will Johnson from the nearby corner for a bang, bang goal in front of the net. Aside from his goal, Freytag isn't overly effective offensively and lost a fair amount of puck battles in the offensive zone and along the boards. It's not an issue with effort for Freytag, it just seemed like plays seemed to fizzle out when the puck got onto his stick or in his corner. However, Freytag was physical, finished most of his checks tonight and did provide good energy to his bench.

WIS #24 RW Soleway, Jedd (AZ, 7th Rd) – Usually Soleway gets his offensive production by using his big body to battle for position in front and bang home rebounds, however tonight Soleway scored with a great shot from the slot, using the defender as a screen. While Soleway continues to be a long term project for the Coyotes and his skating continues to be a work in progress, the other parts of his game seem to be developing more consistency.

WIS #4 RD Sexton, Patrick (Free Agent) – Loved his game tonight. Sexton didn't bring a lot offensively and missed some easy reads on some outlet passes but brought a physical edge to the game all night that his team seemed to feed off of. It was a nightmare for any player either, entering the offensive zone on his side of the ice, dumping the puck in his corner or trying to setup in front of the net because he punished players all over the ice. This was just Sexton's 5th NCAA game and is still getting his feet wet but he has a quick powerful release from the point on a couple of shots I saw and should be an interesting Free Agent Freshman to follow as his season and career progresses.

WIS #17 RW Johnson, Will (2016+) – Tonight Johnson showed a lot of the skill and offensive instincts that had him leading the USHL in scoring last year prior to a season ending knee injury. Setup the goal by Freytag by making a beautiful backhanded pass out of the corner that found the tape of Freytag in front of the net. Johnson still needs to get stronger along the wall and work on his consistency but seems to be settling into NCAA hockey nicely.

WIS #30 G Jurusik, Matt (2016) – Jurusik has started to come into his own, since playing a great two games a couple weeks prior against #1 North Dakota in Grand Forks, and it showed tonight when he was able to settle his game down after giving up back to back goals in the 2nd period to lose a 3-1 lead. Jurusik responded by making some great saves in the 3rd period to earn his team a tie against a very good Denver team. Jurusik took away the lower half of the net very well and showed quick pad movement. He can get out of position and swimming in his crease when the play is in close and makes it difficult for him to track loose pucks, but is very athletic which bailed him out a lot of the time.

DU #7 RW Gambrell, Dylan (2016) – Gambrell had 1 assists tonight, he played well in all situations and areas on the ice. He was physical and battles in the right areas. Showed good offensive skill and playmaking ability by creating a lot of chances in the offensive zone that the Wisconsin goalie was able to make some great saves on. Was very good at getting the puck to scoring area's and didn't waste time doing it.

DU #4 LD Butcher, Will (Col. 5th Rd.) A rare average game for the Sun Prairie, WI native. Butcher, who is known for being an impact defenseman for Denver night in and night out, in his return back to Wisconsin struggled a bit. Butcher struggled on the Power play; he was fairly stagnant and mishandled some passes at the point. He was ok in his own end but far from dynamic on the breakouts and didn't join the rush as much as he usually does. Butcher didn't make any big glaring mistakes but just wasn't the dynamic puck mover that he has shown in the past. I'll chalk this one up to hometown nerves and a one off game for Butcher. (NOTE: Butcher was much better the next night VS Wisconsin, racked up 2 assists and hit two posts on Power plays in route to a 6-2 Denver win)

Final Score 3-3 (OT)

Moose Jaw Warriors at Kootenay Ice, November 20th, 2015

MJW #2 RD Brook, Josh (2017) - Quite mindful defensively, didn't skate the puck forward a lot, preferring quick layoff passes. He got a bit more offensively involved in the third period. His decisions on the offensive blueline are good, however since he played a rather conservative game with skating the puck, he needed someone to get him the puck there to be effective.

MJW #18 C Quinney, Landon (2016) - He got an assist off his faceoff win. Too inconsistent shift to shift, didn't find ways to get involved into the flow of the game. Had a shift or two where he was effective with long lulls inbetween.

MJW #21 C Howden, Brett (2016) - His compete level was good. Very reliant on his work ethic to get things done offensively, didn't entirely convince me he had top 6 qualities with the puck on his stick. He got his nose dirty working deep in his own zone as well as on the boards in the offensive zone, likeable effort.

MJW #22 C Gregor, Noah (2016) - He started on Howden's left wing before moving to a different line and playing C. His edgework is good and he uses it well to win races and fend off checkers as he moves around the offensive zone. Won some puck races and didn't mind going to the middle of action full speed. Tied the game late in third picking up the puck off a faceoff before cutting to the middle and ripping a wristshot into the net.

MJW #71 LW Popugaev, Nikita (2017) - Impressive toolset and commendable compete level, but he forced the play too much. Tried to skate through people with poor results. He tried taking the puck from the boards to the middle but Kootenay defended well against those attempts as well.

KTN #4 RD Fleury, Cale (2017) - He plays all situations and logs significant minutes and did a good job with it. Had two big open ice hits. His ability to carry the puck was on display throughout. Sometimes a bit lost defensively. Scored the OT winner by reading a Moose Jaw change and receiving the pass at the blueline with an empty lane to the goalie.

KTN #8 LD Hines, Dallas (2016) - Solid defensively, consistent in his positioning, good outlets, simple offensive game with quick point shots. Played a low-risk game throughout, the type of quiet yet effective game you expect out of a defenseman who does his job.

KTN #10 LW Dymacek, Roman (2016*) - Had several chances off the rush in first period by doing a good job pressuring the point in his own zone and creating turnovers. Good chemistry with Luke Philp in offensive zone with Dymacek distributing the puck from the left side.

KTN #18 C Loschiavo, Vince (2016) - Had some opportunistic scoring chances. Found himself alone in front of the goalie off a Fleury pass but couldn't convert. A couple of other instances of him sniffing around the net. Didn't control the puck in his shifts, but was looking more for a chance to strike quickly reading opportunities to do so.

Vancouver Giants at Kelowna Rockets, November 21st, 2015

VAN #7 RW Ronning, Ty (2016) - Reads the offensive zone well and can anticipate the play jumping into scoring positions. He was one of the few Vancouver players that had something going offensively though it was more isolated chances than sustained pressure. Not convinced that he did enough to offset the lack of size.

VAN #17 LW Benson, Tyler (2016) - He has only recently got back from missing extended time with an injury. He scored a goal in the third period by outmuscling the defenseman in the slot and getting his stick on the puck. He had two or three checks on the forecheck but not as consistent in that regard as I've seen before from him. He struggled for most of the game, his ability to protect the puck was rarely seen and he played with less jump than usual. He had long lulls without having any sort of impact.

VAN #24 LD Barberis, Matt (2016) - He struggled to find lanes to get his shot through from the point, often being forced to simply dump it back deep. He was less effective offensively than usual.

KEL #9 LW Wishnowski, Tanner (2016*) - Not the most talented or biggest player on the ice but he worked his butt off, especially in the first period. Smaller buzzsaw, was relentless in hounding the opponents and played at a pace that was challenging for Vancouver's defense. Thought he set the tone well.

KEL #15 C Soustal, Tomas (2016*) - Had an assist picking up a loose puck on the wall before dishing off a centering pass to the slot. He knows size is his advantage, however his balance and center of gravity didn't look that great in this game. He would need a wider lower base on his skates for it to be effective against men.

KEL #16 RW Lind, Kole (2017) - He did a good job getting open and he had a couple opportunities where he got free from coverage in the slot but nobody got him the puck. His play with the puck was mostly to the outside as he'd get pushed to the perimeter.

KEL #25 RD Foote, Cal (2017) - He played a pretty mature game on the blueline logging significant minutes. Got his stick on pucks defensively and did a good job of moving the puck out. Offensively involved, though nothing elaborate with the puck. Thought he made better decisions with the puck under pressure than in the last game I saw him.

Scout's notes: Lucas Johansen and Dillon Dube (both Kelowna) were not in the lineup.

HPK U20 at Sport U20, November 21st, 2015

SPO #74 RD Salo, Robin (2017) - Didn't play much but played decent game. Robin is a good all-round d-man with good size and mobility. He has played safe game in professional level and doesn't ry to do big things.

HPK #82 RW Tuulola, Eetu (2016) - He played only 3 minutes and 20 seconds. He was benched in the last two periods. His offensive skills are tremendous but he's not ready to play in pro level. His quickness is the main reason for that but he should also use his size better. At the moment pure offensive player and nothing more.

Ottawa 67's at Hamilton Bulldogs, November 21, 2015

OTT #19 LW Barron, Travis (2016) - Good scoring chance in the slot, but got rocked before he could pull the trigger. Missed a few shifts afterwards. Simple play on second power play unit, stands in the slot and creates traffic for the most part. Skating is average or slightly below. Had a great chance in the slot later on in the game but fanned on it. Covered for punching defender well.

OTT #83 LW Warnholtz, Connor (2016) - Decent size/speed combination, but doesn't finish checks, leads with his stick on the forecheck.

HAM #17 C Saigeon, Brandon (2016) - Great play in neutral zone to steal puck and accelerate up the middle for scoring chance. Moves puck well in neutral zone and very good in transition getting the play going the other way quickly. Jammed home 4-1 goal after being stopped on his first attempt that looked like a sure goal on a bad puck play by the goaltender.

HAM #20 D Candella, Cole (2016) - Good skating, smooth mobility. Got out of position getting ahead of the rush allowing his man to walk right in undefended on the turnover. Second penalty killing unit.

HAM #28 RW Mizzi, Joseph (2016) - Strong skater, good speed, rushes the puck well, good power in shot but shot way too much when he didn't have a lane to the net. Good forecheck pressure. A little undersized.

HAM #42 D Gleason, Benjamin (2016) - Nice wrister from point, got deflected for 2-0 power play goal. Top power play unit. Very good skating ability. Defensive reaction time isn't great putting him at a disadvantage down low. Only draft eligible on either side to see ice on the last minute of a 4-2 game.

Val-d'Or Foreurs vs Drummondville Voltigeurs, November 21st, 2015

VDO #12 RW Gauthier, Julien (2016): Had a bit of sluggish start to the game, but got going by generating three scoring chances on one shift midway through the first period. On that sequence, he was able to show how fast of a skater he is by exploding between two Drummondville defensemen, taking two solid shots on net in the process. On the power play, he played a simple game. Once in the zone, he was in front of the net, screening the goaltender and when his team rushed the puck, he was at the DRU blueline waiting for passes. I didn't see him rush the puck once while on the power play. He created all sorts of problems for the Drummondville defense; he's a horse down low and protected the puck well.

VDO #26 LD Galipeau, Olivier (2016): Un-Drafted last year, Galipeau was the most used defenseman on the Foreurs today, playing in all situations of the game. He was beat early in the game one-on-one, but played a more stable game the rest of the way. He played a good physical game down low in his zone. Decent puck movement on the point, he was the lone defenseman on the VDO 1st power play unit. He did score a key goal on the PP with 10 seconds left to play in the 2nd period, making a nice read by moving into the slot to become a target for his teammate behind the Drummondville net.

VDO #61 C Rafuse, Cole (2017): Didn't get much ice time today, though I saw him more in the 3rd when the game was out of hand. He showed on some sequences that he's strong on his skates and can use his big frame along the walls. He does not the quickest feet, however, and will need some work on his skating over the next couple of years.

DRU #22 C Sevigny, Mathieu (2016): As usual, Sevigny played in every facet of the game today, working hard in all three zones. He did a good job along the wall, but didn't generate much offense during the game. He struggled a bit in the faceoff circle, going 10 for 24.

DRU #4 LD Gagne, Benjamin (2017): Played on both special teams, including the 2nd power play unit during the game. He used his feet nicely to rush the puck when needed and was able to get the puck out of his zone when pressured on the forecheck. Saw a tough 3rd period defensively, as VDO was all over DRU in that period. He finished the game minus 4.

DRU #8 LW Carcone, Michael (2016): The un-drafted '96-born forward was one of the few Voltigeurs to have a good game. He used his speed to challenge VDO defensemen, often trying to beat them on the outside. He scored the lone Drummondville goal on the power play by being well-positioned at the side of the net for an easy tap-in into an empty net. Carcone's speed is above-average, but he's very agile as well, and this helps him to avoid defenders.

DRU #19 C Barre-Boulet, Alex (2016): He made a nice defensive play covering top VDO forward Anthony Richard one-on-one down low in the first period, giving him little room to manoeuver. On the power play, he controlled the puck from the half-wall, but overall in the game (mostly at even-strength) he didn't generate much offense. He lost too many one-on-one battles during the game to be really efficient.

DRU #90 LW Poirier, William (2018): Poirier's skating was a bit rough today, and he will need to work on his acceleration. He wants to play a physical game, but lost equilibrium too many times trying to lay out hits. Played on the 4th line with no special team ice-time, made a shot-block in the 3rd period with the game already out of hand.

Niagara Ice Dogs at Windsor Spitfires, November 22, 2015

OHL Regular Season

NIA #14 C Paquette, Christopher (2016) - Good skater, particularly for his size. Goes to the right places but struggles to create much. Had trouble beating defenders one on one.
WSR #17 D Stanley, Logan (2016) - Top unit power play and penalty kill today. Did a pretty good job one on one making sure opponents didn't get around him. His first pass was pretty consistent with accurate east options up ice, not trying to do too much. Blocked shots.

WSR #22 RW Carter, Cole (2016) - Drew power play using his speed on a puck race and was interfered with. Second power play unit.

WSR #28 D Nother, Tyler (2016) - Hurt mid first on a hit in the corner. Stuck with the play despite in obvious pain until it left the zone. Didn't return.

WSR #31 D Sergachev, Mikhail (2016) - On the top penalty killing unit, he's not great at clearing bodies out front, but does a very good job getting into passing lanes. Gets his shots through from the point. Good one on one play taking the body on opponent going wide. Good backwards skating combined with size helps him hold off opponents. Likes to finish his checks hard and did so on multiple occasions today.
WSR #64 G DiPietro, Michael (2017) - Consistently does a great job getting himself set in position. Always gets set extremely fast. Calm and focused under pressure. Gets across well on cross crease passes.

Final Score: Niagara Ice Dogs: 3 - Windsor Spitfires: 0

Calgary Hitmen at Prince Albert Raiders, November 24, 2015

CAL #2 LD Bean, Jake (2016) – Continued to show good footwork and anticipation, especially when quarterbacking the powerplay. Doesn't necessarily look like a speedster, but has excellent all-directional agility and is certainly fast enough to rush the puck up ice and to lead the rush on his own. Made some really crisp and smart passes in the offensive zone. Especially good at moving the puck off of his backhand, able to deliver long distance dishes from his off side. Made some great one-on-one plays to strip guys of the puck and prevent scoring opportunities.

CAL #3 LD Lapointe, Jakob (2016) – Saw considerable ice-time and was very dependable in his own end. Looked strong and physically engaged. Really physical along the boards, throwing some nice hits to break up the opposition's offense.

CAL #10 RW Stukel, Jakob (2016*) - Looked very fast and far more confident than I've previously seen him. Used his footwork to drive the Raiders defence wide and to open up holes. Scored two goals, one from in tight and one from out wide. Has always been fast in terms of both foot and hand speed, but is showing more with Calgary than he did with Vancouver, simply because he's being fed the puck in the important scoring areas and appears to have more confidence in his finishing abilities.

CAL #11 LW Malenstyn, Beck (2016) – A powerful straight-ahead skater who appears to have good hop and leg strength in his first few strides. Can be a bit awkward and uneconomical at full-stride but still more than fast enough. I liked his backchecking efforts. Drew several penalties. Does an admirable job of skating to the scary areas but protecting himself when hit from dangerous angles. A really good hitter in his own right, too.

PRA #6 LD Budik, Vojtech (2016) – A really good defencemen in all areas, but especially when defending in reverse or when engaged in a one-on-one battle along the boards. Played on the top penalty killing unit. Passing and puckhandling skills looked much better along the blueline than I'd previously noted. Showed off a decent set of shooting options with well-timed releases. Although his shot selection could have been better.

PRA #23 LW Stransky, Simon (2016) – Played on the second line and also saw less minutes in this one than I'm accustomed to seeing. Game appeared a bit one-dimensional at times, as his backchecking lacked the full effort on some shifts. Continued to look elusive in the attacking end though. Stole the puck away with real ease in the offensive zone. And once he had the puck, he was very elusive and creative with it. Had some horrendous fumbles with the puck, however, in what seemed like an 'off night.'

Acadie-Bathurst Titan vs. Gatineau Olympiques, November 25th, 2015

Robert Guertin Arena

BAT #31 G Pickard, Reilly (2016) – He was outstanding tonight, made 33 saves in the first 2 periods and only allowed 2 goals, ended the night with 56 shots against, very athletic goalie, has really quick feet and quick lateral movement, tracked the puck really well and battled through screens to make the save, covers the lower net extremely well but got caught a few times on the goals by being down to soon and Gatineau player going upstairs, made a couple highlight reel glove saves on the power play keeping Gatineau of the scoreboard, would like to see him a little more quieter in the net and not scrambling as much.

BAT #88 C Morand, Antoine (2017) – Other than Pickard, he was the best player on ice for Bathurst, skated really well, smooth skating stride not a lot of effort, played a really good 2way game, broke up a scoring chance by back checking hard and lifting the players stick, scored a beautiful end to end goal undressing the D and making a nice move on the goalie going upstairs, smart hockey player, looked really good on the PP setting up players and finding the open man, his age showed a little bit tonight by being knocked around off the puck a lot and was getting beat on draws a lot.

BAT #98 LW Kuznetsov, Vladimir (2016) – Big Body forward, skated well tonight, but needs to compete hard every shift, he wasn't affected when he wasn't moving his feet,
Showed some good speed on the PP carrying the puck into the zone and beating defenders wide, showed some skill on the PP, has a really good shot but needs to use it more often and hit the net more, has good hockey sense, see's the game well and understands it, he wasn't engaged physically

tonight and with a kid his size he should be going hard to the net, he used his big frame to control the puck and was good at uses his body to protect the puck but he didn't turn it into offensive chances.

GAT #11 LW Abramov, Vitali (2016) – Played a good 1st and 3rd period but struggled in the 2nd period, he was too soft along the boards and caused too many turnovers which one turned into a goal, tried to do too much in the 2nd period and wasn't effective, very skilled forward and very smart player, used the D as screen and scored a nice goal top corner with a hard wrist shot, other than his turnovers he was all over the ice creating chances and the puck seemed to follow him all night, was good in his dzone, didn't panic with the puck with defenders coming down on him, has very good speed and knows when to use it.

GAT #13 C Dostie, Alex (2016) – Was really good tonight, he was a hard man to check tonight because he was moving his feet and has really good speed and acceleration, and can stickhandle really good at that speed and make defenders miss, small forward so he doesn't like to go into the dirty areas, but also doesn't put himself in bad situations to get hurt, smart hockey player and is really good at putting the puck in good areas for his teammates, quick wrist in close as well.

GAT #37 G Taylor, Bo (2016) – had a solid game tonight in the nets, very positional type goalie, allows puck to hit him and he doesn't give up much 2nd chances, really good lateral movement post to post, struggled a bit tonight tracking the puck from the point and with screens in front of him, rebound control was good tonight, wasn't overly tested tonight with high quality chances but made the save when he needed too.

Final Score: Acadie-Bathurst 3   Gatineau 4 SO

Waterloo Blackhawks at Madison Capitols, November 25th, 2015, USHL

WTL #15 LW, Bowers, Shane (2017) – Bowers was effective at both ends of the ice all evening long and was the best forward on the ice for either team. He has a long powerful stride that makes him deceivingly quick to loose pucks. He showed great hand eye coordination, deflecting a lot of point shots which resulted in one goal. Bowers liked to give up the puck as he enters the offensive zone then head straight for the front of the net looking for tips and rebounds and isn't shy about battling for positioning in front. Played a dynamic 2-way game and made an impact on the game in all 3 zones. Finished the game with 1G and +1

WTL #17 LW, Wait, Garrett (2016) – Wait didn't show a lot tonight. He wasn't necessarily a liability for his team but also didn't create a lot in way of offense, playing mostly 4th line minutes tonight. His skating ability allows him to play an effective defensive game and showed sound fundamentals on the back check and in his own zone.

MAD #5 LW, Messner, Mick (2017) – Was given more of an opportunity offensively tonight by playing on the 2nd line. While Messner didn't find the back of the net he did create some chances in front by battling and digging for rebounds. Messner was physical on the fore check, finishing a lot of his checks. His speed allows him to force defenseman to move the puck quickly.

Sault Ste. Marie Greyhounds at Niagara Ice Dogs, November 26, 2015

OHL Regular Season

SSM #11 D Hollowell, Mac (2017) - Strong skating to stick with speed/skill in the offensive zone. Used skating to rush puck out of trouble. Good one on one plays using skating and his stick to frustrate opponents. Moves feet well on point opening himself up as an option.

SSM #12 LW Katchouk, Boris (2016) - Good size and takes smart routes but lack of speed got him in trouble at times. Struggles to generate speed. When play went end to end he couldn't keep up but with puck below the dots on the offensive zone he made a lot of smart plays and created a few chances. Good stick in defensive zone then quick pass to set up breakaway. Drew power play protecting the puck down low. Played some penalty kill. Nice play early third taking the puck to the net, very hard/deceptive shot for scoring chance. Stepped it up in the final period creating several chances.

SSM #38 C Verbeek, Hayden (2016) - Strong skater, good speed, plays a very high paced game. Competed in all three zones. Tremendous work ethic. Smart play on 2 on 1 rush, passing option was taken away and quickly fired a difficult shot for the goaltender. Second unit penalty kill.

SSM #52 LW Kopacka, Jack (2016) - Struggles to build speed. Good puck protection. Capable of making quick decisions with the puck under pressure. Good compete in the defensive zone to force turnovers. Second power play unit. Very good passing; hard and accurate. Displays good hockey sense.

NIA #17 D Lochead, William (2016) - Pretty good mobility helps him one on one. Let's guys think they have the outside then closes the gap quickly so they can't beat him in either direction. Keeps it simple with the puck and makes the smart simple play. Bad shot decision blocked and taken for a breakaway.

Final Score: Niagara Ice Dogs: 4 - Sault Ste. Marie Greyhounds: 1

USANTDP at Youngstown Phantoms, November 27th, 2015

USA #4 RD Krys, Chad (2016) - Good mobility in all directions, uses skating offensively and defensively. Showed skill with the puck. Sometimes executed a high-end play, other times lost the puck in the process, decision-making lacked consistency. Defensive zone game was average.

USA #7 C Frederic, Trent (2016) - Skating, compete, and off the puck reads were there which makes him useful as a forechecker and backchecker. Had one nice pass but otherwise his play with the puck didn't produce much offense.

USA #8 RD Fox, Adam (2016) - His reads are on point, thought he slowed the game down too much with the puck, looking for openings and a high-end play instead of just focusing on a quick effective play and keeping the pace going.

USA #10 RW Lockwood, Will (2016) - Scored off a breakdown on a backdoor play. Good effort finding soft spots on the ice, though he was not a consistent offensive threat. Scored the empty netter as well.

USA #14 LD Greenway, J.D. (2016) - Offensive instincts looked better than what he could accomplish through his feet and hands. Doesn't wow you with skill or speed, but he seems to find a way to come up with that one effective offensive zone play. Made a nice backhand pass to Bellows in that manner.

USA #18 LD Lindgren, Ryan (2016) - Thought he was slower in his decision-making than what he has shown in other games. The quick puck-movement and anticipation was not there to the same level, which resulted in him spending more time in defensive zone.

USA #19 C Keller, Clayton (2016) - Several nice backhand no-look feeds and subtle little dish-offs, he could have been a bit more decisive in going to the middle of the ice as opposed to operating with passes from the corners and behind the net.

USA #22 LW Bellows, Kieffer (2016) - Scored on a quick-release shot immediately after entering the zone and receiving a pass from Greenway. Doesn't just wait for the puck to get to him, he actively works to obtain good position and will be involved in the play.

USA #30 G Oettinger, Jake (2017) - Had one bad moment giving up a goal on a wristshot from outside, otherwise calm and makes good initial saves, wasn't tested much laterally or on his recovery.

YNG #3 LD McInnis, Luke (2016) - Moved the puck effectively out of his zone. Scored a goal on a low percentage wristshot that made its way through. Smart but not dynamic offensively. Defensive zone coverage was on point, but lacks size.

YNG #26 C Morrison, Cameron (2016) - Effective when he uses his size and did so on a couple of occasions, winning pucks on the wall or bulling through players. It did not result in any goals, but it at least allowed him to keep the puck in the offensive zone for his shift. Was worse in the second half of the game.

YNG #27 LD Myllari, Kris (2016*) - He was Youngstown's best defenseman all things considered. Good puck distribution on PP, could skate the puck up ice, sometimes got smartly involved deeper in offensive zone. Solid if unspectacular defensively.

Moose Jaw Warriors at Seattle Thunderbirds, November 28th, 2015

MJW #2 RD Brook, Josh (2017) - He was a lot more active handling the puck and skating with it. Got beat once by Barzal but otherwise had no glaring defensive zone mistakes. His comfort level with the puck looked a lot better than in my early season viewings.

MJW #21 C Howden, Brett (2016) - Engages in one on one battles, made a key play on the wall that led to the OT winner. Not much creativity with the puck outside of that, struggled to set up possession time and move the play forward.

MJW #22 LW Gregor, Noah (2016) - He scored twice on the powerplay including the OT game-winner. Very quick release. Skating looked good at top speed but felt like he could move his feet more when without the puck. Wasn't a big threat at even strength.

MJW #31 G Sawchenko, Zach (2016) - Handled the puck well when having to go out of the net. No rebounds when his sight is unobstructed. His play in traffic was OK. He got beat by a Gropp snipe that he was partially screened on. Gave up the tying goal with one minute to go after Barzal beat him one on one. Would have liked to see him come up with the big save that his team needed.

MJW #71 LW Popugaev, Nikita (2017) - A pretty disappointing performance for him. Didn't move his feet and wasn't using his size well. Needs to be more engaging to be effective. Didn't see him take a shift in the third period.

SEA #4 LD Ottenbreit, Turner (2016*) - Used his size well in his own zone. Reach helped him when defending against zone entries. Had a solid defensive game. Couple of big shots from the point. Did a good job winning a wall battle against Popugaev.

SEA #5 LD Tyszka, Jarret (2017) - Moved his feet and played with energy. Threw a big open ice hit. Good size, though his game needs to be polished out going forward. Can run around a little bit, would like to see more composure on some outlets as well.

SEA #19 RW Neuls, Donovan (2016) - Smart game in the offensive zone. Several time sneaked up to the front of the net with nobody picking him up. Attempted to make some moves on the wall to lose his check but got stripped of the puck more often than not.

Scout's notes: Nolan Volcan (Seattle) was not in the lineup.

Cobourg Cougars at Georgetown Raiders, November 28, 2015

OJHL Regular Season

COB #11 D Dunn, Sam (BAR/2016) - Good skating for his size, capable of skating the puck out of trouble, protects it well. Played an entire 2 minute penalty kill and didn't look tired. Does a good job out front pushing opponents out of way of goalie and not letting them get their stick on anything. Doesn't have a mean streak and will only use as much force as necessary to make the play. Wears an "A" as a 17 year old. Excellent lateral movement and uses it in a variety of ways to benefit him. Uses stick effectively one on one. Can chase play out of position on occasion. Good hands, smooth with puck. At 90 seconds into a 2 and a half minute shift he made a great end to end rush. During that shift he played shorthanded, 4 on 4 and power play without being taken off the ice.

COB #21 F Carroll, Matthew (NIA/2016) - Huge size, loves to hit, punishes opponents, surprising skill in the slot to create scoring chance.

GEO #23 F Jacome, Jack (2017) - Very shifty, great speed, quick hands, has good skill to create offense. Played last minute down 4-5.

GEO #55 D Cairns, Matthew (PET/2016) - Skating has improved, has a little more jump. Does a good job playing one on one simple keeping opponents outside. Consistently moved the puck well, kept it pretty simple choosing good options. Moved puck well on power play. Good pass setting up 4-0 goal. Last minute down a goal made an excellent pass to set up a great chance.

Final Score: Cobourg Cougars: 5 - Georgetown Raiders: 4

Medicine Hat Tigers at Victoria Royals, December 1st, 2015

MED #16 RW Gerlach, Max (2016) - Had a good third period but was quiet for most of the game. He has good chemistry with Shaw and was often sneaking around the offensive zone looking for bounces or a good pass to convert on. Needs to do more on his own to drive the play.

MED #18 C Shaw, Mason (2017) - Good vision with the puck, made several quick passes setting up dangerous offensive situations. Reacts quickly to what is happening around him.

MED #19 RD Quenneville, David (2016) - He had a ridiculous amount of point shots, though some lacked in power most were accurate and made it through. Kept his game very simple but mostly effective. Was a real offensive threat with his quick point shots.

VIC #4 LD Jarratt, Ralph (2016) - He had a very good effort in his own zone. Won the vast majority of his battles. Especially his ability to break up plays on the wall and to kill any sustained Medicine Hat pressure was apparent.

VIC #11 RW Phillips, Matthew (2016) - He scored by converting on an oddly bouncing puck. Was buzzing around the play, effective as a forechecker with good jump and sniffs out offensive opportunity. Subtle effective plays on the wall despite the lack of size as well.

VIC #17 C Soy, Tyler (2016*) - He was good both on PP and PK. Had two shorthanded chances. Several steals in neutral zone, intercepting Medicine Hat's puck-movement. Smart game though you would expect him to dominate the offensive zone more for him to be worth using a pick on.

Tri-City Americans at Everett Silvertips, December 2nd, 2015

TRI #6 LD Valimaki, Juuso (2017) - Had a shorthanded goal on a two on one play with Rasmussen. Outside of that, he was not as active offensively as in some of the other games. Used his body well defensively pinning forwards down on the wall.

TRI #10 RD Coghlan, Dylan (2016) - Scored on a wristshot joining the play as a trailer. Saw PK time and did well there, positionally solid and cleared the puck several times. Used his skating and size well to interfere and slow down Everett's attack, he picked up an interference penalty once, but was effective for most of the night without crossing that line.

TRI #15 C Rasmussen, Michael (2017) - Displayed very good vision and anticipation setting up Coghlan and Valimaki goals. He was a threat for most of the night using his body to protect the puck and create offensive zone chances and has good skill to go along with it. Though he competed well, he could have used his body to be more effective defensively and on the forecheck.

TRI #31 G Sarthou, Evan (2016) - He had a good if unspectacular game. Wasn't challenged much as Everett's offense was anemic most of the time, though he did well on some PK sequences. Thought he saw the puck well through the traffic, making a couple of saves through screens. Seemed like he could take better control of his crease on some of the jam plays in front of him.

EVE #8 RW Bajkov, Patrick (2016) - Dangerous from the half-wall on the powerplay. Very smart in open ice, anticipates where the puck is going. Utilized fakes and subtle movements to open up space for him. Lost effectiveness when the player checking him managed to close the gap on him.

EVE #17 C Fonteyne, Matt (2016) - Good compete level and moves his feet. Can be a hound off the puck. His problem was that he lost pucks as fast as he stripped them from someone. Forces the play too much with the puck, didn't think he played a very smart game here even if the willingness to work was there.

EVE #70 G Hart, Carter (2016) - He was the main reason why Everett was trailing only by a goal after the first period, as his team didn't bother to show up. Unfortunatley, that only lasted for a period as Hart got pulled in the third afer he let in his fourth goal. He could have done better on Coghlan's goal, but the rest was more a case of him failing to come up big than letting in any soft goals. His focus wasn't as good as in some of the other games of his.

North Bay Battalion at Sarnia Sting, December 4, 2015

OHL Regular Season

NBY #4 D Dineen, Cam (2016) - Took too long down low to make a decision with the puck, got stripped, directly resulted in first goal against. Good mobility overcompensates when trying to protect the puck making it too easy for opponents to steal the puck.

NBY #14 C Poirier, Zach (2016) - Under heavy pressure in defensive zone does a good job flipping puck out without icing. Top penalty kill unit.

NBY #15 LW Sherman, David (2016) - Not very good skating ability. Good neutral zone pass to set up chance.

NBY #25 D Shoemaker, Mark (2016) - Excellent breakout pass set up scoring chances. Usually made good passes up ice.

SAR #5 D Chychrun, Jakob (2016) - Excellent vision and puck movement on the power play. Made some great shot fakes followed by passes to throw off opposition but sometimes overdoes it or will do it when he has a shooting lane available. Beat down low own zone on power play killing time off powerplay.

SAR #13 C Chemelevski, Sasha (2017) - Good positioning skating into the slot and a quick, accurate release for 2-1 goal.

SAR #25 LW Kyrou, Jordan (2016) - Excellent work ethic down low to steal puck and set up 1-0 goal. Varied results down low; sometimes held on to the puck a little too long, other times made quick, accurate passes. Showed flashes of his skill and speed, made a few great rushes. Excellent hands to create chance in close. Pulled up going into corner against big defenseman. Shift by shift play showed a wide range of results.

Final Score: Sarnia Sting: 5 - North Bay Battalion: 2

Sioux City Musketeers at USANTDP, December 4th, 2015

SCM #10 RD Boyle, Michael (2016) - Started out a bit shaky, average decision-making. Competed well and was willing to play physical. Had some good shoving matches and was feisty. More involved after the midpoint of the game, but not much of an offensive threat.

SCM #15 RW Tolvanen, Eeli (2017) - Had a couple of mediocre looks on PP. Shot is a threat and he's better when he moves his feet. Wasn't enough of a factor off the puck. Thought he got too content looking for his shot and not working enough to challenge US's defense.

USA #7 C Frederic, Trent (2016) - Good in the corners and from the hash-marks to the end-boards area as a whole. Hard to handle there with the puck as well as when hounding the opposition. Enough skill and vision to win battles and make plays off it. Dumb offensive zone penalty in third period.

USA #8 RD Fox, Adam (2016) - Good puck-movement. Skating and hands were on display, can manoeuvre around the ice while handling the puck and keeping his head up to see his options.

USA #9 C Pastujov, Nick (2016) - Not many second efforts on plays and a touch too easy to play against when defending. He got better later in the game but his passes ended up dying on his wingers' sticks. Didn't get anything useful back.

USA #14 LD Greenway, J.D. (2016) - Big body, but a bit slow in his reaction time. Felt he struggled with some of the reads early on, using his large frame to get by but not having much control of his position and space. Not flashy offensively but got involved.

USA #17 RW Anderson, Joey (2016) - Good net presence type of game on a line with Keller and Bellows. Kept it simple but was effective in that role, good instincts around the net.

USA #18 LD Lindgren, Ryan (2016) - Good though not elite skating. Uses frame effectively to close down, reads the play well and strong positionally. His processing of the game allowed him to be in the right positions and push the play up ice with effective quick passing. Strong performance, though would like to see him engage more in offensive zone.

USA #19 C Keller, Clayton (2016) - Showed high-end understanding of offensive zone. His ability to find teammates who are skating into open space and hit them with a pass was very good. While having a fluid stride, he didn't show elite elusiveness, his anticipation helped him offset some of that though.

USA #22 LW Bellows, Kieffer (2016) - Shot plenty and shot from everywhere. Certainly willing to go closer to the net, but at times wondered about his shot selection. Still, he ended up scoring the game winner in third period precisely on a hope shot from outside that the goalie wasn't ready for.

USA #25 LD Luce, Griffin (2016) - Big and physical. Worked to be a physical factor on the ice. Skating wasn't horrible, but could improve. Can execute passes if he has enough time but is better off not handling the puck too much.

USA #30 G Oettinger, Jake (2017) - He was solid. He had one bad goal on an unobstructed point shot on the PP, but was otherwise composed and had good rebound control, directing rebounds to the side and making the saves he needed to.

Scout's notes: Chad Krys was not in the lineup.

Waterloo Black Hawks at Dubuque Fighting Saints, December 5th, 2015

WAT #9 LD Rossini, Sam (2016) - Held the blueline in offensive zone several times preventing the opposition from clearing the zone and made plays back deep. Quickly picked up loose pucks in defensive zone and moved them forward. Thought he backed off too much against zone entries, sometimes giving up too much room.

WAT #15 C Bowers, Shane (2017) - Some of his early shifts were on LW. He was moving his feet well. Good compete level, always involved in races for the puck. Played at a good pace and was taking away time and space off the puck, had two assists but also had a couple of quick passes that his linemates didn't recognize in time or couldn't handle properly.

WAT #17 LW Wait, Garrett (2016) - Had a couple of sequences interrupting Dubuque's breakout by anticipating puck-movement. He finds open ice and has good timing in offensive zone to jump into scoring areas. Not enough deception with the puck, was a bit too easy to defend against and didn't challenge the defense much.

DUB #27 RW Knierim, William (2016) - Good support on break-outs and puck-movement through neutral zone. It was clear that he can read the play and anticipate where the puck is going, but he didn't use his size well until the third period. If he used his frame better to fend off checkers, he'd be able to make more plays in the offensive zone, but too many times defensemen managed to get their sticks on the puck and break up plays against him.

Vancouver Giants at Everett Silvertips, December 5th, 2015

VAN #7 RW Ronning, Ty (2016) - He was dangerous when coming into the offensive zone with speed. Didn't mind taking direct routes to the slot and getting his nose dirty. While he did a good job coming into the scoring areas he didn't get the bounces going his way.

VAN #17 LW Benson, Tyler (2016) - He scored on the PP by throwing the puck to the net from an odd angle. Had another good breakaway chance. That said, he didn't establish a physical presence as a checker, nor did he use his size effectively to protect the puck on the cycle. I don't think a wait and see approach makes him all that effective as a player.

VAN #24 LD Barberis, Matt (2016) - He was good early on when using his skating to move the puck out of the zone and through neutral zone, but faded later in the game. Picked up a secondary assist on the PP but was not much of an offensive threat outside of that.

EVE #8 LW Bajkov, Patrick (2016) - He made a key play on Fonteyne's goal and especially came up big late in third period by converting on a rebound and putting his team up by 2 goals. Had a good night distributing the puck in the offensive zone.

EVE #17 C Fonteyne, Matt (2016) - He was one of the better players through the first half of the game. Several strong defensive plays that come from him moving his feet and quickly closing down the puck carrier. Scored the first goal of the game by picking up a loose puck, spinning and firing a wrister.

EVE #70 G Hart, Carter (2016) - Saved a couple of grade A scoring chances including a Benson breakaway. Very good second efforts, though his rebound control on initial shots could be better. Battles hard. Gave up one fluke PP goal by a shot from the side that had almost no angle to go in but bounced off him into the net.

Scout's Notes: Ryely McKinstry (Vancouver) was not in the lineup.

Fargo Force at Madison Capitols, December 5th 2015, USHL

FAR #13 LW Crone, Hank (2016) – Crone shown more willingness to involve his teammates and play more of a complete game then previous viewings when he was playing for Omaha. Crone still showed he is very much a perimeter player who tends to avoid then tough areas of the ice but does have a lot of puck skills and can create something out of nothing.

FAR #17 RW Smirov, Denis (2016) – Finished with one Assist on the night but also rang a rocket of a shot off the post on the Power Play. Knows his way around the offensive zone and finds a way to create chances and find the open ice. Runs the Point on the Power Play. Played a solid power forward style game despite only being 5'10". Didn't shy away from physical play or the hard areas.

Final Score: 4-3 (SO) Fargo

Cape-Breton Screaming Eagles vs Blainville-Boisbriand Armada, December 6th, 2015

CAP #18 RW Dubois, Pierre-Luc (2016): Today Dubois was playing RW on the top line with his two Russian linemates Lazarev and Svechnikov. He played a strong two-way game and was a key contributor on the PK for the Screaming Eagles. He made an excellent play on Clark Bishop's shorthanded goal in the 2nd period, showing great patience with the puck and drawing the defensemen toward him, then making a great feed to Bishop, who was all alone in the slot. He was good on the forecheck, taking good angles in his puck pursuit and didn't hesitate in throwing his body around. He showed very good puck-protection in the offensive zone. The smaller Armada defenders had a tough time taking the puck away from him. He didn't score in the game, but showed that he has a lethal wrist shot, a quick release and lot of velocity behind his shot.

CAP #21 RW Hoyt, Peyton (2017): Played on the fourth line today with no power play ice time. He kept his game simple for most of his shifts by bringing some good energy with his speed and physical game. He didn't get many scoring chances in this game, but had one where he was able to show off a good wrist shot while coming down his off-wing; it had a good, quick release. He had some PK shifts during the game, including a soft clearing attempt in the 3rd that could have been costly, seeing as he was protecting a lead.

CAP #31 G Jessiman, Kyle (2017): A hometown kid playing in front of his friends and family today. He was a bit nervous early in the game handling the puck. Made numerous key saves in the first period where the Armada outplayed the Eagles, and made 13 of his 24 saves in the first period alone. His rebound control got better as the first period went on and he looked very poised once the nerves were gone. He was the same poised goaltender I saw last year in Midget AAA. As a small goaltender, he has to work hard to track pucks with traffic in front of him. The lone goal that was scored on him was from a point shot with traffic in front.

CAP #23 LW Lazarev, Maxim (2016): The un-drafted '96-born Russian had a decent game overall. He got rocked hard early on in the first period by Thomas Pospisil, who was given a five-minute major on the play. He had two good scoring chances after taking passes in the slot where he found open ice. He took two good wrist shots on net and showed a very quick release on those shots. Played LW with Svechnikov and Dubois on his usual line, and saw ice time on the top PP unit.

CAP #6 LD Beaudin, Jeremie (2016): Beaudin had some tough shifts defensively while playing on the 3rd pairing with #20 MacIntyre during the game. On one shift, he lost his footing and then was deked out by #13 Bramwall. This led to 2-3 quality scoring chances for the Armada. In the 2nd half of the game, he had some good battles along the boards and threw some good hits.

BLB #24 LW Teasdale, Joel (2017): He was not as good as in my previous viewings. Teasdale seems to struggle to keep up with the pace of the game today. He was playing LW with top PP ice time; as usual, he did a good job along the wall in the offensive zone. He was a bit hesitant with the puck on his stick on the power play, as he was playing more along the half-wall position than his usual role (in front of the net).

BLB #22 RW Katerinakis, Alexander (2016): He was the only player on his line to be noticeable today, playing with two fellow draft eligible prospects (Hylland and Picard). He made good use of his speed, going wide on CAP defenders on a couple of occasions during the game, and obtained 2-3 decent scoring chances because of this.

Prince Albert Raiders at Edmonton Oil Kings, December 8, 2015

PRA #6 LD Budik, Vojtech (2016) – A good skater with strong crossover technique who cut players off really well along the wall. Took care of the centre of the ice and the prime scoring area as well. Was physical yet remained in good position. Puckhandling skills might be in need of improvement, as he had a hard time handling pucks that arrived on edge. Played on the second powerplay unit.

PRA #23 LW Stransky, Simon (2016) – Looked fast and explosive out of the gate, even though he'll be flying out to attend the Czech national team camp in preparation for the 2016 World Juniors. Didn't appear to be preserving his energy. Showed tremendous vision and was excellent at moving pucks to players positioned advantageously in open-space.

PRA #27 LW Kelly, Parker (2017) – Was fast and very physical. Delivered several hits that easily could have been deemed charging calls as they were powerful and purposeful.

EDM #2 RD Yewchuk, Kyle (2016) – Skating continued to be a bit of an issue, but I liked his puck movement a lot more in this one. Shot has a long release time and could be more accurate. Fought hard for the puck in the corners. Did a good job of getting pucks out of trouble but, once again, I thought his puck movement could use some refinement.

EDM #3 LD Gorda, Brayden (2017) – Looks a lot bigger, stockier, and faster than you'd expect, given that he's one of the youngest players on his club. Played a smart and cerebral game, not afraid to reverse the puck to buy himself some time. Didn't give up on plays in the corner.

EDM #16 RW Koch, Davis (2016) – Handled the puck really well in tight spaces, especially along the boards or in the corner. Didn't look reluctant to crash the net. Played on the first power play unit.

EDM #28 LD Elizarov, Anatolli (2016) – Very tall and lanky yet still fairly graceful on his feet. Not terribly fast but moves up and down the ice in acceptable timing.

Seattle Thunderbirds at Spokane Chiefs, December 9th, 2015

SEA #4 LD Ottenbreit, Turner (2016*) - Slapshot from the point was an asset for him. Used his size in his own zone. Decision making on outlets was a bit slow. Somewhat sluggish first few steps when taking off with the puck.

SEA #7 RD Khaira, Sahvan (2016) - The best that could be said for him in this game is that he has a big frame. He's essentially a defensive defenseman who had a poor defensive game. Got beat between his legs when defending a rush which resulted in a goal against.

SEA #19 LW Neuls, Donovan (2016) - Picked up a nice assist by hiding on the weak-side post and then making a pass to the middle. Otherwise was largely a non-factor in this game.

SPK #10 LW McIndoe, Ethan (2017) - Worked all game long moving his feet to take pucks out of the defensive zone. Really willing to sacrifice his body but the finish in the offensive zone wasn't there for him.

SPK #11 C Anderson-Dolan, Jarret (2017) - I haven't seen a game of his where he wasn't highly competitive yet. Tends to skate himself out of room though. Needs to be more aware of his surroundings and put it into a lower gear on the occasion.

SPK #17 RW Yamamoto, Kailer (2017) - He's a good player on PK which is a bit surprising given that he is a smaller highly skilled wing. He had a great cycle shift with Helewka where he made a nice drop pass into the slot for a Helewka goal.

SPK #26 C Elynuik, Hudson (2016) - He's a 6'5 200 forward that can skate. Played both special teams, on PP he battles in front of the net and provides screens. Decent puck skills for his size and there's hints of offensive vision there. Needs to put it all together on a shift-by-shift basis though.

SPK #28 LW Andersen, Nik (2016) - He's a reasonably smart player that however didn't really show any asset that would legitimize him as an NHL prospect. He was just OK at everything and never really appeared to dictate the play at any point.

Saginaw Spirit at Niagara Ice Dogs, December 10, 2015

Meridian Centre (St. Catharines, Ont.)

NIA #3 Jones, Ben (2017) – He was a very average player at best. He is average in size and did not show any real skill sets and offensive thoughts. He appeared to struggle a bit to keep up with the pace and make the simple plays and passes in breaking puck out or in transition. Perhaps uncomfortable on the wing as believe usually plays center and looked positional out of the play at times. On the only goal against he failed to get the puck in deep on the tip-in dump in the neutral zone and Saginaw quickly transitioned back the other way for a goal. It is only the rookie season for the young '99 Jones, so there will be a learning curve.

NIA #6 Davis, Hayden (2017) – Another rookie in the Ice Dogs line-up in 3rd D-man pairing that is decent size who skates and handles puck adequately. He seemed to keep play simple in making first pass with the limited ice time. He is 2017 NHL Draft eligible that will have plenty more viewings.

NIA #12 Krassey, Evan (2016) – He is a good sized winger that had limited ice time on the 4th line that showed some physical side at times although did not see any true example of offensive skills or thoughts.

NIA #14 Paquette, Christopher (2016) – Paquette was the 3rd line center and seemed to show more skill set and confidence since this scouts last viewing of him in October. He showed good possession with the puck in coming back into the defensive zone and help break puck out. You can see good skill sets in skating/pivots, stop/starts, and handling the puck. He also made some nice rushes with the puck and good zone entries and set-ups for scoring chances. He made good puck decisions in all three zones and looked to win face-offs too. Honestly, really thought his wingers did not give him much to work with on the night. Overall, he played a solid 2-way game and a draft prospect that looks more comfortable in his game and might be a nice mid-round pick with size, skills, and IQ.

NIA #17 Lochead, William (2016) – He played a simple, steady game that did not impress really one way or another. Paired with another OHL rookie #6 Davis as the 3rd pairing he made some outlets and took care of his own zone in limited ice time.

NIA #25 Langdon, Kyle (2016) – He was the center on the 4th line that looked to have a choppy stride and average to below average handle with the puck as well. He did not really do much to stand out and only really noticed as the skating is poor in technique with extension and edges.

NIA #27 Davis, Cal (2017) – He is a decent sized 6-foot winger that was one of the many rookies in line-up for IceDogs who was given 4th line duty. He was given limited ice and did not really exemplify his skill sets and offensive ways.

SAG #9 Gilmour, Brady (2017) – He is '99 OHL rookie that was given limited ice and relegated to 4th line center duties. Gilmour looked to have some nice skill sets in his mind-set with the puck to elude defenders although did not get a ton of ice time. He will need to continue to gain more muscle strength as well as quicker, stronger skating stride to escape pressure at the OHL and eventually the higher levels.

SAG #49 Coskey, Cole (2017) – He played average on the night, yet then again he was another '99 rookie adjusting his game from the Tier 1 HPHL U16 level with the Chicago Mission. He did not look bad as he was taking the puck off the puck board and breaking it out efficiently as well as cycling the puck a bit in the offensive zone. He eventually will start gaining more confidence with the puck and start displaying his offensive side and should start playing stronger in his own zone without the puck. He is average in size. He will need to gain more size and strength so consistently win puck battles and not forced off puck.

SAG #55 Middleton, Keaton (2016) – He certainly has the NHL size and strength in the defensive zone as he will play physical and will battle along the wall and corners. His mobility is decent although the skating in lateral foot speed will need to improve as will his stick handling abilities. He is a decent player with good mind in that he will move puck up ice efficiently in breakout and transition. One example was he caught the puck on a dump-in just inside the defensive blue line, yet quickly found the open teammate #10 Sadowy in neutral zone on the first goal early in the 3rd period. He made a few quick head-man passes that initially created offensive rushes. He is just a raw talent that will certainly continue to gain interest for NHL teams with his size and developing abilities. He possesses a heavy shot from the blue line although the offensive upside seems limited and will fill in as shut-down, aggressive D-man for the next levels.

SAG #56 Niemelainen, Markus (2016) – He is a tall, yet still lanky D-man that could still pack on some muscle to his frame. His mobility is decent although he will need to continue developing his foot speed. You could see here and there when he opens up and pivots the lateral foot speed could be better. He utilizes his long stick well in the defensive zone to break up plays and will outlet puck up well to forwards as makes good puck decisions. He does not play overly physical and could start to do so more often as he did in the 2nd period laying good body checking on boards at the defensive blue to break up Niagara rush. His gap control is decent although a few times he did tend to pivot or turn the wrong way to give free space to his opponent. Niemelainen will need to tighten up this technique and also making sure not overly aggressive through the neutral zone as will be exposed greater at the NHL level. He finds shooting lanes from the point and shot shows to be pretty hard and accurate. There is plenty to like and NHL scouts are starting to pay closer attention.

SAG #62 Falhaber, Tye (2016) – He is not overly tall and his stride looks even more choppy with his lack of size yet shows some speed as gets his legs going quickly even though not the most efficient stride. He works hard in all 3 zones. He was playing 3rd line center and showed some success at the face-off dot. Not overly impressed although he had some scoring success in the OHL last season as rookie. Falhaber did not display the offensive skill sets and know-how on this night. He looked to be an average player on the ice.

SAG #35 Cormier, Evan (2016) – He is a prototypical sized goalie who movements and foot speed seem pretty good. He made some good saves on the night although at times can let a rebound get away as displayed on first goal against. He made a brilliant save on the trailer #21 Jenys coming down the slot 1-on-1 with Cormier off a 3-on-2 rush by Niagara, yet he knocked rebound back into the slot and then was beat by initial passer #10 DiFruscia as he came across the slot and fired into net as Cormier was down. He looked composed on the night showed confidence. Made simple play of stopping puck behind net a couple times for D-man on opposition change to quickly transition up ice are little things that get you noticed. The GWG against was a rocket of a shot by #20 Wesley as he cut to slot on forehand and wired over Cormier's glove. To Cormier's defense it was a 4-on-2 rush by Niagara and well placed shot for sure. Cormier has the tools, technique, and frame for the next level.

Prince George Cougars at Portland Winterhawks, December 11th, 2015

PGC #15 C O'Brien, Brogan (2016*) - Good checking game and uses his stick well to cover lanes and for pokechecks. Some of the scoring chances were created by him forcing the other team into turnovers. Lost the puck behind his net on the third period tying goal by Portland.

PGC #18 LW Bison, Bartek (2016) - Started off slow and looked a bit confused as to what he was supposed to be doing on the ice when he didn't have the puck but settled into the game in the second half. Can pick up speed with puck and attack with his large frame. Threw a couple of hits.

PGC #26 RW McDonald, Kody (2016) - Scored by tipping a shot after he won the wall battle that started the play. Can go shifts without doing anything useful, too often lacking in energy and tempo.

PGC #28 LD Anderson, Josh (2016) - Good defensive move to break up a two on one. Not much there offensively, took a couple of simple shots when he got the puck on the point. Felt like he could close down more effectively when defending on zone entries.

POR #8 C Glass, Cody (2017) - He was outstanding. Played like a seasoned veteran. Involved on both ends of the ice, great reads with and without the puck, very competitive game. Gained the zone with ease and had several shots from high-quality scoring areas. Won battles, made quality give and go plays.

POR #21 RD De Jong, Brendan (2016) - Good forward skating at his size, did a good job joining the rush and being an option on one play. No real physicality to speak of in his own end. His play in his own end was average at best and he wasn't much of an offensive threat either. Ended up questioning whether he knows what he is as a player.

Hamilton Bulldogs at Barrie Colts, December 12, 2015

HAM #17 C Saigeon, Brandon (2016) – Saigeon was very quiet offensively in this game. He generated a good shot in the slot following a power move where he used his size to get to the middle of the ice but other than that he didn't create much. He had a couple solid hits on the forecheck and landed a big one on Adrian Carbonara along the wall. The Bulldogs were often running around in the defensive zone with his unit on the ice.

HAM #18 LW Strome, Matthew (2016) – Strome showed good patience and vision with the puck slowing play down and allowing lanes to open up before making a pass. He setup a couple good chances that way. Though he did make some nice plays he was rather inconsistent on a shift-to-shift basis. He wasn't overly physical although he did battle hard along the walls and also had a good net front presence on the man advantage.

HAM #42 Gleason, Benjmain (2016) – Gleason made a good play on an odd man rush early on by pressuring the puck carrier but keeping his stick in position to intercept a pass. He was poised with the puck and made good outlets. If nothing was available to him he had no problem skating it up ice and was effective doing so. He turned it over on the PP on one occasion but for the most part his decision-making was sound.

BAR #10 D Murray, Justin (2016) – Murray was struggling early as no outlets were available and he resorted to icing the puck several times. As the game progressed he started to rush the puck up ice himself if nobody was open and that helped him get play going in the right direction. He moved the puck effectively in the offensive zone and picked up an assist on a nice passing play that led to a Justin Scott goal. Defensively there were some hiccups but he did a good job of sticking with the play and not letting miscues get to him.

BAR #16 LW Hawerchuk, Ben (2016) – Hawerchuk finished his checks with regularity and landed a couple big hits throughout. One hit on Saban led to a retaliatory penalty although Barrie didn't score on that power play. Hawerchuk had some nice give and go's with Magwood – including one on Barrie's 4th goal – and had a couple nice looks himself in dangerous areas. He didn't score but had five shots and seemed to consistently find seams in the defense throughout the night.

BAR #18 RW Magwood, Zachary (2016) – Magwood was a force on the forecheck in this game. He disrupted several outlet attempts and that led to a plethora of extra chances and shots for Barrie throughout the game. He also forced several turnovers in the neutral zone with a good stick and back checking pressure. There were several shifts where his unit was able to cycle the puck and keep it down low for 30-40 seconds in Hamilton's zone. He scored a beautiful one-touch goal on a nice give-and-go with Hawerchuk in the 3rd period. He played a real strong 200-foot game in this one.

Final Score: 5-1 Barrie

Sudbury Wolves at Guelph Storm, December 13, 2015

OHL Regular Season

SBY #11 LW Lyszczarzyk, Alan (2016) - Nice pass across slot set up 1-0 goal. Carries the puck well with decent speed and good protection. Takes hit to make the play. Reacted quickly to turnover and went to the net for scoring chance.

SBY #98 RW Sokolov, Dmitry (2016) - Great one time shot to score 1-0 goal. Shoot first mentality, has choppy skating, overall below average in skating department. Great power in shot, fairly good accuracy for power. Rang another power play shot off the post. Likes the give and go and will drive the net after giving looking for a pass.

SBY #33 G Timpano, Troy (2016) - Made some big saves on some defensive breakdowns. First goal against was 2 on 1 where pass was blocked, then shot; not much chance. Handled powerplay scramble in the slot well. Second goal against scored right after scramble but was a cross crease one timer, not much chance. Anticipated passes well.

GUE #4 D Carroll, Noah (2016) - Really struggled to clear the puck out of the defensive zone resulting in scoring chances. Liked to jump up and get involved offensively a couple times.

GUE #7 RW Phillips, Brock (2016) - Defenseman playing forward today. Looks for hits and landed a few big ones, one of which the opponent didn't have the puck for an interference penalty. Levelled defender after taking a shot and was high sticked in the face, instead of taking the powerplay he put a beating on the opponents player. Running around a bit after the high stick getting in some shots and getting under the skin of the opposition.
GUE #25 LW Burghardt, Luke (2016) - Good skater, looks off hits. Terrible own zone pass lead to 1-2 goal. Always keeps his feet moving which helps him in some areas but can take him out of position sometimes. Made some blind behind the back passes that were unsuccessful. Good positioning at the side of the net on the powerplay firing one timer for 2-2 goal.

Final Score: Sudbury Wolves: 4 - Guelph Storm: 2

Orebro HK J20 at Sodertalje SK J20, December 13th, 2015

ORE #24 C Johansson, Anton (2017) - He used his speed well on a couple of occasions. Some of his shifts were really played at a good pace, he made it easy a couple of times to gain the offensive zone with speed and pierce through defensive coverage into the slot. He also showed off his skill on a spinorama move that he pulled off with ease and retained possession of the puck.

ORE #28 LD Anderberg, Alexander (2016*) - He was very willing to play a physical game. You could see him immediately going for physical contact when defending one on one against forwards. This worked well on the wall and on more stationary plays. However, defending against speed and in situations where he had to use his positioning and lateral ability proved to be a bit more challenging for him.
ORE #50 G Marmenlind, Daniel (2016) - Was certainly not his best game. Gave up four goals, three alone in the first period. His defense also did quite a bad job as most of the goals were either odd-man rushes or resulting from poor coverage in the crease. However Marmenlind didn't really do anything to stop any of those. Looked slow, almost lethargic for most of the game, and his game really lacked focus and detail. You could see him gliding out of position and out of ideal angles and there was a notable lack of jump on second efforts.

SOD #30 G Eriksson, Filip (2016) - He only gave up one goal where the puck slowly trickled behind him from a fanned slapshot and a body in front of him. Otherwise, had a strong game. Real good quickness in his crease. His recovery and reaction time on shots looked good. He also had good stability and control on explosive side-by-side movements. One thing that was lacking was rebound control, as he seemed to block shots far more often than make saves, with pucks sometimes bouncing right back into the middle of the slot.

SOD #59 LD Carlsson, Lukas (2016) - He was the best defenseman on the ice. Really smart game, though he has good size he didn't go out of the way to throw big hits. Picked his spots as to when to engage physically. Good positioning when defending on zone entires. Easily tracks and picks up his man. Not a big threat from the offensive blueline in, but did most of the puck-movement in his zone and in the neutral zone. Best thing about him was the fact that he anticipated the play a step ahead and set himself up to be in good positions when defending.

Vancouver Giants at Victoria Royals, December 13th, 2015

VAN #7 RW Ronning, Ty (2016) - He was the recipient of a couple of good stretch passes. Had some chances coming into the offensive zone with speed but failed to establish any secondary efforts, was mostly a one and done type of night for him.

VAN #17 LW Benson, Tyler (2016) - Once he started playing with jump it was evident that he can win pucks, use his frame and skill to gain space towards the middle and set up his linemates. Went to the front of the net as well and had a couple of good tips. Good passing vision overall. Didn't like how he glided around in defensive zone. While he did throw his body around on a couple of occasions, his effort in closing down gaps and pursuing his man left a lot to be desired. Rarely had a shift where he put all of his tools together.

VAN #24 LD Barberis, Matt (2016) - An unremarkable game for him. I remember him being a shot threat from the blueline early in the season but none of that happened. He did ok on first passes and had one or two good pinches to keep the puck in the offensive zone. Average in defensive zone, not lost in his coverage but not much of a factor either.

VIC #4 LD Jarratt, Ralph (2016) - Struggled to adjust when defending against speed. Had some errant passes out of his zone and in neutral zone. Positioning was mostly on point, but skating can be problematic for him. Had one good offensive zone chance sneaking backdoor past Benson.

VIC #11 RW Phillips, Matthew (2016) - This kid continues to sacrifice his small frame to be a factor. Took abuse in front of the net and yet came up with scoring chances. Even engaged with Benson on one wall play and held his own. Smart player too and can make plays while skating at speed. Like Hannoun, the tiny frame really hurts him.

VIC #17 C Soy, Tyler (2016) - Good at both ends of the ice, lacks the dynamic ability to lose the player checking him off his back. Real smart reads, several times he started the play in his own zone and was then the guy responsible for creating a scoring chance in the offensive zone as well.

VIC #19 C Hannoun, Dante (2016) - Tiny and I simply didn't see anything that would suggest he can outplay the lack of size. Good hands in-tight and decent vision allowed him to be dangerous a couple of times.

Scout's Notes: Ryely McKinstry (Vancouver) was not in the lineup.

Czech Republic vs Canada West, WJAC, December 13th, 2015

CZE #3 LD Sirota, Jakub (2017) - Good size and held his own. Skating for his size is good. Reads the play well and doesn't take himself out of position when defending, became more offensively active later in the game and didn't struggle handling the puck and making plays in those situations.

CZE #6 LW Zachar, Marek (2016) - Although a good skater, didn't think he played with the kind of motor needed to make his game work. Needs to keep his feet moving consistently and hound the puck to be effective.

CZE #7 LD Kachyna, Ondrej (2016) - Agility isn't that good, but skating isn't completely horrible at his size. Though not an offensive defenseman, he did an OK job making passes and handling the puck when he had to while logging considerable minutes.

CZE #8 RD Valik, Dominik (2016) - Thought he was positionally solid in his own zone making sure he controls the area around the net and the middle of ice. Didn't handle the puck a lot.

CZE #20 LW Havranek, Tomas (2016) - Played as a 13th forward but did a good job in all of his shifts. Good energy and was taking the play to Canada's defensive zone. Was a bit of a sparkplug out there, felt like he deserved more minutes.

CZE #22 C Reichel, Kristian (2016) - He was good at playmaking and finding options to pass the puck up ice, though there wasn't really anything dynamic with the puck in terms of beating players or manipulating defensive coverage. Faded considerably after the first period.

CZE #23 LD Doudera, Lukas (2016) - One of the better Czechs on the ice. Good puck-movement, can skate with the puck and maintain possession. Battled in his own end, doesn't have a huge frame but was stingy enough.

CZE #28 RW Kousal, Pavel (2017) - Kept his feet moving and played a direct straight line game which actually caused some problems for Canadian D, pushing them back and giving his team some offensive options.

CAW #6 LD Pasichnuk, Brinson (2016) - Thought he played an up-tempo game that made him involved at both ends of the ice. A couple of slapshots from the point and he was engaged in his own zone, getting his body on players.

CAW #8 RD Fabbro, Dante (2016) - Sloppy for his standard and body language looked slightly disinterested. He had some uncharacteristically poor decisions with the puck and some of his pinches looked pretty sloppy in execution as well.

CAW #9 LD Cholowski, Dennis (2016) - Good mobility, used his stick well defensively and was positionally solid. Didn't overextend in trying too hard to make things happen offensively but let the game naturally come to him. Had one bad lateral pass on the offensive blueline that got intercepted.

CAW #10 C Jost, Tyson (2016) - The best offensive weapon on the ice, had an assist on a nice offensive zone effort and scored a goal by escaping coverage and receiving a pass into the slot. Did a good job making things happen offensively and has the skills and intelligence to cause quick-strike attacks that result in scoring chances.

CAW #20 LW Van Tetering, Troy (2016*) - He moved his feet coming down the wing, played a pretty competitive game, gained the zone well coming out of netural zone with speed. Was buzzing around the play, effective in one and one battles.

CAW #30 G Murray, Matthew (2016) - Doesn't look like the biggest guy in goal, but he played a pretty composed game, not giving up a lot of rebounds, and not having a lot of excess movement in the crease.

Canada East vs Russia, WJAC, December 14th, 2015

CAE #2 RD Grant, Owen (2016) - He's done a good job utilizing his skating to bring the puck up ice on a couple of occasions. Had one careless outlet in his zone that got intercepted and turned into a penalty for his team.

CAE #11 RD Dunn, Sam (2016) - He was good early on making simple decisions with the puck and focusing on quick passes. Faded later in the game once Russia started to take over.

CAE #15 C Dickinson, Josh (2016) - Reads the play well, had an opportunity after quickly recognizing a Russian turnover and fired a shot from the slot. Didn't create a lot with the puck but was using his awareness and timing well to show up for offensive opportunities.

CAE #17 LW Murray, Brett (2016) - Good effort on PP, twice preventing Russian D from clearing the puck by quickly establishing pressure and keeping possession for his team. Was good at bringing the puck into offensive zone. Battles well on the wall and below the hashmarks as well. Good size.

CAE #20 LD Cairns, Matt (2016) - Had a couple of errant passes from the point. Thought he struggled to get his puck-moving game going in this game.

CAE #31 G Latinovich, Nicholas (2016*) - Hardly at fault for any of the goals, had a nice effort making a save after a scrum. Didn't however really come up big at any moment, Russia converted on most of their best scoring chances.

RUS #8 RD Alekseev, Dmitrii (2016) - Scoring opportunity sliding into the high slot and firing a shot after a Kayumov pass. Had several other big shots from distance. Competes defensively but his gaps and positioning weren't always great.

RUS #10 LD Makeev, Nikita (2016) - Smart and competitive in his own zone, plays bigger than his size. Good balance on skates when battling against bigger players. Did well distributing the puck on PP. Will need to show more offensive upside at his size.

RUS #11 LW Maltsev, Mikhail (2016) - Has size and keeps his feet moving which can make him a handful to handle. Scored by finding the puck in a scrum and putting it home. Willing to go to the net and use his body. Good effort on empty net goal.

RUS #12 LW Ivanyuzhenkov, Artem (2016) - Scored after receiving a pass off a 2 on 1 play. Didn't use size to his advantage with any consistency.

RUS #15 C Ivanov, Georgii (2017) - Had a nice wristshot goal coming from behind the net turning his body and roofing it. Really smart in reading offensive zone opportunities and making quick decisions, uses his feet well to throw off checkers and has some deception to his game as well.

RUS #17 C Rubtsov, German (2016) - Solid defensively and off the puck. Had one great move coming down the right side and cutting to the middle. Can get his stick on pucks and strip the opposing player. Didn't convince me on the offensive side of it, only showed any sort of dynamic offensive ability in isolated flashes. Wasn't a challenge for the defense to handle.

RUS #19 RW Slepets, Kirill (2017) - Struggled to get much time with the puck but he knows where to go. Was actually quite solid at checking and he'd open up for plays in the offensive zone but rarely got the puck to make anything happen.

RUS #25 C Mescheryakov, Mikhail (2016) - He's got good tools, can buy time for himself in the offensive zone but several times had no idea what to do with the puck once he got to that point. His tools looked better than his hockey IQ.

RUS #51 RW Kovalenko, Nikolay (2018) - Had a nice cut from the wall to the front of the net creating a scoring chance. Nice read and a pass to Maltsev on a 2 on 1 as well. Small, but showed some upside for the future. Seems stronger on his skates than size would suggest.

RUS #77 G Sukhachev, Vladislav (2016) - Flashed his ability with the glove. Was rarely challenged from close but he had no problem making saves on shots from further out. Did a good job handling the puck and actually picked up a primary assist by flinging the puck into open space and a rushing Ivanov. Only goal he gave up he seemed to lose track of the puck by being partly screened on a point shot.

Canada West vs United States, WJAC, December 15th, 2015

CAW #6 LD Pasichnuk, Brinson (2016) - Gets into position quickly and was again quite aggressive against the puck-carrier, takes away time and space from forwards. His shot selection from the point could be better, sometimes forced a slapshot when the lane wasn't there. Decent breakout passes, but can be slightly frantic with the puck forcing plays that aren't there.

CAW #8 RD Fabbro, Dante (2016) - Had sequences where he showed high-end two way play, defending well then dishing off the puck with ease even making long accurate passes on his backhand. That said, he was pretty inconsistent shift-to-shift, some sloppiness in his game and at times lackadaisical execution. Had a weak drop pass that was intercepted and resulted in a dangerous turnover.

CAW #9 LD Cholowski, Dennis (2016) - Mostly solid though not as adventurous in puck-movement as his partner Fabbro. Had one chance to finish on a backhand after sneaking up into the slot. No glaring mistakes. Preferred simple decisions with the puck, though he wasn't flawless.

CAW #10 C Jost, Tyson (2016) - Nice pass into the slot recognizing a linemate sliding into open ice. Good puck-handling, has natural ability to use his own movement to dictate the play, uses his feet well to change angles of attack and uses deception to throw defensemen off-guard. Very fast at recognizing open space and open lanes both for passing and scoring plays.

CAW #20 LW Van Tetering, Troy (2016*) - Had a nice drive around Reinke using the top hand on his stick to protect the puck before cutting to the net. Another good effort on the backcheck lifting a stick and stealing the puck. Was useful defensively as well taking the puck out of the zone after his team got stuck in their own end.

CAW #29 LW Betts, Kyle (2016) - Had a good checking game, thought he was especially good at reading the neutral zone and pressuring US movement up the ice. Was good at quickly joining the rush after turnovers committed by US. Pretty simple offensive zone game, was driving to the post both with and without the puck.

CAW #31 G Murray, Matthew (2016) - Made saves on unobstructed shots and didn't give up any bad rebounds. Thought he could have challenged the shooter a bit more by coming out of his crease on some shots, but it was a pretty solid game for him.

USA #6 LW Zimmer, Max (2016) - Good lateral ability, skating made him challenging to be picked up by defensemen. Liked to take the puck wide and circle the offensive zone looking for passes to the middle, though he would take it there himself if there was no other option. One of his stronger shifts led to a goal by Chase Pearson.

USA #9 RD Peeke, Andrew (2016) - He competed well and was moving his feet consistently, he was better at utilizing his skating on defense than as an offensive threat. Was willing to get involved physically in battling for pucks. Had a point shot that took a big rebound off the boards and was cleaned up into the net.

USA #15 LW Jozefek, Grant (2016) - He was below average in defensive zone, too much puck-watching and gliding around. Better in the offensive zone, flashes of skill and skating but not enough to get by without a consistent off-the-puck effort in this game.

USA #24 RW Knierim, William (2016) - Had one good chance in front of the net but couldn't control the puck in time to finish the play. Threw a big hit in response to Canada's physical play. Had one bad play losing the puck in his feet in neutral zone that resulted in a turnover, then failed to clear the puck out of his zone. His shifts were pretty sparse.

Kelowna Rockets at Moose Jaw Warriors, December 16th, 2015

KEL #7 LD Johansen, Lucas (2016) - Good first pass and has awareness to find open lanes. He was good in transition but didn't' really show much as far as being a defensive presence in his own end or an offensive threat from the offensive zone blueline.

KEL #16 RW Lind, Kole (2017) - He and Dube were setting each other up for scoring chances, he had a couple of good passes hitting players sliding into the slot. Pretty smart game but clearly a support player to Dube who drove the line.

KEL #19 C Dube, Dillon (2016) - He scored the only goal of the game with a one timer from the right circle on the PP. Good pace to his game, battled well and made some accurate passes despite being tackled by the player checking him. Got robbed by Sawchenko on a 2 on 1.

KEL #25 RD Foote, Cal (2017) - Big size, skating will need to improve, good smarts, even saw some PP time. Puck-handling was average. A lot to like for the 2017 NHL draft, he already logs considerable minutes and doesn't look out of place at all.

MJW #2 RD Brook, Josh (2017) - This is the second consecutive game where I saw him take the puck end to end for a scoring chance. His skating game is getting consistently better throughout the season. He wasn't the toughest guy to play against around the net but his positioning was alright.

MJW #18 C Quinney, Landon (2016) - He saw more minutes than usual due to key players missing from the lineup. He had a good checking game moving his feet and racing for pucks, but didn't show the skill needed to create plays with the puck.

MJW #21 C Howden, Brett (2016) - He left the game early in the first period after crashing into the boards and didn't return.

MJW #22 C Gregor, Noah (2016) - With both Point and Howden out of the game he was relied upon to be a key contributor and did really well in that role. He also played centre in this game which forced him to be more involved at even strength. He did a real good job, looked a lot more proactive than in my last viewing where he was waiting for the centre to get him the puck in scoring positions. He was constantly buzzing around the play. More give and go plays with him as the center made the pace of his line better than what I saw previously.

MJW #31 G Sawchenko, Zach (2016) - Never has any wasted movement. He had two strong lateral saves robbing Dube on a 2 on 1 and then Lind on a 3 on 1 play. Rebound control was good most of the time. Like in my other viewings he gives up that one goal that's borderline questionable, this time it was Dube with a one timer that went through his legs, no real screen on the play either. Outside of that, he was really strong though.

MJW #71 LW Popugaev, Nikita (2017) - His puck-decisions need to get better but the potential is apparent. Was prone to losing the puck or skating himself into trouble, tunnel vision on the occasion. Despite a couple of turnovers he was competing well in this game though.

Kitchener Rangers at London Knights, December 16, 2015

OHL Regular Season

KIT #23 LW Mascherin, Adam (2016) - Good end to end rush but a bad pass negated the scoring chance. Scored a bit of a soft one from the point on the power play for 1-0 goal. Took holding penalty on the offensive zone. Good positioning and quick finished to score 3-4 goal with 45 seconds left to give his team a chance in the final minute.

LON #3 D Mattinen, Nicolas (2016) - Jumped in from the point during a scramble at the top of the crease and jammed home 3-2 goal for his first career OHL goal.

LON #17 LW Henderson, Eric (2016) - Feet are heavy which really affects his mobility. Struggled with the pace a bit. Second penalty killing unit. Finished his checks on the forecheck. Good stick placement defensively to get his stick on some passes. Second power play unit.

LON #49 LW Jones, Max (2016) - Will sometimes decide before he gets the puck that he wants to shoot which results in him struggling to get his shots through at times. Great pass through traffic to set up scoring chance. Top unit power play and penalty kill. Good positioning and quick release to score on rebound for 2-1 goal. Not playing nearly as physical as he should be in certain situations. Took the puck along the wall and used his speed and puck protect to drive net then nice move followed by a hard accurate shot to score 4-2 goal. Smart play when team was getting penalized to suck opponent into punching him, quickly hitting the ice making it a 4 on 4 situation.

LON #63 C Pu, Cliff (2016) - Good compete down low in defensive zone. Stopped on one on one chances quick hands and good speed to drive the net, create chance and draw power play. Drew two more power plays in the second once when battling for the puck and again while protecting the puck and was easy to knock down. Was one of the players who really stepped up his game in absence of teammates. Great speed and desire to win races to the puck and turn them into scoring chances. Won about 33 percent in the face-off circle.

LON #98 D Mete, Victor (2016) - Took a pass at the offensive line and carried the puck out to centre forcing whole team to regroup. Rushes puck decisions in the defensive zone at times. Isn't pushing the pace the way someone of his skating and skill should be. Was effective on the powerplay; a good pass helped set up 1-1 goal. Early second he showed off his speed to rush into the zone and made a centering pass that lead to 2-1 goal, got second assist. Played top unit in all game situations.

Final Score: London Knights: 4 - Kitchener Rangers: 3

Kamloops Blazers at Swift Current Broncos, December 19th, 2015

KAM #12 LW Kryski, Jake (2016) - He did well with his speed through the neutral zone, gained the offensive zone well but struggled to establish possession for his team once there. Scored a goal by picking up his own rebound that bounced weirdly off the boards beating the D to the puck. Had another great effort beating Sissons with a diving play on the empty net goal.

KAM #27 LD Kneen, Nolan (2017) - Real solid game in his own zone. Played a physical game and was really engaging in protecting the middle of the ice. Accurate outlets but didn't look like he felt comfortable trying more with the puck just yet.

KAM #32 LW Loewen, Jermaine (2016) - Played limited minutes. Skated well at his size, good on the forecheck. Had a good backcheck too after his D turned the puck over. Not a lot of skill with the puck but he sees the ice and the lanes well enough.

KAM #38 LD Davidson, Dawson (2016) - Not as dangerous offensively as in my other viewings of him. Did really well skating the puck out of his zone. Not the biggest guy but he's quite sturdy, wins battles against bigger players. I thought he had a strong game after the first period.

KAM #41 C Pilon, Garrett (2016) - Quiet night for him overall. One good chance after Swift Current turned the puck over, he picked up the puck and made a nice backhand pass. Supported his defensemen down low. He supports the play really well all over, was always looking to make his linemates' job easier.

KAM #42 LD Vala, Ondrej (2016) - He wasn't terrible but made some questionable decisions with the puck. Not as physical as he can be either. Iced the puck with an inaccurate pass, passed the puck to a linemate who already had a Swift Current player breathing down his neck which led to turnovers...It was a pretty underwhelming game for him.

SWI #2 LD Sissons, Colby (2016) - He looked improved and was a much bigger factor on the ice compared to my intial viewings. He had a couple of skilful plays in the offensive zone and was more involved in bringing the puck out of his own end.

SWI #4 LD Jensen, Kade (2016*) - In this game he effectively had pro-level decision-making amongst junior kids. Didn't see him make one play that wouldn't work at a higher level. However being passed over already once, you would like to see him dominate more than just settling for being a smart low-maintenance player.

SWI #5 RD Minulin, Artyom (2017) - He did a solid job playing his minutes. Good first pass and his ability to read the play is good but he'll have to start using his 6'2 200 frame in his his own zone. Looked too soft for that size.

SWI #17 C Steenbergen, Tyler (2016) - He was excellent through first two periods but really fell of a cliff in the third. Played with great energy and was more physically involved than his size would suggest. Didn't create scoring chances for himself but wins pucks and sniffs around in the offensive zone.

SWI #27 RD Lajoie, Max (2016) - He played the right side at even strength and the left side on PP. Good on powerplay as always. Had more bite in his own zone than what I've previously seen out of him this season. His first pass still looks a bit clunky, there are situations where he either waits too long when he has an open lane or forces a pass where there is nobody open.

Russia at Czech Republic, December 26th, 2015

CZE #28 RW Tomasek, David (2016) - Skilled winger with decent mobility and good size. He flashed couple of times his skills but couldn't do big things.

CZE #25 D Hronek, Filip (2016) - Filip is a decent puck-moving d-man with good mobility. He lacks of toughness which came up against big Russian forwards. Got good vision but need improve his defensive game.

CZE #11 LW Stransky, Simon (2016) - Highly skilled player with great hockey sense. Like most of the guys he wasn't his best at this game but he surely showed his potential. Great player in the o-zone but he needs to improve his quickness.

CZE #27 D Masin, Dominik (Drafted by Tampa Bay Lightning) - Was the best d-man on ice. Great decisions with puck and played flawless game in the d-zone.

CZE #13 C Zacha, Pavel (Drafted by New Jersey Devils) - Pavel had a subpar game but showed his physical ability couple of times giving hard hits. He wasn't that effective in the d-zone even though he made some great passes.

CZE #18 RW Spacek, Michael (Drafted by Winnipeg Jets) - Great plays in the o-zone and scored and scored a shootout goal. Great puck handling skills and vision which really showed at this game.

CZE #20 Zboril, Jakub (Drafted by Boston Bruins) - Showed some toughness and was solid in the d-zone. Decent overall game but made some un-accurate passes.

RUS #22 D Voronkov, Yegor (2016) - Was pretty lost in the d-zone and lost some battles around corners. Good passing skills and mobility and got some all-round ability even though he struggled in own zone.

RUS #28 D Rykov, Yegor (2016) - D-man with good size and skating ability. Yegor is a smart kid with good vision and passing skills. He started the game pretty bad he was getting better. Made some mistakes with out puck couple of times... like positioning in the d-zone.

RUS #13 LW Polunin, Alexander (2016) - Polunin flashed his great speed and puck skills. He's not big kid but got strong lower body and good balance so the size isn't that big problem. Showed couple of times his great playmaking ability.

RUS #26 RW Korshkov, Yegor (2016) - Big winger with good skillset and vision. Like his teammates he got a slow start but was better in the third period. Big kid who protects the puck well and doesn't afraid to get his nose dirty. Good around corners.

RUS #8 C Svetlakov, Andrei (2016) - Andrei is a fast centerman with great puck-handling skills. Pure offensive weapon who can create scoring opportunities to his line mates. Got also hard and accurate shot. He reads the game well and got some great allround ability.

RUS #16 RW Lazarev, Maxim (2016) - Not a big kid but got decent offensive instincts. Good finisher with solid shot but more important he reads the game well and can find scoring opportunities. Physicalness is a concern and doesn't stand out with his quickness. This really wasn't his best game and from time to time you didn't even notice him on ice.

RUS #9 D Provorov, Ivan (Drafted by Philadelphia Flyers) - Had troubles in the d-zone and didn't play at his level. Showed his great passing skills and blueline skills tho.

RUS #25 C Dergachyov, Alexander (Drafted by Los Angeles Kings) - Played gritty game but wasn't that effective. Played decent two way game and worked hard but his offensive game was below average.

RUS #16 C Kamenev, Vladislav (Drafted by Nashville Predators) - He was the most dangerous forward of his team. Used his size, speed and puck-handling skills creating great scoring opportunities but missed some great chances.

RUS #17 RW Kaprizov, Kirill (Drafted by Minnesota Wild - Skilled winger who got great offensive instincts. Played really mature game and was dangerous in the o-zone.

RUS #7 LW Svechnikov, Yevgeni (Drafted by Detroit Red Wings) - Used his size and quickness a lot but missed some scoring chances. Played with passion and worked hard.

Belarus at Finland, December 26th, 2015

FIN #4 D Juolevi, Olli (2016) - Scored two assists and played a steady game. Calm puck-moving d-man who made great decisions with puck.

FIN #9 RW Puljujärvi, Jesse (2016) - One of the best players on ice. Used his speed and created scoring chances to his line mates. He recorded two goals and a one primary assist.

FIN #29 LW Laine, Patrik (2016) - Played great together with Puljujärvi. Always tried to find a way to shoot and succeeded well. Scored a one goal. He used his size good and handled the puck in small places very well.

FIN #23 RW Repo, Sebastian (2016) - Played in the fourth line but also in the first powerplay unit. Didn't show much but scored a one beautiful goal by using his size and protecting skills. Good speed and great player in front of the net.

FIN #12 LW Björkqvist, Kasper (2016) - A grinder who did that job well. Good speed and has some puck skills but played in the fourth line and didn't got that much ice time. He worked hard and didn't do any mistakes.

FIN #30 GK Vehviläinen, Veini (2016) - It wasn't easy game for him but succeeded well. Recorded 10 saves in whole game.

FIN # LW Rantanen, Mikko (Drafted by Colorado Avalanche) - Was pretty lost whole game. Scored a empty net goal.

FIN # C Hintz, Roope (Drafted by Dallas Stars) - Played strong two way game and showed his playmaking ability.

FIN #24 RW Kapanen, Kasperi (Toronto Maple Leafs) - Couple of great shifts but made false some bad mistakes. Flashed his skillset and speed.

FIN # D Saarijärvi, Vili (Drafted by Detroit Red Wings) - Amazing first passes and good plays in the blueline. Wasn't as good as usually on powerplay.

FIN # LW Saarela, Aleksi (Drafted by New York Rangers) - Strong kid who was good around corners and worked hard. Scored an assist.

FIN # C Nättinen, Julius (Drafted by Anaheim Ducks) - Calm centerman who made good decisions with and without puck. He's role is quite small which u can in his game. Tries to play simple way.

FIN # C Sebastian Aho (Drafted by Carolina Hurricanes) - Great passing game for the whole night and played strong two way game. One of the best players on ice.

BLR #3 D Vorobey, Pavel (2016) - Big d-man with good mobility and vision. Played very well and didn't do mistakes. Got along with fast Finns and can play good game with puck.
BLR #8 C Sharangovich, Yegor (2016) - Couldn't do much but Yegor got a good speed and puck-handling skills. Lost the puck couple of times in bad places. Lack of hockey sense.

Rouyn-Noranda vs. Gatineau Olympiques, QMJHL, December 28th, 2015

Robert Guertin Arena

ROU #3 RD Neveu, Jacob (2016) – Big body stay at home defensemen, played well tonight, good skating defensemen, struggled tonight in the 1st period getting lost in his own zone, he got caught standing still and watching the puck and lost his man and turned into a goal against, played physical tonight, kept everything simple tonight, low maintenance defensemen, he doesn't like to hang out with the puck a whole lot, no options coming out of the zone he would use the glass effectively, has a good stick and broke up a few cross ice passes in the dzone, good first pass out of zone, has a good shot from the point, low hard shot and gets the puck through, didn't show any signs of an offensive upside.

ROU #6 RD Myers, Philippe (PHI) – Played a solid game tonight, big stay at home D, that plays every situation, hard nose player to play against, physical in his own end, good first pass tonight, has a good hard shot and he uses it on the power play, tries to carry the puck too much which turned into turnovers, needs to keep it simple and not try to do too much, uses his big frame well on the penalty kill and didn't give Gatineau much chances offensively.

ROU #10 LW Dzierkals, Martin (TOR) – Was outstanding tonight, showed his very high hockey skill and hockey IQ, he was excellent with the puck on his stick, very smooth stickhandle with the puck and could stickhandle in a phone booth, really good acceleration with the puck, and he uses his edges really well especially in transition, was the power play qb tonight, was really good at finding the open player and making it look effortless, would like to see him shoot the puck more, he passed up a couple quality scoring chances for the pass, not physical but got into a few mixed up after the whistles, took a couple shifts off and wasn't effective would like to see him compete hard every shift.

GAT #8 RD Carrier, Alexandre (NSH) – He played a great 2 way game tonight, moved the puck good, crisp hard passes, when he has the puck he slows the game and always makes the right decisions, very smart player and read's plays well, played in every situation and was good in every situation, he isn't physical but has good body positioning on defenders and always came away with the puck, had really good gap control not allowing Rouyn to gain the zone, has a good shot, always shoots for the tip.

GAT #11 LW Abramov, Vitali (2016) – Was good tonight, generated 4-5 good quality scoring chances by using his speed and hockey smarts, when he gets his feet moving he is a tough person to contain with or without the puck, made some nice moves on defenders turning them inside out and using his quick release and good shot for chances, would like to see him shoot the puck more he gave up a couple chances to try and make pretty play, got caught a few times with his head down along the boards and was hit hard, he is really good at controlling the play on the PP and sucking people too him and finding the open man for the scoring chance.

GAT #31 G Bellemare, Mathieu (2016) – Played well tonight, wasn't tested a whole lot tonight, but when needed the save he made it, very agile goalie and moves side to side really well and has quick feet, small goalie but makes himself look big in the nets, has a quick glove hand, and was very calm in nets tonight not a lot of movement in the crease, battled through screens and tracked the puck well.

Final Score: Rouyn-Noranda 1   Gatineau 4

Sherbrooke Phoenix vs Quebec Remparts , December 28th 2015

SHE # 10 LW Gilbert, Kevin (2016): Sherbrooke forward had a nice game, scored a beautiful goal by accessing quickly the offensive zone and finding himself alone in front of Quebec goalie and beating him with a backhand shot on the stick side. He played a few times shorthanded, but lost a few battles along the boards by more physically imposing opponents than him.

SHE # 20 RW Johnston, Logan (2017): Played limited minutes doing some appearances during the game especially late in the game when the scores was 4-1 Sherbrooke. He is a decent skater and played a conservative game.

QUE # 91 LW Boucher, Matthew (2016): The fast forward player had a good game. He played a sound positional game in the offensive zone, which allowed him to score the only goal for Quebec today. He played on both special teams and did well particularly shorthanded when he was exercising a lot of pressure on the defense with his speed on the forecheck.

QUE # 14 LW Garneau, Olivier (2016): Remparts winger did well defensively. He played regularly shift 5 on 5 and in addition to shorthanded ice time. He got involved along the boards and was focus in his positioning in the defensive zone.

QUE # 21 RW Thierus, Lucas (2016): The forward was physically involved in the game battling along the boards and going for a few hits. He played a few times on the power play and positioned himself well in the slot without being able to capitalize.

QUE # 82 C Sutton, Jesse (2016): The big center player has played a few times on the power play on the second wave. He used his size to protect the puck along the boards. He positioned himself in front of the net on the power play. However, he lost control of the puck during some of his possessions.

Tri-City Storm at Green Bay Gamblers, December 28th, 2015

TRI #12 RW Duehr, Walker (2016) - Thick frame but hasn't played much of a heavy game at his size. Scored after the puck got loose into the slot after Washe created the turnover. Was not really much of a factor in this game.

TRI #15 C Washe, Paul (2017) - Really stood out for his compete level. Played a stingy game on both ends of the ice. Really got involved physically in one on one battles, not many big hits but his physicality definitely had a purpose. Picked up an assist after a great forechecking shift, where he killed Green Bay's puck-movement twice, the second the puck got loose into the slot and his linemate converted on his effort.

TRI #18 RW Meyer, Carson (2016*) - Scored on PP by tipping the puck on a shot from the blueline. Had another good chance in the slot but couldn't get a handle on the puck before losing his balance. The rest of his shifts he was mostly kept to the outside.

TRI #19 RW Allison, Wade (2016) - Had a good move on his blueline moving the puck past a pinching defenseman and getting a scoring chance out of it. Another great chance on an up-close one-timer on the far side post, didn't seem to get much on the puck though as the goalie got 'across in time to make the save.

TRI #20 LW Wahlin, Jake (2016*) - Made a nice pass to Meyer who would have been left with a great scoring chance if he got a proper handle on the puck. Moved his feet well, but there was no real impact coming out of it, didn't get the puck much on his stick. A secondary assist on PP on a routine pass back to the point.

TRI #26 C Limoges, Alex (2016) - His linemate Allison was doing most of the driving on that line, but Limoges had one or two opportunities just by being the late guy and reading the traffic and where the puck was. I thought he played an OK game as far as his reads as a center, but didn't do much to make himself stand out with any physical tool of his.

TRI #31 G Rasmussen, Dayton (2017) - He came into the net a couple of mins into second period after the starter got pulled. Thought he played well. Good rebound control on shots he could see, a heads-up game in traffic and tracked the puck well with bodies in front of him. Stopped Murphy's dekes on a 1 on 1. Had another quick reaction after the puck was trickling past the goal line and managed to somehow keep it out of the net with his defenseman also making an effort. Thought he gave his team a chance to stage a comeback.

GBG #20 RD Peeke, Andrew (2016) - Good backwards and lateral mobility, beautifully presented an easy pass to his D partner when he was under pressure. Crisp on-tape outlets to forwards with speed. Used his size defensively on the wall when needed. A very solid low-maintenance game overall.

Saskatoon Blades at Regina Pats, December 29th, 2015

SAS #9 C Hebig, Cameron (2016*) - Picked up an assist after Connor Gay scored off his faceoff win. Pretty quiet night for him offensively, didn't have a lot of offensive pressure nor any high-end scoring chances. His compete level as a checker was good.

SAS #23 RD Higson, Schael (2016) - He had a bad shift failing to clear the puck twice and then followed it up with a lazy play on his coverage of the player in the slot. Was pretty underwhelming defensively. Didn't do much offensively either, outside of one nice move to evade two forecheckers in the neutral zone which gave his team numerical advantage coming into the offensive zone.

SAS #25 LD Hajek, Libor (2016) - He started on RD and struggled in the first period. Blindly rimmed the puck around the boards which got intercepted. While protecting the front of the net area he had forwards sneaking behind his back that he was not aware of. Skated himself into trouble in the offensive zone, Brooks scored after his poor pinch and an errant pass. He settled into the game once he got moved back to LD and followed it up with a strong third period. Flashed his ability to move the puck up ice with a quick first few steps and was solid defensively from that point on.

SAS #47 RD Reid, Nolan (2016) - He was not much of a factor outside of one or two shifts where his quick release from the point caused some trouble to Regina.

REG #10 LW Berg, Adam (2016*) - He was effective on the forecheck and is a good player on the wall. Scored a goal on a 2 on 1 play off a Brooks pass.

REG #23 C Steel, Sam (2016) - A couple of good passes when coming into the zone and cutting back at the half wall looking to distribute the puck towards the middle. He scored on the PP coming off that same area and cutting to the middle. His offensive and defensive reads are generally on point. He's not much of a factor defensively or on the wall and is a bit too easy to play against. Although smart, he settled for just making plays that were there and rarely truly dictates the play on ice.

REG #39 RW Zablocki, Lane (2017) - He had a couple of good chances waiting for Steel to get him the puck near the far side post. Got involved in a couple of scrums.

REG #55 LD Schioler, Liam (2016) - Big frame but he was not very physical. Not the fastest with his feet but he had good patience with the puck and didn't force plays. Seemed rather comfortable handling the puck and was even useful with his delays letting the forwards to re-group before making a pass. Not much there offensively, the one time he tried to shoot it got blocked.

U.S.A. U20 vs. Switzerland U20, WJC, Round Robin, December 30, 2015

USA #4 LD Krys, Chad (2016) - A good all-directional skater who combined above-average footwork with slick hands. Not afraid to take his time with the puck as he has good stickhandling skill. Waited with the biscuit before making the right play.

USA #7 RW Tkachuk, Matthew (2016) - A good but not great skater who does a fantastic job of getting to the good areas. Owns a fantastic wristshot. Received a drop pass from Matthews and picked his shot blocker high from the top of the slot to put his team up 5-0. Good hands in tight, finishing a netfront feed from Matthews for his second goal of the game.

USA #34 LC Matthews, Auston (2016) - Great balance and power in his skating stride. Simply could not be knocked off his feet by smaller opponents. Able to split the defence with pure speed and power and earned himself a breakaway in the first period. Later, he set up a play and then finished all on his own; showed good hand-eye coordination batting a puck out of the air and into the net after a sweet deke move a and wristshot created some second chance opportunities. Carelessly tried to carry the puck out from behind the net resulting in a turnover and a goal against. Came back moments later to feed Tkachuk for his second goal of the game.

SWI #19 LW Hischier, Nico (2017) - Didn't give up on this game which is nice to see. Good skater with strong stickwork along the wall and down low. Also showed good vision on the rare occasion Switzerland saw some offensive zone possession time. Forced a turnover before feeding the puck into the slot for Timo Meier.

Guelph Storm at Kitchener Rangers, January 1, 2016

OHL Regular Season

GUE #2 D Tetrault, Levi (2016) - Made some excellent plays down low to contain but sometimes slow to react to where he's supposed to be.

GUE #4 D Carroll, Noah (2016) - Good pinch to keep play going. Puts pucks deep, made sure he got the red line and didn't shortcut. Good stick on rush to breakup play. Good hit one on one. Opponent split both defenders (Carroll and Garcia) and neither defended properly. Took hit to keep play going.

GUE #23 RW Hotchkiss, Matthew (2016) - Struggled to get much going with speed and struggled to get around opponents as well. Jumped on goaltender puck mistake to quickly finish 1-1 goal. Good path to the net and good scoring chance. Good penalty killing puck pressure to force opponents into rushing their plays. Good position in slot on the power play to jam home 2-1 goal.

GUE #24 RW Smith, Givani (2016) - Heavy feet and wide turns affected his puck pursuit but finishes his checks the first chance he gets.

GUE #25 C Burghardt, Luke (2016) - Compete level is off the charts. Good skating ability.

KIT #23 LW Mascherin, Adam (2016) - Nice pass to set up 1-0 goal. Laser release with great accuracy to score 3-2 goal. Showed off his vision creating offense.

Final Score: Kitchener Rangers: 3 - Guelph Storm: 2

London Knights at Sarnia Sting, January 2, 2016

OHL Regular Season

LON #2 Bouchard, Evan (2018) - Quick puck movement, consistent first pass.

LON #3 D Mattinen, Nicolas (2016) - Keeps it simple with the puck. In the second period he unloaded a big blast from the point to score 2-3 goal.

LON #17 LW Henderson, Eric (2016) - Skating is heavy which effected his forecheck. Gets pucks deep. Second power play unit.

LON #49 LW Jones, Max (2016) - Took puck for 2 on 0 short handed break but didn't look at teammate and goalie played the shot for easy save. Another short handed chance, this one 2 on 1 and he again put his head down and fired puck on goal for an easy save. Good dive to draw power play but was overdoing it a little much today resulting mostly in no calls. Nice move in overtime and with defender falling on play walked in and scored the 5-4 OT winner.

LON #98 D Mete, Victor (2016) - Struggled defensively early on facing big puck protecting forwards. Multiple solid rushes, some of which he passed and others he took to the net using his unique ability to fly back into position when it looks like he's caught. Top power play unit. Fired a decent wrister from the point to score 4-4 goal.

SAR #13 C Chmelevski, Sasha (2017) - Showed quick hands and pick patience to create offence. Great evasiveness to shake defender, then perfect pass to set up 2-0 goal. Great play in slot to bang home 3-0 goal.

Final Score: London Knights: 5 - Sarnia Sting: 4 – OT

Finland vs Canada, WJC U20 quarter-finals, January 2nd, 2016

FIN #3 LD Keskitalo, Miro (2016**) - Was guilty of two horrible turnovers in the first period. One of his passes got intercepted on the breakout and he fumbled the puck on his stick on another occasion. Not the best game with the puck on his stick but did reasonably well on PK and has good positioning and awareness around his net.

FIN #4 LD Juolevi, Olli (2016) - He was the best defenseman on the ice. Very fluid skating, calm even under pressure. Executed accurate and crisp passes on the breakout, consistently moving the puck up ice. Ran the point on the PP and did a good job there. Had a couple of nice offensive zone moves going around players and opening up space before dishing a pass to an open teammate.

FIN #9 RW Puljujarvi, Jesse (2016) - He played a good competitive game on both ends of the ice. A polished defensive game for a draft eligible player at this level. Works on the backcheck. Good vision with the puck, can win battles and then make high-end skill plays to find open linemates. Did a good job getting open and finding scoring chances but didn't quite manage to convert.

FIN #21 LW Kalapudas, Antti (2016**) - He showed some upside when picking up speed in the neutral zone. Didn't have much possession time in offensive zone. He scored a wristshot goal after Fleury blew a tire giving him a clear lane to the net.

FIN #29 LW Laine, Patrik (2016) - Flashed all of his tools – skating, size, physicality, shot, and vision. He scored twice with one timer blasts from the high-slot area. Made a great stretch pass from his own blueline to a rushing Puljujarvi with Aho then finishing on the play. Some of his puck control in-tight could be better and he could stand to use his size on the wall but his upside is very high and his shot is already elite. Skating is improving, wouldn't say it looked like a weakness at his size. On his line, Puljujarvi did most of the digging in the corners while Laine laid back a bit more and approached the game in a more cerebral manner.

FIN #30 G Vehvilainen, Veini (2016*) - He had a tough game. Looked shaky from the drop of the puck and never managed to come up with a big save. Couldn't freeze the puck on Strome's goal, Crouse wristshot was from ways out. Didn't seem like it was his night on either shots from outside or with traffic in front of him, struggled at both.

CAN #4 LD Fleury, Haydn (2014 Carolina) - He fell down when defending a zone entry play against Kalapudas which resulted in a clear lane to the net and a goal against Canada. Good physical tools, but his defensive zone game needs to be further polished out. A player with his size and skating should be able to keep his coverage tighter and push the play to the outside more effectively than he did. Can skate with the puck.

CAN #6 RD Hickey, Brandon (2014 Calgary) - Had a real smart game. Especially in transition he makes quality decisions with and without the puck. Whether it's defending his blueline or making a first pass out of the zone, he did well at both.

CAN #9 C Strome, Dylan (2015 Arizona) - He was Canada's best forward in the first half of the game. His wristshot was a threat. Scored a goal jamming a puck past Vehvilainen after he didn't manage to cover it up. Thought he showed some lack of maturity later in the game as he seemed to get a bit rattled and overly emotional with the way the game was going.

CAN #11 LW Perlini, Brendan (2014 Arizona) - At times he looks like he's a bit too passive looking for scoring chances instead of getting involved, but he had a decent game. He won't run the line for you, but he protected the puck well on the wall and came up with several scoring chances by reading the play. Lacked the finishing touch in this game though.

CAN #12 LW Gauthier, Julien (2016) - Clearly already looks up to par when it comes to physical ability. Big body, skates well. He had two good chances in front of the net. Real nice play that he started in neutral zone then got the puck back while driving the net with speed. There looked a bit too much start-stop type of skating in his game, felt like he could maybe use gear changes a bit differently and find better angles to get involved up and down the ice.

CAN #16 RW Marner, Mitch (2015 Toronto) - He was very quiet early on but came up with a big effort in the third period. Canada didn't have much going for them in the third period, but you could say Marner was single-handedly keeping them in the game. If Marner finished on all of the scoring chances he created, he might have even put them into the lead.

CAN #17 RW Konecny, Travis (2015 Philadelphia) - He scored the first goal of the game for Canada. Plays his heart out on his shifts. Didn't see tons of time but when he was out there he did his job. Good skater, good skill level, and can give you a grinder-style look as well with his ability to hound the puck.

CAN #18 RW Virtanen, Jake (2014 Vancouver) - He was having a good first half of the game. His ability to extend plays in the offensive zone looked better than in his draft year and his puck-support looked improved. He did take two very stupid penalties that had a key outcome on the game though, first taking a penalty on what would have been a 5 on 3 for Canada and taking another offensive zone penalty late in the game that ended Canada's PP. Not sure what he was thinking on those plays.

CAN #20 RD McKeown, Roland (2014 Carolina) - Thought he was Canada's best defenseman in their own zone. He didn't have much going for him offensively but his compete level was very good. Blocked shots, got his stick on pucks, used his body... Good mobility and real sturdy game in his own end.

Final score: FIN 6 CAN 5

Red Deer Rebels at Prince Albert Raiders, January 5th, 2016

RED #11 C de Wit, Jeff (2016) - He surprised me with his puck-distribution on PP early in the game as that same component of his game is not as commonly seen even strength. Saw PK time as well. He's a pretty consistent player shift-to-shift, competes at both ends of the ice. At this point he's mostly useful utilizing his size on the wall, on the forecheck and in the defensive zone. He struggled to create much with the puck.

RED #14 RW Pratt, Austin (2017) - Big frame, skating and a hard-nosed game will make him alluring in next year's draft. Had a good chance early in the game trying to jam the puck into the net from up-close.

RED #22 LW Hagel, Brandon (2016) - Had a tough night. Struggled handling the puck and receiving passes in the offensive zone. The positive was that he had a couple of good plays clogging lanes and getting his stick on the puck in the neutral zone.

RED #27 RW Rattie, Taden (2016) - Played the role of a pest. Physical. Had a chance late on a loose puck in front of the net but didn't manage to convert on it.

PRI #6 LD Budik, Vojtech (2016) - Him and Bleackley seemed to have a couple of good battles. Budik got beat wide by Bleackley who cut to the middle and somehow got the puck to go through into the net. The second time on a similar play Budik did a real good job intercepting a lateral pass with his stick to break up the play. Budik also showed some willingness to engage as he got involved in a scrum with Rattie. His play with the puck was good, he shows good comfort level making passes on his backhand as well. Sometimes he could have made his outlets at a higher pace. Continues to be good at retrieving loose pucks with his skating.

PRI #19 RW Gardiner, Reid (2016**) - He picked up a goal and an assist on the PP. The goal was a nice one-timer from the faceoff dot area. He had one good play stealing the puck from behind from a careless defenseman but was otherwise underwhelming even strength.

PRI #25 C Montgomery, Sean (2016) - He failed to get into a rhythm and be involved in the game. There might have been one or two good shifts, but the lack of physical tools and a just average skill level hurts him in games like these. His positioning is good, his ability to see the play is good but he simply couldn't do much with it. The lack of size limited his ability to win defensive battles, the average speed and skill level limited him offensively.
PRI #27 C Kelly, Parker (2017) - Had a key interception in offensive zone that led to Tkatch's goal which put Prince Albert up by one in third period.

PRI #28 LW Coleman, Luke (2016) - I really liked him in my first viewing of the year but he has never shown that level of play since. He did a good job trying to be a net presence with his large body in the first period but was underwhelming outside of that. Shaky execution with the puck, his passes got intercepted. His skating was only ever utilized to gain zone entry but he not once used a cut-back or changed the angle of attack in a manner that would allow for his teammates to catch up and get open.

Scout's Notes: Simon Stransky (Prince Albert) and Josh Mahura (Red Deer) were not in the lineup.

Sweden vs USA (WJC U20 Bronze Medal Game), January 5th, 2016

SWE #16 LW Grundstrom, Carl (2016) - He scored his first goal of the tournament by driving the net while Eriksson-Ek hit him with a pass from the left circle area. He was utilized on PK and did a good job there as his aggressive up-tempo game serves him well with pressuring players. Finished his checks and was physical both dishing it out as well as sacrificing his body to battle and to make plays. He sometimes rushes decisions with the puck and is prone to forcing passes that aren't there.

SWE #18 C Asplund, Rasmus (2016) - Active stick on back-check. His ability to read the ice looked very good at both ends of the ice. Competed well too even though he will need to bulk up. His line had a defensive zone breakdown that led to Bjork's goal but Asplund was generally in correct positions defensively. He's smart about his shot selection and seems to easily switch between being a playmaker and a shooter depending on the play that is there.

SWE #19 LW Nylander, Alex (2016) - He had a somewhat quiet game compared to what he has done in previous games, especially in group stage. USA defended him well and he was forced to the outside a lot. Good puck-handling allows him to alleviate forechecking pressure. Can change angles of attack at speed while keeping control of the puck.

USA #4 LD Krys, Chad (2016) - He was the 7th defenseman and saw limited minutes. Didn't really hurt his team in any manner but didn't contribute much either. Can skate with players at this level but has some further development ahead in order to be a contributor.

USA #7 LW Tkachuk, Matthew (2016) - Nothing new with him, he dominates the areas around the net. Skating is average and will probably need to improve if he wants to be a factor all over the ice at the next level. Did exactly what everyone expected him to do with being a scoring threat in front of the net, scoring twice. His ability to see the ice and find those goals in high-quality scoring areas remains a positive for him against any kind of competition.

USA #14 RW Eansor, Scott (2016**) - He moved his feet, competed and was a bit of a pest on the ice. Good on the forecheck, worked his butt off in his own zone. He did his job.

USA #21 LW Hitchcock, Ryan (2016**) - He played on a line with Schmaltz and Boeser and managed to keep up just fine. Had some nice give and go plays with Schmaltz and plays bigger than his size on the wall.

USA #25 RD McAvoy, Charles (2016) - He was average in his own zone. Decent vision and passing game. He had one nice play coming from the point to the boards and then cutting inside towards the net for a scoring chance with Swedish D caught flat-footed. Did not really excel in any one aspect of the game but held his own as a 2016 draft eligible. It would be fair to say that he can already provide some quality minutes at this level.

USA #34 C Matthews, Auston (2016) - It was a quiet night for him with other USA forwards filling up the scoreboard. He started off a bit slow with just flashes of brilliance but picked it up in the second period. There was a type of feeling with him that it's all just a part of routine for him, almost as if he was bored as USA started to take the game into their hands. Had a couple of great shifts that immediately made it obvious he's the best player on the ice.

Scout's Notes: The game's tempo and the competitive spirit was somewhat lacking. It only got worse once USA started running up the score late in the second period.

Final score: SWE 3 USA 8

Windsor Spitfires at Barrie Colts, January 7, 2016

Final score: 3-1 Barrie
WSR #17 D Stanley, Logan (2016) – Stanley had a good stick in the defensive zone and used it effectively to steer players wide and disrupt passing lanes. His one-on-one defense as a whole was excellent as he played the man and didn't over commit or panic. He showed good defensive awareness getting back and clearing a puck off the goal line before it crossed. Stanley made a good first pass, was smart with the puck and kept everything simple. On the 2nd power play unit he did a good job of moving the puck around and also showed the ability to get pucks through traffic. He was pick pocketed a couple times in the defensive zone but as a whole he was very solid at both sides of the ice.

WSR #21 C Brown, Logan (2016) – Brown showed good vision finding open teammates in this game and for the most part his passes found tape. He used his size effectively early on when protecting the puck but he wasn't very physical and certainly didn't assert himself. He had a couple chances but was pretty quiet and had an underwhelming game as a whole.

WSR #26 RW Carter, Cole (2016) – Carter had a couple controlled entries but didn't accomplish much beyond that in his limited ice. He was on the receiving end of a big hit when he was caught with his head down and he struggled to create offensively. Carter had a couple shot attempts but failed to get any on target. He was sealed off easily a couple different times and really didn't make an impact at either end of the ice.

WSR #31 D Sergachev, Mikhail (2016) – Sergachev showed great poise and patience in this game. He didn't force anything that wasn't there and made a lot of good passes under pressure. His outlets were accurate and when no lanes were available he had no problem carrying the puck up ice himself. He made some firm passes and also showed great touch feathering pucks through tight lanes. On the power play he moved the puck very fluidly and he did a nice job of walking the line and waiting for lanes to open up. Sergachev didn't go out of his way to hit someone but he didn't shy away from physicality.

BAR #10 D Murray, Justin (2016) – Murray was hit and miss in this game. He had a big hit on Brendan Lemieux and played with an edge for much of the night. He also had a couple nice zone exits and did a good job of holding the line and pinching to keep plays alive. On the negative end of things he missed a few outlets and iced the puck a couple times as a result.

BAR #16 LW Hawerchuk, Ben (2016) – Hawerchuk wasn't at his best in this game. He didn't create much offensively and he missed the few chances he did get. Hawerchuk also had a couple defensive zone turnovers.

BAR #18 LW Magwood, Zach (2016) – Magwood had a couple careless giveaways in the neutral zone and defensive zone. He struggled to get the puck out and spent a lot of time chasing play in his own zone. He showed good speed through the neutral zone and made a couple nice plays with the puck but as a whole more bad than good happened with him on the ice.

Ohio State University at University of Wisconsin, Janaury 8th 2016, NCAA

WIS #9 LW Kunin, Luke (2016) – Kunin showed good physicality and willingness to battle for pucks along the wall and generate space in front of the net. Luke Did try to do too much on his own at times and could have added more simplicity to his game tonight. Displayed good speed and skill through the neutral zone and drove the net hard all night.

WIS #15 LW Freytag, Matthew (2016+) – Freytag was really good tonight and his line created most of Wisconsin's scoring chances. Brought a physical element, finished his checks and created turnovers on the fore-check. Showed good stick work and anticipation by picking the pocket of the Ohio State's defenders on a couple of occasions. Protected the puck along the wall and was good on the cycle.

WIS #30 G Jurusik, Matt (2016) – Jurusik kept Wisconsin in the game for the first two periods, making a number of great 1 on 1 saves and showed the ability to get from side to side to make some back-door saves. A couple of poor turnovers by his team in the 3rd period resulted in a 2-0 loss. Jurusik is starting to look more calm and poised in the crease and is progressing as the season moves along.

WIS #17 RW Johnson, Will (2016+) – Johnson continues to show good puck possession ability. Had a couple of nice deflections in front of the net that just missed. Played with a lot of pace and physicality.

WIS #4 LD Sexton, Patrick (Free Agent) – Sexton left the game with a lower body injury after going into the boards feet first but prior to the injury Sexton was having a pretty good game. Like most nights the physicality is a key part of Sexton's game. He initiates contact in most situations, was very strong on his skates and made good simple outlet passes.

Final Score: 2-0 Ohio State

Windsor Spitfires at Barrie Colts, January 9, 2016

OHL Regular Season

WSR #17 D Stanley, Logan (2016) - Good puck play to advance it up ice. Puck skills have advanced a lot over the course of the season. Took a penalty but on the delay made a huge play to sweep the puck off the goal line to save a goal. Simply overpowers opponents at times in the offensive zone. Fired an nice wrister through traffic from the point, rang off the post, had some net if it was a couple inches to the right. Good job in offensive zone moving puck making smart simple decisions. Got stick on centring pass but went right to opponent for 1-1 goal. Top penalty killing minutes and secondary power play minutes. Played final minute down 2-1.

WSR #21 C Brown, Logan (2016) - Lost battles down low and didn't show much urgency on back check. Has a decent shot, fired a scoring chance off the post. Good puck movement when on top power play unit utilizing the additional time and space to execute passes. Played final minute down 2-1.

WSR #31 D Sergachev, Mikhail (2016) - Great job on penalty kill clearing zone. Excellent play taking a pass in his skates, kicking it up to his stick then quickly walked in from point creating scoring chance. Played final minute down 2-1.

WSR #32 G Culina, Mario (2016*) - Stays low, very good quickness. Good recovery. Cut down angles very well on partial breaks and did very well taking away the net on shots down the middle in general. Very quick.

BAR #3 D Lizotte, Cameron (2016*) - Multiple big hits early. Took an undisciplined penalty cross checking opponent down out of frustration, resulted in a Windsor power play goal. Played top unit penalty kill when not in the box. Chased the big hit constantly. Good stick on a 2 on 1 rush to break up scoring chance. Was regularly out of position defensively

BAR #10 D Murray, Justin (2016) - Good stick one on one. Fired puck for icing. Second penalty killing unit. Competes but sometimes outmatched down low.

Final Score: Barrie Colts: 3 - Windsor Spitfires: 1

Youngstown Phantoms at Madison Capitols, January 9th, 2016, USHL

YNG #26 LW Morrison, Cameron (2016) – It was a bit of a strange game for Morrison tonight. He seemed to battle the puck and was easy to separate from the puck at times but had moments where he showed how dominate he can be with his size along the wall and in front of the net. Morrison had 1 Assist tonight, making a great backhanded pass from behind the goal line, along the wall with a defender right on him to #12 Hirano in front of the net for a tap in goal. Didn't look incredibly strong on his skates in the open ice.

YNG #3 LD McInnis, Luke (2016) – McInnis is a smaller defenseman that used his skating ability to defend efficiently and move the puck well. McInnis didn't register any points tonight, but was calm with the puck, moved the puck north quickly using his skating ability or making quick outlet passes. McInnis made really good 10-15 foot passes all night to relieve pressure. Took care of the puck all night and was good at both ends of the ice. Picked his spots well on when to join the rush and didn't get caught deep in the offensive zone.

Final Score 5-3 Youngstown

Drummondville Voltigeurs vs Quebec Remparts, January 9th 2016.

DRU #22 C Sevigny Mathieu (2016): A good two way game for the Drummondville forward. He supported his defensemen down low in the defensive zone to help them out and also had good execution speed. He played a few times on the second wave on the power play. He has good vision of the game and distributed the puck well.

DRU # 4 LD Gagné, Benjamin (2017): Played on a regular basis and with confidence. He was reliable defensively but needs to improve his speed. He contributed offensively by directing some good shots on net.

QUE # 91 LW Boucher, Matthew (2016): He had another good game offensively. Well positioned in front of goal to deflect shots from the point. He used his speed effectively to overflow opposing defense in his second goal in this game with a great move to put the puck top net in right corner. After taking a 10 minutes penalty in the third period, he was back with battling hard around the net.

QUE # 21 RW Thierus, Lucas (2016): After a slow start, he finished the game strong. He distributed solid body checks, won his battles along the boards and some good sequences during incursions into the offensive zone. He often created great opportunities near the goal.

QUE #16 LD Huntley, Christian (2017): The young offensive defenseman played on a regular basis in addition to being used on the power play. He used his speed well, has good hockey sense and a good vision of the game despite some improper defensive coverage.

Shawinigan Cataractes vs Drummondville Voltigeurs, January 10th, 2016

SHA #28 C Gignac, Brandon (2016): Gignac was all over the ice in the 2nd period. He started using his speed while in possession of the puck, and Drummondville had no answer for him. He can reach his top speed in two to three strides; he beat several Drummondville defensemen wide during the game. He centered the 2nd line, with Pawelczyk and Daoust as his linemates. He had many scoring chances during the game but couldn't get one past the Drummondville goaltender. He played on the 2nd power play unit, playing on the half-wall where he was able to show some his playmaking abilities.
SHA #3 RD Sylvestre, Gabriel (2016): Paired with Girard, Sylvestre had a tough first period, but settled down in the 2nd and 3rd. He started playing with more confidence in the 2nd period, where he controlled the puck with more ease. In the first, he had a horrible giveaway trying to rush the puck and ended up turning the puck over after a bad pass just inside in his own zone.

SHA #42 G Denisov, Mikhail (2016): Denisov was the surprise starter, as on the game sheet it was indicated that Cadorette would be the starter. The Russian goaltender had a decent game. On the first goal, his lateral movement was a bit slow. On the 2nd goal, he had no chance on a great passing play while shorthanded. Not a big goaltender, he was quick to get on his kneed. However, he did fairly well with rebound control in this game.

SHA #94 LD Girard, Samuel (2016): Girard played a decent game today. He didn't stand out, but just by his smart plays he was able to contribute offensively. He made good passes to activate Shawinigan's transition game; he rushed the puck a couple of times out of his zone, including one that led to Shawinigan's 1st goal. He was also good on the power play. I started to see some chemistry being built between him and Timashov on the man-advantage.

DRU #4 LD Gagne, Benjamin (2017): Playing on the right side once again today on Drummondville's 3rd pairing, Gagne had a tough first period, mostly versus D'Aoust of Shawinigan who had two great scoring chances due to Gagné's errors. Decision-making was not his strong point today, as he tried to force the play a bit too much. He didn't get any power play time, but had a regular shift on the PK.

Good footwork was shown, but decision-making has been an issue for him this year in my viewings and it was again this time.

DRU #8 LW Carcone, Michael (2016): The '96-born forward continues to impress with each viewing. Speed was a big factor in this game. He was the best player on the ice in the first period, scoring a power play goal after a nice exchange between Laliberté and Barré-Boulet. Carcone has really good chemistry on the power play with Barré-Boulet, and there were some real nice passing plays between those two as a result. His speed allowed him to attack the offensive zone with terrific ease, which gave Shawinigan defenders a ton of problems.

DRU #19 C Barre-Boulet, Alex (2016): As previously mentioned, the 2nd-year eligible forward was dangerous on the power play today with Carcone. He does a good job creating offense from the half-wall position on the power play. With added free space, he was able to show off his playmaking abilities more than at even-strength today. He scored a power play goal from a one-timer after a great feed from Laliberté from the top of the faceoff circle. He could have had two to three goals in this game on the power play alone.

DRU #22 C Sevigny, Mathieu (2016): Sevigny worked hard as usual today, and didn't create much offense but did a good job of supporting his defense deep in his zone. He was involved along the boards and took the puck to the net on a couple of occasions. He got his nose dirty in the tougher areas of the ice. He had some shifts on the 2nd power play unit and on the PK.

DRU #9 RW Afanasyev, Kristian (2016): The Russian forward had two back-to-back scoring chances in the first period and disappeared (at least offensively) after that. He's never far from the net and gets involved there as well as in the corners. He showed good team spirit defending a teammate after a bad hit. Afanasyev played on the 2nd PP unit today.

Kingston Frontenacs at Kitchener Rangers, January 10, 2016

KGN #6 D Paquette, Jacob (2017) - Good quickness and mobility to hang with shifty forwards along the wall. Good reaction time on plays. Showed some escapability with the puck when under pressure in his own zone. Good play on penalty kill when outnumbered to pin the puck then get it down the ice. Good body positioning and reaction time to win some dump and chase races. Good positional play on second penalty kill unit and stick always in the right place. Walked in and blasted a big accurate slap shot top shelf for 1-3 goal. Good skating and good stick to break up a potential breakaway against a quick skater.

KGN #11 C Dorval, Zack (2016) - Got stick on shots in the defensive zone. Went to the net and made a decent deflection for scoring chance. Good zone clears playing on the second penalty killing unit. Skating is average, shot is below average.

KGN #21 RW Cranford, Ryan (2016) - Good forecheck pressure but sometimes chases the hit when he should use his stick. Loves the physical game and made the Rangers feel the pressure when he forechecked. Great pressure on the penalty kill, forced turnovers and killed time. Good diving play in the defensive zone to break up chance. Got in passing lanes in defensive zone well. Second unit penalty kill.

KIT #23 LW Mascherin, Adam (2016) - Good positioning on the rush anticipating pass and unloaded a big one timer for 2-0 goal. Skating is slightly above average but not where we'd like it to be considering his size. Had a 2 on 1 chance early third and shot first, firing a heavy shot over the net. He would fire hard and high on three different scoring chances in the third. Stripped defender down low to create scoring chance but when he centred the puck into his linemates feet it negated the chance.

Showed good vision and patience on the power play making some skilled passes but missed at times as well. His vision is good and he sees the passes but doesn't always execute as desired.

KIT #74 LW Bunnaman, Connor (2016) - Forced turnover but lacked separation and settled for low percentage shot and an offensive draw. Good hustle on forecheck to use his big frame to protect the puck well. Good effort on the second penalty killing unit clearing the zone several times. Showed some puck control ability down low. Fired an odd angle shot for chance, lost balance and crashed into the wall hard. He hurried back to break up puck possession on the back check before going off. Won the only two face-offs he took.

KIT #98 D Roberts, Elijah (2017) - Quick passes up ice. Excellent acceleration to rush puck. Great play off the bench on the second penalty killing unit to take away stick of player driving net on 2 on 1 scoring chance.

Final Score: Kitchener Rangers: 3 - Kingston Frontenacs: 1

Everett Silvertips at Spokane Chiefs, January 10th, 2016

EVE #8 RW Bajkov, Patrick (2016)- Smart player but not a good game for him. Have seen him exhibit all of his downsides in this performance. No pull-away ability got him rubbed out of the game. Lost pucks at the wall. Inexplicably complicated some easy passes. His instincts still looked good on some offensive zone plays.

EVE #17 C Fonteyne, Matt (2016)- Thought he did alright. Was a bit more patient with the puck than in my previous viewings. Left himself some time for the play to open up as opposed to trying to skate through defense. This allowed him to make some dangerous passes but nobody converted on it.

EVE #30 G Hart, Carter (2016)- Had a good game. Couple of big saves robbed Johnson 1 on 1. Then flashed his glove in third period stopping Ross on a good scoring chance and giving up no rebound. Was strong when Spokane pulled the goalie. There were a couple of flinged shots or passes to the front of the net area where he looked a bit shaky with traffic but nothing too serious.

SPK #10 LW McIndoe, Ethan (2017)- His compete is good and he used his frame to battle for pucks. Didn't get a lot done with the puck, kept it simple for the most part but it was reasonably effective. Pretty responsible game.

SPK #11 C Anderson-Dolan, Jaret (2017)- Thought he struggled in the first, had a hard time receiving a pass from his defense and getting out of his zone. Did better later on, had one big slapshot in dying seconds that was quite dangerous.

SPK #17 RW Yamamoto, Kailer (2017)- For some reason, in the first period he was forcing slappers from the blueline as soon as entering the offensive zone. Did quite good after that though. Has innate sense of finding soft spots and the timing to get into them without taking physical contact. Set up a couple of chances for his linemates later in the game but no finish on his line.

SPK #26 C Elynuik, Hudson (2016)- Quickness, first few steps and edgework looked decent for his size, stride needs to improve at top speed, looks a bit slow on the backcheck through neutral zone. Some very good quick drop passes on his backhand, assisted on Johnson's goal in that similar manner. Good stick, uses his reach well to strip pucks as well as to sweep the puck around the boards. Needs to start using his frame better, looks too upright and not as strong in the corners as he should be. Needs to push back against contact more.

Chicago Steel at Madison Capitols, January 15th 2016, USHL

CHI #2 LD Kiersted, Matt (2016) – Kiersted was Chicago's most steady defenseman all night. His Combination of smooth hands and good skating ability allowed him to elude fore checkers and get the puck going north quickly. Ran the point on the Power play effectively, made quick decisions when under pressure, showed good agility to move laterally along the blue line in order to open up lanes and get the puck to the net. Made a slick move to get around opponent in the slot and get a shot towards the net. Kiersted did make one errant pass from behind his own net that was nearly picked off for a Grade "A" scoring chance in front, luckily for him the opponent couldn't handle it cleanly and the puck harmlessly ended up covered by his goalie. Other than the one turnover Kiersted was effective at both ends of the ice, showed the skating ability to challenge the rush at his own blue line and still keep players to the outside and not get turned around, even against some of Madison's more steady forwards.

CHI #6 LW Zimmer, Max (2016) – Zimmer's speed was on full display all night tonight. Especially through the Neutral zone with the puck. Zimmer really got his feet moving quickly and can get the puck up ice. His first few strides were a step above anyone else on the ice which allowed him to take time and space away from players and create turnovers. Zimmer showed great ability to shoot in stride and has a really quick release. Zimmer didn't get on the score sheet tonight but Registered 3 SOG and showed a good nose for the net.

CHI #36 LD Parsells, Adam (SJ, 2015, 6th Rd.) – Parsells game has made strides since earlier in the season before being traded from Green Bay. Showed a good stick in the defensive zone, uses his long reach to force plays to the outside. Blocked some key shots on a 5-3 PK. Parsells showed smarter decision making with the puck, keeps his game simple.

CHI #10 C Laczynski, Tanner (2016+) – Laczynski did score the game winner in OT on a great shot from the slot, he shows good offensive instincts and plays a good 200 foot game, worked hard on the back check to get back in the play and is good at picking up his man but there are shifts throughout the game where he wasn't noticeable at either end of the ice. Consistency shift to shift is something Laczynski needs to continue to work on.

CHI #12 C Lewandowski, Mitch (2016) – The smaller center played a 3rd line role and was effective. Won a lot of his draws, his line along with FLA draft pick Karch Bachman did a good job in a checking role all game long. Lewandowski was good on the PK as well.

Val-d'Or Foreurs at Victoriaville Tigres, January 15th, 2016

VAL #12 RW Gauthier, Julien (2016) - He scored a goal with pure effort using his large frame to maintain his position and pretty much jamming the puck through the goalie. Showed real good strength and balance there as he absorbed a pretty hard check. Good movement in the slot to open up for scoring opportunities. His play with the puck was decent but not impressive, saw him force a pass to the middle into a clogged lane instead of playing it to the point or playing it back around the boards and continuing the cycle both of which wouldn't result in loss of possession.

VAL #20 RW Tremblay, Nathan (2016) - He looked to be struggling with the pace, his reads seemed a bit slow. Tried to be physical but both threw checks that were way behind the play only resulting in more open space for Victoriaville to play with.

VAL #26 LD Galipeau, Olivier (2016*) - Pretty competitive game around the net, was a physical presence in his own zone. Had one poor play letting himself be dragged out of position and opening up space behind him but quite solid outside of that.

VIC #19 LW Goulet, Alexandre (2016**) - Scored a PP goal with a backhand top-shelf cleaning up a rebound. Good straight-line speed and jump, had some dangerous quick-strike attacks. Really looked to get involved as a shooter.

VIC #44 RW Comtois, Maxime (2017) - He picked up the assist on Goulet's goal. Comtois had a real strong offensive game. His ability to read how the play develops in the offensive zone and where he has to go was very good. He had three opportunities finding himself one on one against the goalie but lacked finish. One of those was a shorthanded breakaway.

Scout's Notes: Pascal Laberge (Victoriaville) not in lineup.

Val-d'Or Foreurs at Sherbrooke Phoenix, January 16th, 2016

VAL #12 RW Gauthier, Julien (2016) - Came down on his off-wing and cut to inside successfully using his size and skating. Spent a lot of time in front of the net. Beats defenseman at obtaining inside body position and smartly opens up his blade facing the play. Really willing to drive the net with speed as well. D-zone coverage could be better. I would like him to do a better job of sustaining offensive zone time for his team, I think he only had two passess that were aimed at that goal. Almost too direct in his approach, needs to show a bit more patience in puck-movement.

VAL #26 LD Galipeau, Olivier (2016*) - Up and down game for him. Good physicality and first pass was OK. Poor pinch left a 2 on 1 going his own way and a goal by Poulin. Got caught flat footed on the offensive blueline late in third period. Hasn't shown much outside his own zone.

VAL #45 LD Henley, David (2016*) - Lack of quickness left him a step behind on coverage, usually started in correct position but struggled to close down forwards or make adjustments on the fly. When he does get the body on the forward, he can be quite effective. Good effort with his stick on poke-checks.

SHE #1 G Fitzpatrick, Evan (2016) - Held his position on net drives. Side to side movement and recovery looked slightly sluggish. Saw pucks well through traffic. He gave up 3 goals in the third but it's hard to blame him when the D lets cross-ice passes through the slot and leaves players unchecked directly in front of the net. Good play with the puck, nothing flashy but was calm.

SHE #2 RD Gregoire, Thomas (2016) - Struggled with Pepin's size several times just bouncing off him. Skated well and kept his feet moving. First pass was accurate when he wasn't under pressure. He got checked off the puck twice by having his head down in his own end.

SHE #10 RW Gilbert, Kevin (2016) - Good effort clearing the puck on PK. Had a deke on Galipeau making him miss with the pokecheck then throwing a nice backhand dish to his linemate for a scoring chance. Pretty quiet overall, no real consistent offensive pressure in his shifts.

Chicoutimi Sagueneens vs Victoriaville Tigres, January 16th 2016

CHI #58 RD Allard, Frédéric (2016): Great game from Allard today, playing with 16 year old Jeremy Groleau. He made some great passes during the game, which really helped the Sags' transition game. He made three to four excellent stretch passes during the game. He controlled the puck well and was a big help for his young D-partner, rushing the puck plenty of times out of his zone with confidence. He was not shy to go deep in the offensive zone, trying to make something happen offensively for his team. He played in every situation during this game; he was on for every PP and did well on the PK as well, with a quick stick to win possession of the puck along the boards.

CHI #77 LD Groleau, Jeremy (2018): Groleau, who turned 16 in late November, was really good today alongside Krief. He made a lot of smart plays in the defensive zone. Not a flashy performer or skater, but Groleau did a lot of small things well today. He was really good along the boards and won a lot of battles, showing good puck poise and a willingness to take hits to move the puck. He moved the puck out of his zone on a regular basis, keeping his game simple and being efficient on the ice. Didn't get PP time, but was a regular on the PK unit.

CHI #3 LD Krief, Alexander (2017): Krief was playing on the 3rd pairing and saw time on the 2nd power play unit. He was able to show some of his offensive skills during the game, including a good slapshot from the point and a very good release on his wrist shot. He earned an assist after taking a shot after which the Saguenéens scored on the rebound. Krief is a big kid that moves very well on the ice, and has an extra gear when he rushes the puck.

VIC #30 G Povall, James (2016): Gave up 7 goals today. He had some bad luck on possibly two of these goals, but the rest were stoppable. He didn't get much help from his defense, but he was not challenging shooters enough and was too deep in his net. Even with his size, he was struggling to track the puck. Not a good day at the office.

VIC #5 RD Lalonde, Bradley (2016): Lalonde was a regular on the Tigres' PP today, either on the first or 2nd unit. He was not shy in terms of rushing the puck into the offensive zone and taking shots on net. On the power play, he was often in position to take one-timers, as his teammates would set him up for those. Unfortunately, he didn't get to score, and missed some of those one-timers despite being in a good scoring position.

VIC #7 RD Beck, Guillaume (2017): Limited ice time for Beck today, and he didn't get to play much on the special teams. He's still trying to find his game after missing a ton of hockey in the past year or so because of concussion problems. His lack of footspeed was on display a bit today against the quick Chicoutimi forwards. However, he was involved physically and in some scrums as well. Didn't get a ton of chances to touch the puck during the game.

VIC #44 LW Comtois, Maxime (2017): Comtois was injured in the first period after taking a hit from behind. It looked like he hurt his neck on the play. In the time that he was on the ice, he was able to show some of his smarts and vision with the puck on his stick. He sees the ice very well and made an excellent backhand pass to a teammate at the side of the net. On the power play, he was used in front of the net to screen the goaltender.

VIC #47 LW Lapierre, Jacob (2017): The big winger didn't have the best of games. He didn't work hard and was often a second late to react to plays. He was not involved physically and was invisible on the ice for the most part of the game.

VIC #48 C Lauzon, Félix (2016): Lauzon had some good shifts in the 2nd half of the game when the game was out of hand. He had two or three good scoring chances in the game, created space for himself in the slot, but couldn't beat the Chicoutimi goaltender. Made some smart plays in the neutral zone. Lauzon is a smart forward with good anticipation, and was able to cut some passes in the neutral zone and create turnovers.

VIC #96 LW Huber, Mario (2016): The big Austrian winger was like Lapierre today, he was invisible for the most part of this game. He didn't use his size well enough and his lack of speed was most evident against the quick Chicoutimi team. He has a good, heavy shot, but didn't use it enough. He played a regular shift on the power play, but was not involved enough to be a factor.

Green Bay Gamblers at Madison Capitols, January 16th 2016, USHL

GB #20 RD Peeke, Andrew (2016) – Played an effective shutdown style tonight. Kept the play to the outside by using good body and stick positioning. Peeke usually very strong on his skates took two hard hits while going for 50/50 pucks and took the brunt of both hits. Saw limited time on the #2 PP unit tonight and made simple plays with the puck at the point. Peeke didn't join the rush much tonight, seemed content handling things in his own end and letting his D-partner join the rush when possible, which isn't uncharacteristic of his game. Peeke didn't register any points or SOG and finished the evening +1.

MAD #31 G Edquist, Ryan (2016) – Edquist played as well as a goalie could have in a 5-2 loss after not seeing game action in a while. Edquist made some really good saves on a couple 2 on 1's as well as on some great scoring chances in tight in the crease. Many of his goals against were due to terrible mistakes made by the team in front of him. Edquist has improved his puck tracking ability since earlier in the year and is quicker to find pucks in traffic. The Capitols currently have 3 goalies on their roster so it's up in the air ho w many starts Edquist might get the rest of the season.

Red Deer Rebels at Swift Current Broncos, January 17, 2016

RED #2 LD Strand, Austin (2016*) - A fantastic straight-ahead skater who can handle the puck fairly well. In fact, had one end-to-end rush in the first period that was absolutely brilliant, thanks entirely to great skating and above-average stickhandling ability. Didn't score, but the rush itself looked marvelous. Sometimes over-extended himself and strays away from his proper position on the ice.

RED #22 LW Hagel, Brandon (2016) – Did a good job of assisting on a teammate's goal by crashing the net and occupying the opposition defence with power and speed. A bit of an awkward skater but gets to the right areas in a hurry. Played a simple but effective game that wasn't always pretty. Got some good chances towards the net.

SWI #17 Steenbergen, Tyler (2016) – Not a great skater by any means, but gets enough initial propulsion to glide meaningfully from south-to-north. Threw some nice hits on the forecheck. Didn't show the greatest of poise when he passed up a great scoring opportunity from the mid-slot. A good puck mover who had a couple brilliant passes into the slot, racking up two assists, and making up for that original blunder.

SWI #27 LD Lajoie, Max (2016) – All-around mobility is well above-average. Good in the corners thanks to quick feet and hands, even if he isn't particularly powerful at this point. Rarely if ever made positional mistakes in his own end. A good stickchecker who makes it hard to chances on net when he's defending against you. Not overly physical, however. Played in all situations. Appeared highly versatile and coachable.

Youngstown Phantoms at USNTDP, January 18th, 2016

YNG #3 LD McInnis, Luke (2016) - Good first pass, doesn't panic under pressure but finds open lanes and distributes the puck swiftly out of his zone. Tries to play bigger than his size in his own zone, even had a big hit on Sanchez but got his elbow up which resulted in a penalty.

YNG # 26 LW Morrison, Cameron (2016) - He had an underwhelming game, scored on a shot from up-close after Pearson created the turnover, but outside of that he was getting stripped of the puck a lot, seemed to have some trouble handling it even when nobody was on him as well.

USA #2 RD Martin, Luke (2017) - He played a quality mistake-free game though he did not really try to do much outside of moving the puck up ice from his own end. Faded a bit later down the stretch.

USA #3 LD Campoli, Michael (2016) - A pretty quiet night, thought he had some good defensive plays breaking up the attack, but didn't really show up much with the puck.

USA #4 RD Krys, Chad (2016) - He had a couple of nice plays showing off his skating and passed the puck around on the PP but did not really put his stamp on the game. I was wishing that he would exhibit more control over the outcome of his shifts but he never really raised the bar.

USA #7 C Frederic, Trent (2016) - A consistent game with him moving his feet offensively and defensively. Was good on PK as well. I thought he was working hard, pressuring the puck-carrier and looking to get his nose dirty by going to scoring areas without the puck.

USA #8 RD Fox, Adam (2016) - He was the best defenseman on the ice. Smart little delays, sees the ice well, good puck distribution from the point. Can join the attack or sneak in back-door. Had a nice backhand goal on an EN firing it all the way from his own zone.

USA #14 LD Greenway, J.D. (2016) - He was average at best the entire game, having little impact or any sort of engaging effort until he had a fantastic one man effort to put USA back into lead late in the third.

USA #15 RW Walker, Zach (2016) - He did a great job winning races to pucks, especially on dump-ins he was often good at beating the defenseman with speed or using his body to gain inside position and retrieve the puck and then make plays off that, was able to make plays coming out of corners with the puck while under pressure.

USA #17 RW Anderson, Joey (2016) - Hit the post twice coming into the high-slot area trailing the play and looking for a pass. Good wristshot there. Didn't do a lot to create offense as a playmaker though.

USA #18 LD Lindgren, Ryan (2016) - He was just OK. Rarely out of position defensively, moves the puck well. Broke up plays on some of the zone entries, but no real offensive impact to speak of.

USA #19 C Keller, Clayton (2016) - He was flying out there. I think Youngstown got the body on him exactly once in the entire game, he just craftfully avoided checks and was dominating the offensive zone. Good defensive performance too, took good angles on the forecheck and has a real nice active stick that is annoying to deal with. Good on PK, too.

USA #22 LW Bellows, Kieffer (2016) - I thought he was real strong early on with his ability to shoot the puck. He can release it while being off-balance, or has no space for the wind-up, finds ways to get it on net with sticks and bodies around him.

USA #25 LD Luce, Griffin (2016) - He got in trouble when not moving the puck quickly, attempted to pull off a move on his own blueline and got quickly stripped of the puck. Had a big hit that got him ejected for head contact.

USA #29 G Woll, Joseph (2016) - Not much work for him in this game. He did his job for the most part, could have done a bit better making the save on PK goal after Luce got ejected, but was OK outside of that. Nothing he could do on Morrison's goal as the defenseman turned the puck directly in front of him.

Shawinigan Cataractes at Quebec Remparts, January 21st 2016

SHA # 94 LD Girard, Samuel (2016): The small defenseman was mobile and agile on skate. He took good accurate shots on goal. He moved the puck very well and had a good vision of the game. He spotted his teammates well and successfully carried the puck out of his own zone.

SHA # 28 C Gignac, Brandon (2016): Use a few times on the power play and playing regularly during the match, the forward took some good shots on goal without scoring. He had a good acceleration, particularly in zone entries. However, he had some difficulties with the accuracy of his passes and sometimes he lacked intensity in his back checks.

SHA # 3 RD Sylvestre, Gabriel (2016): The big defenseman played a little bit in the shadow of his teammate Girard but had a decent game. He is physically involved along the boards and in front of his net, but lacked a bit of speed as with his skating and his decision making with the puck on his stick.

QUE # 91 LW Boucher, Matthew (2016): The speedy forward played a good game. He showed a great combativity along the boards and was involved in the heat of the action. He took several good wrist shots. Although his shots were sometimes predictable, they forced the goalie Cadorette to make good saves. He also had nice shifts defensively and brought speed and energy to his team.

QUE # 66 LD Woods, Dakota (2016): The 6' 5" defenseman used his big size to clean the front of his net and gave a chance to his goalie to see shots from the point. However, he lacked a bit of speed and stability on his skates.

Erie Otters at Kitchener Rangers, January 22, 2016

ERI #6 D Sambrook, Jordan (2016) - Pinch was hit or miss at times but usually good. Excellent outlet, two-line pass created rush then jumped up to receive a pass and good shot for scoring chance. Good plays down low defensive zone to win battles and take puck up ice. Good first pass then gets to the offensive line quickly. Stepped in on loose puck and fired a cannon for 3-3 goal. Good wrister from the point for 4-3 goal. Played the final minute up one goal.

ERI #13 LW Neumann, Brett (2017) - Great compete, uses his speed at both ends of the ice.

ERI #17 RW Raddysh, Taylor (2016) - Went to the right spot in the slot and quickly fired a laser for 2-1 goal.

KIT #7 D Hall, Connor (2016) - Scored 2-2 goal driving wing and fired a wrister off defenders stick and in. Closed gaps quickly. Takes away opponents stick in slot on incoming shots and passes well.
KIT #74 LW Bunnaman, Connor (2016) - Showed good defensive awareness and positioning. Good puck decisions to set up chances.

Final Score: Erie Otters: 5 - Kitchener Rangers: 3

University of Minnesota at University of Wisconsin, January 22nd, 2016

WIS #9 W/C Kunin, Luke (2016) – In a game where not much went his teams way tonight, Kunin showed good effort and jam to his game all night. Was engaged physically in front of the net and in the corners but did take a couple bad penalties and seemed to let his emotions get the better of him at times, in what is always a big rivalry game for both teams. Kunin showed a good stick in the defensive zone and the ability to read and anticipate the play well. Didn't generate a lot of offensive chances tonight and Minnesota did a good job of defending his line and keeping them contained.

MIN #24 RW Fasching, Hudson (Buf.) – Was a dominating player for Minnesota tonight. Played in all situations and made an impact in all of them. Fasching showed terrific hockey IQ in knowing where to be on the ice, the puck seemed to follow him all night long. Finished the night with 1 goal and 2 assists.

Final Score: 4-0 (Minnesota)

Genève-Servette HC at ZSC Lions, NLA, January 23rd 2016

GSHC #9 LW Riat, Damien (2016*) – Riat saw some time on the penalty kill and took regular shifts on the powerplay, mostly positioned on the right side of the umbrella, where he was able to move the puck quickly. Made a one-time pass to reach a teammate open in the slot immediately exposing a missed coverage by the penalty killers. Later on wasted no time to shoot the puck into the net from the right faceoff circle when he had the chance to tie the game on the PP. Good effort skating at even strength.

GSHC #96 LW Rod, Noah (SJ) – Took a minor six seconds into the game throwing out a knee at Malgin in the neutral zone. Then went for a big hit inside the offensive zone but missed it for the most. Received some time on the PP but didn't get opportunities. Didn't accomplish much overall, his best plays were a steal in the neutral zone and a deep backcheck in the slot.

ZSC #13 C Malgin, Denis (FLA) – Centering the 4th line he only got one chance in the whole game to transition the puck, was only dangerous the few times he was able to settle down the play in the offensive zone with quick turns, buying himself time to use his playmaking skills. Made a nice feed in front from below the goal-line.

ZSC #34 C Matthews, Auston (2016) – Had a rather quiet game against the most physical team in the league, and a couple of poor plays in the offensive zone: a turnover and a misfired shot from the slot. His best plays were a couple of nice passes where he showed tremendous anticipation. On one of them he immediately found Herzog open in the slot for the opening goal. Better effort in the 3rd period with a couple of good looking shifts, eventually added an empty net goal.

ZSC #44 LW Suter, Pius (2016*) – Saw regular shift on the penalty kill. He had a bit of a slow start and didn't look at his best skating wise, but competed throughout the game and brought his contribution.

ZSC #61 LW Herzog, Fabrice (TOR) – The third wheel of the top line alongside Matthews and Nilsson, Fabrice had an active game and opened the scoring using his good reach to receive a pass in the slot and promptly beat the goalie. Made a very nice play using his reach again to break out at his defensive blueline and launch the counter attack. Had a good drive into the slot after winning a puck along the side boards in the neutral zone.

ZSC #97 LD Siegenthaler, Jonas (WSH) – Smooth and efficient puck-moving in his own end. Made a couple of mistakes in the 2nd period, in particular got caught after he unnecessarily stepped up along the side boards in the neutral zone, which resulted in a 2-on-1 chance for the opponents. Go beaten cleanly on one play at the end boards by Jim Slater, but played a good game overall.

Final Score: GSHC: 2 – ZSC Lions: 4

Barrie Colts at Mississauga Steelheads, January 24, 2016

OHL Regular Season

BAR #10 D Murray, Justin (2016) - Moving the puck quickly on the defensive line. Good one on one plays using his stick to stop and body to drive opponents into the wall. Second penalty killing unit. Good positionally. Took the puck to the net on rush creating scoring chance then kept the puck in the zone while getting back into position showing good hand/eye. Good skater, good variation of passes.

BAR #31 G Badenhorst, Ruan (2016) - Made some big saves. Excellent quickness, kicked away. Lot of rebounds. Great save late on 2 on 0 break.

MIS #92 LW Nylander, Alexander (2016) - Good speed on puck race but lost to bigger defender who outmuscled him. Great shot on rush, let goalie drop down then roofed laser 1-1 goal.

Final Score: Barrie Colts: 4 - Mississauga Steelheads: 2

Farjestad BK at Vaxjo Lakers, January 26th, 2016

FBK #29 LW Steen, Oskar (2016) - Good balance on his skates and wide frame despite lacking height, doesn't look overpowered against men. Was surprisingly effective in corners and in absorbing contact. Had some bite to his game. One or two wristshots coming down the wing that the goalie easily swallowed up as there was no traffic.

FBK #74 C Asplund, Rasmus (2016) - Good game in all three zones. His line had some key shifts midway through the first period after Vaxjo scored, that started turning the momentum into Farjestad's favor. Took really smart routes, opens up easily, makes smart plays with the puck. Engages in puck-battles, already effective on the forecheck and backcheck with his active stick. Always keeps his feet moving. Will need to fill out to battle effectively down-low in his zone.

Chicago Mission U18 vs Milwaukee Jr. Admirals U18, January 29th, 2016

MIL #21 C/W Cruikshank, Grant (2016) – Cruikshank's team was overmatched tonight but Grant showed great speed with and without the puck and was the best skater on the ice for either team. His great first few strides allowed him to get to loose pucks quickly and create separation with the puck. Worked hard at both ends of the ice and did a good job getting in lanes on the back check and breaking up plays. Cruikshank liked to stretch the ice by getting behind the defense, looking for a stretch passes. Hit the post with a quick release from the slot.

CHI #45 LW Abate, Joseph (2017) – Abate could be playing in the USHL right now. Played a solid power forward game tonight, took the puck to the net at will. Abate scored on a snap shot from the right circle beating the goalie on the far post.

Final Score: 5-1 Chicago Mission

Chicoutimi Saguenéens vs Shawinigan Cataractes, January 29th 2016

CHI #48 RD Maltsev, Artem (2016): Maltsev got involved in rushes at times during the game. He is not a pretty skater, but showed a willingness to help out offensively. He played on the power play on the 2nd unit and didn't shy away from taking shots on net, mostly slapshots. Most of his shots got blocked in front of the net, though. He was involved physically as the game got chippy in the 2nd half- he didn't throw any big hits, but was involved after whistles and in scrums.
CHI #58 RD Allard, Frédéric (2016): A good game from Allard offensively, as he finished with three points in this game. He was good on the power play, scoring a goal in the 3rd period and setting up another one. He had a couple of nice rushes and was good at moving the puck out of his zone with a good first pass. He competed hard in his zone versus Shawinigan's top line, and was often paired with a 16 year old, either McIsaac or Groleau.

CHI #7 LD McIsaac, Keenan (2017): The young defender saw ice time on the power play today (1st unit) with top defender Frédéric Allard. In the first period he rushed the puck two or three times out of his zone using his good footwork. On the power play he kept his game simple and made safe plays when moving the puck. He was a bit out of position when he was in his zone and physically overmatched versus older and bigger Shawinigan forwards.

CHI #77 LD Groleau, Jeremy (2018): He was often paired with Allard today and had a regular shift on the PK, but no PP time for him today. Not a pretty skater but does well, even at his young age, along the boards, winning a lot of puck battles. He made smart plays most of the time and kept his game simple. He had one major mistake when he fumbled the puck in his zone that almost led to a Shawinigan goal. He has a good, quick stick that helps him in one-on-one confrontations.

CHI #61 LW Lavigne, Zachary (2018): Love his compete level. He does great work along the boards and protects the puck well. He scored a goal in the game after finishing the play on a two-on-one opportunity. He didn't get the most out of the puck, but eventually it found his way to the back of the net. A good, smart game out of him today.

CHI #30 G Billia, Julio (2016): Un-Drafted twice mainly due to his average size, Billia, coming back from an injury, had a strong game today, leading the Sags to an upset win in Shawinigan. He was strong in his crease and never seemed out of position. Even with traffic in front of him, he made numerous saves, showing a good sense for tracking the puck. Also did very well handling rebounds during the game, as there were not many 2nd chances for Shawinigan forwards in front of the net.

SHA #3 RD Sylvestre, Gabriel (2016): Sylvestre played on both special teams today, on the 2nd PP unit and as a regular on the PK unit. On the 1st Chicoutimi goal, he made a bad pinch by being too aggressive, leading to a two-on-one where Zachary Lavigne scored. On Chicoutimi's 2nd goal after a turnover from his D-partner, he couldn't get the puck out of his zone and was out of position because of it, which led to the Jake Smith goal.

SHA #72 C Asselin, Samuel (2016): Did some good work on the PK. In one sequence, he stole the puck from Nicolas Roy at his blueline. His good anticipation makes him a valuable penalty killer. His good, low center of gravity helps him protect the puck. Lacks the top-end speed at this moment to be a factor offensively with the Cataractes.

SHA #97 RW Taillon, Charles (2017): On the 4th line today, Taillon was not very noticeable because of his lack of ice time. He was involved physically when on the ice, but took a bad penalty for a hit from behind. He went to the net for his only scoring chance of the game.

Saint John Sea Dogs vs Acadie-Bathurst Titan, January 30th, 2016

SNB #55 RD Green, Luke (2016): Green was all over the offensive zone in the first period, taking many shots on net and jumping in the play, creating scoring chances. He rushed the puck with ease thanks to his excellent skating ability. He made good decisions with the puck. He had one bad shift in the defensive zone where he got lazy in retrieving pucks, but overall, he did well today defensively.

SNB #23 LD Felixson, Oliver (2016): His decision-making is still slow and will need to improve. Did a good job in a shutdown role and on the PK, using his size along the boards and in front of the net. Good active stick and made a nice play blocking a pass on a two-on-one opportunity.

SNB #10 C Noel, Nathan (2016): Noel played an intense game, mostly in the first period, where he used his speed and finished hits on the forecheck. He was quick to put pressure on the puck carrier with his great wheels. He often was the player carrying the puck in the offensive zone.

SNB #9 C Veleno, Joseph (2018): Veleno is very elusive along the boards to avoid hits; he still lacks strength at this age but still had an impressive game along the boards for a 2000-born player. He scored the 3rd Saint John goal by tipping a shot in front of the net, showing good hand-eye coordination. He made good use of his speed on puck-pursuits and on the forecheck.

AB #98 LW Kuznetsov, Vladimir (2016): The big Russian only played in the first two periods, getting hurt late in the 2nd period after getting hit in the face by a puck. He was not very involved in the play and didn't move his feet enough. He had his best scoring chance in the first period in the goalie crease. He's tough to move from the front of the net, as he is strong on his skates.

AB #16 C Maher, Jordan (2016): Maher was arguably the top Titan forward today. He made good use of his speed on the forecheck and his speed gave Sea Dogs' defensemen headaches. He scored Bathurst's 2nd goal with a wicked wrist shot coming down with speed on his off-wing. He did a good job on Bathurst's 3rd goal, controlling the puck along the boards and getting the puck into a scoring area. Good job on the backcheck during this game as well.

AB #31 G Pickard, Reilly (2016): He did a fine job being square to shooters and challenging them in the game. Gave up five goals in the defeat, but couldn't be faulted on any of them (aside from the 4th, where he gave puck away).

AB #62 RW Miromanov, Danill (2016): He showed good anticipation in the neutral zone by intercepting passes. He did a fine job of protecting the puck, using his size along the boards, often with only one hand on his stick. An average skater who scored Bathurst's 3rd goal on a rebound late in the game.

AB #44 C Rafuse, Cole (2017): The 2017 draft-eligible prospect was playing center today on a line with Theede and Lemay-Champagne. Rafuse didn't see any special team ice time today. He is a big, strong kid who's tough to knock down, but lacks speed and was often late on plays due to his lack of quickness.

Tappara at Sport, January 30th, 2016

TAP #29 LW Laine, Patrik (2016) - Laine was one of the best players on ice and scored a goal and an assist. Was willing to battle around the boards and won one-on-one battles by playing tough. Showed again fancy moves and was really dangerous almost every time he got the puck in the o-zone. Recorded over 20 minutes ice time.

Djurgardens IF J20 at HV 71 J20, January 31st, 2016

DJU #10 C Davidsson, Marcus (2017) - Really smart offensive zone positioning and reads. Great hand-eye coordination tipping two hard Bernhardt point shots into the net. Completed a hat-trick with a nice quick shot from the slot after receiving a pass from behind the net.

DJU #39 G Larsson, Filip (2016) - Started off a bit shaky giving up two goals in 4 minutes but put himself together by the end of the first period. Tracked the puck well and keeps his eyes on the puck while adjusting angles. Left a bit more room upstairs.

DJU #41 RW Jonsson-Fjallby, Axel (2016) - Two of his reads resulted in two goals. First intercepting a D to D pass that he finished himself, and on second occassion making a nice pass from behind the net to an open Davidsson that sneaked into the slot.

DJU #49 LD Bernhardt, David (2016) - He showed off his shot from the point. His slapper lacked accuracy, but had several good wristshots that had some power and got through, two of those were tipped and resulted in goals. Decent passing but a bit iffy when pressured. Was physical in his own end a couple of times. His poor pinch lead to a goal against. Feet look sluggish at times. Sometimes doesn't know where he should be positioned defensively.

HV71 #26 LD Brannstrom, Erik (2017) - Nice feet and lateral movement in walking the blueline and finding lanes. More dangerous on powerplay than even strength.

HV71 #33 RD Cederholm, Jacob (2016) - His mobility and stick are quite good. Was noteable with his reach and the way he controls space with his stick leaving forwards that attack him with speed with little options. He allowed himself to skate with the puck a couple of times but didn't try anything too fancy. Not a lot there offensively.

HV71 #71 C Andersson, Lias (2017) - He was outstanding. A never-ending engine that comes in waves shift-after-shift, really drove the play for his team. Wins battles, excellent at fending off checks and moving the puck despite having players hanging on his back. Good passing.
HV71 #72 LD Moverare, Jacob (2016) - Had a couple of close-calls in his own zone when trying to use his skating to open up a lane but instead skated himself into trouble. Thought he could have moved the puck quicker there. He did a good job bringing the puck up ice on PP. Good defensive positioning, competed but was not really aggressively physical.

HV71 #73 LW Lestan, Filip (2016) - He can really skate at his size and used it to hunt players down on the forecheck. Didn't do much with the puck, needed to find better ways to utilize his frame and speed offensively.

Sudbury Wolves at Windsor Spitfires, February 4, 2016

OHL Regular Season

SBY #12 RW Pataki, Brady (2017) - Big body who hits hard, every chance he gets, very tough in corners. Skating needs improvement.

SBY #13 C Pezzetta, Michael (2016) - Assistant captain. Big hit but interfered with opponent without the puck resulting in penalty. Loves to take the body and took on anyone. Huge shot block, visibly hurt but stayed with play until whistle. Drilled Brendan Lemieux at the end of the second period after the horn, took a penalty, Windsor scored their 3-1 goal on the ensuing power play.

SBY #18 LW Carson, Macauley (2017) - Dropped gloves with fellow 16 year old and absolutely destroyed him.

SBY #71 C Levin, David (2018) - Great move to split defenders and create chance. Has the tools, skating, hands but tried to do too much. Will take a simple scoring chance and try to do something extra fancy with it which in the end negates the play.

SBY #98 RW Sokolov, Dmitry (2016) - Took hit to make the play. Struggled to create much offense, was stopped one on one a few times. Defensive play hit or miss would sometimes float around the red line looking for passes, other times he's all over the opposition.

SBY #33 G Timpano, Troy (2016) - Fought the puck a little bit today. Made a few solid cross crease saves. Leaves holes when he over commits. First GA a rocket top shelf didn't have much of a chance. Second GA he overcommitted too far and was exploited. Let in four goals in the third all were middle of the road in terms of difficulty.
WSR #13 C Vilardi, Gabriel (2017) - Good anticipation to force turnovers. Quick hands and creativity to set up some scoring chances. Chances speeds well on rush. Very quick release.

WSR #17 D Stanley, Logan (2016) - Won some battles down low. Nice puck movement on the rush. Carries the puck well for a big defender and knows when to carry and when to pass off.

WSR #21 C Brown, Logan (2016) - Skating has improved, showed good puck protection down low. Skating and speed much better and made some nice end to end rushes.

WSR #26 RW Carter, Cole (2016) - Gets dominated below the hash marks in the offensive zone. Small, good skater, showed some passing ability. Finished on pass to score 5-1 goal.

WSR #28 D Nother, Tyler (2016) - Took penalty punching opponent in the face then selling the retaliation. Kept it simple at both ends. Tried to go end to end but got destroyed going wide on defender, however 5-1 goal was scored on the sequence.

WSR #31 D Sergachev, Mikhail (2016) - Good pinch to keep play going. On rush skated puck out of trouble evading two checkers then took the hit to make the outlet pass. Great move to beat defender, walk in and roof the puck locked side firing into a small space top shelf to score a high skilled goal, was waved off despite the puck going in. After having that goal negated he took it a step further beating three opponents then fired a perfect wrister to score. After the first goal got negated, next shift went out and levelled opponent in open ice. Only defenseman on top power play unit. Calmly makes good passes on the power play. Good strength one on one to shut opponents down.

WSR #32 G Culina, Mario (2016*) - Faced two shots in the first period, 10 by the end of the second. Not tested much but when he was he made some outstanding saves. Great quickness. Made an unbelievable save on a centering pass getting to the top of the crease in a hurry. Only goal allowed he made the first two saves and had no chance for the third.

Final Score: Windsor Spitfires: 6 - Sudbury Wolves: 1

Saginaw Spirit at Guelph Storm, February 5, 2016

OHL Regular Season

SAG #9 C Gilmour, Brady (2017) - Shook checker and good pass to set up 1-0 goal.

SAG #55 D Middleton, Keaton (2016) - Playing very physical in his own zone. Jumped up to battle for puck but lost, resulting in a 2 on 1 rush. Playing more of a big mans game which is making him more successful down low. Good stick one on one.
SAG #56 D Niemelainen, Markus (2016) - Had open net pinching in and took his sweet time on the wind up and got robbed instead, letting goalie get back into position. Defended a 2 on 1 rush perfectly. Good passing on second power play unit. Completed passes under pressure. Gets shots on net. Needs to get more on the puck when trying to clear the defensive zone. Showed some physicality landing some good hits. Great puck protection ability. Tried to go wall and out but kept turning the puck over. Great two like pass set up scoring chance. In 3 on 3 overtime was able to go end to end with the puck, protecting it all the way.

SAG #35 G Cormier, Evan (2016) - Fighting the puck a little bit. First goal through screen. Second goal a short handed breakaway. Made excellent cross crease save. Third goal no chance, a slap pass redirection. Made some good point blank saves. Great saves in overtime stopping a point blank centring one timer.

GUE #4 D Carroll, Noah (2016) - Lost puck battles he should have won. Good play to jump up in 2 on 1 rush. Backwards skating is good and showed a good stick one on one. Stripped down low resulting in a scoring chance against. Played big minutes in all game situations.

GUE #7 D Phillips, Brock (2016) - Huge hit to finish one on one play. Tough/fearless going after opponents. Good plays at offensive line kept the play going and made smart passes. Plays game with a nasty edge finishing checks and will get some two handed slashes in there when he could.

GUE #11 LW Sicoly, Nicolas (2016) - Good play on top penalty killing unit to chop the puck past defender and good breakaway move for 2-1 short handed goal.

GUE #23 C Hotchkiss, Matthew (2016) - Good move to shake checker but perimeter shot after. Good puck protection ability and went to the net. Made a great deflection to score 3-3 power play goal. Top power play minutes.

GUE #24 RW Smith, Givani (2016) - Showed a lack of awareness work the puck a few times early on. Doesn't have great hands but can maintain possession with power and will also force opponents off the puck. Rushed ahead of play. Skating below average. Showed a little skill through patience and good decision making with the puck. Huge open ice hit.

GUE #25 C Burghardt, Luke (2016) - Nice puck patience and good wrist shot through traffic for 1-1 goal. Good backcheck. Played second unit all situations.

Final Score: Guelph Storm: 4 - Saginaw Spirit: 3 - OT/SO

Victoriaville Tigres vs Saint John Sea Dogs, QMJHL, February 6th 2016

VIC #9 RW Laberge, Pascal (2016): Saw a quiet first half of the game from Laberge, who made some bad passes in the neutral zone early in the game. Started playing better halfway through the 2nd period; he made a great play on the Huber goal by coming back from the corner and feeding him the puck at the side of the net. He made a similar play with Goulet later in the game. He had some good flashes in one-on-one confrontations in the 2nd half of the game, showing quick and agile hands trying some good dekes.

VIC #44 LW Comtois, Maxime (2017): Comtois made good reads during the game, showing good anticipation when he doesn't have the puck in the neutral zone. On the power play, he's used in front of the net and has a strong compete level. He goes to the net every chance he gets and doesn't mind the rough stuff. Did a great job on the game-winning goal, screening the goaltender without taking an interference penalty.

VIC #48 C Lauzon, Felix (2016): Lauzon was a key player defensively today for the Tigres. He often acted as a 3rd defenseman, doing a good job supporting his defensemen deep in the defensive zone. He was a key player on the Tigres' PK unit as well, where he had some good blocked shots. Almost scored a goal after creating a turnover, but hit the post in front of the goaltender. Even at his size, he was battling hard in front of the net, showing he was not afraid.

VIC #96 C Huber, Mario (2016): Scored a nice goal after taking a pass from Laberge at the side of the net. Huber is a very strong player who plays physical and had some good hits during this game. However, he is a below-average skater and will need to work on his quickness. With the puck on his stick, he's tough to handle, and protects the puck very well.

SNB #55 RD Green, Luke (2016): Green made nice, accurate tape-to-tape passes during the game and rushed the puck often from his zone. He showed good anticipation in cutting passes in the neutral and defensive zones. He scored a highlight-reel goal going end-to-end, making a nice deke and scoring on a perfect shot from a bad angle.

SNB #23 LD Felixson, Oliver (2016): Made a nice play in the neutral zone in the first period, cutting a pass in the neutral zone with a good read. Outside of that, he was not a player who was really noticeable today. He didn't get to play with the puck a lot, and when he did, his decision-making was still slow. He's big and heavy and does well in his zone in PK situations with his reach and strength.

SNB #9 C Veleno, Joseph (2018): Veleno is very shifty and tough to contain as a result, combined with his explosiveness. He created a scoring chance for himself when he won a puck race, but was not able to beat the Victoriaville goaltender. He still showed a great burst of speed on that sequence. He was willing to play a physical game, but was outmuscled a bit in the corners. Strong forechecking and backchecking from him; he showed that he can play a strong two-way game. He had another good scoring chance late in the game where he showed great velocity on a backhand shot.

SNB #10 C Noel, Nathan (2016): He made good use of his speed, flying down the wing and controlling the puck in the offensive zone. He had a tendency to hold onto it too long in the offensive zone instead of trying quick puck-distribution to his teammates, and Victoriaville players were able to take the puck away from him. He played with a high level of energy and was shooting the puck well. He played hard and was intense all game long. Noel made a nice play on the Sea Dogs' 4th goal of the game by taking the puck to the net with speed on the left side, ending up burying the rebound after a scramble in front of the net.

Val D'Or Foreurs vs Blainville-Boisbriand Armada, QMJHL, February 6th 2016

VDO #12 RW Gauthier, Julien (2016): Good game from Gauthier today, who scored two goals and used his speed well by attacking the offensive zone. He had one shift where he took off from the neutral zone, showing great acceleration and crashing the net. He made good use of his reach to protect the puck and the Blainville-Boisbriand defenders had a tough time dealing with him. He scored his first goal of the game by jumping on a rebound in front of the net on an easy tap on his backhand. For his second goal, he took a quick wrist shot from the faceoff circle after his centerman Anthony Beauregard won the faceoff cleanly. On the power play, he was used either in front of the net or in the slot where he would position himself for one-timers. He could have scored two or three more goals today; he had many quality scoring chances.

VDO #20 RW Tremblay, Nathan (2016): It was also a good game from Tremblay, who was effective on the forecheck and involved all over the ice. He had his best scoring chance of the game while taking advantage of a turnover. He played a simple game with the puck, taking shots from different angles in the offensive zone without hesitation. He worked hard at both ends of the ice.

VDO #45 LD Henley, David (2016): Un-Drafted last season, Henley threw a couple of hits during the game, but his physical play was not a highlight, as it was in previous viewings. He rushed the puck a couple of times during the game, keeping it simple and simply dumping it deep after crossing the blueline.

VDO #21 C Beauregard, Anthony (2016): Got hurt in the first period after a bad hit from behind. He came back later on and did an excellent job on Gauthier's 2nd goal by winning the faceoff clean, which allowed Gauthier enough time shoot the puck. A strong effort without the puck, Beauregard worked hard on the backcheck and made good use of his quick stick to strip pucks from his opponents.

VDO #24 LD Pyrochta ,Filip (2016): Pyrochta played on the wrong side most of the game, but had an overall good showing for the Foreurs and was arguably their best defender today. Not the prettiest skater, but he was confident enough to rush the puck in the offensive zone a couple of times as well as setting up the plays on the power play. He played mostly on the 2nd power play unit tonight but was more effective at it than Galipeau, who's getting the top power play slot. He showed a strong, accurate shot from the point. He also threw his weight around with some solid hits in the first half of the game.

BLB #92 RD Corbeil, Pascal (2016): Did a good job in the offensive zone at getting his shot through the net; he's good at finding shooting lanes. Doesn't possess the most powerful shot, however, he still gets pucks through with a simple wrist shot. A good skater with good feet, he played on the first PP unit and used his feet to rush the puck in the offensive zone. He was creative in the offensive zone as well, which is something otherwise lacking from his team. He was caught being too aggressive on the power play, which led to Val-d'Or's 4th goal of the game. He was overmatched physically in his zone versus the big forwards on Foreurs.

BLB #91 RW Miller, Shaun (2017): Miller made good use of his speed in this game, notably in the first period as he was involved a lot in the play. He scored a very nice goal with a perfect wrist shot that went top corner; no chance for the Foreurs' goaltender on that one. In addition, he almost scored the tying goal late in the game. He worked hard all game long and saw his ice time increase in the 3rd period as the Armada was attempting their comeback.

BLB #96 RW Pospisil, Kristian (2016): Pospisil was the biggest threat offensively for the Armada today. He scored a very nice goal in the 3rd period to get them back in the game. He's not a fast skater, but used his size and strength to manoeuvre in the offensive zone and was strong along the wall. He also was effective on the forecheck and created turnovers with a good active stick, including one on Joel Teasdale's goal in the 1st period.

BLB #24 C Teasdale, Joel (2017): Teasdale was used at center today and also on the point on the power play (first unit). Didn't look overly comfortable handling the puck on the point, but was still able to show flashes of his good on-ice vision. He scored in the first period after a great job by Pospisil on the forecheck. Once again today, Teasdale was strong along the wall and won a lot of puck battles. He kept his game simple, took some good shots on goal, and always drove to the net to look for rebounds.

BLB #89 C Picard, Miguel (2016): Picard generated two to three scoring chances during the game just because of his hard work and his will to go in front of the net. He was used in a shutdown role all game long, mostly versus the Gauthier line and on the PK as well. He was used in 3-on-5 penalty-killing situations and was a key player for Joël Bouchard's team in every defensive situation. He did, however, lose a key faceoff to Beauregard, which led to Julien Gauthier's 2nd goal.

BLB #22 RW Katerinakis, Alexander (2016): He didn't start the game on a good note after taking a bad penalty (retaliation after getting hit hard in the neutral zone). All game long, he seemed frustrated and received at least four solid hits during the game. He was clearly off his game after those hits, even getting a bad penalty in the offensive zone on the power play. He still showed good bursts of speed on a couple of rushes, but no scoring chances to show for it.

Russia vs Finland, U17 5 Nations Tournament, February 9th, 2016

RUS #1 G Tarasov, Daniil (2017) - Didn't really make any high-end saves, though he was not consistently peppered with shots, he seemed to let in most of the good chances Finland got with a 3:0 score by the end of second period. Didn't inspire any confidence whenever the play was in Russia's defensive zone. Not a strong performance for him.

RUS #6 LD Rubinchik, Mark (2017) - Had periods of really strong play with the puck. Average defensively, but did a good job bringing the puck up ice with his skating, even attacking the net once. Also was firing shots from the point, probably more-so than any other defenseman on the ice.

RUS #7 RD Baranov, Veniamin (2017) - Thought he was solid defensively, looked a bit tentative to create offense or get involved further up ice. Had a nice pass on Chekhovich's goal.

RUS #8 C Demin, Pavel (2017) - A solid two-way game. Wasn't the most creative with the puck but a lot of smart high-percentage plays. Had a nice compete to his game, certainly played bigger than his size. Liked seeing him kill time behind Finland's net against two Finnish players while he battled on the wall.

RUS #9 C Bitsadze, Mikhail (2018) - Had some flashes of good offensive play. Would ramp up his play if he saw a high-end offensive opportunity developing, but wasn't quite as consistent at the less flashy parts of the game. Would have liked seeing some of that same will he got when trying to contribute on scoring plays to also create and start plays for his team.

RUS #12 LW Alekseev, Yaroslav (2017) - Great job stealing the puck from Isiguzo on his blueline and taking off with speed before converting on a nice shot. Had some opportunities utilizing his skating to attack with speed and catching defensemen flat-footed or out of position.

RUS #18 RD Samorukov, Dmitri (2017) - Real smart plays with the puck, and was a very strong defensive presence. Really solid positionally in his own zone as well as when defending in transition. He had a big hit on Nyman at his blueline, and was willing to play physical and close the gap on forwards without taking himself out of position.

RUS #24 RW Kostin, Klim (2017) - Was a real horse out there with his size and skating. Good reach in protecting the puck. Goes around defensemen with ease and can make circles or zigzag around the offensive zone. Didn't really throw his body around much on the forecheck, but he's a tank with the puck.

RUS #25 RW Kovalenko, Nikolai (2018) - Had some good shifts, especially early on. He can be a real slippery guy on his skates with him turning around and changing directions. Especially in corners, despite his smaller size, he showed good elusiveness and liked how he balanced himself on his skates.

RUS #27 C Marushev, Maxim (2017) - Seemed to have solid size and skating but struggled to create anything once he brought the puck into the offensive zone. Most of the time the play died on his stick or immediately after he made the play.

FIN #5 RD Teravainen, Eero (2017) - Good decision-making with the puck, performs his outlets with ease and seems to have no issue finding open forwards. Read the play well defensively, but didn't strike me as a real strong defensive game for him. Good puck-distribution on PP, but a bit too predictable as he almost never seemed to show any interest in shooting.

FIN #12 LW Koskenkorva, Jesse (2017) - Looked like a reasonably smart forward with a decent compete level, but didn't make himself stand out in any particular way. Wasn't physical, nor terribly skilled, but did an alright job with his minutes. Engaging defensively as well.

FIN #13 C Ikonen, Joni (2017) - Scored the first game of the goal with a nice quick wrist-shot. Good stickhandling and can handle the puck while moving his feet. Had some one-timers from the left circle on the powerplay, but felt like his shot selection wasn't very good, at times forced shots that weren't there.

FIN #22 LW Virtanen, Santeri (2017) - Had a nice pass to Heponiemi for his goal. Was a threat a couple of times with his shot. Put the game away in the last minute with a nice move around the Russian goalie. Can struggle catching up on the backcheck due to his skating that needs improvement. Also limits him in bringing the puck up through the neutral zone as Russian D closed on him very fast. Smart game though, still found ways to contribute.

FIN #24 LW Nyman, Linus (2017) - He had a nifty cut-move towards the middle almost beating the goalie as well. Left the game after the Samorukov hit.

FIN #25 RW Heponiemi, Aleksi (2017) - Heponiemi had some good isolated shifts as far offensive zone chances go, did a good job on the PP playing the right side as well. Scored after a Virtanen feed, and was directly involved in creating the last minute goal that put the game away for Finland. He can go for a period of time where he's not doing a lot offensively, but he's a smart player in all three zones.

FIN #27 RD Rasanen, Eemeli (2017) - He really struggled. Slow in his movement and not up to the pace of the game, not with his skating, his hands, or his mind. Certainly appealing tools to look out for down the road though.

FIN #30 G Lehtinen, Lassi (2017) - He had a strong game. A really even-keel demeanour, rarely gets flustered. Very fluid movement in his crease and positions himself well for shots. Not a big goalie. The goals he gave up were both high-end one-on-one scoring chances.

Czech Republic vs USA, U17 5 Nations Tournament, February 9th, 2016

CZE #2 G Vomacka, Tomas (2017) - Vomacka was frustrating USA shooters all game long as they could not find ways to turn their possession into goals. Vomacka always seemed to get some part of his body on pucks and made several good saves both up-close on jam plays in traffic and on lateral passes, as well as on outnumbered rushes against. Vomacka played an intense game in the net and was the key player that allowed the Czechs to win this game.

CZE #4 RD Kral, Filip (2018) - Kral showed himself to be adept at making accurate first passes as well as being an offensive threat. He stripped Mishmash of the puck and produced a good scoring chance for himself skating the length of the ice. His rush in OT also drew the penalty that produced the GWG for the Czechs. Was more than willing to be active offensively.

CZE #8 RD Rutar, Ludvik (2017) - Rutar did not do much offensively, but had a solid game in defensive zone, especially around the net and on the wall. Did a good job protecting the slot and pushing USA offense to outside.

CZE #9 LD Salda, Radim (2017) - He had a very average game, he was paired with Kral and played a more conservative game as Kral was looking to get offensively involved. Salda did not have many mistakes, but did not have a big impact defensively either.

CZE #12 C Kern, Jan (2017) - Though Czech Republic did not have much offensive zone time, Kern had a relatively solid two-way game. On PK he seemed to back off a bit too much which allowed USA to easily move the puck around, but outside of that Kern seemed to compete well over the ice. He also came up big in key moments, converting a horrible Barratt turnover into a goal and scoring the OT winner on a rebound from a Mikyska slapshot.

CZE #13 RW Safin, Ostap (2017) - Big size and showed some good offensive zone instincts when he got the puck. Seemed a bit sluggish with his skating, especially his agility and first few steps lacked jump.

CZE #16 RW Svoboda, Matyas (2017) - Had a good sequence killing time on PK using his big body to protect the puck on the wall from a couple of USA players. Quiet game at even strength for the most part.

USA #31 G Scheel, Adam (2017) - He had no real work for most of the first period. Gave up a bad goal from a poor angle with the puck bouncing from the back of his leg into the net and then gave up another goal on his first real scoring chance against before being pulled.

USA #33 G St. Cyr, Dylan (2017) - Like Scheel, he too had minimal workload, though he at least didn't give up any bad goals. The first goal he gave up was from a horrific turnover directly in front of him and the OT winner was on his juicy rebound that he could arguably direct more to the side. Overall, a very pedestrian night with not much work, certainly didn't come up big for his team either.

USA #37 C Tkachuk, Brady (2018) - He was quite good on faceoffs and seemed to smartly distribute the puck to his linemates. I thought his line as a whole struggled a bit with taking the puck into scoring areas, but that was more a cause of his wingers' trigger-happy shoot from any position approach.

USA #41 RD Maniscalco, Josh (2017) - Not the most offensive blueliner on his team, but I thought he was US's best blueliner at breaking up plays. Engaging physically and very positionally solid with getting his stick and body on pucks. Seemed to quickly end whatever attempts Czech Republic had at gaining offensive zone entry against him.

USA #42 RW Dhooghe, Sean (2017) - Relentless all game long, was surprised he only ended up with an assist based on the amount of scoring chances he produced for himself and others. Was consistently getting into scoring areas with ease and despite his small size, he had no problem attacking the net.

USA #43 LD Hughes, Quinn (2018) - Great puck-handling and skating from the back-end. Really intelligent offensive player. Sees the ice very well, and was very good at bringing the puck up ice as well as moving around the offensive zone and distributing the puck. Had a very good chance deking his way to the net late in third period but couldn't convert. Sometimes overhandled the puck instead of taking advantage of open space.

USA #46 LW Mismash, Grant (2017) - Not a bad game, but I thought he was forcing too many of his shots. Would have liked to see more patience with the puck from him, a lot of his shots were from outside or from poor angles and simply resulted in loss of possession if his linemates didn't manage to get to the puck first.

USA #51 RD Farrance, David (2017) - Had a solid puck-moving game, not as flashy as Hughes but seemed to be a core compoment of USA's puck-movement out of their zone and through the neutral zone which was one of their strong points that allowed them extensive offensive zone time and Farrance was a key part of that.

USA #52 LW Tortora, Jacob (2017) - Tortora scored on a great effort in the last minute of second period, taking off from his own end and deking out Vomacka. Tortora had real good jump throughout and was especially dangerous with his speed.

USA #56 LD Gildon, Max (2017) - Thought he was pretty underwhelming. No real offensive or defensive impact. Took a lot of time to make decisions with the puck which was slowing the pace down. His defensive gaps and positional play weren't that good either.

USA #57 C Reedy, Scott (2017) - Came out flat in the first period. His game improved in the second, but he was still just OK from that point on. His release looks good, though his shot selection could have been better. A couple of good shifts in the second half, keeping the puck in Czech Republic's zone.

Sweden vs Russia, U17 5 Nations Tournament, February 10th, 2016

SWE #1 G Eriksson-Ek, Olle (2017) - Eriksson-Ek made the saves he needed to but failed to come up big on any grade A scoring chances against. His rebound control was good for the most part. He had one erratic play in his crease losing his balance. Sometimes looked flustered by quicker lateral puck-movement to which he responded by retreating deeper into his net.

SWE #2 RD Hedberg, Tom (2017) - Had a good offensive zone move pinching deep and making his way to the net, producing a rebound that Ringsby easily cleaned up into the net. Hedberg was active offensively and would often get involved in the offensive zone.
SWE #5 LD Ehrnberg, Calle (2017) - A really slight but fluid defenseman. Did a good job skating the puck out of his zone on a couple of ocassions, but lacked punch in offensive zone.

SWE #9 LD Walfridsson, Sebastian (2017) - Walfridsson provided some muscle on the back-end, as he played a sturdier game in comparison to some of their slighter defensemen. He was mostly just OK logging his minutes, not a lot there offensively and had one bad defensive zone pass missing his partner.

SWE #11 LW Aterius, Erik (2017) - Good play off the puck. Went to the net and screened the goalie. Also knows how to get open and was decent on the forecheck. Didn't get much done with the puck, struggled to string passes together.
SWE #24 C Ringsby, Jakob (2017) - Good on faceoffs. Scored a goal cleaning up Hedberg's rebound. Smart game down the middle, used open lanes and moved the puck, capable of keeping possession for his team. His game looked a bit vanilla as far as creating scoring chances goes, wasn't really much of a consistent threat.

SWE #26 RW Zetterlund, Fabian (2017) - He was the best Swedish forward. Good speed, had some pace to his game and was one of the few Swedes who were consistently creating plays in offensive zone. Scored a goal on a wristshot from a bit further out with the goalie screened.

SWE #29 C Tjernstrom, Max (2017) - I thought he competed really well, especially early on. Effective defensively and on the forecheck, brought puck up ice as well. Saw some PK time and did well there. Tailed off later in the game.

RUS #4 LD Alexeev, Aleksandr (2018) - Good skating and size. Will engage the forward once he enters into his zone of control. Thought he was a bit tentative overall, his tools shoudl allow him to do more.
RUS #6 LD Rubinchik, Mark (2017) - Thought he had a great defensive game. Maybe not quite as offensively involved as in his previous game of the tournament, but he used that same energy he has for defense. Quickly closed down on Swedish forwards, won the majority of his battles and quickly moved the puck out.

RUS #8 C Demin, Pavel (2017) - He'll do whatever he needs to do to help his team. Plays the whole ice all situations, offensively, defensively, faceoffs...really a high level of attention to details. Not skilled enough to be consistently dangerous offensively, but did a real good job on zone entries in the third period. Set up some offensive zone time for his team.

RUS #9 C Bitsadze, Mikhail (2018) - Started off with a good tempo to his game. Competed well for pucks, but got himself in trouble when trying to deke through players. Mixed results there. Tailed off quickly after the first period. Some good one on one moves, but his game lacked any semblance of control and patience with the puck. Had EN goal.

RUS #10 C Lipanov, Alexey (2017) - An alright mistake-free game, thought he was almost too conservative in his approach. Too passive of a game where he didn't take any chances, ended up limiting himself by observing the play too often.

RUS #12 LW Alekseev, Yaroslav (2017) - Among the quietest three point performances I've seen this year. Doesn't have consistent shift-to-shift impact but he can really sting you with one of his quick strikes. Has good off the puck reads. Read a turnover beating the D to the far-side post and finished with authority. Good pass from side of the post to Kostin for first goal of the game as well. An assist on the EN as well.

RUS #15 LW Maximov, Kirill (2017) - Important goal last minute of second period to tie the game up. Made a nice move to the inside before finishing. Had a couple of good offensive chances in the game.

RUS #18 RD Samorukov, Dmitri (2017) - Solid positionally, quite physical. A bit sloppier with moving the puck out of his zone in this game. Seen him flatten another forward on his blueline. Slapshot bomb late in third put his team up by one with just a minute to go.

RUS #24 RW Kostin, Klim (2017) - Set up a dominant offensive zone shift that lead to his goal with Y. Alekseev passing him the puck for an accurate snapshot from up-close. Does whatever he wants to do with the puck, was almost too easy for him to keep the puck to himself at his size, skill, and mobility. That said, seemed to lack the drive to really bring it shift after shift. Thought he was at times a bit lazy without the puck as well.

RUS #25 RW Kovalenko, Nikolai (2018) - Not much of a factor in this game. Had one very nice move in the corner, throwing the Swedish D off and producing a good scoring chance.

RUS #26 LD Rarov, Alexey (2017) - Saw both PP and PK time. Moved the puck well, panic-free game and really contributed to Russia's breakouts. Can keep the puck in the offensive zone holding the blueline, but was not much of a threat with his shot.

RUS #30 G Zhukov, Maxim (2017) - He had a decent game. Gave up goals on a rebound, a screen, and an odd bounce. Good when he has clear sight of the puck, thought he was at times a bit unsure with traffic and on obstructed shots. Can also come up with a good save on second efforts.

USA vs Finland, U17 5 Nations Tournament, February 10th, 2016

USA #33 G St. Cyr, Dylan (2017) - St. Cyr had a strong game, thought he held the forth there for USA a couple of times. Some good saves on quality scoring chances, especially him getting across in time on a 2 on 1 to make the save really stood out. Thought he was seeing pucks well and battled in traffic despite being a smaller goalie.

USA #37 C Tkachuk, Brady (2018) - Tkachuk is a real leader out there for this team. Was great on faceoffs, saw both PP and PK time, he establishes control for his team on every shift. Competes, goes to the hard areas, wins battles, good passing vision. He brought the same game every shift. Scored the first goal of the game reading that the Finnish goalie was out of position.

USA #42 RW Dhooghe, Sean (2017) - Among the most competitve players on the ice, his shorthanded goal with him taking off and beating Ikonen to the puck was pretty much his game in a nutshell. His feet never stop moving.

USA #43 LD Hughes, Quinn (2018) - Not quite as offensively active as in some other viewings but still a very strong game for him. His skating ability, vision and puckhandling is obvious every time he takes off from his own zone. Had a tremendous rush and a backhand dish to Reedy who didn't manage to finish.

USA #46 LW Mismash, Grant (2017) - He scored a goal taking off from neutral zone with the Finnish D being caught flat footed and scored on a wrister. Mismash didn't have the flashiest game, but he he had a good knack for finding some scoring opportunities.

USA #52 LW Tortora, Jacob (2017) - Had a great move exploding with speed from neutral zone and leaving Teravainen in dust. Would have liked seeing him do more with the puck on the cycle, a couple of good chances with his reads and speed though.

USA #53 C Barratt, Evan (2017) - Thought he was one of the better players on the ice. Might have had the most puck touches in the game overall, he did a real good job at being an open potion for the puck-carrier in all three zones. Real smart 10 foot passes with the puck, too.

USA #57 C Reedy, Scott (2017) - His best chance was off a Hughes pass, he didn't manage to convert though. He had an OK game, would have liked seeing him utilize his shot more, his feet can at times look a bit sluggish, too. In some of my viewings he shot more than he should, I thought he deferred too much in this one.

FIN #1 G Luukkonen, Ukko-Pekka (2017) - Big goalie, too reactive at times. Didn't cover the post on the first goal which resulted in Tkachuk beating him from a bad angle. He had a couple of high-end saves, but thought he was far too passive overall, played back on his heels more than anything.

FIN #5 LD Teravainen, Eero (2017) - Great first pass, consistently finds open lanes and executes accurate crisp outlets. Would have liked seeing more punch out of him defensively as well as in the offensive zone. He had one shot that immediately produced a good rebound, but other than that he semmed to hang back quite a bit.

FIN #6 RD Isiguzo, Bernard (2017) - Wasn't really impressed with Finnish D in this game, but he was probably the best one of them in his own zone. Actually seemed to close down forwards effectively and get his body on them, breaking up attacks.

FIN #7 RD Vesterinen, Saku (2017) - He had some flair to his game and did well on the PP. Can handle the puck, though a few times he tried fancy stickhandles in his own zone resulting in dangerous situations as opposed to just executing a smart quick pass.

FIN #13 C Ikonen, Joni (2017) - Showed off his skill and skating ability a couple of times, gaining the offensive zone then circling back for open passing lanes. He had an incredibly careless if not lazy play on the PP just slowly skating to the puck in his own zone before Dhooghe stole it and scored.
FIN #25 RW Heponiemi, Aleksi (2017) - Had a real nice move coming off the wall into the slot area and delaying his shot which allowed him to drag the puck further and change the angle before finishing.

FIN #27 RD Rasanen, Eemeli (2017) - He had one hit late in third period that plastered a USA forward to the wall. Tried handling the puck once with a forward pressuring him and immediately coughed it up. Will need to improve his quickness and the pace at which he executes. Didn't seem like he has a terribly poor hockey IQ though.

Halifax Mooseheads vs Gatineau Olympiques, Feb 10th, 2016, QMJHL

Robert Guertin Arena

HAL #3 RD Flower, Walter (2017) – Played a very good game tonight, made a lot of good decisions with the puck, his first pass coming out of the zone was good missed a few easy passes, has really good size for a 16 year old and should fit into his body as he gets older, has a really good stick as well he knows when to get it in the lanes whether it's on the PK or in the dzone, plays in a lot of situations tonight, not physical enough for his size, not a lot of panic in his game either, his gap control was ok again would like him to set up more and trust his teammates are covering for him.

HAL #41 RW Foriter, Maxime (2016) – Played an ok game tonight, has really good speed and acceleration and used it well on a few occasion going wide on defenders, but he stop every time and looked for the trailer coming in instead of going hard to the net with his momentum to create some chances, he played too much on the perimeter tonight, has a long reach and can be effective in tight, showed some skill on the power play coming off the half wall, struggles with his positioning in the DZone and got running around too much instead of staying in his position, -2 tonight,

HAL #89 C Somppi, Otto (2016) – Played ok tonight as well, didn't notice him at all in the first period and a half, he got his feet rolling on a power play and then showed his skill, distributes the puck nice to his teammates, really good and touch passes coming off the rush on the wall, and sees the ice really well, other than a few spurts in the 2nd and little in the 3rd he didn't generate anything on a consistent basis, wasn't engaged offensively or physically, kept everything to the outside, was ok on the draws, needs to get stronger and needs to compete every shift to be more effective.

GAT #11 LW Abramov, Vitali (2016) – He was very good tonight, he was all over the ice offensively and it seemed like every time he was on the ice the puck would follow him around everywhere, very smart hockey player, high hockey IQ, reads plays really well and understands where his teammates should be on the ice, made a beautiful no look backhand pass to #91 for a nice goal, he showed very good speed tonight with the puck, and he really protects the puck well against defensemen leaning on them while he still manages to control the puck away from defender and then generates chances, really quick wrist when stickhandling and is able to get the puck off quick making these moves, competes hard every shift, he does tend to stay out too long on his shifts and needs them to be shorter, and needs to keep working on his dzone positioning and get better along the boards.

GAT #31 G Bellemare, Mathieu (2016) – He wasn't tested a whole lot tonight, but when he had to make a save he did, he's a small goalie but is very effective at making himself big and not giving Halifax anything to shoot at, his lateral movement is really good and quick, he can get post to post real quick, tracks the puck well and battles to find the puck good, really good rebound control tonight didn't give Halifax any second chances.

GAT #44 RD Bilodeau, Gabriel (2016) – Didn't play a lot tonight, but when given his ice he played well, good size Defensemen needs to be more physical with his size, move the puck well tonight, didn't miss a lot of passes coming out of the zone, joined in on a couple rushes tonight and showed some offence, needs to get stronger and more engaging in the dzone lost too many battles in his own zone down low, and he struggles with speed needs to get better at body positioning.

Final Score: Halifax 0   Gatineau 6

Finland vs Sweden, U17 5 Nations Tournament, February 11th, 2016

FIN #5 LD Teravainen, Eero (2017) - Thought he was the best defenseman on the ice. As before in the tournament, really good first pass. He got credited for a goal with a shot from the point, though it looked like it was tipped. He was shooting more from the point. What also stood out is that he had a real strong defensive game, getting his sticks on puck and even effectively using his body which was lacking in some of his other games here.

FIN #7 RD Vesterinen, Saku (2017) - Vesterinen had a good game. Him and Teravainen formed a pairing and were really solid throughout. Vesterinen like his partner was quite adept at moving the puck out of his zone which gave Finland a big advantage in quickly turning the play out of their zone off

Swedish attacks and not getting pinned down in their own end. Vesterinen gave a good effort playing a smart controlled game on the back-end.

FIN #10 RW Engberg, Teemu (2017) - He played a real hard checking game. Real good as the first guy on the forecheck. Thought he was key in setting the tone early and putting Sweden back on their heels from which they never quite recovered. Engberg was a pesky, physical presence on the ice.

FIN #13 C Ikonen, Joni (2017) - Thought he had a good game. Scored with a quick release off a Nyman pass. Looked like one of the faster and more skilled players on the ice. Worked hard, too. Struggled a bit with his one timer on PP, didn't look the most comfortable being set up for one timers and his execution wasn't that good either.

FIN #24 LW Nyman, Linus (2017) - Nyman was involved offensively both on Ikonen's goal as well as scoring himself with a slapper from the left circle. He has shown good vision and skill with the puck, but felt like he could work harder to create his own chances.

FIN #25 RW Heponiemi, Aleksi (2017) - Was an up and down game for him. He had some jump in the offensive zone and was good at creating a couple of chances, but too many shifts went by where he was not really involved.

FIN #27 RD Rasanen, Eemeli (2017) - Might have been his best game of the tournament so far. He did a bit better moving the puck and handling it than before. Seemed like he got a bit more ice time as well. Nothing to write home about though, still has a long way to go with skating and pace.

FIN #30 G Lehtinen, Lassi (2017) - Continues to play well. In my viewings of him so far a rather typical game of his in that he was calm and made the saves he had to and has a fluid controlled movement in his crease. Not the most challenging shutout you'll see, Sweden didn't get much done at all.

SWE #1 G Eriksson-Ek, Olle (2017) - He came into the net midway through second period with Sweden down by three. Thought he played an OK stretch of hockey, better at tracking the puck and getting into position in time than I've seen before. Gave up a goal from the left-circle area on a Nyman slapshot, though. Would have been a reasonably good game outside of that.

SWE #9 LD Walfridsson, Sebastian (2017) - Again probably the most mature defenseman on a completely underwhelming Swedish defense. Walfridsson had a couple of good sequences, he protected the puck well, can sustain contact in one and one battles and can lean into players, definitely has some strength to him at least at this level.

SWE #18 C Johansson, Anton (2017) - One of the few Swedish player that played with any jump in this game. Like the rest of the team, Johansson did not have great scoring chances but at least worked his butt off towards that goal. His jump would at least back off Finnish defense and he was not glued to the perimeter like the majority of Swedish forwards were.

SWE #21 LW Sveningsson, Filip (2017) - Tough game for him. Some dumb decisions with the puck, where he'd get the puck in the offensive zone and make a stupid pass to the middle trying to hit a player through tons of sticks in the lane.

SWE #24 C Ringsby, Jakob (2017) - He had one good chance with a Berg stretch-pass hitting him in the neutral zone. Nothing much there outside of that, a bit of a passenger.

SWE #26 RW Zetterlund, Fabian (2017) - Good speed and skill with the puck. Zero help from his linemates, he tries to create plays but he can only do so much on his own. Continues to jump out as the best Swede on this team.

SWE #29 C Tjernstrom, Max (2017) - Tjernstrom was pretty much a non-factor offensively, the good part of his game was that he didn't cheat on the effort part of it. Couple of good efforts on PK as well.

SWE #30 G Soderblom, Arvid (2017) - He got pulled after his third goal in the second period. Certainly could have done better on some of those, especially the second one he seemed to react late. Thought he was a bit unlucky outside of that, his movement and angles seemed OK, didn't come away thinking that he had horrible athletic ability or lack of technique.

West Kelowna Warriors at Penticton Vees, February 12, 2016

PEN #17 LC Jost, Tyson (2016) - Yet another standout offensive performance from Jost. Sniped two goals on the first period. Wristshot is a cut above the rest in this league. Can pick his spots and score cleanly. Continued to quarterback the first powerplay unit alongside Fabbro. Also proved very useful on the penalty kill tonight. Has improved leaps and bounds in the faceoff circle.

PEN #23 LC Sillinger, Owen (2017) - Looks quicker and more agile with each viewing. Not terribly fast in terms of straight-ahead acceleration, but works really hard on the backcheck whilst remaining fairly disciplined. Has an active stick on the defensive side of the puck. Doesn't back down from the post-whistle shoving game, even though he's a bit undersized.

PEN #57 RD Fabbro, Dante (2016) - A relatively quiet game by Fabbro's standards in terms of offense, but a good game nonetheless. Played in all situations. First passes were powerful and smartly directed. Made some great passes across the ice to set up teammates in the offensive zone. Threw his body around, and looked like a brickhouse. Didn't make any noticeable mistakes.

PEN #77 RD Mendell, Griffin (2017) - Straight-ahead acceleration only slightly above-average. But he pivots from forward to backwards quickly, easily able to recover when caught a step behind. Good gap control. Dependable when hounding the puck down in the corner. An excellent penalty killer. Good shot blocker. Good pokecheck.

Kärpät at Sport, February, 12nd, 2016

KAR #9 RW Puljujärvi, Jesse (2016) - Jesse had a subpar night. played 17 minutes and recorded zero shots. He didn't win battles and usually lost his balance when the game got rough. He used his speed challenging opponent but made usually bad decisions with in the o-zone.

University of Michigan at University of Wisconsin, February 12th, 2016

UW #30 G Jurusik, Matt (2016) —Tonight was one of Jurusik's best games of the season. He made a number of point blank saves on the evening, Made a great save on a 3 on 2 on a shot from the slot by Kyle Connor. Jurusik kept his team in the game, which looked overmatched tonight. Michigan eventually got a power play goal and an empty netter in the 3rd period to pull away. Jurusik tracked the puck well and showed good poise and positioning in the crease and got more confident as the game went on. Jurusik was under siege in the 3rd period, facing 19 shots and turning away 18 of them. On the evening Jurusik turned away 37 of 40 shots.

UW #9 C/W Kunin, Luke (2016) – Threw some big open ice hits and played with an edge around the puck all night. His line with Cameron Hughes (BOS '15) and Grant Besse (ANA ' 13) could not keep up with Michigan's top line as a unit tonight, but Kunin stayed above the puck for most of the night which has been an issue at times in his freshman year.

UW#15 LW Freytag, Matthew (2016+) – Physical on the fore-check and in front of the net. Battled hard in the corners and was agitating all night. Effort has hardly been an issue for Freytag this season as he finds a way to contribute even when left of the score sheet.

MICH #18 LW Connor, Kyle (WPG, 2015) – Connor had 1 Assist tonight but his line with JT Compher (Buf' 13) and Tyler Motte (CHI '13) was dominate all night. Connor had a number of great scoring chances that UW goalie Jurusik made some terrific saves on. Connor's speed through the Neutral zone was difficult for Wisconsin to handle, and seemed to get the puck to the net at will. Kyle showed every bit the skill that had him selected in the first round in last year's draft and looked like one of the best players in all of college hockey as a freshman.

MICH #13 LD Werenski, Zach (CLB' 15) –Werenski didn't jump into the play a lot tonight but moved the puck up the ice with quick passing and decision making. His pairing along with Joseph Cecconi (DAL '15) was the steady hand that took care of things in his own end and controlled the game well as a pairing.

Final Score: 4-1 Michigan

Cape-Breton Screaming Eagles at Drummondville Voltigeurs, February 13th 2016

CAP #18 LW Dubois, Pierre-Luc (2016): Good game overall from Dubois. While he didn't register any points, he was strong in all three zones today. He was involved physically, even after whistles, as Drummondville players were trying to take him off his game. He was really good at protecting the puck in the offensive zone along the boards and behind the net. He showed great strength and technique, using his back to shield his opponents away. He had a couple of nice scoring opportunities, including in the first period when he hit the post from a great wrist shot just after making a zone entry. He was involved in front of the net and gave Drummondville defensemen some headaches. He also played a shift or two in the 2nd period on the point on the power play, showing some versatility.

CAP #21 RW Hoyt, Peyton (2017): The 16 year old rookie started the game on the 4th line, but saw his ice time increase in the 2nd and 3rd periods. He started using his speed and grit in the 2nd period, including on a couple of nice rushes where he would take the puck wide and cut to the net. He showed good intensity and played a feisty game. In the 3rd period behind the net, he made a couple of nice passes, showing good vision with the puck on his stick.

CAP #23 LW Lazarev, Maxim (2016): The 19 year old Russian scored a nice goal in this game, he showed a very good release on his shot and also good patience, waiting an extra second before releasing it. He played on the 2nd line today, as in previous viewings he was usually on the Dubois/Svechnikov line, and was also playing on his off-wing. With the puck on his stick, Lazarev usually looks for passing options first, as was often the case today.

DRU #90 LW Poirier, William (2018): The young forward was promoted to the top line once team captain Joey Ratelle went down with an injury. He scored the opening goal of the game finishing a great passing play at the net from Carcone and Barré-Boulet. He showed his smarts in the defensive zone, playing sound hockey with a good active stick and winning his battles. Will need to work on his speed, as he lacks agility and explosiveness.

DRU #19 C Barré-Boulet, Alex (2016): The 18 year old centerman was not a standout offensively today for the Voltigeurs, aside from the nice pass he made on Poirier's goal at the beginning of the game. He did a good job coming back deep in his zone to help his defensemen out. But overall, he was not very noticeable out there.

DRU #8 RW Carcone, Michael (2016): This was one of the quietest performances I saw from Carcone all year long. He was manhandled physically at times during this game versus bigger Cape Breton players. He made some nice plays with the puck in the offensive zone, mostly as a playmaker. Didn't skate well today, looked a bit slow out there.

DRU #22 LW Sevigny, Mathieu (2016): Sevigny was one of the better Voltigeurs today; he worked hard as usual at both ends of the ice but was able to create more scoring chances than he usually does. He did a lot of nice things while in possession of the puck in the offensive zone including some good passes. He was strong on the puck and made good use of his frame to protect the puck down low.

DRU #9 C Afanasyev, Kristian (2016): Not a gifted skater, Afanasyev worked hard today and showed good commitment on the backcheck. I saw a good compete level from him at both ends of the ice. He had some sequences where he was able to show off a very good wrist shot. He will often finish his shift near the opposing goaltender, getting his nose dirty in the slot.

DRU #4 LD Gagné, Benjamin (2017): Liked his passing game in the first period. He made quick decisions and was quick to counter-attack. A left-shooting defenseman playing on the right side today, as he has for most of the season with the Voltigeurs, on their 3rd pairing. He was less noticeable in the 2nd and 3rd periods with the puck. Not the biggest defenseman, but always competes hard and who finds himself in PK situations often.

Slovakia vs Germany, U18 Dzurilla Tournament, February 13, 2016

GER #24 C Eder, Tobias (2016) - Really strong game today, captained his team well. Eder consistently finds weaknesses in his opponents and exploits them. Had a shorthanded breakaway, shot five-hole with a quick release, but the goalie made a great save. Set up his power play line mate with a drop pass assist after he raced down the wing, cut across the high-slot. Coach had him start in the dzone more than any player on the roster. Despite that, he struggled in the face-off dot. Eder needs to get stronger, big weakness in his overall game. Took a hard hit in the first period - rattled him - he went to the bench and through his stick and sat down. But, next shift he came out a finished a check, but wasn't that hard of a hit. He tried to lay some hits tonight, but bounced off very easily. One timer today was lacking some juice. His shot release is quick and deceptive - high end skill here. Head butted a puck on net like a soccer player in from to the net, wouldn't count but it was a interesting play. Was passing really well, setting up his line mates. He has a good hockey IQ, saw opportunities really well tonight. Didn't score, but was effective in all three zones.

GER #21 LW Kiefersauer, Christoph (2016) - never gives up on the back check. Worked hard in all three zones today. Stopped a great scoring opportunity on the back check in the first period. Great effort on the penalty kill.

GER #8 LW Ratmann, Marvin (2017) - Did a great job finding openings in the defensive zone. Scored two goals that had him slipping the far side/back door, catching a pass and getting a quick shot on net. Sneaky player.

GER #14 C Jahnke, Charlie (2016) - hard not to mention this kid. He doesn't quit. Despite his slender frame, he throws whatever weight he has into every hit, almost every chance he gets. When he gets the puck, he is hard to knock off, surprisingly. Appears to really enjoy working hard below the goal line, digging pucks out, taking them to the net. Good competitor.

GER #30 G Pantkowski, Mirko (2016) - didn't get to see much of him as Germany split their goalie duties tonight. But he has a noticeably strong technique and good patience. Angles are right on, plays on top of his crease. Good athletic posture in his stance. One goal against him - penalty kill, deflected shot from the point that snuck through his five hole. He was awarded goalie of the tournament. Had a scare puck playing incident that almost led to a goal. But he plays with lots of confidence.

GER #1 G Steinmann, Jonas (2017) - Steinmann had a terrific game today. Made some ridiculous saves tonight, really kept his team in the game. Very strong lateral pushes, powerful. Made a huge glove save on a 2-on-1, laterally sliding from his right to left. Was very solid in tight, his legs are quick and seal up the ice very well. Stopped at least four shots that should have ended up in the back of the net, including one very late in the game pushing across and getting his leg out. He doesn't have a physically dominating presence in the crease, but his quick on his feet and knows his angles.

SVK #3 LD Zelenak, Vojtech (2016) - He came to play today. His puck decisions were, again, smart and simple. Was on the point for the first power play goal, slid a puck back to his partner and he shot it for a deflection into the net. But also played in front of the net on the power play (with his big frame, goalies must hate him). Yelled at himself a couple of times tonight after some errors - loud. When Eder came down on him, Zelenak gave him too much of a gap allowing Eder to get some speed.

SVK #6 LD Fehervary, Martin (2018) - Poked in a lose puck to get Slovakia's second goal on the power play. There is a lot to like about Fehervary - size, footwork is strong and balanced, puck decisions are consistently right. He is certainly an intriguing prospect for the 2018 draft being a late '99 birth year. Played a lot of ice tonight and was used also in front of the net on the powerplay.

SVK #11 RD Krempasky, Martin (2016) - Simple, nothing fancy defensemen and was reliable tonight except one hiccup at the end of the game. Was seeing passing lanes well and hitting his targets tape. Was under heavy pressure in the third and shot the puck out of the ice for a delayed game call.
SVK #8 LW Ruzicka, Adam (2017) - Showed some speed tonight, has a high gear, and was creating offensive opportunities. Had a breakaway in the third but goalie had to make a big save to stop him. Worth tracking his progress.

University of Michigan at University of Wisconsin, February 13th, 2016, NCAA

UW #9 CW, Kunin, Luke (2016) – Tonight was one of Kunin's best games of the season. He registered 2 goals tonight; one was to tie the game in the final 30 seconds by driving the net and banging home a loose puck on the backdoor. Kunin was engaged physically and played a controlled nasty game, got under the opponent's skin on almost every shift.
Final Score: 4-4 OT

Sweden vs Czech Republic, U17 5 Nations Tournament, February 13th, 2016

SWE #1 G Eriksson-Ek, Olle (2017) - Thought it was a disappointing showing for him. Both the Svoboda and Safin goals were not impossible to save. And he somehow put a flubbed Kral point shot that was going high over the net into his own goal. Not sure about his focus in this game, didn't look comfortable.

SWE #5 LD Ehrnberg, Calle (2017) - Played with confidence with the puck and got involved offensively, good at gaining space as he can skate well and handle the puck while moving up the ice, wasn't scared of doing an extra stickhandle or two and it worked out for him more often than not. His shot late in the third got redirected for a tie game.

SWE #10 RD Berg, August (2017) - Had a couple of real good rushes, there was a sequence where he left the forwards behind him and skated it into offensive zone himself taking it directly to the net. Thought he did a good job defensively as well. The only blemish on his record were a couple of inaccurate passes.

SWE #16 RW Bemstrom, Emil (2017) - Thought he was the best Swedish forward. He was buzzing out there, kept his feet moving and went to scoring areas with authority. Real good compete level out there and was involved in the play a lot.

SWE #17 RW Emanuelsson, Jesper (2017) - Had some nifty one on one moves and isolated chances but thought he was way too passive overall. He flashes enough talent that makes you believe he could have done more on a consistent basis.

SWE #21 LW Sveningsson, Filip (2017) - His offensive reads were off for most of the game. Struggled to get open, when he did get the puck he would quickly lose it. Constantly put himself into situations where he couldn't do much either with or without the puck.

SWE #23 C Wennlund, Max (2017) - Thought he had a good game but failed to really get those high-end scoring chances. He did tie the game in the second period redirecting a Zetterlund slapshot/pass.

SWE #26 RW Zetterlund, Fabian (2017) - Not necessarily a bad game, but he is capable of better. Thought he played a perimeter game, failing to get pucks or take pucks into scoring areas with any consistency. Had an assist on Wennlund's tip after his slap/pass to the far-side post.

SWE #29 C Tjernstrom, Max (2017) - Pretty quiet game for him. No glaring mistakes, but was not invovled much offensively for most of the game. Did have a key goal late in third redirecting an Ehrnberg shot tying it up.

CZE #1 G Skarek, Jakub (2018) - Had a strong game with a high volume of shots, though wouldn't say a high amount of quality scoring chances against. Good size and movement. Thought he was sliding out of position a bit excessively early in the first period but he cleaned that up. Looked quick with his recovery after dropping down. He did get beat one on one by a Johansson wristshot but no real bad goals to speak of.

CZE #4 RD Kral, Filip (2018) - Was impressive with the puck on his stick, can move the puck out but also has a good skill level when creating in the offensive zone. He scored an odd goal by a Eriksson-Ek mistake on his flubbed shot from the point.

CZE #6 LD Mikyska, Dalimil (2017) - One of the better defensive players, especially early on. Mikyska used his pokecheck well and was also using his body to block shots. Did a good job with puck-movement, too.

CZE #12 C Kern, Jan (2017) - Kern's forechecking lead directly to the first goal of the game. Really liked Kern's situational reads. He did look like a good skater with some skill, but I liked his awareness and the willingness to work to turn different defensive and offensive scenarios to his advantage even if it was not particularly flashy.

CZE #13 RW Safin, Ostap (2017) - Thought he had some jump in this game but still too hit or miss on a shift by shift basis. He flashes his combination of skill, size, and shot but doesn't impact the game every shift. He scored on a one-timer from the left circle.

CZE #16 LW Svoboda, Matyas (2017) - Can really lean on players. Scored the first goal of the game with a wristshot after Kern created the turnover. His puck protection along the wall was very good, controlled the puck and produced a lot of offensive zone time on several occasions.

CZE #17 LW Machala, Ondrej (2017) - Most notable asset was his speed. Was dangerous a couple of times flying into offensive zone.

CZE #22 RW Pour, Jakub (2017) - Worth noting for his ability to keep his feet moving and his work-ethic, but didn't get much done in this game. You can expect him to work his every shift, though.

NAHL Selects vs Midwest (Top Prospects Game), February 15th, 2016

NAHL #15 RD Clarke, Cameron (2016**) - Clarke was the best defenseman on the ice, exhibiting high amounts of two-way control on the back-end. Clarke would position intelligently and used his stick and body to push forwards wide when they tried to cut inside. He moved around the ice well and had patience with the puck, making strong passes out of his zone. Clarke also made a great move going to the net giving Burgess an easy tap-in goal from his rebound.

NAHL #3 LD Jansons, Gvido (2016*) - Jansons had a solid defensive game, he also displayed some of his skating ability along with the big frame, especially when bringing the puck forward up ice. Though, he didn't always find an open man after skating the puck out. Overall mobility also did not look too impressive outside of forward motion.

NAHL #4 RD Fear, Erich (2016*) - Towering defenseman who kept it simple and didn't put himself into trouble with the puck. Not an liability on the ice, had a couple of solid defensive plays but not much with the puck.

NAHL #10 RW Bender, Koby (2016*) - Good skating ability. Made a nice play gaining the zone and delaying then making an accurate pass back to the point for a Russell shot that made it through into the net.

NAHL #12 C Goodsir, Adam (2017) - Showed some upside with his ability to distribute the puck, though it was more around the perimeter and give-and-go plays rather than setting someone up for a scoring chance. Had one physical shift on the forecheck, finishing both of his checks on defensemen that were trying to make an outlet.

NAHL #21 LD Russell, Rourke (2016) - Played a bit more of a defensive game, preferring to stay back and play it safe. Showed good compete in a battle with a forward around the net, working to push him out. Stood up for himself and gave him a couple of whacks. Scored on a wristshot from the point late in the game.

NAHL #27 C Burgess, Todd (2016**) - Played a smart game on both ends of the ice. Was involved in supporting the puck and making sure he was open for outlets and puck-movement through neutral zone. Had a nice backhand dish on a partial-break for Gorowsky's goal and scored a goal himself putting Clarke's rebound into the net.

NAHL #30 G Johnson, Tyler (2016) - Started the first half of the game. Not a lot of workload, though he did a good job handling the pucks with his stick and moving them. Gave up one goal to an uncontested shot from up-close after his D failed to cover a forward driving the net.

NAHL #45 G LaFontaine, Jack (2016) - Started the second half of the game. He moved well in his crease especially at 6'3, covered his angles well. The goal he gave up was a 2 on 1 SH chance against. Thought he was better after that goal, being a bit more active with some momentum on Midwest's side.

WEST #20 LW Sardina, Joey (2016*) - He scored a goal with a nice effort driving the net. Thought he competed well off the puck and was looking to make things happen with his drive and compete level.

WEST #30 G Nappier, Tommy (2016) - He started the second half of the game. Gave up three very quick goals late in second period. They weren't really soft, but it would be good if he came up with a big save or two there to keep his team in it. Was just OK from that point on, team Midwest had some momentum in the third, so he didn't have quite as much work either.

WEST #35 G Kivlenieks, Matiss (2016**) - He started the first half of the game and did a good job providing some stability in net, saw pucks well through traffic and didn't panic but kept his position. Only gave up one goal on a lateral pass and a quick finish with his defense having a breakdown.

Saginaw Spirit at Sarnia Sting, February 15, 2016

OHL Regular Season

SAG #55 D Middleton, Keaton (2016) - Was able to make plays on the puck down low because a lot of opponents wouldn't engage him. Good play one on one. Good toughness on the wall. Top penalty killing unit.

SAG #56 D Niemelainen, Markus (2016) - Good stick two on two rush. Chased play a little too much and was out of position for some 2 on 1 chances in the slot including the 0-3 goal. Quick on the wall holding puck but doesn't have great hands. Doesn't try to get too fancy with puck on rush and will make a good pass off if he doesn't have a clear lane. Too aggressive on loose puck in neutral zone, not getting there in time resulting in a 3 on 1 chance. Kept chasing play even after it cost a goal.

SAR #5 D Chychrun, Jakob (2016) - Good stick down low, in position but passes still find its way through sometimes. Protects puck well with frame and advances it quickly. Made some good one on one plays but lateral movement is a little slow affecting his ability to consistently defend rushes against skilled players. Had occasional mental lapse in offensive zone but was usually good with the puck.

SAR #10 C Salinitri, Anthony (2016) - Great pass on rush to send White in alone for 2-0 goal. Shot into screens.

SAR #19 LW McGregor, Ryan (2017) - Great move to beat defender and nice shot to score 9-4 goal.

Final Score: Sarnia Sting: 11 - Saginaw Spirit: 4

NAHL Selects vs USNTDP U17 (Top Prospects Game), February 16th, 2016

NAHL #15 RD Clarke, Cameron (2016**) - Clarke had another showing where he displayed good skating with the puck as well as accurate outlets. His ability to read the play and move the puck played a key role in establishing controlled zone exits for his team. Overall, he also had a strong defensive performance, although he was prone to relying too much on his stick when defending laterally, in those situations he could do a better job getting his body on the player as well.

NAHL #21 LD Russell, Rourke (2016) - Russell was more active offensively than in yesterday's showing. He was often seen taking more chances while moving up the ice and sometimes even penetrating deep into offensive zone. He had a nice move in the offensive zone making a backhand pass to an open Burgess who would convert on the play.

NAHL #27 C Burgess, Todd (2016**) - A slippery game that made him challenging to get a hold of. Showed a nice spin move through the neutral zone that changed the point of attack. Had another great move deking out Hughes and Kemp for a scoring chance. Burgess also scored on a top corner wristshot from the slot after a Russell pass. Overall, a good display of his hands and deceptive moves, though he did have one sloppy turnover in his own zone.

NAHL #30 G Johnson, Tyler (2016) - Johnson started the second half of the game. He came up big a couple of times with US pressuring. Did a good job not getting overwhelmed with traffic in front and held his position while US tried to jam the puck behind him. Was great on a critical PK sequence. Saved Reedy's wrist-shot on a 1 on 1 rush. He wasn't exactly outstanding but did an alright job with US putting on some pressure.

NAHL #45 G LaFontaine, Jack (2016) - LaFontaine started the first half of the game. Thought he had a strong performance, quick-movement through the crease and good size. His lateral movement looked controlled and his recovery from dropping down looked quick as well. He didn't face a lot of high-end scoring chances, but was good throughout. Did make a stop on a Hernandez one on one break.

USA #31 G Scheel, Adam (2017) - He did face quite a big volume of shots, but I thought he never really seemed to have the comfort level down. Played slightly back on his heels and overly reactive, not really challenging the shooters much. Felt he was lucky that the puck hit him on some of his saves. Was slow to get across the crease on a weak cross-ice pass.

USA #32 LD Inamoto, Tyler (2017) - Good defensive zone performance in slowing down opponents and not giving up space, but not a lot of control on his outlets, felt he was happy to just rim the puck out of danger on some occassions.
USA #37 C Tkachuk, Brady (2018) - His best shifts were in key moments in third period when the score was close. Went to the dirty areas of the ice and was looking to make things happen. Good vision with the puck as well, thought he struck a good balance between working hard to get the puck into scoring areas without forcing plays and committing turnovers. Scored the first US goal, getting behind D's back and scoring five hole off a Reedy pass.

USA #41 RD Maniscalco, Josh (2017) - He struggled with the pace and his reads a little bit, thought his penalties were a result of him trying to make up for time and space lost. Seemed a step behind when defending and didn't move the puck quick enough when he got it.

USA #42 C Dhooghe, Sean (2017) - Pushes back D with his speed. Good at entering the zone and works hard. He scored a key goal late in second on the PP and made the pass to Mismash for his goal in the third which tied the game. Overall, was one of the better US players, though he could have done a better job turning his speed and jump into controlled possession for his team.

USA #43 LD Hughes, Quinn (2018) - Would have liked seeing more shots out of him, but his ability to take off the puck from his own end and weave through traffic was very apparent. At the point, he could simplify his game and look to get pucks on net with more quickness.

USA #46 LW Mismash, Grant (2017) - He scored the tying goal early in the third period. Had a couple of good passing plays after that, but was largely a disappointment for me through the first two periods. Not really much of a offensive factor.
USA #55 RD Kemp, Phil (2017) - Struggled throughout the game. Intercepted outlets, his passing lacked accuracy resulting in icing as well. Got turned pretty badly by Burgess on one occassion. Not a strong defensive performance and quite poor in his puck-movement in this game.

USA #57 LW Reedy, Scott (2017) - Was making a lot of plays. His feet looked a bit on the slower side, but he had several nice dishes to linemates who were getting into scoring areas. Real good vision there, accurate passing with his backhand as well. Thought he was one of the better playmakers on the ice. Assisted on the first US goal with a nice pass to a rushing Tkachuk.

Sault Ste. Marie Greyhounds at Windsor Spitfires, February 18, 2016

OHL Regular Season

SSM #12 RW Katchouk, Boris (2016) - Good pass under pressure. Does a good job giving his linemates the puck quickly if he doesn't have a lane. Tried to do too much with the puck on the penalty kill in his own zone for turnover. Good passes on the rush for scoring chance. Has a bit of a heavy stride to start but picks up speed quickly and deceptively. Better penalty killing clears later on. Drew a penalty with his penalty killing forecheck pressure. Good power in shot. Good defensive zone coverage and killed time off the clock late with a two goal lead.

SSM #22 C Hawel, Liam (2017) - Big forward, good skating for size. Dump and chase effectively.

SSM #26 LW Gettinger, Tim (2016) - Good frame, protects the puck and passes off well. Lost several defensive zone battles. Slow to the wall and doesn't react quickly enough to situations at times. Went to the net on an odd man rush but fanned on his scoring chances. Didn't make good shot decisions in this game as he got blocked a lot.

SSM #38 C Verbeek, Hayden (2016) - Great forecheck pressure on penalty kill. Plays a high energy game every shift

SSM #52 LW Kopacka, Jack (2016) - Skating still needs work. Finished checks. Went to the net on the draw and nice deflection for scoring chance.

WSR #17 D Stanley, Logan (2016) - Great pass up ice under pressure. Hard/accurate passes. Good stick one on one and doesn't panic. Uses his size on the rush. Knows when to make the simple puck play and when to go for the more difficult options. Half committed to pinch resulting in a loss of possession and out of position on the rush.

WSR #21 C Brown, Logan (2016) - Has a great ability to look causal with the puck then quickly unload a hard wrist shot which can surprise some goaltender. Got involved a few times but was otherwise pretty subdued tonight.

WSR #28 D Nother, Tyler (2016) - Skating has improved a lot this year's. Plays a conservative game and doesn't put himself in bad spots playing safe. Good patience on the point and got his shots through. Good puck patience on the point. Good first pass.

WSR #31 D Sergachev, Mikhail (2016) - Likes to use his size in baffles and in one on one match ups. Cut into his own slot with the puck, lost control but drew a power play out of it. Played puck carrier too much in two on one's. Made some solid one on one plays. Nice touch pass through a seam to set up a scoring chance. Smart passes on the rush. Can make the occasional mental mistakes but generally made good decisions.

WSR #91 C Luchuk, Aaron (2016*) - Looked good tonight using his speed end to end to create chances and made some good passes to set up scoring opportunities.
Final Score: Sault Ste. Marie Greyhounds: 4 - Windsor Spitfires: 1

Sault Ste. Marie Greyhounds at Sarnia Sting, February 21, 2016

OHL Regular Season

SSM #12 RW Katchouk, Boris (2016) - Anticipates defensive zone plays well and is quick on passes. Good backcheck and hard hit on opponent along the wall. Good forecheck pressure. Playing a very inspired game. Crashed into side of the net chasing the puck, missed a few shifts before returning. Went to the net and scored on rebound for 2-2 goal. Great pressure on the penalty kill, played top unit. Had great scoring chance but passed instead when he should have shot.

SSM #52 LW Kopacka, Jack (2016) - Nice one on one move going wide, then good centring pass to set up 1-1 goals. Playing point on Greyhoinds top power play unit. Gets pucks deep. Took puck from battle in overtime walked into the slot for great scoring chance.

SAR #5 D Chychrun, Jakob (2016) - Made some skilled plays carrying the puck up ice. At his best when squaring up one on one. Can sometimes back up too much giving too much gap space. Half committed in puck in neutral zone, didn't get puck and wound up out of position.

SAR #10 C Salinitri, Anthony (2016) - Good defensive play on penalty kill 2 on 1 to break up chance then drew penalty.

Final Score: Sarnia Sting: 4 - Sault Ste. Marie Greyhounds: 3 – OT

Canada vs USA, Youth Olympic Games – Gold Medal Game, February 21st 2016

Final Score: CAN 2 USA 5

CAN #1 G Gravel, Alexis (2018) - Gravel did OK on open looks where he had clear sight of the puck, but struggled a bit more with traffic and jam plays in front of him. With that said, his D committed quite a few errors in front of him. Questionable coverage on the first goal against left an open lateral pass for an easy tap-in while Gravel played the shot. Second goal was a blown coverage in front of the net and there were other examples. However, Gravel never really made that big save that would turn momentum into his team's favor. By the end of the game he gave up three goals, while two were empty netters.

CAN #2 RD Woo, Jett (2018) - Woo had a quiet game aside from one or two flashes of brilliance. His effort in the offensive zone where he showed off good skating ability, especially his edgework, started the sequence that resulted in the first Canada goal that was however overturned.

CAN #5 C Groulx, Benoit-Olivier (2018) - He started at center but was later moved to Focht's left wing with Dudas on RW. Had a slow first period outside of a couple of shifts on PP but did his best work on Focht's wing in the second half of the game. With Focht connecting the defense and offense down the middle, Groulx was left to play a more opportunistic offensive game. His skill level and skating were both apparent, however he also did a good job making plays in corners and on the wall and didn't mind crashing into the slot or towards the net when he sniffed out a scoring chance.

CAN #6 LD Smith, Ty (2018) - I thought he played a really steady game. High-percentage decision-making and was not the flashiest guy out there but provided a steady game from the back-end. Especially in the first period, where USA seemed to dominate, he could be counted on to provide a reliable shift.

CAN #7 RW Dudas, Aidan (2018) - A bit small, but found a role on a line with Groulx and Focht. Couldn't drive the play on his own but he did make a couple of quick skill plays that were dangerous including setting up Focht in front of the net with a great pass.

CAN #8 RD Merkley, Ryan (2018) - Didn't have the best first couple of minutes but got better with every ensuing shift. He scored the first Canadian goal in the game just by wiring a slapper from the blueline with 5 seconds to go on PP. Good heads-up puck-movement, later in the game with Canada chasing the score he became really active with his skating as well and made several high-end offensive plays. Partly at fault in the PK breakdown that left two open USA forwards directly in front of the net.

CAN #10 C Burzan, Luka (2018) - Like many of his temmates, he too had a slow start but picked it up later. Was one of the key players early in the third period with Canada pressing to tie the game. He did a good job with his speed entering the zone and adjusting his angles to maneuver around sticks. Made the pass from behind the net to McShane for the goal that put Canada down by one with minutes to go.

CAN #20 C Focht, Carson (2018)- He scored the first goal that got overturned. Had another good chance later by going to the net but shot the puck up high over the crossbar. I thought he was the best Canadian forward through the first half of the game or so. Really smart player, thought his defensive positioning and how he supports the puck out of the zone was very good. Skill level didn't look as high as a Wise or a Groulx but his instincts both offensive and defensive really stood out positively and he competed well.

USA #1 G DeRidder, Drew (2018) - Thought he had a real strong game. Calm between the pipes, even with traffic and bodies around him, he gets into position and holds his ground. He really came up big a couple of times when Canada had momentum. Big save on late PK on McShane and did well with the clock winding down as well.

USA #2 LD Krygier, Christian (2018) - Played a pretty solid game. A nice move in the offensive zone, dragging the puck from the left circle area to change the angle of the release, avoiding the body in front of him and beating the goalie on a wristshot. Put USA back up by 2 after Merkley scored on PP.

USA #5 LD Samuelsson, Adam (2018) - Big body and defended decently well, feet looked a bit slow, especially his agility in-tight and having to quickly adjust to plays seemed like it could use some improvement. Not much there offensively.

USA #6 LD Samuelsson, Mattias (2018) - Thought he was the best USA defenseman overall. Big framed two-way blueliner. His puck-movement was pretty simple but effective, he doesn't complicate plays. Long defensive stick and will use body, too. Just a solid overall game for him. Didn't see much shooting from him, even though he did log some PP time.
USA #8 LW Walsh, T.J. (2018) - Came ready to play and was the key player setting the tone early. He played like a skilled sparkplug, with his combination of skills, smarts and compete, he was effective despite not being the biggest guy on the ice. Scored the first goal of the game with a smart read opening up on the far side post for an easy tap-in goal.

USA #9 LW Weiss, Tyler (2018) - He had some quick-strike attacks in the offensive zone that resulted in scoring chances. Thought he used pace and speed to his advantage. He had one shift where he circled the offensive zone and set up his linemate for a chance, but outside of that sometimes it felt like he could do a better job setting up offensive zone time. There was a bit of that one and done type of scoring opportunities, where the puck is as quickly out of the zone as it is in it. Good game overall, though.

USA #12 C Wise, Jake (2018) - While you couldn't clearly point to him as the best player on the ice in this game, he nevertheless displayed high-end upside. He was the key player on US's PP, though he sometimes opted for wristshots from outside that didn't really produce anything. Liked his ability to control the play by protecting the puck both in open ice and in the corners and finding options for passing plays.

Scout's Notes: Not dressed – Oliver Wahlstrom (USA)

Cedar Rapids RoughRiders at Chicago Steel, February 26th, 2016

CED #10 C DeRoche, Johnny (2016) - Showed off his vision and passing on a few occasions. Not very physically involved, though. Very cerebral game. Had a nice backhand shot off a spinorama after coming down the wing on the right side.
CED #12 LW Filipe, Matt (2016) - Good puck protection, had good handling while moving his feet. Can change angles of attack without being stopped by the D, can also circle the offensive zone bringing the puck out of corners or playing on the cycle. At one point he had a clear shot from up close but opted to curl back and look for a pass that wasn't there. Hit the post on an EN attempt.

CED #16 LW McGing, Hugh (2016) - Could have easily put a couple of points on the board with his play. Good compete and skating ability. Drove the net as if he were much bigger, got to a rebound first on a Burke shot. Worked on the backcheck. Can be elusive on the wall and made some long accurate passes in the offensive zone, often from the wall into the slot or cross-ice passes.

CED #17 RW Sternschein, Sam (2016) - Good frame and played a smart game. Good at bringing the puck out of his own zone and through neutral zone. Finds space where he can open up in the offensive zone but didn't have any high-end scoring chances in this game, but a combination of simple 10 foot passes and some work on the forecheck, that resulted in more offensive zone time for his team. Had a fight with Austen Long.

CED #22 RW Colton, Ross (2016**) - Two great scoring chances, both from a stretch pass with him camping in the neutral zone. Converted on the first one with a nice snapshot. Got stopped on the second one when he tried to deke the goalie out, though it was a good attempt.

CHI #2 LD Kiersted, Matt (2016) - Good first pass, doesn't look to just get rid of it either, will use his skating to delay a little bit and find a better angle. Got more offensively active chasing the score later in the game.

CHI #4 RW Long, Austen (2016) - Scoring chance shorthanded by working hard in his own zone. Later had a big block on that same PK. Fought Sternschein.

CHI #6 LW Zimmer, Max (2016) - His smarts and skating jumped out as positives for him. Set up a few scoring chances for his linemates, but didn't really start imposing his will on the game until later on. Seemed at times just content to play an OK game, but did pick it up when it became obvious more will be needed to tie the game with the clock running down. Saw some shifts at C and looked good there as well.

CHI #25 LW Bucek, Samuel (2017) - At times he's too eager to chase the puck-carrier head-on instead of trying to take away a lane and approach at an angle and with some timing. Compete level was good, though he seemed a bit sluggish with his feet not generating much speed despite a lot of movement. His play with the puck looked best on PP and he looked good when being used as a screen in front of the net as well. Some poor plays at even strength though, fanned on a pass and got stripped of the puck more than he should. Inklings of skill mixed with size but execution overall was lacking.

North Bay Battalion at Hamilton Bulldogs, February 27, 2016

OHL Regular Season

NBY #4 D Dineen, Cam (2016) - Good passes up ice early. Lost puck races in his own zone. Shot is average. Aggressive trying to keep puck in, but usually didn't work and was out of position with the play going the other way. Generally made good first pass, but panic's with pressure and will turn the puck over on heavy forechecks. Walked one on one.

NBY #22 D Lyle, Brady (2017) - Walked line on the power play and a nice wrister from point to score 5-1 goal, his first career OHL goal.

NBY #25 D Shoemaker, Mark (2016) - Chooses good paths with puck and gets it deep. Plays simple game both ways. Good one on one plays. Finishes his checks. Good reaction time to get to the wall quickly in his own zone. Top penalty killing unit.

HAM #18 LW Strome, Matthew (2017) - Went to the net as the trailer and scored 1-2 goal. Lazy on back check leaving opponent all alone for 1-3 goal. Good release. Lacks compete at times. Top power play unit.

HAM #42 D Gleason, Benjamin (2016) - Caught puck in slot and tried to skate with it a bit but was stripped and ended up well out of position on second goal against. Turnover resulted in goal. Walked in from point for scoring chance. Walked in from point with nice move for scoring chance. Hard shot. A few solid rushes. Top power play unit.

HAM #33 G Fulcher, Kaden (2017) - Pulled after 2 shots, 2 goals. First was a rocket bar down. Second was a bad turnover by defender. Little to no chance on either goal.

Final Score: North Bay Battalion: 6 - Hamilton Bulldogs: 1

Spokane Chiefs at Kelowna Rockets, Feb 27, 2016

Final Score KEL4 SKP3 SO

KEL #15 LW Soustal, Tomas (2016)
Continues to show improvement in his offensive game, was a strong net front force in this contest and showed a willingness to battle hard in front of the net, is tough to defend when his feet are planted. A times looks slow of foot but does show good coordination when pivoting from a stand still. Was hard on pucks tonight and showed and increase in drive to pursuit loose pucks and attack scrums. Tonight lacked some finish but still had a number of chances that showed his ability to create strong scoring chances. A couple of times had a strong back check to hold the puck into the offensive zone and keep plays alive.

KEL #7 LD Johansen, Lucas (2016)
Was a fixture on the point for the 1-3-1 power play setup. Shows good timing for his pinches in the offensive zone, often looks for a shot on the pinch with the ability to score. Can rush a decision when the puck is on his stick, looks to force plays at times and can get caught deep and a play is breaks up, more patients is needed for plays to develop or to reset and hold the zone to minimize turnovers. Relatively stationary when on the point, would like to see more lateral mobility out of his feet to keep options open, again can rush a decision if his first option isn't there, resorts to a dump-in off the boards.

KEL #19 C Dube, Dillon (2016)
Shifted to center for this game after playing most of the second half at LW, despite liking him in the middle I believe shifting his position consistently has lead to some struggles, was relatively quite for this game. Looked dangerous at times on the power play off the right wall on the 1-3-1 formation, scored a one-timer from the right circle on a quick shot, that looks powerful, when his shot is accurate its one of the tops on the team.

KEL #6 LD Smart, Jonanthan (2017)
Smart player (pun intended) with a young body that shows its physical limitations at times, a strong forecheck can get him off his game and cause turnovers. Makes a good first pass out of the zone and plays with a good awareness of his surroundings, which leads to sneaky tendencies. Pinched for a goal into an open cage going completely unnoticed as he used effective timing to find the open space that developed. Skating has looked better as the season progressed, with a smooth stride and agility, showed some good jump in this contest.

SPK #10LW Mcindoe, Ethan (2017)
Not provided a ton of offensive opportunity looking at mostly 3rd line assignments. Reads the play well and shows good game awareness with more of a quite approach that leads to good positions, doesn't run around or chase when defending. Plays with a head on a swivel as he always looks to have knowledge of his surroundings and other positions.

SPK #11 C Anderson-Dolan, Jaret (2017)

Jumps out as a player who wants to make plays, not a passive approach to the game shows a fearless ability to push the puck up the ice and attack the middle with speed. Has elusive moves when carrying the puck that create space and time for him to make plays, shows a desire to have the puck on his stick. Couple instances where a separation gear would have helped him finish a play by giving him more space, has a good top speed but doesn't always burst off consistently yet. Started a fair number of shifts in the offensive zone but saw minimal special teams in this game, which is a change from earlier viewings this year.

Rogle BK at Farjestad BK, March 2nd, 2016

RBK #18 RD Liljegren, Timothy (2017) - Liljegren did a good job on the powerplay, starting breakouts, making passes for zone entries and playing the point on PP. He did not see a lot of even strength time, but especially on PP his reads, skill, and skating ability were apparent. Very good feel for the game and can easily adjust on the fly to his lanes being taken away. He picked up a secondary assist on PP.

RBK #20 RW From, Mathias (2016) - From had a couple of good shifts, especially early in the game. His size already looks reasonably pro-ready and he skates well. He had a good play offensively utilizing those two skills to skate wide around the defense bring the puck from behind the goal and fire a shot while turning around. He also competed well off the puck so his skating and size allowed him to have a pretty decent checking game. His game faded down the stretch though.

FBK #29 RW Steen, Oskar (2016) - Steen showed off his vision hitting a teammate trailing into the slot and picking up the assist on the play. He displays good sense for offensive openings, but his physical tools don't quite look developed enough to have an impact on a consistent basis yet.

FBK #74 C Asplund, Rasmus (2016) - His feet keep moving and he displays a good work-ethic on every shift. Asplund had a couple of scrums in front of the net offensively and was quite active in sniffing around for rebounds and chances directly in front of the goalie. In transition, he did a good job opening up for his defenseman to make an outlet. Good on the forecheck, but in his own zone he sometimes focused on following the puck too much as opposed to tracking players, which was opening up space in the middle and behind him.

Shawinigan Cataractes vs Victoriaville Tigres, March 3rd 2016

SHA #94 LD Girard, Samuel (2016): Really liked his poise with the puck today. He always buys himself time on the ice by holding onto to the puck for an extra second or faking a shot to create openings for himself in the offensive zone. He did well on the power play, moving the puck well and scoring Shawinigan's 3rd goal of the game using a wrist shot from the point with a lot of traffic in front of the net. Defensively, he did well; I noticed a good play early in the game where he used his stick to poke the puck away from Laberge in a one-on-one sequence.

SHA #28 C Gignac, Brandon (2016): He made good use of his speed and shiftiness in the first period to make good zone entries for his line. He was not as noticeable during the rest of the game, outside of two scoring chances in the third period. He played on both the PP and the PK and did well in the faceoff circle.

SHA #3 RD Sylvestre, Gabriel (2016): Tough first period for Sylvestre, as he was beaten wide by Laberge on the first goal of the game. He was beaten fairly easily twice in one-on-one sequences, where he notably had bad stick position and played the puck instead of the man. He had some good hits during this game, including a good one on Mario Huber. He played better in the 2nd and 3rd periods by not making big mistakes on the ice. He did a good job on the PK unit clearing the front of the net.

VIC #9 RW Laberge, Pascal (2016): He had two quick goals in a great first period. The first one was a thing of beauty, beating Sylvestre on the outside and taking a quick shot while going to the net. The 2nd goal was on the power play and from the slot, it was a good enough shot (though not his best) to beat Povall with traffic in front of the net. Throughout the rest of the game, he was inconsistent with his passing. He did make two sweet passes late in the 3rd period to Comtois and Goulet, but during the game he made a number of bad passes and turned the puck over with them.

VIC #44 LW Comtois, Maxime (2017): Comtois played on both the PP and PK units today. Early on in the game, he showed good playmaking skills with some good passes, including an excellent backhand pass in the slot. He made quick decisions with the puck. On the PP, he was used in front of the net. He almost got a goal late in the game, but was robbed by Cadorette after a great feed from Laberge. On the PK he did some good work late in the game, keeping the puck pinned along the wall and battling alone versus three Shawinigan players.

VIC #96 C Huber, Mario (2016): The 19-year-old Austrian had a good game, using his body to play a physical game but also as a workhorse along the wall with a strong puck-protection game. As a center, he always takes care of his own zone; you can always see him giving good support down low to his defensemen. He always works hard on the backcheck, showing good commitment in the defensive aspects of the game. He scored an easy goal on the backhand all alone in front of the net after taking a pass from Lanoue. Before that goal, he and his line did an amazing job cycling the puck down low.

VIC #48 C Lauzon, Felix (2016): Lauzon, like Huber, is very efficient in the defensive aspects of the game; he always gives good support to his defensemen deep in the defensive zone. In the first half of the game, he was involved physically, even with his lack of strength. He scored a goal by jamming the puck behind Cadorette after a nice play by Goulet in in front of the net. His lack of high-end speed at his size hurts him, as he can't create separation on the ice and has less room to work with.

VIC #5 RD Lalonde, Bradley (2016): He was the main option on the back end on the power play. He was very noticeable out there, either by taking shots from the point or by rushing the puck into the offensive zone. His passes were crisp and accurate. He created a nice play (a shot that turned into a pass) at the side of the net to Lapierre, but Lapierre couldn't finish the play. Good first pass from him today to get the puck out of his zone.

VIC #30 G Povall, James (2016): Overall, he did a decent job with his rebound control out there today. Some shots were tougher, as he was facing a lot of traffic in front of him. He had some issues with point shots with traffic in front; he had a hard time tracking the puck. He gave up two PP goals with Pawelcyck in front of him. He probably wants to have the 2nd Shawinigan goal back (beginning of the 2nd period), as it was a weak shot from Beauvillier from the blueline. Overall, at least three of the goals scored against him had heavy traffic and made it such that he couldn't see anything.

SC Bern at ZSC Lions, NLA playoffs 1st Rd Game #1 , March 3rd 2016

ZSC #13 C Malgin, Denis (FLA) – Malgin did not play in this game.

ZSC #34 C Matthews, Auston (2016) – In his first pro playoff game his determination to lead his team was obvious from the beginning. Played a high-paced game with his linemate Robert Nilsson and the duo combined nicely more than once. He was dangerous around the net and more in general in the offensive zone from start of finish, overtime included, but was consistent and really effective in his defensive efforts as well. Among others, his best chance came halfway through the 3rd when he drove the net after a drop pass, got the eventual rebound but Stepanek deflected his shot and the puck bounced off the post. Was double-shifted throughout the 20 minutes overtime and was up to the task. Played an impressive game, unfortunately missed both his attempts in the shootouts (hard to blame him on the second, decisive one, as Stepanek pulled a perfect personification of his countryman Hasek).

ZSC #44 LW Suter, Pius (2016*) – Was used as a LW all game alongside Ryan Shannon, usually paired with him on the PK too. Played a smart and effective game. Drew a penalty beating a defenseman one on one and later on earned a penalty shot on a counter attack and tied the game. Was very dangerous in the 2nd period, had two more looks after the goal. He was stopped on his shootout attempt.

ZSC #61 LW Herzog, Fabrice (TOR) – Played all game on a line with Matthews and Nilsson but was not able to take advantage of their strong game. Was not nearly as good as his linemates and more importantly didn't manage to convert any of the scoring chances he got. Could have had more luck when he hit the post one on one against the goalie after he nicely made himself available in the neutral zone and received Rundblad's pass, or when he beat the defense to a rebound and his shot was stopped, but his other shooting attempts were rather weak. Better effort in the overtime.

ZSC #97 LD Siegenthaler, Jonas (WSH) – Jonas was good without the puck but struggled with it several times and could have used more patience in a couple of situations in his zone that ended up in turnovers. Also made a bad pass at the offensive blueline that was intercepted by Cory Conacher and resulted in a scoring chance against at the end of the odd men rush. Conacher proved to be too fast for him again in this game when he stripped him of the puck jumping on him at the right faceoff circle before Jonas could play the puck.

SCB #13 Hischier, Luca (2016*) – Nico's older brother and youngest player on the ice for Bern played a mature game and never looked out of place in his first career pro playoff game.
Final Score: SC Bern: 4 – ZSC Lions: 3 (SO)

Sioux Falls Stampede at Dubuque Fighting Saints, March 4th, 2016

DUB #19 C O'Leary, Michael (2016) - O'Leary was the best player on ice through the first two periods. He scored a goal by planting himself in front of the net and getting his stick on the puck past the player checking him. He also had a great on-tape backhand pass from behind the net to an oncoming linemate who scored. Several times he set up players in the slot with his passing and also produced a dangerous chance while on PK. Overall, he played a smart playmaking game, displayed a mature approach to defense and competed well by using his frame. The only downside to his performance was the fact that he seemed to fade in third period.

DUB #22 RW Makitalo, Petter (2016*) - Despite a somewhat choppy stride he seemed to have good pace to his game. He was often first to the net in the offensive zone, dragging the defense along him, he would also do a good job on the forecheck. He had two or three good scoring chances but no finish. His best one was him finding himself all alone in the slot and opting for a big slapshot that Stezka saved without even giving up a rebound.

DUB #27 RW Knierim, William (2016) - Knierim was a physical presence on the ice. He seems to be much stronger than just about anyone he goes up against, as players tend to bounce off him and even a seemingly slight push from Knierim threw them off balance. After Knierim's goalie got bumped on the play, he also fought Warpecha. His play with the puck was a mixed bag, he did have a couple of good shifts but no consistent impact. Like in some of my other viewings of his, he did a good job finding himself with loose pucks around the net but he was slow to react with his stick or struggled to control the puck.

SFS #4 LD Wells, Justin (2016) - Big body but hasn't shown much in his game other than him possessing a large frame. He got beat wide badly after being caught flat footed. Looked shaky defensively, and had nothing going on offensively either.

Sault Ste. Marie Greyhounds at London Knights, March 4, 2016

OHL Regular Season

SSM #12 LW Katchouk, Boris (2016) - Cycles the puck well down low and protects it well. Great power forward move protecting the puck with a big defender all over him and driving the net for scoring chance. Penalized for a clean hit on an opponent six inches bigger than him. Next shift he got cheap shot by Martenet and challenged him to a fight. Katchouk challenged him to a fight, ducked and landed a big shot and got the takedown. Played final minute down a goal.

SSM #26 LW Gettinger, Tim (2016) - Bad defensive positioning on the rush, taking away lane from no one. Gets more out of his first few steps than he used to. Pretty quick hands for a big guy. Good positioning in the slot but he gets pushed around a little too much. Good defensive play to block a pass then nice long distance pass to set up scoring chance. Played last minute down a goal.

SSM #52 LW Kopacka, Jack (2016) - Inconsistent physicals play. Decent cycling ability. Tenacious pressure caused turnovers and created scoring chance. Good give and go on the rush driving the net. Got the puck back and scored 4-5 goal.

LON #4 D Juolevi, Olli (2016) - Great long distance pass on penalty killing set up short handed chance. Walked in from the point and pit a good shot on to score a bit of a soft 4-2 goal. Playing a little tougher in the defensive zone winning more battles. Misplayed a 2 on 2 which lead to a 2 on 1 chance for goal.

LON #49 LW Jones, Max (2016) - Stole a bad pass and quickly skated it out of trouble on the penalty kill. Second penalty killing unit. Used his size on the cycle. Great move in open ice that few big power forwards can pull off.

LON #98 D Mete, Victor (2016) - Does a good job of getting low and taking away passing lanes, but struggles once opponent starts protecting the puck. Played last minute up a goal.

Final Score: London Knights: 6 - Sault Ste. Marie Greyhounds: 4

Vernon Vipers at Penticton Vees, March 4th, 2016

Playoffs - Round1 Game1

PEN #57 RD Fabbro, Dante (2016) Began this game by taking a 10 minute misconduct 10 seconds in for an open ice check to the head. Consistently makes turns to be the furthest defenseman back remaining in the most defensively responsible position as possible while having the entire play in front of him usually until the rest of his team has completed the zone entry and begun a sustained attack. Held the first until powerplay spot on the right point in this game. Showed a good instinct for attacking in this game, will always look at the net for a shot right away, if he doesn't take the shot, puck is quick on, quick off his stick. Would like to see more of a "QB" style play and use a little more range at the top zone to command the ice, nonetheless a very effective player on the powerplay. Has a great knack for keeping attackers to the outside when defending, shows a strong position, not a ferocious checker but a very effective defender. Holds a great position when skating in reverse all they way through the NZ, always remains square to his attacker. Skating was on display to break up a 2 on 1, closed a gap and used a textbook stick check to ruin a likely goal. Doesn't poses a big booming point shot, lacks velocity, far more effective shooting a quick wrist shot to get pucks on net forcing a save.

PEN #17 C Jost, Tyson (2016) Takes face-offs in all situations, in all position over the ice with good results, exhibits responsibility as a high scoring 2-way line. Skating is one of his best assets, played with a lot of jump tonight looking assertive and explosive. Edging is elite level, pivots, stops and first movement are lightning quick and contribute to one of the best multi directional movers in the draft. Scored from the goal line while taking a bounce off the back boards, not a lucky goal, saw the goaltender cheating expecting a pass out front and put a puck in a small area on the near post. Awareness on the attack is really good, pulled off an elite move on a drop pass to give a teammate a wide open net. Finished the night with 3 points showing off a versatile attacker that thinks with a high hockey IQ and has the elite skill to match his quick intelligent thinking.

Final Score: PEN 6 VER 3

Rouyn-Noranda Huskies vs Blainville-Boisbriand Armada, March 5th 2016

RN #3 RD, Neveu Jacob (2016): It was a quiet game from Neveu today, who did a decent job in his zone clearing pucks and clearing the front of the net. Strong kid who used his size well along the wall. Doesn't take many risks and plays a very safe game. He had some shifts on the PK and none on the PP, and didn't get to touch the puck many times in the game.

RN #1 G Harvey, Samuel (2016): Decent game from Harvey, who gave up three goals and would probably have liked to have the first one back (it was still a great shot from Pospisil). A bit early on his knees on that first goal, this seemed to hurt Harvey more as an average-sized goalkeeper. Overall, he did a fine job with his rebound-control in the game, as there were not a lot of juicy rebounds in the slot. Good reflex saves from him today; I liked his poise as well and how he always looks like he's in control.

RN #4 C Fontaine, Gabriel (2016): Not a flashy game from Fontaine, other than on one great rush where he blew by an Armada defenseman and provoked a penalty by going hard to the net. He did a good job along the boards, with his body always on a good angle to keep possession of the puck. Often acted like a 3rd defenseman in the defensive zone. He was always there to support his defense deep in the defensive zone. He was also the only forward on the ice on a 5-on-3 PK. He did really well in terms of retrieving pucks along the boards, using his size and a quick stick.

BLB #6 LD Crête-Belzile, Antoine (2017): The young defenseman played on both special team units today and got better as the game went on. He looked much more confident in the 3rd period while in the offensive zone. He made some good one-on-one plays, defending versus Rouyn's top-two forwards (Meier and Perron) in the game, showing a good active stick. He will need to work on the level of explosiveness in his skating abilities.

BLB ##92 RD Corbeil, Pascal (2016): Corbeil did a good job on the PP, keeping his feet alive and moving laterally trying to find a better shooting lane. He also did well carrying the puck, showing good footwork and acceleration to help him in that aspect. However, he is an undersized blueliner, and it showed in the defensive end versus the big Rouyn forwards. He also didn't get as much ice time as he usually does.

BLB #24 RW Teasdale, Joel (2017): As usual, Teasdale was a workhorse along the boards, getting involved in the play and not being shy to throw some hits. Good effort on the backcheck. A key member of the Armada PK unit. He didn't do a whole lot offensively during the game but had his best scoring chance in the three-on-three overtime period, taking advantage of the free space available on the ice.

BLB #96 LW Kristian Pospisil (2016): Amazing first period from the Slovakian forward, who scored two goals and was involved physically with some big hits. His first goal came from a perfect shot that went high-glove on Harvey. His second goal was a good tip in front of the net. However, the rest of his game was not as good as the first period, but he still worked hard (which was an improvement, since he has had a tendency to disappear this season). On the power play, he was often set up to use his one-timer, but couldn't get his 3rd of the game.

BLB #91 RW Miller, Shaun (2017): Miller was very involved in the play, playing on a line with Pospisil in this game. He used his speed very well on the wing and was able to beat Rouyn-Noranda defensemen wide on a couple of occasions. Good on the forecheck, he also played a strong puck-pursuit game. In the offensive zone, he was able to get open in the slot on a couple of occasions that led to scoring chances. He finished the game with two assists.

Kamloops Blazers at Kelowna Rockets, Mar 5th, 2016

KAM #38 Davidson, Dawson (2016)   Played in all situations this game, has rounded into a fundamental part of the breakout for Kamloops, and is a big part of the transition game when he is looking up ice toward the offensive zone. Gathering pucks below the goal line and starting a breakout deep in his own end can be a challenge for him as size and strength is currently a concern. Appears fluid on his skates with a good burst out of his first three strides, shows strong on ice awareness when moving up ice, consistently has head up and uses effective lateral bursts to elude obstruction through the NZ, and in-turn displays solid individual efforts to gain the zone. Made several tape to tape passes that showed strong outlet passing ability that are accurate and flat, ability to hit players in motion is evident even at high speeds

KAM #42 LD Vala, Ondrej (2016) A defender with limited offensive ability and a slower skating stride, lumbers in his pivots and maintains a large gap due to limited jump in his reverse stride. Was tasked as a first pair guy in this game and is effective around the crease imposing his physical stature on players who come close to the net, deterred forwards from high percentage shots and shows a good ability to direct play away from the net with a long reach a good positioning; a strong shot blocking presence in this game.

KEL #19 Dube, Dillon (2016) Showed positive puck pursuit tonight winning battles and showing good jump with a willingness to engage in contact to come out with the puck, consistency in this skill set would be a big asset especially if he remains on LW and is the F1 in on the forecheck. Displayed good puck handling in tight space and holds the puck well alone the wall, squeezes between the boards and a defenders well and can draw penalties this way, did so in this game. Shows varying levels of effective play at the LW position but played well in the retrieval game, showing high energy, has the ability to be effective without the puck and get to shooting positions, create havoc and distraction for defenders

KEL #15 RW Soustal, Tomas (2016) Tasked with a less offensive role in this game was put on the 3rd line which could explain his lack of puck touches. Was a little over zealous with the physical game including a roughing call in the 2nd period, looks more effective battling in front of the net for scoring position and standing his ground instead of going after players. Held his typical spot in front of the net on the power play, good read as puck shifted along the blueline used a very effective moving screen to block Ingram's view and make a very good tip for a goal.

KEL #7 LD Johnasen, Lucas (2016) Game appeared calm tonight, played methodical and looked like his hockey IQ was stronger than usual, has a tendency to lose his next move and stop thinking ahead. Strong offensive instincts were displayed tonight, reads the motion and the flow of play throughout the offensive zone really well. Took a few strides when a shot was placed on goal, lead to a rebound scoring chance. More relaxed on the offensive blueline, keeps his game simpler than earlier in the year looks to work the play to his forward on the half boards instead of prolonged moments trying to make a decision on the point

Final Score: KAM 3 KEL 2

Edmonton Oilkings vs Saskatoon Blades, Mar 7, 2016

SAS #25 D, Hajek, Libor (2016) This was a tale of two games for Hajek, he started off the game very slow struggling to outwork and out battle his man as he took the puck strong to the net for the opening goal. Just minutes later he over played the puck carrier to deep into the corner and was chasing the play leaving the slot wide open. He was then benched for the majority of the first period. He continued to struggle defensively being a step behind most of the game. It was obvious to see his upside as he is a strong, powerful skater who has great agility and moves very well laterally. Has a good escape-ability, which allows him to make a great first pass out of his zone. He continued to try to impact the game by joining the rush and on a change going end to end but failed to create anything. This may have been an off night for this player but I would like to see him compete more away from the puck and on the defensive side especially one on one battles in the corner and in front of his own net.

SAS #9 FW, Hebig, Cameron (2015) Was very noticeable every time he was on the ice. Each shift he found a new way to impact the game, whether it was making a hit, winning a battle on the wall or using his size and speed to win puck battles in open ice, this player stood out. He is a very powerful skater that is always moving and goes very hard to the net. He has a very high hockey IQ coupled with his desire to compete makes him dangerous every time he steps on the ice. Loves to carry the puck and does a great job of using the ice and changing the point of attack which makes him difficult to defend.

EO #16 FW, Koch, Davis (2016) Koch had two goals in this game and both were identical as he is not afraid to play in traffic and go hard to the net. On the first goal he stayed with the play while battling for position with the Dman and drove the puck to the net and it deflected up and over the goalie. He continued to drive the net all game and was rewarded with his second goal that deflected off of him in the crease. He really played to his strength using his speed and agility to gain the zone then moving the puck and going hard to the net paid off for him on this night.

Final Score Saskatoon Blades: 5 Edmonton Oilkings: 2

SC Bern at ZSC Lions, NLA playoffs 1st Rd Game #3 , March 8th 2016

ZSC #13 C Malgin, Denis (FLA) – Couldn't beat the goalie with his forehand all alone in front of the net early in the game. Played a strong skating game, showed nice playmaking ability and patience when he set up a linemate for a great chance in front after using his agility to come away from the side boards with the puck. Denis made probably the best play of the entire overtime when he nicely cut to the inside to beat out a defenseman in the offensive zone but his pass was deflected and didn't reach his teammate for the tap-in.

ZSC #34 C Matthews, Auston (2016) – It was a high intensity game and Matthews fit right in. He was buzzing in the offensive zone in the first part of the game. Jumped on a loose puck beating out two opponents, took it to the net in stride, but his one on one move to the forehand was stopped by the goalie. Consistently went through the high traffic areas and was often driving the net after dishing the puck to teammates. Got called early on for a trip in the offensive zone behind the play. Recorded a secondary assist on the tying goal in the 3rd period when he won a puck battle along the boards at the offensive blueline. Made a nice immediate little pass to the front on the PP for a great chance wasted by a teammate. Looked tired late in the game, just before Bern GWG he had a good chance in the slot but went five-hole and couldn't beat the goalie.

ZSC #44 LW Suter, Pius (2016*) – Steady effort and key penalty killing minutes for Pius in this game. Made a couple of good reads on the PK but he seemed to miss some explosiveness to be able to indeed force the turnover. Was beaten by an opponent in a race without the puck which resulted in a legit scoring change against.

ZSC #61 LW Herzog, Fabrice (TOR) – Opened the scoring using a toe-drag move down low to get into the slot and beat the goalie short side. Found the rebound in front of the net and scored again to give his team a two goals lead halfway through. Looked slow and disappeared in the 2nd half of regulation. Resurfaced in OT making a couple of good plays in the neutral zone when he set up a scoring chance and then when he created a legit shot for himself by quickly jumping on a loose puck.

ZSC #97 LD Siegenthaler, Jonas (WSH) – Played a sound game, aside from when he fell at the offensive blueline while trying to keep the puck in, which created a big chance against. It was not an easy game to play for an 18 yrs old defenseman, but he was up to the challenge.

SCB #13 Hischier, Luca (2016*) – Became more noticeable in the 3rd period, he set up Bern's 3rd goal making a great play: entered the offensive zone along the right boards gaining room for himself, delayed and perfectly hit the trailer with a nice centering pass. Mishandled the puck in the slot with 3 minutes left in regulation as he tried to change the angle and shoot from the slot, but later in the same shift won a puck battle vs Matthews at the other end to regain possession.

Final Score: SC Bern: 4 – ZSC Lions: 3 (OT)

Chicoutimi Sagueneens at Quebec Remparts, March 10th, 2016

CHI # 58 RD Allard, Frédéric (2016): The d-man had a very good game. Despite some difficulties in his defensive coverage, he distinguished himself offensively with excellent vision of the game. He made beautiful accurate passes, and well spotted his teammates. He also got assists on four goals for his team and got the first star of the game. He played regularly shorthanded, even at 3 against 5 and he was effective in part of the game

CHI # 61 LW Lavigne, Zachary (2017): In addition to playing regularly, the rookie evolved shorthanded. Despite his lack of speed and some difficulties in his passes reception, he got involved physically, offered a good performance and a good effort every shift. He scored the insurance goal into an empty net.
CHI # 48 RD Maltsev, Artem (2017): The Russian rookie had a good overall game. He remained focused on the game and took very good shots on the opposing net. He played on the man advantage and shorthanded, he showed great versatility in his game. He had some difficulty in his passing game but stood out to block the passing and shooting lanes in the defensive zone
QUE # 27 C Gentile, Derek (2017): Evolving regularly on the powerplay, he showed incredible footwork by being very agile, mobile and quick on skate. He has also shown great vision by finding Auguste Impose on the first goal. He had good hands and was creative with the puck.

QUE # 91 LW Boucher, Matthew (2016): Evolving with his teammate Gentile on the powerplay, both generated a lot of speed. Boucher got several good scoring chances and was involved along the boards despite his small stature. He also illustrated himself shorthanded putting quick pressure on the puck carrier.

QUE # 16 LD Huntley, Christian (2017): The young defenseman shown great skills in his stick handling with beautiful dekes and pass receptions. He was mobile and has a nice vision despite some deficiencies in his physical and defensive play.

Gatineau Olympiques at Quebec Remparts, March 11th, 2016

GAT # 44 RD Bilodeau, Gabriel (2016): The defenseman had a good game. He was well positioned defensively and he also illustrated offensively. In the third period, he received a pass to the point and takes a great shot to beat the Remparts's goalie. He has had some difficulties in his speed defensively, but did well when playing on the power play

GAT # 30 G Grametbauer, Mark (2016): The goalie didn't had a busy evening receiving only 18 shots. He stay concentrated in the game despite the low shots on goal, he reacted well particularly short-handed and made a big save on a 2 on 1 in the second period. He seemed a bit surprised on the first goal on butterfly shot, but made good saves at the right time thereafter.

QUE # 23 LW Côté, Louis-Filip (2017): Côté has had one of his best games with the Remparts this season. He was part of the starting line-up and played regularly on the powerplay during the game. He showed good hockey sense in making beautiful passes and got involved in the action during the game. He also scored his first goal in the Remparts uniform.

QUE # 91 LW Boucher, Matthew (2016): He played on all the special teams during the game. He had some good scoring chances and showed a good vision of the game by making beautiful passes. He earned an assist on the first goal of his team and brought a lot of speed in the attack. Even with a score of 5-2 for Gatineau late in the game, he continued to work hard along the boards and skated with energy.

Kamloops Blazers at Kelowna Rockets, March 11th, 2016

KAM #38 LD Davidson, David (2016) Shows a smooth stride with a quick acceleration going both forward and backwards, reads the offence well shows well times pinches while playing with a heads up awareness of the flow within the offensive zone. Showed good battle and jump to get to loose pucks quickly, when engaged lost out to large more physical players a few times, did not back down from contact or battles. Got beat on a 1 on 1 rush because he stopped moving his feet, threw a hip check but didn't fully connect to stop a Baillie scoring chance. Gathered a puck at the red line and sent a good pass to the middle for a zone entry leading to a 2nd assist on the power play. In a game where they had to mount a comeback, rushed couple zone clears or breakout passes looking for open teammates. Was part of a 3 on 1 rush showing good foot speed,
orchestrated a give and go for the GWG, shifting his feet to a reverse stride to open his blade for a tap in.

KAM #12 C Kryski, Jake (2016) Shows good 3-step acceleration and strong overall speed. Looks hesitate to use his speed to drive the middle of the ice in the offensive zone, noticed him drifting away from the middle of the ice a few time and passing off or taking himself out of the play.

KAM #42 LD Vala, Ondrej (2016) Looked slow tonight in footraces as he skates with a labored stride, looses races to pucks but follows up with a punishing physical game and a strong ability to battle, holds up players and make things difficult on his opponents, clears the net with a strong physical presence makes it difficult for forwards around the crease.

KAM #41 C Pilon, Garrett (2016) Had a flash of what he can provide placed a shot on goal through a screen for an assist from a tip on the power play. Showed good awareness and patients for the screen developing in front of the net and put it on goal quickly. Started the breakout for the OT winner, got the 2nd assist starting the rush.

KEL #19 Dube, Dillon (2016) Had the point on the power play, darted into the slot and drew two penalty killers no look passed off to the right side for a suberb assist on Chartier's powerplay goal. Showed poise manning the point on powerplay situations, was an asset on zone entries protecting pucks and staying in motion to wait for teammates to set up. An emotional game for him showed a lot of frustration on the bench and on the ice, calls and chances weren't going his way throughout the night and had difficulty keeping his composure.

KEL #7 LD Johansen, Lucas (2016) Showed his strong ability to read offence off the rush and created a prime scoring chance for himself. Darts into seams and soft spots in the defense and exploits them very well, puts himself in a good position to receive passes, especially when defenders are collapsing around the net. Tends to chase in the defensive zone at times and lose position, however had an effective game and looked quieter than usual in his positioning.

KEL #15 RW Soustal, Tomas (2016 re-entry) Tracked pucks well while screening the goalie in this game, was a strong net presence and put pressure on the defense to create room for the goalie and clear his view. Showed off soft hands as he picked a puck out from goalie on a rebound and tucked it in on the powerplay surrounded by some traffic. Has been showing good chemistry as a complimentary player on the top line allowing puck possession line mates time and space to work.

Saginaw Spirit at Sarnia Sting, March 11, 2016

SAG #55 D Middleton, Keaton (2016) - Handled the puck in his skates well. Made some puck playing mistakes on the power play. Used his size and strength well showing a bit of a mean streak as well. Gave too much space one on one backing up too far when in the defensive zone. Made some good defensive plays in the slot to tie up his man and prevent scoring chances including a late chance with a tie game.

SAG #56 D Niemelainen, Markus (2016) - Stripped rushing the puck in the neutral zone. Bad pass for icing. Bad shooting selections. Was stripped of the puck on several occasions. Taking too long to make decisions at times was a make reason for this. Good rush into the zone going wide on defender not forcing the play and protecting while an option opened up for him. Only defenseman playing on Saginaw's top power play unit. Made several puck mistakes on point.

SAG #62 LW Felhaber, Tye (2016) - Great pass to set up 1-0 goal. Used speed and fell on breakaway when he felt contact to draw a big power play. Good skater created scoring chance with speed.

SAR #10 C Salinitri, Anthony (2016) - Good pass and good finish on quick pass play in slot for 1-1 goal. Played second penalty killing unit.

SAR #25 RW Kyrou, Jordan (2016) - Good hands and creative passing in neutral zone. Quick and accurate pass set up 2-1 goal. Great pass to set up 3-3 goal.

SAR #26 D Sproviero, Franco (2016) - Good skating ability. Good puck plays on the offensive line. Made quick decisions with pressure. Excellent two line pass to set up partial breakaway chance. Got down to block shots, blocked about a half dozen shots or more tonight. Excellent play in slot to break up chance. Lacking size and strength.

Edmonton Oil Kings vs Calgary Hitmen, March 11, 2016

CH #2 D, Bean, Jake (2016) Bean had a quite game for the most part but was solid. He is a very efficient and controlled skater that uses his skating to make a great first pass. His head is up and he is always thinking and making plays. On numerous occasions he showed great instincts and the willingness to engage and activate into the rush. One thing that was very evident was his quick accurate release and the ability to get pucks through and on net. He has great composure with the puck and gets himself into good shooting positions. Will need to continue to work on his battle level and improve on his footspeed, especially his first couple steps.

CH #10 LW, Stukel, Jakob (2015) Had one goal when the game was out of reach for the other team. Stukel has great hands and the ability to make plays off the rush and on the power play. He is solid on his skates with good balance and creates offensive opportunities. His one glaring weakness in this game was his ability to compete away from the puck and willingness to play a 200 foot game. I saw on a couple of occasions where he got caught up ice and did not back check when the other team was attacking.

CH #11 C, Malenstyn, Beck (2016) Had a dominant game though it did not show on the scoreboard. He was competing and battling for lose pucks on every shift. Is a very strong and powerful skater that plays with an edge and is very physical making 3 huge hits in his first couple of shifts. The thing that caught my eye with this player is he was always first to the puck. He was strong in the corners and below the goal-line. He played in all situations and was also very effective on special teams especially on the PK.

CH #17 C, Stallard, Jordy (2016) Jordy finished the game with 2 goals and really capitalized on his chances. The first goal was a gift as the goalie mis-played the puck behind the net and it bounced into the slot where he was all alone. On the second goal his teammate stole the puck behind the net and Stallard was once again going hard to the net and scored with a wrist shot through traffic. He is a big skilled forward who loves to goto the net and was rewarded. He is very willing to engage in battles and used his size and speed numerous times to win possession for his team.

CH #24 LW, Twarynski, Carsen (2016) 1G, 1A: Carsen was a force all game long using his size and great skating ability to set the tone for this game. He is a fast agile skater who prides himself with being first to the puck. He was physical and won battles on both sides of the puck. In the second he was hard in on the forecheck and capitalized on a turnover feeding his teammate for an easy goal in the slot. He has composure and the ability to slow things down while maintaining a high battle and compete level. His willingness to the go to the tough areas and his 200foot game really made him stand out in this contest.

Final Score: Calgary Hitmen: 5 Edmonton Oilkings: 0

Youngstown Phantoms at Madison Capitols, March 12th, 2016

YNG #12 RW Hirano, Yushiroh (2016) – Hirano is a 95' Birthdate but Draft eligible being this is his first year playing in North America. Hirano continues to put up good numbers in his first USHL season and had 2 Goals on the night. Hirano Played with a lot of pace and drives the net hard, which resulted in his first goal after finding a rebound in the slot. Put a lot of pucks toward the net. Not a lot of physicality to his game tonight, he wasn't first in on a lot of puck in the offensive zone but showed good offensive instincts and awareness of where to be. Game Stats (2-0-2, 5SOG)

YNG #3 LD McInnis, Luke (2016) – McInnis was solid with his outlet passes tonight, didn't try to force passes or take risks. Luke supported the play well all night and was quick getting pucks out of the D-zone. Showed a quick and powerful release on his snap shot from the top of the circle. Took a couple poor penalties in the 2nd period but all in all had a pretty steady game and distributed the puck well. Didn't see a lot of time on the #1 Power Play units tonight in comparison to earlier in the season. Game stats (0-0-0, 1SOG, 4 PIMS)

YNG #26 RW Morrison, Cameron (2016) – Pretty average game tonight for Morrison, didn't create the offensive chances that he has been accustom to all season. Morrison showed what he is capable of on one play skating through the neutral zone with the puck up the wall and as he moved into the offensive zone he was able to use his size and reach to cut to the middle of the slot and get a good back hand on net that the goalie was able to fight off but the rebound was eventually put into the net by #12 Hirano as he drove the net. Morrison also lost a few puck battles along the wall due to some lack of physicality and poor body positioning but Morrison was much more willing to engage physically in front of the net and on the Power play. Skating has improved over the course of the season but still room for improvement but looks to be progressing. Game Stats (0-1-1, 2SOG)

MAD #31 G Edquist, Ryan (2016) – Edquist finally looks to be settling in down the stretch for Madison as he gets more starts in the second half of the season since the Capitols traded away their Starter Garrett Metcalf. Edquist was more aggressive and on top of his crease tonight. Made a number of great point blank saves from the slot early in the game. Seemed to be more poised and sound fundamentally for the full 60 minutes. Game State (23/26 saves)

MAD #5 LW Messner, Mick (2017) – Messner has seen limited games and playing time this year, splitting his time between AAA and USHL but saw a decent amount of ice time and even some Power Play time tonight. Messner showed his speed tonight by beating the YNG Dman #3 to a puck race in the corner and taking himself and the puck to the net that eventually resulted in a goal. Messner was all over the ice tonight, won a lot of puck battles along the wall and was good on the fore-check. Was good on the Power Play on the half wall, didn't panic when pressured and made good plays with the puck on the cycle down low. Game Stats (0-1-1, 3SOG)

MAD #94 LW Buinitsky, Dmitri (2016) – Showed good anticipation on his goal by picking off an outlet pass and generating possession in the offensive zone, eventually scoring on a net mouth scramble. Buinitsky skating allows him to play at a quick pace in all 3 zones. He tracked back into the play hard, disrupted plays and created turnovers with good back pressure. Game Stats (1-0-1, 1SOG)

Final Score: 5-3 Madison

Oshawa Generals at Mississauga Steelheads, March 16, 2016

OSH #12 C Commisso, Domenic (2016) - Displayed great vision in offensive zone and on the rush making some very skilled passes leading to scoring chances. Played second power play unit. On power play he serves up some solid one-timer passes. Good deflection to win the game in overtime.

OSH #16 D Stillman, Riley (2016) - Jumped up on rush. Good skating ability. Second power play unit. Can rush the puck effectively, knows when to pass off. Great one on one plays against good puck protection forward. Stripped opponent in neutral zone then carried the puck into the offensive zone for a scoring chance. Mishandled puck with pressure resulting in a scoring chance against with 3 minutes left in a 3-3 goal. Played last minute on the penalty kill of a 3-3 game.

MIS #9 C McLeod, Michael (2016) - Quick hands pressured opponents quickly. Outstanding moves to split two defenders then walk in and fire a laser shot. Good open ice hit, got stripped in neutral zone. Landed a few hard hits. Played the final minute of a 3-3 game.

MIS #14 RW Bastian, Nathan (2016) - Good puck protection then pass off to set up scoring chance. Had open net in slot but missed wide. Played final minute of 3-3 game. Terrible attempted zone clear on the penalty kill in overtime.

MIS #41 D Hague, Nic (2017) - Good stick down low. Has reach to stand on the side of the net and use his reach to break up possession behind the net.

MIS #74 RW Tippett, Owen (2017) - Outstanding play to beat defender. Good shot but quickly scored on his own rebound for 3-2 goal. Highlight reel goal.

MIS #92 LW Nylander, Alexander (2016) - Lined up as a defenseman in 4 on 4 and unloaded a shot from the point. Played last minute of 3-3 game.

Final Score: Oshawa Generals: 4 - Mississauga Steelheads: 3 - OT

Edmonton Oil Kings vs Red Deer Rebels, March 17, 2016

RD #11 C, De Witt, Jeffery (2016)- Was effective down low on board battles. Brings a physical edge. Was 50% in the draws that he took. Was chasing the play most of the night. Missed his check on the first goal and didn't see the ice much after that.

RD #23 LW, Hagel, Brandon (2016)- Battles hard and is consistently around the puck and in battles. Makes good plays in transition. Lost possession on a couple occasions in battles with bigger physical players. Good puck skills along with great vision.

RD #3 D, Bobyk, Colton (2016)- Was dominant in all areas of the game. Strong on the puck and likes to engage physically in battles in both zones. Has a hard, heavy shot that he gets off quickly. Strong in transition gets up ice quickly in transition. Scored a goal in the second off a heavy shot in the high slot.

EO #3 D, Gorda, Brayden (2017)- Had a very solid, noticeable game. A strong, physical presence. Engaged in battles winning the majority. Was not flashy but very consistent always making the safe simple play.

Final Score: Red Deer Rebels: 4 Edmonton Oilkings: 1

Green Bay Gamblers at Madison Capitols, March 18, 2016

GB #20 RW Peeke, Andrew (2016) – Andrew played a pretty reliable and safe game tonight. Listed on the 3rd pairing as Green Bay rotated their full D-core all night long, however Peeke saw significant Power play time on the #1 Unit and handled the point well. He made clean moves with the puck and distributed the puck well to the open guy on the Power Play. When Peeke took a shots toward the net it was a quick release snap or wrist shot, didn't waste a lot of time with a big slap shot. Peeke's body and stick position in his own end was solid all night, I could see his footwork being exposed against shifty agile forwards, however it wasn't challenged against a lesser skilled set of forwards tonight. On a few occasions tonight I felt Peeke was a tad conservative at the offensive blue line and could have pinched in the Offensive zone, even with support and keep the puck in the zone and decided to concede the blue line and allow the play to come to him. Assisted on the game tying goal late in the 3rd.

MAD #31 G Edquist, Ryan (2016) – Edquist is at his best when he is confident and challenging at the top of his crease and he did that for most of the night. Edquist saw a number of point blank chances, especially in the first period and did a good job challenging the shooter and making the saves. Edquist looked big in the crease by keeping an upright posture while in the butterfly. Edquist continues to get better and better the more starts he gets down the stretch.

MAD #27 C Jerry, Billy (2016) – After a pretty successful season at St. Thomas Academy (MN-HS) Jerry has joined the Capitols for the remainder of this season. Jerry showed good offensive instincts and high hockey IQ with and without the puck. His very lanky build leads to an awkward looking skating stride and the tendency to get bumped off the puck fairly easily. Showed pretty good patients with the puck at both ends of the ice, made some good passes in the neutral zone to relieve pressure and keep the play going north.

MAD #94 LW Buinitsky, Dmitri (2016) – Got out of some tough situations by using his quick puck skills and stick handling ability. Showed good offensive instincts and knows where he needs to be to get chances. Was rarely the first into the offensive zone to retrieve the puck or get on the fore check, avoided a lot of the hard areas, came away with the puck a lot mainly because he would be 2nd into the battles.

Des Moines Buccaneers at Madison Capitols, March 19th, 2016

MAD #94 LW Buinitsky, Dmitri (2016) – Dmitri was very good tonight. Registered 2 assists and showed the ability to utilize his teammates. He made a nice pass on a 2-1 to setup Madison first goal. Showed a little more willingness to go to the hard areas tonight than in previous viewings and it paid off with more puck battles won and more possession. Still wasn't overly physical in puck battles but came away with a lot of pucks. Buinitsky ended with 2 assists on the night, one on a goal late in the 3rd for Force OT.

MAD #27 C Jerry, Billy (2016) – Tall and Lanky build causes him to get bumped off the puck easily but has been puck skills and uses his reach and positioning to possess the puck but if a defender got him lined up he was easily separated from the puck. Jerry scored by circling the perimeter of O-zone with the puck, finding some open ice by the faceoff circle and beating the goaltender with a nice wrist shot.

MAD #5 LW Messner, Mick (2017) – Was a force on the fore check and on the back check tonight. Created a lot of turnovers using good positioning and anticipation. Gets going North quickly with a good first few strides, liked to play at a quick pace but still needs to learn to show some patients and stay with the play, as soon as a line mate would get possession Messner would immediately take off toward the offensive end and a lot of the time it eliminated him as an option to get the puck. Registered 1 assist on the night and was knocking at the door for a couple goals in close by the net.

DM #27 C Pelton-Byce, Ty (2016*) – Pelton-Byce was also draft eligible last year and dominated the Wisconsin Prep scene but was looked over mostly due to the fact he was never really challenged at the High School level. Pelton-Byce has put together a very solid rookie USHL campaign this season. Despite his line mate Patrick Grasso Registering a Hat Trick tonight, Pelton-Byce was Des Moines best forward. Pelton-Byce was put out for every key faceoff at both ends of the ice, showed a really good 200 foot game and made plays all over the ice to help his team, whether it be winning a key battle when his team was hemmed in their own end or making a good pass through the Neutral zone to send a forward in on a line rush. Showed good skill and vision by making a beautiful, quick cross ice pass from blue line to blue line through some sticks to spring a teammate in on a breakaway. Ty was especially dangerous behind the offensive goal line by finding the open man in front or at the point. Registered 2 assists tonight and factored into a couple other goals by making some good plays without the puck.

DM #24 RW Johnson, Isaac (2017) – Along with line mate Mark Senden (2016), Isaac Johnson was playing his first USHL game tonight after a solid junior season at Anoka (MN-HS). Despite playing limited minutes on the 4th line Johnson registered 1 goal tonight and played a solid game at both ends. Worked hard on all his shifts and didn't seem timid or intimidated against much old players.

Windsor Spitfires at Kitchener Rangers, March 26, 2016

Game #2 - OHL Western Conference Quarter-Finals

WSR #13 LW Vilardi, Gabriel (2017) - Great stick check in the slot to break up scoring chance. Excellent shot blocking. Great positioning in the slot on the top power play unit causing major disruptions in front, resulted in goals. Good compete, constantly involved in puck battles.

WSR #17 D Stanley, Logan (2016) - Good puck protection on the rush to take it end to end. Terrible own zone giveaway directly resulted in 2-3 goal against. Next shift took an interference penalty on a dump and chase. Got stripped a few times in his own zone. Definitely an off game for him.
WSR #21 C Brown, Logan (2016) - Skilled, hard cross off pass on power play for scoring chance. Played top power play unit. Massive hit on the forechecking. Good moves with the pick on rush to maintain control and create scoring chances. Has elevated his game big time the past few viewings.

WSR #31 D Sergachev, Mikhail (2016) - Excellent breakout pass set up scoring chance. Made quick decisions with pressure. Only defenseman on the top power play unit. Great agility and acceleration changing speeds and accelerating to drive the net. Crashed net with puck on his stick. Multiple strong puck rushes. Shot from point deflected in by a defender to score 1-1 goal. Great evasiveness shaking forecheckers. Great end to end rush showing quick hands. Excellent one timer form the point on the power play to score 4-5 goal. Top penalty killing unit, saved a side goal with a good stick in the passing lane. Took the body very well one on one. Finds ways to get his shot through.

KIT #7 D Hall, Connor (2016) - Uses skating to create time instead of forcing pass. Great two like pass tape to tape. Showed good vision moving the puck. Excellent gap control. Doesn't give too much space, then closes in quickly to make the play. Won battles down low. Physical. Great shot blocking on the penalty kill to prevent scoring chances.

KIT #23 RW Mascherin, Adam (2016) - Great positioning to get open on scoring chance. Excellent backhand pass. Forcing shot from low percentage angles, but has velocity to create chances regardless. Won some battles on the wall.

KIT #74 LW Bunnaman, Connor (2016) - Excellent forechecking pressure to force turnovers. Made smart, simple decisions with the puck. Outstanding hand/eye to bat the puck out of mid air in the slot to score the eventual game winner 5-3 goal

Final Score: Kitchener Rangers: 6 - Windsor Spitfires: 4

Val-d'Or Foreurs vs Blainville-Boisbriand Armada, March 29th, 2016

VDO #12 RW Gauthier, Julien (2016): Decent performance from Gauthier tonight, even though he didn't register any points. He was able to create some chances for himself in different ways, off the rush with his speed and reach he had three to four good sequences. On the power play in front of the net he did his job well, as he is tough to move from there. He won position battles and had two or three good chances to score from the goalie crease. When the Foreurs were looking for goals, he tried to do a bit too much with the puck, trying too much on his own. He showed good puck skills one on one and also an excellent shot with a quick release.

VDO #26 LD Galipeau, Olivier (2016): He had a real strong first period in his zone, including many solid hits and attempts to set a tempo for his team. He was good at anticipating the play and stepping up for good hits in the neutral zone. He played tough in his own end and in front of his net. He played in every situation, including the top-D pairing, top PP unit and top PK unit. On the power play, he was the lone defenseman but his play selection was average at best. He is not a natural puck-mover and his decision-making was slow. He played most of the game on the right side on the PP and at even-strength.

VDO #20 RW Tremblay, Nathan (2016): Played more of a depth role, mostly on the 3rd line, but didn't get to play on special teams. Good anticipation away from the puck; he read the play well and was quick to put pressure on puck-carriers. Good work along the boards; he was strong on his skates and protected the puck nicely. However, not many scoring chances came from him during the game.

VDO #51 LW Beauchemin, Francois (2016): The '96-born forward had an excellent game for the Foreurs, including probably the hit of the game on Crête-Belzile in the 2nd period. He had many scoring chances in the the game, including a breakaway in the 2nd period. Solid on his skates with good smarts.

BLB #6 LD Crête-Belzile, Antoine (2017): Got hit really hard in the second period by Francois Beauchemin, but showed good courage by taking the hit and moving the puck out of his zone. He played a sound, effective game with not a lot of flash, but he was efficient in moving the puck out of his zone. He kept his game simple, didn't take risks but made simple breakout plays. Defensively, he did well. On one particular sequence, he made good use of his stick when matched up one-on-one versus Julien Gauthier.

BLB #24 C Teasdale, Joel (2017): Playing center tonight, Teasdale had a tough night in the faceoff circle, going 9/25. He played his typical game along the boards, winning battles and in front of the net. He played in every situation, almost scoring in the first period off a two-on-one chance during a PK, but was robbed by the glove of Étienne Montpetit. Great work ethic.

BLB #89 C Picard, Miguel (2016): Scored the game-winning goal, diving by crashing the net and getting the puck past Montpetit. He did good job on the PK, always supporting his defensemen well and blocking passing lanes with his good stick. His skating is rough, and he will need to improve his acceleration.

BLB #22 RW Katerinakis, Alexander (2016): Katerinakis was involved a lot in the play in the first period, showing good quickness and creating offensive scoring chances with his speed. His play dropped off in the 2nd and 3rd periods.

Sault Ste. Marie Greyhounds at Sarnia Sting, April 2, 2016

Game #5 - OHL Western Conference Quarter-Finals

SSM #12 LW Katchouk, Boris (2016) - Good release driving the wing. Great work ethic down low. Competes hard for picks in battles despite having to wear a full face mask.

SSM #26 LW Gettinger, Tim (2016) - Great play down low to set up scoring chance. Quick hands and good pass. On power play he made life difficult for the goaltender on the power play, who couldn't see past him.

SSM #38 C Verbeek, Hayden (2016) - Great forecheck pressure but when opponent hesitated and curled off he drilled them from behind in the offensive zone down 0-2 for penalty. Grabbed opponents stick behind the net and wouldn't let go, which allowed a Sarnia player to easily walk into the slot and score.

SAR #5 D Chychrun, Jakob (2016) - Great move walking in from the point, beat defender, created chance. Didn't force shot from the point. Great lateral movement, but opponent still beat him as he was late on the pivot, play lead to a penalty.

Final Score: Sarnia Sting: 5 - Sault Ste. Marie Greyhounds: 1

Barrie Colts at Mississauga Steelheads, April 3, 2016

Game #6 - OHL Eastern Conference Quarter-Finals

MIS #4 D Day, Sean (2016) - Landed multiple big hits down low. He protected the puck and levelled and opponent. Great one-timer from the point to blast home 2-0 goal.

MIS #9 C McLeod, Michael (2016) - Good moves going to the net with the puck for scoring chance. Good move in close and went forehand/backhand and rang one off the post. He celebrated as if the puck was in, but it hit post, goalie and in to eventually score 3-0 goal.

MIS #61 LW Harrogate, Brendan (2016) - Outstanding first shift, landed a big hit to force an offensive zone turnover, then made a great move to beat the defender then a skilled pass to set up scoring chance. When the shot missed he jumped on the rebound off the glass and fired a bad angle shot for 1-0 goal.

MIS #74 RW Tippett, Owen (2017) - Finished his checks. Competes hard for pucks. Good positioning in the slot and quick release. Rebound resulted in an assist on the 4-0 goal.

Final Score: Mississauga Steelheads: 7 - Barrie Colts: 0

Victory Honda U16 vs Honeybaked U16 USA Hockey Nationals, April 3rd, 2016

HB #91 F, Ellis, Max (2018) – Played at a high pace the entire game, showed maximum effort on every shift. His first could strides are very good and allowed him to be first or get position on a lot of loose pucks and pressure the puck all over the ice.
HB #77 LD, Semik, Jacob (2018) – Wasn't great in this game with the puck. Committed a couple of turnovers in his own end that resulted in goals against. Defended and used his size pretty well, showed good stick and gap on his own blueline. Jacob has a big slap shot from the point but didn't show a dynamic offensive game today either.

VH #88 W, Danol, Chase (2017) – One of the older players in this tournament and showed his dominance in this game. Had 2 Goals and 1 Assist on the day. Showed a good nose for the front of the new and ability to capitalize on his chances. Showed pretty good puck skills for a bigger forward and good vision in the offensive zone. Skating and foot speed are a work in progress.

VH #27 F, Moyle, Nolan (2017) – Big frame player who used it well to protect the puck and win battles. Not overly physical in the gritty area's however. Registered 2G and 2A in t his game. Made some good plays in the neutral zone with the puck to find the open teammate and relieve pressure. Good finishing ability and quick release on his shot.

FINAL SCORE 6-2 (Victory Honda)

Shattuck vs Oakland Jr. U18, T1EHL USA Hockey Nationals, April 3rd, 2016

SSM #3 RD, Johnson, Kenny (2016) – Was Solid all around in this game. Was active in joining and leading the rush up the ice, used his size and long reach to protect the puck coming out of his own end. Was quick to getting back to his position and didn't allow himself to get caught deep in the offensive zone. Johnson defended the rush well, using his reach and positioning to forced plays outside. Wasn't as physical as he has been in other viewings but defended well in his own end and didn't get caught out of position chasing the play

SSM #22 W, Wahlstrom, Oliver (2018) – Despite being the youngest player on the ice, Wahlstrom didn't have any trouble handling the game physically, however wahlstrom was pretty quiet tonight. Oliver went unnoticed for stretches throughout the game. Picked up 1 assist on SSM first goal.

SSM #17 F, Blueger, Robert (2016) – Had an up and down game tonight, looked good in his play without the puck by winning battles and gaining puck possession but didn't like some of his decision with the puck. Seemed rushed with the puck and tried to do too much himself and didn't use his teammates enough. Showed good anticipation breaking up and D to D pass in the defensive zone and showed good breakaway speed to go in all alone on a breakaway that the goalie made a good save on.

SSM #9 F, Weber, Noah (2016) – Was all over the puck in this game, worked hard all over the ice and the puck seemed to find him. Made the right reads with the puck and made some good dump ins and put the puck in area's that gave the forechecker the best chance for possession. Good effort all over the ice.

SSM #14 F, De May, Vincent (2016) – Liked his 200 foot game tonight and he continues to improve his play and compete level in his own end. De May did pass up a few opportunities to dive the puck to the net, instead he would shoot off the rush then follow up his shot to the net.

FINAL SCORE 3-2 OT (Oakland Jr. Grizzlies U18)

Val-d'Or Foreurs vs Blainville-Boisbriand Armada, QMJHL playoffs, April 3rd, 2016

VDO #12 RW Gauthier, Julien (2016): Gauthier did a good job driving the net on Val-d'Or's 1st goal, creating room for his two linemates. He used his strength well down low to keep possession of the puck and to take it to the net with one or two players on him. He didn't get many scoring chances in the game; there was one good chance in the first period where he was all alone in the slot, but overall, the Armada did a great job taking space away from him. In a big game like this one, I wish he would have made more of a statement with a big play or big hit.

VDO #26 LD Galipeau, Olivier (2016): Galipeau was great in the first period, throwing lots of hits and taking a lot of space away by being very aggressive on the puck-carrier. He made two nice plays with a good active stick blocking passes on two odd-man rushes. On the PK, he worked hard in front of the net, clearing the front and blocking a couple of shots. He played on the first PP unit but was not a factor on the point.

BLB #6 LD Crête-Belzile, Antoine (2017): The young rookie had some difficulty tonight playing one-on-one versus top Foreurs' forwards. His lack of footspeed was on display, as he was beaten on the outside and also played the puck instead of the man a couple of times. He did well on the power play, though, and there was some good smart puck-moving from him on the point.

BLB #24 C Teasdale, Joel (2017): Scored two goals today and was impressive. Both goals came near the net (one at the side of the net and the other right in front of the net). He worked hard along the boards and got his nose dirty in front of the net. He's strong on his skates and did well along the boards, keeping possession of the puck. I liked his effort in his zone, where he was always backchecking hard and providing good support down low for his defensemen.

BLB #18 LW Hylland, Tyler (2016): Great work on the PK from Hylland, who created some scoring chances for his team, at least two chances that I noted. On the PK, he created those chances with his speed and good active stick. He also created another chance at even-strength on a two-on-one with Sanche, but they couldn't get a goal from that sequence.

BLB #96 LW Pospisil, Kristian (2016): In the offensive zone, he's likely the most talented player on the Armada. However, he was seen often trying to do too much with the puck. He kept possession too long, not using his teammates enough. He has good puck skills and showed some good dekes tonight. He was good along the boards as well, using his size to keep possession of the puck. He's big and skates well, but didn't show enough of a team game tonight. He was hit hard by Alex Pepin during the game because he was skating with his head down behind the net.

BLB #22 RW Katerinakis, Alexander (2016): He was quiet in the first two periods, but came alive early in the 3rd with two or three good chances, created due to his good speed down the wing. He was robbed by the Val-d'Or goaltender with a low shot that looked like a sure goal. He looked more involved in that 3rd period and the overtime periods than he did in the first two periods.

Quinnipiac vs Boston College, Frozen Four, April 7, 2016

BC #5 Fitzgerald, Casey (2016*) – The game did not start well for the re-entry eligible Dman. He looked a bit nervous in the early going and that came out about 3 minutes into the game when he tried to pass to partner behind net. The puck was turned over and then quickly in the back of BC's net. He did make up for mishap in 1st period by getting puck to net from the point early 2nd period which led to deflection by #18 White and rebound goal by #10 Tuch. Overall he quarterbacks BC power-play unit as he handles and distributes the puck well, along with the ability to show good poise in puck possession. He can be a good puck moving Dman and although a tad undersized he plays a tough game. Fitzgerald isn't afraid to play physical style when needed. He could benefit from added muscle and strength as at times out worked in defensive zone. His shot is accurate although not heavy. He shows good intelligence from the back end and although comparisons are difficult, the style, RH shot, and size resembles Dan Boyle.

QU #2 Priskie, Chase (2016*) – He is decent sized second year draft re-entry prospect that makes nice outlets and puck decisions. He made a couple good puck decisions with the puck at the offensive blue in the 1st period that led to Bobcats 2nd goal. He held the blue line well twice by making pass into space for teammate and getting SOG. He has good mobility and handles puck pretty well. Shows a good hard, accurate point shot too. The lapse in the game looks in the defensive zone with positioning. Although he is good with stick and anticipates plays, he sometimes plays a tad too much with offensive instinct risk instead of being reliable on the D-side as will at times leave defensive zone prematurely. This is certainly a teachable skill and thought process. Priskie does play the body effectively and solid in defending the 1-on-1 situations. You like the potential as shows offensive side in the game and will continue to develop in strong Quinnipiac program.

North Dakota vs Denver Pioneers, Frozen Four, April 7, 2016

DU #7 Gambrell, Dylan (2016*) – He is decent sized centerman that moves well with good stride and edges. He isn't explosive though strong on skates with decent speed. He showed nice hands and ability to stick handle the puck and ability to read & see plays to make soft little touch passes. He also played solid defensive game and took care of his responsibilities in his own end. You like the offensive instincts and IQ in the offensive zone as plays PP. He certainly benefited in playing on a line with #20 Danton Heinen (Boston Bruins) as he the player on the line that stirs the drink with his abilities. Gambrell could develop into a bottom 6 dependable 2-way center. Not sure he is a pure goal scorer as a few times he mishandled the puck with scoring opportunity and that is the difference.

Kitchener Rangers at London Knights, April 8, 2016

Game #1 - OHL Western Conference Semi-Finals
KIT #7 D Hall, Connor (2016) - Bad turnover in the slot directly resulted in 0-1 goal. Mishandled the puck several times in the defensive zone. Great penalty killing positioning pressured opponent but didn't get too far out of position to get back and deflect away a sure goal. Top penalty killing unit.

KIT #23 RW Mascherin, Adam (2016) - Very quiet through the first two periods of this game. Showed great positioning in the slot and an excellent release to score 3-4 goal late in the third to give his team a chance.

KIT #74 LW Bunnaman, Connor (2016) - Good play on forecheck to force turnover and pressure defender, turned it into a scoring chance. Great play in the slot with great timing to score 4-2 goal. Doing all the little things well. Cycling the puck, smart pass, good forecheck.

LON #4 D Juolevi, Olli (2016) - Played his man well along the wall, quick skating and direction changes, then closed in on the wall to shut down possession. Nice pinch from the point and good one-timer to score 4-1 goal. Does a great job pinching undetected by opposition.

LON #7 LW Tkachuk, Matthew (2016) - Great back check on a quick transition to break up a scoring chance. Good vision, made some great passes, one of which set up London's 4-1 goal.

LON #63 C Pu, Cliff (2016) - Good move cutting through traffic and beat defender for scoring chance. Took the puck to the net several times for scoring chances. Good hands taking the puck to the net but can sometimes get knocked off the puck due to a lack of strength and balance on the puck protection.

LON #1 G Parsons, Tyler (2016) - Excellent reflected to make multiple saves in close on a defensive turnover. Made some great saves in succession in this game. Good composure on puck mistakes by defenders to come up with some big saves.
Final Score: London Knights: 6 - Kitchener Rangers: 3

Kitchener Rangers at London Knights, April 10, 2016

Game #2 - OHL Western Conference Semi-Finals

KIT #7 D Hall, Connor (2016) - Quickly gets puck on net when pressured. Does a great job of getting his shot through, one of which resulted in a rebound that created Kitchener's 3-1 goal. Good stagger for his defensive partner making him an easy option. End of shift will skate his lane and get pucks deep. Good body and stick one on one when opponent tried to drive wide. Good reaction time and reach to get to loose pucks in the defensive zone. Top penalty killing unit. Risky pass own zone.

KIT #23 RW Mascherin, Adam (2016) - Blind pass in slot on power play cleared zone. Top power play unit. Went to the net and made no mistake on a pass to score 2-1 goal.

KIT #74 LW Bunnaman, Connor (2016) - Good passing on rush. Second penalty killing unit. Great lane rushing through the neutral zone, then made a nice pass two on one to set up 2-1 goal.

LON #2 D Bouchard, Evan (2018) - Top power play unit, sets up one-timers well and has good power in his shot.

LON #4 D Juolevi, Olli (2016) - Didn't take away passing lanes very well on the penalty kill. Top power play unit. Good hands and decision making on the point.

LON #7 LW Tkachuk, Matthew (2016) - Top power play unit. Good puck decisions on the power play with the goalie out of position sent the fake shot pass cross crease to give Dvorak an one net to shoot at for 1-0 goal. Drove the wing with great spacial awareness to ensure his shot didn't get defend, opened up, received the pass and fired 2-3 goal top shelf.

LON #27 RW Thomas, Robert (2017) - Good speed and can beat defenders one on one. Great move taking the puck to the net, was stopped but rebound directly created 4-3 goal.

LON #63 C Pu, Cliff (2016) - Stayed stick length away in battles on the wall. Great speed and nice inside out move to beat defender for scoring chances. Went to the net and buried 4-3 goal off a rebound.

LON #98 D Mete, Victor (2016) - Didn't move his stick or skates in the slot area on the penalty kill resulting in several passes being completed right through him. Great speed to get puck up ice. Bad no look behind the back pass down low in his own zone lead to scoring chance against. Jumped up with an empty net and took a pass going to the net to early score the 5-3 empty net goal.

Final Score: London Knights: 5 - Kitchener Rangers: 3

Russia vs USA, U18 World Championships, April 14th, 2016

RUS #2 RD Sergachyov, Mikhail (2016) - Showed off skating ability bringing the puck up ice. Used his frame defensively but had a couple of moments where he was not being as engaging as he could. Had a big blast from the point on one occasion but was not all that involved offensively. Flashes of high-end upside mixed with some lackadaisical moments. Too much dangle. Not himself today overall.

RUS #12 LW Alexeyev, Yaroslav (2017) - Found lose puck in crease after Samorukov's shot and put it into the net for Russia's first goal of the game. Stepped up and closed a gap. Big hit. Took away pass nicely on 2 on 1. Great puck control. Went wide with speed and shot off.

RUS #14 RW Svechnikov, Anderi (2018) - Good size and skating and positioned intelligently without the puck, but his line really struggled to get anything going in this game. Showed some smarts.

RUS #18 RD Samorukov, Dmitri (2017) - Played a solid defensive game, liked his smarts and he flashed a shot. Good skating and reads and protected the middle of the ice well. His shot resulted in a rebound that would get cleaned up into the net to put Russia on board. Had one bad moment defensively where Keller escaped his coverage on a stretch pass that lead to a goal against.

RUS #20 RW Kuznetsov, Vladimir (2016) - Had a couple of good moments where he entered the zone with energy but would quickly get blocked out of the play by US defense with loss of possession, as neither he or his linemates could retrieve the puck back. Around the puck. Nice awareness in the Dzone.

RUS #24 RW Kostin, Klim (2017) - Had some strong shifts showing off his reach and skating ability. Protected the puck well at times but also had some bad turnovers.. His drive and shot started the sequence that lead to Russia's first goal. Kid can shoot the puck.

RUS #30 G Zhukov, Maxim (2017) - Struggled making saves on his blocker side, both of first period goals could have been played better in that respect and he would have given up another high blocker-side if not for the bar stopping it. Scored on himself redirecting an odd-angle backhand shot into his own net. Tough game for him.

RUS - #17 LW Kozlov, Ivan (2017) - Had a great shift controlling the puck. Had a wrap around goal.

USA #7 C Frederic, Trent (2016) - Just a honest hard-working physical game on both ends of the ice. He'll engage in every battle and makes sure he's putting in work to get to loose pucks. Not as prominent offensively, as Keller and Brown lines did most of the work there.

USA #8 RD Fox, Adam (2016) - Great play on Keller's goal, first Fox intercepted the pass skated it forward to open up a better lane and hit Keller with an accurate stretch pass. Good passing game throughout and shows skill with puck. Skating still on weak side and his shot looked weak today.

USA #18 LD Lindgren, Ryan (2016) - Played a solid game outside of one or two questionable coverage decisions. Got quite involved offensively which isn't always a consistent part of his game and wasn't shy about skating the puck forward and being decisive with the puck. Knocked Kozlov on his ass.

USA #19 C Keller, Clayton (2016) - Great vision with the puck to find linemates as well as without the puck to open himself up. Set up Bellows several times. Had one high-end play walking through Russia's defense and deking out the goalie but lacking finish on the play. Just a very solid offensive game overall.

USA #20 LW Mittelstadt, Casey (2017) - Had some good shifts of high-end skill with the puck through which he displayed his upside. Good puck-handling and moves his feet, some isolated skill efforts of his created quick scoring chances.Quick, shifty. Fast release on his shot.

USA #22 LW Bellows, Kieffer (2016) - Started out a bit slow but got involved as the game progressed. Scored just seconds after Keller's goal on an odd man rush. Did a good job battling and finding spots in scoring areas. Still a distinct feel that Keller is the straw that stirs the drink, although Bellows also had a good contribution. He shoots, shoots and shoots some more. Flashed a bullet one-timer.

USA #23 RW Yamamoto, Kailer (2017) - Had some nifty passing work looking to set up linemates including a slick little dish along the wall in Ozone.. Despite his smaller stature, he didn't mind playing in the middle and going to scoring areas which is how he scored the goal to put his team up by three in third period.

USA #27 C Brown, Logan (2016) - Big size and used it well to protect the puck. At his size he had some really smooth skill plays, whether it was stickhandling or making give and go plays with Yamamoto and Mittelstadt, he executed both of those with ease. Also played an active engaging game.

USA #30 G Oettinger, Jake (2017) - Didn't have as much work as his Russian counterpart but played an OK game. He gave up one bad goal not managing to close his legs on a wraparound with the puck squeezing through. Big second effort on a rebound to stop Bitsadze while the score was still close.

USA #10 RW Locwood, William (2016)- Wasn't smart today. Selfish play as well.

Final Score: RUS 2 USA 8

Kitchener Rangers at London Knights, April 14, 2016

Game #4 - OHL Western Conference Semi-Finals

LON #2 D Bouchard, Evan (2016) - Great work on the power play making solid accurate outlet passes. Consistent good puck decisions on the point on the power play.

LON #4 D Juolevi, Olli (2016) - Walked in off the point at the right time during a bit of a scramble for scoring chance.

LON #7 LW Tkachuk, Matthew (2016) - Took undisciplined hooking penalty in the offensive zone on the power play. Shows off smarts without the puck, great body position making it tough for defenders to get past him into the battle. Smart simple plays with puck in transition to get the play going. Playing physical but leading with his elbow to the head a lot.
LON #63 C Pu, Cliff (2016) - Drove the wing and put the puck on goal to score a soft 3-4 goal.

LON #1 G Parsons, Tyler (2016) - First goal allowed didn't play the angle well on wing and beat by a great shot. Recovered well making some good saves afterwards. Second goal not much chance on great passing play.

KIT #7 D Hall, Connor (2016) - Excellent cross ice pass initiated the tic-tac-toe 2-0 goal for a well deserved second assist. Great recovery as power play ended, London player out of the box had breakaway and he closed in and negated the breakaway chance. Quick to loose pucks. Sticks with his man well, even through traffic.

KIT #23 RW Mascherin, Adam (2016) - When he has the puck below the goal line he will blindly throw it into the slot hoping for the best. Forced shot and it got blocked.

Final Score: London Knights: 6 - Kitchener Rangers: 4

Canada vs Czech Republic, U18 World Championships, April 16th 2016

CAN #1 G Fitzpatrick, Evan (2016) - Fitzpatrick was one of the better players on the ice, especially in second period where he saw a high volume of shots and also made several key saves on high-end scoring chances against. Among those, he stopped Zadina both on an in-close jam play as well as on a 1 on 1 stickhandle that came off the rush. Fitzpatrick was good at making the initial save and also did a good job in traffic and on second efforts.

CAN #4 RD Fabbro, Dante (2016) - A lazy tunover early but Fabbro displayed a high-end passing game as he distributed the puck with ease. His backhand passes under checking pressure were fantastic, smooth and on-tape to his partner. He also did a good job hitting forwards with speed. Skating looked fluid but not explosive today, his defensive positioning was good and he defended well with his anticipation. Made a fantastic cross-ice pass for Howden's goal.

CAN #5 LD Chychrun, Jacob (2016) - Chychrun had a bit of a rocky start to the game, making some questionable decisions with the puck. Some of his passes got intercepted and at times he opted to skate the puck through bodies when there was a better passing option available, or the other way around force a pass when it wasn't there. He did eliminate those quirks as the game progressed and several times flashed his skating ability in creating offense.

CAN #7 C Jost, Tyson (2016) - A heads-up game in all three zones with good compete level. Jost displayed a smart game with high-end offensive anticipation, where he had a couple of chances coming off speed plays that he created with Bitten and Kyrou. That said, his offensive impact was a bit lesser in this game than what he is usually capable of. Did a good job in the faceoff circle and played a strong game on both ends of the ice.

CAN #10 C Howden, Brett (2016) - Leans into guys on the wall and doesn't cheat on either side of the puck. Scored two goals. First one was scored inside post off a great cross-ice feed by Fabbro and second one was him driving the lane and beating the defenseman to the puck and cleaning up the rebound.

CAN #20 RD Stanley, Logan (2016) - Stanley used his reach well defensively, also displayed an encouraging level of comfort with the puck in both skating the puck forward as well as being calm under pressure. Particularly impressive for a player his size was the play where his passing lane got blocked and he had a smooth curl back moving the puck back to his partner with ease.

CAN #22 C McLeod, Michael (2016) - He had flashes of his speed, where he pushes the defense back and opens up considerable space. He made a couple of good passes in those instances. With his tools he could have done more, had some plays where he skated himself into problems and wasn't much of a factor in the corners or on the cycle. Some bad turnovers.

CAN #23 RW Morrison, Cameron (2016) - Had a strong first period being an engaging presence on the wall and taking pucks to the net. Positioned himself well in the slot looking for tips, rebounds, and shots. Faded down the stretch. Bad turnover.

CAN #12 Comptois, Maxime (2017) Drove the net hard with the puck.

CZE #30 G Korenar, Josef (2016) - Played well for stretches but the two late first period goals really deflated Czech Republic's efforts. Those goals were hardly his fault, but unlike Fitzpatrick, Korenar never really saved his team's bacon. His best stretch came in third period by the time the Czechs were already down by three.

CZE #3 RD Hajek, Libor (2016) - Thought he battled well in his own end, showed the will to be physical. Skating looked strong both in offensive and defensive situations. Had some good wristshots from the point, including one that produced the rebound for the Czech's only goal in the game.

CZE #9 RD Budik, Vojtech (2016) - Defensive reads were generally on point, though I wouldn't classify his game as a particularly great defensive performance. He did a good job skating the puck out of trouble a couple of times but made some poor outlet passes. Offensively he was quiet if not underwhelming.

CZE #10 C Najman, Ondrej (2016) - One of the better Czechs on the ice. He displayed good skill with the puck and especially his playmaking stood out. Several times he quickly recognized his open linemates and set them up, but they lacked any kind of finish. Smart game, but could stand to have a bit more bite.

CZE #14 LD Vala, Ondrej (2016) - Looked like he was trying harder not to make a mistake than to contribute positively to his team. Big body, feet looked average at best. Got beat by Howden to the rebound that resulted in a goal against.

CZE #23 LD Doudera, Lukas (2016) - Had some good offensive shifts where he would utilize his skating to get involved further up ice. Has some skill with the puck. Defensively he was just OK, no glaring mistakes but not much of a presence either.

CZE #24 LW Zadina, Filip (2018) - Scored the lone Czech goal by putting the rebound from Hajek's point shot into the net. Had several good scoring chances including being stopped by Fitzpatrick on a 1 on 1. Zadina battled well, his skating looked good and he showed a good nose for the net. As a 2018 eligible, he not only didn't look out of place but was one of the better Czech players in the game.

Final Score: CAN 3 CZE 1

USA vs Sweden, U18 World Championships, April 16th, 2016

USA #4 RD Krys, Chad (2016)- Thought he stepped up well in neutral zone a couple of times. Not with a big hit but just anticipated where the puck was going well. Did a good job on PP keeping the puck in as well. Other than that, played a pretty average game, several other defenseman on his own team had better impact.

USA #8 RD Fox, Adam (2016)- Continues to impress with heady game and puck-skills, when involved deeper in offensive zone at times looks like a forward the way he picked up speed and skated around the D. Showed good compete and balance in absorbing contact on forecheck but still got bumped off the puck too easily a couple of times.

USA #14 LD Greenway, James (2016)- Came out of nowhere with a fantastic SH effort receiving a pass in neutral zone, deking out the defenseman and using his reach to finish around the goalie. Felt like he had more in his game than he bothered to show on a per-shift basis.

USA #18 LD Lindgren, Ryan (2016)- Good read sneaking in back-door on far-side post to finish on a McPhee pass.

USA #19 C Keller, Clayton (2016)- Excels in all situations with his smarts. Not big, but got sticks on pucks defensively, stripping players. Great PK sequence skating around with the puck to kill off several seconds. Fantastic pass to an open Greenway for SH goal after he dragged Swedes' attention to himself.

USA #20 LW Mittelstadt, Casey (2017)- His hands in-tight looked very good, first goal of the game he just comes off the wall beating his check and finishes on a quick-release, made it look easy for him.

USA #22 LW Bellows, Kieffer (2016)- Threw a couple of good hits on the forecheck. Sneaked behind Swedish D and finished on a nice top-shelf shot off the bar and in. Finds ways to get scoring chances.

USA #27 C Brown, Logan (2016)- Buys time for himself well, skated well and used his size and hands. Maybe not quite explosive, but played a smart game. Showed he could do everything you want out of a big skilled center down the middle. Nice vision. Nice passes.

USA #29 G Woll, Joseph (2016)- Woll had a good game, giving up the lone late goal by the time the US win was already firmly secured. Woll did a really good job on initial shots which most often came from further out as the Swedes struggled to establish any secondary efforts in the crease. The odd time the Swedes did manage to get some bounces and traffic going, Woll stood his ground and competed well. Squared up nice.

SWE #3 RD Cederholm, Jacob (2016)- There's not much there offensively so he needed to play a good defensive game but was average in that regard. I think he did OK moving the puck out and not getting pinned endlessly into his own end.

SWE #6 LD Moverare, Jacob (2016)- Did a good job handling the puck and trying to move it out of danger, but the lack of skating ability meant he usually had to dump it pretty quickly as US forecheck closed in on him fast.

SWE #11 RW Nylander, Alexander (2016)- Struggled. Didn't get the puck with speed or in any good scoring areas from his linemates and I didn't think he did much to work for his own pucks either.

SWE #19 RD Liljegren, Timothy (2017)- Showed good shot from the point hitting a post early on. Scored the lone Swedish goal of the game with a snipe from further out. Good mobility and smarts, defensive game isn't bad but at times looked a bit overwhelmed. Keller beat him one on one gaining the inside route towards the net.

SWE #26 C Andersson, Lias (2017)- Had some good shifts, looked good bringing the puck up ice on his own and had a bit of power to his game. Was the best player on his line with Nylander and Wahlgren, but they didn't get much done as a unit.

SWE #28 C Lindstrom, Linus (2016)- Played both ends with a good compete level. Leans into guys on the boards and tries to tie them up and get a good body position on the wall but lacks the strength to execute. Needs to use better angles on the forecheck instead of always using the direct line with starts-stops as it puts him behind the play once the puck gets moved.

SWE #30 G Larsson, Filip (2016)- Hung out to dry by his defense. Gave up 6 goals but nearly all of those were either 1 on 1 plays with blown defensive assignments or soft Swedish defense in front of him. Thought he actually did pretty well making saves he was expected to make.

Red Deer Rebels vs Brandon Wheat Kings, May 25, 2016 – Memorial Cup Final Score RD2 BDN1 OT

RD #5 LD Mahura, Josh (2016) - Looks to have rounded into game shape after missing all but 2 games in the regular season, skating didn't look at its peak. He didn't show any obvious signs of lack of conditioning, had a good full speed stride but was a touch choppy or labored in his opening steps. Impacted the game with a good physical presence and a strong ability to battle down low, did not give up much time and space, closed on players quickly and clogged up play behind the net. Showed strong finish on his body checks, has the ability to pushing and inflict uncomfortable but clean contact. Showed a couple of good rushes up ice through the neutral zone, kept his head up, didn't rush plays and looked observant of the ice and developing play in front of him. Had a couple of turnovers when trying to pass through traffic, was a result of rushed decisions after gaining possession in deep. Was not a factor in scoring but didn't give up much when on the ice.

RD #11 C de Witt, Jeff (2016) - A 4th line center that was playing an energy role, showed a couple good physical plays and was creating energy on the forecheck. A few times his line was hemmed into their own zone and could gain possession long enough to clear. Missed coverage on the only Brandon goal getting crossed up with the defense after a turnover. I like his reach and ability to use his stick as a defensive weapon to pick at pucks and make forwards adjust to him.

BDN #19 C Patrick, Nolan (2017) - Was incredibly defensive minded in this game, consistently supporting his defense and circling back to avoid any rushes the other way; especially after they gained the lead. Skating is solid, stance is wide and top speed is very good, would like to see a slightly quicker burst getting up to full speed, didn't see much of separation gear tonight. Showed really good puck pursuit, battled hard for loose pucks going into scrums with an extra charge and used his body intelligently to separate players away. High hockey IQ was on display he showed a strong ability to create shots and find open teammates, especially with a bit more open space on the powerplay. Although held scoreless he was creating and had a couple nice scoring chances that could easily have been converted if not for very strong goaltending. Liked the way his offensive game is unpredictable, he read the ice so well tonight that it was hard to tell if he was going to shoot or pass, deceptive and versatile.

BDN #12 RW Mattheos, Stellio (2017) - There was a few thinks I really liked about Mattheos tonight but overall he had somewhat of a quiet game where he disappeared for stretches. When he carried the puck down the wing he looked slippery and dynamic. Had a few rushes that came out of traffic where he really looked like he could have made something happen but plays ended up breaking down, this was a tightly played game but we would have liked to see more driving of the offense to complete plays. I like the way he comes out of small spaces with the puck, he works well in tight but didn't go to the net often enough to utilize this strength. Would appreciate him shooting the puck more especially in stride.

BDN #10 RD Clague, Kale (2016) - Was far more involved continuously throughout the game than in past viewings, looks as though he was really interested in making a difference instead of deferring to teammates. Did observe him a couple times chasing in the defensive zone and straying out position, he recovered well because he is a strong skater, something that stood out tonight in both defending and pushing the play up ice. More of an asset on zone exits than expected, showed assertive play to be the first defended out and helping create quick transition through the neutral. When he pushes that play he can make turnovers at his own blue line, so there was some risky play in a high stakes game but showed good puck pursuit and back check to recovery from a couple of mistakes that end up on the other teams stick. Skating stood out tonight looks quick and compact in reverse, fluid with long stride going forward and his quickness gets him to full speed easily. Shoots well in stride and got pucks to the goalie with regularity. Was impressive tonight after looking indifferent in past viewings.

Rouyn-Noranda at Red Deer, May 27th, 2016 – Memorial Cup

RD #5 LD Mahura, Josh (2016) - Looked a little lost defensively through out he first period, ended up pinned in his own zone a few times. Took a bad penalty in the 2nd period and subsequently the Huskies scored the insurance goal to put the game out of reach. Reverse stride looked slow tonight, takes an extra few steps to get up to speed and was giving forwards more space that he should. Didn't look very confident with the puck in this offensive zone, decision making looked off tonight, much prefer when he's assertive and thinking ahead. Conditioning could be a factor in his skating issues because he hadn't played throughout the regular season and was forced to play catch up.

RD #11 C de Witt, Jeff (2016) - Speed was good tonight looked quick and kept up with fast team. As a 4th line center he was defending well and his line was effective in keeping play outside the middle of the ice. Showed good read off a turnover and beat his man cleanly to the net for a good scoring chance. Did have a glaring turnover in the neutral zone on a risky pass that backed up his line and lead to some extended zonetime for the opposition. Like his speed and could see a considerable jump in production with more opportunity, understands how to use his reach to protect and create.

RN #22 C/RW Abbandonato, Peter (2016) - Didn't play a ton of minutes tonight and what minutes he did play were somewhat protected, took only the face-offs on his strong side but faired well going 4/6 as somewhat of hybrid center with a few starts in offensive zone. Liked his speed again in this game, looks light on his feet and move fluidly on his edges. He's undersized and gets knocked off puck pretty easily.

RN #3 RD Neveu, Jacob (2016) - Gets a chance to play in some high leverage situations, was on the ice for the final 1:30 defending a lead with the oppositions goalie pulled. Got lots of penalty kill time and some offensive zone starts, didn't see much from an offensive stand point but doesn't look lost when working the offensive zone, makes simple plays. Uses his stick a fair amount and a couple times looked a little lost hacking away at pucks close to the crease and ended up giving up a couple scoring chances in a row. Does use his stick effectively to clog lanes and disrupt players moving and shooting pucks.

CREDITS

First off, this year will be the first year my father won't be reading this book. He passed away in November, so if it's possible to dedicate an NHL Draft book, this one is for him.

Thanks again this season to our scouts who helped put this book together. Ryan Yessie, Jérôme Bérubé, Mik Portoni, Nik Funa, Scott McDougall, Russ Bitely, Dusten Braaksma, Toni Rajamäki, Justin Sproule, Stephan Comeau, Todd Cordell, Alex Stewart, Tyler Bilton and our mid season rookies Jason Wiwad and Andy Levangie. I appreciate your hours in the rinks and the time put into writing reports.

Once again for the 2016 NHL Draft, we travelled across Canada, USA and Europe. Our goal is to mirror what NHL scouting staffs do, albeit with a much smaller travel budget. In essence we try to act as though we are a 31st NHL team. With scouts based all over Canada, USA and Europe we are able to scout hundreds of prospects. I travelled to Grand Forks to attend the World Under 18 Championship again this year. We also made our regular trips to all the other large events that take place during the scouting season.

I attended the NHL Combine again this year. Prior to going to the testing on the Saturday, I touched base with some scouts during the week. I'm always able to get some info on player interviews. In general, this year the feedback was very positive.

I want to thank Kathy Kocur for all her help all season long. Kathy assists with editing and also serves as our staff photographer. Her photos are used on our website.

Thanks to Paul Krotz and all the other media staff from around the NHL, CHL, the USHL who help us out and are a pleasure to deal with.

Mark Edwards
Founder & Director of Scouting

www.ingramcontent.com/pod-product-compliance
Lightning Source LLC
Chambersburg PA
CBHW062123160426
43191CB00013B/2185